THE JOSEPH SMITH PAPERS

Dean C. Jessee
Ronald K. Esplin
Richard Lyman Bushman
GENERAL EDITORS

PREVIOUSLY PUBLISHED

Journals, Volume 1: 1832–1839

Revelations and Translations: Manuscript Revelation Books, Facsimile Edition

Revelations and Translations, Volume 1: Manuscript Revelation Books

Revelations and Translations, Volume 2: Published Revelations

THE
JOSEPH SMITH
PAPERS

JOURNALS
VOLUME 2: DECEMBER 1841–APRIL 1843

Andrew H. Hedges
Alex D. Smith
Richard Lloyd Anderson
VOLUME EDITORS

THE CHURCH
HISTORIAN'S
PRESS

Copyright © 2011 by Intellectual Reserve, Inc. All rights reserved.

THE CHURCH HISTORIAN'S PRESS is an imprint of the Church History Department of The Church of Jesus Christ of Latter-day Saints, Salt Lake City, Utah, and a trademark of Intellectual Reserve, Inc.

www.josephsmithpapers.org

The Joseph Smith Papers Project is endorsed by the National Historical Publications and Records Commission.

Art direction: Richard Erickson.
Cover design: Scott Eggers. Interior design: Richard Erickson and Scott M. Mooy.
Typography: Riley M. Lorimer and Alison Palmer.

Library of Congress Cataloging-in-Publication Data

Smith, Joseph, 1805–1844.
Journals series / Dean C. Jessee, Mark Ashurst-McGee, Richard L. Jensen, volume editors.
p. cm. — (The Joseph Smith papers)
Includes bibliographical references.
ISBN 978-1-57008-849-0 (hardbound: alk. paper; v. 1)
ISBN 978-1-60908-737-1 (hardbound: alk. paper; v. 2)
1. Smith, Joseph, 1805–1844—Diaries. 2. Mormon Church—Presidents—Biography.
3. Church of Jesus Christ of Latter-day Saints—Presidents—Biography. 4. Mormon Church—History—Sources. 5. Church of Jesus Christ of Latter-day Saints—History—Sources.
I. Jessee, Dean C. II. Ashurst-McGee, Mark. III. Jensen, Richard L. IV. Title. V. Series.
BX8695.S6A3 2008   289.3092—dc22   [B]   2008037101

Printed in the United States of America on acid-free paper.
10 9 8 7 6 5 4 3 2 1

The Joseph Smith Papers

EXECUTIVE COMMITTEE
Marlin K. Jensen
Paul K. Sybrowsky
Richard E. Turley Jr.

EDITORIAL BOARD
Richard E. Turley Jr.
Reid L. Neilson
Matthew J. Grow
Max J. Evans

NATIONAL ADVISORY BOARD
Stephen J. Stein
Harry S. Stout
Mary-Jo Kline
Terryl L. Givens

MANAGING EDITOR
Ronald K. Esplin

ASSOCIATE MANAGING EDITOR
Jeffrey N. Walker

ASSOCIATE EDITOR
Ronald O. Barney

PROGRAM MANAGER
David L. Willden

PRODUCTION MANAGER
R. Eric Smith

RESEARCH AND REVIEW EDITOR
Richard L. Jensen

PROJECT ARCHIVIST
Robin Scott Jensen

EDITORS CONTRIBUTING TO THIS VOLUME

PRODUCTION EDITORS
Constance Palmer Lewis, Lead Editor
Alison Palmer
Rachel Osborne
Kathryn Burnside
Heather Seferovich
Caitlin Shirts
Jed Woodworth

DOCUMENT SPECIALISTS
Mark Ashurst-McGee
Sharalyn D. Howcroft
Christy Best

RESEARCH SPECIALISTS
Noel R. Barton
Brian P. Barton
Steven Motteshard

Contents

List of Illustrations and Maps	viii
Timeline of Joseph Smith's Life	x
Map: Joseph Smith's Residences	xi
Volume 2 Introduction:	
Nauvoo Journals, December 1841–April 1843	xiii
Editorial Method	xxxiii

Journals, December 1841–April 1843

Journal, December 1841–December 1842	3
Journal, December 1842–June 1844	185
Book 1, 21 December 1842–10 March 1843	189
Book 2 (First Part), 10 March–30 April 1843	303
Appendix 1: Missouri Extradition Attempt, 1842–1843,	
Selected Documents	377
Appendix 2: William Clayton, Journal Excerpt, 1–4 April 1843	403

Reference Material

Chronology for the Years 1839–1843	409
Geographical Directory	414
Maps	427
Pedigree Chart	438
Biographical Directory	439
Organizational Charts	
Ecclesiastical Officers and Church Appointees	505
Nauvoo City Officers	510
Nauvoo Legion Officers	514
Glossary	522
Essay on Sources	527
Works Cited	529
Corresponding Section Numbers in Editions of	
the Doctrine and Covenants	549
Acknowledgments	556

Illustrations and Maps

Textual Illustrations

Nauvoo Journals	xiv
First Nauvoo Journal	2
Title Page of the Book of the Law of the Lord	6
First Pages of Journal Entries and Donation Records	12
Journal Entries and Donation Records	22
Large "Journal" Heading	28
Example of Shorthand in First Nauvoo Journal	61
Transfer of Journal from Willard Richards to William Clayton	72
Eliza R. Snow Handwriting	144
Contemporaneous and Noncontemporaneous Journal Keeping	162
Transfer of Journal to Memorandum Books	182
Second Nauvoo Journal	184
First of Four Memorandum Books	187
Title Page of Second Nauvoo Journal, Book 1	190
First Page of Journal Entries	192
Penciled Draft beneath Penned Inscription	201
Notes of Habeas Corpus Hearing	229
The "Mormon Jubilee"	238
Cancellations and Insertions	269
Examples of Significant Insertions	270
Shorthand in Second Nauvoo Journal	298
Second of Four Memorandum Books	304
Observations in the Night Sky, Initial Diagram	311
Observations in the Night Sky, Corrected Diagram	315
Parhelia	317
Unidentified Symbols	322

Contextual Illustrations

Scribes of Joseph Smith's Nauvoo Journals	xx
Red Brick Store	23
Book of Abraham, Facsimile 1	35
Book of Abraham, Facsimile 2	41
John C. Bennett	59

ILLUSTRATIONS AND MAPS

Map of Nauvoo with Profile of Joseph Smith	69
Orson Pratt	76
Key Figures in Missouri Extradition Attempt	82
Sidney Rigdon	98
Joseph Duncan	98
Tomb of Joseph Smith	118
Arlington House	134
Portraits of Joseph and Emma Smith	158
Stephen A. Douglas	175
Thomas Ford	180
Lyman Trumbull	202
State Capitol, Springfield, Illinois	207
Legal Counsel for Joseph Smith	217
Sketch of Joseph Smith	221
Nathaniel Pope	226
Nauvoo House	272
Drawing of Nauvoo Temple	328
Brigham Young	366
Thomas Reynolds, Requisition	376

Maps

Joseph Smith's Residences	xi
Map of Nauvoo with Profile of Joseph Smith	69
Detailed Reference Maps	427

Other Visuals

Timeline of Joseph Smith's Life	x
Citation Format for Joseph Smith Revelations	xxxix
Chronological Index to Journal Entries	9
Pedigree Chart	438
Ecclesiastical Officers and Church Appointees	505
Nauvoo City Officers	510
Nauvoo Legion Officers	514
Corresponding Section Numbers in Editions of the Doctrine and Covenants	549

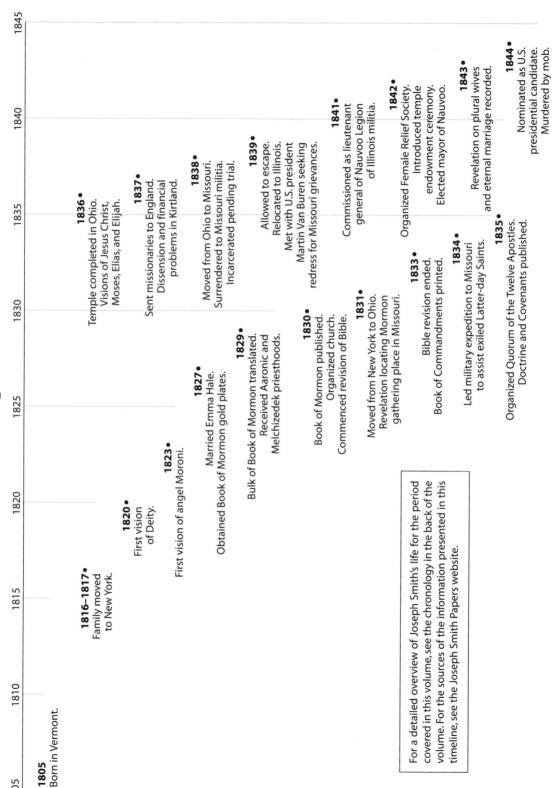

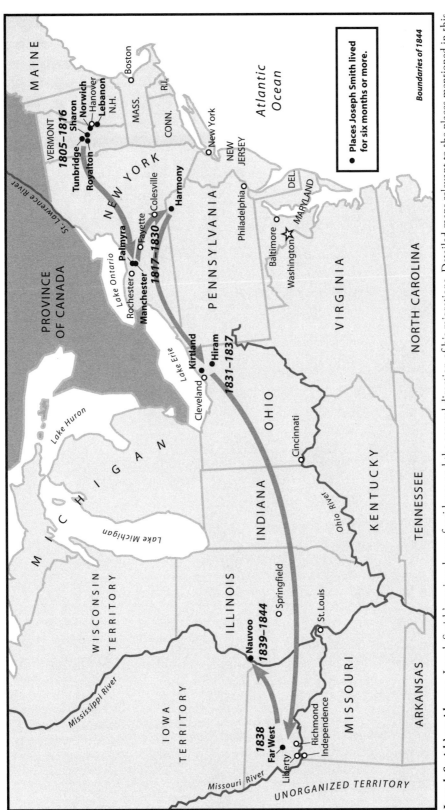

Joseph Smith's residences. Joseph Smith's major places of residence and the general direction of his migrations. Detailed maps relevant to the places mentioned in this volume appear on pages 427–437. (Design by John Hamer.)

VOLUME 2 INTRODUCTION

Nauvoo Journals, December 1841–April 1843

The journals presented in this volume cover a seventeen-month period marked by the continued growth of the church, significant doctrinal developments, the ongoing settlement of the Nauvoo community, and the maturing of Joseph Smith as a political and religious leader. Like most of the journal entries found in volume 1 of the Journals series, the Nauvoo journals were written entirely by scribes who accompanied Joseph Smith, not by the Mormon leader himself. Though not a comprehensive history of events, the journals are an essential source for reconstructing Joseph Smith's life and the history of the church he founded.[1]

The journals in volume 1 ended as the Latter-day Saints, having been driven from Missouri, began to gather at Commerce, Illinois. Shortly after Joseph Smith left Commerce for a journey to Washington DC in autumn 1839, James Mulholland, the scribe who was keeping Smith's journal, died.[2] Smith asked Robert D. Foster, who accompanied him on part of the trip east, to keep a journal, but the extent to which Foster complied is unclear; Joseph Smith wrote him in March 1840 that he wanted "to get hold of your journal very much," but no record is known to exist.[3] Scribes were employed to compile and write the history of the church and to copy Joseph Smith's correspondence, but there is no evidence that anyone was keeping a record of his daily activities in Nauvoo until Willard Richards's appointment in December 1841.

Richards arrived in Nauvoo in August 1841 after a four-year mission to England. Joseph Smith found him to be "a man after his own heart, in all things, that he could trust with his business" and appointed him temple recorder and "Scribe for the private office of the President" on 13 December 1841. Richards began "the duties of his office" immediately, apparently writing the first entry of Joseph Smith's journal on the day of his appointment.[4] Richards kept the journal for the remainder of Smith's life, with the exception of the

---

1. For additional biographical context, see "Joseph Smith and His Papers," in *JSP*, J1:xv–xli.
2. Emma Smith, Nauvoo, IL, to JS, Washington DC, 6 Dec. 1839, Charles Aldrich Autograph Collection, State Historical Society of Iowa, Des Moines.
3. JS, Nauvoo, IL, to Robert D. Foster, Beverly, IL, 11 Mar. 1840, JS Collection, CHL.
4. Willard Richards, Nauvoo, IL, to Jennetta Richards, Richmond, MA, 26 Feb. 1842, CHL; JS, Journal, 13 Dec. 1841, p. 11 herein.

Nauvoo journals. Willard Richards kept Joseph Smith's journals with help from William Clayton and others between 1841 and 1844. The large book, the first of Smith's journals begun in Nauvoo, is titled "The Book of the Law of the Lord" and covers the period from December 1841 to December 1842. The four small memorandum books together make up the second Nauvoo journal, titled "President Joseph Smith's Journal," which covers the period from December 1842 to June 1844. This volume of *The Joseph Smith Papers* includes the journal entries in the Book of the Law of the Lord, the first memorandum book, and part of the second (through April 1843). (Church History Library, Salt Lake City. Photograph by Welden C. Andersen.)

period from 30 June through 20 December 1842, when he moved his wife and son from Massachusetts to Nauvoo. During Richards's absence, William Clayton kept the journal, with occasional assistance from Eliza R. Snow and Erastus Derby. References in the journal to the recorder, scribe, or secretary always refer to Richards;[5] the other scribes did not make reference to themselves.

During the two-year interruption in journal keeping, much happened to set the stage for the events detailed in the Nauvoo journals. In October 1839, Joseph Smith left Commerce for Washington DC, seeking government redress for the Saints' losses in Missouri. Failing to win any promises of support from either United States president Martin Van Buren or Congress, Smith returned to Illinois in March 1840. Shortly after, the post office at Commerce changed its name to Nauvoo, a word derived from a Hebrew word meaning "beautiful."[6] The Illinois legislature granted Nauvoo a city charter in December 1840, and Joseph Smith was elected a member of the city council in the first municipal election in February 1841.

In many ways, Nauvoo's charter was similar to other city charters in Illinois at the time.[7] Each limited the terms of office for city officials to either one or two years, for example, and the legislative powers granted to the Nauvoo City Council were essentially the same as those granted to Springfield and Quincy.[8] On the other hand, Nauvoo's charter required a much shorter residency period for voters and aspiring officeholders than many other charters and also eliminated the citizenship requirement for the same—the first, perhaps, in an effort to allow recently returned missionaries to participate in politics, and the second in response to the anticipated growth in the number of

---

5. See, for example, JS, Journal, 22 Dec. 1841; 17 and 21 Jan. 1842; 26 Dec. 1842; and 9 Jan. 1843, pp. 17, 27, 29, 194, 242 herein.

6. Notice, *Times and Seasons,* May 1840, 1:106; Robert Johnston to Richard M. Young, 21 Apr. 1840, in JS Letterbook 2, p. 135; Richard M. Young, Washington DC, to Elias Higbee, 22 Apr. 1840, in JS Letterbook 2, pp. 135–136; Seixas, *Hebrew Grammar,* III; Zucker, "Joseph Smith as a Student of Hebrew," 48. In September 1839, Joseph Smith, Hyrum Smith, Sidney Rigdon, and George W. Robinson submitted a plat for the town of Nauvoo. (Hancock Co., IL, Surveyors Record, 1836–1884, microfilm 954,775; Hancock Co., IL, Plat Books, vol. 1, microfilm 954,774, U.S. and Canada Record Collection, FHL.)

7. See Bennett and Cope, "City on a Hill," 33–40. Between 1837, when Chicago was chartered as a city by the Illinois General Assembly, and 1840, when Nauvoo's charter was drafted, four other Illinois cities—Alton, Galena, Springfield, and Quincy—were granted charters. (Kimball, "Nauvoo Charter," 68–70; An Act to Incorporate the City of Chicago [4 Mar. 1837], *Laws of the State of Illinois* [1836–1837], pp. 50–80; An Act to Incorporate the City of Nauvoo [16 Dec. 1840], *Laws of the State of Illinois* [1840–1841], pp. 52–57.)

8. Kimball, "Nauvoo Charter," 70, 77–78.

foreign-born residents.⁹ Other important differences were various powers granted the city council, such as the authority to organize a university and a city militia, and the authority granted the municipal court to issue writs of habeas corpus "in all cases arising under the ordinances of the city council."¹⁰ Broad in its scope and forward-looking in its provisions, the Nauvoo charter gave the Mormons in Nauvoo the authority and autonomy necessary to integrate newcomers into the city, establish civic order, and provide for the safety, education, and prosperity of the city's inhabitants.

Strong support from Democrats for the Nauvoo charter had important ramifications for the Mormons' political life in Illinois. Most members of the church voted the Whig ticket in 1840 in both national and local elections, in part as a result of their disappointment with Democrat Martin Van Buren and his failure to help them obtain redress for their losses in Missouri. Several months before the 1842 gubernatorial elections in Illinois, however, Joseph Smith published a lengthy article endorsing Democratic candidates Adam W. Snyder and John Moore (running for Illinois governor and lieutenant governor, respectively), citing their support for the charter as a primary consideration. Snyder and Moore were "free from the prejudices and superstitions of the age," Smith wrote, "and such men we *love*, and such men will ever receive our support, be their *political predilections* what they may. . . . We will never be justly charged with the sin of ingratitude—they *have* served us, and we *will* serve them."¹¹ State supreme court justice Thomas Ford replaced Snyder as the gubernatorial candidate after the latter's untimely death shortly before the election and received, predictably, a significant majority of the Mormon vote.¹² Whig leaders chafed at the Saints' apparent political capriciousness, and Whig papers like the *Sangamo Journal* excoriated the Mormons in spirited editorials and articles throughout 1842.

For all there was to do in Illinois, Joseph Smith's trip to Washington DC in 1839–1840 demonstrates his continued preoccupation with Missouri. A revelation dated 19 January 1841, however, marked a turning point in his history. In effect, the revelation released Smith and the church from their obligation—for

---

9. An Act to Incorporate the City of Nauvoo [16 Dec. 1840], *Laws of the State of Illinois* [1840–1841], p. 54, sec. 7; Bennett and Cope, "City on a Hill," 22; Kimball, "Nauvoo Charter," 70–71.

10. An Act to Incorporate the City of Nauvoo [16 Dec. 1840], *Laws of the State of Illinois* [1840–1841], pp. 55–57, secs. 17, 24, 25. Some Illinois cities' charters provided for the establishment of common schools (although not universities), and most chartered cities had volunteer militias that, while not organized by the city council, could nevertheless be called out, as in Nauvoo, by the mayor. Alton, Illinois, had a provision allowing the judge of the municipal court to issue writs of habeas corpus. (See Bennett and Cope, "City on a Hill," 23–29.)

11. JS, "State Gubernatorial Convention," *Times and Seasons*, 1 Jan. 1842, 3:651; italics in original.

12. Leonard, *Nauvoo*, 294–297.

the time being, at least—to build a city and temple in Missouri and refocused their attention on Illinois. "When I [the Lord] give a commandment to any of the sons of men, to do a work unto my name," the revelation read, "and those sons of men go with all their mights, and with all they have, to perform that work, and cease not their diligence, and their enemies come upon them, and hinder them from performing that work; behold, it behoveth me to require that work no more. . . . Therefore for this cause have I accepted the offerings of those whom I commanded to build up a city and a house unto my name, in Jackson county, Missouri, and were hindered by their enemies."[13] Freed from the immediate responsibility to build a temple and the city of Zion in Missouri,[14] Joseph Smith and the church turned their attention to Nauvoo.

The same revelation identified several priorities for the Saints in Illinois, including the need to construct two buildings in Nauvoo—neither one of which Joseph Smith would live to see completed. One, the Nauvoo House, was to serve both as a residence for Joseph Smith and his family and as a "house for boarding, a house that strangers may come from afar to lodge therein . . . that the weary traveller may find health and safety while he shall contemplate the word of the Lord."[15] Money for construction was to come through selling stock in the project for at least $50 per share, with the amount one person could invest limited to $15,000.[16] George Miller, Lyman Wight, John Snider, and Peter Haws were appointed as trustees of the newly created Nauvoo House Association on 23 February 1841, and the cornerstone of the building was laid 2 October 1841.[17]

The other building was the Nauvoo temple—an edifice dedicated to God in which the "fulness of the priesthood" could be restored. The revelation declared that the various ordinances and ceremonies that would be performed in the temple were the "foundation of Zion" and the means through which God would bestow "honor, immortality, and eternal life" upon the faithful. Like the Israelites' wilderness tabernacle and Solomon's temple, the Nauvoo temple was to be built of the finest materials available and would demonstrate that the church would faithfully perform "all things whatsoever" the Lord commanded

---

13. Revelation, 19 Jan. 1841, in Doctrine and Covenants 103:15, 1844 ed. [D&C 124:49, 51].

14. Church leaders and members continued to appeal to Congress to redress their losses in Missouri, however. (See Elias Higbee et al., Memorial to Congress, 10 Jan. 1842, photocopy, Material Relating to Mormon Expulsion from Missouri, CHL; JS et al., Memorial to U.S. Senate and House of Representatives, 28 Nov. 1843, in Records of the U.S. Senate, Committee on the Judiciary, Records, 1816–1982, National Archives, Washington DC.)

15. Revelation, 19 Jan. 1841, in Doctrine and Covenants 103:9, 1844 ed. [D&C 124:23].

16. Revelation, 19 Jan. 1841, in Doctrine and Covenants 103:19, 1844 ed. [D&C 124:64–66].

17. An Act to Incorporate the Nauvoo House Association [23 Feb. 1841], *Laws of the State of Illinois* [1840–1841], pp. 131–132; JS, Journal, 29 Dec. 1841, p. 19 herein.

them.¹⁸ With sixteen companies of local militia looking on and thousands of people vying for a view, Joseph Smith directed the laying of the temple cornerstones on 6 April 1841.¹⁹

One of the specific ordinances to be performed in the temple was vicarious baptism for deceased persons. Briefly referenced in the New Testament,²⁰ the doctrine of "baptism for the dead," as it came to be called, was taught by Joseph Smith in his funeral sermon for Seymour Brunson on 15 August 1840.²¹ Smith later elaborated: "The Saints have the privilege of being baptized for those of their relatives who are dead, whom they believe would have embraced the Gospel, if they had been privileged with hearing it, and who have received the Gospel in the spirit, through the instrumentality of those who have been commissioned to preach to them" in the afterlife.²² Such baptisms were performed in the Mississippi River by September 1840.²³ Revelation dictated that the ordinance be performed in a temple and that God would accept such baptisms performed elsewhere only for a time; otherwise, the revelation read, "ye shall be rejected as a church with your dead, saith the Lord your God."²⁴ Taking the words seriously, church members dedicated a baptismal font in the basement of the unfinished temple on 8 November 1841, a mere seven months after laying the cornerstones.²⁵

During the two years preceding the commencement of these journals, important changes were made in church leadership as well. Canadian convert and businessman William Law took the place of Hyrum Smith, Joseph Smith's older brother, as counselor in the First Presidency. Hyrum, in turn, was appointed "a prophet and a seer and a revelator" to the church, to "act in concert" with Joseph Smith, who would "shew unto him the keys whereby he may ask and receive, and be crowned with the same blessing, and glory, and honor, and priesthood, and gifts of the priesthood, that once were put upon . . . Oliver Cowdery." Hyrum Smith was also appointed patriarch, in which office he held

---

18. Revelation, 19 Jan. 1841, in Doctrine and Covenants 103:10–17, 1844 ed. [D&C 124:25–55].

19. The sixteen companies of militia included the Nauvoo Legion and two volunteer militia companies from Iowa Territory. ("Celebration of the Anniversary of the Church," *Times and Seasons,* 15 Apr. 1841, 2:375–377.)

20. See 1 Corinthians 15:29. For a brief discussion of this reference in its historical context, see "Baptism for the Dead: Ancient Sources," in *Encyclopedia of Mormonism,* 1:97.

21. Simon Baker, "15 Aug. 1840 Minutes of Recollection of Joseph Smith's Sermon," JS Collection, CHL.

22. JS, Nauvoo, IL, to "the Twelve," Great Britain, 15 Dec. 1840, JS Collection, CHL.

23. Jane Neymon and Vienna Jacques, Statement, 29 Nov. 1854, Historian's Office, JS History Documents, ca. 1839–1880, CHL.

24. Revelation, 19 Jan. 1841, in Doctrine and Covenants 103:11, 1844 ed. [D&C 124:32].

25. JS, Journal, 30 June 1842; Clayton, History of the Nauvoo Temple, 6, 20–21.

"the keys of the patriarchal blessings" for individual members of the church.[26] Joseph Smith received additional assistance from the Quorum of the Twelve Apostles, whose members began returning to Nauvoo in July 1841 after a two-year mission in England. Before the apostles' English mission, their responsibilities had been limited to overseeing scattered branches of the church lying outside the organized stakes. Upon their return, however, Joseph Smith explained to a conference of the church on 16 August 1841 that the Twelve "should be authorized to assist in managing the affairs of the Kingdom in this place [Nauvoo]." A sustaining vote of the conference formalized the new arrangement, allowing Smith to delegate an increasing number of church administrative responsibilities to the Twelve in the coming months and years.[27]

Shortly after the Quorum of the Twelve assumed their new responsibilities, members of the church who had been involved with Freemasonry prior to the church's move to Illinois requested the establishment of a Masonic lodge in Nauvoo. Seeing the Mormons as potential allies who might help him obtain his political goals, Abraham Jonas, Grand Master of the Columbus Lodge, endorsed the request and created a temporary lodge in Nauvoo on 15 October 1841. Joseph Smith, who had not been a Mason earlier, was not involved with these early efforts to establish a local lodge, although he served as Grand Chaplain at the installation of the permanent Nauvoo lodge on 15 March 1842. He and Sidney Rigdon were admitted as members of the lodge that same day. Perhaps attracted to the ideals of "brotherhood, justice, learning, and character development" Masons espoused, Smith occasionally participated in the proceedings of the lodge throughout the remainder of his life.[28]

The period between journals (1839–1841) had its share of challenges as well. One of the most significant came in 1840 when Missouri governor Thomas Reynolds issued a requisition to the governor of Illinois, Thomas Carlin, to extradite Joseph Smith to Missouri as a fugitive from justice. This requisition arose from alleged treason and other charges brought against Joseph Smith, Lyman Wight, and others during the 1838 Mormon conflicts in Missouri. Carlin signed the extradition order in September 1840, but no arrest attempt

---

26. Revelation, 19 Jan. 1841, in Doctrine and Covenants 103:29, 1844 ed. [D&C 124:91–95]. Cowdery, whom Hyrum Smith replaced, had received the keys of the priesthood in connection with Joseph Smith, had been ordained as the second elder of the church on 6 April 1830, and had served in the church's presidency from December 1834 to April 1838 under the titles "assistant President" and "assistant Councillor." (JS History, vol. A-1, 18, 27, 37; JS, Journal, 5 Dec. 1834, in *JSP*, J1:47–48; Minute Book 1, 3 Sept. 1837.)

27. General Church Minutes, 16 Aug. 1841; Esplin, "Emergence of Brigham Young," 482, 500–506. In his journal, Willard Richards summed up the new arrangement in the words "Business of the church given to the 12." (Richards, Journal, 16 Aug. 1841.)

28. Leonard, *Nauvoo*, 313–321; JS, Journal, 15 Mar. 1842; Nauvoo Masonic Lodge Minute Book.

Scribes of Joseph Smith's Nauvoo journals. Willard Richards (top left) and William Clayton (top right) were the principal scribes who kept Joseph Smith's Nauvoo journals. Eliza R. Snow (right) and Erastus Derby (not shown) assisted William Clayton in copying correspondence into Smith's first Nauvoo (second Illinois) journal. (Church History Library, Salt Lake City.)

was made until 5 June 1841. Joseph Smith obtained a writ of habeas corpus in Quincy, Illinois, and was discharged five days later in Monmouth after circuit court judge Stephen A. Douglas ruled that the arrest warrant was invalid.[29] Adding to Smith's difficulties that summer were the deaths of his young son Don Carlos, his brother Don Carlos, and another of his clerks, Robert B. Thompson.[30]

When Willard Richards began writing the journals in this volume, Nauvoo and the surrounding area were experiencing a population boom. In 1839, Joseph Smith identified Nauvoo as an important gathering place for the Saints; by January 1843, he estimated that twelve thousand Saints lived in the area.[31] Many lived on land the church had purchased from Isaac Galland and brothers William and Hugh White in 1839; others lived on the five hundred acres known as "the Flats" that Smith had contracted to purchase from Connecticut land speculators Horace R. Hotchkiss, John Gillett, and Smith Tuttle. Joseph Smith planned to make the required payments for some of these properties by selling lots to those moving into the city. Speculators holding land in nearby areas such as Warsaw, Ramus, and Shokokon also solicited Joseph Smith, leading to similar land contracts in some of these areas. Other land speculators who owned land in Nauvoo on "the Hill" or "the Bluffs," located to the east of the Flats, however, sold their land to new arrivals at a lower price, making it difficult for Smith to meet the terms of his real estate contracts and creating tensions between the competing interests. The numerous references throughout the journals to the buying and selling of these lands reflect the frontier nature of Nauvoo, the growth of the church, and Joseph Smith's prominent role in developing the community.

Many journal entries deal with building the Nauvoo temple and the Nauvoo House. Despite support from many church members, both undertakings suffered from a lack of capital, complaints of mismanagement, and competition with private developers' projects. The economic jealousies between promoters of the Flats and the Hill that plagued Joseph Smith's efforts to pay off land debts also affected the building of the temple and the Nauvoo House. As a result, Joseph Smith publicly denounced other developers like Robert D.

---

29. "The Late Proceedings," *Times and Seasons*, 15 June 1841, 2:447–449; Requisition for JS, 1 Sept. 1840, State of Missouri v. JS for Treason (Warren Co. Cir. Ct. 1841), JS Extradition Records, Abraham Lincoln Presidential Library, Springfield, IL.

30. Obituary for Don Carlos Smith, *Times and Seasons*, 1 Sept. 1841, 2:533; General Church Minutes, 16 Aug. 1841; Richards, Journal, 16 Aug. 1841; "Death of General Don Carlos Smith," *Times and Seasons*, 16 Aug. 1841, 2:503–504; "Death of Col. Robert B. Thompson," *Times and Seasons*, 1 Sept. 1841, 2:519–520.

31. "Proceedings of the General Conference," *Times and Seasons*, Dec. 1839, 1:30–31; JS, Journal, 5 Jan. 1843, p. 233 herein.

Foster, Amos Davis, and Hiram Kimball, whose business enterprises, he believed, impeded these church building projects.[32] Addressing workers' concerns, improving the methods for collecting funds, and keeping church members on task with these construction projects occupied much of the Mormon leader's time and energy.

At the same time, concerns for the temporal well-being of his family and members of the community vied for Joseph Smith's attention. By the end of 1842, Joseph and Emma Smith had four children to support, as well as others who lived in their home as household help or as wards. One means of providing for the family was Smith's store on Water Street.[33] While Joseph Smith seems to have spent relatively little time directly managing or operating the store, journal entries indicate his continued involvement in stocking the store with hard-to-find goods. Similarly, although he turned the management of his farm over to Cornelius Lott, Joseph Smith rode the three miles from Nauvoo to visit Lott and hoe potatoes during the summer. Both the store and the farm—as well as his other business concerns and the building projects he oversaw as trustee for the church—affected the economic lives of numerous Nauvoo residents. "Let me assure you," wrote Emma to Illinois governor Thomas Carlin in August 1842, "that there are many whole families that are entirely dependant upon the prosecution and success of Mr Smiths temporal business for their support."[34]

Administrative concerns also occupied a large part of Joseph Smith's time. As lieutenant general of the Nauvoo Legion, he oversaw the training, staffing, and supplying of more than two thousand troops of the Illinois militia. As a city councilman and later as mayor of Nauvoo, he helped draft ordinances and resolutions, attended city council meetings, and served as a judge for both the mayor's court and Nauvoo Municipal Court.[35] Cases involving slander, assault, petty thievery, and disorderly conduct occupied much of the court docket, although more specialized and technical cases occasionally appeared, such as the *Dana v. Brink* medical malpractice suit. The forty-one pages of the journal dedicated to recording the graphic testimony of witnesses in this trial probably reflect scribe Dr. Willard Richards's interest in the medical details more than Smith's, but the technical language about legal precedents and procedure illustrates how Joseph Smith understood and applied the law.

---

32. See JS, Journal, 21 Feb. and 13 Apr. 1843, pp. 271–273, 355–356 herein.
33. See "Store," in Geographical Directory.
34. Emma Smith to Thomas Carlin, [17] Aug. 1842, p. 113 herein.
35. See Nauvoo City Officers, p. 510 herein.

Through all of this, and especially during the year 1842, Joseph Smith directed and oversaw important developments in the doctrine and organization of the church. These included publishing writings of the biblical patriarch Abraham that Smith said he translated from papyri he had obtained from an antiquities dealer several years earlier in Kirtland, Ohio. Written as a first-person account of Abraham's experiences, the record recounts the patriarch's calling to the priesthood, his escape from idolatrous priests in "the land of the Chaldeans," and his and Sarah's journey toward Egypt.[36] Teachings about the priesthood, the Abrahamic covenant, premortal life, astronomy, and the Creation overshadow the more familiar elements of the biblical narrative and were considered significant enough for the church to accept the record into its official canon in 1880. The same status was eventually given to two lengthy letters Joseph Smith wrote during this time that further discuss the doctrine and practice of baptism for the dead. Explaining the need and procedure for making an official record of each baptism, the letters—both of which were copied into the journal[37]—discuss the ordinance in terms of an unfolding objective to provide for the salvation of the whole human family through priesthood ordinances whose efficacy reached beyond the grave.[38]

During the years covered in these journals, Joseph Smith also delivered important discourses on a variety of topics ranging from gospel basics, such as obedience and gaining knowledge, to the second coming of Christ, the nature of God, and the ultimate destiny of the earth. Some of these discourses were copied into his journal, and a few, such as the writings of Abraham and the letters about baptism for the dead, were eventually canonized.[39] Smith also shared with a few trusted associates new rituals that would later be performed in the Nauvoo temple and that added to the ceremonies that had earlier been introduced in the Kirtland temple. Building on Sarah Kimball's efforts to create a women's benevolent society, Joseph Smith also assisted in organizing the Female Relief Society of Nauvoo during this period. At the society's initial meeting, he charged the women with "searching after objects of charity" and "correcting the morals and strengthening the virtues of the female community," after which John Taylor ordained Emma Smith to preside over the

---

36. "The Book of Abraham," *Times and Seasons*, 1 Mar. 1842, 3:704 [Abraham 1:1].

37. JS to "all the saints in Nauvoo," 1 Sept. 1842, p. 131 herein [D&C 127]; JS to "the Church of Jesus Christ," [7] Sept. 1842, p. 145 herein [D&C 128].

38. See *JSP*, J1:222n478; and Revelation, 12 July 1843, in Revelations Collection, CHL [D&C 132:7–20].

39. Instruction, 2 Apr. 1843, in JS, Journal, 2 Apr. 1843, pp. 324–326 herein [D&C 130]; see also Clayton, Journal, 2 Apr. 1843, pp. 404–405 herein.

organization.⁴⁰ The Relief Society, as it came to be called, quickly grew to a membership of over one thousand Mormon women in the Nauvoo area.⁴¹

By December 1842, the end of the first year covered in these journals, Joseph Smith had explained the doctrine of plural marriage to a few of his closest associates and was practicing it himself.⁴² Glimpses into the reasons for introducing the practice and his understanding of the doctrine behind it are provided in some of his translations and revelations. The Book of Mormon, for example, taught that monogamy was the rule but that it was permissible for one man to have multiple wives when God commanded.⁴³ A revelation recorded 12 July 1843—the general outlines of which were reportedly understood much earlier⁴⁴—accordingly taught that Abraham, who was married to Sarah, was under no condemnation for taking Hagar as a second wife because the Lord had commanded him to do so.⁴⁵ According to the revelation, other ancient prophets in addition to Abraham had the keys or authority from God to participate in or perform plural marriages, and those who received plural wives under the direction of these prophets stood blameless before God. The stipulation of prophetic direction meant that the practice was carefully controlled, however, and those who took plural wives on their own initiative faced serious consequences.⁴⁶ Joseph Smith believed that this ancient authority had been conferred upon him as part of the latter-day restoration of the keys and power of the priesthood⁴⁷ and that his authorization of plural marriages was justified before God.⁴⁸ With these checks in place,⁴⁹ a man might legitimately take plural

---

40. Relief Society Minute Book, 17 Mar. 1842.

41. Ward, "Female Relief Society of Nauvoo," 88.

42. Among the best-documented examples of plural marriage involving Joseph Smith during this period are his marriages to Sarah Ann Whitney and Eliza R. Snow. (Revelation, 27 July 1842, in Revelations Collection, CHL; Blessing, JS to Sarah Ann Whitney, Nauvoo, IL, 23 Mar. 1843, Whitney Family Documents, CHL; Sarah Ann Whitney Kimball, Affidavit, Salt Lake Co., Utah Territory, 19 June 1869, in Joseph F. Smith, Affidavits about Celestial Marriage, 1:36, 4:36; Snow, *Biography and Family Record of Lorenzo Snow,* 68; Eliza R. Snow, Affidavit, Salt Lake Co., Utah Territory, 7 June 1869, in Joseph F. Smith, Affidavits about Celestial Marriage, 1:25; Beecher, *Personal Writings of Eliza R. Snow,* 16–17. For evidence that others were practicing it as well, see Clayton, Journal, 27 Apr. 1843.)

43. See Book of Mormon, 1840 ed., 125 [Jacob 2:27–30].

44. Orson Pratt, in *Journal of Discourses,* 7 Oct. 1869, 13:193; Bachman, "Ohio Origins of the Revelation on Eternal Marriage," 19–32.

45. Revelation, 12 July 1843, in Revelations Collection, CHL [D&C 132:34–35].

46. Israel's king David, for example, who had received several wives under the direction of the prophet Nathan, lost his exaltation when he took Uriah's wife. (See 2 Samuel 11–12; Revelation, 12 July 1843, in Revelations Collection, CHL [D&C 132:38–39].)

47. See Revelation, 12 July 1843, in Revelations Collection, CHL [D&C 132:45]; and Vision, 3 Apr. 1836, in JS, Journal, in *JSP,* J1:219–222 [D&C 110].

48. See Revelation, 12 July 1843, in Revelations Collection, CHL [D&C 132:44, 48].

49. Although reminiscent accounts must be used with caution (see note 51 below), later affidavits attest

wives "to multiply & replenish the earth, . . . & for thire exaltation in the eternal worlds," while plural relationships that were undertaken without Joseph Smith's direct approval were unauthorized and adulterous.[50]

The nature of the extant sources precludes a thorough understanding of the extent to which Joseph Smith and others practiced plural marriage in Nauvoo and the nature of the relationships between the men and women in these marriages. Most of the information on the practice during this period comes either from later affidavits and reminiscences or from reports of disaffected members of the church at the time—none of which, for a variety of reasons, can be considered entirely reliable historical sources for delineating how plural marriage was understood and practiced by those involved at the time.[51] William Clayton provides the best contemporaneous evidence that at least some plural marriages in Nauvoo during Joseph Smith's lifetime involved conjugal relations[52]—just as they did later in Utah—and nothing in the 12 July 1843 revelation on plural marriage provides any doctrinal reason for why any authorized plural marriage could not have included such relations. At the same time, there is insufficient evidence to conclude that all Nauvoo plural marriages or sealings were consummated.[53] Although Joseph Smith had many children

---

to the highly regulated nature of plural marriage during Joseph Smith's lifetime. The most complete accounts generally refer to a specific ceremony, performed on a specific date, by an acknowledged holder of the priesthood, in the presence of witnesses, and according to specific regulations. Eliza R. Snow's affidavit, for example, notes that "on the twenty-ninth day of June A.D. 1842 . . . she was married or sealed to Joseph Smith . . . by Brigham Young, President of the Quorum of the Twelve Apostles of said Church, according to the laws of the same regulating marriage, in the presence of Sarah M. Cleaveland." (Eliza R. Snow, Affidavit, Salt Lake Co., Utah Territory, 7 June 1869, in Joseph F. Smith, Affidavits about Celestial Marriage, 1:25, CHL. For a description of rules regulating plural marriage as they were understood in 1853, see Orson Pratt, "Celestial Marriage," *The Seer,* Feb. 1853, 1:25–32.)

50. See Revelation, 12 July 1843, in Revelations Collection, CHL [D&C 132:41–43, 63]; and Book of Mormon, 1840 ed., 125 [Jacob 2:27–33].

51. Many accounts about plural marriage in Nauvoo during Joseph Smith's lifetime were recorded decades after the events they describe. Similarly, most of the affidavits about plural marriage that authors cite were collected decades after the church left Nauvoo. Given the selective and social nature of human memory and its susceptibility to being influenced by more recent events, such reminiscent accounts must be used with caution when attempting to reconstruct past events and practices. Moreover, most of these affidavits were gathered in response to a concerted effort by the Reorganized Church of Jesus Christ of Latter Day Saints to deny that Joseph Smith practiced plural marriage and to lay the practice at the feet of Brigham Young after Smith's death. In response, a number of women who had been sealed to Joseph Smith in Nauvoo prepared formal statements about their marriages. As with the affidavits, personal motives influenced the reports of disaffected members of the church in Nauvoo as well. (See Thelen, "Memory and American History," 1117–1129.)

52. William Clayton married Margaret Moon as a plural wife on 27 April 1843. Margaret gave birth to a baby boy on 18 February 1844. (Clayton, Journal, 27 Apr. 1843 and 18 Feb. 1844.)

53. Similarly, the fact that a number of women were sealed to Joseph Smith after his death, when there was no opportunity for conjugal relationships, suggests that plural marriage was instituted for reasons

with Emma, no progeny from any of his plural marriages have been identified.[54]

Given the sensitivity of the topic, it is no surprise that clear references to plural marriage are virtually absent from Joseph Smith's Nauvoo journals. Some entries, however, may be best understood—or at least partially understood—in light of the practice, although a significant amount of ambiguity remains even after a careful examination of the context and supporting sources. For example, a revelation dated 2 December 1841 for Marinda Nancy Johnson Hyde (recorded in a 25 January 1842 entry of Smith's journal) closes by counseling her to "hearken to the counsel of my servant Joseph in all things whatsoever he shall teach unto her, and it shall be a blessing upon her and upon her children after her."[55] Decades later, Hyde reported that this revelation had been delivered to her shortly after Joseph Smith had taught her the "doctrine of celestial marriage" and that she "followed the council of the prophet Joseph as above instructed" and continued to hope for "the fulfilment of the promises and blessings" contained in the revelation.[56] In addition, a 1 May 1869 affidavit signed by Hyde attests that she was "married or sealed" to Joseph Smith in May 1843.[57] Assuming Hyde's memory accurately reflects events of 1841–1843 and that the "doctrine of celestial marriage" about which she learned included plural marriage, it would be reasonable to conclude that the revelation's reference to "all things whatsoever" Smith would teach her included a marriage or sealing to the Mormon leader. But Joseph Smith could have counseled Hyde about many other issues in 1841 as well. Her husband, Orson Hyde of the Quorum of the Twelve, for example, had left on a mission to Europe and the Middle East in April 1840, leaving Hyde and her children to rely on others for much of their support until his return in December 1842.

Several later documents suggest that several women who were already married to other men were, like Marinda Hyde, married or sealed to Joseph Smith.

---

beyond simply "multiplying and replenishing the earth." For records of some of these posthumous sealings, see Brown, *Nauvoo Sealings, Adoptions, and Anointings,* 281–286.

54. Ugo A. Perego and his associates have recently used DNA testing to rule out, to a high degree of probability, Joseph Smith's paternity of five individuals traditionally identified as his possible children through plural wives. (See Perego et al., "Reconstructing the Y-Chromosome of Joseph Smith: Genealogical Applications," 70–88; Perego et al., "Resolving the Paternities of Oliver N. Buell and Mosiah L. Hancock through DNA," 128–136.)

55. JS, Journal, 25 Jan. 1842, p. 37 herein.

56. Marinda Nancy Johnson Hyde, Statement, [ca. 1880], CHL. This document is undated, but a reference to the death of Orson Hyde in the statement indicates it was written after his death on 28 November 1878. Marinda Hyde died 24 March 1886.

57. Marinda Nancy Johnson Hyde, Affidavit, Salt Lake Co., Utah Territory, 1 May 1869, in Joseph F. Smith, Affidavits about Celestial Marriage, 1:15. A notation in Joseph Smith's journal in the handwriting of Thomas Bullock dates the event to April 1842. (JS Journal, 14 July 1843.)

Available evidence indicates that some of these apparent polygynous/polyandrous marriages took place during the years covered by this journal. At least three of the women reportedly involved in these marriages—Patty Bartlett Sessions, Ruth Vose Sayers, and Sylvia Porter Lyon—are mentioned in the journal, though in contexts very much removed from plural marriage.[58] Even fewer sources are extant for these complex relationships than are available for Smith's marriages to unmarried women, and Smith's revelations are silent on them. Having surveyed the available sources, historian Richard L. Bushman concludes that these polyandrous marriages—and perhaps other plural marriages of Joseph Smith—were primarily a means of binding other families to his for the spiritual benefit and mutual salvation of all involved.[59]

More definitive echoes of plural marriage are apparent in several journal entries that refer to men attempting to seduce women by telling them that Joseph Smith sanctioned extramarital affairs. In these cases, though, the connection is an indirect one, and reflects an abuse or misrepresentation of the practice as reflected in Smith's translations and revelations rather than the practice itself.[60] Chief among those who invoked Joseph Smith's name "to carry on their iniquitous designs"[61] was John C. Bennett. Bennett had helped obtain the charter for the city and was a major general in the Nauvoo Legion, a prominent Mason, the mayor of Nauvoo, and a member of the First Presidency of the church. While the journal and other documents indicate that Joseph Smith initially reproved Bennett privately for his immoral behavior,

---

58. Sessions is mentioned in the 2 and 3 March 1843 entries in connection with a court case. Sayers appears in a business transaction in the 7 March 1843 entry, while Joseph Smith visited Lyon shortly after the death of her baby on 24 December 1842. Sessions married David Sessions on 28 June 1812 and reported being "sealed" on 9 March 1842 "for time and all eternity" to Joseph Smith.[a] Sayers married Edward Sayers on 23 January 1841 and signed an affidavit dated 1 May 1869 attesting that she was "married or sealed" to Joseph Smith in February 1843.[b] Evidence for a marriage or sealing between Lyon (who had married Windsor Lyon in March 1838) and Joseph Smith is less compelling, as it is based on an unsigned, unnotarized affidavit-in-the-making incompletely dated to 1869. Two copies of this incomplete affidavit are known; both say that Lyon was "married or sealed" to Joseph Smith, although one gives 8 February 1842 as the date and the other gives 8 February 1843.[c] (a. Smart, *Mormon Midwife*, 276. b. "Hymenial," *Times and Seasons*, 15 Feb. 1841, 2:324; Ruth Vose Sayers, Affidavit, Salt Lake Co., Utah Territory, 1 May 1869, in Joseph F. Smith, Affidavits about Celestial Marriage, 1:9, 4:9. c. Sylvia Porter Lyon, Statements, 1869, in Joseph F. Smith, Affidavits about Celestial Marriage, 1:60, 2:62.)

59. Bushman, *Rough Stone Rolling*, 437–446.

60. The abuse extended beyond Nauvoo and beyond Joseph Smith's lifetime. In May 1845, Parley P. Pratt of the Quorum of the Twelve issued a carefully worded statement in New York warning church members in the East of unauthorized relationships between men and women while reaffirming the reality of properly performed "sealings, and covenants" designed "to secure the union of parents, children and companions in the world to come." (Parley P. Pratt, "This Number Closes the First Volume of the 'Prophet,'" *The Prophet*, 24 May 1845, [2].)

61. JS, Journal, 10 Apr. 1842.

Bennett was eventually expelled from the Masonic lodge, dishonorably discharged from the Nauvoo Legion, and excommunicated from the church.[62] Faced with censure from many directions, Bennett resigned as mayor, left Nauvoo, and wrote emotionally charged letters to the *Sangamo Journal* and other newspapers accusing Smith and other church leaders of a variety of crimes and improprieties.[63] Bennett also lectured for pay against Joseph Smith and Mormonism in several eastern cities and eventually published a book attacking the church and its leader.[64]

The willingness of the *Sangamo Journal* and others to publish John C. Bennett's claims, and the inclination of more recent authors to accept those allegations at face value, obscures the contempt in which many others at the time—including some who opposed Joseph Smith and the church he led—held Bennett and his reports. The *Boston Courier,* for example, had little regard for the "pretended revelations of J. C. Bennett . . . an offender against decency, who having been punished for his faults now wishes to take vengeance upon his judges for their righteous decisions."[65] Thomas Ford remembered Bennett as "probably the greatest scamp in the western country," while Horace Greeley, editor of the *New York Tribune,* saw Bennett's book as "nothing more than a collection of all the newspaper trash about the Mormons that has been published for the last few years."[66] Similarly, the editor of the *Boston Investigator* made it clear that although he questioned the claims of Mormonism, he doubted "the notorious *John C. Bennett*" and his "miserable catch-penny book" even more:

---

62. In the official notice informing the public of Bennett's excommunication, church leaders wrote that they were withdrawing "the hand of fellowship" from Bennett. ("Notice," *Times and Seasons,* 15 June 1842, 3:830.)

63. See Bennett's letters printed in the 8, 15, and 22 July, 19 August, and 2 September 1842 issues of the *Sangamo Journal*. As a Whig paper, the *Sangamo Journal* had been publishing articles against the church ever since Joseph Smith published his endorsement of the Democratic candidate for Illinois governor. (See p. xvi herein.)

64. In his letters and in his 1842 book, *History of the Saints,* Bennett referred to plural marriage as "spiritual wifery"—a term not employed in Joseph Smith's revelations or in other sources generated by those who participated in plural marriage in Nauvoo. Similarly, Bennett's description of Joseph Smith's plural wives as a "seraglio . . . divided into three distinct orders, or degrees" appears to be a creative account uncorroborated by other sources. James Arlington Bennet, who had recently discussed the forthcoming book with John C. Bennett himself, wrote Smith that he (John C. Bennett) "expects to make a fortune" out of his book. Bennett's book and lectures were a financial success; for two years, his biographer notes, Bennett "had no known revenue other than the royalties from the book and his lecture fees." (Bennett, *History of the Saints,* 218–225; James Arlington Bennet to JS, 1 Sept. 1842, p. 155 herein; Smith, *Saintly Scoundrel,* 127.)

65. "The Mormons," *Boston Courier,* 26 Sept. 1842, [1].

66. Ford, *History of Illinois,* 263; "Literary Notices," *New York Daily Tribune,* 1 Nov. 1842, [1].

We place no sort of reliance . . . upon any testimony of Bennett himself, and indeed the testimony which he says was given by others is rendered suspicious by his own contemptible treatment of the Mormons. He says he went among them a stranger; they gave him a friendly welcome, elevated him to stations of honor and trust, and for years he lived upon their bounty. When he could no longer fleece them, the ungrateful whelp, in return for their kindness, published to the world a large volume of their pretended vices and immoralities. . . . We have no confidence in the statements of a fellow guilty of such consummate meanness and hypocrisy, and we cannot suffer any extract from his vile work to appear in our paper without saying beforehand, that we heartily despise and detest him.[67]

Even William Law, who had served as a counselor to Joseph Smith before turning against him and publishing the *Nauvoo Expositor*, remembered Bennett as a "scoundrel" rather than as an ally whose charges against Smith might be used to sustain his own.[68]

Such assessments by Bennett's contemporaries suggest that historians must be cautious when using Bennett's reports as a means of understanding events in Nauvoo—including some recorded in Joseph Smith's journal. For example, several entries in the journal reference "certain difficulties" and "surmises which existed" between Smith and Sidney Rigdon during this period, as well as the disaffection of Rigdon's nineteen-year-old daughter, Nancy, from the church.[69] Some authors have found the explanation for these difficulties in Bennett's claim that Nancy had refused Joseph Smith's invitation to become one of his plural wives.[70] While the cause of these "difficulties" may have been a rejected proposal of marriage to Nancy, it is far from certain. Other issues also served as a wedge between Rigdon and Smith in Nauvoo, and given the nature of the evidence, it is not certain that such a proposal was even made in the first place.[71] For his own part, Joseph Smith summarily dismissed Bennett's

---

67. "Mormon Bible," *Boston Investigator*, 26 July 1843, [3]; italics in original.
68. "The Mormons in Nauvoo," *Salt Lake Daily Tribune*, 3 July 1887, [6].
69. JS, Journal, 12 May and 21 Aug. 1842, pp. 55, 97 herein.
70. "Astounding Mormon Disclosures! Letter from Gen. Bennett," *Sangamo Journal* (Springfield, IL), 8 July 1842, [2]; "Further Mormon Developments!! 2d Letter from Gen. Bennett," *Sangamo Journal*, 15 July 1842, [2].
71. Some sources corroborate Bennett's charge, while others refute it. For example, Bennett later published portions of a purported letter from Rigdon's son-in-law George W. Robinson to James Arlington Bennet repeating the allegation, and John W. Rigdon, Nancy's younger brother, signed an affidavit more than sixty years later to the same effect. On the other hand, Orson Hyde asserted in 1845 that Nancy created the story of a proposal after Joseph Smith had reproved her for immoral behavior. The well-known "Happiness" letter Bennett published in the *Sangamo Journal* in August 1842 from (Bennett claimed) Joseph Smith to Nancy fails, even if taken at face value, to clarify the circumstances behind its genesis. The letter can be read in light of plural marriage without requiring it to refer to a proposal to Nancy and, given its emphasis on the blessings following obedience, may even have its origin in an issue altogether unrelated to plural marriage. (Bennett, *History of the Saints*, 243–247; John W. Rigdon,

charges as falsehoods and called for elders to "go forth and deluge the States with a flood of truth" to counteract Bennett's influence.[72]

Bennett similarly accused Joseph Smith of seeking an illicit relationship with Orson Pratt's wife, Sarah, while Orson was on a mission.[73] Sarah supported Bennett's charge, sending Orson into a fit of despair and distrust. Orson's subsequent refusal to retract his public statements "against Joseph & others" during the course of a four-day hearing with the Quorum of the Twelve led to his excommunication.[74] Joseph Smith emphatically denied the charge: "She lied about me," he told members of the Twelve. "I never made the offer which she said I did."[75] According to his journal, Joseph Smith at one point also "stated before the public a general outline of J[ohn] C. Bennetts conduct . . . with regard to Sis P[ratt]"[76]—a cryptic phrase possibly clarified by other sources alleging that Sarah had actually been involved with Bennett in an adulterous relationship during Orson's absence.[77] Both Sarah and Orson Pratt were eventually rebaptized and reconfirmed under the hand of Joseph Smith himself, thus setting the issue at rest for the time being.[78]

In another dramatic accusation, Bennett charged Joseph Smith with masterminding the 6 May 1842 assassination attempt on Lilburn W. Boggs, the former Missouri governor who had ordered the removal of the Mormons from the state in 1838.[79] Although others had started this rumor, Bennett actively circulated it through his letters published in the *Sangamo Journal* and the St. Louis *Bulletin*. Missouri authorities could do little on the basis of these claims, but

---

Affidavit, Salt Lake Co., Utah, 28 July 1905, pp. 6–8, in Joseph F. Smith, Affidavits about Celestial Marriage, CHL; *Speech of Orson Hyde,* 27–28; "6th Letter From Gen. Bennett," *Sangamo Journal* [Springfield, IL], 19 Aug. 1842, [2].)

72. JS, Journal, 26 Aug. 1842. A number of affidavits, some of which were collected earlier, attesting to Bennett's immoral conduct were published at this time. (See *Affidavits and Certificates,* [Nauvoo, IL: 31 Aug. 1842], copy at CHL.)

73. "Further Mormon Developments!! 2d Letter from Gen. Bennett," *Sangamo Journal* (Springfield, IL), 15 July 1842, [2].

74. Woodruff, Journal, 10 Aug.–18 Sept. 1842.

75. Quorum of the Twelve Apostles, Minutes, 20 Jan. 1843.

76. JS, Journal, 15 July 1842.

77. *Affidavits and Certificates,* [Nauvoo, IL: 31 Aug. 1842], copy at CHL.

78. JS, Journal, 20 Jan. 1843; Woodruff, Journal, [20] Jan. 1843. In 1875, after she had separated from Orson and left the church, Sarah claimed that she had "not been a believer in the Mormon doctrines for thirty years." Some evidence suggests that Sarah renewed her accusation against Joseph Smith later in life. (Papers in the Case of Maxwell vs. Cannon, H.R. Misc. Doc. 49, 43rd Cong., 1st Sess., p. 32 [1873]; Von Wymetal, *Joseph Smith the Prophet,* 60–61; "Workings of Mormonism Related by Mrs. Orson Pratt," 1884, CHL; Kate Field, "Horrors of Polygamy," *San Francisco Chronicle,* 4 Dec. 1892, 12.)

79. "Further Mormon Developments!! 2d Letter from Gen. Bennett," *Sangamo Journal* (Springfield, IL), 15 July 1842, [2]; "Gen. Bennett's 4th Letter," and "Disclosures—the Attempted Murder of Boggs!" *Sangamo Journal,* 22 July 1842, [2].

when Boggs himself signed an affidavit on 20 July 1842 accusing Joseph Smith of complicity in the attempted assassination, Missouri governor Thomas Reynolds requested that Illinois governor Thomas Carlin deliver the accused to Missouri authorities. Carlin issued an arrest warrant, and on 8 August 1842 Smith was arrested in Nauvoo by Thomas King, undersheriff of Adams County. Joseph Smith petitioned the Nauvoo Municipal Court for a writ of habeas corpus, which was granted. King, unsure of the writ's validity, returned to Quincy with the writ of habeas corpus and the governor's arrest warrant in hand for further direction from Governor Carlin. Unable to hold a prisoner without an arrest warrant in their possession, Nauvoo authorities released Smith, who went into hiding and evaded authorities until federal district judge Nathaniel Pope ruled in early January 1843 that he be discharged from arrest. As more pages and entries in Joseph Smith's Nauvoo journals are devoted to aspects of the extradition attempt than to any other single topic, an appendix providing a summary of the case and the full text of the most important relevant legal documents has been included in this volume.[80]

The journals reproduced here note both the momentous and the mundane. Several of Joseph Smith's dreams find their way into the journals, as do some of his reminiscences, opinions about current events, and various excursions. Mission calls, church disciplinary decisions, and references to local politics, economic developments, and newspaper articles find a place as well. Following the 4 March 1843 entry in which Smith criticized Willard Richards for a failure in "naming or noticing surrou[n]ding objects. weather &c," observations on the weather begin to appear. Other topics covered in these journals include Joseph Smith's petition for bankruptcy, his emerging friendship with James Arlington Bennet, and discussions in the Illinois legislature about repealing or amending the Nauvoo city charter. The journals also include copies of letters, reports of speeches and blessings, and other documents. With the exception of the 16 and 23 August 1842 entries, which include lengthy benedictory statements about individuals who had helped Joseph Smith over the years, it is doubtful that he dictated any portion of these journals. The first-person pronouns that occur in the Nauvoo journals do not appear to be formal dictations but probably reflect the scribes' conscious efforts to make this document Joseph Smith's personal journal and to capture, on occasion, his own language.

The journal as kept by Willard Richards differs markedly from some of Joseph Smith's earlier journals. For example, where Smith's 1832–1834 and 1835–1836 journals contain many lengthy, descriptive accounts of his activities—some in his own hand—Richards's entries are often short and terse and

---

80. See Appendix 1, p. 377 herein.

provide only the barest outlines of Joseph Smith's activities. On numerous occasions, even for several days running, Richards failed to record anything at all. William Clayton, who had primary responsibility for keeping the journal during Richards's absence, also wrote in an abbreviated style at times. Nevertheless, the events, teachings, revelations, ordinances, and organizational changes documented in the journals constitute a significant contribution to foundational Latter-day Saint identity, beliefs, and practices. The journals were also part of Joseph Smith's attempt to fulfill earlier commandments to keep a history—instructions that he took seriously but that often had been beyond his immediate ability to accomplish.[81] Perhaps most important, Joseph Smith's Nauvoo journals provide scholars and other interested readers with a much-needed window into his life, personality, and religious contributions.

---

81. See Revelation, ca. 8 Mar. 1831–B, in Doctrine and Covenants 63, 1844 ed. [D&C 47]; JS, Kirtland, OH, to William W. Phelps, [Independence, MO], 27 Nov. 1832, in JS Letterbook 1, pp. 1–4 [D&C 85].

Editorial Method

The goal of the Joseph Smith Papers Project is to present verbatim transcripts of Joseph Smith's papers in their entirety, making available the most essential sources of Smith's life and work and preserving the content of aging manuscripts from damage or loss. The papers include documents that were created by Joseph Smith, whether written or dictated by him or created by others under his direction, or that were owned by Smith, that is, received by him and kept in his office (as with incoming correspondence). Under these criteria—authorship and ownership—the project intends to publish, either in letterpress volumes or electronic form, every extant Joseph Smith document to which its editors can obtain access. The Journals series of *The Joseph Smith Papers* presents an unaltered and unabridged transcript of each of Smith's known journals.

Rules of Transcription

Because of aging and sometimes damaged texts and imprecise penmanship, not all handwriting is legible or can be fully deciphered. Hurried writers often rendered words carelessly, and even the best writers and spellers left out letters on occasion or formed them imperfectly and incompletely. Text transcription and verification is therefore an imperfect art more than a science. Judgments about capitalization, for example, are informed not only by looking at the specific case at hand but by understanding the usual characteristics of each particular writer. The same is true for deciphering spelling and punctuation. If a letter or other character is ambiguous, deference is given to the author's or scribe's usual spelling and punctuation. Where this is ambiguous, modern spelling and punctuation are favored. Even the best transcribers and verifiers will differ from one another in making such judgments. Interested readers may wish to compare our transcriptions with images of the original manuscripts at the Joseph Smith Papers website, josephsmithpapers.org, to better understand how our transcription rules have been applied to create these transcripts. Viewing the originals also provides other information that cannot be conveyed by typography.

To ensure accuracy in representing the texts, transcripts were verified three times, each time by a different set of eyes. The first two verifications were done using high-resolution scanned images. The first was a visual collation of the journal images with the transcripts, while the second was an independent and double-blind image-to-transcript tandem proofreading. The third and final verification of the transcripts was a visual collation with the original document. At this stage, the verifier employed magnification and ultraviolet light as needed to read badly faded text, recover heavily stricken material, untangle characters written over each other, and recover words canceled by messy "wipe erasures" made when the ink was still wet or removed by knife scraping after the ink had dried. The verified transcripts meet or exceed the transcription and verification requirements of the Modern Language Association's Committee on Scholarly Editions and the National Archives and Records Administration's National Historical Publications and Records Commission.

The approach to transcription employed in *The Joseph Smith Papers* is conservative by historical documentary editing standards. The transcripts render most words letter by letter as accurately as possible, preserving the exact spelling of the originals. This includes incomplete words, variant spellings of personal names, repeated words, and idiosyncratic grammatical constructions. The transcripts also preserve substantive revisions made by the journal keepers. Canceled words are typographically rendered with the strikethrough bar, while inserted words are enclosed within angle brackets. Cancellations and insertions are also transcribed letter by letter when an original word—such as "sparingly" or "attend"—was changed to a new word simply by canceling or inserting letters at the beginning or end of the word—such as "sparing~~ly~~" or "attend⟨ed⟩". However, for cases in which an original word was changed to a new word by canceling or inserting letters in the middle of the word, to improve readability the original word is presented stricken in its entirety, followed by the revised word in its entirety. For example, when "falling" was revised to "failing" by canceling the first "l" and inserting an "i", the revision is transcribed as "~~falling~~ ⟨failing⟩" instead of "fal⟨i⟩ling". Insubstantial cancellations and insertions—those used only to correct spelling and punctuation—are silently emended, and only the final spelling and punctuation are reproduced.

The transcription of punctuation differs from the original in a few other respects. Single instances of periods, commas, apostrophes, and dashes are all faithfully rendered without regard to their grammatical correctness, except that periods are not reproduced when they appear immediately before a word, with no space between the period and the word. Also, in some cases of repetitive punctuation, only the final mark or final intention is transcribed while any other characters are silently omitted. Dashes of various lengths are standardized to a consistent pattern. The short vertical strokes commonly used in early American writing for abbreviation punctuation are transcribed as periods, but abbreviation punctuation is not reproduced when an abbreviation is expanded in square brackets. Flourishes and other decorative inscriptions are not reproduced or noted. Ellipsis marks appear in the featured text only where they occur in the original manuscript and are standardized to a consistent format; they do not represent an editorial abridgment. Punctuation is never added silently.

Incorrect dates, place names, and other errors of fact are left to stand. The intrusive *sic,* sometimes used to affirm original misspelling, is never employed, although where words or phrases are especially difficult to understand, editorial clarifications or corrections are inserted in brackets. Correct and complete spellings of personal names are supplied in brackets the first time each incorrect or incomplete name appears in a journal entry (unless the correct name cannot be determined). Place names that may be hard to identify are also clarified or corrected within brackets. When two or more words are inscribed together without any intervening space and the words were not a compound according to standard contemporary usage or the scribe's or author's consistent practice, the words are transcribed as separate words for readability. Journal entries appear in their original sequence, retaining out-of-order and duplicate entries.

Formatting is standardized. Original paragraphing is retained, except that the first paragraph of the journal entry is always run in with the original dateline. Standardized editorial datelines—typographically distinguishable from the text—have also been added before every entry for convenience of use. All paragraphs are given in a standard format, with indention regularized and with blank lines between paragraphs omitted. Blank space of approximately five or more lines in the original is noted, as are lesser amounts of blank vertical space that appear significant. Extra space between words or sentences is not captured unless it appears the scribe left a blank space as a placeholder to be filled in later. Block quotations of letters, minutes, revelations, and other similar items within entries are set apart with block indentions, even when, as in a few cases, such items are not set off in the original. Horizontal rules and other devices inscribed between entries to mark them off from each other are not reproduced. Line ends are neither typographically reproduced nor symbolically represented. Because of the great number of words broken across a line at any point in the word, with or without a hyphen, end-of-line hyphens are not transcribed and there is no effort to note or keep a record of such words and hyphens. This leaves open the possibility that the hyphen of an ambiguously hyphenated compound escaped transcription or that a compound word correctly broken across a line ending without a hyphen is mistakenly transcribed as two words. As many end-of-line hyphens have been editorially introduced in the transcripts, a hyphen appearing at the end of a line may or may not be original to the document.

Many but not all changes in color of ink are noted. In some cases, the ink color changes mid-entry to match the ink color of the following entry, indicating that the latter portion of an entry likely was added at the time the subsequent entry was inscribed. These and other significant color changes are noted. However, it is apparent in some cases that a scribe had more than one color of ink at hand because the scribe changed colors often, even in the middle of sentences. Such changes in ink color are not generally considered noteworthy. In some entries, cancellations and insertions were made in a different color than the original inscription. Because these cancellations and insertions are already marked as revisions—with the horizontal strikethrough bar for cancellations and with a pair of angle brackets for insertions—the color of the ink used for the revision is not noted.

Redactions and other changes made on the manuscript after the original production of the text, such as when later scribes used the journals for drafting history, are not transcribed. Labeling and other forms of archival marking are similarly passed by in silence.

Transcription Symbols

The effort to render mistakes, canceled material, and later insertions sometimes complicates readability by putting Joseph Smith and his scribes behind the "barbed wire" of symbolic transcription. However, conveying such elements with transcription symbols can aid in understanding the text and the order and ways in which the words were inscribed. Typesetting can never effectively represent all the visual aspects of a document; it cannot fully capture such features as the formation of letters and other characters, spacing between words and between paragraphs, varying lengths of dashes and paragraph indentions, and varying methods of cancellation and the location of insertions. Despite its limitations, a conservative transcription method more faithfully represents the process by which the text was inscribed—especially cancellations and insertions—rather than just the final result.

The following symbols are used to transcribe and expand the text:

/ⁿ	In documents inscribed by more than one person, the slash mark indicates a change in handwriting. A footnote identifies the previous and commencing scribes.
[roman]	Brackets enclose editorial insertions that expand, correct, or clarify the text. This convention may be applied to the abbreviated or incorrect spelling of a personal name, such as Brigham Yo[u]ng, or of a place, such as Westleville [Wesleyville]. Obsolete or ambiguous abbreviations are expanded with br[acket]s. Bracketed editorial insertions also provide reasonable reconstructions of badly miss[p]elled worsd [words]. Missing or illegible words may be

	supplied within brackets in cases where the supplied word is based on textual or contextual evidence. Bracketed punctuation is added only when necessary to follow complex wording.
[roman?]	A question mark is added to conjectured editorial insertions, such as where an entire word was [accidentally?] omitted and where it is difficult to maintain the sense of a sentence without some editorial insertion.
[*italic*]	Significant descriptions of the writing medium—especially those inhibiting legibility—and of spacing between the inscriptions are italicized and enclosed in brackets: [*hole burned in paper*], [*leaf torn*], [*blank*], [*9 lines blank*], [*pages 99–102 blank*].
[*illegible*]	An illegible word is represented by the italicized word [*illegible*] enclosed in brackets.
◊	An illegible character within a partially legible word is rendered with a hollow diamond. Repeated diamonds represent the approximate number of illegible characters (for example: sto◊◊◊◊s).
[p. x]	Bracketed editorial insertions indicate the end of an originally numbered manuscript page, regardless of the location of the written page number on the manuscript page.
[p. [x]]	Bracketing of the page number itself indicates that the manuscript page was not originally numbered and that the number of the page is editorially supplied.
<u>underlined</u>	Underlining is typographically reproduced. <u>Individually</u> <u>underlined</u> <u>words</u> are distinguished from <u>passages underlined with one continuous line</u>.
superscript	Superscription is typographically reproduc^{ed}.
~~canceled~~	A single horizontal strikethrough bar is used to indicate any method of cancellation: strikethrough and cross-out, wipe erasure and knife erasure, overwriting, or other methods. ~~Individually~~ ~~canceled~~ ~~words~~ are distinguished from ~~passages eliminated with a single cancellation~~. Characters individual~~ly~~ canceled at the begi~~nning~~ or end of a word are distinguished from ~~words canceled in their entirety~~.
⟨inserted⟩	Insertions in the text—whether interlinear, intralinear, or marginal—are enclosed in angle brackets. Letter⟨s⟩ and other characters individual⟨ly⟩ insert⟨ed⟩ at the beginning or end of a word are distinguished from ⟨words⟩ inserted in ⟨their⟩ entirety.
bold	Joseph Smith's handwriting is rendered in boldface type. Bracketed editorial insertions made within passages of **Smith's own h[and]w[riting]** are also rendered in boldface type.
[roman]	Stylized brackets represent [brackets] used in the original text.

[shorthand]   Instances of Taylor shorthand—a phonetic system of symbols first published by Samuel Taylor in 1786—are expanded into longhand in the running text and enclosed by ⟦stylized brackets⟧, with precise transliterations and any necessary description or explanation appearing in footnotes.

TEXT   The word TEXT begins textual footnotes describing significant details not comprehended by this scheme of symbolic transcription.

| A line break artificially imposed in an original document is rendered as a vertical line in textual notes.

Annotation Conventions

The Joseph Smith Papers do not present a unified narrative. Annotations—including historical introductions, editorial notes, and footnotes—supply background and context to help readers better understand and use the documents. The aim of the annotation is to serve scholars and students of early Mormon history and American religious history generally, whose familiarity with these fields may vary widely.

The *Papers* cite original sources where possible and practical. Secondary sources of sound scholarship are cited when they usefully distill several primary sources. Quotations from primary sources preserve original spelling but silently emend cancellations and insertions (unless judged highly significant).

Certain conventions simplify the presentation of the annotation. Joseph Smith is usually referred to by the initials JS. The terms *Saint, Latter-day Saint,* and *Mormon*—all used by mid-1834 in reference to church members—are employed interchangeably here. Most sources are referred to by a shortened citation form, with a complete citation given in the Works Cited. Some documents are referred to by editorial titles rather than by their original titles or the titles given in the catalogs of their current repositories. These editorial titles are in some cases similar to informal names by which the documents have come to be known. The editorial titles are listed in the Works Cited along with the complete citations by which the documents can be found in repositories. Page numbers for cross references to other journal entries in this volume are provided when the referenced material may be difficult to find, as in the case of a long entry or entries that do not appear in chronological order; otherwise, only the date of the cross-referenced entry is given. The most important sources used in annotating a volume are discussed in the Essay on Sources preceding the Works Cited.

The volumes in this series use a citation style that lists all source citations at the end of the footnote. Because of the complexity of some footnotes and the difficulty readers might have in determining which source citations document particular statements within such footnotes, superscript letters are sometimes used to key specific statements to their corresponding documentation. Though it goes beyond conventional citation style, this detailed approach may best serve researchers using volumes of the Journals series as reference works.

The annotation extensively cites Joseph Smith's revelations. Many of these revelations were first collected and published in 1833, with numbered chapters and paragraphs (or verses), as the Book of Commandments. An expanded collection, organized into sections and with new versification, was published in 1835 as the Doctrine and Covenants. In 1844, at the time of his death, Smith was overseeing publication of a revised edition of the Doctrine and Covenants, which was published later that year. Since then, the Doctrine and Covenants has been published in several editions, each including newly canonized revelations or other items.

Source citations in this volume identify revelations by their original date and by a citation of the version most relevant to the particular instance of annotation (usually the 1835 edition of the Doctrine and Covenants). In cases in which two or more revelations bear the same date, a letter of the alphabet is appended so that each revelation has a unique editorial title—for example, May 1829–A or May 1829–B. Revelation citations also include a bracketed "D&C" reference that provides the Doctrine and Covenants section and verse numbers that have been standard in The Church of Jesus Christ of Latter-day Saints since 1876. For example, the last portion of the revelation that provided a basis for the Mormon health code is cited as Revelation, 27 Feb. 1833, in Doctrine and Covenants 80:3, 1835 ed. [D&C 89:16–21] (see figure).

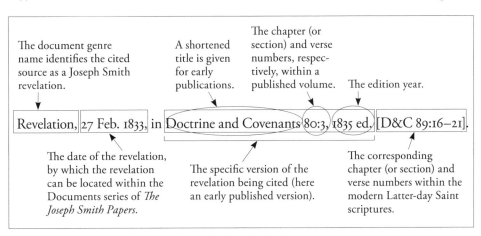

Citation format for Joseph Smith revelations.

Bracketed D&C references are provided for the benefit of Latter-day Saints, who can easily access the revelations in their familiar canon of scriptural works, and other students of early Mormonism who may wish to access the most widely available editions of these revelations. A table titled Corresponding

Section Numbers in Editions of the Doctrine and Covenants is provided following the Works Cited to help readers refer from the cited version of a canonized revelation to other published versions of the same revelation. For more information about revelation citations, see the aforementioned table and the introduction to the Works Cited.

Smith's revelations and revelatory translations published outside of the Doctrine and Covenants, such as the Book of Mormon, are referenced in *The Joseph Smith Papers* to an early published or manuscript version, with references to modern Latter-day Saint publications added in brackets. These books of Latter-day Saint scripture are described in more detail in the introduction to the Works Cited. When the Bible is used in annotation, the King James Version—the version read by Smith and his followers and contemporaries as well as by English-speaking Latter-day Saints today—is referenced.

In addition to the annotation in the main body of a volume, several supplementary resources in the back of each volume aid in understanding the text. As many of the places, people, organizations, and terms mentioned in the journals appear more than once, the reference material serves to remove duplicate footnotes and to otherwise systematically reduce the annotation in the main body. To minimize repetition and interruption, only rarely will annotation within the journals directly refer readers to the reference material in the back.

Many of the people whose names appear in the journals in this series have been identified. In most cases, information about these people appears in the Biographical Directory rather than in the notes. Some names have silently been left without identification either because resources did not permit research or because no information was found. Complete documentation for reference material in the back and for the timeline and map included at the front of the volume may be found on the Joseph Smith Papers website, josephsmithpapers.org, along with other resources.

The Journals series will be indexed cumulatively in the final volume of the series. A printable, searchable index for volume 2 is available at the Joseph Smith Papers website.

JOURNALS
DECEMBER 1841–APRIL 1843

First Nauvoo journal. "The Book of the Law of the Lord" includes Joseph Smith's journal entries as well as revelation transcripts and donation records. The journal entries, which were inscribed for Smith by Willard Richards and William Clayton, cover the period from December 1841 to December 1842. Eliza R. Snow and Erastus Derby assisted Clayton by copying letters into the journal. The inset shows the label affixed to the spine of the volume. Book of the Law of the Lord, Church History Library, Salt Lake City. (Photographs by Welden C. Andersen.)

JOURNAL, DECEMBER 1841– DECEMBER 1842

Source Note

JS, Journal, Dec. 1841–Dec. 1842; handwriting of William Clayton, Willard Richards, Eliza R. Snow, and Erastus Derby; signatures of William Clayton and Willard Richards; 90 pages; in "The Book of the Law of the Lord," Record Book, 1841–1845, CHL. Includes shorthand; also includes redactions and use marks.

JS's journal for December 1841–December 1842 was inscribed in a large, leather-bound blank book made with thick paper. The paper bears a star-shaped watermark in the middle of each leaf and was printed with forty-seven blue lines on each side. The text block was originally formed with thirty gatherings of eight leaves each. The second gathering, however, has only six leaves. This six-leaf gathering was either a binding error or one sheet came loose from the binding before the book was inscribed (the book's inscription and pagination runs through this gathering without skipping any text or page numbers). The gatherings were sewn all along. Each set of front and back endpapers consisted of a gathering of four leaves of unlined paper, but only two leaves are now extant in the back gathering. The trimmed pages measure 16¼ × 10½ inches (41 × 27 cm). Headbands were sewn onto the text block. The exterior pages of the endpapers are joined to the pasteboards with a strip of pink cloth. Marbled papers featuring a shell pattern with green body and veins of red and yellow are glued to the inside covers of the boards and to the exterior page of each gathering of endpapers. The leaf edges are stained green. The text block is bound in a ledger style to the boards. The spine was constructed with four false raised bands demarcating five panels. The boards and spine are covered in suede leather with additional leather strips over the top and bottom of the book. The suede leather was blind tooled on the outside covers, the raised bands of the spine, and the turned-in edges on the inside cover. The additional leather strips, which also cover the first and fifth panels of the spine, are embossed with dual lines and vegetal designs along the borders and have gold line filling. The spine is further embossed with the number "6" in 20-point type on the fifth panel. The second and fourth panels have black-painted squares of paper glued to them. These feature gold lining and decoration at the top and bottom. The completed volume measures 17 × 11 × 2¼ inches (43 × 28 × 6 cm) and includes 244 free leaves. A penciled inscription at the inside top corner of page [ii]—the verso of the front marbled flyleaf—gives what appears to be an expensive price for this high-quality blank book: "bth | 10.00".

Robert B. Thompson inscribed nine revelations in the book on the first twenty-three pages of lined paper. Willard Richards made minor revisions to these revelation texts. Apparently either Richards or Thompson inscribed page numbers on pages 3–18, beginning at the first page of lined paper, in a stylized script. Richards inscribed page numbers on pages 19–25 as well as on the next several dozen pages—which included journal entries for JS and records of donations in cash and in kind for the construction of the Nauvoo temple. At some point page [1], the recto of the last leaf of unlined endpaper in the front of the book, was inscribed with a title: "THE | BOOK | of the | LAW | of the | LORD". Because these words are hand lettered in various ornate styles, the handwriting cannot be identified. A matching title appears on the spine of the volume: the square label of black paper on the second panel of the spine bears a smaller square label of white paper with a hand-lettered inscription: "LAW | — of the — | LORD." Willard Richards inscribed pages 26–126 of the book, with help from William Clayton on pages 27–28 and 72–87. Clayton inscribed the rest of the volume, pages 127–477, with help from Erastus Derby on pages 168–171 and from Eliza R. Snow on pages 189–190 and 192–201. These clerks and scribes generally paginated the book and inscribed dateline page headers along the way as they inscribed its texts.[1]

The donation records constitute the bulk of the volume. The journal entries are inscribed on pages 26, 31, 33, 36, 39, 43, 44, 48, 56–61, 66–67, 88–95, 122–135, and 164–215. As is also the case with the pages bearing donation records, many of the pages bearing journal entries have vertical margin lines inscribed in graphite. The journal entries themselves are inscribed in ink that is now brown. Pages 165–181, however, either include or are entirely in blue ink. Some of the entries begin with a descriptive heading as well as a dateline. The entry for 6 January 1842, for example, features the large heading "The New Year". Page 58 features the large double underlined heading "Journal of President Joseph". Many of the entries are divided by horizontal lines. Where groups of journal entries span several pages, notes written at the beginning and end of these spans reference the previous or succeeding pages of journal entries.[2] At various stages in the production of the volume, Richards and Clayton signed their names to their work (pages 126, 181, 215).

The volume contains a number of redactions that were made as the journal entries were later revised for inclusion in the "History of Joseph Smith" published in Mormon newspapers in the mid-nineteenth century.[3] Most of these redactions, made in graphite, were subsequently erased.[4] The upper left-hand corner of page 3 bears the graphite inscription "6", a redactive note on page 43 is inscribed in purple pencil, and red-penciled "X"s appear in the margins next to entries on pages 164 and 180. Notes written on three white and three blue slips of paper of various sizes have been inserted in various places, as well as a clipped portion of a Nauvoo-era elder's certificate form with no notes (apparently just a placeholder). There are also two leaves of pink paper just inside the front of the volume. All of these slips and leaves of paper are loose and appear to have been added to the book subsequent to its use as a journal.

The book is intricately related to its successor volume, the 1844–1846 donation record, and to a volume that indexed the donation records.[5] The "Law of the Lord" is listed as such in inventories of church records made in Salt Lake City, Utah, in the 1850s. These show that the volume was held for a time in the office of church president Brigham Young.[6] In 1880, John Taylor, president of the Quorum

---

1. The page numbers on pages 19–71, 86–90, and 122–125 are in the handwriting of Willard Richards; on pages 72–85, 91–121, 126–167, and 171–477, in the handwriting of William Clayton; and on pages 168–170, in the handwriting of Erastus Derby. There are two pages numbered 453. Pages 476–477 constitute the last leaf of lined paper. The headers generally consist of a year or a month and year. The headers inscribed on pages 26–27, 29–71, 88–95, 119, and 121–126 are in the handwriting of Richards; the headers inscribed on pages 28, 72–87, 96–118, 120, 127–167, and 172–215 are in the handwriting of Clayton; pages 168–171, which were inscribed by Derby, have no headers. A few other pages are missing headers.

2. For example, page 135 points the reader to page 164, which begins by noting the continuation from page 135.

3. This serialized history drew on the journals herein, beginning with the 4 July 1855 issue of the *Deseret News* and with the 3 January 1857 issue of the *LDS Millennial Star*.

4. Most of these now-erased graphite inscriptions are recoverable with bright white light and magnification. Pages 209–215, which were not erased, represent the state of the journal entries generally when they were used for drafting the "History of Joseph Smith."

5. Tithing and Donation Record, 1844–1846, CHL; Trustee-in-trust, Index and Accounts, 1841–1847, CHL.

6. "Inventory. Historian's Office. 4th April 1855," [1]; "Inventory. Historians Office. G. S. L. City April 1.

of the Twelve Apostles, carried the book to a stake Relief Society conference in Salt Lake City.[7] At some point the book was marked on the spine with an archival sticker, which was later removed. The book eventually was housed with the papers of Joseph Fielding Smith, apparently during his tenure as church historian and recorder (1921–1970), and then became part of the First Presidency's papers when he became church president in 1970.[8] In 2010, the First Presidency gave custody of the book to the Church History Library.[9] This evidence indicates continuous institutional custody and authenticity.

Historical Introduction

Willard Richards, William Clayton, Eliza R. Snow, and Erastus Derby recorded JS's journal entries from 13 December 1841 through 20 December 1842 in a large leather-bound blank book. The book was first used by church recorder Robert B. Thompson to copy revelations. Between January 1841 and his death on 27 August the same year, Thompson recorded nine of JS's revelations, beginning with the 19 January 1841 revelation commanding the building of the Nauvoo, Illinois, temple and a boardinghouse called the Nauvoo House. On 11 December 1841, following his election as "sole Trustee in Trust for the Church" earlier in the year, JS instructed that all donations for building the Nauvoo temple be received directly through his office rather than through the committee overseeing construction of the temple. Two days later, he appointed Willard Richards of the Quorum of the Twelve Apostles as recorder for the temple and as his personal scribe. Richards then became custodian of the book Thompson had used for recording revelations, and Richards apparently began recording journal entries and tithing donations in some manner on that same day. However, the quality of inscription for the journal entries in the book suggests that they are copies of previously inscribed notes, and if Richards began making such notes in mid-December it is less certain when he began copying them into the book.[10] The book apparently was kept in the "counting room" on the lower floor of JS's red brick store on Water Street, where Richards received and entered donations and also inscribed JS's journal.[11]

Journal entries and donations were kept concurrently in the book, alternating sometimes every other page and chronologically leapfrogging each other. This pattern was especially pronounced near the beginning of the book, where donations and journal entries occasionally appear together on a single page. Over time, however, larger and larger blocks of text were dedicated to either donations or journal entries until eventually, in December 1842, the journal was transferred to another book. This slow separation or disentanglement

---

1857," [1]; "Historian's Office Inventory G. S. L. City March 19. 1858," [1]; "Historian's Office Catalogue Book March 1858," [11], Historian's Office, Catalogs and Inventories, 1846–1904, CHL.

7. Emmeline B. Wells, "Salt Lake Stake Relief Society Conference," *Women's Exponent,* 1 July 1880, 9:22.

8. "Inventory of President Joseph Fielding Smith's Safe," 23 May 1970, First Presidency, General Administration Files, CHL.

9. Letter of transfer, Salt Lake City, UT, 8 Jan. 2010, CHL.

10. One of Richards's entries records that he was ill "& did not take notes." Other entries, such as those dictated by JS to William Clayton while in hiding, are clearly copies of previously inscribed notes. (JS, Journal, 17 June 1842; 16 and 23 Aug. 1842.)

11. Clayton, History of the Nauvoo Temple, 16; Brigham Young et al., "Baptism for the Dead," *Times and Seasons,* 15 Dec. 1841, 3:626.

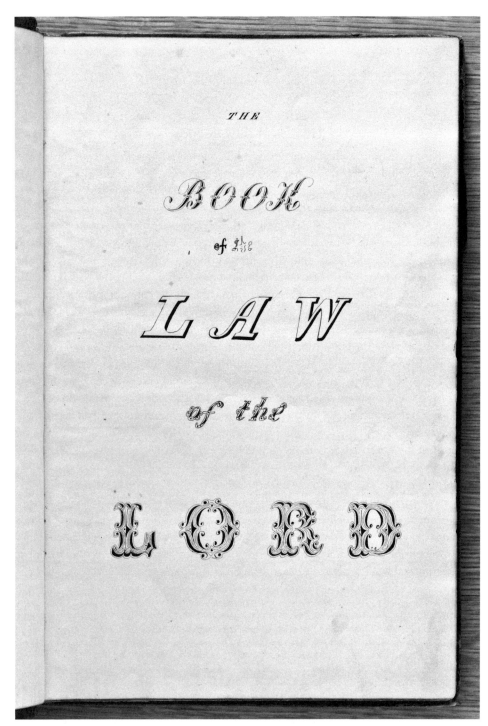

Title page of the Book of the Law of the Lord. Willard Richards and others inscribed revelations, donation records, and journal entries in the Book of the Law of the Lord, which begins with this ornately inscribed title page. Book of the Law of the Lord, p. [1], Church History Library, Salt Lake City. (Photograph by Welden C. Andersen.)

of the journal and donation records—the reasons for which are unclear—was completed long before the volume was filled; indeed, only 90 of the volume's 478 pages include journal entries, and all of these are within the first 215 pages. In several places it is clear that lists of donations were recorded earlier than were the journal entries found on preceding pages; that is, Richards and William Clayton—who was assigned to assist in the recorder's office 10 February 1842—left several pages blank between lists of donations and then later filled in those pages with journal entries.[12] This practice sometimes left the scribes with insufficient space to finish a journal entry before running into the list of donations, requiring them to continue the entry several pages later.[13]

The interspersing of journal entries with pages of donation records, as well as JS's conscious efforts to record the names of people who helped him, suggests that the volume as a whole was understood in terms of an 1832 revelation that "a hystory and a general church record" must be kept "of all things that transpire in Zion and of all those who consecrate properties . . . and also there manner of life and the[ir] faith and works." This record was to be kept in a book called "the book of the Law of God"—a book whose name parallels that of "the book of the law of the Lord" mentioned in the Old Testament.[14] Richards continued the pagination of Thompson's revelation transcripts and, at some point in time, the title "The Book of the Law of the Lord" was inscribed in the front of the book Richards was filling with journal entries and donation records. That the revelation transcripts, donation records, and journal entries appear under the same title and pagination suggests the book's creators understood its title to comprehend all of its parts.

During the first few months of keeping JS's journal, Richards included events that occurred before his appointment as JS's scribe and temple recorder as well as current journal entries. For example, in his 13 December 1841 entry on deteriorating conditions in Warsaw, Illinois, Richards explained what led church members to settle there in the first place. At times these retrospective entries eclipse the events of the day on which they were written and have no apparent connection to surrounding entries. The entries for 17 and 29 December 1841, for example, relate to Brigham Young's July 1841 arrival at Nauvoo following his mission to England and to the October 1841 laying of the cornerstone for the Nauvoo House, respectively, but they record nothing about the events of 17 and 29 December. Multiple entries for individual days, sometimes separated by several pages, add to the complexity of the first part of the journal and also suggest that Richards wrote retrospectively at least part of the time. Only after Richards moved into the Smith home in mid-January 1842 and was able to more closely observe JS's actions did the entries become more regular, and even then multiple entries occasionally occurred. Immediately preceding the entry for 15 January 1842, the header "Journal of President Joseph" appears—showing that by the time he moved into JS's home, Richards considered the daily entries he was keeping as journal entries.[15]

---

12. Clayton, History of the Nauvoo Temple, 18; Clayton, Journal, 10 Feb. 1843.

13. For example, the donation records on pages 136–163 were evidently inscribed before the 16 August 1842 journal entry, which begins on page 135 and is continued on page 164.

14. JS, Kirtland, OH, to William W. Phelps, [Independence, MO], 27 Nov. 1832, in JS Letterbook 1, pp. 1–2 [D&C 85:1–2, 5]; 2 Chronicles 17:9; 34:14; Nehemiah 9:3.

15. See also the entry for 29 June 1842, in which Richards transferred "this Journal" to his assistant

Richards kept JS's journal in the Book of the Law of the Lord through 29 June 1842, shortly after which he left for Richmond, Massachusetts, to bring his family to Nauvoo. Among the numerous topics addressed in Richards's entries are problems relating to the purchase of land in the Nauvoo area, the organization of the Female Relief Society, and the developing rift between JS and two of his close associates, John C. Bennett and Sidney Rigdon. When Richards left for Massachusetts, he transferred the book—and therefore JS's journal—to his assistant, William Clayton, to keep during his absence. Two months later, in early September, Clayton was appointed temple recorder, officially replacing Richards as custodian of the Book of the Law of the Lord. Some of Clayton's entries include accounts of JS's activities during the day as well as his activities later in the evening. In some of these entries, the record of the evening events is inscribed in an ink that differs from the ink he used to record JS's activities earlier in the day yet matches that of the following day's entry. This indicates that he was probably writing in the book about some events the very day they occurred.[16]

Clayton's first entry (30 June 1842) retrospectively records three events dealing with the Nauvoo temple—the dedication of the baptismal font on 8 November 1841, a miraculous healing in the waters of the font in February 1842, and a deposit made in the cornerstone on 25 September 1841. JS may have directed the inclusion of this material after having "heard the Recorder [Willard Richards] Read in the Law of the Lord" the day before;[17] alternatively, Clayton may have recorded it on his own in his role as assistant temple recorder. Either way, its inclusion clearly demonstrates the desire to include information about the temple in the record. The Book of the Law of the Lord was to be kept in the temple when it was completed.[18]

Clayton had kept JS's journal for little more than a month when, on 8 August 1842, JS was arrested as part of an effort to extradite him to Missouri to stand trial for alleged complicity in the attempted assassination of former Missouri governor Lilburn W. Boggs.[19] JS's subsequent efforts to avoid extradition to Missouri were attended by a flurry of letter writing among JS, his associates, and Illinois governor Thomas Carlin. Eliza R. Snow, a private teacher living in the Smith home, and Erastus Derby, who also had clerical skills, assisted Clayton in copying these and other letters into the journal. Among other things, this correspondence provides valuable insight into the thoughts and character of several of Nauvoo's leading citizens. Emma Smith's articulate and thoughtful letters to Carlin, for example, in which she argued against the legality of Boggs's affidavit and the entire extradition proceedings, reveal a woman of ability and resourcefulness. Two of JS's letters written to members of the church during this period provided important instructions regarding proxy baptisms for deceased persons and record keeping. Clayton and Snow also copied into the journal three of the early letters in a lengthy series between JS and his New York correspondent James Arlington Bennet.

William Clayton.

16. Pages 207–209, for example, contain such inscriptions. Willard Richards's entry for 10 March 1842 also indicates contemporaneous inscription.

17. JS, Journal, 29 June 1842.

18. Brigham Young et al., "Baptism for the Dead," *Times and Seasons,* 15 Dec. 1841, 3:626.

19. JS, Journal, 8 Aug. 1842; see also Appendix 1, p. 377 herein.

JS spent much of the last five months of 1842 in hiding to avoid arrest and extradition to Missouri. Periods of enforced solitude gave him time for sustained reflection and opportunity to commit his thoughts to paper. Lengthy recitations of the names and deeds of his loyal friends, and explicit references to his desire to have them recorded in the Book of the Law of the Lord are unique features of this part of his journal and contribute—like the lists of donations for the temple—to the unusual character of the book as a whole.

Although Richards returned to Nauvoo with his family on 30 October 1842, Clayton continued keeping JS's journal in the Book of the Law of the Lord through 20 December of that year. Clayton's entries end with a recital of his, Richards's, and several other men's efforts in Springfield, Illinois, to resolve a bankruptcy case involving JS. While there, they also counseled with Judge Stephen A. Douglas, United States district attorney Justin Butterfield, and newly elected Illinois governor Thomas Ford regarding the effort to extradite JS to Missouri. All three gave suggestions for how JS might safely and successfully proceed in the case against him. On 21 December 1842, the day following the party's return to Nauvoo, JS appointed Richards his "private se[c]retary & historian" and Richards began keeping a new journal for JS in a small memorandum book.[20] As temple recorder, Clayton retained possession of the Book of the Law of the Lord, in which he continued to record tithing and other donations.

Chronological Index to Journal Entries

Journal entries in the Book of the Law of the Lord were not always dated sequentially. In addition, there are several dates for which more than one entry was made, often with entries for other dates intervening. This chronological index helps to locate journal entries. In this index, sequential journal entries are not individually listed, and dates with no journal entry are not noted.

Date	Manuscript Page	Page Herein
December 1841	26, 31, 33, 36, 39, 43–44	10–21
Dec. 1841	36	16
11–13 Dec. 1841	33	14–15
13 Dec. 1841	26, 33	10–11, 15–16
14 Dec. 1841	26	11
15–16 Dec. 1841	31	13–14
17 Dec. 1841	26	11
22 Dec. 1841	36	16–17
24–28 Dec. 1841	39	17–19
29–31 Dec. 1841	43–44	19–21
January 1842	31, 43–44, 48, 56–60, 66–67	14, 21–32, 36–38
1 Jan. 1842	44	21
4 Jan. 1842	48	23–24

---

20. JS, Journal, 21 Dec. 1842.

Date	Manuscript Page	Page Herein
5 Jan. 1842	31, 44	14, 21
6 Jan. 1842	57	25–26
12–16 Jan. 1842	48	24
15 Jan. 1842	58	26–27
16 Jan. 1842	48, 58	24, 27
17 Jan. 1842	43, 56, 58	20–21, 24–25, 27
18–22 Jan. 1842	58	27–30
23 Jan. 1842	59, 66	30, 36–37
24 Jan. 1842	59	30
25 Jan. 1842	59, 66	30, 37
26–27 Jan. 1842	59	30–31
28 Jan. 1842	59, 67	31, 38
29–31 Jan. 1842	60	31–32
February–July 1842	**60–61, 88–95, 122–128**	**32–36, 38–80**
August 1842	**128–135, 164–167, 179–184**	**80–99, 115–124**
3–15 Aug. 1842	128–135	80–92
16 Aug. 1842	135, 164–165	93–96
17–21 Aug. 1842	165–167	96–99
Copied Correspondence	168–178	100–114
23–31 Aug. 1842	179–184	115–124
September–December 1842	**184–215**	**124–183**

―――― ❦ ――――

13 December 1841 • Monday • First of Two Entries

/[21]<u>1841</u> Dec.[r.] 13[th.] A conference was held at Ramus on the 4 & 5th of December 1841. over which the patriarch of the church, Hyram [Hyrum] Smith Presided, and Joseph Johnson acted as clerk; Brigham Young. Heber C. Kimball, Willard Richards & John Taylor of the Quorum of the twelve being present, when it was unanimously Resolved by the whole conference that the organization of the Church at Ramus as a stake be discontinued,[22] & that John Lawson be presiding Elder over the Branch, & Joseph Johnson Clerk; and that William Whiteman [Wightman], The Bishop, transfer all the Church property in Ramus To the Sole trustee in trust Joseph Smith, President of the whole church.[23]

---

21. TEXT: Willard Richards handwriting begins.

22. In a meeting of the church in Ramus three weeks earlier, five members of the stake were excommunicated for larceny and another two for being involved in an assault. Documents pertaining to the illegal activities and the action taken were published in the *Times and Seasons*. (Macedonia Branch, Record, 18 Nov. 1841; "Thieves," *Times and Seasons,* 1 Dec. 1841, 3:615–618.)

23. On 30 January 1841, JS was elected sole trustee-in-trust for the church with power "to receive acquire manage or convey property real personal or mixed for the sole use and benefit of said church," in

December 13th 1841 This day Joseph the Seer, and President of the church, appointed Willard Richards. Recorder.[24] for the Temple, and the Scribe for the private office of the President. Just opened in the upper story of the New Store,[25] and the recorder entered on the duties of his office.

14 December 1841 • Tuesday

December 14th.— Joseph commenced opening, unpacking, and assorting goods in the large front room on the seckond floor of the new Store, situated on the corner of the Lot. bounded north by water Street, & West by Granger Street, this 14th. day of December A.D. 1841. The building. being yet unfinished, the Joiners and Masons. are prosecuting this their labors in the lower part thereof.—

17 December 1841 • Friday

December 17th 1841. Brigham Young, President of the Quorum of the twelve, arrived at his house in Nauvoo, July 1st 1841. from England, having been absent from his family since the 14th. of September 1839.[26] and the following Revelation[27] was given at his house in—

"Nauvoo City. July 9th. 1841.

Dear & well beloved Brother, Brigham Young, Verily thus saith the Lord unto you my servant Brigham. it is no more required at your hand to leave your family as in times past for your offering is acceptable to me I have seen your labor and toil in journeyings for my name. I therefore command you to send my word abroad and take special care of your family from this time henceforth and forever, Amen.[28] Given to Joseph Smith this day." [p. 26]

---

compliance with Illinois law governing business transactions of trustees on behalf of religious corporations. (Appointment, 2 Feb. 1841, Hancock Co., IL, Bonds and Mortgages, vol. 1, p. 97, microfilm 954,776, U.S. and Canada Record Collection, FHL; An Act concerning Religious Societies [6 Feb. 1835], *Laws of the State of Illinois* [1834–1835], pp. 148–149, sec. 3.)

24. According to the published notice of Richards's appointment, it was his responsibility to "receive all property devoted to the building of the Temple and enter the same, at the Recorder's office in the lower room of the new store." (JS, "To Whom It May Concern," *Times and Seasons,* 15 Dec. 1841, 3:638.)

25. The store opened for business on 5 January 1842. (JS, Journal, 1 and 5 Jan. 1842, p. 21 herein.)

26. Young and Heber C. Kimball departed on their proselytizing mission with the Quorum of the Twelve to England on this date. (Allen et al., *Men with a Mission,* chaps. 4 and 12.)

27. This revelation was later canonized as D&C 126.

28. Between his baptism in April 1832 and his return from England in July 1841, Young served eight missions for the church, totaling roughly three and one-half years. The responsibilities of Young and the Quorum of the Twelve were broadened in August 1841 to include working closely with the First Presidency and attending "to the settling of emegrants and the business of the church at the stakes, and

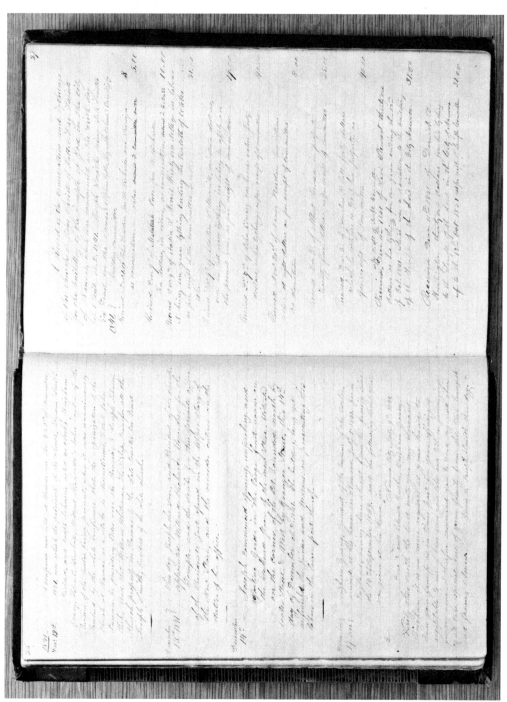

First pages of journal entries and donation records. The journal entries and donation records kept in the Book of the Law of the Lord begin on pages 26 and 27, following the revelation transcripts found in the beginning of the book. Handwriting of Willard Richards. Book of the Law of the Lord, pp. 26–27, Church History Library, Salt Lake City. (Photograph by Welden C. Andersen.)

[pages 27–30, donation records dated 30 November–16 December 1841]

15 December 1841 • Wednesday

Dec 15th. In reply to enquiries concerning Almon Babbitt. the Printing Press. Kirtland, &c contained in a letter written at Kirtland, Nov 16th 1841. by by Lester Brooks & Zebedee Coltrin, acting Prests.— & Thomas Burdick, Bishop. & council. To. Presidents Joseph Smith & Brigham Young &c.[29] it was decided as follows;

> "It remains for Almon Babbitt to offer satisfaction. if he wishes so to do, according to the minutes of the Conference, <u>You are doubtless all well aware that all the stakes except those in Hancock, Co.— Illinois, & Lee county Iowa. were discontinued some time Since by the First Presidency, as published in the Times and Seasons</u>;[30] but as it appears that there are many in Kirtland who desire to remain there. and build up that place, and as you have made great exertions, according to your letter, to establish a printing press, & take care of the poor, &c. since that period, you may as well continue operations according to your designs. & go on with your printing, & do what you can in Righteousness to build up Kirtland but do not suffer yourselves to harbor the Idea that Kirtland will rise on the ruins of Nauvoo.[31] It is the privilege of brethren emigrating from any quarter To come to this place, and it is not right to attempt to persuade those who desire it, to stop short,"

(Extract from the letter of the presidents in reply— Decr 15th 1841.)

---

assist to bear off the kingdom victorious to the nations." (Whittaker, "Brigham Young and the Missionary Enterprise," 86–87; "Conference Minutes," *Times and Seasons,* 1 Sept. 1841, 2:521–522.)

29. The letter acknowledged the action taken in the 2 October 1841 conference in Nauvoo to disfellowship Kirtland, Ohio, stake president Babbitt for teaching "doctrine contrary to the revelations of God and detrimental to the interest of the church" and requested counsel on his case. The letter also explained the hopes of Kirtland church leaders to build up the city and their attempt to establish a printing office. Babbitt had attempted to explain his actions in an earlier letter to the First Presidency. (Lester Brooks et al., Kirtland, OH, to JS et al., Nauvoo, IL, 16 Nov. 1841, JS Collection, CHL; "Minutes of a Conference," *Times and Seasons,* 15 Oct. 1841, 2:577; Almon Babbitt, Kirtland, OH, to JS et al., Nauvoo, IL, 19 Oct. 1841, JS Collection, CHL.)

30. JS, "To the Saints Abroad," *Times and Seasons,* 1 June 1841, 2:434.

31. According to a letter from Babbitt to the First Presidency, approximately five hundred church members lived in Kirtland at this time. At a church conference in Kirtland on 2 October 1841, it was decided that the printing press would publish a periodical titled *The Olive Leaf* and that profits from the proposed printing operation would be used to benefit the church; however, there is no evidence that this press produced any publications. (Almon Babbitt, Kirtland, OH, to JS et al., Nauvoo, IL, 19 Oct. 1841, JS Collection, CHL; "Conference Minutes," *Times and Seasons,* 1 Nov. 1841, 3:587–589.)

16 December 1841 • Thursday

December 16⟨th⟩ 1841 This day William Wightman, of Ramus, deliverd to Pres⟨t.⟩ Joseph ~~Sole~~ Smith, sole Trustee in Trust, the <u>deed.</u> for the unsold ⟨& bonded⟩ Lots of land in the town of Ramus, bearing date Dec⟨r⟩ 8⟨th⟩ 1841:[32] also the plat of the "first addition To Ramus." and the notes which have been received of Individuals who have purchased lots. and the Bonds of William Miller. Sept 21. 1840; & of Uti [Ute] Perkins Nov 26⟨[th]⟩ 1840: & of W⟨m⟩ G. Perkins. Nov 7. 1840. & of John F. charles Nov 16. 1841. for lots of land adjoining Ramus. and which may hereafter be added. to the Town ~~plot~~ plat; (a part of the land included in W⟨m⟩ Millers Bond is included in the first addition to Ramus;) The above described property in Ramus. & the Notes ⟨were⟩ ~~is~~ transferred to the sole Trustee in trust. for the benefit of the whole church. (by a vote of the Ramus Conference Dec⟨r⟩ 4 & 5⟨th⟩. 1841.) after applying sufficient of said property to liquidate the claims of those from whom the Town was purchased,[33] and also paying two notes given by W⟨m.⟩ Wightman for money borrowed to pay for the above property, viz, To Lyman prentice[34] $11.45: & James Cummin[g]s $50.00 and some other small demands against said Wightman which have been contracted for the benefit of the church in Ramus.

5 January 1842 • Wednesday

1842 January 5.⟨th⟩ William Wightman. Signed over & delivered the Town Plot[35] ~~to~~ of Ramus to the sole trustee in Trust Joseph Smith. [p. 31]

[*page 32, donation records dated 17–20 December 1841*]

11, 13 December 1841 • Saturday, Monday

December 11⟨th⟩ Late this evening. Joseph, the prophet. and trustee in trust for the Temple,[36] Commanded Brigham Young. President of the twelve, while

---

32. The deed, signed by Wightman and his wife, Dolly Eaton Wightman, is recorded in the Hancock County Deed Record Book. Wightman was instructed on 13 December 1841 to "transfer all the Church property in Ramus to the Sole trustee in trust Joseph Smith." (Hancock Co., IL, Deed Records, vol. K, pp. 19–20, microfilm 954,599, U.S. and Canada Record Collection, FHL; JS, Journal, 13 Dec. 1841, p. 10 herein.)

33. The branch at Ramus appointed Bishop William Wightman, in a meeting on 15 July 1840, to acquire land on which the town would be built from Miller and from Ute, William, and Absalom Perkins. (Macedonia Branch, Record, 15 July 1840.)

34. Probably Lyman Prentis, a resident of Warsaw, Illinois. (Jacob B. Backenstos, "Names of Carthage Greys & Mobbers," 1846, Historian's Office, JS History Documents, ca. 1839–1880, CHL.)

35. TEXT: Possibly "Plat".

36. On 30 January 1841, JS was elected sole trustee-in-trust for the church in compliance with Illinois law; see 10n23 herein.

sitting in the New store, to go immediately and instruct the building committee[37] in their duty, & forbid their receiving any more property for the building of the Temple Until they received it of himself. and if they committee did not give heed to the instruction, and attend to their duty to put them in the way so to do:[38]

And on monday Morning, Dec[r.] 13[th.], Brigham delivered the above Message. to Reynolds Cahoon. and Elias Higby [Higbee]. while in the committee House. in presence of Heber C. Kimball. Willford [Wilford] Woodruff. and Willard Richards.

13 December 1841 • Monday • Second of Two Entries

1841. Dec[r.] 21[st.] ⟨13[th.]⟩ Some time in the fall of 1839. Daniel S. Witter, of the Steam Mill at Warsaw, solicited the First Presidency of the church to make a settlement on the school section, No 10 16, 1 mile south of Warsaw: and the solicitations were continued by D. S. Witter. Mark Aldrich & others, from time to time, Till the spring or summer of 1841. when articles of Agreement were entered into between Calvin A. Warren. Esq[r.] Witter, Aldrich & others, owners of the school Section;[39] and the First Presidency; giving the saints the privilege of settling on the school. section, which had been surveyed & laid out in town Lots. & called.— Warren, on certain conditions; and willard Richards went to Warsaw on the 8[th.] of September. and spent several weeks to prepare for the receptions of Emigrants;[40] in the mean time the inhabitants of Warsaw. attempted to form an Anti-Mormon Society. & were much enraged because that Esquire [Jacob] Davis, (who had spoken favorably of the Saints) was

---

37. That is, the committee appointed to oversee construction of the Nauvoo temple.

38. Young and the Quorum of the Twelve signed an open letter to the members of the church on 13 December 1841 mandating that all donations to the temple be presented to JS as trustee for the church and recorded in the Book of the Law of the Lord. (Brigham Young et al., "Baptism for the Dead," *Times and Seasons*, 15 Dec. 1841, 3:625–627.)

39. The Land Ordinance of 1785 specified that land in the United States be surveyed into townships of six miles square. Each township was further surveyed into thirty-six one-mile-square sections, one of which was designated the "school section." Proceeds from the sale of the school section were to be used to fund public schools within the township. Warren, Aldrich, Witter, and others contracted to purchase the Warsaw Township school section in 1836 for some $17,000, at an annual interest rate of twelve percent of the purchase price. ("Our Town and County," *Western World* [Warsaw, IL], 13 May 1840, [2]; Gregg, *History of Hancock County, Illinois,* 637–638.)

40. An epistle of the Quorum of the Twelve notified British Saints of the prospects for settlement at Warren, saying: "The church has commenced a new city 20 miles below this [Nauvoo], and 1 mile below Warsaw, called, *Warren,* where many city lots, and farms in the vicinity, can be had on reasonable terms; and it will be wisdom for many of the brethren to stop at that place, for the opportunity for erecting temporary buildings will be greater than at this place, also the chance for providing food, will be superior, to those who wish to labor for it." (Brigham Young et al., "An Epistle of the Twelve," *Times and Seasons,* 15 Nov. 1841, 3:602; see also Quorum of the Twelve Apostles, Minutes, 31 Aug. 1841.)

appointed clerk of the county by Judge Douglass [Stephen A. Douglas]. In Novr about 200 saints arrived at Warsaw, from England, led by Joseph Fielding, and were visited on the 24th of Novr by Richards & [John] Taylor, of the Quorum of the twelve, & counselled To Tarry at Warsaw. according to the instruction of the first Presidency,

December 13th. Isaac Decker. Presiding Elder at Wa[r]saw. stated to the Presidency at Nauvoo. that Mr Witter had risen $1. per barrel on flour. and sold the sweepings of his Mill to the Saints at $2.25 per cwt; and that Witter & Aldrich had forbid the brethren the priviledge of getting the old wood on the school section, which they had full liberty to get; that the price of wood on the wharf had fallen, 25 cents per cord since the arrival of the Saints; that the citizens had risen on their rents; &c, and the First Presidency decided that ~~that~~ the saints should remove from Warsaw To Nauvoo immediately, & that the proceedings at Warsaw be published in the Times & Seasons.—[41] [*7 lines blank*] [p. 33]

[*pages 34–35, donation records dated 20–22 December 1841 and 17 January 1842*]

December 1841 • Undated

Nauvoo December [*blank*] 1841. Elder Amos Fuller, of Zarahemla stated to President Joseph Smith that he had settled all his debts, and made all necessary provision for his family, and desired to know the will of God concerning himself.—

December 22.^d 1841. Verily thus saith the Lord. unto my servants the Twelve, Let them appoint unto my servant Amos Fuller, a mission to preach my gospel unto the children of men, as it shall be manifested unto them by my Holy Spirit.[42] <u>Amen.</u>

22 December 1841 • Wednesday

1841. December 22.^d.

Nauvoo,— Decmber 22.^d 1841. The word of the Lord came unto Joseph the Seer, verily thus saith the Lord, Let my servant John Snider take a mission to the Eastern continent, unto all the conferences now

---

41. In spite of the First Presidency's instructions, no notice of the proceedings at Warsaw was ever published in the *Times and Seasons*. That same day, however, Richards directed Decker to "remove the Saints from warsaw." (JS, Journal, 30–31 Dec. 1841, p. 21 herein; Richards, Journal, 13 Dec. 1841.)

42. On 17 January 1842, the Quorum of the Twelve decided that Fuller should go on a mission to Chicago. (JS, Journal, 17 Jan. 1842, pp. 20–21 herein.)

sitting in that region, and let him carry a package of Epistles that shall be written by my servants the Twelve. making known unto them their duties concerning the building of my houses[43] which I have appointed unto you saith the Lord, that they may bring their Gold, & their Silver, and their precious stones, and the box-tree, and the Fir-tree, and all fine wood to beautify the place of my sanctuary saith the Lord;[44] and let him return speedily with all means which shall be put into his hands,[45] even so;

Amen.

1841. December 22ᵈ· This day commenced ~~received~~ receiving the first supply of Groceries at the new store. 13. waggons arrived from Warsaw loaded with sugar, molasses, glass, salt, tea, coffee, &ᶜ· purchased in St Louis.— The original stock purchased in New Orleans having been detained at St Louis by Holbrook,[46] Inn-keeper under false pretences; & on this evening Joseph the Seer commenced giving instructions to the scribe concerning writing the Proclamation to the Kings of the earth mentioned in the Revelation given January 19. 1841.[47] [*8 lines blank*] [p. 36]

[*pages 37–38, donation records dated 22–27 December 1841*]

24 December 1841 • Friday

December 24. Elder Truman Gillet Juⁿʳ· returned from a short mission to Van. Beuren. [Van Buren] Co. Iowa, where he baptized 14. bringing $20. as a donation to the building of the Temple from James Mo[o]re whom, he baptizd,— Bro Gillet having been disfellowshiped by the elders quorum, is again restored by the first Presidency, & the decision of the Quorum revoked.

---

43. The Nauvoo House and the Nauvoo temple. Snider left for a ten-month mission to England 26 March 1842. On 20 March, shortly before Snider's departure, the Quorum of the Twelve wrote a letter, "To the Church of Jesus Christ of Latter Day Saints, in its various Branches and Conferences in Europe." The letter introduced Snider and explained the objective of his mission, citing this journal entry as the basis for Snider's authority. (JS, Journal, 26 Mar. 1842 and 23 Jan. 1843, pp. 47, 249 herein; Brigham Young et al., "An Epistle of the Twelve," *Times and Seasons,* 1 Apr. 1842, 3:735–738.)

44. See Revelation, 19 Jan. 1841, in Doctrine and Covenants 103:10, 1844 ed. [D&C 124:25–27].

45. Snider returned to Nauvoo with donations for the temple from church members in Great Britain, Ireland, and Scotland totaling £201 14s. 1½d., which William Clayton calculated to be equivalent to $976.25. (Book of the Law of the Lord, 319–325.)

46. Probably Jason Holbrook. (*Saint Louis Directory, for the Year 1842,* 64.)

47. The injunction to write the "Proclamation to the Kings" appeared in Revelation, 19 January 1841, in Doctrine and Covenants 103:1, 1844 ed. [D&C 124:2–4]. The proclamation was ultimately written by Parley P. Pratt and published in 1845. ([Parley P. Pratt], *Proclamation of the Twelve Apostles of the Church of Jesus Christ, of Latter-Day Saints,* [New York: Samuel Brannan and Parley P. Pratt, 1845]; see also Crawley, *Descriptive Bibliography,* 1:294–296.)

December 24th Christmas eve, 11 o'clock. While conversing with Brigham Young and N[ewel] K. Whitney about sending an Agent to England. to establish a cheap & expeditious conveyance for the saints & merchandize. to this place. President Joseph said in the name of the Lord we will prosper if we go forward in this thing.—⁴⁸ Private office.

26 December 1841 • Sunday

December 26th. The public meeting of the saints was at President Joseph Smiths house, on Sunday evening Dec 26th. and after Patriarch Hyram [Hyrum Smith] & Elder Brigham [Young] had spoken on the principles of faith and the gifts of the spirit. President Joseph read the 13th. chap of 1st corinthians and a part of the 14 chap, and remarked that the gift of Tongues was necessary in the church; ⟨but⟩ That if satan could not speak in tongues he could not tempt a Dutchman, or any other nation, but the English, for he can tempt the Englishman, for he has tempted me, & I am an Englishman; but the Gift of Tongues, by the power of the Holy Ghost, in the church, is for the benefit of the servants of God to preach to unbelievers, as on the days of Pentecost. when devout men from evry nation shall assemble to hear of the things of God. let the ⟨elders⟩ preach to them in their own Mother tongue. whither it is German, French, Spanish or Irish. or any other. & let those interpret who understand the tongue ⟨Language⟩ spoken. in their mother tongue. & this is what the Apostle meant. in 1s[t] corinthians 14.27.

27 December 1841 • Monday

Decr 27th. Joseph. was with. Brigham [Young], Heber C [Kimball], Willard [Richards]. & John [Taylor] of the twelve, at his office. instructing them in the principles of the kingdom.⁴⁹ & what the twelve should do in relation to the mission of John Snider. & the European conferences, so as to forward the gathering. means for bulding the Temple & Nauvoo House, & Merchandize; that Brigham might go with John on his mission if he chose. but the object of the mission could be accomplished without.⁵⁰

---

48. A letter from the Quorum of the Twelve directed John Snider to finance the emigration of church members from England to Nauvoo by a system of barter, which would bring British manufactured goods to Nauvoo in exchange for land. The plan was never carried out. (Brigham Young et al., "An Epistle of the Twelve," *Times and Seasons,* 1 Apr. 1842, 3:735–738; JS, Journal, 22 Dec. 1841, pp. 16–17 herein.)

49. Wilford Woodruff, who was also present, noted that at this meeting, "I had the privilege of seeing for the first time in my day the URIM & THUMMIM." (Woodruff, Journal, 27 Dec. 1841.)

50. Young did not accompany Snider on his mission. (JS, Journal, 22 Dec. 1841 and 26 Mar. 1842, pp. 16–17, 47 herein.)

28 December 1841 • Tuesday

Dec.r 28 Joseph baptizd Sidney Rigdon, for and in behalf of his parents. Reynolds Cahoon and others in the Font.⁵¹ [p. 39]

[pages 40–42, donation records dated 27–31 December 1841]

29 December 1841 • Wednesday

December 29ᵗʰ The corner stone of the Nauvoo House was laid by President Joseph Smith. on the 2ᵈ· of October 1841. (At the commencement of the Last General conference of the church. in Nauvoo. previous to the finishing of the Temple,)⁵² And the following articles were deposited therein by the president.

To Wit.—

A. Book of Mormon
A. Revelation given January 19⁽ᵗʰ⁾ 1841.⁵³
The "Times & Seasons" containing the charter of the Nauvoo House.⁵⁴

---

51. Baptisms for deceased persons were first performed in the Mississippi River. After a font in the basement of the unfinished Nauvoo temple was dedicated on 8 November 1841, baptisms for the dead were performed there. Rigdon's father, William, died in 1810, and his mother, Nancy Gallaher Rigdon, in October 1839. (JS, Nauvoo, IL, to "the Travelling High Council," Great Britain, [ca. Dec. 1840], in JS Letterbook 2, pp. 190–196; Jane Neymon and Vienna Jacques, Statement, 29 Nov. 1854, Historian's Office, JS History Documents, ca. 1839–1880, CHL; Clayton, History of the Nauvoo Temple, 20–21; Allegheny Co., PA, Will Packets or Files, 1789–1917, vol. 1, p. 300, no. 216, microfilm 1,653,554, U.S. and Canada Record Collection, FHL; Allegheny Co., PA, Proceedings Index, 1788–1971, vol. 30, p. 312, no. 5, microfilm 877,053, U.S. and Canada Record Collection, FHL; Obituary for Nancy Rigdon, *Times and Seasons,* Dec. 1839, 1:32.)

52. This parenthetical statement reflects a comment JS made 3 October 1841 during the same conference: "There shall be no more baptisms for the dead, until the ordinance can be attended to in the font of the Lord's House; and the church shall not hold another general conference, until they can meet in said house. *For thus saith the Lord!*" Although church leaders continued holding conferences, none was designated a "general conference" until October 1845. ("Minutes of a Conference," *Times and Seasons,* 15 Oct. 1841, 2:578; italics in original; "Conference Minutes," *Times and Seasons,* 1 Nov. 1845, 6:1008–1016; "First Meeting in the Temple," *Times and Seasons,* 1 Nov. 1845, 6:1017–1018.)

53. Among other things, this revelation gave the injunction to build the Nauvoo House and instructions for building the temple in Nauvoo. The water-damaged manuscript also contains a brief revelation dated 20 March 1841, authorizing William Allred and Henry Miller to be stock agents for the Nauvoo House Association. This Allred and Miller revelation is recorded on page 15 of the Book of the Law of the Lord and under the entry of 20 March 1841 in JS's manuscript history. In addition to the two revelations, the last page of the manuscript contains a note recording that JS laid the cornerstone of the Nauvoo House. (Revelation, 19 Jan. 1841, in Revelations Collection, CHL [D&C 124]; see also Revelation, 19 Jan. 1841, in Book of the Law of the Lord, 15 [D&C 124]; and JS History, vol. C-1, 1173.)

54. The charter for the Nauvoo House appeared in the 1 April 1841 issue of the *Times and Seasons.*

Journal of Heber C. Kimball.[55]
The Memorial of Lyman Wight. To the United States'. Senate.[56]
A Book of Doctrine & Covenants.— 1st. Edition.[57]
N[o.] 35. of the Times and Seasons.[58]
The original Manuscript of the Book of Mormon.[59]
The persecution of the Church in the State of Missouri, published in the "Times & Seasons"[60]
The Holy Bible
1 Half Dollar
1 Quarter Dollar
2 Dimes
2 Half Dimes
} Silver Coin
And
1 copper Coin.—[61]

[*donation records dated 2 August–6 October 1841, lines 25–34*]

17 January 1842 • Monday • First of Three Entries

January 17. 1842— Brigham Young, Heber C. Kimball, O[rson] Pratt, W[ilford] Woodruff. John Taylor. Geo. A Smith. & W[illard] Richards of the Quorum of the Twelve assembled in council at the Presidents office. and decided that Elder Amos ⟨B⟩ ~~Fielding~~ ⟨Fuller⟩ take a mission to the city of

---

55. This sixty-page pamphlet, giving an account of Kimball's first mission to England, was dictated to Robert B. Thompson by Kimball and published in 1840 while Kimball was on his second mission to England. (Robert B. Thompson, *Journal of Heber C. Kimball an Elder of the Church of Jesus Christ of Latter Day Saints* [Nauvoo, IL: Robinson and Smith, 1840]; Crawley, *Descriptive Bibliography*, 1:141–143.)

56. This memorial by Wight is probably a copy of his petition describing atrocities committed against the Mormons in Missouri, addressed to "the Honorable Senate of the United States." (Lyman Wight, Petition, ca. 1839, CHL.)

57. *Doctrine and Covenants of the Church of the Latter Day Saints: Carefully Selected from the Revelations of God,* compiled by JS, Oliver Cowdery, Sidney Rigdon, and Frederick G. Williams (Kirtland, OH: F. G. Williams, 1835).

58. "Whole No. 35," dated 1 October 1841, was the most recent issue of the *Times and Seasons*.

59. Warren Foote recalled, "I was standing very near the cornerstone, when Joseph Smith came up with the manuscript of the Book of Mormon and said he wanted to put that in there, as he had had trouble enough with it." (Foote, Autobiography, 2 Oct. 1841; see also Ebenezer Robinson, "Items of Personal History of the Editor," *The Return*, Aug. 1890, 315; John Brown, [Pleasant Grove, Utah Territory], to [John Taylor], [20 Dec. 1879], photocopy, private possession, copy at CHL; and Skousen, *Original Manuscript*, 5–7, 37.)

60. The series titled "A History, of the Persecution, of the Church of Jesus Christ, of Latter Day Saints in Missouri" appeared in issues 2–12 in the first volume of the *Times and Seasons* (Dec. 1839–Oct. 1840).

61. Ebenezer Robinson reported that the objects placed in the cornerstone were "encased in sheet lead to protect the contents from moisture." (Ebenezer Robinson, "Items of Personal History of the Editor," *The Return,* Aug. 1890, 315.)

chicago. in accordance with the Revelation Page 36.[62] and also, that Elder Henry Jacobs. be subjct to the council & presidency of Bro Fuller & accompany him so far on the mission as Bor [Bro] Fuller judge expedient. [p. 43]

[donation records dated 31 December 1841, lines 1–13]

30–31 December 1841 • Thursday–Friday

<u>Visit</u>

Dec 30, & 31st Calvin A. Warren Esqr Mark Aldrich & Daniel S. Witter visited President Joseph, at his office, and after much explanation, and conversation concerning Warren & Warsaw. in which Esqr Warren Manifested the kindest & most confidential feelings, and Aldrich & Witter ~~had~~ expressed their entire approbation of past proceedings of the Presidency; they all agreed that if Joseph did not succeed in the next attempt. to establish and build up Warren. that they would fully excuse him from all censure, & should feel satisfied that he had done all that could reasonably be required of any men in a like case, be the consequence what it might to themselves; and Esqr Warren frankly acknowledged, that his temporal salvation depended on the success of the enterprize, and made liberal proposals. for the benefit of the brethren, to help forward the undertaking. The party retired. manifesting the best of feeling. & expressing the most perfect satisfaction with their visit with the president. & all concrned.—[63]

1, 5 January 1842 • Saturday, Wednesday

1842 January 1. January 1st 1842 Joseph commenced placing the goods on the shelves. of the New Store for the first time assisted by Bishop Newel K. Whitney and others; [64]and on wednesday. January 5th. the doors were opened for trading for the first time; the store was filled continually through the day and Joseph was behind the counter continually waiting upon purchasers.[65] [p. 44]

---

62. The first revelation on page 36 of the Book of the Law of the Lord directed that Fuller be appointed to serve a proselytizing mission. (JS, Journal, Dec. 1841, p. 16 herein.)

63. Two weeks earlier, church leaders, concerned for the economic welfare of Mormons in the Warsaw area, advised the members living there to move to Nauvoo. Despite the optimism expressed at this interview, large-scale Mormon settlement in the Warsaw area never materialized. Aldrich filed for bankruptcy three months after this meeting. (JS, Journal, 13 Dec. 1841, pp. 15–16 herein; Hamilton, "Money-Diggersville," 49–58; Mark Aldrich, Petition for bankruptcy, 22 Mar. 1842, Bankruptcy General Records, [Act of 1841], 3:258.)

64. TEXT: "January 5." appears in the left margin.

65. In a letter to Edward Hunter dated 5 January 1842, JS described the opening of the store: "I rejoice that we have been enabled to do as well as we have, for the hearts of many of the poor brethren & sisters will be made glad. with those comforts which are now within their reach. The store has been filled to overflowing all day. & I have stood behind the counter all day dealing out goods as steady as any clerk you

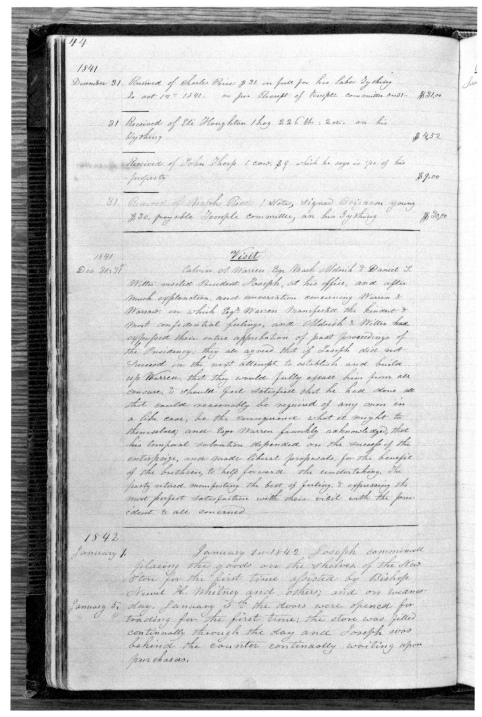

Journal entries and donation records. Page 44 of the Book of the Law of the Lord, one of only two pages that include both journal entries and donation records, illustrates the dual purpose of the book. Handwriting of Willard Richards. Book of the Law of the Lord, p. 44, Church History Library, Salt Lake City. (Photograph by Welden C. Andersen.)

Red brick store. Circa 1886. In addition to serving Nauvoo residents as a general store, Joseph Smith's commodious two-story store housed the private office of Joseph Smith and the tithing office. A large room on the second floor was used as an assembly room for social, municipal, and religious purposes. (Church History Library, Salt Lake City.)

[*pages 45–47, donation records dated 1–6 January 1842*]

4 January 1842 • Tuesday

<u>Prophecy.</u>

 1842 January 4 Thursday evening December 30th· 1841. at the Presidents office, while conversing with Calvin A. Warren Esqr— about the proceedings at Warsaw, President Joseph prophesied in the name of the Lord. that the first thing toward building up Warsaw was to break it down, to break down them that are there, and that it never would be built up till it was broken down, and after that keep them entirely in the dark concerning our movements; and it is best to let Sharpe [Thomas Sharp] publish what he pleases and go to the Devil. and the more lies he prints, the sooner he will get through;[66] not buy him out or hinder him; and after they have been in the dark long enough, let a certain set of men go there who will do as I tell them, a certain kind of men. some of those capitalists from the eastern states, say from Pensylvania; wise men who

---

ever saw to oblige those who were compelled to go without their usual christmas & New year. dinners. for the want of a little Sugar, Molasses, Raisons &c. &c. & to please myself also for I love to wait upon the Saints, and be a servant to all hoping that I may be exalteed in the due time of the Lord." (JS, Nauvoo, IL, to Edward Hunter, West Nantmeal, PA, 5 Jan. 1842, JS Collection, CHL.)

 66. Sharp was the editor of the *Warsaw Signal,* a newspaper openly hostile toward the Mormons.

will take the lead of business, and go ahead of those that are there before they know what we are about. and the place will prosper, and not till then—

12, 14, 16 January 1842 • Wednesday, Friday, Sunday

<u>Coal Mine</u>

1842 January <u>12</u> Wednesday January 12<u>th.</u> 1842 President Joseph. visited his wood-land, about 7 miles South of his residence, accompanied by John Sanders and Peter Maughan, and found and examined ⟨a⟩ vein of coal about 18 inches thick, apparently of a superior quality for the western country.

Friday 14 Maughan and Sanders further examind the coal mine. and a load of coal was drawn to the presidents office. and the room warmed therewith for the first time

16 Maughan and Sanders reported they had continud digging untill the vein of coal was but 6 inches thick. & ceased after getting about 3 waggon loads. [*8 lines blank*] [p. 48]

[*pages 49–55, donation records dated 6–19 January 1842*]

17 January 1842 • Monday • Second of Three Entries

1842 January 17.

A Revelation given at Far West, July 8,<u>th.</u> AD. <u>1838</u>.[67]

Verily thus saith the Lord unto my servants, William Marks, and N[ewel] K. Whitney; Let them settle up their business speedily and Journey from the land of Kirtland before I, the Lord, sendeth snow ⟨again⟩ upon the ground. Let them awake and arise, and come forth and not tarry for I the Lord commandeth it,— therefore, if they tarry it shall not be well with them. Let them repent of all their sins, and all their covetous desires before me saith the Lord; For what is property unto me saith the Lord. Let the properties ~~of~~ at Kirtland be turned out for debts saith the Lord, Let them go saith the Lord, and whatsoever remaineth. let it remain in your hands saith the Lord, for have I not the fowls of Heaven, and also the fish of the Sea, and the beasts of the Mountains?

---

67. Now D&C 117. Following the failure of the church-owned bank and amid dissent and apostasy in Kirtland, Ohio, JS fled Ohio for Far West, Missouri, in January 1838. A revelation dated 26 April 1838 designated Far West and its environs in western Missouri as a new place of gathering for the Saints. However, several prominent church members, including William Marks, president of the Kirtland stake, and Newel K. Whitney, bishop of the church in Kirtland, remained in Kirtland well into the summer, evidently reluctant to leave their property. The other individual mentioned in this 8 July revelation, Oliver Granger, delivered the revelation to Marks and Whitney in Ohio. (Revelation, 8 July 1838–E, in JS, Journal, 8 July 1838, in *JSP*, J1:289–290 [D&C 117]; Revelation, 26 Apr. 1838, in JS, Journal, 26 Apr. 1838, in *JSP*, J1:258 [D&C 115:6–9]; Sidney Rigdon et al., Far West, MO, to William Marks and Newel K. Whitney, Kirtland, OH, 8 July 1838, copy, JS Collection, CHL.)

Have I not made the earth? ⟨Do I not hold the destinies of all the armies of the nations of the earth?⟩ Therefore will I not Make the solitary places to bud and ⟨to⟩ blossom, and bring forth in abundance saith the Lord? Is there not room enough upon the mountains of Adam Ondi Ahman, or upon the plains of Olea Shinihah, or the land where Adam dwelt, that you should not Covet that which is but the drop and neglect the more weighty matters. Therefore, come up hither, unto the Land of My people, even Zion. Let my Servant William Marks be faithful over a few things, and he shall be ruler over many things. Let him preside in the midst of my people, in the city Far West, and let him be blessed with the blessings of my people.— Let My Servant N. K. Whitney be ashamed of the Nicolitans[68] and of all their secret abominations, and of all his littleness of soul before me saith the Lord, and come up unto the land of Adam ondi Ahman,[69] and be a Bishop unto my people saith the Lord, not in name but in deed Saith the Lord. And again, Verily I say unto you I remember my Servant Oliver Grainger [Granger]. Behold, verily I say unto him, that his name shall be had in sacred remembrance from generation to generation. forever and ever Saith the Lord; Therefore let him contend earnestly for the redemption of the First Presidency of My church Saith the Lord; and when he falls he shall rise again, for his sacrifice shall be more sacred to me than his increase saith the Lord; Therefore let him come up hither speedily unto the land of Zion, and in due time he shall be made a merchant unto my name saith the Lord for the benefit of my people; Therefore let no man despise my servant Oliver Grainger. but let the blessings. of my people be upon him forever and ever, <u>Amen</u>.

And. again I. say unto. you let all the Saints in the land of Kirtland remember the Lord their God, and mine house to preserve it holy, and to overthrow the money changers in mine own due time. Saith the Lord. [p. 56]

6 January 1842 • Thursday

<u>The New Year</u>[70]

January— 1842 Thursday 6.— [71]The New Year has been ushered in and continued thus far under the most favorable auspices. and the Saints seem to be <u>influenced</u> by a kind and indulgent Providence in their disposition &

---

68. Nicolaitanism was an early Christian heresy mentioned in Revelation 2:6, 15.

69. Adam-ondi-Ahman, located in Daviess County, Missouri, was identified as "the place where Adam shall come to visit his people, or the Ancient of days shall sit," prior to Christ's return to the earth. (Explanation, 19 May 1838, in JS, Journal, 19 May 1838, in *JSP*, J1:271 [D&C 116].)

70. TEXT: Written in larger handwriting and double underlined.

71. While nothing explicitly identifies the following statement as JS's, its content and tone suggest that it, or its main ideas, originated with him rather than with Willard Richards. As with other retrospective

means; to rear the Temple of the most High God, anxiously looking forth to the completion thereof. as an event of the greatest importance to the Church & the world, Making the Saints in Zion to rejoice, and the Hypocrite & Sinner to tremble, Truly this is a day long to be remembered. by. the saints of the Last Days; A day in which the God of heaven has began to restore the ancient ⟨order⟩ of his Kingdom unto. his servants & his people: a day in which all things are concurring together to bring about the compl[e]tion of the fullness of the gospel, a fulness of the dispensation of Dispensations even the fulness of Times; a day in which God has began to make manifest & set in order in his church those things which have been, and those things, which the ancients prophets and wise men desired to see.— but deid [died] without beholding it. a day in which those things begin to be made manifest which have been hid from ⟨before⟩ the foundations of the world. & which Jehovah has promised should be made known in his own due time. unto his servants, to prepare. the earth for the return of his glory, even a celestial glory; and a kingdom of Priests & Kings to God & the Lamb forever. on Mount Zion.— or the hundred & forty & four thousand ~~which~~ whom John the Revelator. saw;[72] which should come to pass. in the Restitution of all things, [*17 lines blank*] [p. 57]

Editorial Note

After moving in with JS and his family on 13 January 1843,[73] Willard Richards was able to more closely observe and record JS's daily activities than before. The heading "Journal of President Joseph" preceding the next entry may indicate that by this point Richards had written most of the retrospective entries he intended to record and that he had a better idea of his role as "Scribe for the private office of the President."[74]

Journal of President Joseph[75]

15 January 1842 • Saturday

⟨Saturday⟩ January 15. Commenced reading the Book of Mormon at page 54.

---

entries recorded in the journal in December 1841 and January 1842, Richards possibly based this entry on notes about JS's activities that he or others produced earlier.

72. See Revelation 7:4 and 14:1, 3; and Revelation, ca. Mar. 1832, in Revelation Book 1, p. 143, in *JSP*, MRB:259 [D&C 77:11].

73. Richards, Journal, 13 Jan. 1843.

74. See JS, Journal, 13 Dec. 1841, p. 11 herein.

75. TEXT: Written in larger handwriting and double underlined.

⟨American⟩ stereotype edition,[76] (the previous pages having been corrected)[77] for the purpose of correcting the plates, or some errors which escaped notice in the first edition.[78]

16 January 1842 • Sunday

Sabbath. 16 Preached at his own house. morning evening. illustrating the nature of sin, and shewing that it is not right to sin that grace may abound.[79]

17 January 1842 • Monday • Third of Three Entries

Monday 17. Was transacting business in the city. procuring means to assist the printer &c. dined, in company with the Recorder, at. Sister Agnes Smith's; and attended, council of the twelve, (present. B[righam] Young. Prst.— H[eber] C. Kimball. O[rson] Pratt. W[ilford] Woodruff. John Taylor. Geo A smith & W[illard] Richards.) at his private office. in the evening.

18 January 1842 • Tuesday

Tuesday 18 After transacting a variety of business. sleeping an hour from Bodily infirmity. read for correction in the Book of Mormon and Debated, in the evening, with ~~they~~ the Mayor.[80] concerning the. Lamanites.— and Negroes.—[81]

19 January 1842 • Wednesday

Wednesday 19 Read in the Book of Mormon, and in the evening visited Bishop [George] Millers Wife.[82] who was very sick and the Bishop absent.— collecting funds for building the Temple & Nauvoo House[83]

---

76. *The Book of Mormon,* 3rd ed. (Nauvoo, IL: Robinson and Smith, 1840). Page 54 of the "American stereotype edition" begins with the text corresponding to 1 Nephi 20:14 in the 1981 edition.

77. According to Wilford Woodruff, JS began the previous month to proofread the first sixty pages of the Book of Mormon for republication. (Woodruff, Journal, 5 Dec. 1841.)

78. The first stereotype edition of the Book of Mormon (third American edition) was published in 1840. The corrections mentioned here were not included in the fourth American edition, which was published August 1842 in Nauvoo from the same plates as the third edition. (Crawley, *Descriptive Bibliography,* 1:205.)

79. See Romans 6:1–2.

80. John C. Bennett.

81. JS and John C. Bennett debated the same topics the following week. (JS, Journal, 25 Jan. 1842, p. 30 herein.)

82. Mary Fry Miller.

83. JS had asked George Miller to go to Kentucky "on a preaching excursion, and sell some property" Miller owned there, the proceeds of which were to be applied toward building the Nauvoo temple and Nauvoo House. (George Miller, St. James, MI, to "Dear Brother," 26 June 1855, *Northern Islander,* 16 Aug. 1855, [3]–[4].)

Large "Journal" heading. After several pages devoted to donation entries, journal entries resume on page 58 under the heading "Journal of President Joseph." Similar headings, written in a relatively large script, appear on pages 44, 48, and 57 of the Book of the Law of the Lord. Handwriting of Willard Richards. Book of the Law of the Lord, p. 58, Church History Library, Salt Lake City. (Photograph by Welden C. Andersen.)

20 January 1842 • Thursday

Thursday 20 Attended a Special conference of the church at Bro [*blank*] 10 o'clok A.M. concerning D̲ͬ [Isaac] Galland, The conference voted to sanction the revocation of D̲ͬ Galland's Agency dated the 18th of January. as published in the "Times and Seasons."[84] and also, instructed the Trustee in Trust.[85] To proceed with D̲ͬ Gallands affairs in relatian to the church. as he shall Judge most expedient,—[86] 6.—⟨o'ᵏ⟩ evening attended a special council in the upper Room of the New. Store.

21 January 1842 • Friday

Friday 21 Reading at the office, General business in store & city. in the office in the evening with Elder [John] Taylor & Recorder, interpreting dreams &c.—

22 January 1842 • Saturday

Saturday 22 Was very busy in appraising Tything property.[87] and in the evening revised the rules of the City council,[88] attend[e]d council & spoke on

---

84. JS, "Special Notice," *Times and Seasons*, 15 Jan. 1842, 3:667.

85. JS.

86. One of the largest acquisitions of land upon which Nauvoo was to be built occurred on 12 August 1839, when JS, Hyrum Smith, and Sidney Rigdon contracted to purchase "upwards of five hundred acres" from Connecticut land speculators Horace Hotchkiss, John Gillett, and Smith Tuttle for $53,500.*a* In spring 1841, Hyrum Smith and Galland were sent east with a power of attorney to procure means to pay notes that were due. Smith returned to Nauvoo by 1 May 1841, and Galland continued alone.*b* In August, JS learned that Galland had not paid Hotchkiss. By year's end Galland returned to his home at Keokuk, Iowa Territory, without making an accounting of his trip east. In this context, a "Special conference" convened on 20 January 1842. Two days prior to the conference JS revoked Galland's power of attorney to transact business for the church.*c* A week later, on 27 January 1842, Brigham Young and James Ivins "returned a favorable report" from Galland, and JS met with him on 2 February 1842. Although Galland was not actively involved in the church after this time, his relations with JS, Young, and other church leaders remained positive, suggesting that he had satisfied them regarding his activities in the east.*d* (*a*. See Promissory notes, JS et al. to Horace Hotchkiss; and JS et al. to John Gillett and Smith Tuttle, 12 Aug. 1839, JS Collection, CHL; Brigham Young et al., "An Epistle of the Twelve," *Times and Seasons*, 15 Oct. 1841, 2:568. *b*. Editorial, *Times and Seasons*, 1 May 1841, 2:403; Power of attorney, JS to Hyrum Smith and Isaac Galland, Hancock Co., IL, 1 Feb. 1841, private possession, copy at CHL. *c*. JS, Nauvoo, IL, to Horace Hotchkiss, Fair Haven, CT, 25 Aug. 1841, draft, JS Collection, CHL; Horace Hotchkiss, Fair Haven, CT, to JS, Nauvoo, IL, 24 July 1841, JS Collection, CHL; JS, "Special Notice," *Times and Seasons*, 15 Jan. 1842, 3:667. *d*. JS, Journal, 27 Jan. and 2 Feb. 1842; see also Cook, "Isaac Galland," 278–282.)

87. Willard Richards, recorder for the temple, published a notice that the recorder's office would be open for the reception of tithing and consecrations only on Saturdays in order to give the trustee (JS) and the recorder (Richards) the necessary time to "arrange the Book of Mormon, New Translation of the Bible, Hymn Book, and Doctrine and Covenants for the press." (Willard Richards, "Tithings and Consecrations for the Temple of the Lord," *Times and Seasons*, 15 Jan. 1842, 3:667.)

88. The revised rules dealt with the "order of proceeding in Council, the rights & priviledges of the Members, & Duties of the Officers &c"." (Nauvoo City Council Minute Book, 22 Jan. 1842, 42.)

their adoption. and was Elected vice Mayor pro-tem of Nauvoo City.[89] 18 to of 21. votes. [p. 58]

23 January 1842 • Sunday • First of Two Entries

January 23 Sunday With the Recorder in his office most of the day at his house in the eve

24 January 1842 • Monday

Monday 24 This day Reckoned with W^m & Wilson Law in the counting Room.[90] & examined the Lots— on which they are about to build a grain & Sawmill.[91]

25 January 1842 • Tuesday • First of Two Entries

Tuesday 25 Signed the deeds for Bro Law's.[92] transacted a variety of business in the city and office, sent a messenger To Bro John Benbows to inform them. he could not visit them. in the evening debated with J. C. Bennet [John C. Bennett]. & others, to shew that the Indians have greater cause to complain of the treatment of the whites than the Negroes or Sons of Cain.[93]

26 January 1842 • Wednesday

Wednesday 26. Rode out To borrow money to refund for money borrowed of John Benbow to as outfit for Dr [Isaac] Galland in his agency.[94] transacted a variety of business. explained scriptu[r]e to Elder Orson Spencer in his office. read in Book of Mormon in the evening

---

89. The office of vice mayor to which JS was elected was created by an ordinance of the city council passed on this date. The vice mayor was to be elected by the city council, and the principal responsibility of the office was to preside over the city council in the absence of the mayor. (Nauvoo City Council Minute Book, 22 Jan. 1842, 46.)

90. The counting room was in JS's store.

91. William and Wilson Law's combined steam sawmill and flour mill was built along the river, on Sidney Street, between Locust and Marion, on land purchased on this date. The sawmill was in operation by September 1842. (Wilson Law, Purchase record, 24 Jan. 1842, Trustees Land Book B, 266–267 [insert], 275; Notice, *The Wasp*, 11 June 1842, [2]; "Weather, Wind and Works," *The Wasp*, 17 Sept. 1842, [2]; see also Hancock Co., IL, Deed Records, 24 Jan. 1842, vol. K, pp. 490–492, microfilm 954,599, U.S. and Canada Record Collection, FHL.)

92. Hancock Co., IL, Deed Records, 24 Jan. 1842, vol. K, pp. 490–492, microfilm 954,599, U.S. and Canada Record Collection, FHL.

93. The concept of Cain as the progenitor of blacks was an old and prevalent one. (See Goldenberg, *Curse of Ham*, chap. 13; Copher, "Black Presence in the Old Testament," 147–151; Freedman, *Images of the Medieval Peasant*, 89–91.)

94. Galland was sent east in 1841 as an agent for the church. (See 29n86 herein.)

27 January 1842 • Thursday

Thursday 27 Attending to business in general,— in the afternoon in council with the Recorder or giving some particular instructions concerning. the <u>order</u> of the kingdom & the management of business, placed the carpet, given by Carlos Granger. on the Floor of the Presidents office.— Cast Lots.— ~~an~~ with the Recorder. and spent the evening in <u>general council</u> in the upper ~~Chambers~~[95] Room. in the evening.— In the course of the day B[righam] Young. &. James Ivins returned a favorable report [96]from Dr [Isaac] Galland.[97] with his. Letter of Attorny. Letter & papers. which he had receivd of Joseph & the church.—[98]

28 January 1842 • Friday • First of Two Entries

Friday 28 At the office, Sister Emma & Sister [Elizabeth Smith] Whitney spent an hour.— present H[eber] C. Kimball. W[ilford] Woodruff. B[righam] Young. & received instruction concerning John Snider;[99] & E[benezer] Robinson concrning the Times and Seasons as Recorded on 64 page.—[100] and also deliverd a message Elias Higby [Higbee] to arise & work and his household[101] [*6 lines blank*] [p. 59]

29 January 1842 • Saturday

January Saturday 29. Much engaged with the tythings in the afternoon in his office councilling. various individuals. ~~on~~ and in the evening in council with Bro. [Brigham] Young [Heber C.] Kimball. [Willard] Richards and others—

---

95. TEXT: Possibly "~~Chamber.~~".

96. TEXT: "~~Friday 28.~~" appears in the left margin, suggesting that the remainder of this entry might have been written later.

97. Earlier, JS had revoked Galland's power of attorney to transact business for the church. (See 29n86 herein.)

98. The power of attorney given to Hyrum Smith and Galland was signed by JS on 1 February 1841. Other documents retrieved from Galland may have included a 15 February 1841 JS letter to church members informing them of Hyrum Smith and Galland's purpose and authority. (Power of attorney, JS to Isaac Galland and Hyrum Smith, Hancock Co., IL, 1 Feb. 1841, private possession, copy at CHL; Letter of recommendation for Hyrum Smith and Isaac Galland, 15 Feb. 1841, JS Collection, CHL.)

99. After Snider was appointed on 22 December 1841 to serve a mission to England, he hesitated to leave for England unless the Quorum of the Twelve would finance his way. (JS, Journal, 22 Dec. 1841, pp. 16–17 herein; JS History, vol. C-1, 1273; see also Historian's Office, JS History, draft notes, 28 Jan. 1842.)

100. Actually recorded on journal page 67 (p. 38 herein).

101. Willard Richards later recorded another entry, also dated 28 January 1843, that clarifies these matters. The Quorum of the Twelve was directed to take control of the editorial department of the *Times and Seasons* and to send Snider on a mission to England. Higbee was instructed to put his family in order and move forward with construction of the temple. (JS, Journal, 28 Jan. 1842, p. 38 herein.)

shewing forth the kingdom. & the order thereof concer[n]ing many things & the will of God concerning his servants.—

30 January 1842 • Sunday

Sunday 30. preached in the morning after. father coles [Austin Cowles].— & in the evening, at his house, concerning [concerning] Spirits their operation & designs.—

31 January 1842 • Monday

Monday 31. Assisted in prising [appraising] the tithings of Saturday with. Sister Emma. Recived <u>many</u> <u>calls</u>. read in <u>Mormon</u>[102] and in the ⟨evening⟩ was in council with Brigham [Young]. Heber. C. [Kimball]— Orson [Pratt]. Willford [Wilford Woodruff]. & Willard [Richards]. concring [concerning] Bro [John] Snider.[103] & the printing office. spent the evening very cheer[i]ly & retired about 10. o clock. after Dinner visited Bro [Ezra] Chase. who was very Sick.

2 February 1842 • Wednesday

Feb 2ᵈ· Wednesday In council with Dr [Isaac] Galland. and Calvin A. Warren Esqr.—

3 February 1842 • Thursday

3— Thursday In council with Calvin A. Warren Esqʳ·— concerning a Settlement with the estate of Oliver Granger and delivered him ⟨the necessary⟩ papers accordingly[104]

---

102. Perhaps the section titled "Book of Mormon" within the Book of Mormon. (Book of Mormon, 1840 ed., 504–523 [Mormon 1–9].)

103. Snider was called to serve a mission to England. (JS, Journal, 22 Dec. 1841 and 28 Jan. 1842, pp. 16–17, 38 herein.)

104. Granger was in Kirtland, settling debts and other concerns of church leaders, when he died in August 1841. The settlement with Granger's son Gilbert Granger took place on 2 and 3 March 1842. (Certificate, JS to Oliver Granger, 6 May 1839, private possession, copy at CHL; Certificate, JS et al. to Oliver Granger, Commerce, IL, 13 May 1839, in JS Letterbook 2, pp. 45–46; Nauvoo High Council Minutes, 12 Apr. 1840; Obituary for Oliver Granger, *Times and Seasons,* 15 Sept. 1841, 2:550; JS, Journal, 2 and 3 Mar. 1842.)

4 February 1842 • Friday

Friday 4th. Instructed an invoice of [Isaac] Galland's scrip to be made. out.—[105] closed the contract for the printing office by proxy.—[106] attended a debate in the evening.

10 February 1842 • Thursday

Thursday 10th. The President was sick, and kept his bed.

11 February 1842 • Friday

Friday 11th— Convalescent. was at the store twice a few moments

12 February 1842 • Saturday

Saturday 12th. attended city council.—[107] in the afternoon. plead. in an action of slander before the Mayor.—[108] in behalf of the city againts— [Lyman] O. Littlefield.— and obtained Judgment. of $500 bonds to keep the peace.

13 February 1842 • Sunday

Sunday 13th. Council with the Mayor,[109] H[yrum] Smith. the Patriarch.— Recorder &c and visited Sister S. C. Bennet.[110] in co[mpany] with W[m] Law & Lady. . . .[111] [p. 60]

14 February 1842 • Monday

February. Monday 14 At the office. transacting a variety of business

---

105. JS wanted an accounting of Galland's activities. (See 29n86 herein.)

106. Ebenezer Robinson transferred the printing establishment to JS—with Willard Richards as proxy—for $6,600. The printing establishment comprised the printing office, stereotype foundry, bookbindery, house, and 50-by-58-foot lot on the corner of Water and Bain streets. (Ebenezer Robinson, "Items of Personal History of the Editor," *The Return,* Oct. 1890, 346; JS, Journal, 28 Jan. 1842, p. 38 herein; Woodruff, Journal, 4 Feb. 1842; Hancock Co., IL, Deed Records, vol. N, p. 368, microfilm 954,600, U.S. and Canada Record Collection, FHL.)

107. On this date, the Nauvoo City Council passed "An Ordinance Regulating Auctions in the City of Nauvoo." The ordinance was later repealed. (Nauvoo City Council Minute Book, 12 Feb. 1842, 54–58; see also 9 Apr. 1842, 69; and 14 May 1842, 78.)

108. John C. Bennett.

109. John C. Bennett.

110. Selina Bennett, wife of Samuel Bennett.

111. Jane Silverthorn Law.

17 February 1842 • Thursday

Thursday 17 City council. Special Meeting. among other items a A General law licencing marriages[112] in this city. counill [council] in the General office[113] eve.—

18 February 1842 • Friday

Friday 18 Adjourned Council.— Spoke at considerable length in committee of the whole. on the great priviliges of the Nauvoo Charter.[114] & specially on the Registry of Deeds for Nauvoo. And prophecyed in the name of the Lord God that Judge Douglass [Stephen A. Douglas]. and no other Judge of the circuit court will ever set aside a law of the city council establishing a Registry of Deeds in this city.— (Nauvoo)[115]

19 February 1842 • Saturday

Saturday 19 Engaged in the Registers office[116] on the Tythings & in council in the Presidents office with B[righam] Young & H[eber] C. Kimball & others.—

20 February 1842 • Sunday

Sunday 20 Meeting on the Hill.[117]

21 February 1842 • Monday

Monday 21. visiting in the city. and transacting business at the office in the P.M. & evening

22 February 1842 • Tuesday

Tuesday 22 [*3 lines blank*]

---

112. See Nauvoo City Council Minute Book, 17 Feb. 1842, 76–77.

113. The general office was in JS's store.

114. While the Nauvoo charter was similar to other Illinois city charters, some of its provisions were unusual. Most notable were various powers granted to the city council, such as the authority to organize a university and a city militia, and the authority granted the municipal court to issue writs of habeas corpus. (See An Act to Incorporate the City of Nauvoo [16 Dec. 1840], *Laws of the State of Illinois* [1840–1841], pp. 55–57, secs. 17, 24, 25; Kimball, "Nauvoo Charter," 66–78.)

115. The right to establish a registry of deeds was usually the prerogative of the county. Having a registry of deeds in Nauvoo greatly facilitated the process of buying and selling land. The registry of deeds office was established by the city of Nauvoo, with JS appointed as registrar, on 5 March 1842. (JS, Journal, 5 Mar. 1842; Nauvoo City Council Minute Book, 5 Mar. 1842, 66–67.)

116. Probably a reference to the recorder's office.

117. Located near the temple site.

Book of Abraham, facsimile 1. According to Joseph Smith's published text of the Book of Abraham, this drawing illustrates the near-sacrifice of Abraham at the hands of an idolatrous priest in the land of the Chaldeans. (*Times and Seasons,* 1 Mar. 1842.)

23 February 1842 • Wednesday

Wednesday 23 Settled with and paid Bro. Chases' [Ezra Chase's]— and assisted in the counting room[118] in settling with E[benezer] Robinson Esqr—[119] visited the printing office. & gave R. Hadlock [Reuben Hedlock] instructions concerning the cut for the altar & gods in the Records of Abraham. as designed for the Times and Seasons[120]

24 February 1842 • Thursday

Thursday 24. attending to business at the general office. P.M. was explaining the Records of Abraham. To the Recorder. Sisters Marinda [Marinda Nancy Johnson Hyde] Mary and others present. to hear the Explanations

25 February 1842 • Friday

Friday 25 [*2 lines blank*]

26 February 1842 • Saturday

Saturday 26. At the Recorders office. engaged in the tything. and at a court at the office of the Patriarch.[121] Page 88. [p. 61]

[*pages 62–65, donation records dated 20–28 January 1842*]

23 January 1842 • Sunday • Second of Two Entries

January 23 Silenced Elder Daniel Wood. of Pleasant Vale for preaching that the church should unsheath the Sword— and also silenced Elder A, Lits. for preaching that the authoritiees of the church were done away.— &c. and sent the Letters by the hand of Elder William Draper Junior who preferred the charges;[122] & cited A Lits to appear before the High council of Nauvoo

---

118. The counting room was in JS's store.

119. JS was in the process of purchasing Robinson's printing office. (JS, Journal, 28 Jan. and 4 Feb. 1842, pp. 38, 33 herein.)

120. The "cut for the altar & gods" refers to the woodcut used to print a facsimile for the Book of Abraham. ("A Fac-simile from the Book of Abraham. No. 1," *Times and Seasons,* 1 Mar. 1842, 3:703 [Abraham, facsimile 1].)

121. Hyrum Smith.

122. The letter carried to Wood required that he cease functioning in his church appointment until after he appeared before a hearing of the Nauvoo high council. On 5 February, Wood appeared before the high council with evidence proving that the charges against him were false. The high council decided he should be restored to his former standing in the church. (JS and Brigham Young, Nauvoo, IL, to Daniel Wood, Pleasant Vale, IL, 23 Jan. 1842, Nauvoo High Council Papers, CHL; Wiley Watson et al., Statement, 1 Feb. 1842, Nauvoo High Council Papers, CHL; Nauvoo High Council Minutes, 5 Feb. 1842.)

forthwith.— & published the same in the Times and Seasons.[123] in the name of Joseph Smith. P.C.J.C.L.D.S.[124] and B[righam] Young P.QT.—[125] W Ricchards [Willard Richards] C<u>k.</u> [Clerk]

25 January 1842 • Tuesday • Second of Two Entries

Jan— 25—

A. Revelation Given Dc<u>r.</u> 2<u>d.</u> ~~1842~~ 1841. N. M. Hyde [Marinda Nancy Johnson Hyde]

Verily thus saith the Lord unto you my servant Joseph. that in as much as you have called upon me to know my will concerning my handmaid Nancy Marinda Hyde Behold it is my will that she should have a better place prepared for her than that in which she now lives, in order that her life may be spared unto her; Therefore go and say unto my servant Ebenezer Robinson. & To my handmaid his wife,[126] Let them open their doors and take her and her children into their house. and take care of them faithfully and kindly until my Servant Orson Hyde returns from his mission[127] or until some other provision can be made for her welfare & safety: Let them do these things and spare not. and I the Lord will bless them & heal them. if they do it not grudgingly saith the Lord God. and she shall be a blessing unto them,— and let my handmaid Nancy Marinda Hyde hearken to the counsel of my servant Joseph in all things whatsoever he shall teach unto her, and it shall be a blessing upon her and upon her children after her. unto her Justification saith the Lord.[128] [*6 lines blank*] [p. 66]

---

123. A notice was published in the 15 March 1842 issue of the *Times and Seasons* requesting Elder A. Lits "to come to Nauvoo immediately, to answer to charges which may be preferred against him." Four months later, another notice was published in the 15 July 1842 issue: "A notice appeared in the paper some few weeks ago advertizing Elder A. Lits to return to Nauvoo. The notice was inserted by some officious person without authority; we know of no person by that name, but suppose that Elder William A. Lits is the person intended; if so, he is in perfect good standing in the church, and there are no charges preferred against him." ("Notice," *Times and Seasons*, 15 Mar. 1842, 3:734; "Notice," *Times and Seasons*, 15 July 1842, 3:861.)

124. President of the Church of Jesus Christ of Latter Day Saints.

125. President of the Quorum of the Twelve.

126. Angelina (Angeline) Works Robinson.

127. Hyde left Nauvoo on 15 April 1840, being called by church leaders "to be our agent and representative in foreign lands, to visit the cities of London, Amsterdam, Constantinople and Jerusalem; and also other places that he may deem expedient, and converse with the priests, rulers and Elders of the Jews." He returned to Nauvoo on 7 December 1842. (Orson Hyde and John E. Page, Quincy, IL, 28 Apr. 1840, Letter to the editor, *Times and Seasons*, June 1840, 1:116–117; JS, "To All People unto Whom These Presents Shall Come," *Times and Seasons*, Apr. 1840, 1:86; JS, Journal, 7 Dec. 1842.)

128. Upon being informed of this revelation, Marinda Nancy Johnson Hyde immediately moved in with the Robinsons. The Robinsons moved out on 4 February 1842, as part of the terms of the transfer of the printing office to JS. Hyde and her children remained in the house after the Robinsons left. (Ebenezer

28 January 1842 • Friday • Second of Two Entries
January 28.

A Revelation ~~of~~ ⟨to⟩ the twelve concrning the Times and Seasons.
Verily thus saith the Lord unto you my servant Joseph. go and say unto the Twelve That it is my will to have them take in hand the Editorial department of the Times and Seasons according to that manifestation. which Shall be given unto them by the Power of My Holy Spirit in the midst of their counsel[129] Saith the Lord. Amen

⟨1842.⟩ January 28 Joseph decided that Elder John Snider should go out on a mission, and if necessary some one go with him. and raise up a Church. and get means to go to England. & carry the Epistles required in the Revelation[130] page 36.— and instructed the Twelve, B[righam] Young H[eber] C. Kimball. W[ilford] Woodruff. &— W[illard] Richards— being present. to call Elder Snider into their council & instruct him in these things, & if he will not do these things he shall be cut off from the Church. & be damned.—[131]

January 28. Elias Higby [Higbee] of the Temple Comm[i]ttee, came into the Presidents office. and the President said to him The Lord is not well pleased with you, & you must straiten up your loins and do better. & your family also. for you have not been diligent as you ought. and as spring is approaching you ⟨must⟩ arise & shake yourself & be active. & make your children industrious. & help build the Temple. [*12 lines blank*] [p. 67]

[*pages 68–87, donation records dated 28 January–5 March 1842*]

27 February 1842 • Sunday
Sunday 27 [*2 lines blank*]

Robinson, "Items of Personal History of the Editor," *The Return,* Sept. 1890, 324; Oct. 1890, 346–347; JS, Journal, 4 Feb. 1842; see also p. xxvi herein.)

129. According to Wilford Woodruff, "After consulting upon the subject the quorum appointed Elders J[ohn] Taylor & W Woodruff of the Twelve to Edit the Times & Seasons & take charge of the whole esstablishment under the direction of Joseph the Seer." The contract with Ebenezer Robinson for the sale of the printing office was closed one week after this revelation was received. Under the new arrangement, JS would function as editor of the *Times and Seasons,* with Taylor assisting him in writing and Woodruff overseeing "the Business part of the esstablishment." (Woodruff, Journal, 3, 4, and 19 Feb. 1842; JS, Journal, 4 Feb. and 2 Mar. 1842.)

130. On 22 December 1841, Snider was appointed by revelation to serve a mission to England. (JS, Journal, 22 Dec. 1841, pp. 16–17 herein.)

131. Snider departed for England on 26 March 1842. (JS, Journal, 26 Mar. 1842.)

28 February 1842 • Monday

Monday 28 offered a settlement to Father [Oliver] Snow by Jenkings Notes. which he declined. choosing to take land in Ramus. Paid Bro Robert pierce $2.700, the balance due him for a farm Dr [Isaac] Galland Bought of Bro Peirce in Brandywine Township, Chester County, Pensyvania, for $5000. viz— a deed for Lot. 2. Block 94 ⟨$1100.⟩. &. Lot 4. Block 95. ⟨$800.⟩— & Lot 4. Block 78. $800.¹³² The remainder having been previously paid. & the Bond was cancelled. & given up. & Bro Peirce expressed his satisfaction of the whole proceedings in the Times & Seasons.—¹³³

1 March 1842 • Tuesday

March— Tuesday 29 1. During the fore-noon. at his office. & the printing office correcting the first plate or cut. of the Records of father Abraham. prepared by Reuben Hadlock [Hedlock] for the Times & Season.¹³⁴ and in council in his office in the P.M. and in the evening with the Twelve & their wives at Elder [Wilford] Woodruff's.—¹³⁵ where he explained many important principles in relation to progressive improvement. in the scale of inteligent existence

2 March 1842 • Wednesday

Wednesday 2. Read the Proof of the "Times and Seasons" as Editor for the First time, No. 9⁽ᵗʰ⁾ Vol 3ᵈ.¹³⁶ in which is the commencement of the Book of Abraham. Paid taxes. to Bagley [Walter Bagby] in the General Business office, for county & State purposes. but refused to pay the taxes on the City & Town

---

132. Indenture, JS and Emma Smith to Robert Peirce, Hancock Co., IL, 28 Feb. 1842, International Society Daughters of Utah Pioneers, Pioneer Memorial Museum, Salt Lake City.

133. Galland made this purchase while acting as an agent for the church. (Robert Peirce to JS, Nauvoo, IL, 28 Feb. 1842, *Times and Seasons,* 1 Mar. 1842, 3:715; see also 29n86 herein.)

134. The corrected figure was published as "A Fac-simile from the Book of Abraham. No. 1," *Times and Seasons,* 1 Mar. 1842, 3:703 [Abraham, facsimile 1].

135. The occasion was Wilford Woodruff's thirty-fifth birthday celebration. Those present included JS and Emma Smith; Heber C. and Vilate Murray Kimball; John and Leonora Cannon Taylor; John Taylor's mother, Agnes; Willard Richards; and John E. Page. (Woodruff, Journal, 1 Mar. 1842.)

136. A 28 January 1842 revelation indicated the Quorum of the Twelve would "take in hand the Editorial department" of the *Times and Seasons.*ᵃ At this time JS became the editor of the paper, with John Taylor assigned to assist him in writing. While JS's name appears as editor with vol. 3, no. 8, this transitional issue was begun by Ebenezer Robinson and completed by Taylor and Wilford Woodruff. JS's actual responsibility as editor began with vol. 3, no. 9.ᵇ (*a.* JS, Journal, 28 Jan. 1842, p. 38 herein. *b.* Ebenezer Robinson, "Valedictory," *Times and Seasons,* 15 Feb. 1842, 3:695–696; JS, "To Subscribers," *Times and Seasons,* 1 Mar. 1842, 3:710; Ebenezer Robinson, "To the Public," *Times and Seasons,* 15 Mar. 1842, 3:729; Woodruff, Journal, 19 Feb. 1842.)

of commerce.—[137] & Commen[ce]d Settlement with Gilbert Granger,[138] & continud in the Presidents office till 9 O clock evening.— Also visited by General Dudley[139] from Connecticut.

3 March 1842 • Thursday

Thurday 3 Council in the General business office at 9 o clock A.M. in the afternoon continued the settlement with Gilbert Granger. but finally failed to effect any thing but to get Newels Note.[140] Granger refusing to give up. the papers ~~for~~ to the president. which he had recived of his father. the same being church property [*5 lines blank*] [p. 88]

4 March 1842 • Friday

March 4 Friday Exhibeting the Book of Abraham. in the original. To Bro Reuben Hadlock [Hedlock]. so that he might take the size of the several plates or cuts. & prepare the blocks for the Times & Seasons. & also gave instruction concerning the arrangement of the writing on the Large cut. illustrating the principles of Astronomy.[141] (in his office) with other general business

5 March 1842 • Saturday

Saturday 5. City council, among other business of importance the office of Register of Deed's[142] was established in the City of Nauvoo & President Joseph Smith chosen Register [registrar] by the City council.

---

137. Walter Bagby was the Hancock County tax collector. JS refused to pay taxes assessed on behalf of Commerce, "there being no such place known in law; the city & town of commerce having been included in the city plot of Nauvoo." (Walter Bagby, "To Tax Payers," *Times and Seasons,* 1 Mar. 1841, 2:334; Historian's Office, JS History, draft notes, 2 Mar. 1842; see also JS History, vol. C-1, 1286.)

138. The settlement pertained to the estate of Oliver Granger, Gilbert's father, who served as an agent to settle church business in Kirtland, Ohio, before his death in August 1841. (See 32n104 herein.)

139. Possibly Julius Dudley, a brigadier general in the Connecticut state militia. (*Connecticut Annual Register,* 104.)

140. Probably Grandison Newell. On 24 October 1837, the court of common pleas at Chardon, Geauga County, Ohio, ordered JS and Sidney Rigdon to pay $1,000 each to Samuel D. Rounds. Rounds appointed Newell to collect the debt. On 1 March 1838, Newell acknowledged that JS's agents William Marks and Oliver Granger had paid him $1,600 and that he would not seek the remaining $400, thereby settling the debt. (Assignment of judgment, Grandison Newell to William Marks and Oliver Granger, Kirtland, OH, 1 Mar. 1838, Newel K. Whitney, Papers, BYU.)

141. The figure was published as "A Fac-simile from the Book of Abraham, No. 2," *Times and Seasons,* 15 Mar. 1842, 3:720–721 [Abraham, facsimile 2].

142. The importance of having a register of deeds in Nauvoo was discussed two weeks earlier. (JS, Journal, 18 Feb. 1842; see also Nauvoo City Council Minute Book, 5 Mar. 1842, 66–67.)

Book of Abraham, facsimile 2. Joseph Smith published this illustration from the papyri containing the Book of Abraham in connection with its description of cosmography and its accounts of the Creation and of Adam and Eve in the Garden of Eden. (*Times and Seasons,* 15 Mar. 1842.)

6 March 1842 • Sunday

~~Saturday~~ ⟨Sunday⟩ 6. Preached at Elder Orson Spencers on the Hill near the Temple

7 March 1842 • Monday

~~Tuesday~~ ⟨Monday⟩ 7 At the general Business office. Peter Melling. the Patriarch from England brought to the office cash ⟨$13.37:⟩ and clothing ~~to 3 1~~ 65. from P[arley] P. Pratt & Amos Feilding [Fielding] of England.[143] and much general business transacted

8 March 1842 • Tuesday

~~Wednesday~~ ⟨Tuesday⟩ 8 Commenced Translating from the Book of Abraham, for the 10 No of the Times and seasons—[144] and was engagd at his office day & evening—

9 March 1842 • Wednesday

Wednesday 9 Examining copy for the Times & Seasons presented by. [John] Taylor & Bennet [John C. Bennett].—[145] and a variety of other business in ~~this~~ the Presidents office in the morning. in the afternoon continud the Translation [146]of the Book of Abraham. called Bishop Nnights [Vinson Knight] & Mr the ~~Post office~~ ⟨Mr [Amos] Davis's⟩ &c with the Re[c]order. & continued translating & revising. & Reading letters in the evening Sister Emma being present in the office

10 March 1842 • Thursday

Thursday 10 Gave instruction concerning a deed To Stephen Markam [Markham]. & Shadrach Roundy. & Hiram Clark.[147] and Letter of Attorny ⟨fr[o]m⟩ Mrs. [Margaret] Smith To E[dward] Hunter—[148] & a great variety of

---

143. Pratt and Fielding were serving missions in England.

144. In November 1835, JS spent several days translating from the Egyptian papyri that contained the Book of Abraham. (JS History, vol. B-1, 596–597; JS, Journal, 1, 3, and 7 Oct. 1835; 19, 20, and 24–26 Nov. 1835, in *JSP*, J1:67–71, 107–111; "The Book of Abraham," *Times and Seasons*, 15 Mar. 1842, 3:719–722 [Abraham 2:19–5:21].)

145. The next issue of the *Times and Seasons* included a section titled "Universal Liberty," which included correspondence between Bennett and C. V. Dyer in addition to correspondence between Bennett and JS. ("Universal Liberty," *Times and Seasons*, 15 Mar. 1842, 3:722–725.)

146. TEXT: Two illegible words appear in the left margin, probably a day and a date.

147. Nauvoo Registry of Deeds, Record of Deeds, bk. A, pp. 30–31; bk. B, pp. 182–183; Hancock Co., IL, Deed Records, vol. N, pp. 51–52, microfilm 954,600, U.S. and Canada Record Collection, FHL.

148. A Mr. John Guest owed Margaret Smith money, which, by previous arrangement, was to be used to purchase goods for JS's store. Hunter needed Mrs. Smith's power of attorney, certified by an Illinois judge, to collect the funds from Guest. (Edward Hunter, West Nantmeal, PA, to JS, Nauvoo, IL,

other Business—— & Rode out. [149] & in the evening attended Triel at Patriarch Hiram's [Hyrum Smith's] office. The city of Nauvoo, vs, [blank] Davis[150] for indecnt and abusive Language About Joseph while at Mr Davis the day priveo [previous] The charges were clearly substantiated by the Testimo[n]y of Dr [Robert D.] Foster. Mr & Mrs. [Davidson and Sarah Tilton] Hibbard and others. Mr Davis was found guilty by Jury. & by Municepal court bounde over to keep the peace 6 month under $100 Bonds,— after which the— the President retired to the Printing office with his Lady & Dr Supped, ⟨&⟩ with the twelve who had been at the office. closed the evening. & retired to his habitation [p. 89]

11 March 1842 • Friday

March. 11 Friday— The Nauvoo Legion was on parade. commanded by Liutenant Genral Joseph Smith in person The line was formed at 10 'oclock A.M. & soon the Legion ma[r]ched from their usual place of parade. below the Temple. To Water Street. in front of General Smith's house. where the troops were inspectid and after a recess marched west on the bank of the River— & taking a circuetous route resumed their usual Post on the parade ground & closed the day in good order & ⟨with⟩ good feelings & to the fullest satisfaction of the commander in chief.—[151]

In the evening the President attended the Trial of Elder Francis G[ladden] Bishop at his own house, the Prestˢ house, Elder Bishop appeard before the High council of Nauvoo. on complaint of having recived. written & publishd or or taught certain Revelations & doctrines not consistent with the Doctrine & Covenants of the Church. Mr Bishop refusing to present the writtn Revelations. the Mayer[152] issued his warrant & brought them before the council. where parts of the same were ~~written~~ Read by Mr Bishop himself. aloud to Council, the whole mass of which appeard to be the extreme of folly. nonsense, absurdity falsewood [falsehood]. & bombastic Egotism,— so much so as to

---

27 Oct. 1841, JS Collection, CHL; JS, Nauvoo, IL, to Edward Hunter, West Nantmeal, PA, 5 Jan. 1842, JS Collection, CHL; JS, Nauvoo, IL, to Edward Hunter, West Nantmeal, PA, 9 and 11 Mar. 1842, JS Collection, CHL.)

149. TEXT: The remainder of this entry is written in a different ink.

150. Amos Davis was charged on this date with "breach of an Ordinance, entitled, 'an Ordinance Concerning Vagrants & disorderly Persons.'" The jury found Davis guilty and determined he should "give Security of One hundred Dollars, to keep the Peace for Six Months." (City of Nauvoo v. Davis [Nauvoo Mun. Ct. 1842], Nauvoo Municipal Court Docket Book, 4 [second numbering].)

151. JS. Section 3 of the ordinance organizing the Nauvoo Legion specified that the legion would be commanded by a "Lieutenant General, as the Chief Commanding & reviewing officer, & president of the Court Martial." (Nauvoo City Council Minute Book, 3 Feb. 1841, 2.)

152. Mayor John C. Bennett.

keep the saints al[l] laughing, when not over awed by sarrow [sorrow] & shame,— Presidnt Joseph expaind [explained] the nature of the case. & gave a very clear elucedation of the tendency of such Prop[h]ets & propecyings & gave Mr Bishop over to the Buffetings of Satan[153] until he shall learn wisdom. After a few appropriate obsevati [observations] from Patriarch hyram [Hyrum Smith] & some of the council: the council voted unanimously. that F. G. Bishop be removed from the fellowship of the church. president Joseph having previously committed the Revelation[154] above referred to, to the flames.[155]

12 March 1842 • Saturday

Saturday 12 Lieut. Gen. Joseph. Smith. presided at over a courtmartial consisting of the officers of the Nauvoo Legion. at his own house for the purpose of deciding upon the Rank & station of the several officers. & the more perfect organization of the Legion[156] [p. 90]

13 March 1842 • Sunday

Sunday 13 [*2 lines blank*]

14 March 1842 • Monday

Monday 14 Transacted a great variety of business at the office

---

153. At the time, those who were excommunicated were often described as "[given] over to the Buffetings of Satan." The minutes of the Nauvoo high council for this date record that "it was decided that he [Bishop] be expelled from the Church by the unanimous vote of the Council." (Nauvoo High Council Minutes, 11 Mar. 1842; see also Revelation, 1 Mar. 1832, in Doctrine and Covenants 75:3, 1835 ed. [D&C 78:12].)

154. TEXT: Possibly "Revelations".

155. According to Wilford Woodruff, who attended the trial, "Gladden had set himself up as some great thing for 8 or 9 years & the church had been so much troubled with him by his foolish conduct that he had been cut off a number of times from the church & restored, & he had now set himself up as a prophet & Revelator to the church & a number of his revelations were brought forward & red before the congregations & it was the greatest Bundle of Nonsens ever put together it would have taken Gladden Bishop ten thousand Years to have accomplished the work which he said in his pretended revelations he should perform he took the name of God in vain & his crime was so great in his Blaspheming God in his pretended revelations that Joseph the Seer said that nothing would excuse him in the sight of God & angels in commiting the unpardonable sin ownly because he was a fool & had not sens sufficient for the Holy Ghost to enlighten him." Bishop was charged with teaching false doctrine as early as the winter of 1832–1833. He was "reproved, repented, and was reordained" at another high council trial in 1835. (Woodruff, Journal, 11 Mar. 1842; Minute Book 1, 28 Sept. 1835; JS, Journal, 28 Sept. 1835, in *JSP*, J1:66; see also Saunders, "Francis Gladden Bishop," chaps. 3–6.)

156. Minutes and resolutions of this meeting, which indicate a number of decisions in addition to an ordinance consisting of fourteen sections on organization and regulation of the legion, appear under this date in the Nauvoo Legion Minute Book. (Nauvoo Legion Minute Book, 12 Mar. 1842, 10–16.)

15 March 1842 • Tuesday

Tuesday 15 Officiated as grand Chaplin. at the Installation of the Nauvoo Lodge. of Free Masons, ~~on~~ At the Grove. near the Temple. Grand Master [Abraham] Jonas being present.— A Large number of people assembled on the occasion, the day was exceedingly fine, all things were done in order, and universal satisfaction manifested.[157] Admitted a me[m]ber of the Lodge in the evening.[158]

16 March 1842 • Wednesday

Wedy. 16 Continued with the Lodge.[159]

17 March 1842 • Thursday

Thursday 17 Assisted in organizing "The Female Relief Society of Nauvoo"[160] in the "Lodge Room"[161] Sister Emma Smith President. & Sisters ⟨Elizabeth Ann [Smith]⟩ Whitney & ⟨Sarah M. [Kingsley]⟩ Cleveland councillors, ⟨I⟩ gave much instru[c]tion. read in the New Testament & Book of Doctrine & Covenants. concer[n]ing the Elect Lady.[162] & Shewed that <u>Elect</u> meant to be <u>Elected</u> to a <u>certain</u> <u>work</u> &c, & that the revelation was then fulfilled by ~~his~~ Sister Emma's Election to the Presidency of the Society, she having previously been ordained[163] to expound the Scriptures. her councillors[164] were ordaind by Elder J⟨ohn⟩ Taylor. & Emma ⟨was⟩ Blessed by the same.—

---

157. Wilford Woodruff noted that a procession celebrating the lodge's organization formed at JS's store and marched to the grove in front of the temple. Woodruff estimated three thousand people were present. The lodge minutes add that "at the Grove, after the ceremonies of installation the Grand Master delivered a highly creditable and finished address on the subject of Ancient York Masonry, after which the lodges returned to the lodge room in Masonic order." By the end of 1842, the Nauvoo lodge was the largest Masonic lodge in Illinois. (Woodruff, Journal, 15 Mar. 1842; Nauvoo Masonic Lodge Minute Book, 15 Mar. 1842; Hogan, *Vital Statistics of Nauvoo Lodge*, 4.)

158. At this evening meeting JS and Sidney Rigdon were initiated as Entered Apprentice Masons. (Nauvoo Masonic Lodge Minute Book, 15 Mar. 1842.)

159. In the morning JS and Sidney Rigdon were received as Fellow Craft Masons and, later that day, as Master Masons. (Nauvoo Masonic Lodge Minute Book, 16 Mar. 1842.)

160. A few weeks earlier, a group of women in Nauvoo drafted a constitution for a proposed charitable "Sewing Society." When they showed the document to JS, he told them he had "something better" for them and called this meeting. Twenty women, JS, Willard Richards, and John Taylor attended. (Relief Society Record, 29; Relief Society Minute Book, 17 Mar. 1842.)

161. The general business office or "Lodge Room" was located on the second floor of JS's store.

162. A revelation dated July 1830 refers to Emma Smith as an "elect lady." (Revelation, July 1830–C, in Doctrine and Covenants 48:1, 1835 ed. [D&C 25:3]; see also 2 John 1:1.)

163. JS explained that Emma was "ordain'd at the time, the Revelation was given [July 1830], to expound the scriptures to all; and to teach the female part of community." (Relief Society Minute Book, 17 Mar. 1842.)

164. Sarah M. Kingsley Cleveland and Elizabeth Ann Smith Whitney. (Relief Society Minute Book, 17 Mar. 1842.)

18 March 1842 • Friday

Friday 18 [*2 lines blank*]

19 March 1842 • Saturday

Saturday 19 [*2 lines blank*]

20 March 1842 • Sunday

Sunday 20 Baptized 60 or 70 in the River. confirmed them in the grove & baptized in the Font in the P.M.¹⁶⁵

21 March 1842 • Monday

Monday 21 Commenced a Sittlement with W͟m͟ Marks¹⁶⁶

22 March 1842 • Tuesday

Tuesday 22 At the General Business office (Sarah Ann. Whhitney's [Whitney's] Birth day (17. ⟨years of age⟩) celebration, at the Lodge Room. co. waited upon by the Rec͟r͟·¹⁶⁷) ⟨home in the eve.⟩

23 March 1842 • Wednesday

Wednesday 23 At his office in council with H[eber] C. Kimball, Rec͟r͟· &c.

24 March 1842 • Thursday

Thursday 24 At his office. waited on the members of the Female Relief Soci[e]ty. & entered a complaint againts. Clarissa Marvel for Slander¹⁶⁸

---

165. Prior to these baptisms, JS spoke to a large audience in the grove on baptism, death, and the Resurrection. Following the baptisms in the river, JS returned to the grove, where those who had been baptized were confirmed. The same afternoon, members of the Quorum of the Twelve baptized church members for their deceased relatives in the font in the Nauvoo temple. (Wilford Woodruff, "Sabbath Scene in Nauvoo," *Times and Seasons*, 15 Apr. 1842, 3:751–753; Woodruff, Journal, 20 Mar. 1842.)

166. This could be the settlement between JS and Marks that was closed two weeks later. (JS, Journal, 4 Apr. 1842.)

167. The recorder, Willard Richards.

168. At the organizational meeting of the Female Relief Society of Nauvoo on 17 March 1842, JS charged the society with "correcting the morals and strengthening the virtues of the female community." To this end, the organization regularly took roll, voted on the worthiness of its members, and investigated charges of improper behavior. Marvel was here accused of spreading "scandalous falsehoods on the character of Presᵗ Joseph Smith," concerning his relationship with Agnes Coolbrith Smith (wife of his deceased brother Don Carlos), "without the least provocation." On 2 April 1842, following the Relief Society's investigation of the charges, Marvel wrote a statement that she had never "at any time or place, seen or heard any thing improper or unvirtuous in the conduct or conversation" of either JS or Agnes, and that she had never "reported any thing derogatory to the characters of either of them." The report of the Marvel investigation, presented at the meeting of 14 April 1842, cleared Marvel of charges and stated that her testimony of innocence was satisfactorily received. Mary Ann West, who lived with Agnes in Nauvoo,

25 March 1842 • Friday

Friday 25 [*2 lines blank*]

26 March 1842 • Saturday

Saturday 26 [p. 91] Elder John Snider Recivied his final inst[r]uctions from the President, & received his blessing from Prest B[righam] Young. with the Laying on of the hands of Prest. Joseph. J[ohn] E. Page. & W[illard] Richards. & Started for England same day.[169]

27 March 1842 • Sunday

Sunday 27[th] Baptized 107 individuals after speaking on baptism for the Dead[170] and witnessed the landing of 150 English brethren from the Steam boat Ariel[171]

28 March 1842 • Monday

Monday 28 Received P[arley] P. Pratts donations from England.[172] and transacted other business at the office.

29 March 1842 • Tuesday

Tuesday 29 [*2 lines blank*]

---

reported fifty years later that Agnes told her that she (Agnes) had become a plural wife of JS following the death of her husband, Don Carlos. (Relief Society Minute Book, 17 Mar. 1842; 24 Mar. 1842; [31] Mar. 1842; 14 Apr. 1842, 89; Mary Ann West, Testimony, Salt Lake City, Utah Territory, ca. 22 Mar. 1892, pp. 499–500, questions 141–144, pp. 521–522, questions 676–687, 696–699, Reorganized Church of Jesus Christ of Latter Day Saints v. Church of Christ Independence, Missouri, et al. [C.C.W.D. Mo. 1894], typescript, Testimonies and Depositions, CHL.)

169. Although Snider was appointed on 22 December 1841 to serve a mission to Europe, he had not left by 28 January 1842, at which time the Quorum of the Twelve directed him to go. He returned from England 23 January 1843. (JS, Journal, 22 Dec. 1841; 28 Jan. 1842; 23 Jan. 1843, pp. 16–17, 38, 249 herein.)

170. Wilford Woodruff reported that JS said on this occasion that the Bible supported the concept of baptism for the dead and that if persons living could be baptized, those who were deceased could receive the same privilege. Although JS's discourse was on baptism for the dead, at least some of the baptisms performed this day were rebaptisms for living people—including Woodruff and John Taylor. Following the baptisms, the Saints assembled, as on the 20 March occasion, near the temple for confirmations. (Woodruff, Journal, 27 Mar. 1842.)

171. According to *The Wasp*, the *Aeriel* carried "some hundred and fifty or two hundred emigrants . . . from Eng[l]and, accompanied by Elder Lyman Wight and eighty or ninety more from Mississippi." Wight later recalled returning to Nauvoo with "47,500 lbs of sugar & molasses and 10 sacks of coffee, a small quantity of dry goods and 100 mormon passengers." ("Emigration," *The Wasp*, 16 Apr. 1842, [2]; Lyman Wight, Mountain Valley, TX, to Wilford Woodruff, [Salt Lake City, Utah Territory], 24 Aug. 1857, p. 11, Historian's Office, Histories of the Twelve, ca. 1858–1880, CHL.)

172. Pratt, who was presiding over the church's congregations in England, forwarded by the hand of Stephen Nixon seven donations, totaling $250, from church members there. (Book of the Law of the Lord, 103.)

30 March 1842 • Wednesday

Wednesday 30 [*2 lines blank*]

31 March 1842 • Thursday

Thursday 31 In council at his office with. Elders [Brigham] Young. [John] Taylor &ᶜ. & wrote an Epistle to the Female Relief Socity and spake to the Socity in the afternoon.¹⁷³

1 April 1842 • Friday

April¹⁷⁴ Friday 1 at the General Business office

2 April 1842 • Saturday

Saturday 2 Paid Hugh Rhodes $1150. for a Farm¹⁷⁵

3 April 1842 • Sunday

Sunday 3 [*2 lines blank*]

4 April 1842 • Monday

Monday 4 Transacted business at his house with Josiah Butterfie[l]d concerning the Lawrence estates.¹⁷⁶ & closed a Settlement with Wᵐ Marks in the counting Room.¹⁷⁷

---

173. The minutes of the Female Relief Society mistakenly indicate that the meeting was held on 30 March. The "Epistle," recorded following the minutes of the Relief Society meeting on 28 September 1842, cautioned the sisters to be wary of immoral individuals who claimed authority from JS or other church leaders to commit sin. The epistle may have been the "article" that the minutes report Emma Smith as reading during the afternoon meeting. In JS's afternoon discourse, he explained that the society should be "separate from all the evils of the world, choice, virtuous and holy" and that they should be careful to determine the worthiness of those admitted into the society. (Relief Society Minute Book, [31] Mar. 1842, 86–88.)

174. TEXT: "April" is triple underlined.

175. Possibly the final payment for 153½ acres of land in the northeast quarter of Section 8 and northwest quarter of Section 9 within Township 6 North, Range 8 West, that JS contracted to buy from Erie Rhodes on 16 September 1841 for $3,000. Hugh Rhodes was the administrator for the estate of Erie Rhodes, who died October 1841. (Hancock Co., IL, Bonds and Mortgages, vol. 1, pp. 228–229, microfilm 954,776, U.S. and Canada Record Collection, FHL; Hancock Co., IL, Probate Record, vol. A, p. 119, microfilm 954,481, U.S. and Canada Record Collection, FHL.)

176. After the death of Edward Lawrence in November or December 1839, JS was appointed on 4 June 1841 as guardian of the Lawrence children and received title to their assets. Margaret Lawrence, Edward's widow, married Butterfield on 24 December 1840. (Madsen, "Joseph Smith as Guardian," 172–173, 179, 181–187.)

177. A promissory note written by JS on this date stated he would "pay Wᵐ Marks or bearer Two hundrd and eighty nine dollars in goods at the brick store from time to time as my circumstances will admit." (Promissory note, JS to William Marks, 4 Apr. 1842, JS Collection, CHL.)

5 April 1842 • Tuesday

Tuesday 5 Settled with Bro [William] Niswanger[178]

6 April 1842 • Wednesday

Wednesday 6 With his family. and several of the Twelve. viz. B[righam] Young H[eber] C. Kimball. W[illard] Richards. & gave instructions how to ~~open~~ organize & adjourn the <u>special</u> conference.[179] it being so wet & cold that it was not prudent to continue the meeting & the presidents health would not admit of his going out. at his house also. the Patriarch[180] and the Twelve present bore Testimony to the principles of virtue which they had invariably heard taught by Joseph.

7 April 1842 • Thursday

Thursday 7 Spoke to the conference in the grove & replied to Elder John E. Page'.s communication. Shewing the cause of his Seperation from Elder [Orson] Hyde. ~~on~~ in his mission to Jerusalem.[181] first a covenant to communicate to each other all secrets.[182] [p. 92]

8 April 1842 • Friday

Friday 8 [*10 lines blank*]

---

178. William Niswanger paid $800 on this date for land in block seventy-one of the Hotchkiss purchase. (Trustees Land Book A, Hotchkiss Purchase, block 71, lot 2, [124].)

179. This was the first day of a three-day conference held 6–8 April 1842. The conference was not termed a "general conference" because JS announced in October 1841 that there would not be another "general" conference until the completion of the temple in Nauvoo. ("Conference Minutes," *Times and Seasons,* 15 Apr. 1842, 3:761–763; see also 19n52 herein.)

180. Hyrum Smith.

181. In April 1840, Hyde and Page were appointed to serve a mission to London, Amsterdam, Constantinople, Jerusalem, and "other places" to "converse with the priests, rulers and Elders of the Jews, and obtain from them" the "present views and movements of the Jewish people." After "obtain[ing] from them all the information possible," they were to "communicate the same to some principal paper for publication, that it may have a general circulation throughout the United States." The two men started their mission together but separated after a time—Hyde continuing on to Jerusalem and Page eventually returning to Nauvoo. At the April 1842 conference, Page explained that he and Hyde separated during their fund-raising activities and Hyde left for Europe earlier than they had originally intended. After Page's remarks, JS stated there was no great harm done in the separation, and a vote of the conference affirmed that Page was to remain in full fellowship. (JS, "To All People unto Whom These Presents Shall Come," *Times and Seasons,* Apr. 1840, 1:86; "Conference Minutes," *Times and Seasons,* 15 Apr. 1842, 3:761–763.)

182. Hyde and Page evidently made a covenant of secrecy with each other, although the conference minutes do not record a statement by Page to that effect. JS responded that such a covenant was wrong, as it "created a lack of confidence for two men to covenant to reveal all acts of secrecy or otherwise to each other." ("Conference Minutes," *Times and Seasons,* 15 Apr. 1842, 3:762.)

9 April 1842 • Saturday

Saturday 9 Preached at the Funeral of Bro Ephraim Marks in the Morning.[183] and in the eve[n]ing attended city council[184]

10 April 1842 • Sunday

Sunday 10 Preached in the grove after Elder Wm Law. had spoken. a[nd] pronounced a curse upon all Adulterers & fornicators & unvirtuous persons. & those who had made use of his name to carry on their iniquitous designs.[185]

11 April 1842 • Monday

Monday 11 In the Lodge & at his house—

12 April 1842 • Tuesday

Tuesday 12 In the Lodge

13 April 1842 • Wednesday

Wednesday 13 In the Lodge Mr Backinstos [Jacob B. Backenstos]. & [George W.] Stiles. & Robinson [Chauncey Robison] from carthage enterd 1st [1st]. degree &. Joseph assisting P.M. S⟨am^{l.}⟩ H. Smith. Wm Smith. & Vincent [Vinson] Knight. on 3^d degree[186]

14 April 1842 • Thursday

Thursday 14 Calvin A. Warren Esqr arrived and commenced an investigation of the principles of General insolvency.[187]

---

183. Marks, age twenty-four, died on 7 April. JS and Sidney Rigdon spoke about the solemn nature of the occasion, the eternal nature of relationships, and the need to be prepared for death at any time. (Huntington, Cemetery Records, [1]; Woodruff, Journal, 9 Apr. 1842; Lyman O. Littlefield, "Funeral of Ephraim Marks," *The Wasp*, 16 Apr. 1842, [4].)

184. The city council repealed section 6 of "An Ordinance Regulating Auctions in the City of Nauvoo." The remainder of the ordinance and five other related ordinances were repealed the following month. (Nauvoo City Council Minute Book, 9 Apr. 1842, 69; JS, Journal, 14 May 1842.)

185. TEXT: Possibly "design". In this discourse, JS also taught about repentance and the importance of gaining knowledge for salvation. (Woodruff, Journal, 10 Apr. 1842.)

186. Nauvoo Masonic Lodge Minute Book, 13 Apr. 1842.

187. In a notice dated 5 April 1842, Warren's firm—Ralston, Warren & Wheat—stated that it was ready to take applications for bankruptcy and that one of the partners would be at Carthage and Nauvoo "on or about the 14th inst." and would remain several days.^a JS was one of those who applied for bankruptcy, his rationale being "the embarrassments under which we have labord through the influence of Mobs & designi[n]g men. & the disadvantageous circumstancs under which we have been compelled to contract debts in order to [maintain] our existinc [existence] both as Individuals & as a Society."^b In compliance with federal law, notices of the petitions for bankruptcy of JS and more than a dozen others were published in five successive issues of *The Wasp*, beginning 7 May 1842. In early November, JS and other church leaders prepared for a trip to Springfield for a final judicial review of their petitions.^c (*a*. "Ralston,

15–16 April 1842 • Friday–Saturday

Friday 15 & Saturday 16 Busily engaged in making out a list of Debtors & invoice of Property[188] to be passed into the hands of the assignee.[189]

17 April 1842 • Sunday

Sunday 17 At home

18 April 1842 • Monday

Monday 18 To carthage. in company with. Hyrum Smith Samuel H. Smith. & testified to their lists of insolvency before the clerk of the county commissioners.[190] Sidney Rigdon & many more brethren. were at Carthage on the same day & business.—[191] W[illard] Richards was present.

19 April 1842 • Tuesday

Tuesday 19 Rode out in the city. & examined some land near the north limits

20 April 1842 • Wednesday

Wednesday 20 assisted in surveying some land in section 25. sold W^m cross. [p. 93]

Warren & Wheat, Attorneys at Law, Quincy Illinois," *The Wasp*, 16 Apr. 1842, [3]. *b.* JS, Nauvoo, IL, to Horace Hotchkiss, Fair Haven, CT, 13 May 1842, copy, JS Collection, CHL. *c.* An Act to Establish a Uniform System of Bankruptcy [19 Aug. 1841], *Public Statutes at Large,* 27th Cong., 1st Sess., chap. 9, p. 446, sec. 7; JS, Journal, 7 Nov. 1842.)

188. JS's debts, incurred at both Kirtland and Nauvoo, amounted to $107,395.60. JS's assets consisted of notes owed him amounting to $99,797.38, several household items and articles of furniture, and one-third shares of nearly 250 city lots in Nauvoo. The notes included almost $81,000 owed him by Isaac Galland. ("Schedule Setting Forth a List of Petitioner[']s Creditors, Their Residence, and the Amount Due to Each," ca. 15–16 Apr. 1842, CCLA; "Inventory of Property," in Letter to John W. Woods, Nauvoo, IL, ca. 7 Aug. [1842], JS Collection, CHL.)

189. An "assignee," according to the Bankruptcy Act of 1841, was "vested with all the rights, titles, powers, and authorities to sell, manage, and dispose of" the bankrupt's property. At this time, an assignee for Nauvoo had not been appointed by the court. (An Act to Establish a Uniform System of Bankruptcy [19 Aug. 1841], *Public Statutes at Large,* 27th Cong., 1st Sess., chap. 9, pp. 442–443, sec. 3; Calvin A. Warren, Quincy, IL, to JS, Nauvoo, IL, 3 June 1842, JS Collection, CHL.)

190. Samuel Marshall was the clerk of the Hancock County Commissioners Court from 1838 to 1843. (Cochran et al., *History of Hancock County, Illinois,* 624.)

191. Calvin A. Warren processed the bankruptcy applications of at least fifteen Mormons in the early June hearings. While the Bankruptcy Act of 1841 granted primary authority to federal district courts (in this case, the court in Springfield), it stipulated that petitions and depositions could be filed before any commissioner appointed by the federal district court. (Calvin A. Warren, Quincy, IL, to JS, Nauvoo, IL, 3 June 1842, JS Collection, CHL; An Act to Establish a Uniform System of Bankruptcy [19 Aug. 1841], *Public Statutes at Large,* 27th Cong., 1st Sess., chap. 9, pp. 445–446, secs. 6–7; see also the bankruptcy notices published in *The Wasp,* beginning 7 May 1842.)

21 April 1842 • Thursday
⟨April⟩ Thursday 21

22 April 1842 • Friday
Friday 22

23 April 1842 • Saturday
Saturday 23

24 April 1842 • Sunday
Sunday 24 Prea[c]hed on the hill near the Temple. concerning the building of the Temple. and pronounced a curse on the merchants & the rich who would not assist in building it.[192]

25 April 1842 • Monday
Monday 25 Reading. meditation &c. mostly with his family

26 April 1842 • Tuesday
Tuesday 26   "

27 April 1842 • Wednesday
Wednesday 27   "

28 April 1842 • Thursday
Thursday 28 at Two o'clock after-noon met the members of the "Female relief Society" [193]and after presiding at the admission of many new members. Gave a [194]lecture on the pries[t]hood shewing how the Sisters would come in possession of the priviliges & blesings & gifts of the priesthood— & that the signs should follow them. such as healing the sick casting out devils &c. & that they might attain unto. these blessings. by a virtuous life & conversation & diligence in keeping all the commandments[195]

---

192. Obtaining the support of wealthy church members for building the temple continued to be a problem. On 21 February 1843, JS publicly reprimanded wealthy individuals who favored their own construction projects rather than the temple. (JS, Journal, 21 Feb. 1843, p. 271 herein.)

193. TEXT: "29" in left margin.

194. TEXT: "30" in left margin.

195. According to the minutes of the meetings, JS "said the reason of these remarks being made was, that some little thing was circulating in the Society, that some persons were not going right in laying hands on the sick, &c." After referencing the signs that are to follow those who believe (see Mark 16:17–18), JS went on to say "that there could be no more sin in any female laying hands on the sick than in

29 April 1842 • Friday

Friday 29 was made manifest a conspiracy again[s]t the peace of his househould[196]

30 April 1842 • Saturday

Saturday 30 visiting with Judge [James] Adams.— & his own family. & signed deeds to James & Charles Ivins. & many others.[197]

1 May 1842 • Sunday

May Sunday 1 preached in the grove on the keys of the kingdom charity &c.— The keys are certain signs & words by which false spirits & personages may be detected from true.— which cannot be revealed to the Elders till the Temple is completed.— The rich can only get them in the Temple. The poor may get them on the Mountain top as did moses. The rich cannot be saved without cha[r]ity. giving to feed the poor. when & how God requires as well as building. There are signs in heaven earth & hell. the elders must know them all to be endued with power. to finish their work & prevent imposition. The devil knows many signs. but does not know the sign of the son of man. or Jesus. No one can truly say he knows God until he has handled something. & ~~these~~ this can only be in the holiest of Holies.

2–3 May 1842 • Monday–Tuesday

Monday 2) Tuesday 3) with his family

4 May 1842 • Wednesday

Wednesday 4 In council in the Presidents & General offices with Judge [James] Adams. Hyram [Hyrum] Smith Newel K. Whitney. William Marks, Wm Law. George Miller. Brigham Young. Heber C. Kimball & Willard Richards. [*illegible*] & giving certain instructions concerning the priesthood.

---

wetting the face with water that it is no sin for any body to do it that has faith, or if the sick has faith to be heal'd by the administration." (Relief Society Minute Book, 28 Apr. 1842.)

196. The initials "J.C.B." were later inserted lightly in the journal by Willard Richards and probably refer to John C. Bennett.

197. Land sales to Charles Ivins, James Ivins, George W. Harris, Benjamin Bird, Lavina Murphy, and Jessee Turpin were recorded under this date. (Trustees Land Book A, White Purchase, block 117, lots 3–4; block 118, lot 1; block 125, lot 1; block 140, lot 3; Hotchkiss Purchase, block 14, lot 4; block 100, lot 4; block 102, lots 2–4; block 109, lots 1, 4.)

[*illegible*] &c on the Aronic Priesthood to the first [*illegible*] continueing through the day.[198]

5 May 1842 • Thursday

Thursday 5 Judge [James] Adams left for Springfield the others continued in Council as the day previous & Joseph & Hyrum [Smith] were [*illegible*][199] [p. 94]

6 May 1842 • Friday

Friday 6 Attended the officer drill in the morning.[200] & visited Lyman Wight who was sick

7 May 1842 • Saturday

Saturday 7 Commanded the Nauvoo Legion through the day.[201] the Legion one year since consisted of ~~two~~ 6 companies. to day of 26 companies amounting to about Two thousand Troops. The consolidatd Staff of the Legion partook of an excellent dinner at the house of the commander in chief[202] between

---

198. These instructions constituted a substantial change to the "endowment" as understood and practiced earlier by members of the church in Kirtland, Ohio. Richards, who participated in the events of 4 May 1842, made the brief summary of JS's daylong temple instruction in this journal entry and also prepared the following description of the new endowment, which later became part of the JS multivolume manuscript history: JS instructed those present "in the principles and order of the priesthood, attending to washings & anointings, endowments, and the communicatns of keys, pertaining to the Aronic Priesthood, and so on to the highe[s]t order of the Melchisedec Pristhood, setting forth the order pertaining to the Ancient of days & all those plans & principles by which any one is enabled to secure the fulness of those blessings which has been prepared for the chu[r]ch of the first-born, and come up, and abide in the prese[n]ce of Eloheim in the eternal worlds. In this council was institutd the Ancient order of things for the fir[s]t time in these last days." According to Richards, JS's instructions "were of things spiritul, and to be received only by the spiritual minded: and there was nothing made known to these men but what will be made known to all saints, of the last days, so soon as they are prepared to recive, and a proper place is prepared to communicate them, even to the weakest of the saints; therefore let the saints be diligent in building the Temple and all houses which they have been or shall hereafter be commanded of God to build, and wait their time with patience, in all meekness faith, & perseverance unto the end, knowing assuredly that all these things refer[re]d to in this council are always governd by the principles of Revelation." (Historian's Office, JS History, draft notes, 4 May 1842; see also JS History, vol. C-1, 1328–1329.)

199. Willard Richards's notes of this meeting indicate that JS and Hyrum Smith, having officiated in the ordinance the previous day for others, were endowed on this date. (Historian's Office, JS History, draft notes, 5 May 1842; see also JS History, vol. C-1, 1329.)

200. The legion was required to hold an officer drill on the Thursday and Friday preceding a general parade. (Nauvoo Legion Minute Book, 12 Mar. 1842, 12.)

201. On 12 March 1842, the Nauvoo Legion court-martial passed an ordinance requiring the legion to hold a general parade on the first Saturday of May and September. (Nauvoo Legion Minute Book, 12 Mar. 1842, 12.)

202. JS.

one & three. PM.²⁰³ The day was very fine. & passed away very harmoniously. without drunkenness. noise or confusion.— There was a great concourse of spectators. & many distinguis[h]ed Strangers who exp[r]essed much satisfaction.—²⁰⁴ & the commander in chief. in a very appropriate address. remarkd that his soul was never better satisfied than on this occasion. aftre the Legion was dismissed. Rode in Co. with his Lady & ²⁰⁵others around the Temple.

8 May 1842 • Sunday

Sunday 8 Meeting at the Grove. Prest [Sidney] Rigdon Preached

9 May 1842 • Monday

Monday 9 With his family.

10 May 1842 • Tuesday

[*illegible*] Tuesday [*illegible*] 10 Transacted a variety of business at the Store. printing office &ᶜ.

11 May 1842 • Wednesday

[*illegible*] Wednesday [*illegible*] 11 called with the recorder to see a new secreta[r]y at Bro Colledges.²⁰⁶ dictated various letters & business.²⁰⁷ called a few mome[n]ts with Recorder at B. Knights²⁰⁸

12 May 1842 • Thursday

Thursday 12 Dictated a Letter to President Rigden [Sidney Rigdon]. concerning certain difficulties or surmises which existed.²⁰⁹ & attended the meeting of

---

203. Wilford Woodruff added that the wives of the staff also attended the dinner. (Woodruff, Journal, 7 May 1842.)

204. The "distinguished strangers" included Stephen A. Douglas, James Ralston, Almeron Wheat, and Jacob B. Backenstos. (Jacob B. Backenstos and Stephen A. Douglas, Affidavit, 4 Jan. 1843, p. 390 herein; JS, Journal, 4 Jan. 1843 pp. 222–223 herein.)

205. TEXT: "8" in left margin.

206. Probably Joseph Coolidge, a carpenter. (*History of Mills County, Iowa*, 674–675.)

207. On this day a notice was written and signed by the First Presidency, nine members of the Quorum of the Twelve, and bishops Newel K. Whitney, Vinson Knight, and George Miller, stating that they had withdrawn "the hand of fellowship" from John C. Bennett. The notice, asserting that church leaders had labored with Bennett "to persuade him to amend his conduct, apparently to no good effect," was published the following month in the *Times and Seasons*. (JS et al., "Notice," 11 May 1842, JS Collection, CHL; JS et al., "Notice," *Times and Seasons*, 15 June 1842, 3:830.)

208. Probably Vinson Knight, a bishop in Nauvoo.

209. The correspondence between JS and Rigdon has not been located. Some sources suggest that the difficulties between the two men stemmed from an alleged marriage proposal on the part of JS to

the Female Relief Socity. the house being filled to overflowing.—[210] The meeting closed with heavy thunder Storm.

13 May 1842 • Friday

Friday 13 Received answer from S[idney] Rigdon after. a variety of current business. having been in his garden & with his family much of the day. walked in the evening to the P[ost] office with the Recorder. & had a private interview with Prest Rigdon with much apparent satisfaction to all parties. concerning certain evil reports put in circulation by F. M. [*several illegible words*]—[211] about Prest Rigdons family & others[212] after which the Recorder waited on him to his gate.

14 May 1842 • Saturday

Saturday 14. City council. Advocated strongly the necessity of some active measures being taken to suppress. houses & acts of infamy in the city; for the protection of the innocent & virtuous— & good of public morals. shewing clearly that there were certain characters. in the place who were disposed to corrupt the morals & chastity of our citizens & that houses of infamy did exist.— upon which a city ordinance was passed to prohibit such things & published in this days wasp.—[213] ⟨I⟩ Also. spoke Largely for the repeal of the Laws ordinances of the City Licen[s]ing. Merchants. Hawkers Tavern & Ordinaries. desiring that this might be a free people. & enjoy equal rights & Priviliges. & the ordinan[c]es were repealed.—[214] Bro Amos Fielding arrived

---

Sidney Rigdon's nineteen-year-old daughter, Nancy. Other evidence suggests that bad feelings developed after JS reproved Nancy for immoral behavior. The nature of the sources precludes any firm conclusions. (See, for example, "6th Letter from Gen. Bennett," *Sangamo Journal* [Springfield, IL], 19 Aug. 1842, [2]; Bennett, *History of the Saints*, 243–247; John W. Rigdon, Affidavit, Salt Lake Co., Utah, 28 July 1905, pp. 6–8, in Joseph F. Smith, Affidavits about Celestial Marriage, CHL; *Speech of Orson Hyde*, 27–28.)

210. According to Eliza R. Snow's minutes of the meeting (which mistakenly were recorded under the date of 13 May), JS said "that in his opinion, all men now considered in good standing" who refused to pay their debts owed to widows "ought to be discountenanc'd by the Relief Society." (Relief Society Minute Book, [12] May 1842.)

211. TEXT: An erasure. Draft notes compiled by the Historian's Office indicate that this refers to Francis M. Higbee. (Historian's Office, JS History, draft notes, 13 May 1842.)

212. Rigdon and his family openly turned against JS six weeks later. (JS, Journal, 28 June 1842.)

213. "An Ordinance concerning Brothels and Disorderly Characters," The Wasp, 14 May 1842, [3]; see also Nauvoo City Council Minute Book, 14 May 1842, 77.

214. Five ordinances were repealed on this date: "An Ordinance in relation to Hawkers, Pedlars, & Public Shows and Exhibitions," "An Ordinance Regulating Auctions in the City of Nauvoo," "An Ordinance to regulate Taverns & Ordinaries in the City of Nauvoo," "An Ordinance in relation to Stores and Groceries," and "An Ordinance to amend an Ordinance entitled 'An Ordinance to regulate Taverns and Ordinaries in the City of Nauvoo.'" The ordinance passed on this date, repealing those above, was

from Liverpool.—[215] after Council worked in his garden. & walked out in the city & borrowed two Sovereign[216] to make a payment This day it was first hinted in Nauvoo that Ex govenor [Lilburn W.] Boggs of Missouri. had been shot.[217] Page 122 [p. 95]

[pages 96–121, donation records dated 5 March–17 May 1842]

15 May 1842 • Sunday

[218]Sunday May 15 Attended meeting at the grove. Prest [Sidney] Rigdon preached. News of Govenors— [Lilburn W.] Boggs. confirmed By general Report. & published on the stand

16 May 1842 • Monday

Monday 16 Transacting business at the store until 10. A.M.— Then at home & in the P.M. at the printing office withe Bro. [Brigham] Young [Heber C.] Kimball [Willard] Richards &c in council

17 May 1842 • Tuesday

Tuesday 17 At home and about the offices through the day. & in the evening called at Bro Sniders[219] to See clark Leal of Fountain Green about some land. &c

18 May 1842 • Wednesday

Wednesday 18 Rode on horse back with the Recorder in co. with clark Leal. To Bro Benbows [John Benbow's]. & searched out the N.E. Quarter Sec 15. 6 N. 8 W. & contracted for the refusal of the Same at $3 per Acre.

"An Ordinance repealing certain Ordinances respecting Licenses in the City of Nauvoo." (Nauvoo City Council Minute Book, 14 May 1842, 78.)

215. Fielding, an Englishman, was appointed on 2 April 1841 to "superintend fitting out the Saints from Liverpool to America under the instructions of Elder P[arley] P. Pratt." (Woodruff, Journal, 5 Apr. 1841.)

216. A gold coin of the United Kingdom, equal to one pound sterling. ("Sovereign," in *Oxford English Dictionary*, 10:488.)

217. Former Missouri governor Boggs was shot by an unknown assailant on the evening of 6 May 1842 while sitting in his home in Independence, Missouri. Although seriously wounded, he recovered. Initial reports received in Nauvoo were that he was mortally wounded. Within a few weeks rumors connected JS with the crime, and later in the year formal attempts were made to extradite JS to Missouri. (Woodruff, Journal, 15 May 1842; "Assassination of Ex-Governor Boggs of Missouri," *Quincy [IL] Whig,* 21 May 1842, [3]; JS, Journal, 8 Aug. 1842; see also Appendix 1, p. 377 herein.)

218. TEXT: "95 From Page 95" appears at the top of this page.

219. Probably Robert Snyder, who owned and operated a hotel on the southeast corner of Main and Parley streets in Nauvoo. (Nauvoo Books of Assessment, Fourth Ward, 1842, p. 9, Nauvoo, IL, Records, CHL.)

owned by Crawford B. Shelden [Sheldon] of N York.[220] dined at Bro Benbow's. visited Bro Sayres.[221] &c. which with business at the different offices closed the day.

19 May 1842 • Thursday

Thursday 19. Rain. At. home. during A.M.— 1. o clock P.M. City council. The Mayor John C. Bennet[t] having resigned his office.[222] Joseph. was Elected Mayor & Hyrum Smith Vice Mayor of Nauvoo.[223] While the election was going forward in the council. Joseph recived & wrote the following Rev— & threw it across the room to Hiram Kimball one of the Councillors.

[224]"Verily thus saith the Lord unto you my servant Joseph by the voice of my Spirit, Hiram Kimball has been insinuating evil. & forming evil opinions against you with. others. & if he continue in them he & they shall be accursed. for I am the Lord thy God & will stand by thee & bless thee. <u>Amen</u>."[225]

After the Election Joseph spoke at some length concerning the evil reports which were abroad in the city concerning himself— & the nec[e]ssity of counteracting the designs of our enemies. establishing a night [226]watch &c. Where

---

220. Leal wrote to JS the following day and explained that the owner of the land had not authorized that any improvements be made upon it and that JS must not make improvements until Leal received permission from Sheldon. (Clark Leal, Fountain Green, IL, to JS, Nauvoo, IL, 19 May 1842, Helen Vilate Bourne Fleming, Collection, CHL.)

221. Probably Edward Sayers.

222. Bennett resigned from his office as mayor two days earlier, 17 May, the same day Hyrum Smith accused him of immoral conduct. ("New Election of Mayor, and Vice Mayor, of the City of Nauvoo," *The Wasp*, 21 May 1842, [3]; "Affidavit of Hyrum Smith," *Times and Seasons*, 1 Aug. 1842, 3:870–872.)

223. While the election for mayor was normally a general election, the Nauvoo city charter specified that the city council "shall have power to fill all vacancies that may happen by death, resignation or removal, in any of the offices herein made elective." A resolution was passed this date by the city council and signed by JS, thanking Bennett "for the faithful discharge of his Duty while Mayor of [Nauvoo]." (An Act to Incorporate the City of Nauvoo [16 Dec. 1840], *Laws of the State of Illinois* [1840–1841], p. 54, sec. 11; Nauvoo City Council Minute Book, 19 May 1842, 82.)

224. TEXT: "Revelation To Hiram Kimball" inserted in left margin.

225. The "evil opinions" mentioned in this revelation may refer to the growing friction between JS and various Nauvoo businessmen, like Hiram Kimball, over the latter's promoting their own projects ahead of those of the church. Alternatively, or in addition, they may have had something to do with the principle of plural marriage, which JS reportedly taught to Kimball's wife, Sarah Granger, about this time and which she rejected. In spite of their differences, JS and Hiram Kimball remained cordial, and Kimball joined the church the following year. (JS, Journal, 21 Feb. 1843, p. 273 herein; "Plural Marriage," *Historical Record*, May 1887, 6:232; JS, Journal, 14 and 15 June 1842; "Kimball, Hiram S.," in Jenson, *LDS Biographical Encyclopedia*, 2:372.)

226. TEXT: "Night Watch" inserted in left margin.

John C. Bennett. Bennett held important civic, church, and military positions in Nauvoo for a time but left the city after being censured for adultery. He subsequently lectured against Mormonism in several eastern cities and published letters and a book attacking the church and its leader. (Church History Library, Salt Lake City.)

upon the mayor was authorized to establish a Night watch. by city ordinance,[227]

[228]Dr John C. Bennet. Ex mayor, was then called upon by the Mayor to state if he ~~know~~ knew ought against him.— When Dr Bennet replied "I know what I am about. & the heads of the church know what they are about. I expect: I have no difficulty with the heads of the church. I publicly avow that any one who has said that I have stated that General Joseph Smith has given me authority to hold illicit intercourse with women is a a Liar in the face of God. Those who have said it are damned Liars: they are infernal Liars. He ~~neither~~ never ⟨eithe[r]⟩ in public or private gave me any such authority or licence, & any person who states it is a Scoundrel & a Liar. I have heard it said that I should b[e]come a Seckond [Sampson] Avard by withdrawing from the church. & that I was at variance with the heads ⟨& should use an influence against them⟩ because I resignd the office of Mayor: [p. 122] This is <u>false</u>, I have no difficulty with the heads of the church & ~~hope~~ Intend to continue with you. & hope the time may come when I may be restored to full confidence. & fellowship. & my former standing in the chu[r]ch.[229] & that my conduct may be such as to warrent my restoration.— & should the time ever come that I may have the opportunity to test my faith it will then be known whethr I am a ~~true~~ traitor or a true man."

Josep[h]. will you please state difinitely whether you know any thing again[s]t my character either in public or private?

Answer by Gen Bennet, "I do not. in all my intercourse with General Smith. in public & in private he has been strictly virtuous."[230]

Joseph then made some pertinent remarks before the council concerning those who had been guilty of circulating false reports &c & said [231]"Let one twelve months see if Bro Joseph is not calld for to go to every part of the city

---

227. The ordinance establishing a night watch specified that "the number of Persons to compose said Watch, & the regulations & Duties connected therewith, be at the sole appointment & discretion of the Mayor." An editorial in the *Sangamo Journal* reported that the watch was established to protect JS from possible retaliation following rumors that he had been involved in the attempt to assassinate former Missouri governor Lilburn W. Boggs. (Nauvoo City Council Minute Book, 19 May 1842, 82; "The Mormons," *Sangamo Journal* [Springfield, IL], 3 June 1842, [2].)

228. TEXT: "Bennets chara[c]ter of Joseph" inserted in left margin.

229. JS and other church leaders decided to "withdraw the hand of fellowship" from John C. Bennett on 11 May 1842, but notice of the action was not published until the following month. (JS et al., "Notice," 11 May 1842, JS Collection, CHL; JS et al., "Notice," *Times and Seasons,* 15 June 1842, 3:830; see also 55n207 herein.)

230. This conversation was published along with statements concerning Bennett's character in the 1 July 1842 issue of the *Times and Seasons*. ("To the Church of Jesus Christ of Latter Day Saints, and to All the Honorable Part of Community," *Times and Seasons,* 1 July 1842, 3:839–843.)

231. TEXT: "Prophecy" inserted in left margin.

to keep them out of their[232] groves & I turn the keys upon them from this hour if they will not repent [233]& stop their lyings & surmisings. Let God curse them. & let their tongu[e]s cleave unto the roofs of their mouth.[234]

20 May 1842 • Friday

Friday 20 Charges having been preferrd again[s]t D^r R[obert] [D. Foster][235] by Samuel H. [Smith][236] for abusing the Marshall Henry D. [Sherwood][237] [Henry G. Sherwood]. & abusive language towards[238] said Samuel H. [Smith].[239] The Masonic Breth[r]en met at 1 o clock P.M. when the charges were substantatd [substantiated] confession made by Foster. forgiveness granted. Joseph speaking a at considerable length. to accomplish the decision.

Example of shorthand in first Nauvoo journal. Willard Richards used Taylor shorthand in the journal entries for 20 and 23 May 1842. Handwriting of Willard Richards. Book of the Law of the Lord, p. 123, Church History Library, Salt Lake City. (Photograph by Welden C. Andersen.)

---

232. TEXT: Possibly "the ⟨their⟩".
233. TEXT: "a. curse" inserted in left margin.
234. See Ezekiel 3:26 or Psalm 137:6.
235. TEXT: Transliteration from Taylor shorthand: "d f-s-t-r".
236. TEXT: Transliteration from Taylor shorthand: "s-m-th".
237. TEXT: Transliteration from Taylor shorthand: "sh-r-w-d".
238. TEXT: Possibly "towards".
239. TEXT: Transliteration from Taylor shorthand: "s-m-th".

21 May 1842 • Saturday

Saturday 21 At the High council. investigating the case of Robert D. Foster.[240] Chauncy Higby [Chauncey Higbee][241] & others.—

22 May 1842 • Sunday

Sunday 22 At home. called at the Editors office to have letter copied for Qunciy [Quincy] ~~Whig~~ ⟨Argus⟩ ⟨Whig⟩. denying the charge of killing Ex Govener [Lilburn W.] Boggs of Missouri [242]as published in the Quincy whig[243]

23 May 1842 • Monday

Monday 23 A.M. about home. P.M, Walked down the River opposite Bro Hibbards [Davidson Hibbard's] with Dr Charles.[244] N[ewel] K. Whitney

---

240. Foster was charged by Nathan T. Knight for unchristian conduct in refusing to pay for work done by Knight's son. The charges were not sustained and Foster was acquitted. (Nauvoo High Council Minutes, [21] May 1842.)

241. Higbee was charged by George Miller with "unchaste and unvirtuous conduct with the widow Miller and others." Three witnesses then testified that Higbee seduced these women by teaching that it was "right to have free intercourse with women if it was kept secret &c" and that "Joseph Smith therised [authorized] him to practise these things &c." The high council resolved that Higbee be expelled from the church. Two of the witnesses were presumably Margaret and Matilda Nyman, who, with Sarah Miller, formally recorded their testimonies three days later; the testimonies were eventually published in the *Nauvoo Neighbor*. (Nauvoo High Council Minutes, [21] and 24 May 1842; "Chauncy L. Higbee," *Nauvoo Neighbor*, 29 May 1844, [3]; JS, Journal, 24 May 1842, p. 63 herein.)

242. TEXT: The remainder of this entry is written in a lighter ink, which matches that of the following entry.

243. After announcing the 6 May shooting of former Missouri governor Boggs "by an unknown hand," the *Quincy Whig* speculated: "There are several rumors in circulation in regard to the horrid affair. One of which throws the crime upon the Mormons—from the fact, we suppose, that Mr. Boggs was governor at the time, and no small degree instrumental in driving them from the State.—Smith too, the Mormon Prophet, as we understand, prophesied a year or so ago, his death by violent means. Hence, there is plenty of foundation for rumor." JS's letter to *Whig* editor Sylvester M. Bartlett on this date charged Bartlett with having done JS "manifest injustice." JS pointed out that Boggs easily could have been the victim of political intrigue and emphasized, "he died not through my instrumentality," adding, "I am tired of the misrepresentation, calumny and detraction heaped upon me by wicked men, and desire and claim only those privileges guaranteed to all men by the Constitution and Laws of the United States, and of Illinois." While Boggs recovered from his wounds, these same accusations eventually led to an attempt to extradite JS to Missouri. ("Assassination of Ex-Governor Boggs of Missouri," *Quincy [IL] Whig*, 21 May 1842, [3]; JS, Nauvoo, IL, 22 May 1842, Letter to the editor, *Quincy [IL] Whig*, 4 June 1842, [2]; JS, Journal, 8 Aug. 1842; see also Appendix 1, p. 377 herein.)

244. Probably Dr. John F. Charles, a Whig politician and resident of Carthage who settled there in 1834. A week after this entry, the residents of the Nauvoo area held a public meeting and nominated Charles as their choice for the Illinois state senate to represent Hancock County. Charles previously served as representative of Hancock County in the Illinois legislature. (Gregg, *History of Hancock County, Illinois*, 272, 522–523; "Public Meeting," *The Wasp*, 4 June 1842, [3]; "Illinois," *Niles National Register* [Washington DC], 26 Sept. 1840, 57.)

W[ilford] Woodruff. & Recorder & found a [child]²⁴⁵ in the water. called a city council. & Elected Dymic [Dimick] B. Huntington Corener of Nauvoo

24 May 1842 • Tuesday

Tuesday 24 while the High council were taking depositions of Sarah Miller. Sister Nyman's [Margaret and Matilda Nyman] & again[s]t Chauncey Higby [Higbee] & others for illicit conduct. &c²⁴⁶ a prosecution was pending betwe[e]n Joseph & Chauncy before E[benezer] Robinson. in which Chauncey was bound over in $200 Bonds²⁴⁷

25 May 1842 • Wednesday

Wednesday 25 Councilling the Bishops &c. in ferretting out iniquity & much of this week was spent in session by the High Council of Nauvoo—²⁴⁸ [p. 123]

26 May 1842 • Thursday

Thursday 26 Masonic Lodge in the A.M. Dr John C. Bennet[t] confessed the charges preferred again[s]t him concerning. females in Nauvoo. & was forgiven Joseph plead in his behalf.— Dr Bennet was notified the day previous that the first Presidency. Twelve & Bishops had withdrawn fellowship from him & were about to publish him. but on his humbling himself & requesting it the withdrawal was withheld from the paper.²⁴⁹ P.M. Female Releif Soceity.— so full that many could get no admittance.²⁵⁰

---

245. TEXT: Transliteration from Taylor shorthand: "ch-l-d".
246. In addition to these depositions, Margaret and Matilda Nyman gave their testimonies before the Nauvoo high council three days earlier. ("Chauncy L. Higbee," *Nauvoo Neighbor,* 29 May 1844, [3].)
247. Based on an affidavit from JS, Higbee was arrested 24 May 1842 for "slander and defamation" against JS and Emma Smith. Margaret Nyman, Matilda Nyman, and Sarah Miller were subpoenaed as witnesses. Nauvoo justice of the peace Ebenezer Robinson bound Higbee with a $200 bond to appear at the October term of the circuit court. (State of Illinois v. Higbee [J.P. Ct. 1842], Robinson and Johnson, Docket Book, 117.)
248. The Nauvoo high council minutes record meetings on 25, 27, and 28 May at which four additional people—one woman and four men—were charged with unvirtuous conduct. Three of these, all men, were disfellowshipped. (Nauvoo High Council Minutes, 25, 27, and 28 May 1842.)
249. JS and other church leaders withdrew fellowship from Bennett on 11 May 1842. Bennett's remarks on 19 May indicate he knew he was not in full fellowship at that time, although he may not have been aware of the precise action taken against him. Church leaders, having "labored with [Bennett] from time to time, to persuade him to amend his conduct, apparently to no good effect," published a notice of the action in the 15 June issue of the *Times and Seasons*. (JS et al., "Notice," *Times and Seasons,* 15 June 1842, 3:830; JS, Journal, 19 May 1842, p. 60 herein; see also 60n229 herein.)
250. At this meeting, JS admonished Relief Society members to deal mercifully and privately with transgressors and to encourage them to reform. (Relief Society Minute Book, 26 May 1842.)

27 May 1842 • Friday

Friday 27 A billious attack. at home taking medicine

28 May 1842 • Saturday

[251]& Saturday 28 rather better. walked to the store with Emma, and did some business in the city. called at 8 in the eve at the printing office with the night watch. To see the Wasp.—

29 May 1842 • Sunday

Sunday 29 At home

30 May 1842 • Monday

Monday 30

31 May 1842 • Tuesday

Tuesday 31

1 June 1842 • Wednesday

Wednesday June 1 Political Meetings in the Grove for nomination of County officers S[idney] Rigdon. spoke at length. and nominated a Goneral [General] ticket from the county at large. Joseph spoke at length & in confirmation of the nomination excepting for Sheriff,[252]

2 June 1842 • Thursday

Thursday June 2 Rode out with Bro Bowen & Recorder & Sold Lot. 1. Block 143.—[253]

3 June 1842 • Friday

Friday 3 Rode out in city & Sold to Bro [Elias] Harmer Lot 1 Block 123—[254] & in the P.M. Rode to Bro Benbows [John Benbow's] on the Prairie with Sister Emma & others on horse back

---

251. TEXT: Inscribed dateline in left margin "Friday & Saturday", combining this with the previous entry.

252. The following people were nominated for the August election: "Dr. J[ohn] F. Charles for the Senate; Mark Aldridge [Aldrich], of Warsaw, and Orson Pratt, of Nauvoo, for Representatives; William Backenstos, for Sheriff; Sidney Rigdon Esq., for School Commissioner; Hiram Kimball, for County Commissioner; and Daniel H. Wells, for Coroner." It is unclear whether JS opposed an early candidate or the final nomination for sheriff put forth by this "General" or "Union" ticket—a slate of Mormons and non-Mormons. ("Public Meeting," *The Wasp*, 4 June 1842, [3].)

253. Nauvoo Registry of Deeds, Record of Deeds, bk. A, pp. 189–190.

254. Actually, the lot sold to Harmer on this date was block 123, lot 2. (Hancock Co., IL, Deed

4 June 1842 • Saturday

Saturday 4 At the printing office in the morning. heard the Letters from the Grand master [Abraham] Jonas D[r] [Joseph] King & Mr Helme [Meredith Helm] about Bennets [John C. Bennett's] expulsion from the Lodge in Ohio.[255] P.M. Paid E. B. Nourse[256] $5.05. for land bought of [Hugh] Mc Fall.[257] & settled with the heirs of Edward Lawrence at his house[258] N[ewel] K. Whitney & Recorder Present.

5 June 1842 • Sunday

Sunday 5 Preached in the morning.[259]

6 June 1842 • Monday

monday 6 To the Prairie with Bro. Yearsly. [David D. Yearsley] & Recorder dined at Bro Lots [Cornelius Lott's].

7 June 1842 • Tuesday

Tuesday 7 Sold Bro Yeasley [David D. Yearsley] N.E. 1/4 of Section 15.[260]

Records, 3 June 1842, vol. K, pp. 278–279, microfilm 954,599, U.S. and Canada Record Collection, FHL.)

255. This was the Pickaway, Ohio, lodge, although the correspondence to which the text refers indicates that initially there was some confusion about which lodge in Ohio allegedly expelled Bennett. Helm wrote a letter to King dated 7 April 1842 requesting any information King might have on the subject. In his return letter of 17 May 1842, King reported discussing the subject with "Bro Patterson," who had preferred charges against Bennett "in Pickaway Lodge, from whence he was Expelled," and suggested that Helm write to Patterson for more information. Meanwhile, on 4 May 1842, Grand Master Jonas wrote to George Miller, Worshipful Master of the Nauvoo lodge, saying he received a letter from "a most valued and esteemed Brother," informing him that Bennett had been expelled from a lodge in Fairfield, Ohio. On 7 May, Jonas's letter was read in the Nauvoo lodge, which led to an exchange of letters about the alleged expulsion. This correspondence was read and discussed in the Nauvoo lodge on 16 June 1842, at which time it was ascertained that Pickaway was the lodge in question. (Joseph King, Decatur, IL, to Meredith Helm, Springfield, IL, 17 May 1842, Letters regarding Freemasonry in Nauvoo, CHL; Abraham Jonas, Columbus, IL, to George Miller, Nauvoo, IL, 4 May 1842, copy, Letters regarding Freemasonry in Nauvoo, CHL; Nauvoo Masonic Lodge Minute Book, 7 May and 16 June 1842; see also 67n268 herein.)

256. Probably Earl B. Nourse of Butler County, Ohio, from whom JS purchased land in Hancock County. (Nauvoo Registry of Deeds, Record of Deeds, bk. A, pp. 24–25.)

257. This was partial payment on a promissory note to McFall dated 25 March 1842. (Promissory note, JS to Hugh McFall, 25 Mar. 1842, JS Collection, CHL.)

258. By 4 June 1842—the one-year anniversary of JS's appointment as guardian of Lawrence's children—expenses totaling $394.62 had been presented against the estate, including fees associated with collecting notes owed the estate from debtors in Canada, a bill from Josiah Butterfield (who had married Lawrence's widow, Margaret) for boarding at least some of the Lawrence children, payments made for clothing for the children, and "interest" due Lawrence's widow. (Madsen, "Joseph Smith as Guardian," 181–192; JS, Journal, 4 Apr. 1842.)

259. JS's discourse to about eight thousand listeners, taken from Ezekiel 32 and 33, was a call for the nations to repent. ("The Prophet," *The Wasp*, 11 June 1842, [2].)

260. Trustees Land Book B, 7 June 1842, 11.

8 June 1842 • Wednesday

Wednesday 8 Recorder went to carthage. & narrowly escaped with his life. from a fall from or on old charley.[261]

9 June 1842 • Thursday

Thursday 9[262]

10 June 1842 • Friday

[*illegible*] Friday [*illegible*] 10 Went to Bro Hibbards [Davidson Hibbard's] to purchase some land [p. 124]

11 June 1842 • Saturday

Saturday 11 Attended city council[263]

12 June 1842 • Sunday

Sunday 12 Home. Brought some poetry to printing office.[264] & got some Newspapers

13 June 1842 • Monday

Monday 13 a gene[r]al council in Lodge room to devise ways & means to help the poor to labor[265]

---

261. A horse belonging to JS.
262. On this date JS gave a sermon to the Female Relief Society on the importance of being careful to accept into the society only those who were righteous, and the need to be merciful and help others turn away from sin. (Relief Society Minute Book, 9 June 1842.)
263. TEXT: Two illegible words appear in the left margin, probably a day and a date.
264. Poetry, much of it by Eliza R. Snow and William W. Phelps, was a fairly regular feature in both the *Times and Seasons* and *The Wasp*.
265. The concern for the poor was partly a result of the substantial number of immigrating British Saints. George Miller later described the situation: "Early this spring [1841] the English emigrants . . . began to come in, in apparent poverty and in considerable numbers. Besides these, they were crowding in from the States, all poor, as the rich did not generally respond to the proclamation of the prophet to come with their effects, and assist in building the Temple and Nauvoo House. The poor had to be cared for, and labor created that they might at least earn part of their subsistence—there not being one in ten persons that could set themselves to work, to earn those indispensable things for the comfort of their families. My brethren of the Committee of the Nauvoo House Association, and the Committee of the Temple, all bore a part in the employment of laborers, and the providing food for them." Two weeks later, both JS and Brigham Young addressed the topic of providing employment to the poor. (George Miller, St. James, MI, to "Dear Brother," 26 June 1855, *Northern Islander*, 16 Aug. 1855, [3]; JS, Journal, 26 and 27 June 1842.)

14 June 1842 • Tuesday

Tuesday 14 To the mound with Emma & purchasd 3/4 Sections of Land of Hiram Kimball[266]

15 June 1842 • Wednesday

Wednesday 15 visited in different part of the city. the farm in the Prairie[267] with Recorder & Sister [Marinda Nancy Johnson] Hyde. & supped at Hiram Kimball's

16 June 1842 • Thursday

Thursday 16 Special Lodge. John C. Bennet[t] made his defence for the last time[268]

17 June 1842 • Friday

Friday 17 This week the recorder was sick & did not take notes.[269]

---

266. JS purchased the southwest quarter of Section 25, the southeast quarter of Section 26, and the northeast quarter of Section 35, within Township 7 North, Range 8 West, for $1,500 from Ethan Kimball of Orange County, Vermont. Hiram Kimball served as Ethan Kimball's attorney in the transaction. The "mound" was located in the southwest quarter of Section 25. JS paid Kimball two weeks later. (Hancock Co., IL, Deed Records, 27 June 1842, vol. K, pp. 329–330, microfilm 954,599, U.S. and Canada Record Collection, FHL; JS, Journal, 27 June 1842.)

267. JS's farm.

268. At this meeting of the Nauvoo Masonic Lodge, evidence was presented that Bennett had previously been expelled from Masonry by the Pickaway lodge in Ohio. However, when Bennett presented laudatory character references from men in Ohio dated about the time of his alleged expulsion and claimed he was never informed of his expulsion from the Pickaway lodge, his case was postponed. By 7 July, the Nauvoo lodge was "fully satisfied" that Bennett was "an expelled mason" and resolved that the lodge regard him unworthy of fellowship. On 8 August, Bennett was expelled from the Nauvoo lodge "and from all the privileges of Masonry" for seduction, adultery, using JS's name to justify immoral acts, perjury, embezzlement, and for illicit intercourse with a Master Mason's wife. The Pickaway lodge minutes, which were not available to the Nauvoo lodge, indicate that while charges had been preferred against Bennett, no resolution was passed regarding his ultimate standing in that lodge. (Nauvoo Masonic Lodge Minute Book, 16 June 1842; 7 July 1842; 8 Aug. 1842; Hogan, *John Cook Bennett and Pickaway Lodge No. 23*, 9–12.)

269. One event Willard Richards was unable to report because of his illness was the meeting of Nauvoo citizens on 18 June in which JS, among other things, "spoke his mind in great plainness concerning the iniquity & wickedness" of John C. Bennett and "exposed him before the public." Bennett left Nauvoo for Springfield on 21 June 1842 and returned briefly at the end of the month. (Woodruff, Journal, 18 June 1842; [Nauvoo Masonic Lodge], Nauvoo, IL, to Abraham Jonas, [Columbus, IL], 21 June 1842, Letters regarding Freemasonry in Nauvoo, CHL; "Astounding Mormon Disclosures! Letter from Gen. Bennett," *Sangamo Journal* [Springfield, IL], 8 July 1842, [2].)

24 June 1842 • Friday

Friday 24 St John's day. Rode in masonic procession to the grove where a large Assembly of masons & others listend to an address from Prest [Sidney] Rigdon.[270] dined at Bro [Alexander] Mills.[271]

25 June 1842 • Saturday

Saturday 25 Transacted Business with Bro. [Edward] Hunter. Mr Babbit [Almon Babbitt]. & set for the drawing of his profile. for Lithographing on city chart.[272]

26 June 1842 • Sunday

Sunday 26 Brigham young preached. on consecration. & ⟨or⟩ union of action in building up the city & providing labor & food for the poor.[273] Joseph attended meeting, & council at his house at 6 o clock P.M. present. Hyrum Smith. Geo Miller. N[ewel] K. Whitney. Wm. Marks. Brigham Young. Heber C. Kimball. & Willard Richards. To take into consideration the situation of the pine country & Lumbering business[274] and other subjects of importance to the church; after consultation. thereon the Brethrn united in Solemn prayer that God would make known his will concerning the pine country. & that he would deliver his anointed, his people. from all the evil designs of Govenor [Lilburn W.] Boggs. & the powers of the state of Missouri, & of Govenor [Thomas] Carlin. & the authorities of Illinois. & of all presidents. Govenors. Judges Legislators & all in autho[r]ity. and. ⟨of⟩ John C. Bennet[t].[275] & all mobs & evil designi[n]g

---

270. St. John's Day was Masonry's traditional festival of St. John the Baptist. According to Wilford Woodruff, the procession assembled at JS's store and marched to the stand near the temple. He estimated six thousand people were present to hear Rigdon speak. (Woodruff, Journal, 24 June 1842.)

271. Following the morning's procession and meeting at the grove, the Nauvoo lodge adjourned until 2:00 p.m., at which time they reconvened and held another procession accompanied by the Nauvoo band to Alexander Mills's Masonic Hall Tavern, where the company ate dinner. (Nauvoo Masonic Lodge Minute Book, 24 June 1842; see also "Dr. Charles Higbee," *The Wasp*, 21 Jan. 1843, [3]; and "Boots and Shoes," *Nauvoo Neighbor*, 13 Sept. 1843, [4].)

272. The drawing was made by Sutcliffe Maudsley for a map of Nauvoo.

273. JS and others met two weeks earlier to discuss this matter. (JS, Journal, 13 June 1842.)

274. In 1841 the Nauvoo House Association and the temple committee began a joint lumbering venture on the Black River in Wisconsin Territory that eventually included four mills and about six logging camps before it ceased operation in spring 1845. This operation supplied lumber for the Nauvoo House and the temple. By summer 1842, the church members working in the pineries had produced only one small raft of lumber for use in Nauvoo, and the debts of the enterprise were approaching $3,000. On 28 June it was decided that Ezra Chase should lead an expedition to the pine country. (Rowley, "Mormon Experience in the Wisconsin Pineries," 121, 127, 129; George Miller, St. James, MI, to "Dear Brother," 26 June 1855, *Northern Islander*, 16 Aug. 1855, [3]–[4]; JS, Journal, 28 June 1842.)

275. The concern over Bennett was regarding rumors that he was conspiring to have JS kidnapped. (JS, Nauvoo, IL, to Thomas Carlin, [Quincy, IL], 24 June 1842, in JS Letterbook 2, pp. 233–235.)

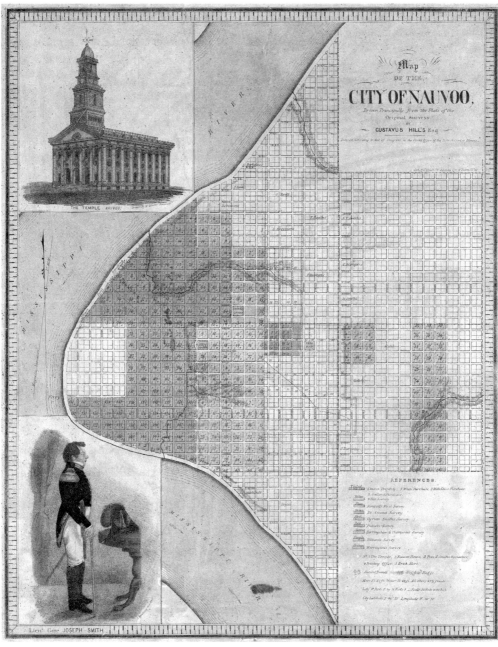

Map of Nauvoo with profile of Joseph Smith. 1842. Sutcliffe Maudsley probably used a pantograph to create a profile of Joseph Smith's head and upper torso; details of the face, as well as the entire lower body, arms, and legs, were added freehand. Willard Richards took Maudsley's portrait of Joseph Smith and other material to John Childs, a printer in New York, who created a lithograph of the portrait, an early rendition of the Nauvoo temple (drawn by architect William Weeks), and Gustavus Hills's map of Nauvoo. (Image courtesy Church History Library, Salt Lake City; information from Glen M. Leonard, "Picturing the Nauvoo Legion," *BYU Studies* 35, no. 2 [1995]: 95–135.)

persons.—— so that his people might continue in peace & build up the city of Nauvoo. & that his chosen might be blessed & live to man's appointed age. & that their households. & the household of faith might. continually be blessed with the fost[er]ing care of heaven.— & enjoy the good things of the earth. abundantly.— adjound [adjourned] to monday evening [p. 125]

27 June 1842 • Monday

Monday 27 Transacting business in general through the day. borrowed money of Bro͛. Wooley.[276] Spencer[277] &ͨ. & made payment To Hiram Kimball for the mound.[278] when the council assembled in the evening. Brothers. [Edward] Hunter. Ivins[,] Wooley. Pierce[279] & others being present. the adjound [adjourned] council was posponed till tuesday eveni[n]g. & Joseph proce[e]d to Lecture at length on the importance of uniting the means of the brethren. for the purpose of establishing manufactories of all kinds. furnishing labor for the poor &ͨ. Brothers Hunter & Wooley offered their goods. toward the general funds.[280] & good feelings were generally manifest. This morning Little. Frederic[k] G. W. Smith.— told his dream to all the house "that the Missourians had got their heads knocked off."—

28 June 1842 • Tuesday

Tuesday 28 payed Brothers Wooley[281] & Spencer.[282] Bro [Edward] Hunters goods were recived at the store & Bro Robins [John R. Robbins] conscirated [consecrated] his goods & money to the general funds.[283] the adgournd [adjourned] council of Sunday eve[n]ing met at the upper Room at Josephs. & were agreed that a reinforcement go immediatly to the pine country Led by Bro Ezra chase.[284] & after uniting in Solemn prayer. to God. for a blessing on themselves & famili[e]s & the chu[r]ch in general. & for the building up of the

---

276. Probably Edwin Woolley.
277. Probably Daniel Spencer.
278. JS purchased the mound two weeks earlier. (JS, Journal, 14 June 1842.)
279. Probably Robert Peirce/Pierce. (JS, Journal, 28 Feb 1842.)
280. Hunter later recalled that he "came to Nauvoo June 1842 with my family. I took with me seven thousand dollars in goods of different kinds, about 4 or 5,000 dollars worth and let Joseph have them all." (Hunter, *Edward Hunter*, 317–318.)
281. Probably Edwin Woolley.
282. Probably Daniel Spencer.
283. Robbins's donation is recorded in the Book of the Law of the Lord, page 147.
284. George Miller ultimately led the party instead of Chase. Under Miller's leadership, the church obtained the use of two mills on the Black River, and within a year the mills produced as much as 157,000 board feet of lumber in a two-week period. (George Miller, St. James, MI, to "Dear Brother," 26 June 1855, *Northern Islander*, 16 Aug. 1855, [3]–[4]; Willard Richards, Nauvoo, IL, to Brigham Young, New York City, NY, 18 July 1843, Brigham Young Office Files, CHL.)

Temple. & Nauvoo House. & city: for deliverance from their enemies. & the sp[r]ead of the work of Righteousnss: & that Bro [Willard] Richards. (who was expecting to go east tomorrow for his family.)[285] that he might have a prosperous Journey. have power of over the winds & elements, & all opposition. & dangers; his life & health be preserved. & be speedily returnd to this place with his family. that their lives & helths might be p[r]eserved. & that they might come up in peace to this place. & that ~~he~~ Bro Richards might be prosprd according to the disire of his heart in all things in relation to his household. & the church. & that the spirit of God might rest upon him continually so that He may act according to the wisdom of heaven, ~~continually~~. the council dispersed. Previous to the council President Joseph in company with Bishop [George] Miller visited Elder [Sidney] Rigdon & his family & had much conversation about J. C. Bennet [John C. Bennett] & others. Much unplesat [unpleasant] feeling was manifested by Elder Rigdon's family who were confounded & put to silence by the truth. from Prst— Joseph[286]

29 June 1842 • Wednesday

Wednesday ~~28~~ 29 Held a long conversation with Francis Higby [Higbee]. Francis found fault with being exposed.[287] but Joseph told him he spoke of him in self defence. Francis was or appeard humble & promisd to reform.

Heard the Recorder[288] Read in the Law of the Lord.[289] paid taxes Rode [290] out in the city on business with Brigham young.[291] The Recorder being about to start east on a Journy. commited the Law of the Lord To Wm Clayton to

---

285. While returning from his mission to England, Richards left his wife, Jennetta, and their young son, Heber, in Massachusetts on 3 July 1841. In summer 1842, he returned to Massachusetts for his wife and son. Richards was authorized to collect money on this trip for the building of the temple and other church projects at Nauvoo. (Richards, Journal, 3 July 1841 and 1 July 1842; JS, Nauvoo, IL, to Jennetta Richards, Richmond, MA, 23 June 1842, JS Collection, CHL; Willard Richards, "To the Eastern Churches," *Times and Seasons,* 1 June 1842, 3:814.)

286. Difficulties between JS and Rigdon were first recorded in the journal 12 May 1842. On 1 July 1842, Rigdon asked JS to go on a ride with him out onto the prairie where they could "settle forever all difficulties, and be again at everlasting peace." Rigdon encouraged JS to invite Hyrum Smith along if he wanted but otherwise asked JS to "say not a word to any person living." (JS, Journal, 12 May 1842; Sidney Rigdon, Nauvoo, IL, to JS, Nauvoo, IL, 1 July 1842, JS Collection, CHL.)

287. A possible reference to JS's earlier interview with Sidney Rigdon about "evil reports" Higbee was circulating about Rigdon's family. (See JS, Journal, 13 May 1842.)

288. Willard Richards.

289. The Book of the Law of the Lord, which includes this journal.

290. TEXT: "~~Tuesday~~" in left margin.

291. According to an affidavit signed by Eliza R. Snow, Young "married or sealed" Snow to JS as a plural wife on this day. (Eliza R. Snow, Affidavit, Salt Lake Co., Utah Territory, 7 June 1869, in Joseph F. Smith, Affidavits about Celestial Marriage, 1:25.)

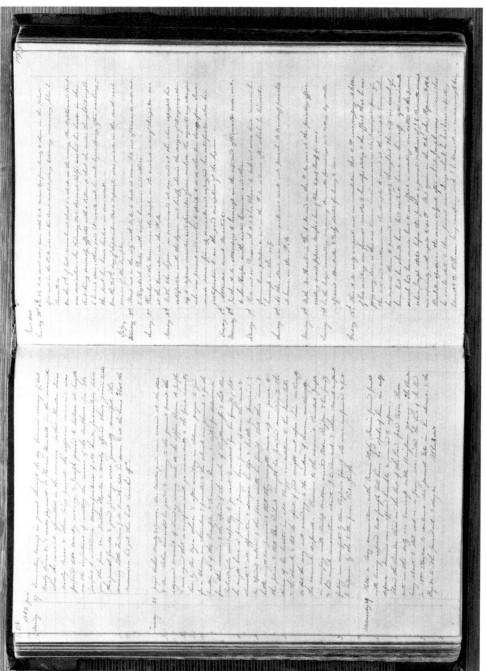

Transfer of journal from Willard Richards to William Clayton. In late June 1842, Willard Richards turned over the Book of the Law of the Lord to William Clayton. Richards's handwriting ends at the bottom of page 126 (left), closing with a note regarding the transfer and his signature. Clayton's handwriting begins on page 127 (right). Handwriting of Willard Richards and William Clayton. Book of the Law of the Lord, pp. 126–127, Church History Library, Salt Lake City. (Photograph by Welden C. Andersen.)

continue this Journal ~~in~~ &c in his absence. & the Keys &c to the president. & claytn

W[illard] Richards [p. 126]

30 June 1842 • Thursday

/²⁹²Thurs-day 30th In the A.M. spent some time with C[alvin] A. Warren Eqr from Quincy & others in the private office and in the P.M. was in the Court martial giving testimony concerning John C Bennett &c.²⁹³

On the 8th. of last November at about 5 o clock in the evening the Baptismal Font was dedicated.²⁹⁴ In February 1842 Samuel Rolfe washed his hands in the Font being seriously affected with a Fellon, so that the Docters thought it ought to be cut open; others said it would not be well before spring. After washing in the Font his hand healed in one week.—

On the 25th. day of September 1841 a Deposite was made in the south east corner of the Temple.—²⁹⁵

2 July 1842 • Saturday

July Saturday 2nd. Went out in the city with W. C. [William Clayton] to look at some lots and afterwards rode out to Hezekiah Pecks with sister Emma and others.—

3 July 1842 • Sunday

Sunday 3rd. Preached at the Grove near the Temple on the ancient order of things &c—²⁹⁶ was at the Grove also in the P.M.

---

292. TEXT: Willard Richards handwriting ends; William Clayton begins.
293. While Nauvoo Legion records for this proceeding have not been located, Bennett was likely cashiered at this court-martial. The following day JS published a statement of "important facts relative to the conduct and character of Dr. John C. Bennett, . . . that the honorable part of community may be aware of his proceedings . . . as an imposter and base adulterer." (Thomas Carlin to JS, 27 July 1842, p. 102 herein; JS, "To the Church of Jesus Christ of Latter Day Saints, and to All the Honorable Part of Community," *Times and Seasons,* 1 July 1842, 3:839–843.)
294. The baptismal font, used for vicarious baptisms for deceased persons, was located in the basement of the unfinished Nauvoo temple.
295. Nancy Alexander Tracy later recalled that "the Bible Book of Mormon doctrine and Covenants hymn book and other Church works as well as the news papers the Times and Seasons and Nauvoo Neighbor that were printed in Nauvoo and money that had been coined in that year" were deposited in the temple cornerstone. Samuel Miles left a similar account of the deposited items. The southeast cornerstone was laid 6 April 1841. (Tracy, Reminiscences and Diary, 41–43; "Recollections of the Prophet Joseph Smith," 174; "Celebration of the Anniversary of the Church," *Times and Seasons,* 15 Apr. 1841, 2:375–377; Robert B. Thompson, "Communication," *Times and Seasons,* 15 Apr. 1841, 2:380–383.)
296. Wilford Woodruff recorded that JS read from Daniel 7 and "explained about the Kingdom of God set up in the last days." Woodruff noted in his journal that about six thousand people were present,

4 July 1842 • Monday

Monday 4th. With the Legion in command all day,297 and at the close expressed his satisfaction with the Legion, and briefly showed the design of its organization viz to defend ourselves and families from mobs &c. He requested any stranger who was present and wished to speak to do so, when Gen. Swa◊◊y [Ezekiel Swazey] from Iowa made some friendly remarks and expressed his satisfaction; also his gratification to see the good discipline of the Legion.—298

5 July 1842 • Tuesday

Tuesday 5th. Attended court Martial.—

6 July 1842 • Wednesday

Wednesday 6th. In the A.M. attending to business in the city and afterwards rode out to La Harpe with sister Emma and others.—

9 July 1842 • Saturday

Saturday 9th. Rode out on Prarie with W. C. [William Clayton] & bro [William A.] Gheen to look out some land. Dined on his farm,299 hoed potatoes &c and in the P.M. returned after which he transacted business in the city

10 July 1842 • Sunday

Sunday 10th. At the stand, was some sick and could not preach. W[ilford] Woodruff preached[.]300 at home in the P.M.—

11 July 1842 • Monday

Monday 11th. With Mr [Edward] Hunter in the A.M. and in the P.M. was at the printing office reading mail papers. Bought a horse301 of [Harmon T.] Wilson Deputy Sheriff for au.$

---

while *The Wasp* reported the attendees numbered "probably 8 or 10,000." (Woodruff, Journal, 3 July 1842; "Life in Nauvoo," *The Wasp*, 9 July 1842, [2].)

297. On 12 March 1842, the Nauvoo Legion court-martial passed an ordinance requiring the legion to hold a general parade on various days, including 4 July. (Nauvoo Legion Minute Book, 12 Mar. 1842, 12.)

298. *The Wasp* reported that between eleven and twelve thousand people were in attendance to witness the day's activities. ("Life in Nauvoo," *The Wasp*, 9 July 1842, [2].)

299. JS's farm.

300. See Woodruff, Journal, 10 July 1842.

301. JS's history identifies this horse as "Jo. Duncan," after Joseph Duncan, former governor of Illinois. Duncan served as governor from December 1834 to December 1838 and was running against Thomas Ford in 1842. Duncan was vigorously anti-Mormon in his 1842 campaign. (JS History, vol. C-1, 1356.)

12 July 1842 • Tuesday

Tuesday 12.th In the lodge consulting concerning [John C.] Bennetts proceedings and taking Esqr [Daniel H.] Wells affidavit.³⁰² Bro's [George] Miller & [Erastus] Derby started for Quincy & Mo—³⁰³

15 July 1842 • Friday

Friday 15.th This A.M. early a report was in circulation that O. P. [Orson Pratt] was missing. A. letter of his writing was found directed to his wife stating to the effect that he was going away;³⁰⁴ Soon as this was known Joseph

---

302. Bennett resigned as mayor on 17 May 1842 and on that date signed a statement before Justice of the Peace Daniel H. Wells that he had not observed misconduct by JS nor heard him condone sexual relations outside of marriage. Bennett later claimed he made the statement under duress. The Wells affidavit referenced in the journal entry was apparently the basis for Wells's sworn statement ten days later, in which he declared he had seen no evidence that Bennett had testified under threat in May. ("To the Church of Jesus Christ of Latter Day Saints, and to All the Honorable Part of Community," *Times and Seasons,* 1 July 1842, 3:840–841; "Astounding Mormon Disclosures! Letter from Gen. Bennett," *Sangamo Journal* [Springfield, IL], 8 July 1842, [2]; Daniel H. Wells, Affidavit, Nauvoo, IL, 22 July 1842, *Times and Seasons,* 1 Aug. 1842, 3:873–874.)

303. By this time Bennett began publicly disparaging those who accused him of immoral behavior. He called on Missouri governor Thomas Reynolds to initiate extradition proceedings against JS on charges related to the Mormon War in 1838. On 12 July 1842, Miller and Derby were sent to Quincy, Illinois, and to Jefferson City, Missouri, to confer with Illinois governor Thomas Carlin and Missouri governor Reynolds, apparently to counter Bennett's initiatives. Thirteen years later, however, Miller recalled the trip was a response to Bennett's accusation that JS was behind the attempt to assassinate Lilburn W. Boggs. ("Astounding Mormon Disclosures! Letter from Gen. Bennett," *Sangamo Journal* [Springfield, IL], 8 July 1842, [2]; Calvin A. Warren, Quincy, IL, to JS, Nauvoo, IL, 13 July 1842, JS Collection, CHL; George Miller, St. James, MI, to "Dear Brother," 26 June 1855, *Northern Islander,* 16 Aug. 1855, [3]–[4]; see also 79n313 herein.)

304. Pratt's wife, Sarah Bates Pratt, was allegedly involved with John C. Bennett in an illicit relationship, which apparently ended quietly upon Orson Pratt's return from a proselytizing mission to Britain in summer 1841.^a When JS publicly exposed Bennett for similar relationships with other women in the 1 July 1842 issue of the *Times and Seasons,* Bennett asserted that JS himself seduced women in Nauvoo and that he (Bennett) was present when JS asked Sarah to be one of his "spiritual wives." Sarah supported Bennett's claim; indeed, that Orson was aware of the allegations against JS on 14 July (see the following letter), while Bennett's claim was not published until 15 July, suggests that Orson first heard of it from Sarah rather than from Bennett.^b JS denied the charge.^c The "letter of his writing," to which the text may refer, was written the evening of 14 July and found on Munson Street, east of Heber C. Kimball's home; it illustrates the difficult position in which these charges and countercharges placed Orson. The unaddressed letter began: "I am a ruined man! my future prospects are blasted! the testimony upon both sides seems to be equal: the one in direct contradiction to the other—how to decide I know not neither does it matter for let it be either way my temporal happiness is gone in this world if the testimonies of my wife & others are true then I have been deceived for 12 years past—my hopes are blasted & gone as it were in a moment—my long toils & labours have been in vain. If on the other hand the other testimonies are true then my family are ruined forever."^d (a. *Affidavits and Certificates,* [Nauvoo, IL: 31 Aug. 1842], copy at CHL. b. JS, "To the Church of Jesus Christ of Latter Day Saints and to All the Honorable Part of Community," *Times and Seasons,* 1 July 1842, 3:839–842; "Further Mormon Developments!! 2d Letter from Gen. Bennett," *Sangamo Journal* [Springfield, IL], 15 July 1842, [2]; JS, Journal, 29 Aug. 1842, pp. 122–123

Orson Pratt. Pratt turned against Joseph Smith for a time and was excommunicated in 1842. Five months later he was rebaptized by Joseph Smith and restored to his position in the Quorum of the Twelve Apostles. (Church History Library, Salt Lake City.)

summoned the principal men of the city and workmen on the Temple to meet at the Temple Grove where he ordered them to proceed immediately throughout the city in search of him lest he should have laid voilent [violent] hands on himself. After considerable search had been made but to no effect a meeting was called at the Grove where Joseph stated before the public a general outline of J[ohn] C. Bennetts conduct and especially with regard to Sis P [Sarah Bates Pratt] Met again in the P.M. when Hyrum [Smith] & H[eber] C. Kimball spake on the same subject after which Joseph arose and said that he would state to those present some things which he had heard respecting Edward & D[avid] Kilbourn being conspiring with J. C. Bennett in endeavoring to bring [p. 127] a Mob upon us, and as Mr E. Kilbourn was then present he would have the privilege of either admitting or denying it. Question by E. Kilbourn "Who did Bennett tell that I and my brother were conspiring to bring a mob upon you" Answer by Joseph "He told me and he told [*blank*] Allred[305] and Orson Pratts wife & others". Q by E Kilboun "Where did he say we were going to bring a mob from". Ans. by Joseph. "From Galena". M[r.] Kilbourn then arose and said, "I was conversing with my brother this morning and he said he had never seen Bennett since he had us before him last year for conspiracy.[306] I have only seen him twice since last fall, I saw ⟨him⟩ once then. I was going to Galena about 2 weeks ago. The Boat I was on stopped at the upper Landing place and I came ashore a little while. The first person I saw was Bennett; we entered into conversation, but there was no mention made of mobs. I have not seen him since. I always regarded Bennett the same as I regard you (Joseph) and thought you were pretty well matched. If any one says that I have conspired to bring a Mob upon you it is false".[307] The meeting was then peaceably

---

herein. *c.* Quorum of the Twelve Apostles, Minutes, 20 Jan. 1843. *d.* Orson Pratt, Letter, [Nauvoo, IL], 14 July 1842, CHL.)

305. Probably William Moore Allred, who married Orissa Bates, sister of Sarah Bates Pratt, on 9 January 1842, with Mayor John C. Bennett officiating. (Allred, Reminiscences and Diary, 8–9.)

306. Sometime prior to 20 September 1841, David and Edward Kilbourne appeared before John C. Bennett in the mayor's court on a charge of conspiring to unlawfully procure an indictment. The charge was based on a complaint by Lorenzo Wasson and Orrin Porter Rockwell after the Kilbournes attempted to catch a group of alleged thieves, including Rockwell, in the act of robbing the Kilbournes' store in Montrose, Iowa Territory. According to the Kilbournes, the charge was "unsustained by a shadow of proof," and they were discharged by Bennett at Nauvoo. (David Kilbourne and Edward Kilbourne, "Latter-Day-ism, No. 1," *Hawk-Eye and Iowa Patriot* [Burlington], 30 Sept. 1841, [1]; see also Bennett, *History of the Saints*, 93.)

307. The Kilbournes wrote three letters attacking the church and JS. On 14 May 1842, David Kilbourne wrote to Missouri governor Thomas Reynolds accusing JS of complicity in the Lilburn W. Boggs assassination attempt and urging his arrest. On 24 June, JS wrote to Illinois governor Thomas Carlin expressing concern about information from Galena, about 160 miles upriver from Nauvoo, that the Kilbournes and Bennett had posted handbills there asking for volunteers to drive out the Mormons

dismissed. O. P. returned at night. He was seen about 2 miles this side Warsaw; set on a log. He says he has concluded to do right.³⁰⁸

16 July 1842 • Saturday

Saturday 16ᵗʰ· Rode out on prairie with W. C. [William Clayton] to show some land to Bro Russel³⁰⁹ from Genessee called at his farm and dined at bro Lots [Cornelius Lott's]. Afterwards went to hoeing potatoes.

17 July 1842 • Sunday

Sunday 17ᵗʰ· At the Grove, was sick. At home the remainder of the day.

18 July 1842 • Monday

Monday 18ᵗʰ· Rode out to bro Kearn's [Henry Kearns's] and to the Farm.—³¹⁰

19 July 1842 • Tuesday

Tuesday 19ᵗʰ· Rode out with Dr [Robert D.] Foster, Henry Kearns & others to look at Timber Land

22 July 1842 • Friday

T̶h̶r̶s̶d̶a̶y̶ ⟨Friday⟩ 2̶0̶ᵗʰ· ⟨22ⁿᵈ·⟩ P̶.̶M̶.̶ ⟨A.M.⟩ At the stand conflicting with O. P. [Orson Pratt] and correcting the public mind with regard to reports put

---

and to assist in kidnapping JS. (David Kilbourne and Edward Kilbourne, "Latter-Day-ism, No. 1," *Hawk-Eye and Iowa Patriot* [Burlington], 30 Sept. 1841, [1]; David Kilbourne and Edward Kilbourne, "Latter-Day-ism, No. 2," *Hawk-Eye and Iowa Patriot,* 7 Oct. 1841, [2]; David Kilbourne and Edward Kilbourne, "Latter Day-ism No. 3," *Hawk-Eye and Iowa Patriot,* 14 Oct. 1841, [3]; David Kilbourne, Montrose, Iowa Territory, to Thomas Reynolds, Jefferson City, MO, 14 May 1842, Thomas Reynolds, Office of Governor, MSA; JS, Nauvoo, IL, to Thomas Carlin, [Quincy, IL], 24 June 1842, in JS Letterbook 2, pp. 233–235.)

308. In spite of this report, two days later Brigham Young wrote in a letter to Orson's brother Parley P. Pratt: "Br Orson Pratt is in trubble in consequence of his wife, his feelings are so rought up that he dos not know whether his wife is wrong, or whether Josephs testmony and others are wrong and due Ly and he decived for 12 years, or not; he is all but crazy about matters." (Brigham Young, Nauvoo, IL, to Parley P. Pratt, Liverpool, England, 17 July 1842, CHL.)

309. Probably Daniel or Samuel Russell, who came with their families to Nauvoo around this time from Newstead Township, Erie County, which borders Genesee County, New York. (1840 U.S. Census, Newstead, Erie Co., NY, 378; "Record of the Names of the Members," [30]; Hancock Co., IL, Deed Records, 27 July 1842, vol. L, pp. 119–120, microfilm 954,599, U.S. and Canada Record Collection, FHL.)

310. Kearns arrived in Nauvoo in early July and purchased a home and farm comprising the north half of the northwest quarter of Section 9—property bordering JS's farm, on the Carthage road—on 14 July 1842. (Henry Kearns, Nauvoo, IL, to Leonard Pickel, Bart, PA, 7 Dec. 1842, Leonard Pickel, Mormon Letters, 1841–1844, Western Americana Collection, Beinecke Rare Book and Manuscript Library, Yale University, New Haven, CT; Trustees Land Book B, 14 July 1842, 13.)

in circulation by [John C.] Bennett & others.³¹¹ In the P.M. a petition was prepared and singed [signed] by the citizens praying the Governor not to issue a writ for the Pres$^{t.\,312}$

24 July 1842 • Sunday

Sunday 24$^{\underline{th}}$ In the A.M. at home sick. In the P.M. at the Grove. Spoke concerning bro. [George] Miller having returned with good news. That [John C.] Bennett could do nothing &c.³¹³

---

311. The meeting was called "to obtain an expression of the public mind" with respect to the efforts of Bennett to defame JS's character. Wilson Law presented a resolution upholding JS's integrity and moral character. The vote by the citizens of Nauvoo, numbering "about a thousand men," was nearly unanimous, but Pratt arose and spoke at length to explain his negative vote, whereupon JS publicly asked Pratt, "Have you personally a knowledge of any immoral act in me toward the female sex, or in any other way?" Pratt replied, "Personally, toward the female sex, I have not."*a* This issue continued until Pratt was excommunicated on 20 August 1842 by the available members of the Quorum of the Twelve Apostles. The same day, Amasa Lyman was ordained in Pratt's stead as an apostle by Brigham Young, Heber C. Kimball, and George A. Smith.*b* In January 1843, Pratt "confessed his sins, and manifested deep repentance" and was rebaptized and reinstated as a member of the Twelve.*c* (*a*. Minutes, *Times and Seasons*, 1 Aug. 1842, 3:869. *b*. Historian's Office, Brigham Young History Drafts, 64; Woodruff, Journal, 10 Aug.–18 Sept. 1842. *c*. Historian's Office, Brigham Young History Drafts, 66–67; JS, Journal, 20 Jan. 1843.)

312. Rumors published as early as 21 May 1842 charged JS with complicity in the attempt to assassinate Lilburn W. Boggs, former governor of Missouri.*a* Bennett made the same accusation in his 2 July letter, published in the 15 July *Sangamo Journal*.*b* In St. Louis, the 14 July 1842 issue of the *Bulletin* published another letter and affidavit from Bennett connecting JS and Orrin Porter Rockwell with the attempted assassination.*c* Soon after, on 20 July, Boggs made a sworn statement that JS "was accessary before the fact" in the assassination attempt and requested that JS be extradited to Missouri.*d* The petition of the Nauvoo citizens urged Illinois governor Thomas Carlin "not to issue a Writ for him [JS] to be given up to the Authorities of Missouri," but to try him in Illinois if Carlin thought JS had broken the law. The petition was drawn up by a committee of the city council, consisting of John Taylor, William Law, and Brigham Young, who were assisted by recorder James Sloan. The petition was "signed by about eight hundred, or upwards" of the citizens of Nauvoo.*e* Carlin received the petition on 26 July but honored the request of governor Thomas Reynolds and issued a writ on 2 August for JS's arrest.*f* (*a*. "Assassination of Ex-Governor Boggs of Missouri," *Quincy [IL] Whig*, 21 May 1842, [3]. *b*. "Further Mormon Developments!! 2d Letter from Gen. Bennett," *Sangamo Journal* [Springfield, IL], 15 July 1842, [2]. *c*. John C. Bennett, St. Louis, MO, 13 July 1842, Letter to the editor, *Bulletin* [St. Louis], 14 July 1842, [2]. *d*. Lilburn W. Boggs, Affidavit, 20 July 1842, p. 380 herein. *e*. Nauvoo City Council Minute Book, 22 July 1842, 95–97. *f*. Thomas Carlin to JS, 27 July 1842, p. 102 herein; Thomas Reynolds, Requisition, 22 July 1842, p. 380 herein; Thomas Carlin, Writ, 2 Aug. 1842, *Ex Parte* JS for Accessory to Boggs Assault [C.C.D. Ill. 1843], copy, Nauvoo, IL, Records, CHL; JS, Journal, 8 Aug. 1842.)

313. Miller and Erastus Derby left Nauvoo twelve days earlier to confer with governors Thomas Carlin of Illinois and Thomas Reynolds of Missouri about rumors concerning an attempt to extradite JS to Missouri. Miller and Derby were told that Bennett's efforts would be ineffectual in reviving the Missouri charges against JS based on the 1838 Mormon War. However, following an affidavit sworn by Lilburn W. Boggs on 20 July implicating JS in the assassination attempt on his life, Reynolds, two days before Miller's arrival in Nauvoo, issued a requisition to Carlin for JS's arrest and extradition. (JS, Journal, 12 July 1842; George Miller, St. James, MI, to "Dear Brother," 26 June 1855, *Northern Islander*, 16 Aug. 1855, [3]–[4]; Calvin A. Warren, Quincy, IL, to JS, Nauvoo, IL, 13 July 1842, JS Collection, CHL;

26 July 1842 • Tuesday

Tuesday 26 Sick. Rode to the farm in the P.M.

27 July 1842 • Wednesday

Wednesday 27th. At the Grove, listening to the electioneering candidates. After they had got through spake some[314]

31 July 1842 • Sunday

Sunday 31st. In council with Bishops [George] Miller & [Newel K.] Whitney, B[righam] Young, Jno Taylor &c concerning Bishop Knights [Vinson Knight's] sickness. Bro Knights has been sick about a week and this morning he began to sink very fast untill 12 o clock when death put a period to his sufferings.

3 August 1842 • Wednesday

August Wednesday 3rd. In the city transacting various business— and in company with General [James] Adams and others.

4 August 1842 • Thursday

Thursday 4th. In the city learning sword exercise under Col. Brewer from St Louis[315] and attending various other business. [p. 128]

6 August 1842 • Saturday

Saturday 6th. Went over the river to Montrose to witness the installation of officers of the Rising Sun Lodge,[316] Iowa in company with Col. Brewer Gen. [James] Adams &c

7 August 1842 • Sunday

Sunday 7th. At home all day

Lilburn W. Boggs, Affidavit, 20 July 1842, p. 379 herein; Thomas Reynolds, Requisition, 22 July 1842, p. 380 herein.)

314. Nominations for the new county officers were made in Nauvoo two months earlier, and the election was held in August. (JS, Journal, 1 June 1842; "Public Meeting," *The Wasp,* 4 June 1842, [3].)

315. Joseph Smith III later recalled a "Colonel Brower," who was one of the drill officers engaged. Brower had lost his lower left arm but "was an excellent horseman and a skillful swordsman and fencer." (Mary Audentia Smith Anderson, "The Memoirs of President Joseph Smith," *Saints' Herald,* 1 Jan. 1935, 15.)

316. A Masonic lodge.

8 August 1842 • Monday

Monday 8th. This A.M the Deputy Sheriff of Adams county in company with two other officers[317] came with a warrant from Governor [Thomas] Carlin[318] and arrested Joseph and O. P. [Orrin Porter] Rockwell. the latter being charged with shooting ex-Governor [Lilburn W.] Boggs of Missouri with intent to kill on the evening of the 6th. of May last and Joseph with being accessary. The city council convened immediately and issued a writ of Habeus Corpus to stop them from taking Joseph & Rockwell away without a trial here.[319] The Deputy Sheriff hesitated complying with the writ of Habeus Corpus for some time on the ground (as he said) of not knowing wether this city had authority to issue such writ but after much consultation on the subject they finally agreed to leave the prisoners in the hands of the city Marshall[320] and returned to Quincy to ascertain from the Governor wether our charter gave the city jurisdiction over the case

Received a letter from Post Office which had been broke open and was much grieved at the meanness of its contents.

---

317. The principal arresting officer was Thomas King, undersheriff of Adams County. King was probably accompanied by James Pitman, constable of Adams County, who played a prominent role in the subsequent efforts to arrest JS. The third officer was most likely Edward Ford, who had been designated to receive the prisoner by the original requisition of Missouri governor Thomas Reynolds. (JS, Petition for writ of habeas corpus, 8 Aug. 1842, copy, JS Collection, CHL; Robison, *Adams County*, E–K:149; L–R:134; JS, Journal, 3 Sept. 1842, p. 125 herein; Thomas Reynolds, Requisition, 22 July 1842, p. 381 herein.)

318. The original warrants from Thomas Carlin for the arrests of JS and Orrin Porter Rockwell were retained by Thomas King; copies made for the Nauvoo Municipal Court date the originals to 2 August 1842. References in JS's journal to Carlin's "writ" or "warrant" are to his 2 August warrant for JS's arrest. (Thomas Carlin, Writ, 2 Aug. 1842, *Ex Parte* JS for Accessory to Boggs Assault [C.C.D. Ill. 1843], copy, Nauvoo, IL, Records, CHL; Orrin Porter Rockwell, Petition for writ of habeas corpus, 8 Aug. 1842, copy, Nauvoo, IL, Records, CHL; JS, Journal, 31 Dec. 1842, p. 200 herein.)

319. Writ of habeas corpus for JS, 8 Aug. 1842, copy, Nauvoo, IL, Records, CHL; Writ of habeas corpus for Orrin Porter Rockwell, 8 Aug. 1842, copy, Nauvoo, IL, Records, CHL. The Nauvoo city charter, which was ratified by the Illinois legislature in December 1840, granted authority to the municipal court to issue writs of habeas corpus "in all cases arising under the ordinances of the city council." Anticipating attempts by "Enemies" to subject the citizens of Nauvoo to "illegal Process," the Nauvoo City Council passed an ordinance in July declaring that "no Citizen of this City shall be taken out of the City by any Writ without the privilege of investigation before the Municipal Court, and the benefit of a Writ of Habeas Corpus." The city council also passed a statute on this date granting the Nauvoo Municipal Court the power to inquire into both proper procedure and merits of the case for any arrest warrant served in Nauvoo. The Nauvoo statutes were attempts to codify the broadest interpretation of the habeas corpus grant in the charter, with the goal to prevent the legal system from being used for "religious or other persecution." (An Act to Incorporate the City of Nauvoo [16 Dec. 1840], *Laws of the State of Illinois* [1840–1841], p. 55, sec. 17; Nauvoo City Council Minute Book, 5 July 1842, 86–87; 8 Aug. 1842, 98–99.)

320. Henry G. Sherwood.

Key figures in Missouri extradition attempt. After being shot by an unknown assailant on 6 May 1842, former Missouri governor Lilburn W. Boggs (top left) signed an affidavit charging Joseph Smith and Orrin Porter Rockwell with the crime. On the basis of this affidavit, Missouri governor Thomas Reynolds (top right) issued a requisition to Illinois governor Thomas Carlin (left) for the extradition of Smith and Rockwell. Carlin subsequently issued an arrest warrant for the two men. (Reynolds image courtesy Missouri State Archives, Jefferson City. Other images: Church History Library, Salt Lake City.)

9 August 1842 • Tuesday

Tuesday 9th. In company with Judge [James] Ralston & Lawyer [Stephen] Powers from Keokuk preparing for the return of the Sheriff. Prepared a writ of Habeus Corpus from the Master in Chancery.[321]

10 August 1842 • Wednesday

Wednesday 10th. The Deputy Sheriff returned but could not find Joseph. He endeavoured to alarm sister Emma & the Brethren by his threats, but could not do it they understanding the nature of the Law in that case.[322]

11 August 1842 • Thursday

Thursday 11th. This A.M. brother Wm. Law entered into conversation with the Deputy upon the illegallity of the whole proceedings in reference to the arrest. After some remarks from both parties the Sherif acknowledged that he believed Joseph was innocent and that Governor [Thomas] Carlins course which he had pursued was unjustifiable and illegal. During the day Joseph who was at this time at Uncle John Smiths in Zarahemla sent word that he wished to see Sister Emma bro's Hyrum Smith, Wm. Law and others, with instructions to meet on the island between Nauvoo and Montrose after Dark. Whereupon Emma, Hyrum, Wm. Law, N[ewel] K. Whitney, George Miller, Wm. Clayton & Dimick B. Huntington met at the water side near the Bricks Store sometime after dark and proceeded in a Skiff to the islands. We proceeded between the islands untill we arrived near the lower end; and then hauled to shore. After waiting a very little while, the skiff arrived from the opposite shore, and in it; Joseph and bro. [Erastus] Derby. A council was then held in the skiffs, and various statements set forth in regard to the state of things. It was ascertained that the Governor of Iowa,[323] had issued a Warrant for the apprehension of Joseph, and O. P. [Orrin Porter] Rockwell;[324] and that

---

321. Illinois law specified that each county have a "master in Chancery"—a magistrate whose responsibilities included taking depositions, administering oaths, and, in the absence of the presiding circuit court judge, authorizing writs of habeas corpus. JS apparently decided against applying for a writ of habeas corpus from the master in chancery, perhaps because this would have been tacit admission that the Nauvoo Municipal Court did not have authority to issue writs of habeas corpus. (An Act to Provide for Issuing Writs of Ne Exeat and Habeas Corpus, and for Other Purposes [11 Feb. 1835], *Laws of the State of Illinois* [1834–1835], p. 32; "Persecution," *Times and Seasons,* 15 Aug. 1842, 3:889.)

322. The city marshal had no authority to keep JS in custody because he did not have the arrest warrant in his possession; Thomas King had taken the warrant back to Quincy, Illinois, to receive instruction from Governor Thomas Carlin. (JS, Journal, 8 Aug. and 31 Dec. 1842, pp. 81, 200 herein; "Persecution," *Times and Seasons,* 15 Aug. 1842, 3:886–889.)

323. The Iowa territorial governor was John Chambers.

324. Church members learned three days later that no arrest warrant had been issued in Iowa

the sheriff of Lee County,[325] was expected down immediately. Very strong evidence was also manifested that Governor [Thomas] Reynolds of Missouri was not acquainted with these proceedings. That Ex-Governor [Lilburn W.] Boggs had made oath before a justice of the peace or a Judge and that the Judge had made the requisition and not Governor Reynolds.[326] Also that the writ issued by Carlin was illigal and unjustifiable[327] [p. 129]

It is very evident that the whole business is but another evidence of the effects of prejudice, and that it proceeds from a persecuting spirit; the parties having signified their determination to have Joseph taken to Missouri wether by legal or illegal means. It was finally concluded that Joseph should be taken up the river in a Skiff and be landed below the farm called Wiggans' [Ebenezer Wiggins's] farm and that he should proceed from thence to brother [Edward] Sayers[328] and their abide for a season. This being concluded upon, the parties separated Joseph and brother Derby being rowed up the river by brother [Jonathan] Dunham and the remainder crossed over to Nauvoo. It was agreed that brother A[lbert] P. Rockwood should proceed up the River on shore unto the place where the skiff should stop and there light up two fires as a signal for stopping place. After the Boat had proceeded some distance above the city a fire was discovered on shore. It was concluded that it was the signal and they immediately rowed to shore. When near the shore one of the company hailed a person on the shore but received a very unsatisfactory answer, whereupon

---

Territory. However, following Missouri governor Thomas Reynolds's requisition of 20 August 1842 to Governor John Chambers, the latter did issue a warrant. Chambers wrote in a letter dated 10 March 1843 that a warrant was issued and returned unserved and that he would take no further action unless Missouri's governor sent another requisition. (JS, Journal, 14 Aug. 1842, p. 90 herein; State of Missouri, Office of the Secretary of State, Commissions Division, Register of Civil Proceedings, vol. A, p. 175; John Chambers, Burlington, Iowa Territory, to John Cowan, 10 Mar. 1843, JS Office Papers, CHL.)

325. Hawkins Taylor. Taylor was replaced four days later by William Stotts. (Lee Co., IA, County Commissioner's Reports, 1840–1856, 15 Aug. 1842, vol. 2, p. 182, microfilm 1,954,904, U.S. and Canada Record Collection, FHL; *History of Lee County, Iowa*, 547.)

326. Boggs swore an affidavit before Jackson County justice of the peace Samuel Weston on 20 July 1842. In spite of what JS's companions had heard, it was Missouri governor Reynolds who made the requisition demanding that Illinois governor Carlin extradite JS to Missouri for trial. (Lilburn W. Boggs, Affidavit, 20 July 1842, p. 379 herein; Thomas Reynolds, Requisition, 22 July 1842, p. 380 herein.)

327. The "writ" refers to the warrant for JS's arrest. The constitutional requirement for extradition was being charged with committing a crime in one state and fleeing to another state. Boggs's affidavit charged JS with being an "accessary before the fact" in the attempt on his life and identified JS as a "citizen or resident of the State of Illinois" but did not charge him with committing a crime in Missouri and then fleeing to Illinois. (Thomas Carlin, Writ, 2 Aug. 1842, *Ex Parte* JS for Accessory to Boggs Assault [C.C.D. Ill. 1843], copy, Nauvoo, IL, Records, CHL; U.S. Constitution, art. 4, sec. 2; Lilburn W. Boggs, Affidavit, 20 July 1842, p. 379 herein.)

328. Sayers's farm, located about two and a half miles northeast of the temple block in Nauvoo. (JS, Journal, 11, 13, and 17 Aug. 1842; Hancock Co., IL, Deed Records, 19 May 1841, vol. I, pp. 309–310, microfilm 954,598, U.S. and Canada Record Collection, FHL.)

they turned about and put to the channel and upon coming near the middle of the river discovered two fires a little higher. They immediately steered towards the fires and was happy to find brother Rockwood awaiting their arrival. [329] They then proceeded through the timber to brother Sayers' house where they were very kindly received and made welcome.

Judge [James] Ralston and Lawyer [Stephen] Powers departed each for home expressing their perfect willingness to aid us in every possible manner. Judge Ralston also promised to ascertain the state of affairs in Quincy and give us the earliest information

12 August 1842 • Friday

⟨Friday 12th⟩ This A.M. it appears still more evident that the whole course of proceedings by Governor [Thomas] Carlin and others is illegal. After some consultation with brother Wm. Law sister Emma concluded to dispatch a messenger with a letter to Lawyer [Stephen] Powers of Keokuk to request him to go to Burlington I. T. [Iowa Territory] and there see the Governor of Iowa and endeavor to ascertain a knowledge of the truth as to wether Gov. [Thomas] Reynolds had made any requisition on him for Joseph & [Orrin Porter] Rockwell.[330] [331] Accordingly Josephs new horse which he rides was got ready and Wm. Walker proceeded to cross the river in sight of a number of persons. One cheif design in this proceedure was to draw the attention of the Sheriffs and public, away from all idea that Joseph was on the Nauvoo side of the river

At night W[illiam] Clayton & John D. Parker left Nauvoo after dark and went to see Joseph and found him chearful and in good spirits.

13 August 1842 • Saturday

⟨Saturday 13th⟩ This A.M. a letter was received by President Hyrum [Smith] from brother [David] Hollister of Quincy[332] stating that Gov. [Thomas] Carlin had said that his proceedings was not legal and he should not pursue the

---

329. TEXT: The remainder of this entry is in a different brown ink matching that of the first two sentences in the following entry.

330. Powers returned two days later and reported that Iowa Territory governor John Chambers had not issued a writ for JS's arrest. Reynolds, however, made a requisition of Governor Chambers on 20 August 1842, after which Chambers issued a warrant for JS's arrest. (JS, Journal, 14 Aug. 1842, p. 90 herein; State of Missouri, Office of the Secretary of State, Commissions Division, Register of Civil Proceedings, vol. A, p. 175; John Chambers, Burlington, Iowa Territory, to John Cowan, 10 Mar. 1843, JS Office Papers, CHL.)

331. TEXT: The remainder of this entry is in a different brown ink matching that of the following entry.

332. David Hollister, Quincy, IL, to Hyrum Smith, Nauvoo, IL, 12 Aug. 1842, JS Office Papers, CHL.

subject any further. The letter allso stated that [Edward] Ford (the agent to receive Joseph from the hands of the Sheriff and carry him to Missouri) had concluded to take the first Boat and start home: and that he was going to fetch a force from Missouri. All this it is thought is only a s[c]heme got up for the [p. 130] purpose of throwing us off our guard that they may thereby come unexpected and kidnap Joseph and carry him to Missouri.

In consequence of President Joseph requesting sister Emma to go and see him that they might consult together &c. She concluded to go in the carriage. But when the carriage was being got ready it attracted the attention of the Sheriff. and they kept a strict watch for some time. Seeing the difficulty of getting away undiscovered sister Emma concluded to go on foot to Mrs [Elizabeth Davis] Durphy's and wait untill the carriage arrived. Accordingly the cover of the carriage being folded up to shew the Sheriffs that she was not in W. C. [William Clayton] & Lorain [Lorin] Walker started down the river— called at Durphys and then proceeded down the river without being discovered. We went about 4 miles the river road and then[333] turned off towards the Prarie. We went round the city about 2 miles from the outskirts and turned into the timber again opposite the Wiggans' [Ebenezer Wiggins's] farm After we got within about a mile from brother [Edward] Sayers sister Emma left the carriage and proceeded on foot. We soon arrived at brother Sayers and was pleased to find President Joseph in good spirits, although somewhat sick. The carriage returned home after we left it.

A report came over the river that there is several small companies of men in Montrose, Nashville, Keokuk &c in search of Joseph. They saw his horse go down the river yesterday and was confident he was on that side. They swear they will have him. It is said there is a reward of thirteen hundred dollars offered for the apprehension and delivery of Joseph and [Orrin Porter] Rockwell and this is supposed to have induced them to search viz. to get the reward.

The sheriff and Deputy[334] have uttered heavy threats several times saying that if they could not find Joseph they would lay the city in ashes They say they will tarry in the city a month but they will find him.

14 August 1842 • Sunday

Sunday 14th. Spent the forenoon chiefly in conversation with sister Emma on various subjects, and in reading this history with her. Both felt in good

---

333. TEXT: Possibly "their".
334. Probably Undersheriff Thomas King and Constable James Pitman. (See Robison, *Adams County*, E–K:149; L–R:132–134.)

spirits and were very chearful. Wrote the following orders to Major Gen.¹ Wilson Law who was reported to be duly elected to that office yesterday,[335] as follows, viz.—

Head Quarters of Nauvoo Legion
Augt. 15— 1842

Major Gen. Law
Dr General—

I take this opportunity to give you some instructions how I wish you to act in case our persecutors should carry their pursuits so far as to tread upon our rights as free-born American Citizens. The orders which I am about to give you is the result of a long series of contemplation since I saw you.— I have come fully to the conclusion both since this last difficulty commenced, as before, that I never would suffer myself to go into the hands of the Missourians alive; and to go into the hands of the Officers of this state is nothing more nor less, than to go into the hands of the Missourians; for the whole farce has been gotten up, unlawfully and unconstitutionally, as well on the part of the Governor as others; by a mob spirit for the purpose of carrying out mob violence, to carry on mob tolerance in a religious persecution. I am determined therefore, to keep out of their hands, and thwart their designs if possible, that perhaps they may not urge the necessity of force and blood against their own fellow-citizens and loyal subjects; and become ashamed and withdraw their pursuits. But if they [p. 131] should not do this and shall urge the necessity of force; and I if I by any means should be taken, these are therefore to command you forthwith, without delay, regardless of life or death to rescue me out of their hands. And further, to treat any pretensions to the contrary, unlawful and unconstitutional and as a mob got up for the purpose as religious persecution to take away the rights of men. And further, that our chartered rights and privileges shall be considered by us as holding the supremacy in the premises and shall be maintained; nothing short of the supreme court of this State, having authority to dis-annul them; and the Municipal Court having jurisdiction in my case. You will see therefore that the peace of the City of Nauvoo is kept, let who will endeavor to disturb it. You will see also that whenever any mob force

---

335. Law was elected major general of the Nauvoo Legion to replace John C. Bennett, who was cashiered two weeks earlier. (Nauvoo Legion Minute Book, 13 Aug. 1842, 22–29; JS, Journal, 30 June 1842; Thomas Carlin to JS, 27 July 1842, p. 102 herein.)

or violence is used, on any citizen thereof, or that belongeth thereunto, you will see that that force or violence is immediately dispersed and brought to punishment; or meet it, and contest it at the point of the sword with firm and undaunted and unyeilding valor; and let them know that the spirit of of old seventysix; and of George Washington yet lives, and is contained in the bosoms and blood of the children of the fathers thereof. If there are any threats in the city let legal steps be taken on the part of those that make the threats: and let no man, woman or child be intimidated nor suffer it to be done. Nevertheless as I said in the first place we will take every measure that lays in our power and make every sacrifice that God or man could require at our hands to preserve the peace and safety of the people without colition. And if sacrificing my own liberty for months and years without stooping to the disgrace of Missouri persecution and violence, and [Thomas] Carlins mis-rule and corruption I bow to my fate with cheerfulness and all due deference in the consideration of the lives, safety and welfare of others. But if this policy cannot accomplish the desired object; let our charter, and our Municipality; free trade and Sailors rights be our motto, and go a-head David Crockett like, and lay down our lives like men, and defend ourselves to the best advantage we can to the very last. You are therefore, hereby authorised and commanded, by virtue of the authority which I hold, and commission granted me by the Executive of this State, to maintain the very letter and spirit of the above contents of this letter to the very best of your ability; to the extent of our lives, and our fortunes; and to the lives and the fortunes of the [Nauvoo] Legion; as also all those who may volunteer their lives and their fortunes with ours; for the defence of our wives, our children, our fathers and our mothers; our homes; our grave yards, and our tombs; and our dead and their tombstones, and our dear bought American liberties with the blood of our fathers, and all that is dear and sacred to man. Shall we shrink at the onset? No, let every mans brow be as the face of a Lion; let his heart be unshaken as the mighty oak, and his knee confirmed as the sappline [sapling] of the forrest; and by the voice and loud roar of the cannon; and the loud peals and thundering of Artillery; and by the voice of the thunderings of heaven as upon mount Sinai; and by the voice of the Heavenly Hosts; and by the voice of the Eternal God; and by the voice of innocent blood; and by the voice of innocence; and by the voice [p. 132] of all that is sacred and dear to man, let us plead the justice of our cause; trusting in the arm of Jehovah the Eloheem who sits enthroned in the heavens: that peradventure he may give us the victory; and if we bleed we shall bleed in a good cause— in the cause of innocence and truth: and from henceforth will their not be a crown of glory for us? And will not those who come after us, hold our names in sacred remembrance? and will our enemies dare to brand us with cowardly reproach? With these considerations, I subscribe myself Yours most faithfully and respectfully with acknowledgements of your high and honored trusts as Major Gen. of the Nauvoo Legion

Joseph Smith— Mayor of the City of Nauvoo and Lieu^t Gen. of the Nauvoo Legion of Illinois. Militia

Wilson Law.
<u>Major Gen. of the Nauvoo Legion.</u>—

P.S. I want you to communicate all the information to me of all the transactions, as they are going on daily, in writing by the hand of my aidecamps. As I am not willing that any thing that goes from my hands to you should be made a public matter, I enjoin upon you to keep all things in your own bosom; and I want every thing that comes from you to come through my Aids. The bearer of this will be able to pilot them in a way that will not be prejudicial to my safety—

Joseph Smith.—[336]

This letter was put into the hands of Sister Emma with a charge to deliver it to Gen. Law tomorrow. After considerable conversation on various subjects and partaking of dinner Sister Emma accompanied by brother [Erastus] Derby & W[illiam] Clayton started for Nauvoo. The morning had been very wet and the roads was very dirty. It was difficult walking. We proceeded to the river and entered a skiff in which we proceeded across the river and then down the side of the islands Soon after we got on the water the wind began to blow very hard and it was with much difficulty and apparent danger that we could proceed. We continued on as well as we could and after considerable toil arrived opposite the City of Nauvoo. We went between the Islands and crossed over the river to Montrose As soon as we landed the wind abated and was near calm. Brother Derby wanted to return up the river without the additional toil of crossing to Nauvoo. We was fortunate in happening to meet with bro. Ivins[337] skiff just about to go over to Nauvoo. We got into that skiff and left brother

---

336. Law's response, dated 15 August 1842, is copied into this journal as part of the following entry for 15 August.

337. Possibly Charles Ivins or James Ivins, brothers who operated a ferry at Nauvoo. (Hancock Co., IL, Deed Records, 9 Nov. 1840, vol. H, pp. 630–631, microfilm 954,598, U.S. and Canada Record Collection, FHL; Walker, "Rachel R. Grant," 20–21.)

Derby to return at his own leasure. Before we could get over the wind arose again considerable but we arrived home safe and well about 6 o clock P.M. We found Mr [Stephen] Powers from Keokuk who had just returned from Burlington. While there he ascertained that there was no writ issued in Iowa for Joseph.[338] The report had evidently originated from the fact of a writ being issued for the apprehension of some horse theives The people enquired if it was not true that Joseph had been commissioned by the United States to visit the Indians and negociate with them for a tract of land, such being the report in circulation. Mr Powers answered that he "was not authorised to assert that the report was true but he thought it was not only possible but very probable.["][339] [p. 133]

15 August 1842 • Monday

Monday 15th. This A.M. several reports were in circulation that the Militia are on their way here, and the same is said to have been stated by the Stage driver; but it is supposed that it is only as scheme to alarm the citizens. Sister Emma presented the forgoing letter to Major Gen. [Wilson] Law to which he responded by the following answer

"Nauvoo City Ill. Aug.t 15th. Afternoon 1842

Lieut Gen. J. Smith
My Dr friend

I this morning received a line from you by the young man ([Lorin] Walker) respecting the Guns[340] &c. One of them is in the stone Shop by the Nauvoo House. One I expect to get put into Mr Ivins' barn and the other I cannot get under lock and key any place I know of yet; but I will have them taken the best care of that I can.

I have also received from the hand of your Lady <u>your orders</u> at len[g]th respecting matters and things, and I am happy indeed to receive such orders from you, for your views on these subjects are precisely my own. I do respond with my whole heart to every sentiment you have so nobly and so feelingly expressed, and while my heart beats, or this hand which now writes is able to draw and weild a sword you

---

338. While Powers's report was accurate, Iowa Territory governor John Chambers later issued a writ, or arrest warrant, after receiving a requisition dated 20 August 1842 from Missouri governor Thomas Reynolds. (State of Missouri, Office of the Secretary of State, Commissions Division, Register of Civil Proceedings, vol. A, p. 175; John Chambers, Burlington, Iowa Territory, to John Cowan, 10 Mar. 1843, JS Office Papers, CHL.)

339. JS was not involved with official negotiations between the United States and the American Indians.

340. These cannon were possibly part of the Nauvoo Legion arsenal.

may depend on it being at your service in the glorious cause Liberty and Truth, ready in a moments warning to defends the rights of man both civil and religious. Our <u>common</u> <u>rights</u> and <u>peace</u> is all we ask and we will use every peaceable means in our power to enjoy these, but our <u>rights</u> <u>we</u> <u>must</u> <u>have</u>, <u>peace</u> we must have if we have to <u>fight</u> for them.— There has nothing worthy of notice come to my knowledge to day, the <u>Gentlemen</u> <u>Officers</u> are seemingly very unhappy and out of humor with themselves more than with any body else, they see we have the advantage of them and that the⟨y⟩ can not provoke us to break the law, and I think they know if they do that we will use them up the right way. I guess they see that in our patience we possess our souls,[341] and I know that if they shed or cause to be shed a drop of the blood of one of the least amongst us that the lives of the transgressors shall atone for it with the help of <u>our God</u>.— I send you the ordinance that was passed by the Court Martial on Saturday last for your approval or otherwise as it cannot become a Law without your approbation.[342]

I also send you the returns of the election for Major General,[343] as you ordered the election,[344] you will please order the War Secretary of the Legion (Col. Sloane [James Sloan]) to send for a Commission.[345]

With the warmest feelings of my heart I remain most respectfully,

Yours—

<u>Wilson</u> <u>Law</u>"

"P.S. Afternoon 6 o clock

I have just learned that Mr Pittman [James Pitman] got a letter about noon and got ready immediately and started off as he said for Carthage but I think for Quincy giving it up for a bad job

W. L"[346]

---

341. See Luke 21:19; and Revelation, 16 and 17 Dec. 1833, in Doctrine and Covenants 97:5, 1835 ed. [D&C 101:38].

342. Ordinance no. 3, passed by the court-martial on 13 August 1842, describes sundry organizational changes to the Nauvoo Legion. (Nauvoo Legion Minute Book, 13 Aug. 1842, 22–29.)

343. Wilson Law was elected as the new major general of the Nauvoo Legion on 13 August 1842. (Nauvoo Legion Minute Book, 13 Aug. 1842, 22–29.)

344. The notice calling for the election, signed by JS, appeared two weeks earlier in *The Wasp*. (Order to assemble, *The Wasp*, 30 July 1842, [3].)

345. Sloan sent a letter to Illinois adjutant general Moses K. Anderson two days later requesting commissions for Wilson Law and thirty-three other officers. (James Sloan, Nauvoo, IL, to Moses K. Anderson, Springfield, IL, 17 Aug. 1842, Thomas Carlin, Correspondence, Illinois State Archives, Springfield.)

346. JS's response to Law, dated 16 August 1842, is copied into this journal on pages 103–104 herein.

About dark brother Woolley[347] returned from Carthage and stated that he had conversed with Chauncey Robison who informed him that he had ascertained that the Sheriffs were determined to have Joseph and if they could not succeed themselves they would bring a force sufficient to search every house in the [p. 134] City, and if they could not find him there they would search the state &c. As before stated the Sheriffs left the City about four o clock saying they were going to Carthage but brother Woolley did not meet them on the road. It is believed they are gone to Quincy. In consequence of these reports it was considered wisdom that some of the brethren should go and inform Joseph accordingly about 9 o clock Hyrum [Smith] Geo. Miller, Wm. Law, A[masa] Lyman, Jno D. Parker, N[ewel] K. Whitney & Wm. Clayton started by different routs, on foot and proceeded to the place where Joseph was. When the statement was made the president prepared to leave the city, expecting he was no longer safe, but upon hearing the whole statement from those present, he said he should not leave his present retreat[348] yet, he did not think he was discovered, neither did he think he was any more unsafe than before He discovered a degree of excitement and agitation manifest in those who brought the report and he took occasion to gently reprove all present for letting report excite them, and advised them not to suffer themselves to be wrought upon by any report, but to maintain an even, undaunted mind Each one began to gather courage and all fears were soon subsided, and the greatest union and good feeling prevailed amongst all present.

Various subjects then was conversed upon and council given by the president which was felt to be both seasonable and salutary. After conversing a while in the grove the company retired into the house and sat and conversed untill 2 o clock at about which time they departed evidently satisfied and much encouraged by the interview It was considered wisdom that the president should have all things in readiness so that if it was necessary he could start immediately for the Pine Country[349] where he would be beyond the reach of his pursuers.

---

347. Probably Edwin Woolley.
348. JS was at Edward Sayers's farm, located about two and a half miles northeast of Nauvoo. (JS, Journal, 11, 13, and 17 Aug. 1842; Hancock Co., IL, Deed Records, 19 May 1841, vol. I, pp. 309–310, microfilm 954,598, U.S. and Canada Record Collection, FHL.)
349. The church's lumber operation near Black River Falls, Wisconsin Territory. (Rowley, "Mormon Experience in the Wisconsin Pineries," 121.)

16 August 1842 • Tuesday

Tuesday 16th. Wrote a letter to sister Emma giving her instructions how to proceed in case he had to go to the Pine Country.[350] Also wrote a letter to Wilson Law asking his opinion about the appearance of things and the best course to be pursued.[351] Brother [Erastus] Derby took the letters and is expected back soon. Brother Erastus H Derby is one among the number of the faithful. souls, who have taken as yet the greatest interest that possibly could have been imagined for the welfare of president Joseph I therefore record the following blessing from the mouth of the president himself.

"Blessed is Brother Erastus H. Derby, and he shall be blessed of the Lord; he possesses a sober mind, and a faithful heart; the snares therefore that are subsequent to befall other men, who are treacherous and rotten-hearted, shall not come nigh unto his doors, but shall be far from the path of his feet. He loveth wisdom, and shall be found possessed of her. Let their be a crown of glory, and a diadem upon his head. Let the light of eternal Truth shine forth upon his understanding; let his name be had in everlasting remembrance; let the blessings of Jehovah be crowned upon his posterity after him, for he rendered me consolation, in the lonely places of my retreat: How good, and glorious, it has seemed unto me, to find pure and holy friends, who are faithful, just and true, and whose hearts fail not; and whose knees are confirmed and do not faulter; while they wait upon the Lord, in administering to my necessities; ⟨See Page 164⟩[352] [p. 135]

[*pages 136–163, donation records dated 18 May–12 September 1842*]

⟨From Page 135⟩ in the day when the wrath of mine enemies was poured out upon me. In the name of the Lord, I feel in my heart to bless them, and to say in the name of Jesus Christ of Nazareth that these are the ones that shall inherit eternal life. I say it by virtue of the Holy Priesthood, and by the ministering of Holy Angels, and by the gift and power of the Holy Ghost. How glorious were my feelings when I met that faithful and friendly band, on the night of the eleventh on thursday, on the Island, at the mouth of the slough, between Zarahemla and Nauvoo. With what unspeakable delight, and what transports of joy swelled my bosom, when I took by the hand on

---

350. The letter is copied into this journal on pages 107–110 herein.
351. The letter is copied into this journal on pages 103–104 herein.
352. TEXT: This insertion and the one that follows are in the handwriting of Willard Richards.

that night, my beloved Emma, she that was my wife, even the wife of my youth; and the choice of my heart. Many were the re-vibrations of my mind when I contemplated for a moment the many ~~passt~~ scenes we had been called to pass through. The fatigues, and the toils, the sorrows, and sufferings, and the joys and consolations from time to time had strewed our paths and crowned our board. Oh! what a co-mingling of thought filled my mind for the moment, Again she ⟨is⟩ here, even in the seventh trouble,[353] undaunted, firm and unwavering, unchangeable, affectionate Emma. There was brother Hyrum [Smith] who next took me by the hand, a natural brother; thought I to myself, brother Hyrum, what a faithful heart you have got. Oh, may the eternal Jehovah crown eternal blessings upon your head, as a reward for the care you have had for my soul. O how many are the sorrows have we shared together, and again we find ourselves shackled with the unrelenting hand of oppression. Hyrum, thy name shall be written in the Book of the Law of the Lord,[354] for those who come after thee to look upon, that they may pattern after thy works. Said I to myself here is brother Newel K. Whitney also, how many scenes of sorrow, have strewed our paths together; and yet we meet once more to share again. Thou art a faithful friend in whom the afflicted sons of men can confide, with the most perfect safety. Let the blessings of the eternal be crowned also upon his head; how warm that heart! how anxious that soul! for the welfare of one who has been cast out, and hated of almost all men. Brother Whitney, thou knowest not how strong those ties are, that bind my soul and heart to thee. My heart was overjoyed, as I took the faithful band by hand, that stood upon the shore one by one. Wm. Law, Wm. Clayton, Dimick B. Huntington, George Miller were there. The above names constituted the little group. I do not think to mention the particulars of the history of that sacred night, which shall forever be remembered by me. But the names of the faithful are what I wish to record in this place. These I have met in prosperity and they were my friends, I now meet them in adversity, and they are still my warmer friends. These love the God that I serve; they love the truths that I promulge; they love those virtuous, and those holy doctrines that I cherish in my bosom with the warmest

---

353. "Seventh trouble" refers to Job 5:19.

354. That is, the book in which this entry is recorded. The wording suggests that this entry and the entry of 23 August were conscious efforts on JS's part to record the names and deeds of faithful and loyal Saints "in the book of the Law of God." (See JS, Kirtland, OH, to William W. Phelps, [Independence, MO], 27 Nov. 1832, in JS Letterbook 1, p. 2 [D&C 85:7].)

feelings of my heart; and with that zeal which cannot be denied. I love friendship and truth; I love virtue [p. 164] and Law; I love the God of Abraham and of Isaac and of Jacob, and they are my brethren, and I shall live; and because I live, they shall live also. These are not the only ones, who have administered to my necessity; whom the Lord will bless. There is brother John D Parker, and brother Amasa Lyman, and brother Wilson Law, and brother Henry G. Sherwood, my heart feels to reciprocate the unweried kindnesses that have been bestowed upon me by these men. They are men of noble stature, of noble hands, and of noble deeds; possessing noble and daring, and giant hearts and souls. There is brother Joseph B. Nobles also, I would call up in remembrance before the Lord. There is brother Samuel Smith, a natural brother; he is, even as Hyrum. There is brother Arthur Millikin also, who married my youngest sister, Lucy. He is a faithful, an honest, and an upright man. While I call up in remembrance before the Lord these men, I would be doing injustice to those who rowed me in the skiff up the river that night, after I parted with the lovely group; who brought me to this my safe and lonely and private retreat; brother Jonathon [Jonathan] Dunham and the other whose name I do not know.[355] Many were the thoughts that swelled my aching heart, while they were toiling faithfully with their oars. The⟨y⟩ complained not at hardship and fatigue to secure my safety. My heart would have been harder than an adamantine stone, if I had not have prayed for them, with anxious and fervent desire. I did so, and the still small voice whispered to my soul, these that share your toils with such faithful hearts, shall reigne with you in the kingdom of their God; but I parted with them in silence and came to my retreat. I hope I shall see them again that I may toil for them and administer to their comfort also. They shall not want a friend while I live. My heart shall love those; and my hands shall toil for those, who love and toil for me, and shall ever be found faithful to my friends. Shall I be ungrateful? verily no! God forbid!["]

The above are the words, and sentiments, that escaped the lips of President Joseph Smith on this the 16th. day of August A.D 1842, in relation to his

---

355. When William Clayton recorded the incident in the 11 August 1842 entry of JS's journal, he mentioned only Dunham and Erastus Derby as accompanying JS. (JS, Journal, 11 Aug. 1842.)

friends;³⁵⁶ and has now quit speaking for the moment, but will continue the subject again.³⁵⁷

Wᵐ· Clayton, Clerk.³⁵⁸

17 August 1842 • Wednesday

Wednesday 17ᵗʰ·— This day president Joseph and brother [Erastus] Derby went out into the woods for exercise and were accidently discovered by a young man. Various questions were asked him concerning the public feeling, and situation of matters around to all which he answered promptly On being requested not to make it known where they were, he promised faithfully he would not and said time would tell wether he did or no.³⁵⁹

several rumors were afloat in the city, intimating that president Smiths retreat had been discovered, and that it was no longer safe for him to remain at brother [Edward] Sayers. consequently sister Emma went to see him at night and informed him of the report. It was considered wisdom that he should remove immediately and accordingly he departed in company with Emma and brother Derby and went to Carlos Grangers who lives on the North East part of the city. Here they were kindly recieved and wel-treated. [p. 165]

19 August 1842 • Friday

Friday 19ᵗʰ· This evening President Joseph had a visit from his Aunt Temperance Mack Spent the day mostly in conversation and reading. At night went to the city and concluded to tarry at home untill something further transpired with regard to the designs of his persecutors.³⁶⁰

20 August 1842 • Saturday

Saturday 20ᵗʰ· Spent the day in the large Room over the Store. Was considerable sick all day. In the evening had an interview with brother Hyrum [Smith], Wilson and William Law, N[ewel] K. Whitney, & George Miller a few hours, conversing on the illegality of the proceedings of our oppressors &c.

---

356. TEXT: The period after "friends" was changed to a semicolon. It appears from changes in ink density that this change and the remainder of the sentence were written later.

357. JS resumed the subject a week later. (JS, Journal, 23 Aug. 1842, p. 115 herein.)

358. TEXT: The ink color changes at this point from dark brown to blue.

359. The young man who discovered JS was Martin Henderson Harris, nephew of Book of Mormon witness Martin Harris. (Harris, Reminiscences and Journal, 4.)

360. Though JS returned to the city, he was still in hiding, spending Saturday, Sunday, and presumably Monday in the store. Four days later he returned to live in his home. (JS, Journal, 20, 21, and 23 Aug. 1842, pp. 96, 97, 119 herein.)

21 August 1842 • Sunday

Sunday 21st. In the Room over the Store. To day Sidney Rigdon went to the grove near the Temple and there related before the congregation the following incident which took place in his family. He stated that his daughter Eliza [Elizabeth Rigdon] had been sick unto death all the skill of physicians having been of no avail. She continued to sink untill finally she appeared to die, and went cold. She continually wished to recover and expressed strong desires to live saying she did not want to die &c. He stated that she appeared to die three times and again recover. When she came to the last time she stated that she had something to say to her father, which was to the effect that he must be faithful in the cause, that this was the cause of truth &c. She also said that George W. Robinson had it in his heart to deny the faith but if he did it would be his damnation, Also that Nancy [Rigdon] had near denied the faith but if she did she would be damned.[361] She also said that Jno C. Bennett was a wicked man. Elder Rigdon that then stated that he felt himself a new man, that his constitution was renewed and his system invigorated. He also bore testimony to the truth of the work; he said he had been in it a number of years and knew for himself that it was the work of God &c. He also said it had been stated that he had said Joseph was a fallen prophet; this he denied in the strongest terms.[362] After he had got through president Hyrum [Smith] arose and spoke at great length and with great power. He cited Elder Rigdons mind back to the Revelation concerning him, that if he would move into the midst of the city and defend the truth he should be healed &c and showed that what Elder Rigdon felt in regard to the improvement in his his health was a fulfilment of the Revelation.[363] He then went on to show the folly of any person's attempting to overthrow or destroy Joseph and read from the Book of Mormon in various places concerning the Prophet who was prophecied should be raised up in the last days, setting forth the work he was destined to accomplish and that he had only just commenced; but inasmuch as we could plainly see that the former part of the prophecy had been literally fulfilled we might be assured that the

---

361. Difficulties between JS and members of Rigdon's family had existed for several months. Rigdon's son-in-law George W. Robinson had recently published his withdrawal from the church, claiming that "SCANDALOUS attacks [had], at several times, been made on myself, in connection with Mr. Rigdon." *The Wasp* responded by publishing statements about Robinson's allegedly dishonest business dealings. (JS, Journal, 12 and 13 May 1842; 28 June 1842; 29 Aug. 1842, pp. 55, 56, 71, 123 herein; George W. Robinson, "Letter from Nauvoo," *Quincy [IL] Whig*, 23 July 1842, [2]; "G. W. Robinson," *The Wasp*, 30 July 1842, [2].)

362. A more detailed summary of Rigdon's sermon was published in the *Times and Seasons* the following month. ("Elder Rigdon, &c," *Times and Seasons*, 15 Sept. 1842, 3:922–923.)

363. The revelation directing Rigdon to move into the city and to be faithful is recorded in Revelation, 19 Jan. 1841, in Doctrine and Covenants 103:32, 1844 ed. [D&C 124:103–110].

Sidney Rigdon. 1873. First counselor in the First Presidency of the church, postmaster of Nauvoo, and a talented orator. Rigdon's years in Nauvoo were beset with chronic poor health and questions about his loyalty to Joseph Smith. (Church History Library, Salt Lake City.)

Joseph Duncan. A member of the Whig party, Duncan served as governor of Illinois from 1834 to 1838. Running again for governor in 1842, he vigorously denounced the Latter-day Saints after Joseph Smith endorsed Democrat Adam W. Snyder. Duncan lost to Thomas Ford, who replaced Snyder as the Democratic candidate after Snyder's death during the campaign. (Courtesy Abraham Lincoln Presidential Library and Museum, Springfield, IL.)

latter part would also be fulfilled and that Joseph would live to accomplish the great things spoken concerning him, notwithstanding his enemies might diligently and continualy seek his destruction;[364] hence the danger of any man's lifting his hand against him, for whosoever did it, would surely come to destruction and could not prosper. He asked if it had not already been proven that this was the fact. and that all who had persecuted the prophet had come to disgrace and shame, and how should any man prosper whilst seeking to injure him whom God had blessed and promised to protect and concerning whom the prophets had prophecied that he should live to fulfil the work committed to him [p. 166]

He concluded his address by calling upon the saints to take courage and fear not, and also told Elder Rigdon that inasmuch as he had seen the mercy of the Lord exerted in his behalf that it was his duty to arise and stand in defence of the truth of and of innocence and of those who were being persecuted innocently and finally called for all those who were willing to support and uphold Joseph and who believed that he was doing his duty and was innocent of the charges &c to hold up their right hand whereupon almost every person present was seen with their hands elevated and their countenances beaming with joy. Afterwards he said if there were any who were opposed to Joseph and would not defend him let them manifest it by the same sign but there was not one opposing witness.

It is evident that this meeting was productive of great good and if there was any treachery and secret combinations of evil and designing characters present, the discourse was calculated to show them their true situation and danger and it is very probable would be the means of bringing them to their senses. The whole congregation appeared highly delighted and strengthened by the circumstance and seemed to be inspired with new zeal and courage. During the day Elder Rigdon went over to President Hyrums and conversed upon various subjects and it is evident he intends to arouse his energies and stand in defence of the truth if Satan do not again darken his mind and fill his heart with evil. Orson Pratt has also signified his intention of coming out in defence of the truth and go to preaching[365] [*25 lines blank*] [p. 167]

---

364. The most notable prophecies regarding the prophet who should be "raised up in the last days" are found in the second book of Nephi and the book of Ether in the Book of Mormon. (Book of Mormon, 1840 ed., 66–67, 108–110, 532 [2 Nephi 3:6–21; 27:6–26; Ether 5:1–4].)

365. Pratt was excommunicated the previous day, 20 August, for publicly speaking "against Joseph & the Twelve" following accusations that JS had proposed to Pratt's wife, Sarah Bates Pratt. Orson and Sarah Pratt were rebaptized on 20 January 1843. (Woodruff, Journal, 10 Aug.–18 Sept. 1842; JS, Journal, 20 Jan. 1843.)

―――― ∽ ――――

Editorial Note

Scribes Erastus Derby and William Clayton here copied eight letters into JS's journal, with occasional explanatory notes interspersed. The letters were written by JS, his wife Emma Smith, Nauvoo Legion major general Wilson Law, and Illinois governor Thomas Carlin. Daily journal entries resumed on Tuesday, 23 August 1842.

―――― ∽ ――――

Copied Correspondence • 30 June–17 August 1842

/[366]Goviner [Thomas] Carlin Letters

[367]Quincy June 30eth 1842

Dear Sir

I have recieved by the last mail your letter of the 24 instant, in which you have thought proper to give me a Statement of charges against the conduct, and character, of Gen, John C Bennet[t] I can say that I regret that any individual should so far disgrace[368] his obligations to his God, and to his fellow man, as to condesend to the commission of the crimes alledged in your letter to have been perpetrated by Gene[ra]l, Bennet, it is however in accordance with representations of his character, made to me more than two years since, and which I then felt constrained to believe ware true, since which time I have desired to have as little intercourse with him as possible, No resignation of his commishion as Mj General of the Nauvoo Legion, has reached me,[369] Some weeks since I recieved a short note from him stating, that, you had reason to believe that a conspiracy was getting up in the state of Mo, for the purpose of mobing the Mormons at Nauvoo, and Kidnaping you, and taking you to that state, and requested to be informed in case of such mob, whether you would be protected by the authorities of this state &c to which I replied, that as all men ware held held ameanable to the Laws so in like maner the rights of all would be

---

366. TEXT: William Clayton handwriting ends; Erastus Derby begins.

367. A copy of this letter in the handwriting of William Clayton appears in JS's letterbook. Carlin wrote this letter in response to JS's letter of 24 June 1842, which discussed rumors of anti-Mormon sentiment and activity as well as proceedings related to John C. Bennett. (Thomas Carlin, Quincy, IL, to JS, [Nauvoo, IL], 30 June 1842, in JS Letterbook 2, pp. 238–239; JS, Nauvoo, IL, to Thomas Carlin, [Quincy, IL], 24 June 1842, in JS Letterbook 2, pp. 233–235.)

368. For "disgrace," the William Clayton copy of this letter has "disregard."

369. The same day Carlin wrote this letter, 30 June 1842, a court-martial was held in Nauvoo in which Bennett was likely cashiered. (JS, Journal, 30 June 1842; Thomas Carlin to JS, 27 July 1842, p. 102 herein.)

protected, and the dignity of the state maintained to the letter of the constitution and laws, the above is in substance the contents of his note to me and my reply to him, hoving [having] destroyed his letter as I considered it of no use— should it be ~~returned~~ ⟨retained⟩,[370]

you state that you have heard that I have of late entertained unfavorable feelings towards you (the Mormons) as a people and especially so with regard to yourself &c &c. if this should be true, you would be pleased to know from me the reasons of such hostile feelings,

In reply I can in truth say that I do not entertain nor cherish hostile or revengeful feelings towards any man or set of men on Earth, but that I may have used strong expressions in reference to your self, at times— when my indignation has been some what aroused by repeated admonitions of my friends, (both before and since the attempt to assassinate ex Gov [Lilburn W.] Boggs) to be upon my guard, that you had prophesied that Boggs should die a violent death— and that I should die in a ditch all this however if[371] true, I looked upon as idle boasting untill since the assassination of Boggs— and ~~ever~~ even since then in reference to my self, I cannot view it in any other light, because whatever your feelings may have been to-wards Boggs, the mere discharge of an official duty on my part ~~enjoins~~ enjoined upon me by the constitution and Laws, of this state, and of the United states could not possibly engender feelings of such deepe malignity, [p. 168]

be assured that this matter Gives me no uneasiness nor would the subject now have been mentioned had you not requested a reply to your enquiries. I have seen your denial of the prediction[372] published in the Wasp[373] attributed to you of the death (or assassination) of Gov Boggs, be that true or false, nothing has contributed more towards fixing the belief upon the public mind, that you had made such prediction than the repeated statements of a portion of your followers,

---

370. In his 24 June letter to Carlin, JS asked about the contents of a letter that JS had requested Bennett write to Carlin. Bennett's letter has not been located. (JS, Nauvoo, IL, to Thomas Carlin, [Quincy, IL], 24 June 1842, in JS Letterbook 2, pp. 233–235.)

371. TEXT: Possibly "of if".

372. The phrase "of the prediction" does not appear in the William Clayton copy of this letter.

373. On 21 May the *Quincy Whig* charged JS with prophesying the death of Boggs "by violent means." The following day JS wrote a response to the *Whig*, which was published in *The Wasp* on 28 May and a week later in the *Whig*. ("Assassination of Ex-Governor Boggs of Missouri," *Quincy [IL] Whig*, 21 May 1842, [3]; "Assassination of Ex-Governor Boggs of Missouri," *The Wasp*, 28 May 1842, [2]; JS, Nauvoo, IL, 22 May 1842, Letter to the editor, *Quincy [IL] Whig*, 4 June 1842, [2]; JS, Nauvoo, IL, to Mr. Bartlett, 22 May 1842, *The Wasp*, 28 May 1842, [2].)

that the maner of his death had been revealed to you, and their exultation that it must needs be fulfilled

In reference to your request to be advised how you should act in case a mob should come upon you, I should feel very much at a loss to recommend any course for you to adopt, other than a resort to the first Law of Nature, viz to defend your own rights, because ware I to advise a quiet submission on your part, I could not expect that you would fold your arms, and silently look on whilst those[374] rights ware violated and outraged, as long as you have the power to protect them,[375]

I however have not the most distant thought that there exists at presant, any real caus for the aprehension of a Mob coming upon you, otherwise I should feel it my duty to endeavor to arrest it,

very respectfully your obedient servant
Tho Carlin

General Joseph Smith

Gov [Thomas] Carlins letter

[376]Quincy July 27th 1842

Dear Sir

your communication of the 25th instant[377] together [with] the petitions of the citizens of the city of Nauvoo both male and female[378] ware delivered to me last evening by Brevet Major General Wilson Law Allso a report of James Sloan Esq Sectry of the Nauvoo Legion of the procedings of a court Martial of Brevet Major Generals had upon charges prefered against Major General John C Bennett upon which trial the court found defendant guilty and sentenced him to be Cashiered[379]

---

374. TEXT: Possibly "thare".
375. TEXT: Possibly "then,".
376. The original of this letter is housed in JS Materials, CCLA.
377. JS's letter to Carlin has not been located.
378. Three petitions were directed to Carlin on JS's behalf. One petition was drawn up at a meeting of the citizens of Nauvoo and "signed by about eight hundred, or upwards" citizens. The petition requested that Carlin not issue a writ for JS's arrest.*a* A second petition, circulated by the Female Relief Society of Nauvoo and signed by "about one thousand Ladies," was delivered to Carlin by Emma Smith, Eliza R. Snow, and Amanda Barnes Smith at the end of July.*b* The third petition, requesting JS's safety and the peace of their families, was drawn up by "many citizens in, and near Nauvoo, who were not Mormons."*c* (*a.* Nauvoo City Council Minute Book, 22 July 1842, 95–97; JS, Journal, 22 July 1842. *b.* Eliza R. Snow, Journal, 29 July 1842; Thomas Carlin to Emma Smith, 24 Aug. 1842, p. 126 herein. *c.* Minutes, *Times and Seasons,* 1 Aug. 1842, 3:869.)
379. Bennett's cashiering probably took place on 30 June 1842. (JS, Journal, 30 June 1842.)

all of which have been considered, In reply to your expressed aprehentions of— the posibility of an attack upon the peaceable inhabitants of the city of Nauvoo and vicinity; through the intreaguees and false representations of John C Bennett and others, and you[r] request that I would inssue [issue] official orders to you, to have the Nauvoo Legion ⟨in⟩ readiness to be caled out at a moments warning in defence of the peaceble citizens &c I must say that I cannot concieve of the least probability or scarcely posability of an attack of violence upon the citizens of Nauvoo from any quarter what ever and as uterly imposible that such attack is contemplated by any sufficient number of persons [p. 169] to excite the least appearance[380] of danger or injury, [and][381] whilst I should consider it my imperative duty to promptly take measures [to][382] suppress and repell any invasion by violence of the peoples rights, I nevertheless think that it is not my province to interpose my official authority gratuitously where no such exigency exists— From the late disclosures as made by Gen Bennett[383] it is not strange that the ~~citzens~~ aprehension of the cit[i]zens of Nauvoo are excited, but so far as I can learn from the expression of public opinion, the excitement is confined to to the Mormons them selves, and only extends to the community at large as a matter of curiosity and wonder,
very respectfully your obedient servent
Tho Carlin

General Joseph Smith jr

[384]Head Quarters of Nauvoo Legion
August 16th 1842

Major General [Wilson] Law

Beloved Brother and friend those few lines which I recieved from you writen on the 15th was to me like apples of Gold in pictures of

---

380. For "appearance," original letter has "apprehension."
381. Omitted word supplied from original letter.
382. Omitted word supplied from original letter.
383. Bennett's attacks against the church were published in the *Sangamo Journal*. ("Astounding Mormon Disclosures! Letter from Gen. Bennett," *Sangamo Journal* [Springfield, IL], 8 July 1842, [2]; "Further Mormon Developments!! 2d Letter from Gen. Bennett," and "Gen. Bennett's Third Letter," *Sangamo Journal*, 15 July 1842, [2]; "Gen. Bennett's 4th Letter," *Sangamo Journal*, 22 July 1842, [2].)
384. A copy of the letter in William Clayton's handwriting is housed in JS Collection, CHL. JS wrote this letter in response to Wilson Law's letter dated 15 August 1842, which is copied into this journal on pages 90–91 herein.

Silver,[385] I rejoice with exceding greate Joy to be associated in the high and responcible stations which wee hold whose mind and feelings and heart is so congenial with my own, I love that soul that is so nobly entabernacled in that clay of yours, may God Allmighty grant that it may be satiated with seeing a fullfilment of evry virtuous and manly desire that you possess, may wee be able to triumph Gloriously over those who seek our destruction and overthrow which I believe weee shall, the news you wrote me was more favorable than that which was communicated by the Brethren, they seamed a little agitated for my safety, and advised me for the pine cuntry[386] but I succeded admirably calming all their fears, but nevertheless as I said in my former letter[387] I was willing to exile myselfe for months and years if it would be for the safety and wellfare of the people, and I do not know but it would be as well for me to take a trip to the pine countries and remain untill arrangements can be made for my most perfect safety when I returned, these are there fore to confer with you on this subject as I want to have a concert of action in evry thing I do, if I knew that they would oppress me alone and let the rest of you dwell peac[e]ably and quietly, I think it would be the wisest plan to absent myself for a little season, if by that means wee could prevent the profusion [of][388] Blood,— Pleas write and give me your ~~views~~ ⟨mind⟩ on ~~this~~ ⟨that⟩ subject and all other information that has come to hand to day, and what are the signs of the times,— I have no news for I am where I cannot get ~~any news~~ ⟨much⟩ all is quiet and peacible around I [p. 170] therefore wait with earnest expectation for your advises I am anxious to know your opinion on any course ⟨that⟩ I may see proper to take for in the multitude of council there is safety[389]

I add no more but subscribe myselfe your faithful and most obedient servant friend and Brother

~~Lieutenant~~ Joseph Smith
Lieutenant General of the Nauvoo
Legion of Illinois Malitia

---

385. See Proverbs 25:11.
386. For "country," the William Clayton copy of this letter has "woods."
387. The referenced letter is copied into this journal on pages 87–89 herein.
388. Omitted word supplied from retained Clayton copy.
389. See Proverbs 11:14; 24:6.

To the forgoing letter I received the following answers To Wit

Nauvoo City Illinois August 17th. 1842

Lieut Gen. J. Smith

Dear Friend— Every thing is moving along in the city in the usual tranquil & industrious manner, there is no change in the appearance of things that a common observer could see, although to one who knows & is acquaint with the countenances of the thinking few, it is evident that their minds are troubled more than common, and I know by myself that they can not help it, and why should it be otherwise when the Lords anointed is hunted like a Lion of forest by the most wicked & oppressive generation that has ever been since the days of the saviour of the world, indeed every movement of this generation reminds me of the history of the people who crucified Christ, it was nothing but mob law, mob rule and mob violence all the time, the only difference is that the <u>Governors</u> then were more just than the <u>Governors</u> now, they were willing to acquit innocent men, but our Governors now despise justice, garble and prevent the law, and join in with the mob in pursuit of <u>innocent</u> <u>blood</u>. I have been meditating on your communication of yesterday & will just add a thought or so on the subject, respecting particularly your going to the Pine country. I think I would not go there for some time if at all. I do not believe that an armed force will come upon us at all unless they get hold of you first & that we rescue you which we would do under any circumstances with the help of God, but I would rather do it within the limits of the city under the laws of the city, therefore I would think it better to Quarter in the city & not long in one place at once. I see no reason why you might not stay in safety within the city for months without any knowing it only those who ought & that as few as is necessary.

I must close for the present remaining as ever your affectionate friend and obedient servant

Wilson Law.

The following is the one designed especially as answers to President Josephs letter dated August 16th. but which through mistake was mislaid and consequently not recorded in the proper place [p. 171]

---

390. TEXT: Erastus Derby handwriting ends; William Clayton begins.

³⁹¹Nauvoo City Ill. one o clock afternoon Aug.ᵗ 16.ᵗʰ· 1842
Lieut. Gen. J. Smith

My Dear Friend— I have just received and read yours of to day & hasten to reply. There is no movements of any kind going on to-day amongst the enemy as far as I can see which helps to strengthen me in my opinion of yesterday, but still it might be a calm before a storm and if so we will meet it when it comes.

You wish my opinion respecting your absenting yourself for some time from those friends that are dear to you as life, and to whom you are also as dear, & from the place and station to which you are call'd by <u>Him</u> who ruleth in the armies of heaven & amongst the inhabitants of the earth.³⁹² I must confess that I feel almost unworthy to give an opinion on the subject, knowing that your own judgment is far superior to mine, but nevertheless you shall have it freely, it is this I think that if they cannot get you peaceably according to the forms of law, that they will not dare to attempt violence of any kind upon the inhabitants of the city, for they are well aware that they cannot insult us with impunity neither use violence only at the risk of their lives, and there are but few men, who are willing to risk their lives in a bad cause, it is the principles & spirit of Liberty, of Truth, of Virtue, & of Religion & equal rights, that make men courageous and valient & fearless in the day of battle and of strife; and just the contrary with the oppressor for nine times out of ten a bad cause will make a man a coward & he will flee when no man pursueth.³⁹³ Now if I am right in thinking that it is you alone they seek to destroy as soon as they find they can not get you, they will cease to trouble the city except with spies; and if we knew that you were completely out of their reach, we could either laugh at their folly, or whip them for impertinence or any thing else, as the case might be, for we would feel so happy in your safety that we could meet them in any shape. On the whole I think it would be better for you to absent yourself till the next Governor takes the <u>Chair</u>,³⁹⁴ for

---

391. Wilson Law wrote this letter in response to JS's letter dated 16 August 1842, which is copied into this journal on pages 103–104 herein.
392. See Daniel 4:35.
393. See Proverbs 28:1.
394. The gubernatorial election was held on 1 August. Thomas Ford, a Democrat, won the election, collecting 46,901 votes, while his Whig opponent, Joseph Duncan, received 38,585 votes. Ford took office on 8 December 1842. Law's recommendation that JS wait until Ford took office before returning to Nauvoo may reflect a hope that Ford would be more sympathetic to JS and the Saints, as church members had overwhelmingly voted for Ford. ("O Yes! O Yes!," *The Wasp*, 16 July 1842, [2]; *Journal of the Senate*...

I do think if you are not here they will not attempt any violence on the city, and if they should they will disgrace themselves in the eyes of the world, and the world will justify us in fighting for our rights, and then you can come out like a Lion and lead your people to glory and to victory in the name of the <u>Lord of Hosts</u>. I know the sacrifice you must make in taking this course, I know it will grieve your noble spirit to do so, for when I think of it myself I feel no desire in life but to fight and to cut off from the earth all who oppress, and to establish that true form of government at once which would guarantee to every man <u>equal rights</u>. I know we have justice on our side in respect of city Laws, & that the acts of municipal court are legal, but the question is are we <u>now</u> able to <u>assert</u> them or had we better wait till we are more able. The latter course will give us peace <u>a</u> <u>little</u> while, by sacrificing <u>your</u> <u>liberty</u> and the feelings of your family and friends and depriving <u>us</u> <u>all</u> of your <u>society</u> and <u>governing</u> <u>wisdom</u>. I will only add that I am ready for either course and may God direct us to do that that is best. [p. 172] If you should conclude to go away for a while I must see you before you go. And for the present I will bid you be chearful and make yourself as happy as you can for the right side of the wheel will soon be up again. And till then and ever I remain under every circumstance your friend &

Ob.[t] servant Wilson Law.

On the same day that the foregoing letter was wrote to Major Gen. Law.[395] President Joseph wrote one to Mrs Emma in the words following To Wit;

Nauvoo August 16.th 1842

My Dear Emma

I embrace this opportunity to express to you some of my feelings this morning. First of all, I take the liberty to tender you my sincere thanks for the two interesting and consoling visits that you have made me during my almost exiled situation.[396] Tongue can not express the gratitude of my heart, for the warm and true-hearted friendship you have manifested in these things toward me. The time has passed away since you left me, very agreeably; thus far, my mind being perfectly reconciled to my fate, let it be what it may. I have been kept from melancholy and dumps, by the kind-heartedness of brother [Erastus]

---

of Illinois, 8 Dec. 1842, 33; "Official Returns of the Hancock County Election," *Warsaw [IL] Signal,* 13 Aug. 1842, [3].)

395. The 16 August 1842 letter from JS to Law is copied into this journal on pages 103–104 herein.

396. Emma visited JS on 11 and 13 August. (JS, Journal, 11 and 13 Aug. 1842.)

Derby, and his interesting chit-chat from time to time, which has called my mind from the more strong contemplations of things, and subjects that would have preyed more earnestly upon my feelings. Last night—in the night—brother Hyrum [Smith], [George] Miller, [William] Law & others came to see us. They seemed much agitated, and expressed some fears in consequence of some manouverings and some flying reports which they had heard in relation to our safety; but after relating what it was, I was able to comprehend the whole matter to my entire satisfaction, and did not feel at all alarmed or uneasy. They think, however, that the Militia will be called out to search the city, and if this should be the case I would be much safer for the time being at a little distance off, untill Governor [Thomas] Carlin could get weary and be made ashamed of his corrupt and unhallowed proceedings. I had supposed, however, that if there were any serious operations taking by the Governor; that Judge [James] Ralston or brother [David] Hollister would have notified us;[397] and cannot believe that any thing very serious is to be apprehended, untill we obtain information from a source that can be relied on. I have consulted wether it is best for you to go to Quincy, and see the Governor; but on the whole, he is a fool; and the impressions that are suggested to my mind, are, that it will be of no use; and the more we notice him, and flatter him, the more eager he will be for our destruction.[398] You may write to him, whatever you see proper, but to go and see him, I do not give my consent at present. Brother Miller again suggested to me the propriety of my accompanying him to the Pine woods, and then he return, and bring you [p. 173] and the children. My mind will eternally revolt at every suggestion of that kind. More especially since the dream and vision that was manifested to me on the last night. My safety is with you, if you want to have it so. Any thing more or less than this cometh of evil. My feelings and council I think ought to be abided. If I go to the Pine country, you shall go along with me, and the children; and if you and the children go not with me, I dont go. I do not wish to exile myself for the sake of my own life, I would rather fight it out. It is

---

397. Ralston and Hollister lived in Quincy, Illinois, and acted as informants. (JS, Journal, 11 and 13 Aug. 1842.)

398. In July, Emma Smith, Eliza R. Snow, and Amanda Barnes Smith took to Carlin a petition from the Relief Society requesting protection for JS. Carlin received them cordially but shortly thereafter issued an arrest warrant for JS on 2 August 1842. (Eliza R. Snow, Journal, 29 July 1842; Thomas Carlin to Emma Smith, 24 Aug. 1842, p. 126 herein; Thomas Carlin, Writ, 2 Aug. 1842, *Ex Parte* JS for Accessory to Boggs Assault [C.C.D. Ill. 1843], copy, Nauvoo, IL, Records, CHL.)

for your sakes, therefore, that I would do such a thing. I will go with you then, in the same carriage and on Horse back, from time to time, as occasion may require; for I am not willing to trust you, in the hands of those who cannot feel the same interest for you, that I feel; to be subject to the caprice, temptations, or notions of any-body whatever. And I must say that I am pre-possessed somewhat, with the notion of going to the Pine Country any how; for I am tired of the mean, low, and unhallowed vulgarity, of some portions of the society in which we live; and I think if I could have a respite of about six months with my family, it would be a savor of life unto life, with my house. Nevertheless if it were possible I would like to live here in peace and wind up my business; but if it should be ascertained to a dead certainty that there is no other remedy, then we will round up our shoulders and cheerfully endure it; and this will be the plan. Let my horse, saddle, saddle-bags, and valice to put some shirts and clothing in, be sent to me. Let brother Derby and Miller take a horse and put it into my Buggy with a trunk containing my heavier cloths, shoes and Boots &c and let brother [John] Taylor accompany us to his fathers,[399] and there we will tarry, taking every precaution to keep out of the hands of the enemy, untill you can arrive with the children. Let brother Hyrum bring you. Let Lorain [Lorin Walker] and brother [William] Clayton come along and bring all the writings and papers, books and histories, for we shall want a scribe in order that we may pour upon the world the truth like the Lava of Mount Vesuvius. Then, let all the goods, household furniture, cloths and Store Goods that can be procured be put on to the Boat, and let 20 or 30 of the best men that we can find be put on board to man it, and let them meet us at Prairie Du Chien; and from thence, we will wend our way like larks up the Mississippi untill the touring [towering?] mountains and rocks, shall reminds us of the places of our nativity, and shall look like safety and home; and then we will bid defiance to the world, to Carlin, [Lilburn W.] Boggs, [John C.] Bennett, and all their whorish whores, and motly clan, that [p. 174] follow in their wake, Missouri not excepted; and until the damnation of hell rolls upon them, by the voice, and dread thunders, and trump of the eternal God; then, in that day will we not shout in the victory and be crowned with eternal joys, for the battles we have fought, having kept the faith and overcome the world. Tell the children that it is well

---

399. James Taylor lived on the Henderson River near Oquawka, Illinois, north of Nauvoo. ("Joseph Smith, the Prophet," 547; Obituary for Agnes Taylor, *Deseret News,* 25 Nov. 1868, 335.)

with their father, as yet; and that he remains in fervent prayer to Almighty God for the safety of himself, and for you, and for them. Tell Mother Smith that it shall be well with her son, wether in life or in death; for thus saith the Lord God. Tell her that I remember her all the while, as well as Lucy [Smith Millikin] and all the rest; they all must be of good cheer. Tell Hyrum to be sure and not fail to carry out my instructions, but at the same time if the Militia does not come, and we should get any favorable information all may be well yet. Yours in haste, Your affectionate husband untill death, through all eternity forevermore

Joseph Smith

P.S. I want you to write to Lorenzo Wasson, and get him to make affidavit to all he knows about Bennett and forward it.[400] I also want you to ascertain from Hyrum wether he will conform to what I have requested. And you must write me an answer per bearer, giving me all the news you have, and what is the appearance of things this morning

J.S.—

To the foregoing Mrs Emma returned the following answer per hand brother [Erastus] Derby.— To Wit;

Dear husband,

I am ready to go with you if you are obliged to leave; and Hyrum [Smith] says he will go with me. I shall make the best arrangements I can and be as well prepared as possible. But still I feel good confidence that you can be protected without leaving this country. There is more ways than one to take care of you, and I believe that you can still direct in your business concerns if we are all of us prudent in the matter. If it was pleasant weather I should contrive to see you this evening, but I dare not run to much of a risk on account of so many going to see you. General [James] Adams sends the propositions concerning his land, two dollars an acre, payments as follows, Assumption of Mortgage say about fourteen hundred, interest included. Taxes due, supposed about thirty dollars. Town property one thousand dollars. Balance, Money, payable in one, two, three and four years. Brother Derby will tell you

---

400. This request was probably prompted by a letter Wasson, Emma Smith's nephew in Philadelphia, wrote to JS and Emma, which was published the previous day in the *Times and Seasons*. In the letter, Wasson offered: "There are many things I can inform you of, if necessary, in relation to Bennett and his prostitutes." (Lorenzo Wasson, Philadelphia, PA, to JS and Emma Smith, Nauvoo, IL, 30 July 1842, *Times and Seasons*, 15 Aug. 1842, 3:891–892.)

all the information we have on hand. I think we we will have news from Quincy as soon as tomorrow.

Yours affectionately forever
Emma Smith.

Joseph Smith.— [p. 175]

According to the hint offered by President Joseph in his letter to Sister Emma she wrote the following letter to Governor [Thomas] Carlin which was dated August 16th. but ought to have been the 17th.—

Nauvoo August 16th. 1842

To His Excellency Governor [Thomas] Carlin.

Sir— It is with feelings of no ordinary cast that I have retired after the business of the day and evening too, to address your honor. I am at a loss how to commence; my mind is crowded with subjects to numerous to be contained in one letter. I find myself almost destitute of that confidence, necessary to address a person holding the authority of your dignified, and responsible office; and I would now offer, as an excuse for intruding upon your time and attention, the justice of my cause. Was my cause the interest of an individual or of a number of individuals; then, perhaps I might be justified in remaining silent. But it is not! Nor is it the pecuniary interest of a whole community alone, that prompts me again to appeal to your excellency.[401] But dear sir, it is for the peace and safety of hundreds I may safely say, of this community, who are not guilty of any offense against the laws of the Country; and also the life of my husband; who has not committed any crime whatever; neither has he transgressed any of the laws, or any part of the constitution of the United States; neither has he at any time infringed upon the rights of any man, or of any class of men or community of any description. Need I say he is not guilty of the crime alleged against him by Governor [Lilburn W.] Boggs.

Indeed it does seem entirely superfluous for me, or any one of his friends in this place, to testify his innocence of that crime; when so

---

401. Less than three weeks earlier, Emma Smith, accompanied by Eliza R. Snow and Amanda Barnes Smith, visited Governor Carlin at his Quincy, Illinois, residence with a petition from the Female Relief Society soliciting protection for JS. Snow wrote: "The Gov. received us with cordiality, and as much affability and politeness as his Excellency is master of, assuring us of his protection, by saying that the laws and Constitution of our country shall be his polar star in case of any difficulty. He manifested much friendship, and it remains for time and circumstance to prove the sincerity of his professions." (Eliza R. Snow, Journal, 29 July 1842; Eliza R. Snow, "Pen Sketch of an Illustrious Woman," *Woman's Exponent*, 15 Oct. 1880, 9:73–74; Thomas Carlin to Emma Smith, 24 Aug. 1842, p. 126 herein.)

many of the citizens of your place, and of many other places in this State, as well as in the Territory; do know positively that the statement of Governor Boggs[402] is without the least shadow of truth; and we do know, and so do many others, that the prosecution against him, has been conducted in an illegal manner; and every act demonstrates the fact, that all the design of the prosecution, is to throw him into the power of his enemies; without the least ray of hope, that he would ever be allowed to obtain a fair trial, and that he would be inhumanly and ferociously murdered; no person having a knowledge of the existing circumstances, has one remaining doubt: and your honor will recollect that you said to me that you would not advise Mr Smith, ever to trust himself in Missouri. And dear Sir, you cannot for one moment indulge one unfriendly feeling towards him, if he abides by your council. Then sir, why is it that he should be thus cruelly pursued? why not give him the privilege of the laws of this State. When I reflect upon the many cruel and illegal operations of Lilburn [p. 176] W. Boggs, and the consequent suffering of myself and family; and the incalculable losses and suffering of many hundreds who survived, and the many precious lives that were lost; all, the effect of unjust prejudice and misguided ambition, produced by misrepresentation and calumny, my bosom heaves with unutterable anguish. And who, that is as well acquainted with the facts as the people of the city of Quincy, would censure me, if I should say that my heart burned with just indignation, towards our calumniators, as well as the perpetrators of those horrid crimes. But how happy would I now be to pour out my full heart in gratitude to Gov. Boggs if he had rose up with the dignity and authority of the cheif executive of the State, and put down every illegal transaction, and protected the peaceable citizens, and enterprising emigrants, from the violence of plundering out-laws, who have ever been a disgrace to the State, and always will, so long as they go unpunished. Yes I say, how happy would I be to render him not only the gratitude of my own heart, but the cheering effusions of the joyous souls of fathers and mothers, of brothers and sisters, widows and orphans, who he might have saved by such a course, from now drooping under the withering hand of adversity, brought upon them by the persecutions of wicked and corrupt men. And now may I entreat your excellency to lighten the hand of oppression and persecution, which is laid upon me and my

---

402. Boggs's affidavit charged JS with being an "accessary before the fact" in the shooting of Boggs on 6 May 1842. (Lilburn W. Boggs, Affidavit, 20 July 1842, p. 380 herein.)

family, which materially affect the peace and welfare of this whole community; for let me assure you that there are many whole families that are entirely dependant upon the prosecution and success of Mr Smiths temporal business for their support. And if he is prevented from attending to the common avocations of life, who will employ those innocent, industrious poor people and provide for their wants. But my dear sir, when I recollect the interesting interview, I and my friends had with you when at your place, and the warm assurances you gave us of your friendship and legal protection, I cannot doubt for a moment your honorable sincerity; but do still expect you to consider our claims upon your protection from every encroachment upon our legal rights as loyal citizens as we always have been, still are, and are determined always to be a law abiding people; and I still assure myself that when you are fully acquainted with illegal proceedings practised against us in the suit of Gov. Boggs[403] you will recall those writs which have been issued against Mr Smith and [Orrin Porter] Rockwell, as you must be aware that Mr Smith was not in Missouri, and of course he could not have left there; with many other considerations which if duly considered will justify Mr Smith in the course he has taken. And now I appeal to your excellency as I would unto a father, who is not only able but willing to shield me and mine from every unjust prosecution. I appeal to your sympathies [p. 177] and beg you to spare me, and my helpless children. I beg you to spare my innocent children the heartrending sorrow of again seeing their father unjustly drag'ed to prison or to death. I appeal to your affections as a son and beg you to spare our aged mother,— the only surviving parent we have left,— the unsupportable affliction of seeing her son, who she knows to be innocent of the crimes laid to his charge, thrown again into the hands of his enemies who have so long sought for his life; in whose life and prosperity she only looks for the few remaining comforts she can enjoy. I entreat of your excellency to spare us these afflictions and many sufferings which cannot be uttered; and secure to yourself the pleasure of doing good, and vastly increasing human happiness; secure to yourself the benediction of the aged and the gratitude of the young and the blessing and veneration of the rising generation.

   Respectfully your most obedient— Emma Smith.—

---

403. Boggs's affidavit charging JS with complicity in the attempt on his life did not meet the constitutional requirements for evidence in an extradition case. (See 84n327 herein.)

Sir I hope you will favor me with an answer[404]
E.S.—

This letter was sent to Quincy by brother Wm. Clayton who presented it to Gov. [Thomas] Carlin on Friday morning the 19th. Inst. in presence of Judge [James] Ralston.[405] The Govr. read the letter with much attention apparently and when he got through he passed high encomiums on sister Emma and expressed astonishment at the judgement and talent manifest in the manner of her address, He presented the letter to Judge Ralston requesting him to read it. Gov. Carlin then proceeded to reiterate the same language as on a former occasion viz. that he was satisfied there was no excitement any where but in Nauvoo "amongst the Mormons themselves" all was quiet and no apprehension of trouble in other places so far as he was able to ascertain.[406] He afterwards stated when conversing on another subject that "persons were offering their services every day either in person or by letter and held themselves in readiness to come against us whenever he should call upon them, but he never had had the least idea of calling out the Militia neither had he thought it necessary. There was evidently a contradiction in his assertions in the above instances and although he said "there was no excitement but amongst them Mormons" it is evident he knew better. He also said that it was his opinion that if president Joseph would give himself up to the Sheriff he would be honorably acquited and the matter would be ended; but on Judge Ralston asking how hee thought the president could go through the midst of his enemies without voilence being used towards him and if acquited how he was to get back? the Gov. was evidently at a loss what to say but made light of the matter as though he thought it might be easily done. He took great care to state that it was not his advice that Mr Smith should give himself up but thought it would be soonest decided. It appeared evident that we have no great things to expect from Carlin as it is evident he is no friend. He acknowledged his ignorance of the law touching the case in plain terms. [p. 178]

---

404. Thomas Carlin responded to Emma's letter one week later, on 24 August. That response is copied into this journal on pages 126–128 herein.

405. Ralston lived in Quincy and acted as an informant for church leaders. (JS, Journal, 11 Aug. 1842.)

406. Carlin used similar language in a 27 July 1842 letter to JS. (See p. 103 herein.)

23 August 1842 • Tuesday

Tuesday 23— This day president Joseph has renewed the subject of conversation, in relation to his faithful brethren, and friends in his own words;[407] which I now proceed to record as follows;

"While I contemplate the virtues and the good qualifications and characterestics of the faithful few, which I am now recording in the Book of the Law of the Lord,[408] of such as have stood by me in every hour of peril, for these fifteen long years past; say for instance; my aged and beloved brother Joseph Knights [Knight] Sen[r], who was among the number of the first to administer to my necessities, while I was laboring, in the commencement of the bringing forth of the work of the Lord, and of laying the foundation of the Church of Jesus Christ of Latter Day Saints: for fifteen years has he been faithful and true, and even handed, and exemplary and virtuous, and kind; never deviating to the right hand nor to the left. Behold he is a righteous man. May God Almighty lengthen out the old mans days; and may his trembling, tortured and broken body be renewed, and the vigor of health turn upon him; if it can be thy will, consistently, O God; and it shall be said of him by the sons of Zion, while there is one of them remaining; that this man, was a faithful man in Israel; therefore his name shall never be forgotten. There is his son Newel Knight and Joseph Knight [Jr.] whose names I record in the Book of the Law of the Lord, with unspeakable delight, for they are my friends. There are a numerous host of faithful souls, whose names I could wish to record in the Book of the Law of the Lord; but time and chance would fail. I will mention therefore only a few of them as emblematical of those who are to numerous to be written. But there is one man I would mention namely [Orrin] Porter Rockwell, who is now a fellow-wanderer with myself— an exile from his home because of the murderous deeds and infernal fiendish disposition of the indefatigable and unrelenting hand of the Missourians.[409] He is an innocent and a noble boy; may God Almighty deliver him from the hands of his pursuers. He was an innocent and a noble child, and my soul loves him; Let this be recorded

---

407. JS began recording the names and deeds of his faithful associates the previous week. (JS, Journal, 16 Aug. 1842, pp. 93–96 herein.)
408. That is, the book in which this entry is recorded.
409. Rockwell fled east after being accused of attempting to assassinate Lilburn W. Boggs; by 1 December 1842 he was in Philadelphia. (Orrin Porter Rockwell per S. Armstrong, Philadelphia, PA, to JS, Nauvoo, IL, 1 Dec. 1842, JS Collection, CHL.)

for ever and ever. Let the blessings of Salvation and honor be his portion. But as I said before, so say I again while I remember the faithful few who are now living, I would remember also the faithful of my friends who are dead, for they are many; and many are the acts of kindness, and paternal, and brotherly kindnesses which they have bestowed upon me. And since I have been hunted by the Missourians many are the scenes which have been called to my mind. Many thoughts have rolled through my head, and across my breast. I have remembered the scenes of my child-hood I have thought of my father who is dead; who died by disease which was brought upon him through suffering by the hands of ruthless mobs. He was a great and a good man. The envy of knaves and fools was heaped upon him, and this was his lot and portion all the days of his life. He was of noble stature, and possessed a high, and holy, and exalted, and a virtuous mind. His soul soared above all those mean [p. 179] and grovelling principles that are so subsequent to the human heart. I now say, that he never did a mean act that might be said was ungenerous, in his life, to my knowledge. I loved my father and his memory; and the memory of his noble deeds, rest with ponderous weight upon my mind; and many of his kind and parental words to me, are written on the tablet of my heart.[410] Sacred to me, are the thoughts which I cherish of the history of his life, that have rolled through my mind and has been implanted there, by my own observation since I was born. Sacred to me is his dust, and the spot where he is laid. Sacred to me is the tomb I have made to encircle o'er his head. ~~that~~ ⟨Let⟩ the memory of my father eternally live. ~~Let the faults, and the follies~~ Let his soul, or the Spirit my follies forgive. With him may I reign one day, in the mansions above; and tune up the Lyre of Anthems, of the eternal Jove. May the God that I love look down from above, and save me from my enemies here, and take me by the hand; that on Mount Zion I may stand and with my father crown me eternally there. Words and language, is inadequate to express the gratitude that I owe to God for having given me so honorable a parentage. My mother also is one of the noblest, and the best of all women. May God grant to prolong her days, and mine; that we may live to enjoy each others society long yet in the enjoyment of liberty, and to breath the free air. Alvin my oldest brother, I remember well the pangs of sorrow that swelled my youthful bosom and almost burst my ~~aching~~ ⟨tender⟩ heart, when he died. He was the

---

410. See Proverbs 3:3; and 2 Corinthians 3:3.

oldest, and the noblest of my fathers family. He was one of the noblest of the sons of men: Shall his name not be recorded in this Book? Yes, Alvin; let it be had here, and be handed down upon these sacred pages, forever and ever. In him there was no guile. He lived without spot from the time he was a child. From the time of his birth, he never knew mirth. He was candid and sober and never would play; and minded his father, and mother, in toiling all day. He was one of the soberest of men and when he died the Angel of the Lord visited him in his last moments. These childish lines I record in remembrance of my child-hood scenes. My Brother Don Carloss [Don Carlos] Smith, whose name I desire to record also, was a noble boy. I never knew any fault in him. I never saw the first immoral act; or the first irreligious, or ignoble disposition in the child. From the time that he was born, till the time of his death; he was a lovely, a good natured, and a kind-hearted, and a virtuous and a faithful upright child. And where his soul goes let mine go also. He lays by the side of my father. Let my father, Don Carlos, and Alvin, and children that I have buried be brought and laid in the Tomb I have built.[411] Let my mother, and my brethren, and my sisters be laid there also; and let it be called the Tomb of Joseph,[412] a descendant of Jacob; and when I die, let me be gathered to the Tomb of my father.[413] There are many souls, whom I have loved stronger than death; to them I have proved faithful; to them I [p. 180] am determined to prove faithful, untill God calls me to resign up my breath. O, thou who seeeth, and knoweth the hearts of all men; thou eternal, omnipotent, omnicient, and omnipresent Jehovah, God; thou Eloheem, that sitteth, as sayeth the psalmist,[414] enthroned in heaven; look down upon thy servant Joseph, at this time; and let faith on the name of thy Son Jesus Christ, to a greater degree than thy servant ever yet has enjoyed, be conferred upon him; even the faith of Elijah; and let the Lamp of eternal life, be lit up in his heart, never to be taken away; and let the words of eternal life, be poured upon the soul of thy servant; that he may know thy will, thy statutes, and thy commandments, and thy judgements to do them. As the dews upon Mount Hermon may the distillations of thy divine grace, glory and

---

411. By this time, JS and Emma had lost five natural children and one adopted child.
412. Evidence suggests that this tomb was located on the south side of the Nauvoo temple block and that it was not completed until 1845. (Johnstun, "To Lie in Yonder Tomb," 163–180.)
413. None of the Smith family members JS mentions here were buried in the tomb. JS resumed this subject on 16 April 1843. (JS, Journal, 16 Apr. 1843, pp. 359–360 herein.)
414. See Psalms 11:4; 103:19.

Tomb of Joseph Smith. Circa 1841–1846. William Weeks's drawings (top view and front view) of a tomb planned for Joseph Smith depict two chambers and a stream of water flowing from underneath the tomb's foundation. The tomb was completed in 1845 and later fell into ruin; it was used for at least one member of Joseph Smith's family but was not used for Smith himself. (Church History Library, Salt Lake City.)

honor in the plenitude of thy mercy, and power and goodness be poured down upon the head of thy servant. O Lord God, my heavenly Father, shall it be in vain, that thy servant must needs be exiled from the midst of his friends; or be dragged from their bosoms, to clank in cold and iron chains; to be thrust within the dreary prison walls; to spend days of sorrow, and of grief and misery their [there], by the hand of an infuriated, insensed and infatuated foe; to glut their infernal and insatiable desire upon innocent blood; and for no other cause on the part of thy servant, than for the defence of innocence, and thou a just God will not hear his cry? O, no, thou wilt hear me; a child of woe, pertaining to this mortal life; because of sufferings here, but not for condemnation that shall come upon him in eternity; for thou knowest O God, the integrity of his heart. Thou hearest me, and I knew that thou wouldst hear me, and mine enemies shall not prevail; they all shall melt like wax before thy face; and as the mighty floods, and waters roar; so shall or as the billowing earth-quake's, devouring gulf; or rolling Thunders loudest peal; or vivid, forked lightnings flash; or sound of the Arch-Angels trump; or voice of the Eternal God, shall the souls of my enemies be made to feel in an instant, suddenly; and shall be taken, and ensnared; and fall back-wards, and stumble in the ditch they have dug for my feet, and the feet of my friends; and perish in their own infamy and shame,— be thrust down to an eternal hell, for their murderous and hellish deeds."[415]

After writing so much president Joseph left off speaking for the present but will continue the subject again. He had a very pleasant visit from mother Smith and aunt Temperance [Mack], who were evidently highly gratified to find him in good spirits and in good health notwithstanding his confinement and lack of exercise. After visiting awhile and hearing read some parts of the Book of the Law of the Lord[416] they departed rejoicing in the blessing and favor of the Almighty.—

In the P.M. president Joseph received a few lines from sister Emma informing him that she would expect him home this evening believing that she could take care of him better at home than elsewhere. Accordingly soon after dark he started for home and arrived safe without being noticed by any person.[417] All is quiet in the city.

---

415. TEXT: A change in ink density indicates that the text following "deeds." (including the closing quotation mark after "deeds.") was written later than the rest of the entry.
416. That is, the book in which this entry is recorded.
417. After returning to Nauvoo on the night of 19 August, JS spent Saturday, Sunday, and presumably

[418]Wm Clayton. Clerk. [p. 181]

24 August 1842 • Wednesday

Wednesday 24th. At home all day. Had a visit from brothers Whitney[419] and Isaac Morley

26 August 1842 • Friday

~~Thursday~~ ⟨Friday⟩ ~~25th.~~ ⟨26th.⟩ At home all day. In the evening in council with some of the Twelve and others, He gave some very important instructions upon the situation of matters, showing that it was necessary that the officers who could, should go abroad through the States; and inasmuch as a great excitement had been raised, through the community at large, by the falsehoods put in circulation by John C. Bennett and others it was wisdom in God that the Elders should go forth and deluge the States with a flood of truth;[420] setting forth the mean, contemptible, persecuting conduct of ex-Governor [Lilburn W.] Boggs of Missouri and those connected with him in his mean, and corrupt proceedings in plain terms, so that the world might understand the abusive conduct of our enemies, and stamp it with indignation. He advised the Twelve to call a special conference on Monday next to give instructions to the Elders and call upon them to go forth upon this important mission, meantime, that all the affidavits concerning Bennetts conduct be taken and printed so that each Elder could be properly furnished with correct and weighty testimony to lay before the public.—[421]

Monday in hiding at the store. (JS, Journal, 19, 20, and 21 Aug. 1842, pp. 96, 97 herein.)

418. TEXT: Beginning with Clayton's signature, the ink color changes from blue to brown.

419. Probably Newel K. Whitney.

420. By this time, articles written by Bennett and others attacking the church had been published in several newspapers throughout the country and in Europe. Many of these articles were copies or excerpts of Bennett's earlier letters in the *Sangamo Journal*. For the Bennett letters, see "Astounding Mormon Disclosures! Letter from Gen. Bennett," *Sangamo Journal* (Springfield, IL), 8 July 1842, [2]; "Further Mormon Developments!! 2d Letter from Gen. Bennett," and "Gen. Bennett's Third Letter," *Sangamo Journal*, 15 July 1842, [2]; and "Gen. Bennett's 4th Letter," *Sangamo Journal*, 22 July 1842, [2]. For examples of other published attacks, see "Trouble among the Mormons," *Daily Atlas* (Boston), 13 July 1842, [2]; "The Mormon Troubles," *Pennsylvania Inquirer and National Gazette* (Philadelphia), 16 July 1842, [2]; "The Mormons," *Louisville (KY) Daily Journal*, 11 July 1842, [2]; "The Mormons—Joe Smith, & c," *Louisville Daily Journal*, 23 July 1842, [2]; "Mormon Developments!" *Louisville Daily Journal*, 25 July 1842, [2]; "To the Editors of the Louisville Journal," *Louisville Daily Journal*, 27 July 1842, [2]; "Mormonism," *Cincinnati Daily Gazette*, 27 July 1842, [2]; "Important from the Far West," *New York Herald*, 27 July 1842, [2]; "To the Editors of the Louisville Journal," *Louisville Daily Journal*, 6 Aug. 1842, [2]; "Great Mormon Explosion!," *Jonesborough (TN) Whig and Independent Journal*, 17 Aug. 1842, [1]; "The Mormons, or Latter-Day Saints," *Liverpool Mercury*, 19 Aug. 1842, 267; and "American 'Items,'" *Freeman's Journal and Daily Commercial Advertiser* (Dublin), 3 Sept. 1842, [4].

421. The affidavits concerning Bennett were published in Nauvoo under the date 31 August 1842.

27 August 1842 • Saturday

Saturday 27th. In the large room over the Store with some of the Twelve and others who were preparing affidavits for the press.—

28 August 1842 • Sunday

Sunday 28th. At home—

29 August 1842 • Monday

Monday 29th. This being the appointed for the conference above referred to,[422] the Elders assembled in the grove near the Temple about 10 o clock A.M. President Hyrum [Smith] introduced the object of the conference by stating

> "that the people abroad had been excited by John C. Bennetts false statements and that letters had frequently been received inquiring concerning the true nature of said reports; in consequence of which it is thought wisdom in God that every Elder who can, should now go forth to every part of the United States, and take proper documents with them setting forth the truth as it is and also preach the gospel, repentance, baptism & salvation and tarry preaching untill they shall be called home. They must go wisely, humbly setting forth the truth as it is in God, and our persecutions, by which the tide of public feeling will be turned. There are many Elders here doing little and many people in the world who want to hear the truth. We want the official members to take their staff and go East, (not West) and if a mob should come here they will only have women and children to fight with. When you raise churches send the means you get to build the Temple, and get the people to take stock in the Nauvoo House. It is important that the Nauvoo House should be finished that we may have a suitable house wherein to entertain the great ones of the earth and teach them the truth.[423] We want the Temple built that we may offer our oblations and where we can ask forgiveness of our sins every week, and forgive one another, and offer up our offering & get our endowment [p. 182] The gospel will be turned from the gentiles to the Jews.[424] Sometime ago almost every person was ordained, the purpose was to have you tried and ready and then to receive their blessings.

(*Affidavits and Certificates*, [Nauvoo, IL: 31 Aug. 1842], copy at CHL.)

422. Three days earlier, JS advised the Quorum of the Twelve to call this conference. (JS, Journal, 26 Aug. 1842.)

423. See Revelation, 19 Jan. 1841, in Doctrine and Covenants 103:9, 18, 1844 ed. [D&C 124:22–24, 60].

424. See Revelation, 8 Mar. 1833, in Doctrine and Covenants 85:3, 1844 ed. [D&C 90:9].

Every one is wanted to be ready in two or three days, and expects there will be a liberal turnout."

After president Hyrum had got nearly through president Joseph came up to the stand. The brethren were rejoiced to see him. He had not been seen for three weeks and his appearance amongst the brethren under present circumstances caused much animation and joy, it being unexpected. Some had supposed that he was gone to Europe and some to Washington; and some thought he was in the city, Every one rejoiced to see him ~~one~~ once more When president Hyrum had done speaking president Joseph got up and began his remarks by congratulating the brethren on the victory gained over the Missourians once more.

"He had told them formerly about fighting the Missourians, and about fighting alone. He had not fought them with the sword nor by carnal weapons; he had done it by stratagem or by outwitting them, and there had been no lives lost, and there would be no lives lost if they would hearken to his council. Up to this day God had given him wisdom to save the people who took council. None had ever been killed who abode by his council. At Hauns Mill the brethren went contrary to his council, if they had not there lives would have been spared.[425] He has been in Nauvoo all the while, and outwitted Bennetts associates and attended to his own business in the City all the time. We want to whip the world mentally and they will whip themselves physically. The brethren cant have the tricks played upon them that were done at Kirtland and Far-west, they have seen enough of the tricks of their enemies and know better". Orson Pratt has attempted to destroy himself,— caused all the City almost to go in search of him.[426] Is it not enough to put down all the infernal influence of the Devil what we have felt and seen, handled and evidenced of this work of God? But the Devil had influence among the Jews to cause the death of Jesus Christ by hanging between heaven and earth. O. P [Orson Pratt] and others of the same class caused trouble by telling stories to people who would betray me and 'they must believe these stories

---

425. During the conflict between Mormons and their neighbors in northern Missouri, JS counseled non-Mormon Jacob Hawn to abandon the mill, and John Killian, a Caldwell County militia officer, advised Hawn to move the Saints to safety in Far West. Hawn rejected their counsel, and seventeen church members at Hawn's Mill were killed. (Baugh, "Call to Arms," chap. 9.)

426. Pratt disappeared for a day after learning of accusations that JS proposed to his wife, Sarah. (JS, Journal, 15 July 1842.)

because his wife told him so'! I will live to trample on their ashes with the soles of my feet. I prophecy in the name of Jesus Christ that such shall not prosper, they shall be cut down in their own plans. They would deliver me up Judas like, but a small band of us shall overcome. We dont want or mean to fight with the sword of the flesh but we will fight with the broad Sword of the spirit. Our enemies say our Charter and Writs of Habeus Corpus are worth nothing.[427] We say they came from the highest authority in the States, and we will hold to them. They cannot be disannulled or taken away."

He then told the brethren what he was going to do, viz; to send all the Elders away and when the mob came there would only be women and children to fight and they would be ashamed, He said

"I dont want you to fight but to go and gather [p. 183] tens, hundreds and thousands to fight for you. If oppression comes I will then shew them that there is a Moses and a Joshua amongst us; and I will fight them if they dont take off oppression from me, I will do as I have done this time, I will run into the woods. I will fight them in my own way. I will send bro. Hyrum to call conferences every where through-out the States, and let documents be taken along and show to the world the corrupt and oppressive ⟨conduct⟩ of [Lilburn W.] Boggs. [Thomas] Carlin and others, that the public may have the truth laid before them. Let the Twelve send all who will support the character of the Prophet— the Lords anointed. And if all who go will support my character I prophecy in the name of the Lord Jesus whose servant I am, that you will prosper in your missions. I have the whole plan of the kingdom before me, and no other person has. And as to all that Orson Pratt, Sidney Rigdon or George W. Robinson can do to prevent me I can kick them off my heels, as many as you can name, I know what will become of them".[428] He concluded his remarks by saying "I have the best of feelings towards my brethren since this last trouble began, but to the apostates and enemies I will give a lashing every oppertunity and I will curse them."

---

427. Two editorials by Thomas Sharp in the *Warsaw Signal* attacked the Nauvoo charter and the issuing of writs of habeas corpus by the Nauvoo Municipal Court. Complaints concerning the powers granted Nauvoo by its charter were eventually heard by the state legislature on 9 and 10 December 1842. ("Recent Attempt to Arrest the Prophet," *Warsaw [IL] Signal,* 13 Aug. 1842, [3]; "An Ordinance," *Warsaw Signal,* 20 Aug. 1842, [2]; JS, Journal, 9–20 Dec. 1842, pp. 173–174 herein.)

428. For a variety of reasons, Pratt, Rigdon, and Robinson each had opposed JS over the course of the summer. (See JS, Journal, 12 and 13 May 1842; 75n304 herein; and 97n361 herein.)

During the whole of this address the feelings of the brethren was indiscribable and the greatest joy and good feeling imaginable was manifest. Orson Pratt set behind president Joseph all the time he was speaking. He looked serious and dejected, but did not betray the least signs of compunction or repentance.

About Three hundred and eighty of the brethren volunteered to go out immediately and it is probable they will nearly all be gone in two weeks[429]

30 August 1842 • Tuesday

Tuesday 30th. At home all day—

31 August 1842 • Wednesday

Wednesday 31st. At home in the A.M. In the P.M rode up to the Grove with his lady to attend the Female Relief Society's meeting.—[430]

1 September 1842 • Thursday

September Thursday 1st. In the A.M. in the large room over the Store, P.M. at home attending to business.[431]

2 September 1842 • Friday

Friday 2nd. Spent the day at home. In the P.M. a report came to the effect ~~the~~ that the Sheriff with an armed force, was on his way to Nauvoo.

3 September 1842 • Saturday

Saturday 3rd. In the A.M. at home in company with John Boynton. A letter was received from brother [David] Hollister[432] to the effect that the Missourians were again on the move and that two requisitions were issued, one on the

---

429. Wilford Woodruff noted that "three or four hundred Elders were called upon to go into the vineyard & about 400 Elders have since gone & many others are going their has never at any time been as great a turn out into the vineyard since the foundation of the Church." (Woodruff, Journal, 10 Aug.–18 Sept. 1842.)

430. This was the last time JS addressed the Female Relief Society of Nauvoo. He talked about overcoming those who spoke falsely against him and persecuted him. He also commended the Relief Society for their aid, particularly in petitioning Governor Thomas Carlin to protect him. (Relief Society Minute Book, 31 Aug. 1842; Minutes, *Times and Seasons*, 1 Aug. 1842, 3:869.)

431. JS wrote a letter on this date to "all the saints in Nauvoo" regarding baptism for the dead, which was published two weeks later in the *Times and Seasons* and was canonized in the 1844 edition of the Doctrine and Covenants. (JS, to "all the saints in Nauvoo," 1 Sept. 1842, pp. 131–133 herein; "Tidings," *Times and Seasons*, 15 Sept. 1842, 3:919–920; JS, Nauvoo, IL, to "all the Saints in Nauvoo," 1 Sept. 1842, in Doctrine and Covenants 105, 1844 ed. [D&C 127].)

432. The letter from Hollister was written two days earlier and addressed to William Clayton. Hollister acted as an informant for church leaders. (David Hollister, Quincy, IL, to William Clayton, Nauvoo, IL, 1 Sept. 1842, JS Office Papers, CHL; JS to Emma Smith, 16 Aug. 1842, p. 107 herein.)

Governor of ~~the~~ this State and the other on the Governor of Iowa.[433] There movements were represented as being very secret and resolute. Soon after 12 o clock [James] Pitman the Deputy Sheriff and two other men came into the house.[434] It appeared that they had come up the river side and hitched their horses below the Nauvoo House and then proceeded on foot, undiscovered untill they got into the house. When they arrived president Joseph was in another apartment of the house eating dinner with his family. John Boynton happened to be the first person discovered by the Sheriffs and they began to ask him where Mr Smith was. He answered that he saw him [p. 184] early in the morning; but did not say that he had seen him since. While this conversation was passing, president Joseph passed out at the back door and through the corn in his garden to brother Newel K. Whitney's. He went up stairs and undiscovered.[435] Meantime Sister Emma went and conversed with the Sheriffs. Pitman said he wanted to search the house for Mr Smith. In answer to a question by sister Emma he said he had no Warrant authorising him to search but insisted upon searching the house. She did not refuse, and accordingly they searched through but to no effect. This is another testimony and evidence of the mean, corrupt, illegal proceedings of our enemies Notwithstanding the constitution of the United States says Article 4$^{th.}$ "The right of the people to be secure in their persons, houses, papers, and effects, against unreasonable searches and seizures, shall not be violated; and no warrants shall issue, but upon probable cause, supported by oath or affirmation, and particularly describing the place to be searched, and the persons or things to be seized." Yet these men audaciously, impudently, and altogether illegally demanded, and searched the house of president Joseph, even without any warrant or authority whatever. Being satisfied that he was not in the house they departed. They appeared to be well armed, and no doubt intended to take him either dead or alive; which we afterwards heard they had said they would do; but the Almighty again delivered his servant from their blood-thirsty grasp. It is rumored that there are fifteen men in the city along with the Sheriffs and that they dined together to day at Amos Davis's. Soon after Sun down Tho$^{s.}$ King[436]

---

433. Illinois governor Thomas Carlin and Iowa Territory governor John Chambers. (Thomas Reynolds, Requisition, 22 July 1842, p. 380 herein; State of Missouri, Office of the Secretary of State, Commissions Division, Register of Civil Proceedings, vol. A, p. 175.)

434. One of the two men who accompanied Adams County constable Pitman was Edward Ford, who had been designated by Governor Thomas Reynolds's requisition to receive JS. (Eliza R. Snow, Journal, 4 Sept. 1842; Thomas Reynolds, Requisition, 22 July 1842, p. 381 herein.)

435. The Whitneys were living in the upper story of JS's red brick store on Water Street. ([Elizabeth Ann Smith Whitney], "A Leaf from an Autobiography," *Woman's Exponent,* 15 Nov. 1878, 7:91; 15 Dec. 1878, 7:105.)

436. King was the undersheriff of Adams County. (Robison, *Adams County,* E–K:149.)

and another person arived at the house and demanded to search, which they immediately did; but finding nothing they also went towards Davis's. Some of them was seen about afterwards but at about 10 o clock all was quiet. It is said that they started from Quincey yesterday expecting and fully determined to reach Nauvoo in the night and fall upon the house unawares but report says they lost the road, and got scattered away one from another, and could not get along untill daylight.[437] This in all probability is true as they appeared much fatigued and complained of being weary and sore with riding. President Joseph, accompanied by brother Erastus H. Derby, left brother Whitneys about nine o clock; and went to brother Edward Hunters where he was welcomed and made comfortable by the family, and where he can be kept safe from the hands of his enemies.

I will now proceed to record the following letter from the Governor to Sister Emma dated

[438]"Quincy August 24th. 1842

"Dear Madam— Your letter of this date[439] has just been handed to me which recalls to my mind your great solicitude in reference to the security and welfare of your husband; but I need not say it recalls to my mind the subject matter of your solicitude, because that subject except at short intervals, has not been absent from my mind. I can scarcely furnish you a justifiable apology for delaying a reply so long, but be assured Madam, it is not for want of regard for you, and your peace of mind, that I have postponed; but a crowd of public business, which has required [p. 185] my whole time; together with very ill health since the receipt of your former letter, and it would be most gratifying to my feelings now, if due regard to public duty, would enable me to furnish such a reply as would fully conform to your wishes— but my duty in reference to all demands made by Executives of other States, for the surrender of fugitives from justice, appears to be plain and simple; consisting entirely of an executive, and not a judicial character leaving me no discretion— or adjudication, as to the innocence, or

---

437. Edward Ford's report to Governor Thomas Reynolds confirms this unexpected delay en route: "on friday evening layte we left Quincy for nauvoo but unfortunatly for us it rain[ed] verry hard and turnd quite dark so that we was compeld to stop we however started verry earley next morning to nauvoo." (Edward Ford, St. Louis, MO, to Thomas Reynolds, 8 Sept. 1842, microfilm, Missouri Historical Society, Selected Papers Pertaining to Mormonism, 1831–1859, CHL.)

438. Thomas Carlin wrote this letter in response to Emma Smith's letter dated 16 August 1842, which is copied into this journal on pages 111–114 herein.

439. No 24 August 1842 letter from Emma Smith to Carlin has been located.

guilt, of persons so demanded and charged with crime, and it is plain that the constitution and laws of the united States in reference to fugitives from justice, presumes, and contemplates, that the laws of the several States, are ample to do justice to all who may be charged with crime. And the statute of this State simply requires, "That when ever the Executive of any other State, or of any Territory of the united States, shall demand of the executive of this State any person as a fugitive from justice, and shall have complied with the requisitions of the act of congress in that case made and provided, it shall be the duty of the executive of this State to issue his <u>warrant</u> under the seal of the State, to apprehend the said fugitive" &c.[440] With the Constitution and laws before me, my duty is so plainly marked out, that it would be impossible to err, so long as I abstain from usurping the right of adjudication. I am aware that a strict enforcement of the laws by an executive,— or a rigid administration of them by a judicial tribunal, often results in hardship to those involved, and to you it doubtless appears to be peculiarly so, in the present case of Mr Smith. If however as you alledge, he is innocent of any crime, and the proceedings are illegal, it would be the more easy for him to procure an acquital. In reference to the remark you attribute to me that I "would not advise Mr Smith ever to trust himself in Missouri" I can only say— as I have heretofore said on many occasions that I never have entertained a doubt that if Mr Smith should submit to the laws of Missouri, that the utmost latitude would be allowed him in his defence, and the fullest justice done him, and I only intended to refer (in the remark made to you when at my house)[441] to the rabble. and not to the laws of Missouri.

Very much has been attributed to me in reference to Genl Smith that is without foundation in truth, a knowledge of which fact, enable⟨s⟩ me to receive what I hear as coming from him, with great allowance. In conclusion Dear Madam I feel conscious when I assure you, that all my official acts in reference to Mr Smith have been prompted by a strict sense of duty, and in discharge of that duty have studiously pursued that course, least likely to produce excitement and alarm, both in your community, and the surrounding public, and I

---

440. An Act concerning Fugitives from Justice [6 Jan. 1827], *Revised Code of Laws, of Illinois* [1826–1827], p. 232, sec. 1. The "act of congress" that the Illinois law refers to is An Act respecting Fugitives from Justice, and Persons Escaping from the Service of Their Masters [12 Feb. 1793], *Public Statutes at Large*, 2nd Cong., 2nd Sess., chap. 7, pp. 302–305.

441. In July, Emma Smith went to Quincy with Eliza R. Snow and Amanda Barnes Smith to see Governor Thomas Carlin regarding protection for JS. (See 111n401 herein.)

will here add that I much regret being called upon to act at all, and that I hope he will submit to the laws, and that justice will ultimately be done. Be pleased to present my best respects to Mrs— [Amanda Barnes] Smith & Miss [Eliza R.] Snow your companions when at Quincy, and accept of my highest regard for yourself, and best wishes for your prosperity & happiness—

Your obedient servant Tho. Carlin.["]

Mrs Emma Smith [p. 186]

To the foregoing letter Sister Emma sent the following by way of answer.

"Nauvoo August 27th 1842

"To His Excellency Gov. Carlin

Dear Sir— I received your letter of the 24th in due time, and now tender you the sincere gratitude of my heart, for the interest which you have felt in my peace and prosperity; and I assure you, that every act of kindness, and every word of consolation have been thankfully received and duly appreciated by ~~my~~ me and my friends also; and I much regret your ill health, and still hope that you will avail yourself of sufficient time to investigate our cause, and thoroughly acquaint yourself with the illegality of the prosecution instituted against Mr Smith.— And I now certify that Mr Smith, my self, nor any other person, to my knowledge, has ever, nor do we at this time wish your honor to swerve from your duty, as an executive, in the least. But we do believe that it is your duty to allow us in this place, the privileges and advantages guaranteed to us by the laws of this State and the United States; this is all we ask, and if we can enjoy these rights unmolested, it will be the ultimate end of all our ambition; and the result will be peace and prosperity to us and all the surrounding country, as far as we are concerned. Nor do we wish to take any undue advantage of any intricate technicalities of law; but honorably and honestly to fulfil all of the laws of this State, and of the United States, and then, in turn, to have the benifits resulting from an honorable execution of those laws.

And now, your Excellency will not consider me assuming any unbecoming dictation; but recollect that the many prosecutions that has been got up unjustly, and pursued illegaly against Mr Smith, instigated by selfish and irreligious motives, has obliged me to know something for myself; therefore, let me refer you to the eleventh Section of our city Charter. "All power is granted to the City council, to make, ordain, establish, and execute all ordinances, <u>not</u> <u>repugnant</u> to the constitution of the State or of the United States, or, as they may deem necessary for the peace and safety of said city."[442] Accordingly there is an ordinance passed by the City Council to prevent our people from being carried off by an illegal process.[443] And if any one thinks he is illegally seized, under this ordinance he claims the right of Habeus Corpus under section 17th. of the charter, to try the question of identity, which is strictly constitutional.[444]

These powers are positively granted in the charter over your own signature; and now, dear sir, where can be the justice in depriving us of these rights which are lawfully ours, as well as they are the lawful rights of the inhabitants of Quincy and Springfield and many other places where the citizens enjoy the advantages of such ordinances, without controversy.[445] With these considerations, and many more which might be adduced, give us the privilege and we will show your Honor, and the world besides, if required, that the Mr Smith referr'd to in the demand from Missouri, is not the Joseph Smith of Nauvoo, for he was not in Missouri; neither is he [p. 187] described in the writ, according as the Law requires; and that he is not a fugitive from justice.[446] Why then, be so strenuos to have my husband taken, when you know him to be innocent of an attempt on the life of Governor [Lilburn W.] Boggs, and that he is not a fugitive from justice? It is not the fear of a just decision against him, that deters Mr Smith from going into Missouri; but it is an actual knowledge that it was never intended he should have a fair trial. And now Sir, if you were not aware of the fact; I will acquaint you with it now, that there were lying ⟨in⟩ wait, between this place and Warsaw, twelve men from Jackson County, Missouri, for the purpose of taking Mr Smith out of the hands of the officers who might have him in custody. Also those two

---

442. See An Act to Incorporate the City of Nauvoo [16 Dec. 1840], *Laws of the State of Illinois* [1840–1841], p. 54, sec. 11.

443. Nauvoo City Council Minute Book, 5 July 1842, 86–87.

444. Carlin's response to this letter, dated 7 September 1842, is copied into this journal on pages 151–153 herein. In his response, Carlin stated that the Nauvoo Municipal Court's authority to issue writs of habeas corpus applied only to cases arising out of city ordinances—not in cases involving actions of higher levels of government.

445. Like Nauvoo, both Quincy and Springfield were granted authority to pass ordinances that did not conflict with the United States Constitution. Similar to the situation in Nauvoo, the judge of the municipal court of Alton could issue writs of habeas corpus for a time. (Kimball, "Nauvoo Charter," 73, 75; Bennett and Cope, "City on a Hill," 39.)

446. The constitutional requirement for extradition was being charged with committing a crime in one state and fleeing to another state. (U.S. Constitution, art. 4, sec. 2.)

men from Missouri that were here with Messrs [Thomas] King and [James] Pitman, divulg'd the most illegal and infernal calculations concerning taking Mr Smith into Missouri the evidence of which, we can furnish you at any time, if required. And dear Sir, our good feelings revolt at the suggestion that your Excellency is acquainted with the unlawful measures taken by those engaged in the prosecution— measures which, if justice was done to others, as it would be done to us, were we to commit as great errors in our proceedings, would subject all concerned in the prosecution to the penalty of the law, and that without mercy.

I admit Sir— that it is next to an impossibility, for any one to know the extent of the tyranny, treachery, and knavery of a great portion of the leading characters of the State of Missouri: yet it only requires a knowledge of the constitution of the United States, and Statute of the State of Missouri; and a knowledge of the outrages committed by some of the inhabitants of that State upon the people called Mormons, and that pass'd unpunished by the administrators of the law; to know that there is not the least confidence to be placed in any of those men that were engaged in those disgraceful transactions.

If the law was made for the lawless and disobedient, and punishment instituted for the guilty, why not execute the law upon those that have transgressed it, and punish those who have committed crime, and grant encouragement to the innocent, and liberality to the industrious & peaceable. And now I entreat your honor to bear with me patiently while I ask, what good can accrue to this state or the United States, or any part of this State or the United States, or to yourself, or any other individual, to continue this persecution upon this people, or upon Mr Smith— a persecution that you are well aware, is entirely without any just foundation or excuse. With sentiments of due respect I am your most obedient servant

Emma Smith

To His Excellency Thomas Carlin
Governor of the State of Illinois.
P.S. Sir. You will please tender my best respects and considerations to your wife and family, and tell them I greatly desire to see them with yourself in our place as soon as can be convenient. <u>Emma Smith</u>.["] [p. 188]

4 September 1842 • Sunday

Sunday 4th. This day President Hyrum Smith & president Wm. Law started for the East accompanied by brothers [Erastus] Derby & [Edwin] Woolley.447 President Joseph sent the following letter to W[illiam] Clayton by brother Erastus H. Derby. The president wrote it and requested it to be read before the saints when assembled at the Grove near the Temple for preaching which was done according to his request.

448"September 1st. 1842

"To all the saints in Nauvoo.—

Forasmuch as the Lord has revealed unto me that my enemies, both of Missouri and this State were again on the pursuit of me; and inasmuch as they pursue me without cause, and have not the least shadow, or coloring of justice, or right /449on their side, in the getting up of their prosecutions against me; and inasmuch as their pretensions are all founded in falsehood of the blackest die; I have thought it expedient and wisdom in me to leave the place for a short season, for my own safety and the safety of this people. I would say to all those with whom I have business, that I have left my affairs with agents and Clerks, who will transact all business in a prompt and proper manner; and will see that all my debts are cancell'd in due time, by turning out property or otherwise as the case may require, or as the circumstances may admit of. When I learn that the storm is fully blown over, then, I will return to you again: and as for the perils which I am call'd to pass through; they seem but a small thing to me, as the fury and wrath of

---

447. At a conference in late August, several hundred men were called to serve missions in various parts of the United States in an effort to spread the gospel and counter John C. Bennett's accusations against JS and the church. Contemporary news accounts reported Hyrum Smith and William Law working in Salem, Massachusetts, and visiting Hyrum's uncle Solomon Mack in Gilsum, New Hampshire. They returned in November and reported that Bennett's publications had, ironically, generated publicity favorable to the church. (JS, Journal, 26 and 29 Aug. 1842; 4 Nov. 1842, pp. 120, 121, 166 herein; Erastus Snow, Journal, 1841–1847, 34; Hyrum Smith, Nauvoo, IL, to Harriett M. Whittemore, Pontiac, MI, 9 Apr. 1843, Whittemore Family, Papers, Bentley Historical Library, University of Michigan, Ann Arbor; Anderson, *Joseph Smith's New England Heritage*, 235n87.)

448. This letter was first published in the *Times and Seasons* and was later published with minor alterations in the 1844 edition of the Doctrine and Covenants. Another manuscript copy of the letter, entirely in William Clayton's handwriting, is housed in Revelations Collection, CHL. ("Tidings," *Times and Seasons,* 15 Sept. 1842, 3:919–920; JS, Nauvoo, IL, to "all the Saints in Nauvoo," 1 Sept. 1842, in Doctrine and Covenants 105, 1844 ed. [D&C 127].)

449. TEXT: William Clayton handwriting ends; Eliza R. Snow begins. Snow lived with the Smith family from 18 August 1842 to 11 February 1843. (Eliza R. Snow, Journal, 14 and 18 Aug. 1842; 11 Feb. 1843.)

man have been my common lot all the days of my life; and for what cause, it seems mysterious, unless I was ordained from before the foundation of the world, for some good end, or bad, as you may choose to call it: Judge ye for yourselves, God knoweth all these things whether it be good or bad; but nevertheless, deep water is what I am wont to swim in; it all has become a second nature to me and I feel like Paul, to glory in tribulation,[450] for unto this day, has the God of my fathers delivered me out of them all, and will deliver me from henceforth; for behold and lo! I shall triumph over all my enemies, for the Lord God hath spoken it.

Let all the saints rejoice therefore and be exceeding glad, for Israel's God[451] is their God and he will meet out a just recompence of reward upon the heads of all your oppressors. And again, verily, thus saith the Lord, let the work of my Temple, and all the works which I have appointed unto you, be continued on and not cease; and let your diligence and your perseverence, and patience and your works be redoubled, and you shall in no wise lose your reward saith the Lord of Hosts. And if they persecute you, so persecuted they the prophets and righteous men that were before you: for all this, there is a reward in heaven.[452]

And again, I give unto [you][453] a word in relation to the baptism for your dead. Verily, thus saith the Lord unto you concerning your dead; [454]Let there be a Recorder, and let him be eye-witness of your baptisms; let him hear with his ears that he may testify of a truth saith the Lord; that in all your recordings, it may be recorded in heaven; ⟨that⟩ whatsoever you ~~loose~~ ⟨bind⟩ on earth may be bound in heaven, and whatsoever you loose on earth may be loosed in heaven;[455] for I am about to restore many things to the earth pertaining [p. 189] to the Priesthood saith the Lord of Hosts. And again, let all the Records be had in order, that they may be put in the archives of my holy Temple, to be held in remembrance from generation to generation, saith the Lord of Hosts.

I will say to all the saints, that I desired with exceeding great desire, to have address'd them from the Stand, on the subject of baptism for

---

450. See Romans 5:3.
451. For "for Israel's God," the William Clayton copy of this letter has "for Israel. God."
452. See Matthew 5:11–12.
453. Omitted word supplied from the version published in the *Times and Seasons*.
454. At this point the Clayton copy of this letter adds, "when any of you are baptized for your dead."
455. See Matthew 16:19; 18:18.

the dead, on the following sabbath: But inasmuch as it is out of my power to do so, I will write the Word of the Lord from time to time, on that subject, and send it you by Mail, as well as many other things.

I now close my letter for the present, for the want of more time; for the enemy is on the alert, and as the Savior said, the prince of this world cometh, but he hath nothing in me.[456] Behold! my prayer to God, is, that you all may be saved and I subscribe myself, your servant in the Lord, prophet and Seer of the Church of Jesus Christ, of Latter-Day Saints.

Joseph Smith.["]

/[457]When this letter was read before the brethren it cheered their hearts and evidently had the effect of stimulating them and inspiring them with courage, and faithfulness.

6 September 1842 • Tuesday

Tuesday 6th. This evining W. C. [William Clayton], Newel K. Whitney, Brigham Young, Heber C. Kimball & Amasa Lyman visited President Joseph, the three latter especially to council concerning their mission &c[458] and the two former concerning a settlement with brother Edward Hunter. The evening was spent cheerfully but nothing of special importance transpired.

7 September 1842 • Wednesday

Wednesday 7th. Early this morning Elder [George J.] Adams and brother [David] Rogers from New York visited president Joseph and brought several letters from some of the brethren in that region. One letter from Dr. Willard Richards[459] I will mention in this place. When speaking concerning his interview with Mr James Arlington Bennett [Bennet] Esqr of New York he says. "He would be happy to receive a letter of his (president Josephs) own dictation, signed by his own hand".

General J. A. Bennett had wrote a letter and sent it by mail which was received a few days ago, and when president Joseph read the foregoing clause in

---

456. See John 14:30.
457. TEXT: Eliza R. Snow handwriting ends; William Clayton begins.
458. The purpose of this proselytizing mission was to rebuff John C. Bennett's attacks against the church. Of the twelve apostles, only Wilford Woodruff and John Taylor, both of whom were ill and were assigned to continue the printing business, did not go on missions at this time. (JS, Journal, 29 Aug. 1842, p. 121 herein; Woodruff, Journal, 10 Aug.–18 Sept. 1842.)
459. Willard Richards, New York City, NY, to JS, Nauvoo, IL, 9 Aug. 1842, JS Collection, CHL.

Arlington House. 1839. Long Island residence of James Arlington Bennet, prominent New York publisher, educator, and author. Bennet's fair-minded treatment of the Mormons led Joseph Smith to write to him on 30 June 1842. Bennet responded, and the two men subsequently exchanged letters discussing a variety of topics. (Courtesy Library of Congress, Washington DC.)

D̲ͬ Richards letter he concluded to write him an answer. I will now record the letter from Gen̲ˡ Jas Arlington Bennett which is as follows—

⁴⁶⁰"Arlington House August 16ᵗʰ· 1842

"Dear Sir—

Your polite and friendly note was handed to me a few days since by D̲ͬ W[illard] Richards,⁴⁶¹ who I must say is a very fine specimen of the Mormon people if they are all like him, and indeed I think him a very excellent representative of yourself, as I find he is your most devoted admirer and true disciple. He spent two days with me, and from his arguments and extremely mild and gentlemanly demeaner almost made me a Mormon.

You have another representative here, (who spent a day with me some time since) of the name of [Lucian] Foster, who is I think president of the church in New York and most unquestionably a most excellent and good man, [p. 190] and would be so if he were Turk, Jew or Saint. He is <u>Ab initio</u> a good man and to you a most true, enthusiastic and devoted disciple. He has no guile. Dr [John] Bernhisel of New York too, is a most excellent man and true christian. These are men with whom I could associate forever, even if I never joined their church or acknowledged their faith.

General John C. Bennett called on me last friday and spent just two hours when he left as he said for the Eastern States. Being aware that Elder Richards was here he had very little to say. He however proposed to me to aid him, wether serious or not, in arranging materials for publishing "an exposition of Mormon Secrets and practices"— which I peremptorily refused on two grounds. 1ˢᵗ· That I had nothing to do with any quarrel that might arise between you and him, as I could not be a judge of the merits or demerits of the matter and 2ndly that inasmuch as he himself had proposed to you and your council to confer on me honors which I never sought, yet which I highly prize,⁴⁶² it would be the height of ingratitude as well as inconsistent with every principle of common honesty and propriety, for

---

460. The original of this letter is housed in JS Materials, CCLA.
461. Two months earlier JS dictated a letter to Bennet introducing Richards and inviting Bennet to open a correspondence with him (JS) and visit him in Nauvoo. (JS, Nauvoo, IL, to James Arlington Bennet, Arlington House, Long Island, NY, 30 June 1842, CHL.)
462. James Arlington Bennet was appointed inspector general of the Nauvoo Legion, with the rank of major general, on 12 April 1842. (Certificate, Moses K. Anderson to James Arlington Bennet, Springfield, IL, 30 Apr. 1842, Thomas Carlin, Correspondence, Illinois State Archives, Springfield.)

me to join him in an effort to lower <u>my own honors</u> by attempting to lower in public estimation the people from whom those honors emanated. He gave [James Gordon] Bennett of the Herald his commission which I opposed from the very first, and you now see by that paper the sport which that man has made of it.[463] I tell you there is no dependance on the friendship of that Editor when his interest is at issue. I am assured that J. G. B. [James Gordon Bennett] is going to publish conjointly with J. C. B. [John C. Bennett] on half profit, the exposition against you and your people, which is going to contain a great number of scandalous cuts and plates. But dont be concerned, you will receive no injury whatever from any thing that any man or set of men may say against you. The whole of this <u>muss</u> is only extending your fame and will increase your numbers ten fold. You have nothing to expect from that part of community who are bigotedly attached to the other churches. They have always believed, and still believe every thing said to your disadvantage; and what General J. C. Bennett is now saying in the papers is nothing more than what was common report before, throughout this whole community, insomuch that I had to contradict it in the Herald under the signature of "Cincinatus",[464] and even requested the Elders at the Mormon Church to do so long ago. You therefore have lost not a whit of ground by it. I must in charity forbear commenting on the course of Genl Bennett in this matter— considering all things, delicacy forbids such a course. There are some things however, I feel very sorely and could wish they had not transpired He and the Herald will make money out of the Book and then the matter will end, as you will find that the Herald will puff it to the skies.[465] The books which I sent you, you will retain in your hands for the present. My respects to your amiable lady and all friends and believe me as ever, tho, not a Mormon, your sincere friend—

James Arlington Bennett [Bennet] [p. 191]

P.S. I know of no reason why the Wasp was not continued to be sent to me. <u>I dont like the name</u>. Mildness should characterise every thing that comes from Nauvoo and even a name as Paley says in his

---

463. James Gordon Bennett was elected aide-de-camp to the major general of the Nauvoo Legion and given the rank of brigadier general on 28 May 1842. Bennett reprinted his commission, accompanied by a mocking editorial, in the *New York Herald*. (James Gordon Bennett, "Rising in the World," *New York Herald*, 13 Aug. 1842, [2].)

464. [James Arlington Bennet], "The Mormons," *New York Herald*, 16 May 1842, [2].

465. John C. Bennett's book, *History of the Saints: or, An Exposé of Joe Smith and Mormonism*, was published not by the *New York Herald* but by Leland and Whiting in Boston in fall 1842.

Ethics[466] has much influence on one side or the other. My respects to your brother its Editor.[467] I would just say that Gen. J. C. Bennett, appeared to me to be in very low spirits. And I find that many communications intended for you from me, has never reached you. Those Books were made over to J C. B. on the presumption that he would in his own name present them for the benifit of the Temple[468]

J. A. B."

In consequence of president Joseph not having the foregoing with him he concluded to write his answer tomorrow. He however wrote—or rather dictated a long Epistle to the Saints which he ordered to be read next Sabbath and which will be recorded under that date.[469]

In the P.M. brothers Adams & Rogers came to visit him again. They conversed upon the present persecution &c president Joseph in his discourse to brothers Adams and Rogers shewed the many great interpositions of the Almighty in his behalf not only during the present trouble, but more especially during the persecution in Missouri &c. The remarks drop[p]ed on this occasion was truly encouraging and calculated to increase the confidence of those present.

8 September 1842 • Thursday

Thursday 8th. This A.M president Joseph dictated the following letter to Gen. James Arlington Bennett [Bennet] as before stated— The letter is as follows.—

[470]"Nauvoo September 8th. 1842

Dear Sir—
I have just received /[471]your very consoling letter dated August 16th.

---

466. Possibly William Paley, *Principles of Moral and Political Philosophy*, first published in Dublin in 1785.
467. William Smith was editor of *The Wasp* from its inception on 16 April 1842 until 3 December 1842, after which John Taylor's name appears as editor.
468. James Arlington Bennet earlier sent one hundred copies of his own *American System of Practical Book-keeping* (the twenty-first edition of which was published in 1842) through John C. Bennett, specifying that the proceeds from ten copies be used to pay for his subscriptions to the *Times and Seasons* and *The Wasp*. Bennet here indicates that his intent was to donate the proceeds from the remaining ninety books to the temple fund, but according to JS, John C. Bennett had directed that those proceeds be sent back to Bennet. Bennet made an additional donation of ninety copies of his book the following year, recorded 11 March 1843 in the Book of the Law of the Lord. (James Arlington Bennet, Arlington House, Long Island, NY, to Willard Richards, Nauvoo, IL, 24 Oct. 1842, Willard Richards, Papers, CHL; JS to James Arlington Bennet, 8 Sept. 1842, p. 142 herein.)
469. JS to "the Church of Jesus Christ," [7] Sept. 1842, p. 143 herein [D&C 128].
470. A copy of this letter in the handwriting of William Clayton is housed in JS Collection, CHL.
471. TEXT: William Clayton handwriting ends; Eliza R. Snow begins.

1842; which I think, is the first letter you ever addressed to me; in which you speak of the arrival of D[r.] W[illard] Richards, and of his person very respectfully. In this I rejoice; for I am as warm a friend to D[r.] Richards as he possibly can be to me: And in relation to his almost making a Mormon of yourself, it puts me in mind of the saying of Paul in his reply to Agrippa, Acts ch. 26th v. 29th, "I would to God that not only thou, but also all that hear me this day; were both almost, and altogether such as I am, except these bonds." And I will here remark, my dear Sir; that Mormonism is the pure doctrine of Jesus Christ; of which I myself, am not asham'd.[472]

You speak also of Elder [Lucian] Foster, President of the Church in New-York, in high terms: and of D[r.] [John] Bernhisel of New-York. These men I am acquainted with by information; and it warms my heart, to know that you speak well of them; and as you say, could be willing to associate with them forever, if you never joined their church, or acknowledged their faith. This is a good principle; for when we see virtuous qualities in men, we should always acknowledge them, let their understanding be what it may in relation to creeds and doctrine; for all men are, or ought to be free; possessing unalienable rights, and the high, and noble qualifications of the laws of nature and of self-preservation; to think, and act, and say as they please; while they maintain a due respect to the rights and privileges of all other creatures; infringing upon none. This [p. 192] doctrine I do most heartily subscribe to, and practice; the testimony of mean men, to the contrary, notwithstanding. But Sir, I will assure you, that my soul soars far above all the mean and grovelling dispositions of men that are dispos'd to abuse me and my character; I therefore shall not dwell upon that subject.

In relation to those men you speak of, referred to above; I will only say that there are thousands of such men in this church; who, if a man is found worthy to associate with, will call down the envy of a mean world, because of their high and noble demeanor; and it is with unspeakable delight that I contemplate them as my friends & brethren. I love them with a perfect love; and I hope they love me, and have no reason to doubt but they do.

The next in consideration is John C. Bennett. I was his friend. I am yet his friend; as I feel myself bound to be a friend to all the sons of Adam; whether they are just or unjust, they have a degree of my

---

472. See Romans 1:16.

compassion & sympathy. If he is my enemy it is his own fault; and the responsibility rests upon his own head; and instead of arraigning[473] his character before you, suffice it to say, that his own conduct wherever he goes, will be sufficient to recommend him to an enlightened public, whether for a bad man, or a good one. Therefore whosoever will associate themselves with him, may be assured that I will not persecute them; but I do not wish their association: And what I have said may suffice on that subject, so far as his character is concern'd.

Now in relation to his book that he may write, I will venture a prophecy; that whosoever has any hand in the matter, will find themselves in a poor fix, in relation to the money matters. And as to my having any fears of the influence that he may have against me; or any other man or set of men may have, is the most foreign from my heart; for I never knew what it was, as yet, to fear the face of clay, or the influence of man. My fear, Sir, is before God. I fear to offend him, and strive to keep his commandments. I am really glad that you did not join John C. in relation to his book, from the assurances which I have, that it will prove a curse to all those who touch it.

In relation to the honors that you speak of, both for yourself and James Gordon Bennett of the Herald,[474] you are both strangers to me, and as John C. Bennett kept all his letters, which he receiv'd from you, entirely to himself; and there was no correspondence between you and me, that I knew of; I had no opportunity to share very largely in in the getting up of any of those matters. I could not, as I had not sufficient knowledge to enable me to do so. The whole, therefore, was at the instigation of John C. Bennett, and a quiet submission on the part of the rest, out of the best of feelings.

But as for myself, it was all done at a time when I was overwhelm'd with a great many business cares, as well as the care of all the churches. I must be excus'd therefore, for any wrongs that may have taken place, in relation to this matter: And so far as I [p. 193] obtain a knowledge of that which is right shall meet with my hearty approval.

I feel to tender you my most hearty and sincere thanks, for every expression of kindness, you have tendered towards me or my brethren; and would beg the privilege of obtruding myself a little while upon your patience, in offering a short relation of my circumstances. I am at

---

473. For "arraigning," the Clayton copy of this letter has "reigning."
474. James Arlington Bennet was appointed major general and James Gordon Bennett brigadier general in the Nauvoo Legion (James Arlington Bennet to JS, 16 Aug. 1842, pp. 135–136 herein.)

this time persecuted the worst of any man on ⟨the⟩ earth; as well as this people, here in this place; and all our sacred rights are trampled under the feet of the mob.

I am now hunted as an hart, by the mob, under the pretence or shadow of law, to cover their abominable deeds. An unhallowed demand has been made from the Governor of Missouri, on oath of Governor [Lilburn W.] Boggs; that I made an attempt to assassinate him on the night of the sixth of May; when on that day, I was attending the officer Drill, and answered to my name when the roll was call'd: and on the seventh, it is well known by the thousands that assembled here in Nauvoo, that I was at my post in reviewing the Nauvoo Legion in the presence of twelve thousand people: And the Governor of the State of Illinois, notwithstanding his being knowing to all these facts, yet he immediately granted a Writ; and by an unhallowed usurpation, has taken away our chartered rights, and denied the right of Habeas Corpus; and has now about thirty of the[475] blood-thirsty kind of men[476] in this place, in search for me; threatening death and destruction, and extermination upon all the Mormons; and searching my house almost continually from day to day; menacing and threat'ning, and intimidating an innocent wife and children, & insulting them in a most diabolical manner; threatening their lives &c. if I am not to be found, with a gang of Missourians with them; saying they will have me dead or alive; and if alive, they will carry me to Missouri in chains, and when there, they will kill me at all hazards. And all this, is backed up, and urged on, by the Governor of this State, with all the rage of a demon; putting at defiance, the Constitution of this State—our chartered rights—and the Constitution of the United States: For not as yet, have they done <u>one thing</u> that was in accordance to them.

While all the citizens of this city, <u>en mass</u>, have petitioned the Governor with remonstrances, and overtures, that would have melted the heart of an adamantine, <u>to no effect</u>.[477] And at the same time, if any of us open our mouths, to plead our own cause; in the defiance[478] of law and justice, we are instantly threatened with <u>Militia</u> and <u>extermination</u>. Great God! When shall the oppressor cease to prey and glut itself upon innocent blood! Where is Patriotism? Where is Liberty?

---

475. At this point the Clayton copy of this letter adds "most."
476. At this point the Clayton copy of this letter adds ", now."
477. Three petitions were sent to Illinois governor Thomas Carlin on JS's behalf. (See 102n378 herein.)
478. For "defiance," the Clayton copy of this letter has "defence."

Where is the boast of this proud and haughty nation? O humanity! where hast thou fled? Hast thou fled forever?

I now appeal to you Sir, inasmuch as you have subscribed yourself our friend; will you lift your voice and your arm, with indignation against such unhallowed oppression? I must say, Sir that my bosom swells with unutterable anguish, when I contemplate the scenes of horror that we have passed through in the State of Missouri; and then look, and behold and see the storm and cloud [p. 194] gathering ten times blacker; ready to burst upon the heads of this innocent people! Would to God that I were able to throw off the yoke. Shall we bow down and be slaves? Are there no friends of humanity, in a nation that boasts itself so much? Will not the nation rise up and defend us? If they will not defend us, will they not grant to lend a voice of indignation, against such unhallowed oppression? Must the tens of thousands bow down to slavery and degradation? Let the pride of the nation arise and wrench these shackles from the feet of their fellow citizens, and their quiet, and peaceable, and innocent and loyal subjects. But I must forbear, for I cannot express my feelings. The Legion would all willingly die in the defence of their rights; but what would this accomplish? I have kept down their indignation and kept a quiet submission on all hands; and am determined to do so at all hazards. Our enemies shall not have it to say, that we rebel against government, or commit treason; however much they may lift their hands in oppression and tyranny, when it comes in the form of government— we tamely submit altho' it lead us to the slaughter, and to beggary: but our blood be upon their garments: And those who look tamely on and boast of patriotism, shall not be without their condemnation. And if men are such fools, as to let once the precedent be established, and through their prejudices, give assent to such abominations; then let the oppressor's hand lay heavily throughout the world, until all flesh shall feel it together; and until they may know that the Almighty takes cognizance of such things. And then shall church rise up against church; and party against party; mob, against mob; oppressor against oppressor; army against army; and kingdom against kingdom; and people against people; and kindred against kindred. And where, Sir, will be your safety, or the safety of your children; <u>if my children can be led to the slaughter with impunity by the hands of murderous</u> rebels? <u>Will they not lead yours to the slaughter, with the same impunity</u>? Ought not then, this oppression Sir, to be check'd in the bud; and to be looked down with just indignation by an enlightened world, before the flame become unextinguishable, and the fire devour the stubble?

But again I say I must forbear, and leave this painful subject. I wish you would write to me in answer to this, and let me know your views.[479] On my part, I am ready to be offered up a sacrifice, in that way that can bring to pass the greatest benefit and good, to those who must necessarily be interested in this important matter.[480] I would to God, that you could know all my feelings on this subject, and the real facts in relation to this people, and their unrelenting persecution: And if any man feels an interest in the welfare of their fellow-beings; and would think of saying or doing anything in this matter; I would suggest the propriety of a committee of wise men, being sent to ascertain the justice or injustice of our cause—to get in possession of all the facts; and then make report to an enlightened world, whether [p. 195] whether we individually, or collectively, are ~~destroying~~ ⟨deserving⟩[481] such high-handed treatment.

In relation to the books that you sent here, John C. Bennett put them into my Store, to be sold on commission; saying, that when I was able, the money must be remitted to yourself. Nothing was said about my[482] consecration to the Temple.[483]

Another calamity has befallen us. Our Post Office in this place, is exceedingly corrupt. It is with great difficulty that we can get our letters to, or from our friends.[484] Our papers that we send to our subscribers, are embezzled and burned, or wasted. We get no money from our subscribers, and very little information from abroad; and what little we do get, we get by private means, in consequence of these things: and I am sorry to say, that this robbing of the Post Office of money, was carried on by John C. Bennett; and since he left here, it is carried on by the means of his confederates.[485]

---

479. No response from Bennet has been located.
480. At this point the Clayton copy of this letter adds, "I have dictated this letter, while my clerk is writing for me; and."
481. TEXT: Insertion in handwriting of William Clayton.
482. For "my," the Clayton copy of this letter has "any."
483. Willard Richards's letter to JS of 9 August and James Arlington Bennet's letter of 16 August, both of which JS had just received, indicated that money from the sale of the books was to be "for the benifit of the Temple." (Willard Richards, New York City, NY, to JS, Nauvoo, IL, 9 Aug. 1842, JS Collection, CHL; James Arlington Bennet to JS, 16 Aug. 1842, p. 137 herein.)
484. At this point the Clayton copy of this letter adds, "Our letters are broken open and robbed of their contents."
485. In a letter to Horace Hotchkiss two months later, JS blamed the current postmaster, Sidney

I now subscribe myself your friend, and a patriot and lover of my country, pleading at their feet for protection and deliverance, by the justice of their Constitutions.

I add no more.[486]

            Your most obedient servant,
                Joseph Smith.["]

9 September 1842 • Friday

/[487]Friday 9th. This P.M. after dark president Joseph received a very pleasant visit from Sister Emma, Wilson Law, Amasa Lyman & George A. Smith.

10 September 1842 • Saturday

Saturday 10th. This being the Training day[488] for the companies composing the Legion president Joseph kept very close and still; lest on account of the quantity of people passing two and fro he should accidently be discovered. After dark sister Emma sent word by a Messinger that she wished him to come home, as she thought he would be as safe at home as any where for the present. Brother Wilson Law also went and carried the same report; consequently the president left for home where he arrived safe and undiscovered.——

11 September 1842 • Sunday

Sunday 11th. At home all day— At president Josephs request the following letter which himself dictated which [was?] read to the saints at the Grove near the Temple./[489]

            [490]Journeying, Septr. 6th 1842.[491]

Rigdon, for the problems of the post office. On 8 November, the citizens of Nauvoo made out affidavits about the illegal activities being committed in the post office and drafted a petition to Postmaster General Charles A. Wickliffe requesting Rigdon's removal from office. (JS, Nauvoo, IL, to Horace Hotchkiss, 26 Nov. 1842, in JS Letterbook 2, pp. 241–242; JS, Journal, 8 Nov. 1842.)

486. In the left margin of the final page, the Clayton copy of this letter notes, "P.S. I have dictated this letter while my clerk is writing for me."

487. TEXT: Eliza R. Snow handwriting ends; William Clayton begins.

488. On 13 August 1842, the Nauvoo Legion court-martial passed an ordinance requiring training maneuvers to be held on three consecutive Saturdays in April and September, beginning with the second Saturday of the month. The second Saturday in September was to feature a company parade, the third Saturday a regiment parade, and the fourth Saturday a legion parade composed of the entire legion. (Nauvoo Legion Minute Book, 13 Aug. 1842, 23.)

489. TEXT: William Clayton handwriting ends; Eliza R. Snow begins.

490. A copy of this letter in the handwriting of William Clayton is housed in Revelations Collection, CHL.

491. The letter was first published in the *Times and Seasons* and was later canonized in the 1844 edition of the Doctrine and Covenants. While the earliest manuscript versions of this letter, including the

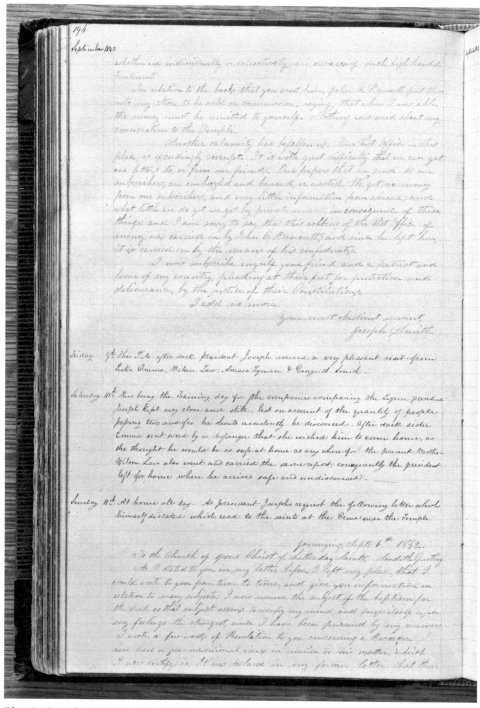

Eliza R. Snow handwriting. Eliza R. Snow assisted William Clayton in keeping Joseph Smith's journal during early September 1842. Snow transcribed portions of several letters into the journal. Handwriting of Eliza R. Snow and William Clayton. Book of the Law of the Lord, p. 196, Church History Library, Salt Lake City. (Photograph by Welden C. Andersen.)

To the Church of Jesus Christ of Latter-day Saints;— Sendeth Greeting.

As I stated to you in my letter before I left my place,[492] that I would write to you from time to time, and give you information in relation to many subjects: I now resume the subject of the baptism for the dead as that subject seems to occupy my mind, and press itself upon my feelings the strongest, since I have been pursued by my enemies, I wrote a few words of Revelation to you concerning a Recorder. I have had a few additional views in relation to this matter, which I now certify; ie. It was declared in my former letter that there [p. 196] should be a Recorder who should be eye-witness, and also to hear with his ears that he might make a Record of a truth before the Lord. Now, in relation to this matter; it would be very difficult for one Recorder to be present at all times and to do all the business. To obviate this difficulty, there can be a Recorder appointed in each ward of the City,[493] who is well qualified for taking accurate minutes; and let him be very particular and precise in making his Record and taking the whole proceeding; certifying in his Record, that he saw with his eyes, and heard with his ears; giving the date, and names &c. and the history of the whole transaction, naming also some three individuals that are present, if there be any present who can at any time, when call'd upon, certify to the same; that in the mouth of two or three witnesses, every word may be established.[494] Then let there be a general Recorder[495] to whom these other Records can be handed, being attended with certificates over their own signatures; certifying that the Record which they have made, is true. Then the General Church Recorder can enter the Record on the general Church Book with the Certificates and all the

---

transcription here, are dated 6 September 1842, it is likely that the correct date of the letter is 7 September 1842. William Clayton's entry in JS's journal for 7 September states that JS "wrote—or rather dictated a long Epistle to the Saints which he ordered to be read next Sabbath and which will be recorded under that date." ("Letter from Joseph Smith," *Times and Seasons,* 1 Oct. 1842, 3:934–936; JS, Nauvoo, IL, to "the Church of Jesus Chr[i]st," 7 Sept. 1842, in Doctrine and Covenants 106, 1844 ed. [D&C 128]; JS, Journal, 7 Sept. 1842, p. 137 herein.)

492. JS's earlier letter to the Saints, dated 1 September 1842, is copied into this journal on pages 131–133 herein.

493. A resolution passed the previous month by the Nauvoo high council dictated that the city of Nauvoo be divided into ten ecclesiastical divisions called "wards," with a bishop appointed over each ward. Additionally, three "districts," each with a bishop, were designated immediately outside the city. (Nauvoo High Council Minutes, 20 Aug. 1842.)

494. See Matthew 18:16.

495. James Sloan served as the "general church Clerk" beginning 2 October 1841. ("Minutes of a Conference," *Times and Seasons,* 15 Oct. 1841, 2:577.)

attending witnesses, with his own statement that he verily believes the above statements and Records to be true, from his knowledge of the general character and appointment of those men by the Church. And when this is done on the general Church Book; the Record shall be just as holy, and shall answer the ordinance just the same as if he had seen with his eyes and heard with his ears, and made a Record of the same on the general Book.

You may think this Order of things to be very particular: But let me tell you, that they are only to answer the will of God by conforming to the ordinance and preparation, that the Lord ordained and prepared before the foundation of the world for the salvation of the dead who should die without a knowledge of the Gospel. And further, I want you to remember that John, the Revelator was contemplating this very subject in relation to the dead, when he declar'd, as you will find recorded in Revelations Chap. 20th v. 12; And I saw the dead, small and great, stand before God: and the books were opened: and another book was opened, which is the book of Life; and the dead were judg'd out of those things which were written in the books, according to their works. You will discover in this quotation, that the books were opened, and another book was opened which is the book of life; but the dead were judg'd out of those things which were written in the books according to their works; consequently, the books spoken of, must be the books which contained the record of their works, and refers to the Records which are kept on the earth: And the book which was the book of Life, is the Record which is kept in heaven; the principle agreeing precisely with the doctrine which is commanded you in the Revelation contained in the letter which I wrote you previous to my leaving my place, "that in all your recordings it may be recorded in heaven".[496] Now the nature of this ordinance consists in the power of the Priesthood by the revelations of Jesus Christ, wherein it is granted that whatsoever [p. 197] you bind on earth, shall be bound in heaven, and whatsoever you loose on earth shall be loosed in heaven:[497] Or in other words, taking a different view of the translation, whatsoever you record on earth shall be recorded in heaven; and whatsoever you do not record on earth, shall not be recorded in heaven; for out of the books, shall your dead be judg'd according to their works, whether they, themselves have attended to the ordinances in their own propria

---

496. JS to "all the saints in Nauvoo," 1 Sept. 1842, p. 132 herein [D&C 127].
497. See Matthew 16:19; 18:18.

persona, or by the means of their own agents according to the ordinance which God has prepared for their salvation, from before the foundation of the world, according to the records which they have kept concerning their dead. It may seem to some, to be a very bold doctrine that we talk of; a power which records, or binds on earth, and binds in heaven. Nevertheless, in all ages of the world, whenever the Lord has given a dispensation of the Priesthood to any man, by actual revelation, or any set of men; this power has always been given: Hence, whatsoever those men did in authority, in the name of the Lord, and did it truly and faithfully, and kept a proper and faithful record of the same, it became a law on earth and in heaven; and could not be annull'd according to the decree of the great Jehovah. This is a faithful saying: Who can hear it? And again for a precedent, Matt. chapter 16 verses 18, 19, "And I say also unto thee, that thou art Peter, and upon this rock I will build my church; and the gates of hell shall not prevail against it. And I will give unto thee, the keys of the kingdom of heaven; and whatsoever thou shalt bind on earth, shall be bound in heaven; and whatsoever thou shalt loose on earth, shall be loosed in heaven.["] Now the great and grand secret of the whole matter, and the sum and bonum [*summum bonum*] of the whole subject that is lying before us consists in obtaining the powers of the Holy Priesthood. For him, to whom these keys are given; there is no difficulty in obtaining a knowledge of facts in relation to the salvation of ~~men~~ the children of men; both as well for the dead as for the living. Herein is glory, and honor, and immortality and eternal life. The ordinance of baptism by water, to be immers'd therein in order to answer to the likeness of the dead, that one principle might accord with the other to be immers'd in the water, and come forth out of the water is in the likeness of the resurrection of the dead in coming forth out of their graves: hence, this ordinance was instituted to form a relationship with the ordinance of baptism for the dead; being in likeness of the dead. Consequently, the baptismal Font was instituted as a simile of the grave, and was commanded to be in a place underneath where the living are wont to assemble, to show forth the living and the dead; and that all things may have their likeness, and that they may accord one with another; that which is earthly, conforming to that which is heavenly, as Paul hath declar'd 1st Corinthians, Chap. 15, verses 46, 47 & 48. "Howbeit, that was not first which is spiritual, but that which is natural, and afterward, that which is spiritual. The first man is of the earth, earthy: the second man, is the Lord from heaven. [p. 198] As is the earthy, such are they also that are earthy: and as is the heavenly, such are they also that are heavenly:["] And as are the records on the earth in relation to your dead, which are truly made out; so also are the records in heaven. This, therefore, is the sealing and binding power; and in one sense of the word the keys of the kingdom, which consists in the key of knowledge.

And now my dearly and beloved brethren and sisters, let me assure me[498] that these are principles in relation to the dead and the living; that cannot be lightly passed over, as pertaining to our salvation; for their salvation is necessary and essential to our salvation; as Paul says concerning the fathers, "That they without us, cannot be made perfect";[499] neither can we without our dead, be made perfect. And now, in relation to the baptism for the dead; I will give you another quotation of Paul, 1 Cor. 15 chap. verse 29 "Else what shall they do which are baptized for the dead, if the dead rise not at all? Why are they then baptized for the dead?" And again in connexion with this quotation I will give you a quotation from one of the prophets, which had his eye fix'd on the restoration of the Priesthood— the glories to be reveal'd in the last days, and in an especial manner, this most glorious of all subjects belonging to the everlasting Gospel, viz. the baptism for the dead; for Malachi says, last chap.— verses 5 & 6. "Behold I will send you Elijah the prophet, before the coming of the great and ~~terrible~~ dreadful day of the Lord; And he shall turn the hearts of the fathers to the children, and the hearts of the children to their fathers, lest I come and smite the earth with a curse". I might have rendered a plainer translation to this, but it is sufficiently plain to suit my purpose, as it stands, It is sufficient to know in this case, that the earth will be smitten with a curse, unless there is a welding link of some kind or other, between the fathers and the children, upon some subject or other. And behold! what is that subject? It is the baptism for the dead. For we without them, cannot be made perfect; neither can they, without us, be made perfect. Neither can they or us, be made perfect without those who have died in the gospel also; for it is necessary in the ushering in of the dispensation of the fulness of times; which dispensation is now beginning to usher in, that a whole, and complete and perfect union, and welding together of dispensations and keys, and powers and glories should take place, and be reveal'd, from

---

498. For "me," the Clayton copy of this letter has "you."
499. See Hebrews 11:40.

the days of Adam even to the present time; and not only this, but those things that never have been reveal'd from the foundation of the world; but have been kept hid from the wise and prudent; shall be revealed unto babes and sucklings, in this, the dispensation of the fulness of times.

Now what do we hear in the Gospel which we have received? A voice of gladness— a voice of mercy from heaven— a voice of truth out of the earth— glad tidings for the dead; a voice of gladness for the living and and the dead; glad tidings of great joy! How beautiful upon the mountains, are the feet of those that bring glad tidings of good things; and that say unto Zion, behold! thy God reigneth.[500] As the dews of Carmel so shall the knowledge of God descend upon them. And again, [p. 199] What do we hear? Glad tidings from Cumorah! Moroni, an angel from heaven, declaring the fulfilment of the prophets— the book to be reveal'd! A voice of the Lord in the wilderness of Fayette, Seneca County, declaring the three witnesses to bear record of the Book, The voice of Michael on the banks of the Susquehanna, detecting the devil when he appeared as an angel of light. The voice of Peter, James & John, in the wilderness, between Harmony, Susquehanna County, and Colesville, Broom County, on the Susquehanna river; declaring themselves as ~~having~~ ⟨possessing⟩ the keys of the kingdom, and of the dispensation of the fulness of times, And again, the voice of God in the chamber of old father Whitmer [Peter Whitmer Sr.] in Fayette, Seneca County, and at sundry times, and in divers places, through all the travels and tribulations, of this Church of Jesus Christ of Latter Day Saints. And the voice of Michael the archangel— the voice of Gabriel, and of Raphael, and of divers angels, from Michael or Adam, down to the present time; all declaring, each one their dispensation, their rights, their keys, their honors, their majesty & glory, and the power of their Priesthood; giving line upon line; precept upon precept; here a little and there a little: giving us consolation by holding forth that which is to come and confirming our hope.

Brethren, shall we not go on in so ~~good~~ ⟨great⟩ a cause? Go forward and not go backward. Courage, brethren! and on to the victory. Let your hearts rejoice and be exceeding glad. Let the earth break forth into singing. Let the dead speak forth anthems of eternal praise to the king Immanuel, who hath ordain'd before the world was, that which

---

500. See Isaiah 52:7.

would enable us to redeem them out of their prisons; for the prisoner shall go free. Let the mountains shout for joy, and all ye vallies, cry aloud; and all ye seas and dry lands tell the wonders of your eternal king: And ye rivers, and brooks, and rills, flow down with gladness. Let the woods and all the trees of the field praise the Lord: and ye solid rocks, leap for joy.[501] And let the sun, moon, and the morning stars sing[502] together; and let all the sons of God, shout for joy: And let the eternal creations declare his name forever and ever.

And again, I say, how glorious is the voice we hear from heaven proclaiming in our ears, glory and salvation, and honor, and immortality and eternal life. Kingdoms, ~~principals~~ principalities and powers! behold! the great day of the Lord is at hand, and who can abide the day of his coming, and who can stand when he appeareth? for he is like a refiner's fire, and like fuller's soap: and he shall sit as a refiner and purifier of silver, and he shall purify the sons of Levi, and purge them as gold and silver; that they may offer unto the Lord an offering in righteousness.[503] And let us,[504] present in his holy Temple, when it is finished, a Book, containing the Records of our dead, which shall be worthy of all acceptation.

Brethren, I have many things to say to you on the subject; but shall now close for the present, and continue the subject another time.[505] [p. 200]

I am as ever your humble servant, and never deviating friend,

Joseph Smith.

/[506]The important instructions contained in the foregoing letter made a deep and solemn impression on the minds of the saints, and they manifested their intentions to obey the instructions to the letter.[507]

---

501. At this point the Clayton copy of this letter adds, "And let all creation."
502. In the Clayton copy of this letter, the word "sing" is inserted above "strike hands."
503. See Malachi 3:2–3.
504. At this point the Clayton copy of this letter adds, "therefore, as a church and a people, and as Latter Day saints, offer unto the Lord an offering in righteousness. and let us."
505. JS continued to emphasize the importance of baptism for the dead in many sermons, such as those on 11 June 1843, 21 January 1844, 7 April 1844, and 12 May 1844. (See JS, Journal, 11 June 1843, JS Collection, CHL; Woodruff, Journal, 21 Jan. 1844; General Church Minutes, 7 Apr. 1844; JS, Discourse, 12 May 1844, JS Collection, CHL.)
506. TEXT: Eliza R. Snow handwriting ends; William Clayton begins.
507. While church members kept records of baptisms prior to receiving the instructions in this letter, they had not systematically utilized witnesses, other than the participants. A week earlier JS taught the Female Relief Society the same principle of having a designated witness for baptisms performed on behalf of the dead. Shortly after the letter in this entry was read, certificates were created identifying ward recorders, while additional certificates, listing the names of witnesses, were created to record baptismal

12 September 1842 • Monday

Monday 12th. At home all day in company with brothers [George J.] Adams & [David] Rogers, and councilling brother Adams to write a letter to the Governor. In the P.M sister Emma received a letter from the Governor the following of which is a copy.

"Quincy September 7th. 1842

Dear Madam—

Your letter of the 27th. Ultimo[508] was delivered to me on Monday the 5th. instant, and I have not had time to answer it untill this evening, and I now appropriate a few moments to the difficult task of replying satisfactorily to its contents, every word of which evinces your devotedness to the interest of your husband and pouring forth the effusions of a heart wholly his. I am thus admonished that I can say nothing, that does not subserve his interest that can possibly be satisfactory to you. and before I proceed I will here repeat, my great regret that I have been officially called upon to act in reference to Mr Smith in any manner whatever. I doubt not your candor when you say you do not desire me "to swerve from my duty as executive in the least" and all you ask is to be allowed the privileges, and advantages guaranteed to you by the constitution and laws. You then refer me to the 11th. Section of the Charter of the City of Nauvoo, and claim for Mr Smith the right to be heard by the Municipal Court of said city, under a writ of Habeus Corpus emanating from said court— when he was held in custody under an executive warrant. The charter of the City of Nauvoo is not before me at this time, but I have examined both the charters, and city ordinance[509] upon the subject, and must express my surprise at the extraordinary assumption of power by the board of Aldermen as contained in said ordinance! from my recollection of the charter it authorizes the Municipal Court to issue writs of Habeues Corpus in all cases of imprisonment, or custody, arising from the authority of the ordinances of said city, but that the power was granted, or intended to be granted to release persons held in custody under the

---

ordinances. The names of the persons baptized, the names of the persons for whom they were baptized, the relationship between the proxies and the deceased, the "witnesses and administrators," and sometimes the date of the baptism were then recorded in a record book. (Relief Society Minute Book, 31 Aug. 1842; Nauvoo Temple, Record of Baptisms for the Dead, 1841, 1843–1845, CHL.)

508. Emma Smith's 27 August 1842 letter to Governor Thomas Carlin is copied into this journal on pages 128–130 herein.

509. TEXT: Possibly "ordinances" or "ordinance⟨s⟩".

authority of writs issued by the courts, or the executive of the State, is most absurd & rediculous, and an attempt to exercise it, is a gross usurpation of power, that cannot be tolerated. I have always expected, and desired; that Mr Smith should avail himself of the benefits of the laws of this State, and of course that he would be entitled to a writ of Habeus Corpus issued by the circuit court, and entitled to a hearing before said court, but to claim the right of a hearing before the Municipal court of the city of Nauvoo is a burlesque upon the charter itself. As to Mr Smiths guilt, or innocence of the crime [p. 201] charged upon him, it is not my province to investigate or determine, nor has any court on earth jurisdiction of his case, but the courts of the State of Missouri, and as stated in my former letter both the constitution and laws presumes that each and every State in this Union, are competant to do justice to all who may be charged with crime committed in said State. Your information that twelve men from Jackson County Mo. were lying in wait for Mr Smith between Nauvoo and Warsaw, for the purpose of taking him out of the hands of the officers who might have him in custody, and murdering him, is like many other marvellous stories that you hear in reference to him— not one word of it true, but I doubt not that your mind has been continually harrowed up with fears produced by that, and other equally groundless stories— that that statement is true is next to impossible, and your own judgement if you will but give it scope will soon set you right in reference to it— if any of the citizens of Jackson had designed to murder Mr Smith, they would not have been so simple as to perpetrate the crime in Illinois, when he would necessarily be required to pass through to the interior of the State of Missouri, where the opportunity would have been so much better, and the prospect of escape much more certain— that is like the statement made by Mr Smiths first messenger after his arrest, to Messrs [James] Ralston and [Calvin A.] Warren— saying that I had stated that Mr Smith should be surrendered to the authorities of Mo. dead or alive— not one word of which was true. I have not the most distant thought that any person in Illinois, or Missouri, contemplated personal injury to Mr Smith by violence in any manner whatever.

 I regret that I did not see Genl [Wilson] Law when last at Quincy. A previous engagement upon business that could not be dispensed with prevented and occupied my attention that evening untill dark. At half past 1 o clock P.M. I came home and learned that the Genl had called to see me, but the hurry of business only allowed me about ten minutes time to eat my dinner and presuming if he had business of any importance that he would remain in the city untill I returned. It may be proper here in order to afford you all the satisfaction in my power, to reply to a question propounded to my wife by Gen[l.] Law in referrence to Mr Smith viz. wether any other, or additional demand had been made upon me by the Gov[r] of Mo. for the surrender of Mr Smith— I answer none, no change whatever has been made in the proceedings. Mr Smith is held accountable only, for the charge as set forth in my warrant under which he was arrested. In conclusion you presume upon my own knowledge of Mr Smiths innocence— and ask why the prosecution is continued against him. Here I must again appeal to your own good judgement and you will be compelled to answer that it is impossible I could know him to be innocent— and as before stated it is not my province to investigate as to his guilt or innocence, but could I know him innocent, and were he my own son, I would nevertheless— (and the more readily) surrender him to the legally constituted authority [p. 202] to pronounce him innocent.

With sentiments of high regard and esteem

Your Ob[t.] servant
Tho Carlin"

Mrs. Emma Smith

13 September 1842 • Tuesday

Tuesday 13[th.] At home all day. This day ~~effected~~ ⟨affected⟩ a settlement with Mr Edward Hunter[510]

14 September 1842 • Wednesday

Wednesday 14[th.] At home. Mr [Jacob] Remick of Keokuk gave president Joseph a Deed for one half of the Land and property he owned in Keokuk amounting to many thousand dollars.[511] Had consultation with C[alvin] A. Warren Esqr— In the P.M. received the following letter from Gen[l.] J. Arlington Bennett [James Arlington Bennet]

---

510. On this date Hunter purchased eight lots of land in blocks 127, 130, and 138. (Nauvoo Registry of Deeds, Record of Deeds, bk. A, pp. 48–49.)

511. In August 1842, JS loaned Remick $200 to help him pay a debt. JS took a promissory note from Remick for the money, payable on demand, but Remick was unable to pay JS when he asked for the money later. In lieu of the money, Remick proposed to give JS a quitclaim deed for land in Iowa, and JS accepted. (JS, Journal, 9 Feb. and 6 Apr. 1843, pp. 257, 336 herein.)

[512]"Arlington House Sep[r] 1— 1842

Lieut. Gen. Smith

Dr Sir,— Mrs Smiths letter to Mrs Bennett[513] containing a very lucid account of Dr John C. Bennett has been received and the only thing concerning him that I regard of importance, is, that you found it necessary to expose him. I wish most ardently that you had let him depart in peace, because the public generally think no better of either the one party or the other in consequence of the pretended exposures with which the newspapers have teemed.[514] But then on the long run you will have the advantage, inasmuch as the universal notoriety which you are now acquiring will be the means of adding to Nauvoo three hundred fold.

That you ought to be given up to the tender mercies of Missouri no man in his senses will allow, as you would be convicted on the shadow of evidence when the peoples passions and prejudices are so strongly enlisted against you and under such a state of things how easy it would be to subern [suborn] witnesses against you who would seal your fate. Add to this, too, the great difficulty under which an impartial Jury, if such could be found, would labor in their attempt to render an honest verdict, being cohersed by surrounding public prejudice and malice. And yet as you are now circumstanced it will not do to oppose force to force, for your protection, as this in the present case would be treason against the State and would ultimately bring to ruin all those concerned.

Your only plan I think will be to keep out of the way until this excitement shall have subsided, as from all I can understand even from the D[r] himself, there is no evidence on which an honest jury could find against you and this opinion I have expressed to him. I most ardently

---

512. The original of this letter is housed in JS Materials, CCLA. In the left margin of the first page, the original letter notes, "This letter is to be considered confidential."

513. Emma Smith's letter to Sophia Bennet, wife of James Arlington Bennet, has not been located.

514. John C. Bennett did not begin his anti-Mormon newspaper articles until his notice of disfellowship was published in the *Times and Seasons* on 15 June 1842, followed with full disclosure of his history by JS, with supporting documents, in *The Wasp* on 25 June 1842, which was rerun on 1 July 1842 in the *Times and Seasons*. Bennett retaliated with a series of articles that began in Springfield's *Sangamo Journal* on 8 July 1842. This series was widely publicized and became the basis of his 1842 book, *The History of the Saints; or, An Exposé of Joe Smith and Mormonism*, referred to later in this letter. (JS et al., "Notice," *Times and Seasons*, 15 June 1842, 3:830; JS, "To the Church of Jesus Christ of Latter Day Saints, and to All the Honorable Part of Community," *The Wasp*, 25 June 1842, [2]–[3]; "To the Church of Jesus Christ of Latter Day Saints, and to All the Honorable Part of Community," *Times and Seasons*, 3:839–843; "Astounding Mormon Disclosures! Letter from Gen. Bennett," *Sangamo Journal* [Springfield, IL], 8 July 1842, [2]; see also 120n420 herein.)

wish that you had one hundred thousand <u>true</u> men at Nauvoo and that I had the command of them— <u>Times and things would soon alter</u>. I hope to see the day before I die that such an army will dictate times from Nauvoo to the enemies of the Mormon people. I say this in the most perfect candor ⟨as⟩ I have nothing to gain by the Mormons, nor am I a Mormon in creed, yet I regard them in as favorable a light, (and a little more so) as I do any other sect. In fact I am a Philosophical Christian [p. 203] and wish to see an entire change in the religious world.

I have been long a Mormon in sympathy alone and probably can never be one in any other way,[515] yet I feel that I am the friend of the people as I think them honest and sincere in their faith and these I know as good and honorable men as any other professing Christians.

D<u>r.</u> Bennett has been the means of bringing me before your people, you will therefore see for <u>this act</u> I am in honor bound to say "<u>Peace to his Manes</u>."[516] To act otherwise would be ungrateful and dishonorable, both of which qualities are strangers to my nature. Nevertheless by leaving him as he is I can still be your friend, for be assured that nothing I have yet seen from his pen has in the least altered my opinion of you. I ~~will~~ well know what allowance to make in such cases.

Docter Bennett and [Origen] Bachelor are now delivering lectures in New York against you and your doctrines and asserted practises at Nauvoo.[517] Elder [Lucian] Foster told me this forenoon that the seats have been torn to pieces out of his church in Canal St, and that the congregation had to move to another place. I intimated to you in my last[518] that [James Gordon] Bennett of the Herald was about to publish conjointly with the Dr his Book of Exposures but since have learned that it is about to come out in Boston.[519] He expects to make a fortune out of it, and I presume he needs it, but I feel sure that it will only

---

515. Bennet was baptized the following August, although he later referred to it as a "frolick . . . without a moments reflection or consideration." (Historian's Office, Brigham Young History Drafts, 82; James Arlington Bennet, Arlington House, Long Island, NY, to JS, Nauvoo, IL, 24 Oct. 1843, JS Collection, CHL.)

516. Latin, referring to the honored souls of the departed dead.

517. Bennett and Bachelor gave advertised lectures attacking the church in August and September. (Notice, *New York Daily Tribune*, 31 Aug. 1842, [2]; "Mormonism Overhauled!!!," *Evening Post* [New York], 30 Aug. 1842, [2]; "Mormon Practices," *Evening Post*, 2 Sept. 1842, [2]; "Anti-Mormon Lecture— The Secret Wive System at Nauvoo," *New York Herald*, 4 Sept. 1842, [2].)

518. James Arlington Bennet to JS, 16 Aug. 1842, p. 135 herein.

519. Bennett's book was published in Boston by Leland and Whiting.

make converts to the Mormon faith. He has borrowed largely from Com. Morris' lacivious Poems.[520]

A general Order signed by Hugh Mc Fall; Ag[t.] [Adjutant] General and authorised by you has appeared in the Herald,[521] ordering me to repair to Nauvoo to take command of the Legion, and to bring with me Brig. Gen. J. G. Bennett, which states that if the requisition[522] be persisted in blood must be shed. I have assured Bennett of the Herald that I deem it a hoax but he insists upon it that it is genuine. My reply to it has appeared to day in that paper.[523] I have there stated that I have written to Gov[r.] [Thomas] Carlin for instructions, this is not so, it is only a rub.[524] On the whole you will only be made a greater Prophet and a greater man a great[525] Emperor by the affliction[526] and consideration of your good friends. My respects with those of Mrs B. to your lady

I am Dr Sir your sincere friend.

James Arlington Bennett [Bennet].["]

This letter was placed in the hands of Gen[l] Hugh Mc Fall who immediately wrote a refutation of the clause concerning himself to Governor [Thomas] Carlin, and also one for the Wasp.[527] The general order was not wrote by Mc Fall neither had he a knowledge of its existence untill shown to him in the letter. It is evidently got up by our enemies to increase excitement and anger, and is barely another addition to the many slanderous reports put in circulation by evil and designing men. [p. 204]

---

520. A possible reference to George Pope Morris's *The Deserted Bride; and Other Poems* (New York: Adlard and Saunders, 1838).

521. The fabricated order attributed to McFall appeared in the *New York Herald* two days prior to this letter to JS. ("Late and Important from the Mormon Country," *New York Herald,* 30 Aug. 1842, [2].)

522. The requisition by Missouri governor Thomas Reynolds directed Illinois governor Thomas Carlin to extradite JS to Missouri on charges of complicity in the 6 May 1842 assault on former Missouri governor Lilburn W. Boggs. (Thomas Reynolds, Requisition, 22 July 1842, p. 380 herein.)

523. James Arlington Bennet's letter stated that he was leaving immediately for Nauvoo and expected *New York Herald* editor James Gordon Bennett to accompany him. James Gordon Bennett responded in kind to Bennet's satirical letter. (James Gordon Bennett, "Military Movements," *New York Herald,* 1 Sept. 1842, [2].)

524. For "rub," the original letter has "ruse."

525. For "great," the original letter has "greater."

526. For "affliction," the original letter has "affection."

527. McFall's denial, stating that the order in the *New York Herald* was a fraud and that McFall was "not a Mormon, but a lover of truth and justice," was published ten days later. ("Great Hoax," *The Wasp,* 24 Sept. 1842, [2].)

15 September 1842 • Thursday

Thursday 15.th In council with Esqr [Calvin A.] Warren. Also councilled Uncle John Smith and brother Daniel C. Davis to move immediately to Keokuk and help to build up a city.[528]

16 September 1842 • Friday

Friday 16.th With brother [David] Rogers at home.[529] bro R painting

17 September 1842 • Saturday

Saturday 17.th At home with brother [David] Rogers, painting.

18 September 1842 • Sunday

Sunday 18.th At home. In the evening had a visit from Mother Smith.

19–20 September 1842 • Monday–Tuesday

Monday 19.th & Tuesday 20.th With brothers [David] Rogers. painting at his house.

21 September 1842 • Wednesday

Wednesday 21.st In the large room over the store. In the P.M. had a visit from E[lde]r John Taylor on[e] of the quorum of the Twelve who is just recovering from a severe attack of sickness. He councilled E[lde]r Taylor concerning the printing office— removing one Press to Keokuk &c.—[530]

22 September 1842 • Thursday

Thurday 22.nd At home. Arrangeing with [Jacob] Remick concerning moving printing press to Keokuk; buying paper &c.

23 September 1842 • Friday

Friday 23.rd At home. Had a visit from E[lde]r [John] Taylor.

---

528. The day before, JS received a deed to land in Keokuk, Iowa Territory. The plans to build a Mormon community in Keokuk failed to materialize. (JS, Journal, 14 Sept. 1842, p. 153 herein.)

529. David Rogers arrived from New York with George J. Adams on 7 September. (JS, Journal, 7 Sept. 1842, p. 133 herein.)

530. Wilford Woodruff noted that JS directed him to go to Keokuk and publish a political paper, while Taylor was to remain in Nauvoo to publish the *Times and Seasons*. Less than two weeks later, however, Woodruff was advised to remain in Nauvoo and assist in the printing office there. (Woodruff, Journal, 22 Sept. and 2 Oct. 1842.)

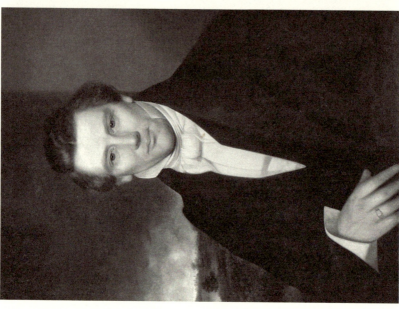

Portraits of Joseph and Emma Smith. September 1842. Church member David Rogers, a New York portrait painter with thirteen years of experience, painted these portraits of Joseph and Emma Smith over the course of several days in September 1842. (Courtesy Community of Christ Library-Archives, Independence, MO.)

24 September 1842 • Saturday

Saturday 24th. At home. Had a visit from old Mr [Joseph] Murdock & Lady[531] concerning land &c

25 September 1842 • Sunday

Sunday 25th. At the Grove. Spake more than two hours chiefly on the subject of his persecution.[532]

26 September 1842 • Monday

Monday 26th. In the Large room over the Store.—

27–28 September 1842 • Tuesday–Wednesday

Tuesday 27th. & Wednesday 28th. At home. Nothing of importance transpired.

29 September 1842 • Thursday

Thursday 29th. This day Sister Emma began to be sick with fever;[533] consequently president Joseph kept in the house and with her all day.

30 September 1842 • Friday

Friday 30th. Sister Emma no better. President Joseph was with her all day.

1 October 1842 • Saturday

October Saturday 1st. This A.M. President Joseph is sick, having a very severe pain in his left side; was not able to be about in consequence. Sister Emma about as usual. The President had previously sent for the Temple Committee to balance their accounts and ascertain how the Temple business was going on. Some reports had been circulated that the committee was not making a righteous disposition of property consecrated for the building of the Temple and there appeared to be some disatisfaction amongst the laborers. After carefully examining the accounts and enquiring into the manner of the proceedings of Committee President Joseph expressed himself perfectly satisfied with them and their works. The books were [p. 205] ballanced between the

---

531. Sally Murdock. Joseph Murdock purchased thirty-five acres in two parcels from JS four days later. (Trustees Land Book B, 28 Sept. 1842, 15.)

532. JS took 1 Kings 19 for his text. (Mendenhall, Diary, 25 Sept. 1842.)

533. Probably malaria, which was common in the summer months in Nauvoo. (Rollins et al., "Transforming Swampland into Nauvoo," 129–130, 133–135.)

Trustee[534] and Committee and the wages of all agreed upon.[535] The president remarked that he was amenable to the state for the faithful discharge of his duties as Trustee in Trust and that the Temple Committee were accontable to him and to no other authority;[536] and they must not take notice of any complaints from any source but let the complaints be made to him if any were needed and he would make things right. The parties separated perfectly satisfied and the president said he would have a notice published stating that he had examined their accounts and was satisfied &c.—[537] It was also agreed that the Recorders Office should be moved to the Temple, for better convenience.—[538]

2 October 1842 • Sunday

Sunday 2nd. About 1 o clock A.M. a messenger arrived from Quincey stating that the Governor[539] had offered a reward of $200 for President Joseph and also $200 for O. P. [Orrin Porter] Rockwell. This report was fully established on receipt of the Mail papers. The Quincy Whig also stated that Governor [Thomas] Reynolds had offered a reward; and published the Governors proclamation offering a reward of $300 for President Joseph and $300 for O. P. Rockwell. It is not expected that much will be effected by the rewards.[540]

Sister Emma continues very sick to day: the President was with her all day.—

3 October 1842 • Monday

Monday 3rd. Sister Emma a little better. The president with her all day.

---

534. JS.

535. The wages of the trustee-in-trust, committee members, and recorder were set at two dollars per day. (Clayton, History of the Nauvoo Temple, 34.)

536. Illinois law specified that every religious organization could elect up to ten trustees who would be legally responsible for the property of their institution. Under provisions of this act, JS earlier filed notice with the county recorder that on 30 January 1841 he was elected "Sole Trustee for said Church to hold my office during life." (An Act concerning Religious Societies [6 Feb. 1835], *Laws of the State of Illinois* [1834–1835], pp. 147–148, sec. 1; Appointment, 2 Feb. 1841, Hancock Co., IL, Bonds and Mortgages, vol. 1, p. 97, microfilm 954,776, U.S. and Canada Record Collection, FHL.)

537. The notice was published in the next issue of the *Times and Seasons*. (William Clayton, "To the Saints in Nauvoo, and Scattered Abroad," *Times and Seasons*, 15 Oct. 1842, 3:957.)

538. The recorder's office was at this time in JS's red brick store. In November 1842 the office moved to a small new brick structure, called the "committee house," near the temple. (JS, Journal, 2 Nov. 1842; William Clayton, "To the Saints in Nauvoo, and Scattered Abroad," *Times and Seasons*, 15 Oct. 1842, 3:957; Clayton, History of the Nauvoo Temple, 35.)

539. Illinois governor Thomas Carlin.

540. Thomas Carlin's proclamation is dated 20 September 1842. Governor Reynolds's offer of a reward of $600—or $300 each for JS and Rockwell—was issued on 19 September 1842. (Thomas Carlin, Proclamation, 20 Sept. 1842, p. 381 herein; News item, *Alton [IL] Telegraph and Democratic Review*, 1 Oct. 1842, [2]; Leopard and Shoemaker, *Messages and Proclamations*, 524–525.)

4 October 1842 • Tuesday

Teusday 4th. Sister E. [Emma Smith] is very sick again to day. President Joseph attended with her all the day, himself being somewhat poorly.—

5 October 1842 • Wednesday

Wednesday 5th. Sister E. [Emma Smith] is worse, many fears are entertained that she will not recover. She was baptised twice in the river which evidently did her much good.[541] She grew worse again at night and continues very sick indeed. President Joseph does not feel well, and is much troubled on account of Sister E's sickness. Elder [Sidney] Rigdon called El'r [Elder] W[illiam] Clayton into his office and said he had some matters to make known. He had been at Carthage and had conversation with Judge [Stephen A.] Douglas concerning Gov. [Thomas] Carlins proceedings &c. He had ascertained that Carlin had intentionally issued an illegal writ expecting thereby to draw President Joseph to Carthage to get acquited by Habeus Corpus before Douglas, and having men there waiting with a legal writ to serve on Prest. Joseph as soon as he was released under the other one and bear him away to Missouri, without further ceremony. E'r [Elder] Rigdon asked what power the Gov'rs. proclamation gave to any man or set of men who might be disposed to take Prest. Joseph. He was answered "Just the same power and authority which a legal warrant gave to an officer".

It is more and more evident that Carlin is determined to have the President taken to Missouri if he can; but may the Almighty Jehovah shield and defend his servant from all their power, and prolong his days in peace that he may guide his people in righteousness untill his head is white with old age. Amen [p. 206]

6 October 1842 • Thursday

Thursday 6th. This day sister Emma is better, and although it is the day on which she generally grows worse yet she appears considerably easier. May the Lord speedily raise her to the bosom of her family that the heart of his servant may be comforted. Amen. Prest. Joseph is comfortable to day.—

---

541. For many years following the organization of the church, the Saints performed baptisms for healing the sick. An epistle from the Quorum of the Twelve to church members dated 14 January 1845 described the original wooden font in the temple as being "for the baptism of the dead, the healing of the sick and other purposes." (Brigham Young et al., "An Epistle of the Twelve," *Times and Seasons,* 15 Jan. 1845, 6:779.)

7 October 1842 • Friday

Friday 7.th This A.M. E'r [Elder] Elias Higbee stated about the same things as were stated by E'r [Elder] [Sidney] Rigdon two days ago, and also that he had been informed that many of the Missourians were coming to unite with the Militia of this State, voluntarily and at their own expense; so that after the court rises at Carthage if they dont take Pres^t Joseph there; they will come and search the city &c. It is likely that this is <u>only</u> report.

Sister E. [Emma Smith] is some better.— Pres^{t.} Joseph is cheerful and well.

From the situation and appearance of things abroad President Joseph concluded to leave home, for a short season untill there should be some change in the proceedings of our enemies; accordingly at 20 minutes after 8 o clock P.M. he started away in company with brothers John Taylor, ~~Shadrach Roundey~~ and Wilson Law and John D. Parker. They travelled through the night and part of

Contemporaneous and noncontemporaneous journal keeping. Some journal entries were evidently written very close to the time of the events they record, sometimes within a few hours. Others appear to be written further from the time they cover, sometimes several days later. The entry for 7 October 1842 exemplifies both cases. The first paragraph of the entry reflects an understanding that rumors of trouble were unworthy of action, while the last paragraph recounts that the threat was real enough that Joseph Smith went into hiding. This suggests that the first paragraph was written earlier in the day on the very day of the events it describes, whereas the last paragraph was written sometime later. The inkflow of the final paragraph in the entry matches the inkflow in the following entry for 10 October, rather than that in the first two paragraphs of the entry. This indicates that the last paragraph of the 7 October entry was not written before 10 October. Handwriting of William Clayton. Book of the Law of the Lord, p. 207, Church History Library, Salt Lake City. (Photograph by Welden C. Andersen.)

next day and after a tedious journey arrived at bro. [*blank*] ⟨James⟩ Taylors well and in good spirits, where he intends to tarry at present.

Editorial Note

In an effort to avoid arrest for his alleged role in the assault on Lilburn W. Boggs, JS spent most of the next three weeks in hiding at the home of James Taylor on the Henderson River some thirty miles or more northeast of Nauvoo. Because JS's clerks were not present, very little was recorded of his activities during this period.

---

10 October 1842 • Monday

Monday 10th. E[lde]r [John] Taylor returned bringing favorable reports concerning Prest. Josephs health, spirits &c. Sister E. [Emma Smith] is yet gaining slowly.

15 October 1842 • Saturday

Saturday 15th. Bro. Jno D. Parker arrived with favorable intelligence from the president. He is well and comfortable.—

20 October 1842 • Thursday

Thursday 20th. Early this A.M. President Joseph arrived at home on a visit to his family. During the day he was visited by several of the brethren, who rejoiced to see him once more. Sister Emma is still getting better and is able to attend to a little business having this day closed contract, and received pay for a quarter Section of Land of brother Job V. Barnum.[542]

21 October 1842 • Friday

Friday 21st. This evening President Joseph returned in company with John D. Parker to father [James] Taylors, judging it wisdom to keep out of the way of his enemies a while longer at least; although all is peace and quiet and a prospect that his enemies will not trouble him much more.

23 October 1842 • Sunday

Sunday 23rd. This day the Temple Committee laid before the Saints the propriety and advantages of laying a temporary floor on the Temple that the

---

542. Barnum purchased land northeast of Nauvoo from JS on 15 October 1842, and the transaction was recorded on 22 October 1842. (Hancock Co., IL, Deed Records, 15 Oct. 1842, vol. K, p. 547, microfilm 954,599, U.S. and Canada Record Collection, FHL.)

brethren could henceforth meet in the Temple to Worship instead of meeting in the grove. This was the instructions of President Joseph: The saints seemed to rejoice at this privilege very much.[543] [p. 207]

28 October 1842 • Friday

Friday 28th. Soon after day-light this morning President Joseph returned home again to visit his family. He found sister E. [Emma Smith] some worse today the remainder of the family are well. In the afternoon he rode out into the city and took a little exercise, From the appearance of thinks [things?] abroad we are encouraged to believe that his enemies wont trouble him much more at present.

This day the brethren finished laying the temporary floor, and seats in the Temple; and its appearance is truly pleasant and chearing. The exertions of the brethren during the past week to accomplish this thing are truly praiseworthy

29 October 1842 • Saturday

Saturday 29th. About 10 o clock this morning president Joseph rode up and viewed the Temple. He expressed his satisfaction at the arrangements made and was pleased the progress made in that sacred edifice. After conversing with several of the brethren and shaking hands with numbers who were very much rejoiced to see their Prophet again, he returned home; but soon afterwards went over to the store where a number of brethren and sisters were assembled who had arrived this morning from the neighborhood of New York, Long Island &c. After E[lde]rs [John] Taylor, [Wilford] Woodruff and Samuel Bennett had addressed the brethren and sisters President Joseph spoke to them considerable, showing them the proper course to pursue and how to act in regard to making purchases of land &c. He showed them that it was generally in consequence of the brethren disobeying or disregarding council, that they became dissatisfied and murmered; and many when they arrived here were dissatisfied with the conduct of some of the saints because every thing was not done perfectly right, and they get mad and thus the devil gets advantage over them to destroy them. He said he was but a man and they must not expect him to be perfect; if they expected perfection from him, he should expect it from them, but if they would bear with his infirmities and the infirmities of the brethren, he would likewise bear with their infirmities. He said, it was

---

543. According to William Clayton, temple committee member Reynolds Cahoon and others visited JS at James Taylor's house and received "glorious instructions." JS also requested that Cahoon have the Saints install a temporary floor in the temple so that meetings could be held there. (Clayton, History of the Nauvoo Temple, 31–32.)

likely he would have again to hide up in the woods, but they must not be discouraged but roll on the city, the Temple &c. When his enemies took away his rights he would bear it and keep out of the way but "if they take away your rights I will fight for you." After speaking considerable and giving them council he blessed them and departed. The company appear to be in good spirits.

30 October 1842 • Sunday

Sunday 30th. This day the saints met to worship in the Temple and notwithstanding its largeness it was well fill'd. It had been expected that president Joseph would address them, but he sent word that he was so sick that he could not meet with them; consequently E[lde]r John Taylor delivered a discourse

In the P.M. President Joseph went to visit sick &c.[544] [p. 208]

31 October 1842 • Monday

Monday 31st. This day president Joseph and his children rode out to his farm, and did not return untill after dark.

1 November 1842 • Tuesday

November Tuesday 1st. A.M. President & sister E. [Emma Smith] rode up to Temple for the benefit of her health she is rapidly gaining. In the P.M. went to see Dr W[illar]d Richards who is very sick;[545] afterwards being accompanied by his children and W. C. [William Clayton] rode out towards the farm. When going down the hill near Caspers the carriage got overbalanced and upset. President Joseph was thrown some distance from the carriage and the children all three almost under it. He arose and enquired if any of the children were killed but upon examination there was no one seriously hurt, Frederic G. W. [Frederick Smith] had his cheek bruised which was about the worst injury received. The horse, so soon as he felt the carriage upset sprang forward but soon entangled himself in some branches and threw himself down on some rails. After some little trouble we succeeded in disengageing the horse from the harness and raising him up. The horse was not much hurt, but the carriage was considerably damaged. It seemed miraculous how we escaped serious injury from this accident, and our escape could not be attributed to any other power than that of divine providence. We felt thankful to God for this instance of his kind and watchful care over his servant and house. Seeing the carriage so much

---

544. TEXT: Ink density in the preceding sentence and in the following entry suggest that both were written at the same time.

545. Richards left Nauvoo on 1 July 1842 and arrived back in Nauvoo from the East with his family on 30 October 1842. (JS, Journal, 29 June 1842; Richards, Journal, 1 July 1842; Woodruff, Journal, 1–5 Nov. 1842.)

broke it was thought best to return home, accordingly leaving the carriage and part of the harness, and putting the children in bro Stoddards Buggy we returned.

In the evening President Joseph and two children rode up to the Temple.

2 November 1842 • Wednesday

Wednesday 2ⁿᵈ· Spent this A.M in removing the books, desk &c from the store over to the house.⁵⁴⁶ In the P.M. rode out to the farm and spent the day in holding plough &c.

3 November 1842 • Thursday

Thursday 3ʳᵈ· Rode out with E[mma Smith] to the Temple.—

4 November 1842 • Friday

Friday 4ᵗʰ· Rode out with Lorain [Lorin] Walker to examine his Timber, north of the City This night President Hyrum Smith and William Law returned from their mission to the East.⁵⁴⁷ They bring very good reports concerning the public feeling, and say that John C. Bennetts expose has done no hurt but much good. Some of the Twelve also returned from their mission⁵⁴⁸

5 November 1842 • Saturday

Saturday 5ᵗʰ· On account of the day being wet president Joseph remained at home He had a very pleasant visit from some of the Indians who were accompanied by a negro interpreter. They expressed great friendship with the Mormon people, and said they were their friends. After considerable conversation and partaking of victuals they departed evidently highly gratified with their visit.— [p. 209]

---

546. The recorder's office was moved to a newly built small brick building near the temple called the "Committee house," where the "property and means" for the construction of the temple were "recorded in due form." (Clayton, History of the Nauvoo Temple, 35; William Clayton, "To the Saints in Nauvoo, and Scattered Abroad," *Times and Seasons,* 15 Oct. 1842, 3:957.)

547. At a conference of the church on 29 August 1842, almost four hundred men volunteered for this mission to preach the gospel and to counter the charges against JS being published by John C. Bennett. Hyrum Smith and William Law started east the following week and preached in Massachusetts and New Hampshire before returning. (JS, Journal, 29 Aug. and 4 Sept. 1842, pp. 121, 124, 131 herein.)

548. Brigham Young and Heber C. Kimball, possibly in company with Amasa Lyman and George A. Smith, returned from preaching in various parts of Illinois on this date. Young started from Nauvoo on 9 September, and the others joined him the following day. Lyman's later published history gives 4 October 1842 as the date of his and Smith's return, while Young's more detailed account has Lyman and Smith preaching with himself and Kimball throughout October. (Amasa Lyman, Journal, 10 Sept. 1842; "Extract from Elder H. C. Kimball's Journal," *Times and Seasons,* 1 Dec. 1842, 4:23–24; "Amasa Lyman's History," *Deseret News,* 15 Sept. 1858, 121–122; Historian's Office, Brigham Young History Drafts, 64–65.)

6 November 1842 • Sunday

Sunday 6th. At home all day. In the P.M. had a visit from Dr W[illard] Richards.—

7 November 1842 • Monday

Monday 7th. Spent this A.M. in Council with Patriarch Hyrum [Smith] and some of the Twelve, and in giving instructions concerning the contemplated Journey to Springfield on the 15th. of December next, and what course ought to be pursued in reference to the case of Bankruptcy.549

In the P.M. C[alvin] A. Warren Esqr arrived, and the president called upon some of the Twelve and others to testify before Esqr Warren what they knew in reference to the appointment of Trustee in Trust &c, shewing also from the records that president Joseph was authorised by the church to purchase and hold property in the name of the church, and that he had acted in all things according to the council given to him.550

8 November 1842 • Tuesday

Tuesday 8th. This A.M. called upon Windsor P. Lyons [Lyon] and others to make affidavits concerning the frauds and irregularities practised in the Post Office.551 A petition was drawn and signed by many and sent by Esqr [Calvin A.] Warren to Judge [Richard M.] Young with a request that the latter

---

549. Attorney Calvin A. Warren advised church members seven months earlier regarding the new federal bankruptcy law, after which JS petitioned, on 28 April 1842, to have his debts discharged.*a* Following an initial hearing that began on 6 June 1842, JS's hearing for "final discharge from all his debts" was set for 1 October 1842.*b* Justin Butterfield, United States attorney for Illinois, objected to the discharge, however, alleging that JS had more assets—especially land—than he had disclosed.*c* Because of Butterfield's opposition, the court reset 15 December 1842 for a final bankruptcy hearing.*d* In spite of continued efforts, JS was not granted bankruptcy before his death. (*a*. JS, Journal, 14 Apr. 1842; see also the bankruptcy notices that appeared in *The Wasp* from 7 May 1842 through 11 June 1842. *b*. Justin Butterfield, Chicago, IL, to Charles B. Penrose, 2 Aug. 1842, microfilm, Records of the Solicitor of the Treasury, copy at CHL. *c*. Oaks and Bentley, "Joseph Smith and Legal Process," 740–741, 756–763. *d*. Justin Butterfield, Chicago, IL, to Charles B. Penrose, 13 Oct. 1842, microfilm, Records of the Solicitor of the Treasury, copy at CHL; JS, Journal, 9–20 Dec. 1842, pp. 177–178 herein.)

550. JS was elected sole trustee for the church on 30 January 1841 in Nauvoo, with authority to "receive acquire manage or convey property" for the church. (Appointment, 2 Feb. 1841, Hancock Co., IL, Bonds and Mortgages, vol. 1, p. 97, microfilm 954,776, U.S. and Canada Record Collection, FHL; see also An Act concerning Religious Societies [6 Feb. 1835], *Laws of the State of Illinois* [1834–1835], pp. 147–149, secs. 1 and 3.)

551. The affidavits charged that "letters had frequently been broken open money detained, and letters charged twice over &c &c." (JS per William Clayton, Nauvoo, IL, to Richard M. Young, Washington DC, 9 Feb. 1843, copy, Newel K. Whitney, Papers, BYU; see also JS, Journal, 8 Sept. 1842, p. 142 herein.)

should present the petition to the Post Master General[552] and use his influence to have the present post master removed and a new one appointed.[553] president Joseph was recommended for the appointment.

In the P.M. sat in court at his house as mayor.[554]

9 November 1842 • Wednesday

Wednesday 9th. Paid E[rie] Rhodes $436.93 being the amount of three notes due for the N.W quarter of section 9— 6 North 8 West.[555]

10–12 November 1842 • Thursday–Saturday

Saturday 12th. This day and also friday and the thursday was spent in the city council—

13 November 1842 • Sunday

Sunday 13th. At home all day

14 November 1842 • Monday

Monday 14th. In the city council—[556]

16 November 1842 • Wednesday

Wednesday 16th. Started in company with John D. Parker up the River

---

552. Charles A. Wickliffe.

553. Sidney Rigdon was serving as postmaster of Nauvoo at the time. JS stated in a letter to Illinois senator Richard M. Young the following February that no response had been received to the petition to the postmaster general. (JS per William Clayton, Nauvoo, IL, to Richard M. Young, Washington DC, 9 Feb. 1843, copy, Newel K. Whitney, Papers, BYU; JS, Journal, 13 Feb. 1843.)

554. According to the provisions of the Nauvoo charter, the mayor served as a justice of the peace and had "exclusive jurisdiction in all cases arising under the ordinances of the corporation." The mayor also served as chief justice of the municipal court. (An Act to Incorporate the City of Nauvoo [16 Dec. 1840], *Laws of the State of Illinois* [1840–1841], p. 55, secs. 16–17.)

555. Erie Rhodes died in October 1841. This payment was likely made to the estate of Erie Rhodes as part of a land puchase on 16 September 1841. (Promissory note, JS to Erie Rhodes, 16 Sept. 1841, JS Collection, CHL; see also 48n175 herein.)

556. On this date, the Nauvoo City Council passed "An Ordinance Regulating the proceedings on Writs of Habeas Corpus." This ordinance followed earlier ordinances on habeas corpus passed by the city council on 5 July, 8 August, and 9 September 1842. The ordinance was the culmination of efforts attempting to protect JS from arrest and trial outside of Nauvoo. Among other things, it empowered the Nauvoo Municipal Court to issue writs of habeas corpus for "any Person or Persons" detained "for any criminal or supposed criminal matter" and to discharge them if the original arrest could be shown, "by hearing the testimony & arguments" of all interested parties, to be invalid. (Nauvoo City Council Minute Book, 5 July 1842, 86–87; 8 Aug. 1842, 98–99; 9 Sept. 1842, 101; 14 Nov. 1842, 119–129.)

22 November 1842 • Tuesday

Tuesday 22nd. This day returned home

23 November 1842 • Wednesday

Wednesday 23rd. At home all day

26 November 1842 • Saturday

Saturday 26th. At home nearly all day. Went to visit E[lde]r. Brigham Young who was taken sick very suddenly.[557] Tarried 2 or three hours in council &c.

27 November 1842 • Sunday

Sunday 27th. At home. Visited E[lde]r B[righam] Young.[558]

28 November 1842 • Monday

Monday 28th. At home all day. Some charges having been instituted by the stone cutter⟨s⟩ against the Temple Committee,[559] at president Josephs request the parties appeared at his house this day to have the difficulties settled. An investigation [p. 210] was entered into before the prest. & his council Wm. Law. Prest. Hyrum [Smith] acted as council for defendents. and E[lde]r H[enry] G. Sherwood on the part of the accusers. The hearing of testimony lasted untill about 4 o clock at which time the meeting adjourned for half an hour. On coming together again prest. Hyrum addressed the brethren at some length showing the important responsibility of the Committee also the many difficulties they had to contend with, He advised the brethren to have charity one with another and be united &c &c. E[lde]r Sherwood replied to prest Hyrums remarks. Prest. H. explained some remarks before made. E[lde]r Wm. Law made a few pointed remarks After which President Joseph arose and gave his dicision which was that the Committee stand as before. He likewise showed

---

557. Young's history records that he was "attacked with a slight fit of apoplexy." (Historian's Office, Brigham Young History Drafts, 66, part B.)

558. Young's history records that he suffered from a "violent fever" this day and that JS and Willard Richards "administered" to him. JS sat by him for six hours. (Historian's Office, Brigham Young History Drafts, 66, part B.)

559. Committee member Alpheus Cutler was not mentioned in the complaint, probably because he spent the previous winter with the church's lumber operations in Wisconsin Territory, returning in July 1842, and had not been as active in the management of the stonecutters. The "principal" charges against Reynolds Cahoon and Elias Higbee were "an unequal distribution of provisions, also giving more iron & steel tools to Cahoons sons than to others. Also giving short measure of wood to father Huntington [William Huntington Sr.]; also letting the first course of stone around the Temple to the man who would do it for the least price &c." (Clayton, Journal, 28 Nov. 1842; Nauvoo High Council Minutes, 30 July 1842.)

the brethren that he was re[s]ponsible to the State for a faithful performance of his office as Sole Trustee in Trust &c.[560] & the Temple Committee were responsible to him and had given bonds to him to the amount of $12000 for a faithful dis-charge of all duties devolving upon them as a Committee &c &c. The trial did not conclude untill about 9 oclock P.M.

29 November 1842 • Tuesday

Tuesday 29th. In council with Prest. Hyrum [Smith], Willard Richards & others concerning the Bankrupt case.[561] P.M. attended court at the trial of Mr [Thomas J.] Hunter before Alderman [Orson] Spencer[562] for Slander. Prest. Joseph forgave Hunter the judgement but he was fined $10.— for contempt of court.[563]

30 November 1842 • Wednesday

Wednesday 30th. A.M. In council in the large Room over the store preparing evidence in the case of Bankruptcy.

P.M. Had Amos Davis brought before the municipal court for slander but in consequence of the informality of the writ drawn by Esqr [Daniel H.] Wells he was nonsuited.[564]

---

560. As trustee-in-trust, JS was legally responsible for all management of church property. (JS, Journal, 1 Oct. 1842; An Act concerning Religious Societies [6 Feb. 1835], *Laws of the State of Illinois* [1834–1835], p. 148, sec. 3.)

561. Three weeks earlier, JS and others met with attorney Calvin A. Warren regarding their petitions for bankruptcy. (JS, Journal, 7 Nov. 1842.)

562. According to the provisions of the Nauvoo charter, city aldermen served as justices of the peace within the limits of the city of Nauvoo. (An Act to Incorporate the City of Nauvoo [16 Dec. 1840], *Laws of the State of Illinois* [1840–1841], p. 55, sec. 16.)

563. JS made a complaint against Hunter before Alderman William Marks the previous day. Hunter was delivered into Spencer's custody on 29 November, after which Spencer issued subpoenas for witnesses. The case was heard by the municipal court, with Alderman Daniel H. Wells presiding pro tem. Hunter pleaded guilty to the charge of "using and making ridiculous and abusive language concerning Joseph Smiths Character . . . contrary to an Ordinance, entitled, 'an Ordinance in relation to religious Societies.'" The court discharged Hunter "without payment of any fine, except the Fine for Contempt of Court, and full Costs of this Suit," making eighteen dollars in total. Hunter's contempt of court was for "using disrespectful and abusive language, & stating that he disregarded the Municipal Court." (City of Nauvoo v. Hunter [Nauvoo Mun. Ct. 1842], Nauvoo Municipal Court Docket Book, 9 [second numbering].)

564. JS filed another complaint later this same day against Davis for making "indecent, unbecoming, abusive and ridiculous language concerning the Acts and Character of Deponent" before Alderman William Marks. Davis was brought to trial three days later before Marks. (City of Nauvoo v. Davis [Nauvoo Mun. Ct. 1842], Nauvoo Municipal Court Docket Book, 12 [second numbering]; JS, Journal, 3 Dec. 1842.)

1 December 1842 • Thursday

December Thursday 1ˢᵗ· This day sister Emma was sick, visited George A. Smith & B[righam] Young of the quorum of the Twelve who were sick. Called on Mr Angels⁵⁶⁵ in company with E[lde]r [Willard] Richards to give some council concerning a sick sister. Called on W[illiam] W. Phelps to get the historical document &c. After which he commenced reading and revising history.⁵⁶⁶

2 December 1842 • Friday

Friday 2ⁿᵈ· Sat as Mayor in the case of Amos Davis who was fined in the sum of $25. for breach of Ordinance by selling spirit⁵⁶⁷ by the small quantity.⁵⁶⁸ In the evening called on E[lde]rs [Willard] Richards & [Newel K.] Whitney to take an apprisal of the printing Office establishment preparatory to a lease to E[lde]rs Taylors [John Taylor] & [Wilford] Woodruff for the term of five years.⁵⁶⁹

3 December 1842 • Saturday

Saturday 3ʳᵈ· Called at the Printing Office several times. In the P.M. attended the municipal court in the case of Amos Davis for breach of ordinance &c.⁵⁷⁰ [p. 211]

---

565. Richards recorded a visit on this date to "Mother Angels." (Richards, Journal, 1 Dec. 1842.)

566. Following the death of Robert B. Thompson on 27 August 1841, Phelps took over the responsibility of writing and compiling the multivolume manuscript JS history. Richards assumed responsibility of the history on 1 December 1842, although Phelps continued to play a role in its development. (Jessee, "Writing of Joseph Smith's History," 464–466; Richards, Journal, 1 Dec. 1842; JS, Journal, 20 Jan. 1843, pp. 246–247 herein; JS, Journal, 7 Nov. 1843, JS Collection, CHL.)

567. TEXT: Possibly "spirits".

568. An ordinance passed by the Nauvoo City Council almost two years earlier prohibited selling liquor in small quantities. The ordinance specified that whiskey must be sold at least by the gallon and other spirits by a quart or more, unless by permission of a physician. Davis appealed the decision of the mayor's court four days later in the Nauvoo Municipal Court. (Nauvoo City Council Minute Book, 15 Feb. 1841, 7–8; Davis v. Nauvoo [Nauvoo Mun. Ct. 1842], Nauvoo Municipal Court Docket Book, 14–15 [second numbering]; JS, Journal, 6 Dec. 1842.)

569. Taylor and Woodruff leased the printing office from JS, who had contracted to purchase it from Ebenezer Robinson earlier in the year. Although this entry states that the lease agreement was being prepared on 2 December, and Woodruff's journal says it was prepared and written on 8, 9, and 10 December, the actual indenture, signed by Taylor, Woodruff, and JS, is dated 1 December 1842. (JS, Journal, 4 Feb. 1842; Woodruff, Journal, 8–10 Dec. 1842; Indenture, JS to John Taylor and Wilford Woodruff, 1 Dec. 1842, JS Collection, CHL.)

570. Davis was charged by JS three days earlier with "indecent, unbecoming, abusive and ridiculous language." The court, over which Alderman William Marks presided pro tem, fined Davis fifty dollars and bonded him to the sum of two hundred dollars to keep the peace. (JS, Journal, 30 Nov. 1842; City of Nauvoo v. Davis [Nauvoo Mun. Ct. 1842], Nauvoo Municipal Court Docket Book, 12–13 [second numbering].)

4 December 1842 • Sunday

Sunday 4th. The day being very wet Prest. Joseph remained at home all day

5 December 1842 • Monday

Monday 5th. A.M. Attendend in council with Prest. Hyrum [Smith] & others on the Bankrupt case.[571] P.M. had conversation with bro. [William A.] Gheen. In the evening attended the Lodge at which time charges were preferred against George W. Robinson for unmasonic conduct towards prest. Joseph.[572]

6 December 1842 • Tuesday

Tuesday 6th. Attended trial of Amos Davis before the municipal Court.[573]

7 December 1842 • Wednesday

Wednesday 7th. This day dined with E[lde]r Orson Hyde & family. E[lde]r Hyde has this day returned home from his Mission to Jerusalem,[574] his presence was gratifying, spent the day with E[lde]r Hyde & drawing wood.

8 December 1842 • Thursday

Thursday 8th. Had a visit from E[lde]r [Orson] Hyde & wife. Spent the day at home.

---

571. See 50n187 herein.
572. According to the minutes of the meeting, Robinson was charged "1st For endeavouring to wrong Nauvoo Lodge by misreprensentations. 2nd For speaking evil of Brethren Master Masons. 3rd For Lying." The hearing was set and received a series of postponements until, on 1 February 1843, Senior Warden Lucius N. Scovil reported that Robinson "had made ample satisfaction to the aggrieved & injured Brethren," and the lodge sustained taking no further action against him. (Nauvoo Masonic Lodge Minute Book, 5 Dec. 1842 and 1 Feb. 1843; JS, Journal, 24 Jan. 1843.)
573. The municipal court, over which JS presided, considered an appeal by Davis of the 2 December verdict of the mayor's court on charges of selling liquor in small quantities. The judgment of the mayor's court, fining Davis twenty-five dollars, was upheld. Davis later appealed to the Hancock County Circuit Court at Carthage, where a jury found Davis guilty of breach of the Nauvoo ordinance and fined him six and one-quarter cents. (JS, Journal, 2 Dec. 1842; Davis v. Nauvoo [Nauvoo Mun. Ct. 1842], Nauvoo Municipal Court Docket Book, 14–15 [second numbering]; Hancock Co., IL, Circuit Court Record, vol. C, p. 475, microfilm 947,496, U.S. and Canada Record Collection, FHL.)
574. Hyde left Nauvoo (at that time still officially called Commerce) on 15 April 1840 to serve a mission to Europe and the Holy Land, where on 24 October 1841 he dedicated the land of Jerusalem for the return of the Jews. (Orson Hyde and John E. Page, Quincy, IL, 28 Apr. 1840, Letter to the editor, *Times and Seasons,* June 1840, 1:116–117; Orson Hyde, "Interesting News from Alexandria and Jerusalem," *LDS Millennial Star,* Jan. 1842, 2:132–136.)

Editorial Note

JS's journal from 9 December through 20 December 1842 chronicles the efforts of several of his friends—including William Clayton, who was keeping the journal at this time—to obtain a discharge of his debts through bankruptcy during a trip to Springfield, Illinois. JS himself remained in Nauvoo during this time. While in Springfield, JS's friends also consulted with state officials and others about a possible course of action JS might pursue in regard to the ongoing effort to extradite him to Missouri to stand trial for his alleged involvement in the assassination attempt on Lilburn W. Boggs. These discussions provided Clayton with access to some of the documents that had been generated during the extradition attempt, as well as to letters to JS from newly elected Illinois governor Thomas Ford and United States district attorney Justin Butterfield, recommending that JS come to Springfield for a judicial review of his case. Clayton copied these documents and letters into this lengthy journal entry. A day-by-day account of JS's activities resumed on 21 December following the party's return to Nauvoo, when JS asked Willard Richards to serve as his private secretary and historian.

9–20 December 1842 • Friday–Tuesday

Friday 9th. This day prest. Joseph went to chopping wood.

On this day President Hyrum [Smith] started in company with Willard Richards. William Clayton, Henry G. Sherwood, Benjamin Covey, Peter Haws, Heber C. Kimball, Reynolds Cahoon & Alpheus Cutler for Springfield. bro. Covey & prest. Hyrum to attend to his case and the others to attend to prest. Joseph's case.[575] [576]We arrived at Springfield on tues-day the 13th. about 3 P.M. Same evening we were visited by E[lde]r William Smith who is a member of the house of Representatives. He stated that the subject of the repeal of our charter had been brought before the house, and the house had referred the subject to the committee on Corporations. He had made a spirited speech before the house on the subject; and thought from the appearance of things that the only way to preserve our charter was, to present a resolution to repeal all the charters in the State, if they repealed the Nauvoo Charter.[577] He stated

---

575. That is, JS's and Hyrum Smith's bankruptcy cases.
576. TEXT: The remainder of the entry is in darker ink and was evidently written later.
577. A report of William Smith's 9 December speech before the Illinois House of Representatives is in "Speech of Mr. Smith of Hancock County," *The Wasp*, 14 Jan. 1843, [1]–[2]. Residents of Illinois had been criticizing the Nauvoo charter for some time.[a] The charter was debated in the Illinois legislature on 9 and 10 December, the issue being that the Mormons were allegedly abusing the powers granted in the charter to keep JS from being extradited.[b] The state senate committee on the judiciary took up the question later and on 19 December reported on the powers given to Illinois chartered cities, concluding that religious prejudice was behind the accusation that Mormons were given special treatment in the Nauvoo charter. However, the committee recommended amending all city charters "to place them all upon an

that we had a many warm friends in both Houses who had determined that if our charter was repealed all the Charters in the State should, especially Springfield, Quincy & Chicago.[578]

It is evident that there would have been little said on this subject before the Houses, had not Governor [Thomas] Ford in his inaugural address, referred to it in strong terms. In that address he says[579] " [*3 lines blank*]

It was expected that Gov[r.] Ford would not have recommended any alteration in our charter, inasmuch as there is no extraordinary privileges granted to the citizens of Nauvoo, more than is granted by the Springfield Charter, to the citizens of Springfield.[580] Such however was not the case, and his remarks have in some measure added a new stimulus to our enemies to agitate the subject. It is, however, evident that Gov[r.] Ford saw that his remarks were not of the wisest as he said to us afterwards that he regretted he had not recommended a repeal of all the charters in the State at the same time. [p. 212] We also had an interview with Judge [Stephen A.] Douglas who appeared very friendly and offered to assist us in our business as much as possible. He recommended us to petition the Gov[r.] to revoke the writ & proclamation by Ex Gov. [Thomas] Carlin for the arrest of pres[t.] Joseph.—[581] On Wednesday the 14[th.] We went to see Mr [Justin] Butterfield the U.S. District Attorney. We stated to him our intention of visiting the Gov[r.] and our object in so doing. He recommended the course and offered to assist us. We requested Mr Butterfield to prepare a petition[582]

---

equal footing."[c] Ultimately, the Nauvoo city charter was not repealed until after JS's death.[d] (a. "The Mormon Plot and League," *Sangamo Journal* [Springfield, IL], 8 July 1842, [2]; "Gov. Duncan," *Times and Seasons*, 1 June 1842, 3:806, 808. b. "Illinois Legislature," *Sangamo Journal*, 15 Dec. 1842, [2]. c. "Report of the Committee on the Judiciary," *Reports Made to Senate and House of Representatives of the State of Illinois*, Senate, 13th Assembly, 1st Sess., p. 4. d. An Act to Repeal the Act Entitled "An Act to Incorporate the City of Nauvoo" [29 Jan. 1845], *Laws of the State of Illinois* [1844–1845], pp. 187–188.)

578. Between 1837, when Chicago was chartered as a city by the Illinois General Assembly, and 1840, when Nauvoo's charter was drafted, four other Illinois cities—Alton, Galena, Springfield, and Quincy—were granted charters similar to Nauvoo's. (Kimball, "Nauvoo Charter," 66–78; Bennett and Cope, "City on a Hill," 20–21, 33–40.)

579. In his inaugural address on 8 December 1842, newly elected Illinois governor Thomas Ford said: "A great deal has been said about certain charters granted to the people of Nauvoo. These charters are objectionable on many accounts, but particularly on account of the powers granted. The people of the State have become aroused on the subject, and anxiously desire that those charters should be modified so as to give the inhabitants of Nauvoo no greater privileges than those enjoyed by others of our fellow citizens." (*Journal of the Senate . . . of Illinois*, 8 Dec. 1842, 33.)

580. Although the Springfield and Nauvoo charters were remarkably similar, a significant difference between the two was the authority held by the Nauvoo Municipal Court to issue writs of habeas corpus. The city of Alton had a similar provision. (Kimball, "Nauvoo Charter," 73–75, 77–78; Bennett and Cope, "City on a Hill," 35; see also 129n445 herein.)

581. Thomas Carlin, Writ, 2 Aug. 1842, *Ex Parte* JS for Accessory to Boggs Assault [C.C.D. Ill. 1843], copy, Nauvoo, IL, Records, CHL; Thomas Carlin, Proclamation, 20 Sept. 1842, p. 381 herein.

582. Three days later Ford wrote a letter in response to the petition stating that after consulting with

Stephen A. Douglas. Circa 1850–1852. Illinois Supreme Court justice, 1841–1842. Friends of Joseph Smith consulted with Douglas on several occasions regarding efforts to extradite Smith to Missouri to stand trial for his alleged involvement in the attempted assassination of Lilburn W. Boggs. (Courtesy Library of Congress, Washington DC.)

which was done & accompanied by an affidavit of each of us present Also a copy of the affidavit of Ex- Gov.ʳ· [Lilburn W.] Boggs of Missouri of which the following is a copy:—[583]

"State of Missouri } ss
County of Jackson

This day personally appeared before me Samuel Weston a Justice of the Peace within and for the County of Jackson the Subscriber Lilburn W Boggs who being duly sworn doeth depose and say that on the night of the sixth day of May 1842 while sitting in his dwelling in the town of Independance in the County of Jackson, he was shot with intent to kill, and that his life was dispaired of for several days, and that he believes and has good reason to believe from Evidence and information now in his possession, that Joseph Smith commonly called the Mormon Prophet was accessary before the fact of the intended murder; and that the said Joseph Smith is a citizen or resident of the State of Illinois and the said deponent hereby applies to the Governor of the State of Missouri to make a demand on the Governor of the State of Illinois to deliver the said Joseph Smith commonly called the Mormon prophet to some person authorized to receive and convey him to the State and county aforesaid, there to be dealt with according to Law.

Sworn to and subscribed before me this 20.ᵗʰ· } Lilburn W. Boggs"
day of July 1842   Samuel Weston J.P.

At 4 o clock P.M. we called upon Mr Butterfield who went with us to see the Gov.ʳ·[584] Mr Butterfield stated the object of our request and read a communication which he had wrote to E[lde]r Sidney Rigdon last October.[585] He then

---

the judges of the Illinois Supreme Court, he did not believe he had power to rescind the action of the previous governor, Thomas Carlin. However, Ford reported that the judges agreed that Reynolds's requisition was "illegal," and promised JS protection if he were to come to Springfield for a judicial review of his case. (Thomas Ford to JS, 17 Dec. 1842, p. 179 herein.)

583. The original affidavit is transcribed in Appendix 1, pages 379–380 herein.

584. Thomas Ford.

585. On 20 October 1842, Butterfield wrote to Rigdon expressing his opinion that the requisition of the governor of Missouri upon the governor of Illinois for the surrender of JS was illegal, and he had "no doubt but the Supreme Court of this State would discharge him upon Habeas Corpus." Butterfield pointed out that the right of the governor of Missouri to demand JS, and the duty of the governor of Illinois to give him up, was imposed by the United States Constitution, "which declares 'that a person charged in any State with Treason, Felony, or other crime who shall flee from Justice and be found in another State; shall on demand of the executive authority of the State from which he fled, be delivered up to be removed to the State having Jurisdiction of the Crime.'" Butterfield stated, "I understand from your

read our petition and presented the papers to the Gov.ᵣ remarking at the same time that the arrest was based upon far weaker premises than he had previously supposed, inasmuch as the affidavit of Ex Gov. Boggs said nothing about Joseph having fled from justice, but plainly said he was a resident of the State of Illinoi◊ and the constitution only authorizes the delivery up of a "fugitives from Justice to the Executive authority of the State from which he fled".⁵⁸⁶ The Gov.ᵣ in his reply stated that he had no doubt but that the writ of Gov. Carlin was illegal, but he doubted as to his authority to interfere with the acts of his predecessor. He finally concluded that he would state the case before the Judges of the Supreme Court⁵⁸⁷ at their counsel next day and whatever they decided on shall be his decision. He then stated his reasons for recommending a repeal of the charter and said he regretted that he had not recommended a repeal of all the charters. &c. [p. 213]

On thursday the 15ᵗʰ· we attended the U.S. District Court being the day appointed for hearing Joseph & Hyrum's cases in Bankruptcy.⁵⁸⁸ At our request the cases was not brought on till tomorrow. During the day we endeavored to satisfy Mr Butterfield with security for the payment of a Judgement against pres.ᵗ Joseph in favor of the United States. That judgement being the only hindrance to pres.ᵗ Joseph receiving his dis-charge.⁵⁸⁹ In the evening we again

---

letter and from the statement of facts made to me by Mʳ [Calvin A.?] Warren . . . that it can be proved that Joseph Smith was not in the State of Missouri at the time the Crime was committed, but was in this State [Illinois]—that it is untrue that he was in the State of Missouri at the time of the commission of the said crime or has been there at any time since he could not therefore have fled from that State since the comission of the said crime." Butterfield added that unless JS "actually fled from the State where the offence was committed to another State the Govᵗ of this State [Illinois] has no Jurisdiction over his person and cannot deliver him up." (Justin Butterfield, Chicago, IL, to Sidney Rigdon, [Nauvoo, IL], 20 Oct. 1842, copy, Sidney Rigdon, Collection, CHL.)

586. See U.S. Constitution, art. 4, sec. 2.

587. The Supreme Court of the state of Illinois.

588. JS met with Hyrum Smith and some members of the Quorum of the Twelve to decide on a course of action for this bankruptcy proceeding the month before. (JS, Journal, 7 Nov. 1842.)

589. The judgment grew out of a case involving the purchase of a steamboat two years earlier. At a public auction in Quincy, Illinois, on 10 September 1840, Captain Robert E. Lee, acting as agent for the United States, sold two keelboats and the steamboat *Des Moines* to Mormon businessman Peter Haws for $4,866.38, due in eight months. The promissory note was signed by Peter Haws, Henry W. Miller, George Miller, JS, and Hyrum Smith—the last four men apparently standing as sureties for Haws's payment. The steamboat, renamed *Nauvoo*, was wrecked later that fall and rendered useless as a source of income, resulting in Haws's inability to pay his note when it came due 10 May 1843. As one of the signers of Haws's promissory note, JS bore at least partial responsibility for payment. Responsibility for collection on behalf of the United States eventually passed to Justin Butterfield, United States attorney for the District of Illinois. On 11 June 1842, a default judgment was entered against JS and three other signers of the promissory note for the amount of the note, $4,866.38, plus damages and court costs, for a total of $5,212.49 ¾. Convinced that JS had the means to pay the United States for the steamboat and that the other signers of the promissory note did not, Butterfield apparently opposed discharging of JS's debts in bankruptcy until

waited on Mr Butterfield[590] who stated that he had attended the council of the Judges, three of whom where of opinion that the Govr ought to revoke the writ and proclamation, and three that he ought not to intefere with the acts of Ex Gov. Carlin. They considered that the present case would be a precedent for cases which might occur hereafter of a similar character consequently it would be best to have it tried on Habeus Corpus. Mr Butterfield said that all the Judges were unanimous in their opinion that pres. Joseph would be acquited on Habeas Corpus, and he thought that would be the best course to be pursued. He said there was no doubt but that the pres.^t might go to Springfield with safety and would certainly be discharged. On Friday the 16.th we again waited on Mr Butterfield and entered into arrangements in the name of the High Council of the church to secure the payment of the judgement.[591] As soon as this was done he withdrew his objections against Pres.^t Hyrum who immediately obtained his dis-charge.[592] Pres.^t Josephs dis-charge could not be obtained until Mr Butterfield had wrote to the solicitor of the U.S. Treasury showing our propositions. If they were accepted a dis-charge will be immediately obtained.[593]

---

he had some assurance that the debt owed the United States would be paid. (Oaks and Bentley, "Joseph Smith and Legal Process," 735–765.)

590. At this point in the text, William Clayton shifts the focus of his narrative from JS's federal bankruptcy negotiations to the contemplated habeas corpus hearing to free JS from extradition to Missouri on the charge that he was an accessory in the shooting of former Missouri governor Lilburn W. Boggs. Legal ethics of the period allowed Butterfield to represent the government's interest in the matter of JS's bankruptcy while simultaneously representing JS in the matter of extradition.

591. By this arrangement, the high council proposed to obtain a bond to cover the amount JS owed the United States, to be paid "in four equal annual instalments with interest" and "to secure the payment of the said Bond, by a mortgage" of Illinois real estate "worth double the amount of the said debt." (Henry G. Sherwood et al., Springfield, IL, to Justin Butterfield, Springfield, IL, 16 Dec. 1842, microfilm, Records of the Solicitor of the Treasury, copy at CHL.)

592. Hyrum Smith's discharge probably means he was considered insolvent, while JS was believed to have assets sufficient to pay the debt owed the United States.

593. Butterfield sent the proposal to Charles B. Penrose, United States solicitor of the Treasury, on 17 December 1842. In January 1843, Penrose directed Butterfield to reject the Mormon proposal, but in a counteroffer he authorized Butterfield to discharge JS of his debts in bankruptcy "if the parties will make a liberal Cash payment in hand, say one third of the debt, and secure the remainder" through the mortgage they proposed to Butterfield, to be paid in three annual, "equal instalments." Apparently Butterfield did not receive Penrose's counteroffer, and JS died before the matter could be resolved. (Justin Butterfield, Springfield, IL, to Charles B. Penrose, 17 Dec. 1842, microfilm, Records of the Solicitor of the Treasury, copy at CHL; [Charles B. Penrose] to Justin Butterfield, Chicago, IL, 11 Jan. 1843, microfilm, Records of the Solicitor of the Treasury, copy at CHL; Oaks and Bentley, "Joseph Smith and Legal Process," 763–766.)

The meanness and animosity of president Josephs enemies may be perceived by comparing the Affidavit of Ex Govr Boggs and the demand of Govr [Thomas] Reynolds of Missouri, the latter is as follows;[594]

"The Governor of the State of Missouri to the Governor of the State of Illinois Greeting:— Whereas:— it appears by the annexed document (the aff.^t^ of Boggs) which is hereby certified as authentic, that one Joseph Smith is a fugitive from Justice, charged with being accessary before the fact, to an assault with intent to kill, made by one O. P. [Orrin Porter] Rockwell on Lilburn W Boggs in this State, and it is represented to the Executive Department of this State, has fled to the State of Illinois. Now Therefore I Thomas Reynolds Governor of the said State of Missouri, by virtue of the authority in me vested by the Constitution and Laws of the United States, do by these presents, demand the surrender and delivery of the said Joseph Smith to Edward R. Ford who is hereby appointed as the agent to receive the said Joseph Smith on the part of this State.

L.S[595] In testimony Whereof, I Governor of the State of Missouri have hereunto set my hand, and caused to be affixed the Great Seal of State of Missouri. Done at the city of Jefferson this 22.nd day of July in the year of our Lord one thousand eight hundred & forty two of the Independance of the United States the sixty seventh and of this State the twenty-third.

By the Governor Tho Reynolds
Ja.^s^ L. Minor Secretary of State." [p. 214]

On Saturday the 17.th Govr Ford wrote the following letter to Pres.^t^ Joseph and sent it by us.

[596]"Springfield Decr 17.th 1842

Dear Sir:— Your petition[597] requesting me to rescind Govr [Thomas] Carlins proclamation and recall the writ issued against you has been received and duly considered. I submitted your case and all the papers relating thereto, to the Judges of the Supreme Court; or at least to six of them who happened to be present. They were unanimous

---

594. The original requisition is transcribed in Appendix 1, pages 380–381 herein.
595. TEXT: Inscription is surrounded by a hand-drawn representation of a seal. "L.S" is an abbreviation of *locus sigilli,* Latin for "location of the seal."
596. The original of this letter is housed in JS Collection, CHL.
597. Butterfield prepared the petition on 14 December 1842. (JS, Journal, 9–20 Dec. 1842, pp. 174–176 herein.)

Thomas Ford. Governor of Illinois, 1842–1846. Ford had been serving as governor less than one month when he recommended that Joseph Smith travel to Springfield for a "Judicial investigation" of his rights following efforts to extradite him to Missouri for his alleged involvement in the attempted assassination of Lilburn W. Boggs. (Church History Library, Salt Lake City.)

in the opinion that the requisition from Missouri was illegal and insufficient to cause your arrest, but were equally divided as to the propriety and Justice of my interference with the acts of Governor Carlin. It being therefore a case of great doubt as to my power, and I not wishing ever in an official Station to assume the exercise of doubtful powers; and in as much as you have a sure and effectual remedy in the courts, I have decided to decline interfering. I can only advise that you submit to the laws and have a Judicial investigation of your rights. If it should become necessary for this purpose to repair to Springfield I do not believe that there will be any disposition to use illegal violence towards you; and I would feel it my duty in your case, as in the case of any other person, to protect you with any necessary amount of force from mob violence whilst asserting your rights before the courts, going to and returning.

I am most respectfully yours

Thomas Ford."

After receiving this letter we went to see Mr [Justin] Butterfield and shewed him the above letter. He immediately set down and wrote the following.—

[598]"Springfield December 17th. 1842

Joseph Smith Esqr.
Dear Sir:—

I have heard the letter read which Govr. [Thomas] Ford has written to you, and his statements are correct in relation to the opinion of the Judges of the Supreme Court. The Judges were unanimously of the opinion that you would be entitled to your discharge under a Habeas Corpus to be issued by the Supreme Court— but felt some delicacy in advising Govr. Ford to revoke the order issued by Govr. [Thomas] Carlin— my advice is, that you come here without delay and you do not run the least risk of being protected while here and of being discharged by the Sup. Court by Habeas Corpus— I have also a right to bring the case before the U.S. Court[599] now in Session here, and there you are certain of obtaining your discharge— I will stand by you and see you safely delivered from your arrest.[600]

---

598. The original of this letter is housed in JS Collection, CHL.

599. During this period, the lowest federal court serviced a district that was part of a multistate circuit. Thus, the federal court at Springfield handled the current functions of a district court and a circuit court of appeals and was properly called the Circuit Court of the United States for the District of Illinois.

600. JS went to Springfield in the last week of December. By the first week of January, Butterfield

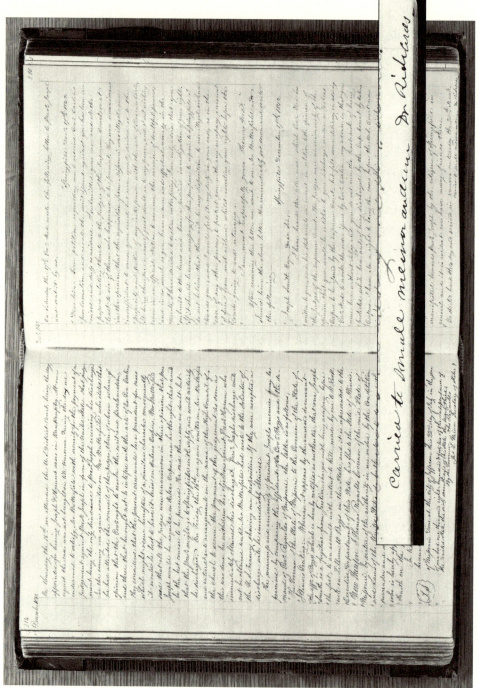

Transfer of journal to memorandum books. At the end of the last page of journal entries in the Book of the Law of the Lord, Willard Richards noted that Joseph Smith's journal would be carried forward in a small memorandum book. Handwriting of William Clayton and Willard Richards. Book of the Law of the Lord, pp. 214–215, Church History Library, Salt Lake City. (Photograph by Welden C. Andersen.)

>   Yours truly
>   J[ustin] Butterfield"

After receiving these letters we considered it best to return as there was no further prospect of doing any thing further to advantage. From what we could learn there seems to be a good feeling manifested towards pres.^t Joseph by the citizens of Springfield in general and it is evident we have many friends there.

We started back this day and arrived in Nauvoo on tuesday the 20th. all well.

⟨carried to small memorandum Dr Richards⟩[601] [p. 215]

---

determined that the federal court was the appropriate venue for this habeas corpus hearing, as it involved the constitutional issue of whether JS could be tried for a crime in Missouri when he had not fled from that state to avoid justice. (JS, Journal, 4 Jan. 1843, p. 220 herein.)

601. TEXT: Insertion in handwriting of Willard Richards.

Second Nauvoo journal. Willard Richards kept Joseph Smith's second Nauvoo journal in four small memorandum books—shown here against the background of a document box and table reportedly belonging to Smith in Nauvoo. The labels on the spines were probably placed on the books in Salt Lake City under the auspices of the Church Historian's Office. The fourth book is labeled as a Willard Richards journal because after Smith's death Richards turned the book over and began using it as his own journal. JS, Journal, Dec. 1842–June 1844, JS Collection, Church History Library, Salt Lake City. (Photograph by Welden C. Andersen.)

JOURNAL, DECEMBER 1842–JUNE 1844

Source Note

JS, "President Joseph Smith's Journal," Journal, 4 vols., Dec. 1842–June 1844; handwriting and signatures of Willard Richards; 1,045 pages; JS Collection, CHL. Includes shorthand and illustrations; also includes redactions, use marks, and archival stickers.

Willard Richards kept "President Joseph Smith's Journal" in four small memorandum books. The paper in book 1 is blue, while the paper in books 2–4 is white. In the first two books, the paper was printed with seventeen blue lines and extra space for page headers, whereas the paper for book 3 was printed with nineteen blue lines and no header space. The first eight gatherings of paper for book 4 were printed with sixteen blue lines and header space, while the last nine gatherings were printed with nineteen blue lines and no header space. The four volumes have 147, 160, 142, and 190 free leaves, respectively, and were sewn with all-along sewing. The leaves in books 1–3 were trimmed to measure 6 × 3¾ inches (15 × 10 cm), while the paper in book 4 measures 6¼ × 3¾ inches (16 × 10 cm). Books 2–4 have the same red-speckled stain on the page edges. All four books were bound with a tight-back case binding and have brown leather over pasteboards. Books 1–3 measure 6¼ × 4 × ¾ inches (16 × 10 × 2 cm); book 4 measures 6⅜ × 4 × ¾ inches (16 × 10 × 2 cm). The outside covers of book 1 feature an embossed pattern around the borders. The cover of book 4 is red and features a gold pattern around the borders on the front and the back.

Willard Richards inscribed most of the journal entries in these memorandum books with a quill pen in ink that is now brown, although he also used blue ink for several entries. Some of the graphite inscriptions in the volumes are also contemporaneous. Richards paginated the first 114 of the 285 inscribed pages in book 1—discounting the title page that precedes the pagination—and the first 20 of the 309 inscribed pages in book 2. There is no pagination in books 3–4. In book 2, pages 11, 17, and 20–21 feature illustrations of celestial observations.

The Richards memorandum books include later inscriptions that are not transcribed in this edition. At the end of book 2, Thomas Bullock added a list of Nauvoo-era plural marriages. A few revisions, additions, or notes are penciled in throughout the volumes. There are also several use marks throughout the volumes—probably made when the journal entries were later revised for inclusion in the "History of Joseph Smith" published in Mormon newspapers in the mid-nineteenth century.[1] The spines of the volumes are now labeled with blue-colored paper stickers that probably date from the early Utah period.[2] Each of the four volumes also bears the mark of a square sticker removed from the upper

---

1. This serialized history drew on the journals herein beginning with the 4 July 1855 issue of the *Deseret News* and with the 3 January 1857 issue of the *LDS Millennial Star*.

2. The labels on the spines of the four volumes read respectively as follows: "Joseph Smith's Journal— 1842-3 by Willard Richards" (book 1); "Joseph Smith's Journal by W. Richards 1843" (book 2); "Joseph

right-hand corner of the outside front cover. Finally, a "Historian's Office Archives" self-adhesive paper sticker appears in the front inside cover or on the first flyleaf of each book.

Willard Richards identified himself as the scribe for the journal on the title pages of books 1 and 4. Because Richards kept the journals for JS and kept his own journal in the back of book 4 after JS's death, the books may be included in the listing of "D^{rs} private books & Papers"[3] in the inventory of church records made in Nauvoo, Illinois, in 1846.[4] The volumes are listed in inventories made in Salt Lake City, Utah, by the Church Historian's Office in 1855, 1858, and 1878, as well as in the 1973 register of the JS Collection.[5] These archival records and the physical evidence of archival stickers indicate continuous institutional custody and authenticity.

Historical Introduction

Willard Richards took over the responsibility of journal keeping from William Clayton on 21 December 1842, the same day JS "made a particular request" that Richards "act as his private se[c]retary & historian."[6] While Clayton—and Richards before him—had kept JS's previous Illinois journal in the large "Book of the Law of the Lord," which also contained records of donations for the Nauvoo temple, Richards began this journal in a much smaller memorandum book. The journal, which Richards kept through 22 June 1844, five days before JS's death, eventually comprised four such memorandum books. The entire first book and part of the second (through April 1843) are presented here; the remainder of Richards's second notebook, as well as the third and fourth books, will be published in volume 3 in the Journals series of *The Joseph Smith Papers*.

Several pieces of evidence indicate that these four memorandum books were considered volumes of the same journal rather than separate journals themselves. For example, whereas JS's journals kept during the 1830s were recorded in bound books or notebooks labeled with different titles—such as "Sketch Book" or "The Scriptory Book"[7]—the first and last of Richards's memorandum books bear virtually identical titles, with the fourth explicitly identified as "vol 4". Similarly, that books 2 and 3 lack titles suggests that each was simply a continuation of the previous book. This suggestion is made even stronger in book 2, in which the first entry commences at 4:00 p.m. on 10 March, with the events of the earlier part of the day recorded at the end of book 1. All four memorandum books are virtually the same size, and the bindings on the first three are similar.

As with nearly all the entries in JS's previous Missouri and Illinois journals, JS neither wrote nor dictated the text of the entries in the memorandum books; they are based on

---

Smith's Journal by W. Richards 1843–4" (book 3); and "W. Richards' Journal 1844 ⟨Vol. 4⟩" (book 4; Richards kept JS's journal in the front of this volume, and after JS's death Richards kept his own journal in the back of the volume).

3. "D^{rs}" in the quotation is a reference to Richards, a Thomsonian doctor. ("History of Willard Richards," *Deseret News*, 23 June 1858, 73.)

4. "Schedule of Church Records," Historian's Office, Catalogs and Inventories, 1846–1904, CHL.

5. "Inventory. Historian's Office. 4th April 1855," [1]; "Contents of the Historian and Recorder's Office G. S. L. City July 1858," 2; "Index of Records and Journals in the Historian's Office 1878," [11]–[12], Historian's Office, Catalogs and Inventories, 1846–1904, CHL; Johnson, *Register of the Joseph Smith Collection*, 7.

6. JS, Journal, 21 Dec. 1842.

7. See *JSP*, J1:53, 225.

First of four memorandum books. The first book of Joseph Smith's second Nauvoo (third Illinois) journal covers the period from 21 December 1842 to 10 March 1843. JS, Journal, Dec. 1842–June 1844, bk. 1, JS Collection, Church History Library, Salt Lake City. (Photograph by Welden C. Andersen.)

Willard Richards's observations. For example, the entry for 22 September 1843 records only that Richards "Saw Joseph pass in a waggon with Hiram."[8] Despite the secondhand nature of the entries, however, Richards, a close associate and frequent companion of JS, was able to capture in detail JS's words and actions on many occasions.

Richards had kept JS's journal in the Book of the Law of the Lord from December 1841 to June 1842 in his earlier capacity as "Recorder. for the Temple, and the Scribe for the private office of the President."[9] When he began keeping this journal on 21 December 1842, however, he did so as JS's newly appointed "private se[c]retary & historian."[10] The change in titles may seem insignificant, but Richards was very much aware of his new role: where he had occasionally identified himself as "recorder" and "scribe" in JS's previous journal, he now referred to himself as the "sec." The shift in titles and responsibilities may have been at least part of the reason the journal was transferred to the memorandum books; William Clayton, who replaced Richards as temple recorder in September 1842,[11] retained custody of the Book of the Law of the Lord and continued its record of temple donations.

The change in Richards's title, as well as the transfer of the journal out of the Book of the Law of the Lord, may have influenced what events Richards recorded in the memorandum books. At least some of the material Richards, as JS's private secretary, included in this journal—such as the detailed record of a medical malpractice suit over which JS presided—probably would have received much less emphasis had Richards, in the capacity of temple recorder and scribe, been keeping JS's journal in the book that also contained records of donations for the temple. Similarly, although the ledger-size Book of the Law of the Lord likely remained in the recorder's office, and most journal entries were probably made there, each of the memorandum books was small enough that Richards could easily carry it with him, allowing him to record many of JS's activities closer to the actual event—both temporally and spatially—than was possible earlier.

Richards's new title of historian was significant as well. On 1 December 1842, Richards began working on the "History of Joseph Smith" that was being serially published in the *Times and Seasons,* and by August 1843 he was drawing on JS's earlier journals for that history.[12] Richards therefore expected that the contemporaneous journal entries he was keeping for JS would eventually be used as the basis for JS's history.

Richards employed various techniques in keeping the journal. For a few entries, he made lightly penciled notes and returned later with a quill pen to expand the entry. In other entries, the morning or afternoon portion of an entry was written in one ink and the evening portion of the entry in a different ink that matches that of the following entry. These changes in writing media and in other aspects of the inscribed text indicate that many entries—or parts of entries—were made on the very day of the events they described. The textual evidence in other entries indicates that they were written several days after the date they bear. Still other entries are a hybrid. Richards's notes of sermons and legal

---

8. JS, Journal, 22 Sept. 1843, JS Collection, CHL.
9. JS, Journal, 13 Dec. 1841, p. 11 herein.
10. JS, Journal, 21 Dec. 1842.
11. Clayton, History of the Nauvoo Temple, 30–31.
12. JS, Journal, 1 Dec. 1842 and 20 Jan. 1843; Richards, Journal, 1 Dec. 1842; Jessee, "Writing of Joseph Smith's History," 441.

proceedings, for example, bear evidence of both contemporaneous inscription and later revision. In some instances, Richards left blank spaces and even blank lines, apparently intending to add details later. Hurried note-taking often resulted in missing words, informal abbreviations, inconsistent spelling, and poorly formed characters. Richards revisited some difficult passages to mend or rewrite characters, revise spelling and punctuation, and add interlineations. Some of the blanks were filled while others were left standing. Richards's notes include both immediate emendations, such as wipe-erasures made while his ink was still wet, as well as later revisions, such as knife-erasures of words written in ink that had dried. The various ways in which Richards wrote and revised entries resulted in the journal's uneven texture but also contributed to its wealth of immediately recorded information and clarifying additions.

Over time, Richards settled somewhat into a pattern of generally recording the events of one day on one page—some pages largely empty and others filled with cramped writing—with weather reported at the bottom of the page. He made an entry for almost every day during the last year and a half of JS's life. The journal ended when JS left Nauvoo on 22 June 1844, five days before he was killed at the jailhouse at Carthage, Illinois. Richards accompanied JS to Carthage and, during the final days of JS's life, kept extensive notes of JS's activities in his personal journal.

Book 1, 21 December 1842–10 March 1843

Editorial Note

Approximately half of Willard Richards's memorandum book 1 focuses on two incidents: JS's effort to avoid extradition to Missouri to face charges of involvement in the shooting of Missouri's former governor Lilburn W. Boggs, and a malpractice suit involving a Nauvoo doctor and his patient in the mayor's court. The reports of the malpractice trial, recorded in this journal and published in *The Wasp*,[13] are the most extensive accounts of any case over which JS presided as judge. Also included in book 1 are reports of three JS sermons and of a variety of JS's daily activities connected with his responsibilities as mayor, municipal court judge, militia commander, church leader, and family man.

———— ☙ ————

President Joseph Smith's
Journal
⟨1843–
as kept by Willard Richards.—⟩[14]
[1/2 page blank] [p. [iii]] [page [iv] blank]

---

13. "Decision," *The Wasp*, 22 Mar. 1843, [2]–[3].

14. TEXT: The first two lines in this four-line heading are inscribed in blue ink, the next two in brown ink; beginning with the first journal entry (21 December 1842), the text reverts again to blue ink.

Title page of second Nauvoo journal, book 1. Willard Richards gave Joseph Smith's second Nauvoo (third Illinois) journal the title "President Joseph Smith's Journal." Handwriting of Willard Richards. JS, Journal, Dec. 1842–June 1844, bk. 1, p. [iii], JS Collection, Church History Library, Salt Lake City. (Photograph by Welden C. Andersen.)

21 December 1842 • Wednesday

~~Januar~~ December 21ˢᵗ· President Joseph at his own house: attending a variety of business Gave instructions about a communication to A. [James Arlington] Bennet.[15] & made a particular request that W[illard] Richards would act as his private se[c]retary & historian

22 December 1842 • Thursday

22— Heard his correspondence with Gov [Thomas] Carlin. as prepared for Gen [James Arlington] Bennet.[16] Recited in German to Elder [Orson] Hyde,[17] Bro Shearer asked the meaning of the Little leaven in 3 measures of meal,[18] Joseph.— said it alludes exp[r]essly to the last days. when there should be little faith on the earth & it [p. 1] leaven the whole world. There shall be safity [safety] in Zion & Jerusalem & the remnants whom the Lord shall call. It refers to the Pristhood.— Truth springing up on a fixd prin[c]iple 3 measures refers to the 3 in the grand Presidency confining the oracles to a certain head on the principle of 3.

23 December 1842 • Friday

23— I[19] visited with Franklin [D. Richards] & his wife[20]

---

15. JS's instructions concerned a letter Richards was writing to Bennet, whom Richards had met in August 1842 in New York. (JS to James Arlington Bennet, 8 Sept. 1842, p. 137 herein; Richards, Journal, 20 Nov. 1842; Willard Richards, Nauvoo, IL, to James Arlington Bennet, 20 Nov. and 22 Dec. 1842, draft, Willard Richards, Papers, CHL.)

16. On this day Willard Richards completed the letter to Bennet mentioned in the previous entry "& in the eve read it to Joseph Emma & Orson Hyde." As instructed by JS, in this second part of his letter Richards referred to the Illinois legislature's recent discussions about repealing the Nauvoo charter and asked for Bennet's thoughts on the constitutionality of a legislature repealing a perpetual charter. He also asked for Bennet's opinion on the "constitutionality, Practicability, & expediency" of the Saints suing the state of Missouri for the recovery of the property they lost there and, insofar as they had determined that the current efforts to extradite JS to Missouri were illegal, for Bennet's opinion on the constitutionality of "bringing a suit or suits" against Carlin or the state of Illinois. The correspondence with Carlin that was prepared to send to Bennet may have included Carlin's letters of 30 June and 27 July 1842 to JS, as well as JS's letters of 24 June and 25 July 1842. (Richards, Journal, 21 and 22 Dec. 1842; see also Willard Richards, Nauvoo, IL, to James Arlington Bennet, 20 Nov. and 22 Dec. 1842, draft, Willard Richards, Papers, CHL; Thomas Carlin to JS, 30 June 1842, p. 100 herein; Thomas Carlin to JS, 27 July 1842, p. 102 herein; JS, Nauvoo, IL, to Thomas Carlin, [Quincy, IL], 24 June 1842, in JS Letterbook 2, pp. 233–235.)

17. Hyde, a member of the Quorum of the Twelve, studied German in Europe during his 1841–1842 mission to Europe and Jerusalem. Hyde returned to Nauvoo on 7 December 1842 and tutored JS in German, as reflected in several entries in JS's journal for February and March 1843. ("Letter from Orson Hyde," *Times and Seasons*, 15 Oct. 1841, 2:570–573; JS, Journal, 7 Dec. 1842.)

18. See Matthew 13:33; and Luke 13:21.

19. In this case, Willard Richards. (Richards, Journal, 18 and 23 Dec. 1842.)

20. Jane Snyder Richards.

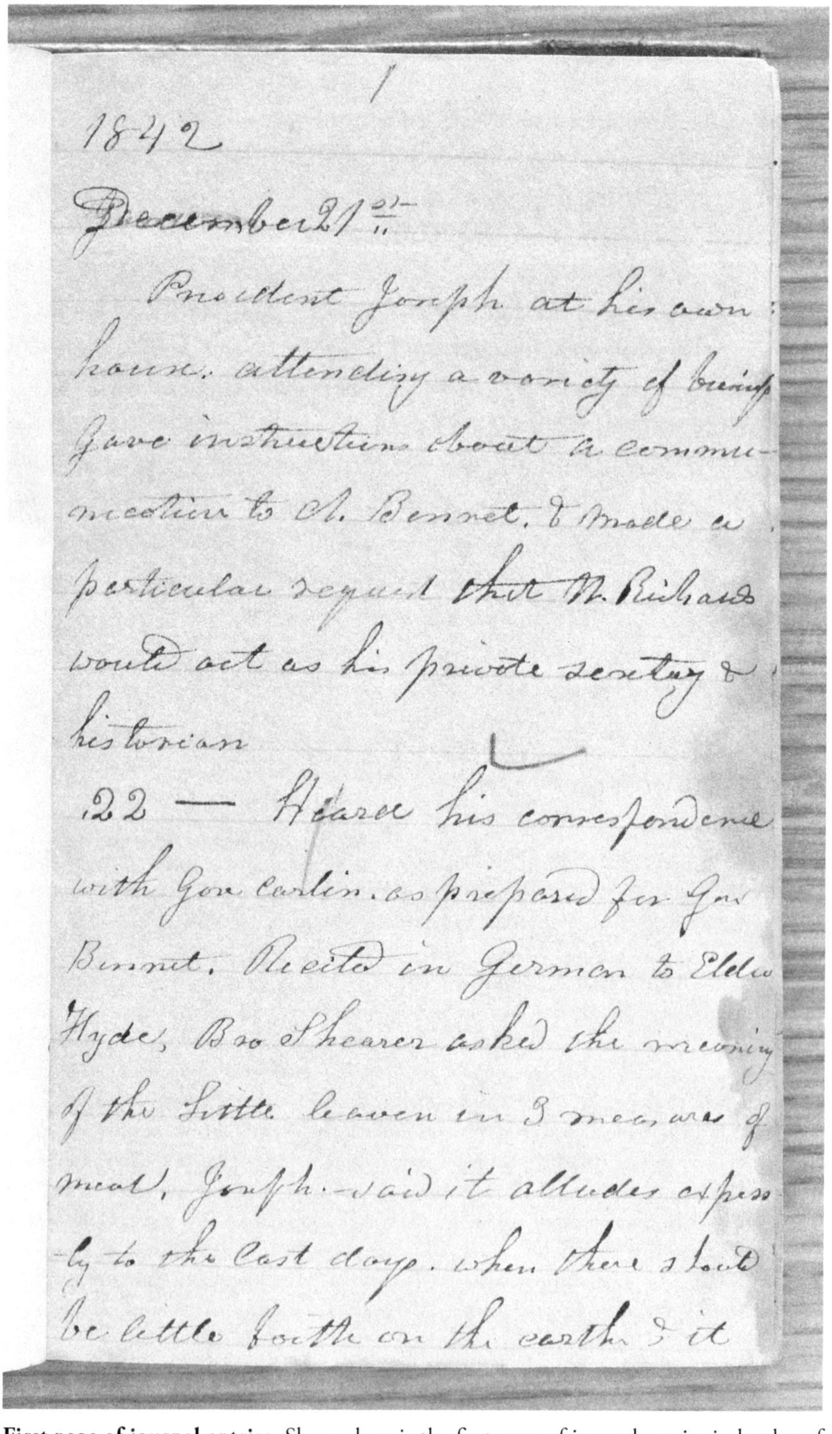

First page of journal entries. Shown here is the first page of journal entries in book 1 of Joseph Smith's second Nauvoo (third Illinois) journal. Many of the pages in the beginning of the book have date headers. Handwriting of Willard Richards. JS, Journal, Dec. 1842–June 1844, bk. 1, p. 1, JS Collection, Church History Library, Salt Lake City. (Photograph by Welden C. Andersen.)

24 December 1842 • Saturday

24— P.M. read & revised history²¹ walked with sec^y. to see sister Lyons [Sylvia Sessions Lyon] who was sick— her babe died 30 minutes before he arrived.²² thence to Bro Sabins [Elijah J. Sabin's] to get some money for expences to Sp[r]ingfield—²³ having Just borrowd $100 of Nehemiah [Jeremiah] Hatch.²⁴ In reply to the [p. 2] question. Do you want a wicked man to pray for you?²⁵ "Yes, if the fervent effectual prayer of the righteous availeth much.²⁶ a wicked man may avail a little when p[r]aying for a Righteous man.— There is none good but <u>one</u>.²⁷ the better a man is the more his prayer will prevail. like the publican & pharisee one was justified rather than the other shewing that both were justified in a degree.²⁸ the prayer of the wicked man may do a Rightioes man good when it does the one who prays no good—["]

25 December 1842 • Sunday

Sunday 25— [*3 lines blank*] [p. 3]

26 December 1842 • Monday

26— Held court. Sis [Sylvia Butterfield] Morey defndat [defendant][.]²⁹ had consultation with Gen W[ilson] W. Law & was arrested by him on

---

21. Three weeks earlier JS resumed actively directing Willard Richards in compiling and writing JS's history. (JS, Journal, 1 Dec. 1842; see also 21 Dec. 1842.)

22. Asa W. Lyon, son of Windsor and Sylvia Lyon, was twelve hours old when he died. His gravestone gives 25 December 1842 as the date of his death. (Cook, *Nauvoo Deaths and Marriages*, 49.)

23. Following the advice of his attorney, Justin Butterfield, JS left the following week for Springfield, Illinois, to obtain a writ of habeas corpus in an effort to avoid extradition to Missouri. (See Justin Butterfield to JS, 17 Dec. 1842, p. 181 herein.)

24. William Clayton wrote: "P.M. went to pres^t Josephs. He was in trouble. At his request I & bro N[ewel] K. Whitney went to Jeremiah Hatch and borrowed $100 for expenses to Springfield. Whitney & I each signed the note for Joseph. We wanted $200 but the old gentleman said he would not let us have more than $100." (Clayton, Journal, 24 Dec. 1842.)

25. Willard Richards asked this question while he and JS were visiting Sabin to borrow money. (Richards, Journal, 24 Dec. 1842.)

26. See James 5:16.

27. See Matthew 19:17; and Mark 10:18.

28. See Luke 18:10–14.

29. According to the court record, the defendant was Sylvia Morey's husband, George Morey. In October 1842 George Morey contracted with John Canfield to have Canfield drive Morey's span of horses and wagon for the winter season, and longer if they could agree. Canfield was also to provide firewood for Morey's family. In return, Canfield would receive "half of what [he] made and room rent free." For unknown reasons Morey later left Nauvoo, after which Sylvia Morey, according to Canfield, took the team away from Canfield, refused to acknowledge the contract, and slandered Canfield in town. On 19 December 1842 Canfield commenced a suit before JS for "Work & labour, & Goods Sold & delivered, or furnished" by Canfield to Morey. With Morey being "absent from home, & it not appearing that he had absented himself to evade service of process," JS dismissed the case at the plaintiff's cost on

Proclomation of Gov. [Thomas] Carlin, & Elders [Henry G.] Sherwood & [William] Clayton startd for carthage after Habeus Corpus to carry him to Spri[n]gfield—[30] visited Sister Morey in custody of Sec.^y & prescribed for her afflictions. spoke very highly of Lobelia—[31] good in its place. was one of the works of God. but Like the power of God or any good it become an evil when improperly used. had lear[n]ed the use & value by his own expirence Home. Sister Emma sick had another chill— had a consultation concerni[n]g her[32] with Secreta[r]y.—[33] while walking up [p. 4] main St Joseph asked Bro [*blank*] Tully[34] if he had aught against him? he replied I have not. Bro [George] Morey gave Joseph a walking stick consisting of whale ivory top. & sperm-whale tooth body— with Mahogany interstice.

Editorial Note

Over the course of the next two weeks, JS and several others traveled to Springfield, Illinois, where JS obtained a writ of habeas corpus and was discharged from arrest for his alleged involvement in the attempted assassination of former Missouri governor Lilburn W. Boggs. JS traveled to Springfield in custody of Wilson Law, who held him by authority of the September 1842 proclamation issued by former Illinois governor Thomas Carlin,[35] the original arrest warrant having been retained by Adams County undersheriff Thomas King. Once JS was in Springfield, Illinois governor Thomas Ford issued a new warrant authoriz-

---

26 December. (John Canfield, Statement, 19 Dec. 1842, Nauvoo, IL, Records, CHL; Canfield v. Morey [Nauvoo Mayor's Ct. 1843], Nauvoo Mayor's Court Docket Book, 43.)

30. Illinois Supreme Court judge Stephen A. Douglas advised that JS's friends arrest JS on the authority of Carlin's proclamation and bring him to Springfield for a hearing on a writ of habeas corpus. Governor Thomas Ford and United States attorney for Illinois Justin Butterfield also suggested, in letters dated 17 December 1842, that JS come to Springfield. Although Clayton and Sherwood were unable to obtain a writ of habeas corpus in Carthage because of the absence of a clerk, federal judge Nathaniel Pope granted one in Springfield two weeks later, on 31 December. (Clayton, Journal, 16 Dec. 1842; Thomas Carlin, Proclamation, 20 Sept. 1842, p. 381 herein; Thomas Ford to JS, 17 Dec. 1842, p. 179 herein; Justin Butterfield to JS, 17 Dec. 1842, p. 181 herein; Clayton, Journal, 26 and 27 Dec. 1842; JS, Journal, 31 Dec. 1842, p. 204 herein.)

31. The wild plant lobelia was used by botanic or Thomsonian physicians for its emetic properties. (Haller, *People's Doctors,* 80.)

32. Numerous journal entries indicate that Emma had been seriously ill since 30 September 1842. JS consulted with secretary Willard Richards about Emma's health since Richards was an experienced botanic physician.

33. TEXT: The ink color changes at this point from blue to brown.

34. Probably Allen Tulley. (Nauvoo, IL, Tax list, district 3, 1842, p. 201, microfilm 7,706, U.S. and Canada Record Collection, FHL; "Special Conference," *Times and Seasons,* 15 Apr. 1844, 5:506.)

35. Thomas Carlin, Proclamation, 20 Sept. 1842, p. 381 herein.

ing JS's arrest by the sheriff of Sangamon County, to whom a writ of habeas corpus could be directed.

---

27 December 1842 • Tuesday

27th. 9 A.M started ~~with~~ in custody of Gen Wilson W. Law for Sp[r]ingfield. in co.— with Hiram [Hyrum] Smith. & John Taylor. William Marks & [*blank*] Maffitt [Levi Moffet]— Peter Hawes. Lorin walker— W[illard] Richards. & orson Hyde & ~~after~~ when 1/2 way to carthage met Bros [Henry G.] Sherwood & [William] Clayton who had obtaind an order from the master of chan[c]ery[36] for Habeus corpus. but the court [p. 5] clerk[37] had been elected Senator therefor they could not obtain the writ but Joined the party.[38] & [after?] watering at the public well in carthage arrived at Bro Samu[e]l Smith's in Plymouth. about sunset ⟨35 mi⟩. [sister [Elizabeth Davis] Durphy & daugter. rode in the carrige][39] one hour after Edward Hunter Theodore Turl[e]y Dr— [Harvey] Tate. ⟨&⟩ Shadrach Roundy arrived & Joined the party Supped with Wms [William Smith's] wife[40]

28 December 1842 • Wednesday

28—— slept with sec— on buffaloes after retiring. J: stated that the peryfying [purifying] of the sons of Levi[41] was by giving unto them inteligince— that we are not capable of meditating ⟨on⟩ & reciving ~~an~~ all the inteligence which belongs [p. 6] to an immortal state. it is to[o] powerful for our faculties. started at 8 oclock— [sis. [Elizabeth Davis] Durphy's Daughter tarrid & Bro Wm Smith wife & little daughter accompanid] before starting Joseph retoled his [dream?]— was by a beautiful stream of water. saw a noble handsome fish. threw it out. soon after saw more threw them out & soon a great many & threw out a gr[e]at abundance. & sent for salt to salt them down. & salted

---

36. Chauncey Robison.

37. Jacob Davis.

38. Illinois law specified that while a master in chancery could order a writ of habeas corpus to be issued, only the court clerk could actually issue it. (An Act to Provide for Issuing Writs of No Exeat and Habeas Corpus, and for Other Purposes [11 Feb. 1835], *Laws of the State of Illinois* [1834–1835], p. 32; People v. Town, 4 Ill. [3 Scammon] 19 [Ill. Sup. Ct. 1841].)

39. "Sister Durphy" is probably Elizabeth Davis Durfee, wife of Jabez Durfee and a friend of the Smith family. In draft material he created when compiling JS's history, Richards stated that William Smith's wife was sick on this date and that "Sister Durfee" came from Nauvoo to "take care of her" on the trip to Springfield. (Historian's Office, JS History, draft notes, 28 Dec. 1842.)

40. Caroline Grant Smith, wife of William Smith, JS's brother. The William Smith and Samuel Smith families lived together in Plymouth at this time. (JS History, vol. D-1, 1430.)

41. See Malachi 3:3.

them— arrived at Rushville. Bell. Tavern by Mrs. Stevenson 3. P.M 20 miles— after supper Joseph with a part of the co[mpany] spent the eve with Mr. & [Uriah] Brown— Joseph stated that to touch the Nauvoo charter was no better than highway robbery that since the [p. 7] creation there never had been a repeal of a perpetual charter by God, Angels, or men. & that he never would submit to lowering our charter—[42] but they might bring others up to it. after retur[nin]g to the tavern. Joseph was measurd 6 feet Hiram [Hyrum Smith] 6. [Edward] Hunter 6. Wilson Law. 6 3/4 in— Moffitt [Levi Moffet] 6 1/2

29 December 1842 • Thursday

29— started 20— 9— arrivd ⟨Capt⟩ Dutches [John Dutch's] ⟨Lancas[t]er. 32 mi⟩ 4 PM. after Supper Gen [Wilson] Law asked why the Sun was masculine & ⟨moon⟩ femini[n]e? ⟨Joseph⟩ The root of masculine is stronger & of femini[n]e weaker Sun is a govening planet to certain planets[43] while the moon borrows her light from the Sun [p. 8] & is less or weaker &c— Let the Governme[n]t of Mo redress the wrongs she has don[e] to the mormons & or let the curse follow them ⟨from generation[44] to generation⟩ till they do it— when ⟨I⟩ we was going up to Missouri in co[mpany] with Elder [Sidney] Rigdon & our families[45] we arrived at Paris. Illinois on a extreme cold day. to go forward was 14 mil[e]s to a house.— & backward nearly as far we applied to all the taverns for admission in vain. we were mormons & could not be recived such was the cold that in one hou[r] we must have perished. We plead for our women & children in vain we councelled together & the breth[r]en agreed to stand by me. & we concluded [p. 9] we might as well die fighting as freeze to death. I went into a tavern & plead our cause to get admission. The Landlord said he could not keep us for love or money. I told him we must & would stay let the consequence be what it might, for we must stay or perish. the Landlord said they had heard the mormons were very bad people & the

---

42. The Illinois state legislature in 1840 granted that the Nauvoo city charter would "have perpetual succession." Three weeks earlier the Illinois House of Representatives debated whether to alter the Nauvoo charter to remove some of the powers granted therein. Governor Thomas Ford also discussed the issue in his inaugural address on 8 December 1842. (An Act to Incorporate the City of Nauvoo [16 Dec. 1840], *Laws of the State of Illinois* [1840–1841], p. 52, sec. 1; JS, Journal, 9–20 Dec. 1842, pp. 173–174 herein; "Gov. Ford's Inaugural Address," *Sangamo Journal* [Springfield, IL], 15 Dec. 1842, [1].)

43. The idea that the sun is a "governing planet" is found in the Book of Abraham, which JS had recently published. ("A Fac-simile from the Book of Abraham, No. 2," *Times and Seasons*, 15 Mar. 1842, 3:720–721 [Abraham, facsimile 2].)

44. TEXT: From the beginning of the entry to this point, Willard Richards wrote first in graphite and then retraced his earlier inscription using brown ink.

45. JS here relates an experience from early 1838 when JS, Rigdon, and others were en route from Kirtland, Ohio, to Far West, Missouri.

inhabitants of the Paris had combined not to have any thing to do with them but we might stay. I told him we would stay but no thanks to him & we went in & all [p. 10] the taverns, I have boys Men enough to take the town & if we must freeze we will freeeze by the burning of these houses— The taverns were then opened & we were accommodatd. & recived many apologies in the morni[n]g from the inhabita[n]ts for their abusive treatment.

(It was reported through the country that a camp of the mormons stole an acre of corn of one man in the neighborhood of Terra haut [Terre Haute])

Much Good music on the Piano with singing in the evening [p. 11]

30 December 1842 • Friday

30— Started at 8— broke one of the carriages & were detaind awhile arrived at Judge [James] Adams[46] 2½ Oclock Joseph said he had decided that he would not vote for a Slave holder— it is giving them power & if they could obtain sufficent power & get a religious peak [pique?] against any religionists— they would subdue them & compel our children to mix with their slaves. By Elder [Orson] Hyde. what would you advice a man to do who came in the having a hundred Slaves? Joseph[:] I have always advised such to bring their slaves [p. 12] into a free county— & set them free— Educate them & give them equal Rights. (the remainder of the co[mpany]— arrived 3½ P.M.) should the slaves be organizd into an independent governme[n]t they would become quarrelsome it would not be wisdom,— ⟨all⟩ the party supped at Judge Adams Justin Butterfield Esqr District Att^y of the United States for Illinois.[47] was introducd by Judge Adams, Bro Wm Smith stated that Pittman [James Pitman]. Sheriff of Adams county had been here some days. but whether he had the writ again[s]t Joseph or not. Tis supposed he has it.—[48] conversation [p. 13] continued on the writ & proclamation[49] Butterfield said that Judge [Nathaniel] Pope would close the court[50] on the marrow [morrow].— had continud it 2 or 3 days on account of Joseph's case, & he should try the case on its Merits & not on any technicality. When Pittman Entered the Secretary's

---

46. At Springfield, Illinois.

47. Although Butterfield, as district attorney, represented the United States government in JS's bankruptcy case, he also represented JS in the habeus corpus hearing for the extradition case. (JS, Journal, 9–20 Dec. 1842, pp. 177–178 herein.)

48. Pitman was the Adams County constable who evidently accompanied Thomas King, undersheriff of Adams County, when King attempted to arrest JS on 8 August 1842. (JS, Journal, 8 Aug. 1842.)

49. Thomas Carlin, Proclamation, 20 Sept. 1842, p. 381 herein.

50. United States district court for Illinois.

office. [Lyman] Trumbull[51] asked him if he had the writ? He replied with a smile it will be forth coming.[52]

It was decided by the council that the old writ should be had if possible in the morning by some one beside Pittman. Joseph be arrestd thereon. & by Habeus Corpus brought [p. 14] before Judge pope in the morning, & he would go clear. & Said Joseph let me have a happy new year⟨s⟩.—

conversation then turned on Missourie[53] Joseph stated that he never had done militry duty in his life. was taken prisoner of war at Far West in his own door yard & the man who took me thrust ~~me~~ my little boy[54] (who was clingi[n]g to my garme[n]ts) f[r]om me by his sword. saying God Damn you get away you little rascal or I will run you th[r]ough.— I was condemd by court martial to be shot at 8 o clock in the Morning[55] there were 18 Priests in the court martial. Gen Donithen [Alexander Doniphan] said it was cold blood[e]d murder would have nothi[n]g to do with it & marched [p. 15] of[f] his Brigade—[56] were marchd to Jackson Co. the soldirs refusd to obey orders. & we were retur[ne]d & thut [thrust] in Prison by Gen [John B.] Clarks orders. kept 6 mo. 5 days[57] with little food & no bed except a little straw, sufferd much with cold.— without p[r]ocess— on charge of Treason.— Larce[n]y & steali[n]g. had a mock trial.[58] witnesses sworn at the point of bayonet. [Judge Austin A.] King sent

---

51. Illinois secretary of state.

52. An arrest warrant, or writ, was needed to begin habeas corpus proceedings.

53. The following paragraphs focus on JS's experiences in Missouri from the time of his arrest at Far West until his arrival in Illinois—events that took place between 31 October 1838 and mid-April 1839.

54. Joseph Smith III. (See JS et al., Liberty, MO, to the church members and Edward Partridge, Quincy, IL, 20 Mar. 1839, in Revelations Collection, CHL [D&C 122:6].)

55. Because JS was a civilian, he was not legally subject to a court-martial of the Missouri militia.

56. After being taken into custody on 31 October 1838 by Missouri militia under the command of Major General Samuel D. Lucas at Far West, Missouri, Mormon leaders, including JS, were sentenced to be shot on the morning of 2 November. Doniphan's denunciation of the sentence and his threat to leave with his troops forced the militia officers to reconsider their decision to use a military court to try civilians. (Baugh, "Call to Arms," 317–326, 337–339; JS History, vol. B-1, 848–849.)

57. Clark ordered the prisoners sent to Richmond, Missouri, where they were confined beginning 9 November 1838. After a preliminary hearing there, JS and five fellow defendants were incarcerated at Liberty, Missouri, to await trial on the charge of treason. JS was incarcerated at Liberty from 1 December 1838 to 6 April 1839, a total of four months and five days. From Liberty, JS and his companions were taken to Gallatin, Missouri, for trial. JS and his companions were allowed to escape on 16 April 1839 while en route to Boone County, where they were being transported after having obtained a change of venue. In all, JS was held prisoner from 31 October 1838, when he was captured in Far West, Missouri, to 16 April 1839, when he escaped—a total of five and one-half months. (JS History, vol. B-1, 848; vol. C-1, 856–858, 913–914, 921–922; JS, Liberty, MO, to Emma Smith, Far West, MO, 1 Dec. 1838, CHL; JS, Journal, 16 Apr. 1839, in *JSP*, J1:336.)

58. The "mock trial" was a court of inquiry, or preliminary hearing, to ascertain whether there was probable cause to prosecute. Judge Austin A. King ruled that JS, Sidney Rigdon, Lyman Wight, Hyrum Smith, Alexander McRae, and Caleb Baldwin were to be tried for treason. Other defendants were to be

summons by Bogerd [Samuel Bogart] methodist Priest. took 50 of our witnesses & put them in Prisone. & then 20 more. we got one witness by beckoni[n]g th[r]ough the window. he was thrust out of court & 2 or 3 soldie[r]s after to kill him.—[59] King was expostulatd with. [p. 16] he repli[e]d Gentlemn you are Mormons & I have pledgd myself to exterminate you f[r]om the state.— 1839.— afterwards trieed by ⟨G[rand]—⟩ Jury. who were our guards at night.— 2 sober at a time. God damn God. & Method[i]st. &c & God damn the Mormons.—[60] when we escaped I was the worst off— Hiram [Hyrum Smith] got one of my boots & I Jumped into the mud. put on my boots without working— & when I got to water after going over 10 [12?] 15 mi Praris [prairies] my boots are full of blood.—

When I arrived at shore opposite Quincy. I saw a man talking with Gov Carlin who said God damn Joe Smith if I could get my eyes on him I^d fix him.— a ferry— beckoned me. & I put off immediately [p. 17] [George M.] Hinkle orderd a retreat[61] I rode through & orderd them to stand. 300 agist [against] 3000. a truce came & said we want Clemenson [John Cleminson] & wife & [blank] & we will protect them—[62] we will massacre all the rest.— they

---

tried for a variety of offenses, including murder, arson, burglary, robbery, and larceny. (Austin A. King, Opinion, Nov. 1838, State of Missouri v. JS et al. for Treason and Other Crimes [Mo. 5th Cir. Ct. 1838], in *Document Containing the Correspondence*, 149–151.)

59. Hyrum Smith referred to this witness as "Mr. Allen." (Hyrum Smith, Testimony, Nauvoo, IL, 1 July 1843, pp. 19–20, Nauvoo, IL, Records, CHL.)

60. At a 9–11 April 1839 hearing at Gallatin, Missouri, the Daviess County grand jury brought indictments against JS and four others. JS was charged with treason, riot, arson, larceny, and receiving stolen goods. Hyrum Smith later stated that these jurors, who aslo served as guards, sang in drunken revelry the words "'God damn God,' 'God damn Jesus Christ, God damn the Presbyterians, God damn the baptists, God damn the Methodists,'" after which they imitated behavior at religious camp meetings and bragged about their exploits against Mormons. (Hyrum Smith, Testimony, Nauvoo, IL, 1 July 1843, pp. 24–25, Nauvoo, IL, Records, CHL. See the indictments issued during the April 1839 term of the Daviess County, Missouri, Circuit Court in the following cases: State of Missouri v. JS et al. for Treason, photocopy, Max H. Parkin, Collected Missouri Court Documents, CHL; State of Missouri v. Jacob Gates et al. for Treason, photocopy, Max H. Parkin, Collected Missouri Court Documents, CHL; State of Missouri v. JS et al. for Riot, Historical Department, Nineteenth-Century Legal Documents Collection, CHL; State of Missouri v. Caleb Baldwin et al. for Arson, Historical Department, Nineteenth-Century Legal Documents Collection, CHL; State of Missouri v. Jacob Gates et al. for Arson, Historical Department, Nineteenth-Century Legal Documents Collection, CHL; State of Missouri v. James Worthington et al. for Larceny, Daviess Co., MO, Courthouse, Gallatin, MO; and State of Missouri v. JS for Receiving Stolen Goods, photocopy, Max H. Parkin, Collected Missouri Court Documents, CHL; see also Baugh, "We Took Our Change of Venue," 63–65.)

61. At this point, the conversation reverted back to events at Far West, Missouri, just prior to Major General Samuel D. Lucas's arrest of Mormon leaders at the end of October 1838.

62. The Missourians offered protection to Cleminson; to his wife, Lydia Lightner Cleminson; and to Adam Lightner Jr. and his wife, Mary Elizabeth Rollins Lightner. Adam Lightner was not a member of the church, and John Cleminson was apparently disaffected from the church at the time, as he testified against JS before Judge Austin A. King at the November 1838 hearing in Richmond, Missouri. ("Mary

refused to go.— I said go tell that army to retreat in 5 minutes or we'll give them hell.— & they run—[63] Ex-Gov. carlin told Butterfield a few days since[64] at Springfield he thought Joseph Smith had left Nauvoo. He[65] was there 3 weeks ago— with Long beard & slouch hat to bye & Bowie knife. & some one present knew— him & he had gone off

8— Joseph said to Judge Adams [p. 18] [66]that christ & the Resurrected saints will reign over the earth, but not dwell on the earth visit it when ⟨go⟩ they please or when necessary to govern it. There will be wicked men ⟨on⟩ the earth during the 1000 years. The heathen nations who will not come up to worship will be destroyed.

Joseph gave a lecture on med[ic]ine salt vinegar & pepper given internally. & plunging in the river when the parozyism[67] [paroxysm] begin. will cure the Cholera [p. 19]

31 December 1842 • Saturday

31— 9 a,m,— Esqr [Justin] Butterfield came in— said Pittman [James Pitman] told Sec of State[68] that [Thomas] King had the writ & he had shewed his letter to King ⟨he⟩ said he was coming up some time & he would bring it.[69] Joseph Signed a pitition to Gov [Thomas] Ford for a new writ. that his case might be tried theron.[70] 11 A.M. esqr Butterfield called with Deputy Ja^s M Maxcy:

Elizabeth Rollins Lightner," 197–199; John Cleminson, Testimony, Richmond, MO, Nov. 1838, State of Missouri v. JS et al. for Treason and Other Crimes [Mo. 5th Cir. Ct. 1838], in State of Missouri, "Evidence.")

63. In pursuit of a Mormon scouting party, General Alexander Doniphan's force of about 250 men halted "within 200 yards" of Mormon troops defending Far West late in the day on 30 October. General Samuel D. Lucas reported that, facing an estimated 800 Mormons, Doniphan's troops withdrew to the militia's main encampment, postponing potential confrontation until the following day. (Samuel D. Lucas, "near Far West," to Lilburn W. Boggs, 2 Nov. 1838, copy, Mormon War Papers, MSA.)

64. At this point, Willard Richards returned to reporting events at hand.

65. JS.

66. TEXT: Willard Richards began this page with notes on lines one and five lightly written in graphite, over which he wrote the journal entry in ink. Penciled notes read: "Nations that do not come up" and "christ & resurrected s[a]ints. [a]bove the earth".

67. TEXT: Possibly "parozyms".

68. Lyman Trumbull.

69. Pitman showed King a letter from secretary of state Lyman Trumbull requesting that Pitman, or whoever was in possession of Thomas Carlin's original writ, bring the writ to Springfield. (Lyman Trumbull, Springfield, IL, to James Pitman, Quincy, IL, Dec. [1842], Secretary of State, General Correspondence, Illinois State Archives, Springfield.)

70. JS came to Springfield in custody of Wilson Law, who had arrested him on 26 December 1842 on authority of Illinois governor Thomas Carlin's proclamation. When it became clear that Carlin's original (August 1842) arrest warrant for JS would not be available, JS sought a new arrest warrant to authorize his custody by the sheriff of Sangamon County, to whom the writ of habeas corpus could be directed. (JS, Journal, 26 Dec. 1842; JS, Petition for New Arrest Warrant, 31 Dec. 1842, p. 382 herein; Clayton, Journal, 31 Dec. 1842.)

Penciled draft beneath penned inscription. Lines one and five on page 19 were drafted in graphite; the entry was then written in ink, covering the penciled notes. Image enhancement and multispectral imaging helped reveal the original inscription. Top: unenhanced photograph. Middle: enhanced photograph. Bottom: multispectral image. Handwriting of Willard Richards. JS, Journal, Dec. 1842–June 1844, bk. 1, p. 19, JS Collection, Church History Library, Salt Lake City. (Photographs by Welden C. Andersen; multispectral image by Gene A. Ware.)

Lyman Trumbull. In preparation for Joseph Smith's 4 January 1843 habeas corpus hearing, Illinois secretary of state Lyman Trumbull requested Adams County constable James Pitman to bring the original warrant for Joseph Smith's arrest to Springfield. When Pitman did not produce the warrant, Trumbull and Thomas Ford, the newly elected governor of Illinois, issued a new warrant to William F. Elkin, sheriff of Sangamon County, for Smith's arrest. (Courtesy Abraham Lincoln Presidential Library and Museum, Springfield, IL.)

having the Gov.r writ— ~~& Habeus Corpus~~ &.— the parties repair immediately to Mess[rs]— [Benjamin] Edwards & Butterfilds office where Butterfild read a Petition to Judge [Nathaniel] Pope of the U. S. C. C.[71] & Joseph Signd. it.[72] Present W.m F. Elkin Sheriff of Sangamo Co[73] [p. 20] enterd court Room before Judge Pope 11½ A.M. heard several decisions in Bankruptcy.— when Esqr Butterfeild read the pitition of Joseph— next stated that the writ & warrant was different from the riqusition [requisition] of the Gov Mo[74] then read Gov Fords Warra[n]t.[75] then watsons [Samuel Weston's] affidavit.[76] next Gov [Thomas] Reynolds ~~of~~ Riquisition on Gov— of Illinois.—[77] nex[t] Proclamati[o]n of Gov [Thomas] carlin.[78] shewi[n]g that Reynol◊d. (with all deffernc [deference] to the Gov of Mo) has made a false statemnt as nothing appears in the affidavit to shew that said Smith ever was in Mo.—[79] Esqr B[utterfield] said all the authority for transpo[r]tation of persons from one state to another [p. 21] rests on the constitution & the Law of congress— we ask for Habeus Corpus because the papers are false & because we can prove that

---

71. United States circuit court, which in this period was both an appellate and a trial court. In the latter situation, the federal district judge could conduct circuit court affairs by himself. Butterfield earlier suggested that JS could present his case either to the Illinois Supreme Court or the United States circuit court. Butterfield's ultimate decision to use the United States circuit court met stiff opposition from Illinois attorney general Josiah Lamborn, who argued that this court had no jurisdiction in this case. Butterfield defended his position, and on 5 January Judge Nathaniel Pope agreed with Butterfield that the federal circuit court had jurisdiction for the hearing. (Justin Butterfield to JS, 17 Dec. 1842, p. 181 herein; JS, Journal, 4 and 5 Jan. 1843, pp. 216, 230 herein; "Circuit Court of the U. States for the District of Illinois," *Times and Seasons*, 16 Jan. 1843, 4:65–71.)

72. The petition to "the Honorable the Circut Court of the United States for the District of Illinois" requested that a writ of habeas corpus be granted whereby JS would be allowed a hearing in the federal circuit court at Springfield on the issue of whether he should be extradited to Missouri. (JS, Petition for Writ of Habeas Corpus, 31 Dec. 1842, p. 385 herein.)

73. At this point JS was arrested by Elkin—on authority of the warrant newly issued by Governor Thomas Ford—and was held in the custody of Elkin and Wilson Law. (See JS, Petition for Writ of Habeas Corpus, 31 Dec. 1842, p. 385 herein.)

74. Missouri governor Thomas Reynolds. (See Thomas Reynolds, Requisition, 22 July 1842, p. 380 herein.)

75. Arrest Warrant, 31 Dec. 1842, p. 383 herein.

76. That is, the affidavit of Lilburn W. Boggs charging JS with being "accessary before the fact" of Boggs's "intended murder," sworn to before Jackson County, Missouri, justice of the peace Samuel Weston. (Lilburn W. Boggs, Affidavit, 20 July 1842, p. 379 herein.)

77. Governor Reynolds's requisition demanding that JS be extradited to Missouri for his alleged complicity in the 6 May 1842 assault on Lilburn W. Boggs. (Thomas Reynolds, Requisition, 22 July 1842, p. 380 herein.)

78. Thomas Carlin, Proclamation, 20 Sept. 1842, p. 381 herein.

79. Reynolds's requisition to Carlin described JS as "a fugitive from justice" and claimed that he had "fled to the State of Illinois." Lilburn W. Boggs's affidavit, however, on which Reynolds's requisition was based, said nothing about JS being in Missouri or a fugitive. (Thomas Reynolds, Requisition, 22 July 1842, pp. 380–381 herein; Lilburn W. Boggs, Affidavit, 20 July 1842, p. 379 herein.)

Joseph Smith was in this State at the time of the commission of the crime— writ is granted.⁸⁰ when will it be returnd.— Esqʳ B.— instanter— it was returnd in one minute— & served.— & Joseph walked up to the bar— after a few mome[n]ts delay.— Esqr— B. read the Habeus Corbus and moved the court take bail till the court hear the case.— Judge[:] is the prisoner in custody of court or officers? Buttefild[:] of the court.— & read the Law[.] Court thought p[r]oper to take bail [p. 22] though it was ~~not~~ only a Misdemeanor.⁸¹ Gen [James] Adams & Gen [Wilson] Law were— baild in the sum of $~~2000~~ 4000— 2000 each⁸² & Monday was set for Trial—⁸³ court rose, & as ~~co~~ the co[mpany] dispersed. (for the room was crowded)— and came to the bottom a row commencd. ⟨one or two rowdies— See Note A. Page 74⟩⁸⁴ swearing &c— which was quelled by interf[er]ence of the marshall after we had tarried above a few minutes— 20 ⟨mi⟩— one. Esqr B. accompanied Joseph to the Govenors room who was sick— said he had a requisition for renewal of Prosecution in the old case of Treason again[s]t Missouri but I happend to know it was all dead.—⁸⁵ dined with Esqr Butterfeld at American House⁸⁶ returnd to Govᵣˢ ⁸⁷

---

80. Writ of Habeas Corpus, 31 Dec. 1842, p. 386 herein.

81. Pursuant to the 1789 federal judiciary act, Illinois in 1827 passed two laws pertinent to JS's case. One allowed a state judge to imprison a fugitive from justice, or to take bail, and the other required a judge in a habeas corpus hearing to require bail if a trial would follow, under penalty of a misdemeanor. (An Act to Establish the Judicial Courts of the United States [24 Sept. 1789], *Public Statutes at Large*, 1st Cong., 1st Sess., chap. 20, pp. 91–92, sec. 33; An Act concerning Fugitives from Justice [6 Jan. 1827], *Revised Code of Laws, of Illinois* [1826–1827], pp. 232–233, sec. 4; An Act Regulating the Proceedings on Writs of Habeas Corpus [22 Jan. 1827], *Revised Code of Laws, of Illinois* [1826–1827], p. 239.)

82. Illinois law required that if bail were admitted in a habeas corpus hearing, as it was in JS's case, the prisoner must "enter into recognizance with one or more securities." Adams and Law were bonded (rather than bailed) to stand as security for JS. (An Act Regulating the Proceedings on Writs of Habeas Corpus [22 Jan. 1827], *Revised Code of Laws, of Illinois* [1826–1827], p. 239, sec. 4.)

83. Technically a habeas corpus hearing rather than a trial. William Clayton reported the morning's activities: "This A.M. Mr Butterfield came and stated that the Sherif of Adams Co did not appear willing to bring forward the writ. This made it necessary to petition the Govᵗ [Ford] to issue a new writ, which was done and put into the hands of the Sherif of Sangamon Co. We then repaired to the U.S. Court now in Session to apply for a writ of Habeas Corpus, which was immediately granted. Monday was appointed for the trial Joseph, Wilson Law, & Judge [James] Adams had to give bail to court of $2000 each." (Clayton, Journal, 31 Dec. 1842.)

84. See manuscript page 74 (page 225 herein). The location of the note in the manuscript indicates that four days later, on 4 January 1843, Willard Richards elaborated on this incident.

85. William Clayton's journal clarifies that this was not another official requisition being made on Governor Ford but merely "some person" who "demanded another writ on the old Missouri affair." Ford, Clayton wrote, "knowing that a nolle prosequi had been entered in the case, refused to do any thing." (Clayton, Journal, 31 Dec. 1842.)

86. The American House, built by Elijah Iles in 1838, was considered the finest hotel in Springfield and was the largest hotel in the state. (Power, *Early Settlers of Sangamon County, Illinois*, 399, 537.)

87. TEXT: Possibly "Govᵗ".

Room. Present Mr [Jonathan] Scammon [p. 23] & Mr Shields,[88] conversation about Nauvoo ⟨& Gov— said he was not a re[li]gionist⟩ Joseph said to the Govenor— I have no creed to circumscribe my mind therefore the people do not like me because I do not cannot circumscribe my mind to their creeds. well said the Gov— from reports we had reason to think the mormons were a peculiar people. different from other people. having horns or something of the kind. but I find they look like other people indeed I think Mr Smith ⟨is⟩ a very good looking man.—— Mr Scammo[n] enquird about the Temple size &c— Mr Shields proposed a question about the Ligion [Nauvoo Legion] ⟨if it was to subdue the state? Jocularly—⟩— Joseph replied We have raised up a Ligeon to defend the [p. 24] state— 2. P.M. returnd to Judg [James] Adams Mr Wm Prentice [Prentiss], Marshall— was very friendly. & expressed much sorrow that he could not have the care of Gen Smith.— Joseph appointed Elders [Orson] Hyde & [John] Taylor to preach on the Morrow Dr Gray called for an introduction & Mr Taylor & Mr Also. after Supper conversation was had on the Nauvoo charter, Joseph Prophecied that before 5 years roled round Judge Duglass [Stephen A. Douglas] will acknowled[g]e that it would have been better for him to have followed my his council— Duglass had been stating to Gen Law & El[der] Taylor that it was possible to revoke political Charters but not Company Charters [p. 25] Joseph argued if a legislature has power to grant a charter for 10 years &[89] has no power to revoke it till the experation thereof, the same principle will hold good for 20. years & for 100 years— & also for a perpetual charter. it cannot be revoked in time.[90]

John Darby, came in said he was going to california[91] Joseph Said I will say as the prophet said to Hezekiah go & prosper— but ye shall not return in peace.—[92] You [James] Brewster may set out for california but he will not get there unless some body shall pick him up by the way feed him &^c—— [Zephaniah] Brewster showed me the Manuscr[i]pts [p. 26] I he enquird of the

---

88. Probably James Shields, state auditor in the administration of Governor Ford, who later served a term in the United States Senate. (Lorimer, *History of Mercer County,* 28, 478–479.)

89. TEXT: Possibly "&c".

90. The perpetual nature of the Nauvoo charter was a topic of discussion three days earlier. (JS, Journal, 28 Dec. 1842.)

91. Darby intended to follow James Brewster. In 1837, at age ten, Brewster claimed to have the gifts of prophesying and receiving revelations. In 1842 he published a pamphlet titled *The Words of Righteousness to All Men,* purporting to be an abridgment of the lost books of Esdras. Brewster and many followers began moving to California in 1850, but most, including Brewster, never reached California. Various difficulties caused the party to instead stop in New Mexico, and a short-lived attempt was made to create a settlement there. Brewster ultimately returned to Illinois. ("Notice," *Times and Seasons,* 1 Dec. 1842, 4:32; Brewster, *Words of Righteousness;* Vogel, "James Colin Brewster," 120–139.)

92. The prophet Micaiah's instructions were to Ahab, not to Hezekiah. (See 1 Kings 22:15; and 2 Chronicles 18:14.)

Lord & the Lord told me the book was not true— it was not of him If God ever cal[l]ed me. or spoke by my mouth. or gave me a revelation he never gave revelations to that Brewster Boy or any of the Brewster race[93]

In the P.M. a team ran away & went past the State house. when the cry was raised, Joe Smith is running away. which produced great excitement & produced a sudden adjournment of the House of Rep[s.] [p. 27]

1 January 1843 • Sunday

1843 January 1.st— Sunday Speaker of the House of Representatives[94] called to inform us we could have the Hall for preaching This day.

Esq[r.] Butterfieeld [Justin Butterfield] called with Esqr— Gilaspie—[95] Judge Douglass [Stephen A. Douglas], Mr Rusk.—[96] Joseph explained the nature of a prophet. Spirit of Prophecy. which is the testimony of Jesus[97] is necessary to constitute a witness or a preacher. or a prophet. 3 Gent[s.] called— one from Cass county (Esqr Pratt[98])

10¾[99] A.M. repaired to House of Repretatives[100]

11½ Elder [Orson] Hyde read the Hymn "Rejoice ye Saints of Latter Days."—[101] Elder [p. 28] [John] Taylor followed in prayr.— The Saints then sung— "The Spirit of God like a fire is burning."[102] &c 3— verses— Elder Hyde then read a portion of the 3[d] Chapter of Malichi— commencing at the beginning— 6 verses.— although strangers permit me to witness wish you all a happy new Year.— though aware ⟨of⟩ the difficultis & prejudices[103] yet we let it all pass by— like the summer threshing floors— for what is chaff to the

---

93. Prior to the publication of James Brewster's book, Brewster's father, Zephaniah, attempted to get JS's opinion of the book during a visit to Nauvoo, but the latter had no time to look at it. In June 1841, Zephaniah again went to Nauvoo with the manuscript, and this time JS examined it over the course of several days. Brewster claimed later that JS told Zephaniah that he had "not received an answer." (James C. Brewster, "The Writings of Esdras," *Olive Branch,* Oct. 1848, 33–36.)

94. Samuel Hackleton.

95. Probably former Illinois state congressman Joseph Gillespie, a Whig politician and jurist from Madison County. William Clayton's journal identifies him as "Senator Gillespie." (Linder, *Reminiscences of the Early Bench and Bar of Illinois,* 121–127; Clayton, Journal, 1 Jan. 1843.)

96. Possibly Benjamin D. Rusk. (McGregor, *Biographical Record of Jasper County, Missouri,* 340.)

97. See Revelation 19:10.

98. Probably John W. Pratt, a lawyer and politician from Cass County, Illinois. (Martin, *History of Cass County,* 2:663–665.)

99. TEXT: Possibly "11 ¾ 10 ¾".

100. TEXT: Beginning with this line, ink is darker.

101. Hymn 82, *Collection of Sacred Hymns,* 91–92.

102. Hymn 252, *Collection of Sacred Hymns,* 274–276.

103. TEXT: Possibly "prejudice".

State Capitol, Springfield, Illinois. 1858. Joseph Smith and his companions held religious services in the Illinois State Capitol on Sunday, 1 January 1843, a few days prior to his habeas corpus hearing. In the background, to the right of the capitol, stands the American House, where Smith and others ate lunch on at least two occasions. (Courtesy Abraham Lincoln Presidential Library and Museum, Springfield, IL.)

wheat saith the Lord—[104] Lord whom ye seek &.[105] supposed to be John Baptist. it was not fulfilled at coming christ. . . . after Jews returnd from Babylon— in a sho[r]t time the prophets were killed. Malachi about 500 years before Christ. last[106] Record. Hosea. sawn asunder[107] in the valley of Jehosaphet [p. 29]

From Malachi to John Baptist voice of Revelation was not heard.— John came to prepare the way.— baptizd many of the different sects.— Lawyers &c were the ones who would not be baptized— were the first to pers[e]cute & recive the curses of the Savior died in Jerusalem & ascended from Mt olivet. Temple built by the commandme[n]t of God. recived the heavenly messengers,— it became polluted.— took a whip of small cords &c.— not one stone shall not be thrown down.— German bible says which shall not be broken—[108] Temple Type of the church— Spirit of God is mind of God— when a lad I went out to feed poultry. when the corn was done eve[r]y one went his own way & sung his own [p. 30] song.— when inspiration ceased. eve[r]y one sung his own song. gross darkness covered the people. let us have this temple purified. how shall I educate my son?——— . . . God no longer speaks— there is primafacia— Evdince he never spake to you.— will send his messenger & Lord shall come suddenly.— objectd Angels no more come?— 4 ange[l]s &c in Rev— where Servants of God are sealed have a mark by which God knowns them.[109] send his angels &c.— The Lord has sent his Angel in these last days——— if the christian chu[rc]h will not be cleansd. God will put his finger on this & on that nation. &c[110] & nation will rise agai[n]st nation.— we are neithr catholic or protestant. but like the Temple [p. 31] we have not passed under the poslishing [polishing] of any denomination & the people think to throw down the Latter Day Saint under the rubbish. but they cannot do without us them.— ⟨Elder Hyde returnd thanks⟩

¼— 1 retired for dinner. ⟨to Judge [James] Adams⟩ 2½ returned to the Representatives Hall.— 3.3. Elder Hyd[e] read Hymn 154 Page,[111] & followd in prayer. Elder Taylor Read Rev 14 C. 6 & 7 verses.— Some object to my Text

---

104. See Jeremiah 23:28.
105. TEXT: Possibly "&c".
106. TEXT: Possibly "lost".
107. An old and widespread tradition names Isaiah (rather than Hosea) as having been sawn asunder by Manasseh, king of Judah. (B. Yebamoth 49b; Martyrdom and Ascension of Isaiah, chap. 5.)
108. Martin Luther's translation of Matthew 24:2 reads: "Es wird hier nicht ein Stein auf dem andern bleiben, der nicht zerbrochen werde." (Die Bibel, Matthai 24:2.)
109. See Revelation 7:1–3.
110. TEXT: Possibly "F".
111. Hyde was reading "Lo the mighty God appearing," which begins on page 154 in Emma Smith's 1841 compilation of hymns. (Hymn 141, *Collection of Sacred Hymns*, 154–155.)

in Rev. because it is so mysterious. whatever is revealed is not a mystery.— Blessed is he that readeth, &c[112] might refer to the minist[er]ing[113] of angels to Noah Abra⟨m⟩ Ezekial— Paul, Peter, [*illegible*].—[114] old. & new Testame[n]t is not the gospel.— as a map is not the country it represents. it tells [p. 32] what the gospel is.— Gospel is good news a savor of life to them that receive or the savor of Death. unto death to those who reject— gospel is the power of God unto Salvation go ye into all the world & preach the Gospel &c these signs shall follow them &c faith. Repenta[n]ce, Baptism, Laying on of hands—[115] certain officers— enough that we have it in the Bible can read of those things which were tong[u]es dreams &c—— a man has a history of a feast in his pocket can read it in the wilderness. to keep from starving.— 4½ Elder Taylor returnd thanks to the audience & the Lord. & meeti[n]g dispersd [p. 33]

went to Bro Bowman's to supper his wife ⟨Julia Stringham⟩ was baptizd at colesville one of the first fruits. Many Saints called to see the President— while supper was preparing Joseph related an anecdote. while young his father had a fine large watch dog. which bit off an ear from David Staffords hog, which stafford had turnd into ~~the~~ ⟨Smith⟩ corn field. Stafford ⟨shot the Dog, &⟩ with six other fellows pitchd upon him unawares. & Joseph whipped. the whole of them.— & escaped unhurt. ⟨which they swore to as recorded in Hurlburts [Doctor Philastus Hurlbut's] or [Eber] Howe'ss Book⟩[116]

while in Kirtland a Baptist Pri[e]st came in my house & abused my family— I turnd him out of doors. he raised his cane to strike me [p. 34] & continud to abuse me. I whipped him till he begged.— he threatend to proscute me— I sent Luke Johnson the cunstable after him & he run him out of the County into Mentor[117]

7 returnd To Judge Adams

2 January 1843 • Monday

January 2d. Monday After breakfast Joseph Prophecid in the name of the Lord God I shall not ⟨go⟩ to Missouri dead or alive. Mr [Abraham] Jonas. from Adams— called conversed on the policy of modifying the city charters

---

112. See Revelation 1:3.
113. TEXT: Possibly "ministiry".
114. TEXT: Illegible word is possibly "paul" or "pool".
115. See Mark 16:15–18.
116. JS was acquainted with Stafford in Manchester, Ontario County, New York, in the 1820s. Stafford's derogatory statement mentioned a fight with JS but did not mention any incident involving a dog or a hog. (Howe, *Mormonism Unvailed*, 249–250.)
117. For a more complete account of this story, see "History of Luke Johnson," 6–7, Historian's Office, Histories of the Twelve, ca. 1858–1880, CHL.

[118]9½ A.M. repaired to the court house. 10— court opend. Judge [Nathaniel] Pope present. Docket read by the clerk in matter of Joseph Smith. & then of various Bankrupts.— [p. 35] when the court opend Joseph was with his Atorny[119] in his office retsed [rested] while the Docket was reading at the close of the reading— The Marshall[120] waited on 7 Ladies who took their seats beside the Judge—[121] The state Attorney ⟨Esqr Lambern [Josiah Lamborn]⟩ requested the case to be continud till tomorrow mor[n]ing out of respect to the officers of State & of the Gov.r of Missouri— Wednesday morning was set for trial.— Esqr [Justin] Butterfield moveed to file some objections to facts set forth in the Habus Corpus——[122] Joseph smith is not a fugitive from Justice. was not in Mo— [p. 36] at that time— has not been for 3 years— &c but was in Nauvoo when the attack was made on Lilburn W. Boggs— filed— Ladi[e]s retired— 10½ repaired to the Senate lobby had conversation with Senator [Jacob] Davis.[123] & Mr Webber.[124] (Resolution lost. to make up the defircit [deficit] of the failure of the state Bank to public offices)[125] Major [Edward] Baker of Sangamon: Senator. appears much like an african Monken [Monkey]. ⟨at ⟨one⟩ moment standing by one stove. the next by another on the opposite side of the chamber. setting down in every senators chair in his way & he never gooes out of his way for his way is every where & his nose in every mans facce. eating apples staring at & pointing & staring at every one. next mome[n]t in the Galery pointing the Ladies to Old Joe.[126] whom. he once drilled his regime[n]t to go again[s]t— & slaugh[t]er him or give him up to Missouri an eavesdropper— a monkey without a monkey's wit⟩ [p. 37]

J[acob] B. Backenstos wishing to return to Carthage gave the names of Witnesses who dined with Josep on the 7[th] of May.[127] James. H. Ralston I. N.

---

118. TEXT: Darker ink begins.
119. Justin Butterfield.
120. William Prentiss.
121. Such was public interest in the proceedings of the Springfield court in the JS case that several "distinguished ladies of Springfield" attended Judge Pope on the bench, including Mary Todd Lincoln (recently married to Abraham Lincoln). Lincoln's law office was located in the same building, owned by Seth Tinsley, in which the hearing was held. ("The Mormon Jubilee," *The Wasp*, 14 Jan. 1843, [1]; Randall, *Mary Lincoln*, 74, 77; Arnold, *Reminiscences of the Illinois Bar*, 5–7.)
122. The objections of the defense were filed in JS, Affidavit, 2 Jan. 1843, p. 387 herein.
123. Davis was formerly a clerk of the circuit court in Hancock County. (See JS, Journal, 13 Dec. 1841, pp. 15–16 herein.)
124. Possibly George R. Weber, publisher of the *Illinois Republican* in Springfield.
125. The resolution would have instructed "the committee on Finance to inquire into the expediency and legality of providing by law for remunerating public officers for losses sustained on account of the depreciation of State Bank paper." (*Journal of the Senate . . . of Illinois*, 2 Jan. 1843, 138.)
126. JS.
127. The witnesses were given as evidence that JS was not in Missouri when Boggs was shot on

[Isaac Newton] Morris. ⟨canal. Com¹²⁸⟩ A ⟨Almeron⟩. Wheat. Rep¹²⁹ ⟨Geo C.⟩ Dixon— at the ⟨Mrs [Salome Paddock] Enos—⟩ brick Hotel. ⟨Jud⟩ ~~dined with G~~ several Senators came & conversed with Joseph, ⟨viz— Chief Justice [William] Wilson—¹³⁰ of Illinois Court.—⟩

A discussion arose in the senate on the propriety of Taxing the rich for repair of Road⟨s⟩. Davis spoke in favor. Bill laid on the Table till 4[th] July.— ~~Mr~~ Repaird 12 oclck to Senator Davis private Room. Mr Nye,¹³¹ called.— dineed at the American [House Hotel] opposite Judge Pope & [Henry] Brown. as we rose from the table Judge Brown invited Joseph to his room. & told him he was about publishing a histo[r]y of Illinois— & wished him [p. 38] to furnish a history of the rise & faith of the Church of Latter Day Saints to add to his histo[r]y.—¹³² 1½ retur[ne]d to Jud[g]e [James] Adams.— A gentlemn from St. Louis told General [Wilson] ⟨Law⟩ that the "General impression was that Joseph was innocent. & it would be a kind of murder to give him up— they thought he ought to be whipt a little & let go."

It is evident that prejudice is giving way. & good feeling is gaining ascendency in the public mind.—

4 o clock Esqrʳ Lambern. states attorny— the Marshall & some 1/2 dozen others called. the Marshall said it was the fi[r]st time in [p. 39] his administrati[o]n that the Ladies had attended court. on a trial.—

Mr [Isaac] Mc Coy of Missourie told the marshall that he tried to pacify the people & keep the peace". it was false he headed a co[mpany]— & was a leader in the Mob—¹³³

---

6 May 1842.

128. Morris became the president of the Illinois & Michigan Canal Company in 1841. (*Biographical Directory of the United States Congress,* 1535.)

129. Wheat served as a representative for Adams County in the Illinois legislature from 1842 to 1843. (*Journal of the House of Representatives . . . of Illinois,* 5 Dec. 1842, 4.)

130. Wilson had served as the chief justice of the Illinois Supreme Court since 1825. (Davidson and Stuvé, *Complete History of Illinois,* 328–330.)

131. Possibly Iram Nye, sergeant-at-arms of the Illinois Senate. (*Journal of the Senate . . . of Illinois,* 5 Dec. 1842, 5.)

132. The history is Henry Brown, *The History of Illinois, from Its First Discovery and Settlement, to the Present Time* (New York: J. Winchester, New World Press, 1844). Chapter 20 and the appendix both deal with JS and Mormonism. JS may have provided Brown with the same information included in Orson Pratt's *Several Remarkable Visions,* or possibly Pratt's pamphlet itself. Alternatively, or in addition, JS may have given Brown the article "Church History," published ten months earlier in the *Times and Seasons*. (Orson Pratt, *Interesting Account of Several Remarkable Visions,* [Edinburgh: Ballantyne and Hughes, 1840]; "Church History," *Times and Seasons,* 1 Mar. 1842, 3:706–710.)

133. McCoy, a Baptist reverend, was involved in a number of activities to drive church members from Jackson County, Missouri, in summer and fall 1833. Although McCoy clearly wanted the Mormons to leave Jackson County, he explained in a contemporaneous journal entry that he joined a company of vigilantes with the intent to prevent death and injury to the Mormons, after he perceived that the

Esqr Lambern remarked "Mr Smith is a very good looking Jovial man["]

Examind his head said ~~he~~ Jocosely I think he is not particularly given to burglery. rape & murder[134]

Esqr Lindsey had much converati [conversation]

Marshall was very Jovial & [p. 40] pleasant & a peculiarly pleasant & conciliato[r]y feeling prevaaield [prevailed] through the compa[n]y— & the Marshall invitd Joseph to a family dinner when he was freed.—

5 ⟨o clock⟩ went to Mr Wm Sollars[135] Mr Bridewood visited. in the eve Elder [Orson] Hyde was present. & after Supper asked what is the situation of the Negro? They come into the world slaves mentally & phy[s]ically. change their situation with the white & they would be like them. they have souls & are subjects of salvation go into cincinati— & find one— educated rid[e]s in his carriage he has [p. 41] risen by the power of his mind to his exal[te]d state. of r[e]spectability. Slaves in washington more refind than the presidents. boys will take the shine off those they brush & wait on.—

Says Elder Hyde put them on the level & they will rise above me.— Joseph[:] if I raised you to be my equal & then attempt to oppress you would you not be indignant, & Try to rise above me? ~~did not~~— Oliver Cowd[e]ry & Peter Whitmer[136] & ma[n]y others say I was fallen & they were cap[a]ble of Leading the people [p. 42] had I any thing to do with the negro— I would confine them ~~to~~ by strict Laws to their own Species put them on a national Equalization

Because faith is wanting the fruits are not.— No man Since the world was ever had faith without having something along with it. The ancients quenched the violence of escaped the edged of the sword women recevd their Dead. &^c by faith the worlds were made.—[137] a man who has none of the gifts— has no faith he deceives himseff if he supposes it. faith has been wanting not only

---

vigilantes were bent on revenge, and that he arranged for the group to remain at a distance from individual Mormon homes while he and a few others asked the Mormons to surrender their arms. (Lewis Abbott, Affidavit, Adams Co., IL, 25 June 1839, photocopy, Material relating to Mormon expulsion from Missouri, 1839–1843, CHL; Lemuel Herrick, Affidavit, Adams Co., IL, 8 Jan. 1840, photocopy, Material relating to Mormon expulsion from Missouri, 1839–1843, CHL; "A History, of the Persecution," *Times and Seasons,* Jan. 1840, 1:33–36; McCoy, Journal, 6 Nov. 1833, quoted in Jennings, "Isaac McCoy and the Mormons," 70–71.)

134. A reference to phrenology.

135. Sollars lived in Springfield from 1840 until his death in 1854. ("Death of Mrs. Eliza Sollars," *Decatur [IL] Daily Review,* 17 Apr. 1887, [4].)

136. Probably David Whitmer, who, along with Cowdery, was excommunicated from the church in April 1838. David's brother Peter died in full fellowship of the church in September 1836. (Minute Book 2, 12 and 13 Apr. 1838; Oliver Cowdery, "The Closing Year," *LDS Messenger and Advocate,* Dec. 1836, 3:425–429.)

137. See Hebrews 11:3, 34–35.

among the heathen but but professed Christedom also.— that Tongues. & heali[n]gs [p. 43] & prophecy. & prophets & apostles & all these gifts & blessings have been wanting.—— Joseph spoke at great length. & edification. to the little co[mpany]

⟨obje[c]tions being made to the prophets meeknss⟩— I am meek & lowly in hea[r]t[138] I will personify Jesus for a moment to illustrate & you ~~inquiry~~ inquirers— Wo unto you ye Doctors Wo unto you ye scribes pharises & Hypocrits—[139]

You cannot find the place where I ever went that I found fault with their food their drink their house[140] or their Lodging— no never, & this is what is meant &[141] by the meekness & Lowliness of Jesus [p. 44]

Mr Sollars stated that James Mullone— carpenter, of Springfield told him he "had been to Nauvoo & seen Joe Smith the prophet. he had a grey horse & I asked him where he got it & the Prophet said, you see that white cloud? yes, well ~~it~~ as it come[142] along I got[143] the horse from that cloud" Joseph replied <u>it was a lie. I never told him so.</u>[144]

⟨In referen[ce] to professors Generally.⟩ what is it inspires us with a hope of Salvation? It is that smooth sophi[s]ticated influence of the Devil by which he deceives the whole world.—

Mr. Sollars says may I not Repent & be baptizd & not pay any attention to dreams & visions. &ᶜ? Joseph said suppose I am Travilling. & I am hungry I'[145] meet [p. 45] a man & tell him I am hungry. he tells me to go yonder, there is a house for Entertainment, go knock, & you must conform to all the rules of the house or you cannot satisfy your hunger— knock call for food. & set down & eat.— & I go & knock— & ask for food & set down to the table— but do not eat shall I satisfy my hunger— <u>No! I must Eat. the Gifts are the food</u>.—

The <u>graces</u> of the spirit are the <u>Gifts</u> of the spirit.—

Joseph[:] When I first commencd this work & had got 2 or 3 indiv[i]duals to believe I went about 30 miles with Oliver Cowdery— one horse between us to see [p. 46] them.[146] When we arrivd a mob of a hundrd came upon us before we had time to eat. & chased us all night & we arrived back again about 60 miles in all. and without food a little after Day light.—— I have

---

138. See Matthew 11:29.
139. See Matthew 23:13–15, 23, 25, 27, 29.
140. TEXT: Possibly "food" or "board".
141. TEXT: Or "&c".
142. TEXT: Possibly "came".
143. TEXT: Possibly "get".
144. TEXT: "so" is double underlined.
145. TEXT: Possibly "&".
146. The events JS describes here took place in summer 1830 during a trip he took with Cowdery to visit the recently baptized Saints in Colesville, Broome County, New York. (JS History, vol. A-1, 47.)

often travelled all night to see the brethren. & often been turnd away without food;— Evening closed by singing & prayer. pr El[der] Hyde— posted the bed on the floor— Joseph. Orson. & willard [Richards]—

3 January 1843 • Tuesday

8 [a.m.?] 3ᵈ ~~Dec~~ Jan— Tuesday ⟨1843⟩ called, after breakfast. on Sister Crane, & blessed the boy, Joseph Smith, retur[ne]d to Judge [James] Adams. present M[r] Trobridge Mr Bears [*blank*] Mr [Abraham] Jonas & Esqr [Orville H.] Browning conversed on the old Missouri case[147] [p. 47] ⟨Esqr Browning expressed the best of feeling⟩

9½ repaired to court Room. presnt Mr Butterfied [Justin Butterfield]. Owen—[148] [Nathaniel] Pope, Prentice [William Prentiss] & Mr Prentice told a very int[er]esting story concerning Bro. Eddy's.[149] debate with Mr Slocum[150] the presbyterian Priest on the Steam boat— Nonpariel[151] in august last. presnt at that time Rev Mr wells. & Mc Coy—[152] affidavits prepard[153] during the P.M.— Joseph at. Judge Adams— at Dusk

the Marshall, Mr Prentice, calld with subpoena's & sat some time & retold the story about Rev Mr Slocum. &c— after he retird Joseph prophcied in the name of the Lord that no very formidable [p. 48] opposition would be raised at the Trial on the morrow.—

---

147. Browning defended JS when the state of Missouri attempted to extradite him in June 1841 on a charge of treason growing from the 1838 conflict. Judge Stephen A. Douglas heard his case on 9–10 June 1841, at Monmouth, Illinois, and discharged JS due to a faulty warrant. ("Letter from the Editor," *Times and Seasons*, 15 June 1841, 2:449; "The Late Proceedings," *Times and Seasons*, 15 June 1841, 2:447–449; Requisition for JS, 1 Sept. 1840, State of Missouri v. JS for Treason [Warren Co. Cir. Ct. 1841], JS Extradition Records, Abraham Lincoln Presidential Library, Springfield, IL.)

148. Possibly Thomas Owen, representative from Hancock County, or James F. Owings, clerk of the United States Circuit Court for the District of Illinois. (Gregg, *History of Hancock County, Illinois*, 736–737; JS, Affidavit, 2 Jan. 1843, p. 387 herein.)

149. Probably Cyrus L. Eddy, a convert to the church who moved from Maine to Lee County, Iowa, in 1842. (*History of Iowa County, Iowa*, 650–651.)

150. Probably Reverend John Jay Slocum, prominent Presbyterian minister from New York whose involvement in the anti-Catholic Maria Monk publications earned him national recognition. (See *Awful Disclosures of Maria Monk, as Exhibited in a Narrative of Her Sufferings during a Residence of Five Years as a Novice, and Two Years as a Black Nun, in the Hotel Dieu Nunnery at Montreal* [New York: Howe and Bates, 1836]; and *Further Disclosures by Maria Monk, concerning the Hotel Dieu Nunnery of Montreal; Also Her Visit to Nuns' Island, and Disclosures concerning That Secret Retreat. Preceded by a Reply to the Priests' Book, by Rev. J. J. Slocum* [New York: Maria Monk, 1837].)

151. The *Nonpareil* was a 176-ton steamship operating between St. Louis and Pittsburgh. It sank in the Mississippi after being snagged in November 1842. ("Another Steamboat Lost," *Boston Courier*, 1 Dec. 1842, [2].)

152. Possibly Isaac McCoy, the Baptist minister from Missouri whose activities JS and others discussed the previous day. (JS, Journal, 2 Jan. 1843, p. 211 herein.)

153. TEXT: Possibly "proposd".

evening spent in a very social manner— the most harmonious feeling prevaild closd by Singing & Prayer by Elder [Orson] Hyde

Joseph Lodged on the soffa— as he has eve[r]y night but one sinc[e] he has been in Springfield [*6 lines blank*] [p. 49]

Mr Butterfield wrote drafts of Affidavits[154]

[155]12 retired to Judg Adams

---------- ☙ ----------

Editorial Note

Willard Richards's scanty notes recorded here in JS's journal are the only record known to have been made during this 4 January 1842 habeas corpus hearing.[156] The hearing debate centered on Illinois attorney general Josiah Lamborn's two objections to the proceedings: first, that extradition was a state matter and, therefore, that the federal court had no jurisdiction; and second, that evidence concerning guilt or innocence could not be heard on habeas corpus. Justin Butterfield challenged these objections by arguing first that the United States circuit court not only had jurisdiction in the case but under the circumstances had exclusive jurisdiction, since extradition is a matter between two states; and second, that presenting evidence concerning JS's whereabouts on 6 May 1842 did not establish guilt or innocence but rather that JS was not a fugitive from justice. For JS's case to fall within the purview of extradition law, he first had to be a fugitive.[157]

Butterfield then showed the illegality of the documents used to arrest JS. He pointed out that Lilburn W. Boggs's affidavit said nothing about JS having fled from justice in Missouri and that Missouri governor Thomas Reynolds had misrepresented the wording of the affidavit in demanding extradition. Boggs's affidavit simply said that JS was "accessary before the fact" and that he was a "resident of Illinois." Reynolds added that it had been represented to him that JS was "a fugitive from justice." Butterfield pointed out that JS had not been in Missouri since sometime before the attempt on Boggs's life and therefore that neither Boggs nor Reynolds had grounds to demand JS's extradition.[158]

---------- ☙ ----------

---

154. The two affidavits Butterfield prepared were statements confirming that JS was in Nauvoo in May 1842 at the time when the attempt was made on Lilburn W. Boggs's life. (Wilson Law and Others, Affidavit, 4 Jan. 1843, p. 388 herein; Jacob B. Backenstos and Stephen A. Douglas, Affidavit, 4 Jan. 1843, p. 389 herein.)

155. TEXT: This sentence is inscribed in lighter ink that matches that in the following entry.

156. Court Ruling, 5 Jan. 1843, p. 390 herein; see also "Circuit Court of the U. States for the District of Illinois," *Times and Seasons*, 16 Jan. 1843, 4:65–71; "Circuit Court of the United States for the District of Illinois," *Sangamo Journal* (Springfield, IL), 19 Jan. 1843, [1]; "Ex Parte Joseph Smith—the Mormon Prophet," 57–67.

157. U.S. Constitution, art. 4, sec. 2; An Act respecting Fugitives from Justice, and Persons Escaping from the Service of Their Masters [12 Feb. 1793], *Public Statutes at Large*, 2nd Cong., 2nd Sess., chap. 7, p. 302, secs. 1–2.

158. "The Release of Gen. Joseph Smith," *Times and Seasons*, 2 Jan. 1843, 4:60.

4 January 1843 • Wednesday

~~Dec~~ ⟨Jan⟩— 4. Wednesday 9 A. Repared to court Room— in [Justin] Butterfield's officce a few moments

court opened—— while Docket was reading the Ladies came in & took their seats by the side of the Judge— [*illegible*]¹⁵⁹ 6 ⟨Ladies⟩ By court "Gentlemn of the Bar any motions. this morning?["] sworn Wilson Law. H[enry] G. Sherwood Theodore Turl[e]y ⟨Shadrach Roundy William Clayton John Taylor William Marks Lorin Walker Willard Richards—⟩ [p. 50] matter of Joseph Smith Mr Butterfield— (2 Ladies come in)

Attory. Gen ~~motion to~~ J. Lambern [Josiah Lamborn] no ~~Justice~~ Jurisdiction ⟨⟨motion of Mr Lambern⟩⟩

no jurisdicti[o]n to enquire into any facts behind the writ

⟨By the court⟩

court will take up the case entire.

Buterfild— Josph Smith is in custody— under color of authority of the Unitd States accesary to the shooting of Gov— [p. 51] [Lilburn W.] Boggs on the 6[th]. of May

Read the affidavit of 10 witnesses.—¹⁶⁰

⟨Stephn A⟩ Douglass [Stephen A. Douglas] & ⟨J[acob] B.⟩ Backenstos sworn to affdavit— affidavit. read.¹⁶¹

Esqr Lambern— I am much at a loss how I got into this case as prosecuti[n]g attorney. I dont. know.— ⟨why th[e]⟩ district attorny— ~~admitted.~~—— ⟨should bring this case in this court. which I contend has⟩ no Jurisdiction ⟨except of common Law.—⟩ of common Law Jurisdiction— 2ᵈ condensed report— p 37 page— Ballman—¹⁶² Courts of U. States have no authoritey where there is no Law. evident on the face of the [p. 52] papers that he is not arrested under the authority of the ⟨Unitd⟩ State— but of our state.— Statute of our own state ⟨has Jurisdiction⟩— not contradictory to unitd states laws— ⟨Read⟩ Gales Statu[t]e 315. Page—¹⁶³ fugitives f[r]om Justice.

whole proceedings illegal untill they can shew ~~is~~ that this law is unconstitutio[n]al— complia[n]ce on the part of the Gov— with State law— ⟨Read⟩ Conklins Treaties 51.— Page—¹⁶⁴ there is no general jurisdiction— in

---

159. TEXT: Possibly "~~No~~" or "~~In~~".
160. One of two affidavits prepared by Butterfield the previous night. (Wilson Law and Others, Affidavit, 4 Jan. 1843, p. 388 herein.)
161. Jacob B. Backenstos and Stephen A. Douglas, Affidavit, 4 Jan. 1843, p. 389 herein.
162. *Ex Parte* Bollman and *Ex Parte* Swartwout, 2 Peters Condensed 37 (1807).
163. Actually, page 318. (An Act concerning Fugitives from Justice [6 Jan. 1827], *Public and General Statute Laws of the State of Illinois* [1834–1837], pp. 318–320.)
164. Conkling, *Treatise on the Organization, Jurisdiction and Practice of the Courts*, 51.

Legal counsel for Joseph Smith. As United States attorney for the district of Illinois, Justin Butterfield (left) represented the interests of the United States in Joseph Smith's bankruptcy case. At the same time, he and Benjamin S. Edwards (right) served as Joseph Smith's counsel at the 4 January 1843 habeas corpus hearing in Springfield. (Courtesy Abraham Lincoln Presidential Library and Museum, Springfield, IL.)

this case— the only autho[r]ity of this court— in the Digest read.— Conklins Treaties 85.—¹⁶⁵ if sheriff refuses to give up a prisoner [p. 53] he has all the force¹⁶⁶ ⟨of the state t̶o̶⟩ to back him ⟨Read⟩ 2ᵈ cond[e]nsed 55.—¹⁶⁷ washi[n]gton reports¹⁶⁸ &c¹⁶⁹

The party attempts¹⁷⁰ to prove an allibi— can such a defence be made here— can the court try this part of the case that smith was in this state.— no court ⟨is⟩ competent to try the case, if ⟨we⟩ go behind the papers then we can try the whole case;— we are trying the guilt or innocencce.— Court. ⟨said the⟩ qustion is not the guilt or innocenc[e]. o̶r̶ but is he a fugitive. . . . ⟨Lambern said⟩ if the court could understa[n]d me. ⟨court⟩ the court does understa[n]d you perfe[c]tly. i̶f̶ [p. 54] Lambern. if the papers are sufficient— you abandon the papers & go into the case. the whole case.— guilt or innocence— did he flee f[r]om Mo? is ⟨he⟩ a fugitive f[r]om Justice? Gov is bound to surrender him as a fugitive. Gov has complied with the statute— ⟨By the⟩ Court: ⟨Do you say the⟩ Judge of the S. C. [supreme court] of Ill[inois] could not issue— a Habus Corpus?— Lambern. [I] dont deny Habeus Corpus.— party brought up has no right ⟨to⟩ go into trial on any of the facts behind Record— ⟨read⟩ Gordons Digest—¹⁷¹ [blank] Charles 2ᵈ— Grant Habeus corpus ⟨Act⟩—¹⁷² Large Majority of English Judges submittd to the 12 by Parliamnt 9 Wendell [p. 55] 2̶0̶1̶ 212 page¹⁷³ if he prophe[s]ied that Boggs should be shot.— where should he be tried? in Mo.— Some instances in N. York, &c Maine &c— on accou[n]t of Slaves &c— one indepedant [independent] state equals anothr indepedat state. decision made for political effect in those cases

Positivily, I take ⟨it⟩ this cou[r]t has no Jurisdiction— no disrespect to court.— party not held by united states Laws. but of Illinois. ⟨subject to the Jurisdiction of⟩ our own Governm[en]t.— if they had a right— it would be only to try the papers. our own Statutes cover the ground. & no other courts have authority. ⟨the⟩ Lawyers agree with me. [p. 56] with few Exception.— no Jurisdicti[o]n— no court has power to try the papers.—

---

165. Conkling, *Treatise on the Organization, Jurisdiction and Practice of the Courts*, 85.
166. TEXT: Possibly "forces".
167. *Ex Parte* Bollman and *Ex Parte* Swartwout, 2 Peters Condensed 55 (1807). TEXT: "55" is possibly an insertion.
168. *Ex Parte* Cabrera, 1 Washington's C.C. Reports 232 (Washington, Circuit Justice, 1805).
169. TEXT: Possibly "⟨&c⟩".
170. TEXT: Possibly "forces".
171. Thomas Gordon, *A Digest of the Laws of the United States* (Philadelphia: By the author, 1827).
172. Commonly known as the Habeas Corpus Act, the "Act for the Better Securing the Liberty of the Subject, and for Prevention of Imprisonments beyond the Seas" was passed by the Parliament of England in 1679 during the reign of Charles II.
173. *In re* Clark, 9 Wendell 212 (N.Y. Sup. Ct. 1832).

⟨Esqr⟩ Edwad [Benjamin Edwards:]. ⟨Esqr Lambern is⟩ in the dark— ⟨does not know⟩ why ⟨he is made the⟩ prosecutor— he ⟨is⟩ not a prosecutor— but ⟨is permitted to come in here—⟩ a matter of corttesy.— fugitives— ⟨must be taken by⟩ virtue of the constituti[o]n of the Unitd ⟨states⟩ Kents Comme[n]taries 2ᵈ vol 32 in th[e] notes.[174] Jud[i]cial power extends in all cases— where the action arises under U.S. laws[175]—— Tremendoeas power of the executive to deliver up an affidavit to enquire— into the fact. greater than any Emperor ever used to be transplantd from his home.— Transplanting of Individuals from these colenies [p. 57] to great Britain— 7 years war f[r]amers of Constitution would vest the Governers of the States with the same powers[176] of oppression.— ⟨suppose he is gui[l]ty in view of the retributive Justice due for the murders &—⟩

Boggs— affidavit.[177] that Joe Smith has been accesary ⟨to the shooting of himself⟩.— this p[e]ople whom he has compelled to flee f[r]om Missouri— ⟨which does the fleeing refer to⟩ f[r]om the shooting of Boggs— or the fleeing of this people from the Mo. Mob

◊[178] Mr Butterfield. 1st question by Attry Gen— ⟨that this court has⟩ no Jurisdict[io]n to relieve— & says that this is the opinion of the bar— ⟨I have a⟩ great respct for the bar— ⟨but a⟩ contempt for out door ⟨& bar room⟩ opinion; ⟨without thought. or reading⟩ this court has exclusive Jurisdiction. ~~Law~~ ⟨Prisonr⟩ is [p. 58] arrested under Con of U. S.— & Law— arising under the Constitution.— ◊◊w ⟨power⟩ 2 sec 4^[th] art[icle] Constitution delive[re]d up on dem[a]nd made ⟨by dema[n]d made under color of U.S. Law—⟩ any Executive of the Union— shall dem[a]nd. & produce copy inditcmnt [indictment] or affidavit. ⟨the fugitive shall be⟩ arrestd & securd—was Jose Smith arrested by law of this state— no "⟨most⟩ untruly has it been statd here" Does Gov Reynols [Thomas Reynolds] call ⟨for him⟩ by authority of the Laws of Mo or Ill.? No!— by contitutin [constitution] & laws of the Unitd States.

⟨Govener [Thomas] Carlin⟩ b[e]ing a good Gov & good Lawyer & says Requsitin [Requisition].[179] f[r]om Gov ~~Ford~~ Reynols gov [Thomas] Ford was reqeted [requested] to issue [p. 59] this copy[180] ⟨because the original writ was out of our reach⟩—— ⟨Constituitn [Constitution] & laws of⟩ United States & of this states. law of this state is a furtherance of the Unted States is a null &

---

174. Kent, *Commentaries on American Law*, 2:32.
175. U.S. Constitution, art. 3, sec. 2.
176. TEXT: Possibly "power".
177. Lilburn W. Boggs, Affidavit, 20 July 1842, p. 379 herein.
178. TEXT: Unidentified symbol, possibly a typographic index or manicule.
179. Thomas Reynolds, Requisition, 22 July 1842, p. 380 herein.
180. Arrest Warrant, 31 Dec. 1842, p. 383 herein.

void.— ⟨the Prisonr looks to⟩ this C. [court?] for redressed— ⟨he is⟩ a prisoner of U. S. ⟨& the⟩ Gov⟨rs⟩— one in issuing Requsitin [Requisition] the other in Warrant.— acted as ~~appointd~~ appointees of the U. States.— bound by oath to support the constituti[o]n of U. States. have done so—— gov⟨r.⟩ in issuing this warrant acts as[181] agent in carr[y]ing into effect th[e] laws of th[e] U. S.—— in custody Under U State— can he apply to to state courts? would not conflict⟨s⟩ ensue which have [p. [60]] been anticipated by opposite Council 12th Wendell ~~301~~ 311[182] a fugitive slave. ⟨in⟩ N. York— Jack negro man ⟨vs⟩ Mary Martin.— fled f[r]om Lousana [Louisiana] to N. Yord [New York]. pu[r]sued ⟨arrestd, & taken on⟩ writ of H[abeus] Corpus— action of congress is exclusive on actions— being under law of Congress— decision of the court was they ⟨⟨State⟩⟩ had no Jurisdicti[o]n:— has not my Client. Joseph Smith. the Rights of a negro?— he has been arrestd under a Law of congress— & must seek redress— before the federal court.—

A war ⟨betwe[e]n betwe[e]n the Slave &⟩ non-Slave holding states ⟨and the non-slave holded states—⟩ have passed laws— & Juries have had— virgin[i]a passed [p. 61] laws— to reqire bonds of masters[183] of vassels— by retaliation.

Priggs— Comweath of Pa—[184] fugitives from Justice & ~~Savvery~~ ⟨Slaves⟩ on the same footing.— Congress having passed Laws— the State laws are void.— 5 wheaten—[185] where Congress has legislatd— it is not competent for State⟨s⟩ to Legislate, all power ⟨is⟩ in congress— in relation to fugitive Slaves— (Story) last January term S. C. of U. States[186] aid of States is not wantd. they cannot intrude themselves.— Federal Governmnt is competent.

This Court has not only Jurisdicti[o]n [p. 62] but. it is the only court I could bring this case.— Judic[i]al power shall extend to all cases arising under the constitution ⟨& laws⟩ of the U. States.—[187] I hope the Gent of the bar— will not give th[e]ir opinons without readi[n]g their books thesee[188] out door opinions— ⟨are a disgrace to the profession.—⟩

Has this court power to issue Habeus Corpus—? it has— is the return suffi[cie]nt to hold the prisoner in custody without furthr testim[o]ny?

---

181. TEXT: Possibly "an".
182. Jack v. Martin, 12 Wendell 311 (N.Y. Sup. Ct. 1834).
183. TEXT: Possibly "master,".
184. Prigg v. Commonwealth of Pennsylvania, 16 Peters 611 (1842).
185. Houston v. Moore, 5 Wheaton 23 (1820).
186. Prigg v. Commonwealth of Pennsylvania, 16 Peters 617 (1842).
187. U.S. Constitution, art. 3, sec. 2.
188. TEXT: Possibly "there".

Sketch of Joseph Smith. Benjamin West sketched this profile of Joseph Smith during the 4 January 1843 habeas corpus hearing in Springfield, Illinois. The cane shown in the sketch may be the one George Morey gave Joseph Smith on 26 December 1842, the day before Smith left for Springfield. (Courtesy Abraham Lincoln Presidential Library and Museum, Springfield, IL.)

unless it appears on th[e] testimo[n]y that he is a fugitive. it is not suf-f[i]cient.— affidivit read.—¹⁸⁹ ⟨it⟩ does not state he ever was in Mo. that he even was in the [p. 63] state of ⟨mo⟩— ⟨it⟩ states nothi[n]g that would bri[n]g him within the Law of the Unitd S. [United States] he must have fled.— shall flee.— Boggs knew what he was about. he knew. that Joe Smith had not been in Mo. since the Mormons were murderd— he dare not perjure himself. he thought his Gov— would certify to a lie & save him from perju[r]y

Representd. ⟨to him⟩ who made the false & foul statem[en]t that Joe Smith had fled? no body! would swear to it. that¹⁹⁰ the citizns of Illinois are not to. be [p. 64] imprisond on reprentatin [representation] to gov Reynols—— sent over the Great father of waters to Gov Carlin.— by some necromancy of. ⟨ajdudictin [adjudication]⟩ beyo[n]d our controol.—

Copy ⟨the⟩ progress of Error. little ⟨Bogs affidavit— says he was in Ill— Reynolds that it ~~is~~ was repre[se]nted to him. who reported it⟩ beyond— Requisiti[o]n— Carlins Writ¹⁹¹ appears from affidavit. sp◊◊d¹⁹² before Carlin— while— writing. no man ought to flee from the Justice of Mo—

1st position ⟨is for⟩. the court ⟨to⟩ examine all the papers— ⟨there is not⟩ a particle of testimony that Joseph has fled from Mo Gov. Carlin would not have givn up his dog on such a requsitin [requisition]— ⟨the⟩ Gent¹⁹³ says ⟨it is⟩ not [p. 65] necessary it should appear ⟨that he had fled.⟩—— th[e] Gov thought it necessary. or why insert the falsehood?

⟨He⟩ is not subjct to be transportd till ⟨it is p[r]oved that he is a fugitive⟩ [*blank*] ⟨they⟩ must prove he has fled— if he is guilty can this court deliver him up?— No!— he must have fled—

the Questi[o]n is whither he shall be transpotd [transported] to anothr state or tried on his own soil? ⟨Traspotd [transported]⟩ ⟨to⟩ Botany Bay¹⁹⁴ or Missouri and very indiff[ere]nt which.—

we have shown we were not in Mo. ⟨he ~~was~~ is⟩ not a fugitivs. [p. 66] fr[o]m. Justice. he was at office[r]s drill— on 6—¹⁹⁵ & ⟨in the⟩ Lodge ⟨from⟩ 6— to 9. ⟨oclck⟩— 7¹ day 300 miles off— ⟨in uniform⟩ reviewi[n]g ⟨of⟩ the Nauvoo.— ⟨Legion⟩¹⁹⁶ insted of runig [running] away from Bogg—— in uniform—

---

189. Lilburn W. Boggs, Affidavit, 20 July 1842, p. 379 herein.
190. TEXT: Possibly "trust".
191. Thomas Carlin, Writ, 2 Aug. 1842, *Ex Parte* JS for Accessory to Boggs Assault (C.C.D. Ill. 1843), copy, Nauvoo, IL, Records, CHL.
192. TEXT: Possibly "spread".
193. Illinois attorney general Josiah Lamborn.
194. A British penal colony established in 1788 in Australia.
195. 6 May 1842, the day Boggs was shot.
196. Nauvoo is approximately three hundred miles from Independence, Missouri. This journal entry records Butterfield's assertion that JS attended a meeting of the Masonic lodge in Nauvoo from six

Judg— Douglass— partook of the hospitality of Gen Smith. ⟨insted of flee[i]ng f[r]om J⟩ flee[i]ng from Justice. ⟨he⟩ Dini[n]g on cou[r]ts.— high[e]st cou[r]ts in ou[r] land.

have I a right to try him, ~~have a right to try~~

power of Habeus corpus.— is pretty well settled— ⟨there is⟩ no proof in ⟨the⟩ writ that he is a fugitiv f[r]om Justice— [p. 67] 3 Peters 193.—[197] Tobias Watkins. convictd of embezzling money.— cannot go behind the Judgme[n]t. where Judmett [Judgment] is not issued, can go behind the writ, ⟨same⟩[198] nature of writ of Error— body of Prisoner & cause of commitment— 3 cranchen [Cranch] 447—[199]

3ᵈ Bacons abridgmnt[200] to qustn [question] proposed to 12 Jud[g]es—— where a person is so imprisond that the cou[r]t cannt discha[r]ge yet unjustly.— manife[s]tly to unwarrantable means,—— ⟨clear on Habus Corpus——⟩

most clear & undoubted testim[on]y this man are not [p. 68] manife[s]tly agai[n]st law & Justice.

⟨is the⟩ Habus Corpus— ⟨a⟩ Civil— or criminal? not crimi[n]al— civil proceeding whithe[r] the law of this[201] state on Habeus Corpus— Statute of this ⟨state⟩ that prison[er] may ~~may~~ make allegation ⟨&⟩ cou[r]t shall hear— in H. Corpus ⟨the⟩ Laws of the State shall be regarded by the cou[r]ts where they are held. statute of this state.[202] prisoner shall be allowed to controvert on trial this as well as promissory note

not only controvert the return but that he is not to be surreded [surrendered] or discharged [p. 69]

⟨Gent[203] Read⟩ 9 Wendell 212.[204] when a person is brought on Habeus C. court is not to enquire ⟨into th[e] guilt or innocen[c]e—⟩ authority is again[s]t it, 9 wendell previous to 12 Wendell. & ⟨is⟩ all set aside. has he fled? & not, is he guilty?— if Smith was in this state, says Attorny General, constructively in that state, ⟨I⟩ dont wish to go into a spiritual disquisition.— ⟨the words⟩ shall

---

to nine o'clock on 6 May 1842; however, JS's name is not among those listed as present in the lodge minutes. According to his journal, JS was involved in activities with the Nauvoo Legion that day. (Nauvoo Masonic Lodge Minute Book, 6 May 1842; JS, Journal, 6 and 7 May 1842.)

197. *Ex Parte* Watkins, 3 Peters 193 (1830).
198. TEXT: Possibly "⟨some⟩".
199. The case actually begins on page 448. (*Ex Parte* Burford, 3 Cranch 448 [1806].)
200. *A New Abridgement of the Law by Matthew Bacon, of the Middle Temple, Esq.*, vol. 3, 1st American ed. (Philadelphia: Farrand and Nicholas, 1813).
201. TEXT: Possibly "the".
202. An Act Regulating the Proceedings on Writs of Habeas Corpus [22 Jan. 1827], *Revised Code of Laws, of Illinois* [1826–1827], pp. 236–244.
203. Josiah Lamborn.
204. *In re* Clark, 9 Wendell 212 (N.Y. Sup. Ct. 1832).

flee occurr 3 times ⟨in the constitution⟩—²⁰⁵ ⟨th[e]⟩ removal ⟨is⟩ not spiritually, but bodily.— look at it.— states have passed Laws to take effect out of the State ⟨where they were passd⟩ but they are void. ⟨suppose⟩ [p. 70] Ill[inois] passed a Law to prevent any person from speaking disrespe[c]tfully of her inability to pay her debts ⟨we⟩ Might have 1/2 the city of N York ⟨before our cou[r]ts⟩ for Saying we could not pay our²⁰⁶ debts.— Alabama ag[ain]st N. York— in case of Williams—²⁰⁷ W⁽ᵐˢ⁾ had been Spiritually there had not fl[e]d— f[r]om the Justice of that state. ⟨the⟩ Right to demand & power to give up coextensive. ⟨Gov Marcys [William Marcy] was not an ab[o]litionist as the Gent wo[u]ld intimate⟩— 2/3 Gov Marcy's Message to abuse abolitionist²⁰⁸

that an attempt should be made to deliver up a man who has never ben out of the state strikes at all the liberty— ⟨of our instituti[o]ns⟩ his fate to day may bee yours tomorrow [p. 71] I do not think the def[e]ndant ⟨ought⟩ under any circumstances to be deliverd up to Mo.— it is a matter of history that he & his people [blank] ⟨have been murderd & drivn from th[e] state— he—⟩ had better been sent to the gallows— he is an innocent & unoff[e]nding man the differnc [difference] is this people beleiv in prophecy & othrs do not old prop[h]ets prophicid in Poet[r]y & the modern in Prose—

⟨went into the Judges room. introduced to one senator— & some Ladies— Mrs [Susanna] Ford⟩ 1/2 Ladies retir[e]d—

---

205. U.S. Constitution, art. 4, sec. 2. The word *flee* actually occurs only once in the Constitution. The word *fled* also occurs once.

206. TEXT: Possibly "their" or "her".

207. In October 1842 Butterfield explained in detail the legal basis of this defense of JS in a letter written to Sidney Rigdon. The *State of Alabama v. Williams* case was the foundation of his argument. Robert G. Williams, an abolitionist residing in New York, was indicted by an Alabama court in 1835 on charges of "intending to produce conspiracy, insurrection and rebellion among the slave population" for distributing his antislavery paper *The Emancipator* in the latter state. In his request for Williams's extradition, Alabama governor John Gayle stated that Williams was not in the state when the crime was committed and had not "fled" as the wording in the Constitution required, "according to the strict literal import of that term." Gayle argued that the term "fled" should be interpreted as "evade" and that Williams should be extradited even though he had not physically fled from the justice of Alabama. New York governor William Marcy, though personally highly critical of abolitionism, rejected this interpretation and refused to extradite Williams, maintaining his stance that a fugitive must physically flee the jurisdiction of the state attempting extradition. The Alabama requisition papers, Gayle's letter, and Marcy's lengthy response were printed in the *Albany Argus*. (Justin Butterfield, Chicago, IL, to Sidney Rigdon, [Nauvoo, IL], 20 Oct. 1842, copy, Sidney Rigdon, Collection, CHL; "Requisition of the Governor of Alabama," *Albany Argus*, 7 Jan. 1836, [2].)

208. The message cited is probably a reference to New York governor Marcy's message to the New York state legislature of 5 January 1836. Marcy made it clear that he had protected New York abolitionist Williams from extradition to Alabama because his alleged seditious acts "arose from acts done within this State." (*Documents of the Assembly of the State of New-York*, no. 2, pp. 29–39.)

Lambern read f[ro]m 12 Wendell case of Williams on th[e] pa[r]t of th[e] Gov to act. no court [p. 72] coult [could] compel him to act

differe[n]ce of opinion of the north & south.

Court adjorn till 9 tomor[ro]w morning for making up opini[o]n

[209]retired to Judge [James] adams,— after Dinner. Joseph was with Hiram [Hyrum Smith] & orson [Hyde] in the chamber & Bro T. Turly [Theodore Turley] & mended the bellows. & dug some horse raddish with Lorin [Walker]— 5½ eve Joseph— Gen [Wilson] Law. & Bro Hyde took their departure in Mr Prentices's [William Prentiss's] carriage to visit his house.— & returnd about 11'o clock.— giving a very intersting account of th[e]ir visit with Mr Prentice & family. Judge Douglas ⟨Esqr Butterfield— & Edwards⟩ Judge Pope's Son—[210] Esqr Lambern. & many others see page 76[211] [p. 73]

⟨See page 23—⟩ Note A.[212] as Gen Law came to the head of the stairs some man observd there goes Smith the prophet and a good looking man he is. & (said another) as damnd a rascal as ever lived. then Hyr[u]m repli[e]d & a good many Ditto.— yes said the man Ditto. D°.— God Dam you & any one that takes his part is as dam[n]ed a rascal as he is— then at the foot of the stairs. Law— says I am th[e] man. & I take his part.— you are a damnd ra[s]cal to[o] ⟨you are⟩ a Liyng ⟨schondrl [scoundrel]⟩ said ~~the man~~ ⟨Law—⟩.— & ⟨the man⟩ began to take of[f] his clothes & went out [p. 74] in the street. & the marshall interferd— &c much credit is due to Mr Prentice the marshall for his dilignc [diligence] in quelling the. mob—

⟨Jan 4⟩

The court Room was crowded the whole of the Trial. & the utmost decorum— & good feeling prevailed— Much prejudice was allayed.— Esqr— Butterfield managd the case very learnd & Judiciou[s]ly. preceded by Esqr Edwads who made some very pathetic. allusions to our suffe[r]ings in Missou[r]i. Esqr Lamborn was not severe apparently saying littl more than the natu[r]e of his situation requird— & no more than would be usefull in satisfying the public mind— that there had been a fair investigation— of the whole matter. [p. 75]

---

209. TEXT: The ink color changes at this point; the new ink in this paragraph matches that used in the insertions in the earlier part of the entry, suggesting that Richards made the insertions after court recessed.

210. William Pope.

211. This sentence from the 4 January 1843 entry continues on manuscript page 76 (page 227 herein).

212. The altercation described in this paragraph took place on 31 December 1842. See manuscript page 23 (page 204 herein), where Richards recorded the events leading up to the altercation and inserted a reference to this "Note A," which describes the dispute in greater detail.

Nathaniel Pope. United States district court judge Nathaniel Pope presided over Joseph Smith's habeas corpus hearing on 4 January 1843 in Springfield, Illinois. The following day, Pope ordered that Smith be discharged from arrest, explaining that both the affidavit of Lilburn W. Boggs and the requisition of Missouri governor Thomas Reynolds were defective. (Courtesy Abraham Lincoln Presidential Library and Museum, Springfield, IL.)

[213]had a Most splindid Supper with many intersting anecdotes.— & every thing to render the visit agreeable. [*14 lines blank*] [p. 76]

Editorial Note

Willard Richards's disjointed phrases in the following entry reflect his efforts to capture Judge Nathaniel Pope's decision as it was given.

In his decision, Judge Pope agreed with Justin Butterfield that extradition was a constitutional matter and that the federal circuit court was an appropriate venue for the hearing. To the objection of Illinois attorney general Josiah Lamborn that the court was not empowered to go behind the writ to look at the merits of the case, Pope stated that "the court deems it unnecessary to decide that point, inasmuch as it thinks Smith entitled to his discharge for defect in the [Lilburn W. Boggs] affidavit. To authorise the arrest in this case the affidavit should have stated distinctly, 1st. That Smith committed a crime. 2d. That he committed it in Missouri.

"It must appear that he fled from Missouri to authorise the Governor of Missouri [Thomas Reynolds] to demand him. . . . The Governor of Missouri, in his demand, calls Smith a fugitive from justice . . . [and] expressly refers to the affidavit as his authority for that statement. Boggs, in his affidavit, does not call Smith a *fugitive from justice,* nor does he state a fact from which the Governor had a right to infer it. Neither does the name of O. P. [Orrin Porter] Rockwell appear in the affidavit, nor does Boggs say Smith *fled*. Yet the governor says he has *fled* to the state of Illinois. But Boggs only says he is a *citizen* or *resident* of the state of Illinois.

"For these reasons," Pope concluded, "Smith must be discharged."[214]

---

5 January 1843 • Thursday

January 5, 1843 8½ repaired to Mr [Justin] Butterfields room. 9. enterd Cort Room— the room was crowded— before the[y] Entered, with spectators. Mostly of a very respctable class in society. anxious to hear the decision— although the public exp[r]ession was decididly in favor of an acquittal

9 & 10 mituts [minutes] the Judge. [Nathaniel] Pope. enterd preceded by 2 ladises [ladies].— court opend—

Docket called— 4 more Ladises enterd and took seat beside th[e] Judge while the docket was reading (four councillors sworn &c) ⟨in⟩ matter of J Smith ⟨the cou[r]t⟩ has taken occasion to examine

[215]thanks to gentlemn of th[e] bar [p. 77]

---

213. This sentence is a completion of the last sentence on manuscript page 73 (page 225 herein).

214. Court Ruling, 5 Jan. 1843, p. 401 herein; italics in original.

215. For the remainder of this entry, phrases are disjointed, with irregular spacing. Blank lines in the journal are represented by wider spacing between lines.

move[216] it is more. [*blank*] any other case

the fnd [founders?] of th[e] Constituti[o]n of the [*blank*] states of this

bloodshed— causd by collisi[o]n

nati[o]nal & p◊◊◊tiald [impartial?] Govmt take cha[r]ge

―

Congress— power to regulate commerc[e] & fugitive [p. 78]

Reat[217] fo◊ this provisi[o]n of constutin [Constitution] of th[e] U. S.—

crime was comm[i]tted in mo if th[e] P. had escaped— f[r]om Mo to Ill—

duty of congress—
Laws of its own creation—
not of Partake of th[e] Passions— &

power shoud be [p. 79]

J.—S. appled [appealed?] to the— court.
sangamo[n] Co—

Requisiti[o]n—

gov Ill. professes to

Laws of th[e] U. S. & Ill

court deemed it.— Repctful [Respectful] that the Gov— be informd

Ex[e]cutive & Atty. Gen were info◊d [informed] Atto[rne]y Gen appeard. [p. 80]

& objected. when th[e] p◊◊◊◊◊ [prisoner?]— was— under [*illegible*] [oath?]—

under Author[i]ty of S[tate]. Ill.

congress— of U. S.— had no power to confer the Authority in th[e]
2d Sec 4 art read.

will be perceivd this clause cannot executee itseeff [itself]

what testimony. shall— [p. 81] [*pages 82–83 blank*]

the power of congress to pass &c

---

216. TEXT: Possibly "more".
217. TEXT: Possibly "but".

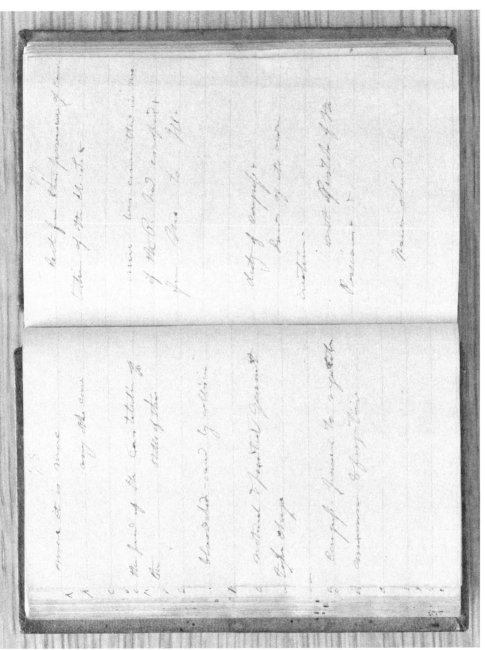

Notes of habeas corpus hearing. Willard Richards attended Joseph Smith's January 1843 habeas corpus hearing in Springfield, Illinois, and hurriedly took notes in the courtroom as part of the journal he kept for Joseph Smith. Handwriting of Willard Richards. JS, Journal, Dec. 1842–June 1844, bk. 1, pp. 78–79, JS Collection, Church History Library, Salt Lake City. (Photograph by Welden C. Andersen.)

shortly after. [*blank*] ex[e]cutive to

testim[o]ny copy of indictmnt or affidavit

Clause of aff[i]davit c◊◊p◊◊◊ [complies?]

claimed by ex[e]cutive of the state Indictmnt of Affi[davit]—

where Congress has power to Legislate [p. 84]

~~on~~ ⟨in⟩ the <u>Gov</u> of the state of Ill.

in order to maintain the Postin [Position] of th[e] Atty Gen— that congress of

the Law had any effect. power only to carry into effect the Law—

no power to carry th[e] Constituti[o]n
duty of th[e] govener[218] to obey.
authority confirmd by Con[gress]
& laws of U. [S.] [p. 85]

therefor this Cou[r]t has Juris[di]ction— &—
power to issuee Habus Corpus.

been contended by U. S. Atto[rne]y Gen. has st Atny
Cou[r]t has no auth[orit]y to— try writs by Gov—

encrochmt [encroachment] from the [*illegible*]—[219]

It was not for petty crime—
but these high [p. 86]

offences. cha[s.] 2[d] Magna Chata [Carta]

howe[220] free it may be its without Habus Corpus. act offered means to evry[221]
man of enj[oy]ing that libe[r]ty
no mattr how mean the prisoner. [*blank*] how high the keeper—

fr[o]m Garret to Dungeon

duty of evry court into full

deny it does not entrd to G◊◊◊.

---

218. TEXT: Possibly "goveners".
219. TEXT: Illegible word is possibly "court" or "creed".
220. TEXT: Possibly "power".
221. TEXT: Possibly "any".

[Govr.?] is ridiculus [p. 87]

ben contended court cannot go behind the warr[a]nt unnecessary to Go behi[n]d into that poi[n]t

& if ever the impotace [importance] of a scrutiny into th[e] acts of the executive

Constituti[o]n. flee m[a]y
be by Indictm[en]t or affidavit
a crime in th[e] state [o]f Mo.—
court will turn
Bogg [Lilburn W. Boggs] swears [p. 88]

on 6 m[a]y 1842
was shot & his life was dispard.
good reason to beli[e]ve

does not say that he was a fugitive fr[o]m Justice
does not say who he was accessory to
this is evide[n]ce
wh[a]t does th[e] Gov Mo say
Gov Mo knew. no arresti[n]g[222] without pr[i]nciple
accused. accessory to Mr [Orrin Porter] Rockwell—
not a w[o]rd of his flig [fleeing] f[ro]m Jus[t]ice. [p. 89]
Gov— Ill. actd on affidavit.
Mr Bogg was shot by Mr R[ockwell].
smith accessory
how cautious Judges shud be [blank] & how loosely Executives officers do act
Boggs was shot.
Smith accesory
Citizen of Illinois—
warrant [blank] issue for Joseph— S.
2 parts
Can a citizen of Ill be transp[o]rted to Mo. to be [p. 90]

tried for a off[e]nce committed

cannot violate a law he has not promisd to obey

Man naturally is a sovereign but when he enter into a state of soci[e]ty up[o]n princ[i]ple of consent that soci[e]ty shall protect

---

222. TEXT: Possibly "accesry".

has that society a right to give him up
by tribunals he has
never created
place him befor tribunals [p. 91] [2 *unnumbered pages blank*]
from witnesses
would violate every contract.
this is th[e] princ[i]ple
no man here but may be[223] admitt
deliver up Jos Smith. any indiv[i]dual

true every writer— every state should be

responsible shall review no ann[o]yance for the[i]r neighbor Ill. [*blank*] Mo— [p. 92]

right of Territ[o]rial bou[n]dary

home[224] his castle when depatd [departed?] f[r]om[225] var [various?] crimes Mo. may complain of Ill if ther has been aggressi[o]n

United States bou[n]d to see that no annoyan[c]e is suffered by any state. [*blank*]
milatay [military] ⟨Expediti[o]n⟩ agai[ns]t may bring nations amenab[l]e
if J. Smith aided & abetted Rockwell might be the duty to provide for acts of th[e] kind that Mo has[226] nothi[n]g to [p. 93]
J. S. cannot be trieed in Mo. offence must be committed where— what would necssarly [necessarily] be the acti[o]n Congress. & laws? the evidence should be so specifice as to leave no doubt— a crime was committd.
where the crime was committd— to the state where th[e] crime
the Gov of th[e] state wher crime was committd gov— Mo. is the p[r]oper [p. 94]

if ever there was a case where th[e] Judge ought to scrutinize this is th[e] case—
Court ◊◊◊◊◊◊t [correct?] so any auth[o]rity why he should be gov
Affidavit defntion [definition] J S. is accessory befor th[e] fact.
who constitutd Bogg competnt to advise this cou[r]t
quetin [question] of Law— facts cort has to do with
must affirm crime was [p. 95]

---

223. TEXT: Possibly "he".
224. TEXT: Or "house".
225. TEXT: Or "for".
226. TEXT: Possibly "her".

committed. Believes & has good reason to believe now in his possession
who ever heard of a mans being arrested.
reasons may have ben futile—
court might not think them very good

another Qu[e]stion now— familiar princ[i]ples own opinion. charged with treason felony or othr crime shall be delivrd suspects J S. as accessory [p. 96]

cou[r]t must put a constrctin [construction]
where there is fear of escapee.
issue a warrant to detain for examination cou[r]t dont concur process on mere suspicion motive fear that he will escape is done away— parties have time to collect testim[o]ny submit it to Grand Jury impeach congress—— only an impechmt [impeachment] charged us[e]d in this Constrctin [Construction]. positive not suspic[i]on [p. 97]

Bogg says he was shot on 6[th] May. (Ladies— [*blank*]) & his affidavit made 20 July following— shall not find a indictment befor Judgm[en]t.
had time to bring a S◊◊◊◊◊◊ [Securing?] of the Citizens of those[227] U. States.—
should be transported. unless on positive charge. not on Suspici[o]n—
mature reflection Affidav[i]t so impefits so imperf[e]ct.—
J. Smith be dischar[ge]d & the entry be made so that [p. 98]

⟨he shall be⟩ to secure him from any ⟨from any further⟩ furthr arrests on this ⟨troubled ⟨no more⟩ in this matter.— in relati[o]n to this ⟨the⟩ matter touchi[n]g this⟩ prosecuti[o]n—— (Joseph arose & bowed to the cou[r]t.—) Spctatrs [Spectators] retired. & court adjornd to 10 o'clock Tomorrow.—

Joseph repared to Judge Popes romm [room] & spent 1 hour in conversation with his honor. showing that he did not profess to be a prophet then evry man ought. who professes to be a preacher of Righteousness— that the testim[o]ny of Jesuss is the spirit of Prophecy.[228] & preached to the Judge— Esqr Butterfield asked him to Proph[e]cy how [p. 99] ma[n]y inhabita[n]ts would come to Nauvoo,— Joseph repli[e]d I will not tell you how ma[n]y inhabita[n]ts will come to Nauvoo but. I will tell you what I said when I came to Commerce, I told them I could build up a city— & the old inhabitants said— we'll be damnd if you can So I prophecid that I could build up a city. & the inhabtns [inhabitants] prop[h]esied I could not. we have now about 12000 inhabtnts. I will prophecy we will bu[i]ld a great city. for we have th[e] stakes. & we have only to. [p. 100] fill up the interstices.— Joseph came in the

---

227. TEXT: Possibly "these".
228. See Revelation 19:10.

Clerks office after he left the Judge who by the bye— was very attentive & agreeable,— & said to the clerks. that he had been disappntd in one thing.— which appeard to allay their pleasure for the moment. but said he I have met with less prejudice & better & more noble & liberal feelings on the part of the people generally than I expected.— befor I came. which lighted evry countena[n]ce. with Joy— after maili[n]g letters to Liverpool [p. 101] Philadelphia & St Louis— retird to Gen [James] Adams— when Secretary went to prep[ar]ing the Judjes Decision for the press on request of Judge Pope. per Presidnt Joseph.[229]

visited Mr Butterfield— with Wm Clayton.— had conversations concerning the abuse which had been received from Mo & the officers— Joseph askd Butterfield if he or the assigneee[230] could sell the Lots on the Hotchkiss purchase in Nauvoo. Butterfield[:] neithr can sel. all the assignee can sell is Josephs Right. the conveyance [p. 102] has not ben made by Hothkiss [Horace Hotchkiss] therefore it reverts back again to him.— Joseph has nothing to do with paying the rema[i]nder which is due Hotchkiss in the event he is discharged on bankruptcy.—[231]

visited at Mr Mc Graws[232] in the eveni[n]g had a very social visit.— & had a disquisiti[o]n on ph[r]enology. Slept in the front chamber with Secreta[r]y. [*5 lines blank*] [p. 103]

6 January 1843 • Friday

January 6^t 1842 [1843] after finishing a copy of Judge Popes's [Nathaniel Pope's] decision. went with Joseph & presentd the same to the Judge

we were in the court Room with [Justin] Butterfield & the Clerk Joseph gave Butterfild 2 notes of $230. each for his fees bind— ⟨Note signd by Joseph

---

229. At Pope's request, Willard Richards used his hastily written notes to prepare a draft copy of the decision, which Pope used as a resource for drafting his published decision. (Court Ruling, 5 Jan. 1843, *Ex Parte* JS for Accessory to Boggs Assault [C.C.D. Ill. 1843], draft, JS Collection, CHL; see also Court Ruling, 5 Jan. 1843, p. 390 herein.)

230. An "assignee," according to the Federal Bankruptcy Act of 1841, was "vested with all the rights, titles, powers, and authorities to sell, manage, and dispose of" the bankrupt's property. (An Act to Establish a Uniform System of Bankruptcy [19 Aug. 1841], *Public Statutes at Large,* 27th Cong., 1st Sess., chap. 9, pp. 442–443, sec. 3.)

231. Much of the land on which Nauvoo was built was purchased by JS, Hyrum Smith, and Sidney Rigdon from Hotchkiss and his associates. As trustee-in-trust for the church, JS sold lots from this land to the Saints. However, Hotchkiss retained title because he had not received payment in full. (Horace Hotchkiss, Fair Haven, CT, to JS, Nauvoo, IL, 27 May 1842, JS Collection, CHL; see also 29n86 herein; and JS, Journal, 14 Apr. 1842, p. 50 herein.)

232. Probably Charles G. McGraw, who was married to Vienna M. Adams, the only living daughter of Judge James Adams, host of JS during this trip to Springfield. (Power, *Early Settlers of Sangamon County, Illinois,* 76, 501–502.)

Smith Hyrum Smith Moffat [Levi Moffet]— & [Edward] Hunter⟩ $40 he had reivd [received]— $500 in the whole— took certified copiees of the Affidavit of [Lilburn W.] Boggs [Thomas] Reynolds Requ[i]sition, [Thomas] Carlins Writ as reissu[e]d by [Thomas] Ford and Joseph Petition petition, Carlins Proclamati[o]n, Habeus Corpus. order of Court Josephs affidavit. and aff[i]davits of Eleven othrs— and all the [p. 104] doings of the court certified by the the clerk— & the order of the govenor theron— shewing that Joseph is discharged from all prosecuti[o]n on the case of the arrest on Requisiti[o]n from Missouri,[233]

Joseph visited Judge Pope to request a copy of his decision for the wasp & not let Mr [Simeon] Francis have the fir[s]t chance as he has publishd much again[s]t us & we have a little pride in being the first. Judge Pope said he could not well. deny Mr Francis but he would give Gen. [James] Adams the first chance of copying the decision as soon as it should be written[234] [p. 105]

After the Govenor[235] had certified the decision of court & the papers[236] he offered a little advice to Joseph that he refrain from all political electioneeri[n]g—— Joseph shewed him that he always had acted on that p[r]inciple & & proved it by Gen [Wilson] Law. & Sec$_y$. qu[i]te to the satisfaction of the govenor— as it appeared that the Mormons were driven to union in their elections[237] by perscution & not by the influence of Joseph. & that the Mormons actd on the most perfect principles of liberty, in all their moveme[n]ts. [p. 106]

In the court room Mr Butterfield enquired the price of lots in Nauvoo said if he became a mormon he should want to come & live with us.— had conversation on the subject of Religion—— Judge Popes son[238] wishd me well. &

---

233. See the following documents in Appendix 1, pages 379–390, 402 herein: Lilburn W. Boggs, Affidavit, 20 July 1842; Thomas Reynolds, Requisition, 22 July 1842; Arrest Warrant, 31 Dec. 1842; JS, Petition for New Arrest Warrant, 31 Dec. 1842; JS, Petition for Writ of Habeas Corpus, 31 Dec. 1842; Thomas Carlin, Proclamation, 20 Sept. 1842; Writ of Habeas Corpus, 31 Dec. 1842; JS, Affidavit, 2 Jan. 1843; Wilson Law and Others, Affidavit, 4 Jan. 1843; Jacob B. Backenstos and Stephen A. Douglas, Affidavit, 4 Jan. 1843; and Thomas Ford, Order Discharging JS, 6 Jan. 1843. William Clayton made copies of all of these documents. (Clayton, Journal, 6 Jan. 1843.)

234. Simeon Francis was editor of the *Sangamo Journal*. Judge Pope's decision was published in the 16 January 1843 issue of the *Times and Seasons*, three days before its appearance in the *Sangamo Journal*. It was also published in the 28 January 1843 issue of *The Wasp*. ("Circuit Court of the U. States for the District of Illinois," *Times and Seasons*, 16 Jan. 1843, 4:65–71; "Circuit Court of the United States for the District of Illinois," *Sangamo Journal* [Springfield, IL], 19 Jan. 1843, [1]; "Circuit Court of the United States for the District of Illinois," *The Wasp*, 28 Jan. 1843, [1]–[2]; see also Court Ruling, 5 Jan. 1843, p. 390 herein.)

235. Thomas Ford.

236. Ford's certificate is contained in his order discharging JS, page 402 herein.

237. TEXT: Possibly "election".

238. William Pope.

hoped I should not be perscutd [persecuted] him[239] any more I Jo[s] Blessed him— conversd with Owens. Catholic.—[240] when we retired the Lawyers were laughing at him saying that he would be a mormon in 6 weeks if he would go to Nauvoo. Mr Butterfield said Joseph must deposite his discharge & all th[e] papers in the archives of [p. 107] the Temple, when it was completed.— 3½ P.M. retired to Judge Adams— eveni[n]g W[m] Smith calld said [John] Cochran Representative f[r]om. Union[241] had brought charges or insinutins [insinuations] again[s]t the mormons. saying certain things false in[242] the Mormon Bible.— The Man[a]ger[243] of the Theatre sent a ticket for ⟨Gen⟩ Joseph Smith to attend the theatre this eve— but the action was dispensed with on account of the weather.—[244] [p. 108] [*page 109 blank*]

7 January 1843 • Saturday

January 7.— Saturday 8½ left Judge [James] Adams on our way to Nauvoo. & arrivd at Mr Dutches [John Dutch's] 4 P.M. Travelling very bad much of the way snow fell the ev[en]ing previous on th[e] mud which had not frozen— though extremely Cold. so as to turn the horses white with frost. while riding Gen [Wilson] Law sung[245] the following Hymn.[246]

  And are you sure the news is true?
  and are you sure he's free?

---

239. TEXT: Possibly "here".
240. Possibly Thomas Owen, representative from Hancock County—although he was Baptist rather than Catholic—or James F. Owings, clerk of the United States Circuit Court for the District of Illinois. (Gregg, *History of Hancock County, Illinois,* 736–737; JS, Affidavit, 2 Jan. 1843, p. 387 herein.)
241. Union County, Illinois.
242. TEXT: Possibly "on".
243. TEXT: Possibly "Monger".
244. William P. Hastings was the manager of the theater directly south of the American House, where the drama "Wenlock of Wenlock, Or, The Spirit of the Black Mantle" was performed on 5 and 6 January. ("Theatre," *Sangamo Journal* [Springfield, IL], 5 Jan. 1843, [3]; "Theatre," *Illinois Register* [Springfield], 6 Jan. 1843, [3].)
245. TEXT: Possibly "sang".
246. William Clayton wrote that Law composed the lyrics, while Willard Richards later wrote in the draft material for JS's history that both he and Law composed them. The song, which came to be known as the "Mormon Jubilee," was to be sung to the tune of "Auld Lang Syne" or "There's Na Luck about the House." The first two lines of the Jubilee are taken almost verbatim from "There's Na Luck about the House." A comparison between the version recorded in this journal and two other versions—a manuscript copy dated 7 January 1843, and the version published in *The Wasp*—shows slight differences in wording and indicates that the order of verses underwent some change before the song was published. Numbers at the head of most of the verses in the journal entry correspond with the final verse order in the published version. (Clayton, Journal, 7 Jan. 1843; Historian's Office, JS History, draft notes, 7 Jan. 1843; "The Mormon Jubilee," *The Wasp,* 14 Jan. 1843, [1]; "The Mormons Farewell," 7 Jan. 1843, Historian's Office, JS History Documents, ca. 1839–1880, CHL.)

Then let us Join with one accord,
And have a Jubilee.
    Chorus
We'll have a Jubilee. my frie[n]ds [p. 110]
We'll have a Jubilee
With heart & voice we'll all rejoice
~~Because~~ ⟨In that⟩ our Prophet's free
    2ᵈ
Success unto the Federal Court.
Judge Pope[247] presiding there;
And also his associates too,
So lovely & so fair
    3 Chorus
~~Also~~ ⟨And⟩ to our learn'd councillors
We owe our gratitude
Because that they in freedom's cause
Like valiant men have stood
    4 Chorus
In the defence of Innocence,
They made the truth to bear; [p. 111]
Reynold's & Carlin's[248] baseness both
Did fearlessly declare
[*illegible*]   5 Chorus   see B 114 page[249]
~~The names of Pope & Butterfield~~ ⟨Edwards & Butterfield & pope[250]⟩
We'll mention with applause
Because that they like champions bold
Support the Federal Laws
    ~~6~~ 7 Chorus
One word [*illegible*] in Praise of Thomas Ford[251]
That Democrat so true;
He understands the people's Rights
And will protect them too.
    ~~7~~ 8 Chorus
There is one more we wish enrol'd

---

247. Nathaniel Pope.
248. Thomas Reynolds, governor of Missouri, and Thomas Carlin, former governor of Illinois.
249. See "Note B" on manuscript page 114 (page 239 herein).
250. Benjamin Edwards and Justin Butterfield, JS's defense attorneys, and Judge Nathaniel Pope.
251. Governor of Illinois.

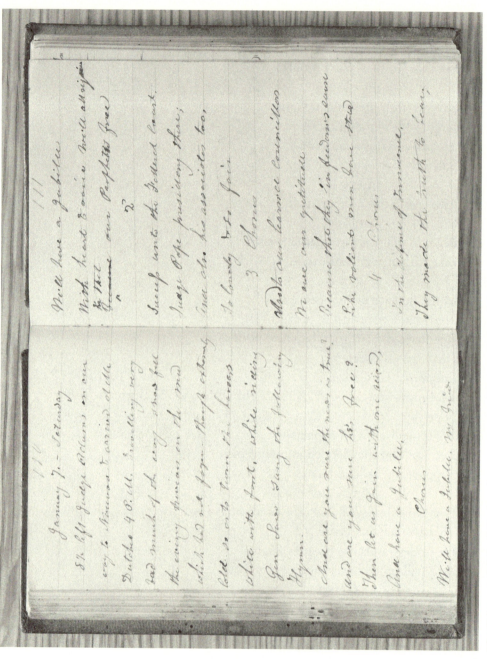

The "Mormon Jubilee." During their return trip to Nauvoo, Illinois, following Joseph Smith's habeas corpus hearing in Springfield, William Law and Willard Richards composed the "Mormon Jubilee" to celebrate Smith's discharge. Handwriting of Willard Richards. JS, Journal, Dec. 1842–June 1844, bk. 1, pp. 110–111, JS Collection, Church History Library, Salt Lake City. (Photograph by Welden C. Andersen.)

Upon the book of fame
That Master spirit in all Jokes
And— 'Printice[252] but in name [p. 112]
   8 Chorus   see C. 114[253]
⟨12⟩
With warmest hearts we bid good bye
To those we leave behind
The citizens of Springfield all
So courteous & So kind.
   9 ⟨15⟩ Chorus
And now wer'e bound for home my fri[en]ds
A. band[254] of brothers true.
To cheer the heart of those we love
In beautiful Nauvoo
We'll have a Jubilee my Fri[en]ds
We'll have a Jubilee
With heart & voice we'll all rejoi[ce]
In that our prophets's free [p. 113]
Note B. 6.— [Chorus]
The Attorny General of the State[255]
His duty nobly did
And ably brought those errors forth
from which we now are fre[e]d.
   9 C— chorus
The sucker State[256] we'll praise in song
She's succour'd us in deed
And we will succour her again
in evry time of need
   10 Chorus
Our Charter'd Rights she has Maintaind

---

252. United States marshall William Prentiss.
253. See "C" on manuscript page 114 (page 239 herein).
254. TEXT: Possibly "bond".
255. Josiah Lamborn.
256. Thomas Ford, in *A History of Illinois,* presented two early and equally plausible traditions for the origin of the term "suckers" in reference to the citizens of Illinois. The first referred to the miners who traveled up the Mississippi River in spring to work the lead mines and then returned back down the river to their homes in fall, thus resembling the migratory habits of the sucker family of fish. The second referred to the poor early immigrants to southern Illinois who came from the tobacco regions of the South and were likened by the Missourians to the sprouts, or "suckers," on tobacco plants that would be stripped from the main plant and destroyed. (Ford, *History of Illinois,* 68.)

Through opposition Great
Long May her Charter Champ[i]ons live
Still to protect the state,
            chorus [p. 114]
              ~~11~~ ⟨13⟩
And Captain Dutch we cannot pass
Without a word of Praise
For he's the king of comic Song
As well as ~~common~~ comic ways.—
            Chorus
And the fair Ladies of his house
~~To~~ ⟨th[e]⟩ ~~thank them we take pains~~ ⟨flowers of Morgan's plains[257]⟩
Who from the soft Piano bring
Such soul enchanting strains,[258]
We'll have a Jubilee my friends
Well have a Jubilee
With heart & voice we'll all rejoice
In that our prophet's freee
              11—
We'll stand by her through sun & shade
Through calm & sunshine too
And when she needs our Legions Aid
'Tis ready at Nauvoo.
            Chorus [p. [115]]

which was writtn and sung[259] repeatedly during the evining with many other songs & stories and the whole party were very cheerful. and had a rich entertainment.—

we retired at a late hour and rose early

8 January 1843 • Sunday

Sunday January 8. 1843. 8 oclk & rode th[r]ough Geneva.[260] past Beardstown crossed the Illinois River on the ice and arrivd at Rushville 4. P.M.—

---

257. Morgan County, Illinois, home of John Dutch.
258. Charles Allen recalled that JS and his party stayed overnight with Dutch "& were very kindly entertained by the family. The women played the piano & sang songs, while Captain Dutch recited his humorous recitation & sang songs." (Allen, Autobiography, 6; see also Clayton, Journal, 7 Jan. 1843; and "A/c of Expenses to Springfield Dec^t 1842," Newel K. Whitney, Papers, BYU.)
259. TEXT: Possibly "sing".
260. Willard Richards's reference to Geneva was probably a naming error for Virginia, in Cass County, Illinois. The state road from Springfield to Rushville passed through Lancaster (where John

soon after a man, Mr Royalty²⁶¹ [p. [116]] 6½ feet high called to see us.— after supper— we repair to Mr [Uriah] Browns & sung the Mormon Jubilee.— Mr Brown repo[r]ted his invention for national dfenc [defense]——— no prospect of the nation adopting²⁶²

virul invulnerable

greek fire²⁶³

agai[n]st the dstrutin [destruction] instantly seald.— turnd my attention to Land operatin compositi[o]n by mineral 100 ft f[l]ame or steam— engins²⁶⁴

300 yr— [p. [117]]

some plans & diagrams behind movable battris [batteries] cutters²⁶⁵ &ᶜ on wheels— by steam if level. confidence of an individ[u]al at St Louis— [*blank*] made a propositi[o]n— for operatin in the South.— Northe[r]n Provinces of Mexico— with a small force— if it was not commitd²⁶⁶ with the Unitd States. Some othe[r] power will avail itself vessel contain machine ball cannot get at it. cannon ball— will dest[ro]y [p. [118]] 300 ft— by land. by. <u>breast</u> works

---

Dutch's establishment, mentioned in the 7 January journal entry, was located), Virginia, and then Beardstown. Richards made the same mistake in his own journal when describing his trip to Springfield in December 1842, but on the return journey of that trip he placed Geneva between Rushville and Nauvoo. At the time, the closest community named Geneva to the route was in Scott County—far enough out of the way that the party could not realistically have traveled there. (Richards, Journal, 11, 18, and 19 Dec. 1842.)

261. Possibly Thomas Royalty, about twenty-two years of age, living at Mount Sterling, a few miles from Rushville, who was later known as a miller. (1840 U.S. Census, Brown Co., IL, 176; 1850 U.S. Census, Mount Sterling, Brown Co., IL, 97B.)

262. Sometime during the War of 1812, inventor Uriah Brown "conceived the plan of a ship to be propelled by steam, to be proof against cannon shot, and to throw liquid fire upon the ships of the enemy, by the means of an ejecting fire apparatus of very great force, placed within the vessel." Congress showed some interest in Brown's idea at various times and passed a resolution in 1828 authorizing funds to test the invention's "practical utility" and an act in 1847 authorizing further tests of the invention. In 1848, however, the Committee on Naval Affairs gave an "unfavorable report" on his "liquid fire." ("On the Expediency of Testing Uriah Brown's System of Coast and Harbor Defence, by Fire Ships," *American State Papers: Naval Affairs*, 3:201; "System of Defense, by Land or Water, by the Use of Inflammable Fluid," *American State Papers: Naval Affairs*, 1:353; A Bill Authorising the President of the United States to Cause Experiments to Be Made, to Test the Utility and Practicability of a Fire-Ship, the Invention of Uriah Brown, H.R. 296, 20th Cong. [1828]; A Bill Authorizing the Secretary of the Navy to Cause Experiments to Be Made to Test the Efficient Properties of a Liquid Fire Discovered by Uriah Brown, H.R. 621, 29th Cong. [1847]; *Journal of the House of Representatives of the United States*, 29 Feb. 1848, 472.)

263. TEXT: Instead of "greek fire", possibly "spech for".

264. TEXT: Possibly "any in" or "evry in".

265. TEXT: Possibly "cutter".

266. TEXT: Possibly "connectd".

account f[r]om [Samuel] Colt. N. York[267] proposd the same thing to Mr Madison,— services of Rand.—[268] explode their magazine by conducti[o]n,—

to determ[in]e precisely— method of determ[in]ing when the vessel comes over magazine.— land[269] explosions.—[270] [*blank*] will not effect[271] our shipping— but an enemy— [*blank*] obse[r]vation by Telescope—— [*blank*] meet an army. Batt[e]ry moved up touch off—— [*blank*] approach an enemy undd [under] cover of sand bags [p. [119]] engine for beseiging city defedd [defended] by india Rubber &c

Joseph said he had thought that the Lord had designd the apparatus for some more magnificnt purpose than for the defence of nations.—[272] [*9 lines blank*] [p. [120]]

9 January 1843 • Monday

Monday January 9. Started 8½— o clock for Plymouth roads pretty good but smooth or icy. when 2 miles beyond Brooklyn at 12½ noon— while Bro [Willard] Richards— & Lorin Walker was in the covered carriage. & ~~going~~ descending a steep hill. the horses Boltd. the carriage slipped & capsized— & feell off the side of the bridge 5 feet descent broke the cariage— some on the Top & the fore axletree which we soon splicd & withed— & went on no one being injured— which we considered a special inte[r]position [p. [121]] of Providence. & agre[e]d that Lilburn W. Boggs. should pay the damage [*5 lines blank*]

arrivd at Bro [Samuel] Smith's in Plymouth 4. P.M.— after supper. Josph went to see his sister Catharine [Katharine Smith] Salisbury with Sister [Elizabeth Davis] Durphy & Sec$_y$. The first time he had visited her in the State of Illinois while there ~~the~~ Joseph spoke [p. [122]] of his friends particularly his fathers family— in general. & particularly of his brother Alvin. that he was a very handsome man. Surpassd by none but Adam & Seth. & of great strength. while 2 Irish-men were fighting & one was about to gouge the others eyes, Alvin took him by his collar. & breeches & threw him over the ring which had

---

267. Colt, famous for manufacturing his patented revolver, had lobbied Congress for acceptance of a system of harbor defense by underwater mines activated through insulated wire. Brown summarizes Colt's work in the next sentences and evidently refers to a public experiment on the previous 4 July, when Colt remotely exploded a ship off Castle Garden, in lower Manhattan. ("The Fourth and Its Events," *New York Herald*, 6 July 1842, [2]; "Celebration of the Fourth in New York," *Daily National Intelligencer* [Washington DC], 8 July 1842, [3]; Lundeberg, *Samuel Colt's Submarine Battery*, 25–26.)

268. TEXT: Instead of "Rand", possibly "Bond".

269. TEXT: Possibly "bond".

270. TEXT: Instead of "explosions", possibly "explosives".

271. TEXT: Possibly "affect".

272. TEXT: Instead of "nations", possibly "nation".

been formd to witness the fight.——— ²⁷³while there my heart was paind to witness a lovely wife & sister of Joseph. almost barefoot & four lovely children entirely so— in the middle of winter [p. [123]] Ah! thought I what has not Joseph & his fathers family sufferd to bring forth the work of the Lord? ~~we~~ I sang the Mormon Jubilee— to cheer our hearts. & we retur[ne]d to Bro [Samuel] Smiths— Ju[s]t before the close of the meeting in the school house— where Bro [John] Taylor preached.— soon after. as some had calld to see the prophet we all collected & sang the Jubilee. & retired.— [*5 lines blank*] [p. [124]]

10 January 1843 • Tuesday

Januay 10 Tuesday 8½ started for Nauvoo. had a prosperous journy— stopping only to water our horseses at the public well in carthage. arrived at General Smith['s] at 2½ P.M. when this family & fri[e]nds assembld together— & sang the ⟨Mormon⟩ Jiubilee soon after his mother came in & got hold of his arm before he saw her which produced a very agreeable surprize on his part. & the Olde Lady was overjoyed to behold her son free once more [p. [125]]

11 January 1843 • Wednesday

11 Wednesday Joseph rode out in his sleigh with his wife startd to go to Bro Russels²⁷⁴ to apologize about the broken carriage. broke sleigh shoe. & retur[ne]d— visitd by a co[mpany] of Ladies & Gentlemen. f[r]om Farmington [Iowa Territory]. on the Desmoin [Des Moines] River— left. at 2½ P.M.— directed ⟨written⟩ Invitations to be given to Wilson Law.— Wm Law, Hyrum Smith. Saml Bennet[t], John Taylor Wm Marks [*blank*] Moffat [Levi Moffet], Peter Hawes [Haws]. Orson Hyde. H[enry] G. Sherwood, Wm Clayton, Jabez. Durphy, H[arvey] Tate. Edwa[r]d Hunter, Theodore Turl[e]y, Shadrach Ro[u]ndy. W[illard] [p. [126]] Richards, Arthur Mil[l]ikin with their Ladies, & Mrs Lucy [Mack] Smith,— to a dinner Party on wednedy [Wednesday] next at 10. A.M. ⟨x⟩ Brigham Young. Wilford Woodruff, Geo A. Smith. Eliza Snow

---

273. At this point Willard Richards describes his own feelings about meeting with JS's sister Katherine Smith Salisbury.

274. An insertion in the draft notes of JS's multivolume manuscript history for this date identifies this as Isaac Russell, although in the history "Isaac" is crossed out and "should be Daniel" is inserted in another hand. (Historian's Office, JS History, draft notes, 11 Jan. 1843; JS History, vol. D-1, 1453.)

Mr [Carlos] Granger Sisters Ells.[275] Partrige[276] Alpheus Cutler. Reynolds Cahoon, H[eber] C. Kimball. wer afterwa[r]ds added [*9 lines blank*] [p. [127]]

12 January 1843 • Thursday

Thurday 12 January At home all day [*15 lines blank*] [p. [128]]

13 January 1843 • Friday

Janury 13 Friday at home till near sun set When Bro Russel [Samuel M. Russell] called to see if $20 had been recived said he put it in his brothers [Daniel Russell's] bag where both their monies were deposited & his bro said if there was $20 due the chu[r]ch he must make it good.—[277] then went to bro Wm Marks to see Sophia [Marks][278] who was sick heard her relate the vision or dream of a visit fr[o]m her two brothers who were dead.— Touching the associati[o]ns & relations of anothr wolrd [p. [129]]

———— ✑ ————

Editorial Note

Willard Richards, who was keeping JS's journal, indicated in his own journal that he was ill much of the time between 14 and 31 January 1843. This may account for the abbreviated nature of some of the entries in JS's journal during this time.

———— ✑ ————

14 January 1843 • Saturday

[*7 lines blank*] January 14. Saturday Rode out with Emma in the forenoon. evening in special council in the chamber—[279] to pray for Sophia Marks [p. [130]]

---

275. Probably Hannah Ells, a Nauvoo dressmaker. According to later sources, Ells was "sealed to Joseph the Prophet before his death." ("Millinery and Dress Making," *Times and Seasons,* 1 Oct. 1841, 2:560; Eliza R. Snow, Salt Lake City, Utah Territory, to John Taylor, 27 Dec. 1886, John Taylor, Collection, CHL.)

276. Probably either Eliza or Emily Partridge (or perhaps both), both of whom were living in JS's home at the time as hired help and both of whom later indicated that they were "married or sealed" to JS in March 1843. (Young, Diary and Reminscences, [315]–[317]; Emily Dow Partridge Young, Affidavit, Salt Lake Co., Utah Territory, 1 May 1869, in Joseph F. Smith, Affidavits about Celestial Marriage, 1:11; Eliza Maria Partridge Lyman, Journal, 13; Eliza Maria Partridge Lyman, Affidavit, Millard Co., Utah Territory, 1 July 1869, in Joseph F. Smith, Affidavits about Celestial Marriage, 2:32, 3:32.)

277. JS related further details about the Russell brothers and the twenty dollars three months later; he used the incident to illustrate the need for implementing better accounting procedures for temple donations. (JS, Journal, 6 Apr. 1843, p. 332 herein.)

278. William and Rosannah's daughter, who was in her midteens at the time. (Ward, "Female Relief Society of Nauvoo," 154.)

279. The "chamber" here might refer to the upper room in JS's store—or to the second floor in JS's

15 January 1843 • Sunday

Sunday Janry 15 at home— [*15 lines blank*] [p. [131]]

16 January 1843 • Monday

Monday January 16 [*16 lines blank*] [p. [132]]

17 January 1843 • Tuesday

Tusday Jannuay 17 at home fast day[.][280] Meeting in the court Room. ⟨Refere[n]ce[281] ⟨with 6. other⟩ on D^r [Robert D.] Fosters Land case⟩[282] [*12 lines blank*] [p. [133]] [*page [134] blank*]

18 January 1843 • Wednesday

January 18th. 1843 party ⟨began to⟩ assembld at the time appointd & before 12 oclock the Julibee songs— by Gen [Wilson] Law & Miss [Eliza R.] Snow were distributed[283] by the govenr of the feast[284] to fifty indivduals.— the party invited except Mr Moffat [Levi Moffet].[285] who were seated in the Court Room. who sung the same— Elder [John] Taylor then read a vision from a New orleans paper Bro & Sister Marks[286] came in.—

Gen ⟨S⟩. I will call your atte[n]tion to one of the most enticing cases you ever saw.——— he then arose & read a letter f[r]om John C. Bennt [Bennett] to. To Pratt[287] & [Sidney] Rigdon dat[e]d Sprigfild [Springfield] Janury 10 1843.

---

home, where JS and close associates had held special prayer meetings in the past. (JS, Journal, 26 and 28 June 1842.)

280. Six days before, on 11 January, the Quorum of the Twelve issued a proclamation that a fast was to be held on 17 January to thank the Lord for the defeat of Missouri officials' attempt to extradite JS. The Saints were also asked to make contributions to assist the poor and to help defray the legal and travel expenses JS incurred in connection with his habeas corpus hearing in Springfield. (Brigham Young, "Proclamation to the Saints in Nauvoo," *The Wasp*, 14 Jan. 1843, [3]; see also Woodruff, Journal, 17 Jan. 1843.)

281. "Reference" is a legal term meaning arbitration. ("Reference," in *American Dictionary*, 681.)

282. TEXT: Insertion in graphite in unidentified handwriting—probably Willard Richards. This added inscription may postdate the journal-keeping effort.

283. The two jubilee songs distributed on the occasion were one composed on 7 January 1843, as JS and his party were en route from Springfield to Nauvoo, and one produced by Snow for this occasion. (JS, Journal, 7 Jan. 1843, p. 236 herein; Historian's Office, JS History, draft notes, 7 Jan. 1843; Eliza R. Snow, "Jubilee Song," *Times and Seasons*, 1 Feb. 1843, 4:96; Clayton, Journal, 18 Jan. 1843.)

284. JS.

285. According to a list made by William Clayton, Moffet was not the only invitee absent: Carlos Granger and Sister Partridge also did not attend. Clayton did not list William Marks as an attendee, perhaps because of Marks's late arrival. The draft material for JS's history also notes that Hyrum Smith's wife was sick and absent. (Clayton, Journal, 18 Jan. 1843; Historian's Office, JS History, draft notes, 18 Jan. 1843; see also JS, Journal, 11 Jan. 1843.)

286. William Marks and his wife, Rosannah Robinson Marks.

287. TEXT: Possibly "Pratts".

Stating that Bennett was [p. [135]] soon going to hav Joseph arre[s]ted on the old score f[r]om Mo. &c for murder. &c.—[288] Mr [Orson] Pratt shewd Josph the Letter. Mr Rigdon did not want to have it known that he had any hand in shewing the letter— Joseph said he had sent word to Gov— [Thomas] Ford by [Jacob B.] Backenstos that before he would be troubld any more by Mo— he woud fight first—

Dreamed that a sheriff came after me. a man put a musket in my hand & told me to keep him. I took the musket & walked round him. when he went to go [p. [136]] away I would push him back & if others came to trouble him I would keep them off—

conve[r]sation continued freely until 2 oclock when 21. sat down to dinner. the Govenor & Goveness[289] in waiting— while thus serving the table. Joseph stated that this was not only a Jubibee but commemoration of his marriage to Emma. Just 15 years[290] this day.

20 sat at the 2ᵈ table

18 at the 3ᵈ table including Joseph & Emma. with many Jokes

⟨15 at the 4ᵗʰ table including children—⟩

H[enry] G. Sherwood prea[c]hed a Methodist Sermon. & [p. [137]] rec[e]ived a votee of thanks from the company. & he continud to tell story. Elder [Orson] Hyde told the Eddy Story[291] [*13 lines blank*] [p. [138]] [*page [139] blank*]

19 January 1843 • Thursday

Thursday Jan 19, At home through the day except. out in the city a little while in the fore noon. [*12 lines blank*] [p. [140]]

20 January 1843 • Friday

Friday Jan 20— visited President [William] Marks returnd at 10 oclock— & gave some inst[r]uctions about [William W.] Phelps & [Willard] Richards

---

288. In his letter to Sidney Rigdon and Orson Pratt, Bennett announced that new indictments were being filed against JS and others "on the old charges" of "murder, burglary, treason—, &c. &c." dating back to the Missouri conflict of 1838–1839. He assured his correspondents, "The war goes bravely on, and altho' Smith thinks he is now safe— the enemy is near, even at the door." (John C. Bennett, Springfield, IL, to Sidney Rigdon and Orson Pratt, Nauvoo, IL, 10 Jan. [1843], Sidney Rigdon, Collection, CHL.)

289. JS and Emma Smith.

290. TEXT: Possibly "years". JS and Emma Hale Smith were married sixteen years earlier, in South Bainbridge, New York, on 18 January 1827.

291. This story was one told by United States marshal William Prentiss while JS was at Springfield. (JS, Journal, 3 Jan. 1843.)

uniting in writing the history of the chu[r]ch.—²⁹² Bro Phelps presnted some poetry. to Joseph Smith. the Prophet.— "Will you go with me in—["]²⁹³

Joseph told his dream in council—²⁹⁴ I dreamd. this morni[n]g that I was in the Lobby of the Representative Hall. at Springfield. when some of the members who did not like my being there. began to mar & cut. & pound my shins with pieces of Iron.— I bore [p. [141]] it as long as I could. then Jumped over the rail into the hall. caught a rod of Iron. & went at them cursing & swearing at them in the most awful manner. & drove them all out of the hou[s]e I went to the door & told them to send me a clerk & I ~~will~~ ⟨would⟩ make some laws ⟨that would do good⟩

There was quite a collection aro[u]nd the ⟨state⟩ house trying to raise an army to take me.— & there were many horses— tied round the square. I thought th[e]y would not have the privilige of getting me so. I took a rod of Iron & mowed my way. through their ~~way~~ ⟨ranks⟩ [p. [142]] looking after their best race horrse thinki[n]g they might catch me when the[y] could find me when I was awake.)

To dream of flying signifies prosperity & delivenc [deliverance] f[r]om Enemies

Swimming in deep waters signifies success among Many people,— the word will be accomp[an]ied with power.— told Elder [Orson] Hyde when he spoke in the name of the Lord. it should prove true. but do not cu[r]se²⁹⁵ the people

prop[h]ecy in the nam[e] of the Lord God as soon as we get that temple built so that [p. [143]] we will not be obliged to exhaust our means. thereon we will have means to gather the sai[n]ts by thousnds & tens of thosnds

Elder Hyde told of the excellnt white wine he drank in the east.²⁹⁶ Joseph prophcid in the name of the Lo[r]d— that he would drink wine with him in that country.—

---

292. In December 1842 Phelps turned over to Richards the historical documents for compiling the history of the church. Phelps identified, in his own journal, Thursday the 19th as the day on which he commenced work on the history. (171n566 herein; Phelps, Diary and Notebook, 19 Jan. 1843.)

293. Phelps's "Vade Mecum," or "Go with Me," dated January 1843, is dedicated to JS and describes a blissful state, free from the cares of the world, to be attained in the afterlife. A seventy-eight-stanza response attributed to JS and dated the following month, titled "A Vision," recounted the themes of JS's 16 February 1832 vision. The poems were later published in the *Times and Seasons* and the *New York Herald*. ("Ancient Poetry," *Times and Seasons*, 1 Feb. 1843, 4:81–85; "A Vision of Joseph Smith, Prophet of the Latter Day Saints," *New York Herald*, 8 Mar. 1843, [2]; JS, Journal, 30 Mar. 1843.)

294. This was a meeting of the Quorum of the Twelve, with JS and Hyrum Smith attending. (Quorum of the Twelve Apostles, Minutes, 20 Jan. 1843.)

295. TEXT: Possibly "cure".

296. Hyde returned from his mission to Europe and Jerusalem on 7 December 1842. (JS, Journal, 7 Dec. 1842.)

Joseph— From the 6th day of April next. I go in for preparing with all present for a mission thogh [through] the Unitd States. & when we arrive [p. [144]] at maine we will take ship— for England. & so on to all countries where we are a mind for to go.—[297] pr[es]ent H[yrum] Smith B[righam] Young. H[eber] C. Kimball. Orson Hyde. Orson Pratt. John Taylor, W[ilford] Woodruff— Geo A. Sm[i]th. W— Rihads [Willard Richards].—

we must write for John E. Page[298] we must have the whole. Quorum— we must Send Kings & Queens to Nauvoo—[299] & we will do it.

We mu[s]t all start f[r]om this place

Let the 12' be calld in on the [p. [145]] 6[th] of April— & a notice be givn by for a special confenc [conference] at on the platform on House of the Lord.—[300] We are sure to go as we[301] live till spring.—

If I live I take these breth[r]en through these united States. & th[r]ough the world.— & I will make Just as big a wake as god Almighty will let me

⟨4. P.M.⟩ Baptizd. Orson Pratt. & wife & Lydia [Dibble] Granger. & confirmd them. ordaind Orson to all the authority. of his former office.—[302] [p. [146]] [*page [147] blank*]

21 January 1843 • Saturday

[303]Saturday January 21— went out in the City with Elder [Orson] Hyde to look at some Lots[304] [*6 lines blank*]

---

297. William Clayton recorded Hyrum Smith's explanation that JS would preach "through the States" and then the group would probably travel to England "and through Europe probably to Jerusalem and thus raise a great excitement through the whole world." (Clayton, Journal, 20 Jan. 1843.)

298. Page, a member of the Quorum of the Twelve, was serving a mission in Pittsburgh, having been called to serve there during a conference held in Nauvoo on 7 April 1842. ("Conference Minutes," *Times and Seasons*, 15 Apr. 1842, 3:762.)

299. See Revelation, 19 Jan. 1841, in Doctrine and Covenants 103:3, 1844 ed. [D&C 124:11].

300. A notice calling for the April conference and requesting the presence of the Quorum of the Twelve was printed in the 16 January issue of the *Times and Seasons*. Rather than going to Europe, members of the Twelve were called at the April conference on a mission within the United States to procure funds for the Nauvoo House and the temple. ("Special Conference," *Times and Seasons*, 16 Jan. 1843, 4:80; "Special Conference," *Times and Seasons*, 1 May 1843, 4:180–185.)

301. TEXT: Possibly "are".

302. Pratt was excommunicated on 20 August 1842. (Woodruff, Journal, 10 Aug.–18 Sept. 1842; see also 79n311 herein.)

303. TEXT: Blue ink commences.

304. William Clayton recorded that he accompanied JS "to sell a lot to E. J Sabin." (Clayton, Journal, 21 Jan. 1843.)

22 January 1843 • Sunday

Sunday January 22ᵈ Preached at the Temple on the setting up of the Kingdom[305] [*5 lines blank*] [p. [148]]

23 January 1843 • Monday

Monday January 23 [306]visited with Emma in the evening Bro [Willard] Richards who is sick

Bro John Snider came home from England. where he had been sent by the Twelve acc[o]rding to Revelati[o]n to procure help for the Temple[307]

24 January 1843 • Tuesday

[308]Tuesday January 24 At home till P.M. Rode out with Emma.— eve at Lodge— for trial of Geo. W. Robinson.— which was posponed.— &ᶜ till Tuesday eve next.[309] [*5 lines blank*] [p. [149]]

25 January 1843 • Wednesday

Wednesday January 25 [*7 lines blank*]

26 January 1843 • Thursday

Thursday January 26 [*8 lines blank*] [p. [150]]

27 January 1843 • Friday

Friday January 27 [*7 lines blank*]

---

305. In this discourse, JS taught that the kingdom of God is present whenever a man able to receive the oracles of God is present, and that John the Baptist had the oracles of God with him and baptized for the remission of sins. (Woodruff, Journal, 22 Jan. 1843; Clayton, Journal, 22 Jan. 1843.)

306. TEXT: Brown ink commences.

307. Snider was called by a revelation on 22 December 1841 to go to England to obtain funds for the building of the Nauvoo House and Nauvoo temple. He departed for England on 26 March 1842. In June 1843, William Clayton recorded donations totaling £201 14s. 1½d. (or $976.25, according to Clayton's calculations), brought back by Snider from "various branches of the Church in the Islands of Great Britain, Scotland and Ireland and designed as consecrations for the building of the Temple." (JS, Journal, 22 Dec. 1841 and 26 Mar. 1842, pp. 16–17, 47 herein; Book of the Law of the Lord, 319–325.)

308. TEXT: Blue ink commences.

309. Robinson was charged at a lodge meeting on 5 December 1842 with "Misreprensentations," "speaking evil of Brethren Master Masons," and "Lying." At the lodge meeting held Tuesday, 31 January 1843, Robinson "desired that he be furnished with specifications of the Charges preferred against him," after which the lodge adjourned to the following day. On 1 February 1843, Lucius Scovil reported that Robinson "had made ample satisfaction to the aggrieved & injured Brethren on whose account he had preferred the charges, and desired . . . that no further action be taken on the charges." The lodge members agreed to Scovil's proposition. (Nauvoo Masonic Lodge Minute Book, 5 Dec. 1842; 31 Jan. 1843; 1 Feb. 1843; JS, Journal, 5 Dec. 1842.)

28 January 1843 • Saturday

Saturday Januay 28⁽ᵗʰ⁾· Played ball & rode round the city with Mr Taylor.³¹⁰ land agent f[r]om New. York

³¹¹Snowed some

steamer went from Montrose over the falls to Keokuk.³¹² [p. [151]] [*page [152] blank*]

29 January 1843 • Sunday

³¹³Sunday Jany— ⟨29⟩ meeting am [a.m.] florr of³¹⁴ the Temple Joseph Read the parable of the prodigal Son³¹⁵ after prayer by John Taylor. then singing by the Quoir

I feel thankful to Almigty God. for the privilege of stanndig [standing] before you this mor[n]ing it is necessary that the hearers³¹⁶ should have good & honest heart as well as the speakers³¹⁷ I rise to address you on the important subjct. of the Prodagal Son

2 Items I wish— to noticce Last sabbath.— 2 questions³¹⁸

saying of Jesus concerning John. a greater prophet. than Jonh [John]. [p. [153]]

2,— least in the kingdom of God Greater than he.—³¹⁹

some so blind they wont see. I dont expect I can wo[r]k mira[c]les enough to open

---

310. Probably Frederick Taylor, former secretary of the Illinois Land Company in New York City. Taylor advertised his November 1842 departure from New York to the "Military Bounty Tract of Illinois," which included all of Hancock County and the surrounding counties. While he advertised a willingness to perform any business service required of him, he particularly mentioned "paying taxes upon lands, making sales, examining titles, recording deeds, and surveying land." William Clayton added that Taylor was "Clerk for the Ill[inois] Land Agency" and that Taylor and JS "viewed the Draft of the Temple; the Temple &c." ("Illinois Lands," *New York Herald*, 29 Oct. 1842, [2]; Frederick Taylor, "To Persons Having Land in the Far West," *New York Herald*, 29 Oct. 1842, [4]; Clayton, Journal, 28 Jan. 1843; see also Taylor, *Sketch of the Military Bounty Tract of Illinois*, 1–12.)

311. TEXT: Brown ink commences.

312. The "falls" refer to the Des Moines rapids, an eleven-mile stretch of the Mississippi River above Keokuk, Iowa, where the river dropped some twenty-two feet in elevation. The rapids were unnavigable during seasons of low water. (Hunter, *Steamboats on the Western Rivers*, 188.)

313. TEXT: Blue ink commences.

314. TEXT: Possibly "on".

315. See Luke 15:11–32.

316. TEXT: Possibly "hearer".

317. TEXT: Possibly "speaker".

318. JS addressed two questions that were posed in a recent lyceum meeting: "1ˢᵗ Did John Baptize for remission of sin? 2ⁿᵈ Wether the kingdom of God was set up before the day of Pentecost or not till then?" (Clayton, Journal, 22 Jan. 1843; Woodruff, Journal, 22 Jan. 1843; JS, Journal, 22 Jan. 1843.)

319. See Matthew 11:11.

greatest propht. what constitudd him.—— no prop[h]et, if do no miracles. John did no miracles.—

How is it John was considerd one of the Greatest of Prophe[t]s? 3 things

1ˢᵗ he was trusted with a divine missoin [mission] of preparing the way before the face of the Lord.— [*blank*] Trust before or since? no man!—

2ᵈ He was trusted & it was reqird at his ha[n]ds to baptize the son of Man. who evr did that? who [p. [154]] had so gr[e]at a privelige & glory?—

son of God into the waters of baptism & beholding the Holy Ghost.— in ⟨in the sign⟩ the form of a dove.—³²⁰ [*blank*]— [*blank*] with the sign of the dove. institutd before the creation Devil could not come in sign of a dove.— Holy Gh[o]st is a personage in the form of a personage.— does not confine itself to form of a dove.— but in sign of a dove.— No man holds the book more sacred than I do.—

3ᵈ. John at that time was the only legal admini[s]trator holding the keys of Power thr [there] was on Earth.

the keys the kingdm the power the glory from the Jews son of Zachari[a]h by the holy anoi[n]ting decree of heaven [p. [155]] these 3 constitutd him the greatest born of woman.

He that is least. in the Kingdom is gre[a]ter than he?³²¹ who did ~~the~~ Jesus have refere[n]ce to?— Jesus. was looked up[o]n as ~~the~~ having the least claim in all gods kingdom.—

He that is considerd the least among you. is greater than John! that is myself.—³²²

anothr qestin [question], Law. & prophts were until John. since which time the kingdom of heaven is ~~preaching~~ preachd & all men pass into it.—³²³

additional proof— to what I offered you on the last sabbath. that that was³²⁴ the beginn[in]g of the Kingdom [p. [156]]

Prodigal Son.— when you have heard go & read your bible. if the things are not verily true.—

great deal of speculation. Subjct I never dwelt upon.— understood by many— to to³²⁵ one of the intricate subjects.— Elders in this church preach.— no rule of interpretation.— what is the rule of interpretati[o]n? Just no

---

320. See Matthew 3:13–17.
321. See Matthew 11:11; and Luke 7:28.
322. That is, Jesus.
323. See Luke 16:16.
324. TEXT: Possibly "even".
325. TEXT: Possibly "be".

interpretati[o]n at all. understand[326] precisely as[327] it read.— I have Key by whi[c]h I understa[n]d the scripture—— I enqire what was the question whi[c]h drew out the answer.——

nati[o]nal. Ab[r]aham. &c as some suppose 1st. place dig up the root— what drew out the saying out of Jesus? Pharises & scribes murmured? this man [p. [157]] recevess [receives] sinners & eatheth with them.[328] this is the key word.— to answer the murmuring & qustioning of Saducees & Pharisee how is it this man ⟨is⟩ as great as he pretends to be. & eat with publican & sinners.—— Jesus not put to it so but he could have found somthing if the had discerned it for nations.—[329] Men[330] in an individaul capacity. all straining on this point is a bubblee.— Boy ⟨Boyys⟩[331] say ought to be hanged can tell it to you.

big folks Presbyterins. Methodists. Baptists &c. [blank] despise the ignorance & abomination of this world.—

this man reciveth sinners— he spoke this parable.— what man of you having an hundrd. sheep ⟨&c⟩[332] 100 saducees & Pharisees [p. [158]] If you pharisees & saduce[e]s are in the sheepfold. I have no mission for you sent to look up sheep that are lost will back him up.— & make joy in heaven— hunting after a few individuals Laying it on his Shoulder— one publican you despise.— [blank] one piece of Silver— the piece which was lost.—[333] Joy in presence of the angels over one sinner that repe[n]teth so rightous they will be damned any how you cannot save them. rain off f[r]om a gooses back— G[r]eat I. little you—

certain man had two sons.—[334] &c

am a poor publican a sinner— humble themselves. spending their bread. & living— &c Ill return to my fathrs house. to Jesus you pharises so righteous you cannot [p. [159]] be touched.—[335] I will arise &c— claim not be a pharisee or saducee. I claim not to be a son do not let me starve— nothing about. Eph[r]aim Abraham— is not mentind [mentioned]. all that is meet. is brought to bear upon the pharisee. saducee. the publican & sinner, Eldst son, pharisees & Saducees murmuring & complaini[n]g.— because Jesus sat with publicns &

---

326. TEXT: Possibly "understood".
327. TEXT: Possibly "at".
328. See Luke 15:2.
329. According to William Clayton, JS's point was that Jesus's parable of the prodigal son "did not refer to any nation, but was merely an answer to the remark 'he receiveth the sinners and eateth with them.'" (Clayton, Journal, 29 Jan. 1843.)
330. TEXT: Possibly "Man".
331. TEXT: Possibly "Bog ⟨Boggs⟩".
332. See Luke 15:3–7.
333. See Luke 15:8–10.
334. See Luke 15:11–32.
335. See Luke 18:10–14.

Sinners— father came out & entreated when John came baptizd all. when Jesus came they were angry & would not go in. [*blank*] dealing of God with individuals men always Righteous always have access to throne of God— eats in his fathers house If we interpret this to nationl. view. where is the eldest son?— [p. [160]]

likend the kingdom to an old womans milkpan— how could Jesus take the kingdom f[r]om them who bore no fruit & give it to another.— is an apple tree no longer a tree because it has no apples? parable of Prodigal son spoken to illustrate the sinner in—[336] from the mome[n]t John's voice was fir[s]t heard. he was the person on the earth entitld to salvation. on the earth.

Servants of God of the last day,[337] my[s]elf & them I have ordaind. have the pristhood & a mission—[338] to the publicans. & sinners.— & if the Presbyterins & [*blank*] are in the kingdom [p. [161]] if they are not righteous— what is the result. they are sinners & if they rej[e]ct our voice they shall be damnded.

If a man was going to hell I would not let any man disturb him.—

while we will be the last to oppress. we will be the last to be driven from our post.— peace. be still. bury the hatchet & the sword.— the sound of war is dredfull in my ear. any man who will not fight for his wife & childrn is a coward & a bastard

Mahometans. Presbyteria[n]s. &c. if ye will [p. [162]] not embrace our religion embrace our hospitalities.— [*15 lines blank*] [p. [163]]

30 January 1843 • *Monday*

[339]Monday January 30 at home

evening city council— closing the old Election.[340] Storm of snow. [341]Mr Taylor gave a Fractional Section[342] of land near Alton

31 January 1843 • *Tuesday*

[343]Tuesday January 31 Severe blowing of Snow. at home all day. [*6 lines blank*] [p. [164]]

---

336. TEXT: Instead of "in", possibly "is".
337. TEXT: Possibly "days".
338. TEXT: Instead of "mission", possibly "missions".
339. TEXT: Brown ink commences.
340. This was the last city council meeting held until 11 February 1843, when the newly elected officers were sworn in. (Nauvoo City Council Minute Book, 30 Jan. and 11 Feb. 1843, 159; JS, Journal, 11 Feb. 1843.)
341. TEXT: Blue ink commences.
342. A section of land surveyed as less than 640 acres—or one square mile—usually because part of it is cut off by a river or other physical boundary.
343. TEXT: Brown ink commences.

1 February 1843 • Wednesday

Wednesday February 1 [*7 lines blank*]

2 February 1843 • Thursday

Thursday Feb. 2 at home. towards evening went onto the hill. to see about the caucus the previo[us] evening.³⁴⁴ Davidson Hibbard Presiding. [Benjamin] Clapp chief speaker. reporting that Joseph & Hiram [Hyrum Smith] had attempted to take away the rights³⁴⁵ of the citizens. referring to the slim Election on the last council.—³⁴⁶ Esqr [Elias] Higbee. Dʳ [Robert D.] Foster &ᶜ H[iram] Kimball being concernd—³⁴⁷ gave those present a blowing up ³⁴⁸The spirit maketh. intercession &ᶜ better &c, "The spirit maketh intercession for us with striving which cannot be exp[r]essed:["]³⁴⁹ [p. [165]]

3 February 1843 • Friday

³⁵⁰Friday Feb 3ᵈ— at home attending To Lesson in German 11. walked out a few mintutes [minutes]. retur[ne]d 12¼ ⟨o'clock⟩ & paid Mr Peck— $100. for Wᵐ Manhard³⁵¹ Read proof of Doctrins & covenants³⁵²

⟨Bro⟩ John Mabery [Mayberry] Sent me a cow To assist in bearing my expences to Springfield.— 2½ Rode out with Emma to purchase Trimmings for a new carriage.— conversed with Elder [Orson] Hyde. & others [*5 lines blank*] [p. [166]]

4 February 1843 • Saturday

Saturday Feb— 4ᵗʰ· 1843 at home— 1 o clock P.M. attended the General

---

344. The caucus was in preparation for the biennial city election, which was held, according to ordinance, four days later on the first Monday in February. (JS, Journal, 6 Feb. 1843.)

345. TEXT: Possibly "right".

346. The Nauvoo City Council.

347. Higbee, Foster, and Kimball were among those who were nominated but not elected to city offices in the February 1841 election. Those who won the election were "elected by majorities varying from 330 to 337 votes." ("Municipal Election," *Times and Seasons,* 15 Jan. 1841, 2:287; "Municipal Election," *Times and Seasons,* 1 Feb. 1841, 2:309.)

348. TEXT: Blue ink commences.

349. See Romans 8:26.

350. TEXT: Brown ink commences.

351. An account book records this transaction under Manhard's account: "Feby 5ᵗʰ— order on C. Peck— 100—." "Mr Peck" is possibly Cyrus Peck, who owned a store in Montrose, Iowa Territory, or Chauncey Peck, a resident of Nauvoo. (Account for William Manhard, Newel K. Whitney, Papers, BYU; Nauvoo, IL, Tax list, district 3, 1842, p. 197, microfilm 7,706, U.S. and Canada Record Collection, FHL; "Burglary!!!," *Times and Seasons,* 1 Apr. 1841, 2:368–369.)

352. According to Wilford Woodruff, who with John Taylor was leasing the printing office from JS, work commenced Monday of this week (30 January) on stereotyping what became the second (1844) edition of the Doctrine and Covenants. (JS, Journal, 2 Dec. 1842; Woodruff, Journal, 1–4 Feb. 1843.)

city Election caucus at the Temple, where all things were amicably settled & mutual good feelings were restored to all parties. Bro [Benjamin] Clapp made a public confession. for the speech which he made at a former caucus³⁵³ ⟨4¼⟩ told Amasa Lyman he had restord Orson Pratt to his former standing, that he had concluded to make Amasa councillr to the fir[s]t Presidency.—³⁵⁴ ³⁵⁵[council Municipal court in the eve on a case of assault & Battery.³⁵⁶] [p. [167]]

5 February 1843 • Sunday

Sunday Feb. 5ᵗʰ 1843.— home all day studying German.

6 February 1843 • Monday

Monday Feb 6. at the fore-noon at the city election of Mayor Aldermn & council for next two years.³⁵⁷ at Prest Hirams [Hyrum Smith's] office.³⁵⁸ One

---

353. Clapp was the chief speaker at a caucus held three days earlier. (JS, Journal, 2 Feb. 1843.)

354. Following the excommunication of Orson Pratt on 20 August 1842, Lyman was "ordained an apostle in his place."ᵃ He functioned as a member of the Quorum of the Twelve during the five-month interim between Pratt's excommunication and his rebaptism and reinstatement in the quorum, though Lyman was not sustained to a formal position in the quorum by the membership of the church. After Pratt was rebaptized 20 January 1843 and ordained "to all the authority. of his former office,"ᵇ Lyman ceased to function as a member of the Quorum of the Twelve and was appointed as a counselor to the First Presidency.ᶜ While Lyman was not sustained to this position in subsequent conferences, he was recognized as having been a counselor in the First Presidency by those present at the 8 August 1844 special meeting following JS's death. At that meeting, Lyman was sustained as a counselor to the Twelve and in the October 1844 general conference as "one of the Twelve, just in the same relationship as he [was] sustained to the first presidency."ᵈ (a. Historian's Office, JS History, draft notes, 20 Jan. 1843; Amasa Lyman, Great Salt Lake City, Utah Territory, to Wilford Woodruff, 23 Aug. 1866, Historian's Office, Histories of the Twelve, ca. 1858–1880, CHL. b. JS, Journal, 20 Jan. 1843. c. Woodruff, Journal, [20] Jan. 1843. d. "Special Meeting," *Times and Seasons*, 2 Sept. 1844, 5:637–638; Clayton, Journal, 8 Aug. 1844; Woodruff, Journal, 8 Aug. 1844; "October Conference Minutes," *Times and Seasons*, 1 Nov. 1844, 5:692.)

355. TEXT: Blue ink commences.

356. A fight at a singing school in Nauvoo two days earlier resulted in two separate lawsuits between the parties involved. According to William Clayton, Josiah Simpson began the fight by attacking Stephen Goddard, William Cahoon, and William Riley. Goddard pressed charges on 3 February, and Simpson was fined three dollars plus court costs for assaulting Goddard. Simpson, in turn, charged Goddard, Cahoon, and Riley with assault and battery. The charge against Cahoon was dismissed, and a judgment was later made against Goddard and Riley for three dollars each and court costs. (Clayton, Journal, 2, 3, 4, and 6 Feb. 1843; State of Illinois v. Goddard et al. [Nauvoo Mun. Ct. 1843], Nauvoo Municipal Court Docket Book, 17–19 [second numbering].)

357. The Nauvoo city charter stated that elections were to be held on the first Monday in February, every two years, beginning with the first general election on 1 February 1841. At the Nauvoo city election on this day, JS was elected mayor; Orson Spencer, Daniel H. Wells, George A. Smith, and Stephen Markham, aldermen; and Hyrum Smith, John Taylor, Orson Hyde, Orson Pratt, Sylvester Emmons, Heber C. Kimball, Benjamin Warrington, Daniel Spencer, and Brigham Young, councilors. (An Act to Incorporate the City of Nauvoo [16 Dec. 1840], *Laws of the State of Illinois* [1840–1841], pp. 53–54, secs. 6 and 11; "City Election," *The Wasp*, 8 Feb. 1843, [2].)

358. The city council passed a lengthy ordinance three weeks prior to this 6 February 1843 election

o clock dined at home. after dinner Thomas Mo[o]re came in. & & enquired about a home.— & recived this blessing. "God bless you forever & ever. May the blessings of abraham. Isaac & Jacob rest upon you forever. & may you be set on th[r]ones high & lifted up in the name of Jesus Christ amen.— retur[ne]d to city Election [p. [168]]

7 February 1843 • Tuesday

Tuesday Feb 7th. 1843 at a council of the Twelve at B[righam] Youngs. in the afternoon sent a warrant to Hiram Kimballs for the book of blessings given by father Smith.[359] which was stolen from Far West. the affidavit Warrant was issued on affidavit of Johnathn Holmes. & the book obtaind. when Hiram Kimball came to Josephs & heard a general expose of the pocedig [proceeding] of Oliver Granger.—[360] [*5 lines blank*] [p. [169]]

8 February 1843 • Wednesday

Wednesday Feb. 8. Lesson in German. visited with breth[r]en & Sisters from. Michigan "A Prophet is not always a Prophet" only when he is acting as such. after. dinner Bro Parly [Parley P.] Pratt come[361] in f[r]om England.—[362] Conversati[o]n. [363]a bill was reported in the Legis[la]ture to divorce a man or woman. Wm Smith said they could not repeal the Nauvoo. Charter & the divorc[e] had better be referred to the courts. one Gentlemn said he understood it was very f[r]uitful at Nauvoo. two women from his neighbo[r]hood who had no children went to Nauvoo [p. [170]] & since have families. W^m

---

providing further detail about the election process, as well as a resolution identifying Hyrum Smith's office as the appointed and posted location for the 1843 election. (Nauvoo City Council Minute Book, 14 Jan. 1843, 132, 140.)

359. Joseph Smith Sr.

360. Reference is to a book containing patriarchal blessings mostly given by the first patriarch, Joseph Smith Sr., to Latter-day Saints in Ohio. Contrary to what is stated in this journal entry, the blessing book was not stolen "from Far West." When Patriarch Smith left Ohio for Missouri in spring 1838, Cyrus Smalling, a church dissenter, stole the book from him in Kirtland. About two years later, the volume was purchased from Smalling by Oliver Granger, the church's agent at Kirtland. But when Granger suddenly died in August 1841, the record fell into the hands of his son Gilbert, who claimed it as his own property. Gilbert Granger sent the book to Hiram Kimball at Nauvoo, "authorizing him to sell it to the church." When JS learned that Hiram Kimball had the book, he recovered it with a warrant on 7 February 1843. (George A. Smith and Wilford Woodruff, "A History of This Record," in Patriarchal Blessings, vol. 1; see also JS, Journal, 2 and 3 Mar. 1842.)

361. TEXT: Possibly "came".

362. When others of the Quorum of the Twelve returned from their British mission in 1841, Pratt remained to preside over the mission and supervise the church's publications there. He returned to Nauvoo on 7 February 1843. (Allen et al., *Men with a Mission,* chap. 12; Clayton, Journal, 7 Feb. 1843.)

363. TEXT: Brown ink commences.

Smith said he would explain the[y] lived in the Gentlemens neighbo[r]hood before they came to Nauvoo.—[364]

John C. Bennet[t] was like Jonah's Gourd. he came up like Jonah out of the whales belly. but when the sun arose. he witherd.—[365]

[366]4 P.M. went out. with Frederic [Frederick Smith] to slide on the ice [*7 lines blank*] [p. [171]]

9 February 1843 • Thursday

[367]Thursday Feb 9. 1843 was at the "Masonic Hall. some time in the forenoon. conversing with Mr [Jacob] Remick. & trying to effect a Settlement. Remick promisd to let Joseph have some notes on a paper Maker in Louisville. to pay him. & then went off contrary to promise.[368] ⟨conversation with Master [Jonathan] Nye & W[illiam] W. Phelps went to Keokuk⟩— Read Many letters. one f[r]om Judge [Richard M.] Young.—[369] Gave a relation of the Mob in Hyrum [Hiram, Ohio] which was writtn for the history[370]

Parley Pratt & othe[r]s came in & Joseph explai[ne]d the followi[n]g [p. [172]] there are 3 adminitater [administrators] Angels. Spirits Devils— one

---

364. The conversation here focused upon a recent exchange on the floor of the Illinois House of Representatives. William Smith presented a petition from a Mr. M'Boove for divorce. When a motion was made to postpone the petition, Smith took the opportunity to argue that it was just as inappropriate for the legislature to repeal city charters—which was a topic of recent debate—as to dissolve a marriage. Hall Sims, the Edgar County representative, commented that "singular results sometimes followed an association with Mormons," noting that when two childless couples in his neighborhood joined the Latter-day Saints they were blessed with children. William Smith retorted, "This is easily accounted for.— These families resided in the same county with the gentleman from Edgar." ("House of Representatives," *Sangamo Journal* [Springfield, IL], 2 Feb. 1843, [2]; see also 196n42 herein.)

365. See Jonah 4:6–8.

366. TEXT: Blue ink commences.

367. TEXT: Brown ink commences.

368. In August 1842, JS loaned Remick $200 to help him pay a debt. Remick paid JS back by deeding to him "one half of the Land and property he owned" in Keokuk, Iowa, but had then "calld for some more favors" from JS. JS let him have some six or seven hundred dollars' worth of "cloths," apparently on credit. Whatever payment JS ultimately managed to obtain from Remick—either for the original $200 loan, the "cloths," or perhaps additional debts—was unsatisfactory; JS reported in April 1843 that Remick had taken "most $1100 from me, . . . he is a thief." (JS, Journal, 14 Sept. 1842 and 6 Apr. 1843, pp. 153, 336 herein.)

369. JS responded to Young with a letter this day, discussing a loan and requesting information about the petition that JS sent to Young through Calvin A. Warren, requesting the appointment of a new postmaster for the city of Nauvoo. (JS per William Clayton, Nauvoo, IL, to Richard M. Young, Washington DC, 9 Feb. 1843, copy, Newel K. Whitney, Papers, BYU; JS, Journal, 8 Nov. 1842.)

370. The incident in Hiram, Ohio, refers to the mobbing of JS and Sidney Rigdon on the night of 24–25 March 1832. The history refers to the history of the church that Willard Richards was writing and compiling. (JS History, vol. A-1, 205–208.)

class in heaven Angels the spir[i]ts of Ju[s]t men made perfect.— innumerable co[mpany] of angels & Spirits of Ju[s]t Men made perf[e]ct.

An angel appears to you how will you prove him. ask him to shake hands if he has flesh & bones— he is an Angel. "spirit hath not fl[e]sh & bones"[371]

spirit of a Ju[s]t man made perf[e]ct. person in its tabernacle could hide its glory. [p. [173]]

if David Patten or the Devil came. how would you determi[n]e should you take hold of his hand you would not feel it. if it were a false administrtin[372] he would not do it.

true spirit will not give his hand
the Devil will. 3 Keys—[373]

a man came to me in Kirtland & told me he had seen an angel dressed so & so. I told him he had seen no angel there was no such dress in heaven he got mad & went out in the street & commanded fire to come down out of heaven & consume me [p. [174]] I laughed at him & told him he was one of Baals prophets his God did not not hear him. Jump up & cut yourself—[374] & he comma[nde]d fire f[r]om heaven to consume my house.—

when I was preaching in Philadelphia a quaker wanted a sign— I told him to be still. after sermon he wanted a sign. I told the congregati[o]n the man was an adulterer, "A wicked & adulterous geneatin [generation]."[375] & the Lord to me in a revelation that any man who. wantd a sign was adulteros person.— "It is true [p. [175]] said one for I caught him in the very act.— which he afterwards confessed when he was baptized[376]

Parley Pratt asked for some council. & tomorrow evening was appointed before the Quorum of the Twelve [*9 lines blank*] [p. [176]]

10 February 1843 • Friday

Friday February 10,th. 1842 conversation with strangers & others. reviewed the history of the Mob in Hyrum [Hiram, Ohio]. & the first Journey to Missouri[377]

---

371. See Luke 24:39.

372. TEXT: Possibly "administrtor".

373. In 1839, JS gave similar instruction to the Twelve. William Clayton's account of this 9 February 1843 meeting was later canonized. (Woodruff, Journal, 27 June 1839; Instruction, 9 Feb. 1843, in Clayton, Journal, 9 Feb. 1843 [D&C 129].)

374. See 1 Kings 18:22–29.

375. See Matthew 16:4.

376. This event likely took place during JS's stay in Philadelphia during December 1839 and January 1840, while on a trip to Washington DC, seeking redress for losses sustained by church members in Missouri. (See JS History, vol. C-1, 1003, 1012.)

377. A mob attacked JS and Sidney Rigdon at Hiram, Ohio, the night of 24–25 March 1832; JS,

3 o, clock P.M. in court room with B[righam] Young H[eber] C. Kimball. Orson Hyde. P[arley] P. Pratt Orson Pratt Wilford Woodruff John Taylor. Geo. A. Smith. & W[illard] Richards. according to previous appointmnt. by Pret Joseph at 3½ P.M.³⁷⁸

Let business be presented in short. no explanati[o]ns³⁷⁹

had an interview with Mr [John] cowan this morning. he is a [p. [177]] delegate from the inhabitants 20 miles above this, opposite Burlington ⟨viz. Shokokon—⟩ to come to Nauvoo & petition that a talented Mormn preacher take up his residence with them & they would find him a good house. & give him suppo[r]t with liberty to invite as many Mormons to settle in that place as May please to so to do—³⁸⁰ Decided that Bro Bear³⁸¹ go and preach to them, Observation concerning theiving & the Post Office. & suggested that a general meeting be called.—³⁸² & that Elder Geo. J. Adams be silencd & called to Nauvoo with his family—³⁸³ Requested that all business be presentd without comments.— [p. [178]]

5 o clock P.M. adjourned. & immediately— Oliver Olney & Newell Nurse were brought in by Sheriff J[ohn] D. Parker as prisoners for Stealing Goods f[r]om the Store of Moses Smith on the night of the 23ᵈ of January. last.— Olney confessed before the Mayors court that he had been visited many times

---

Rigdon, and others visited Missouri in summer 1831 to determine the location of the city of Zion.

378. See Quorum of the Twelve Apostles, Minutes, 10 Feb. 1843.

379. TEXT: Possibly "explanation".

380. The concern of the inhabitants of Shokokon, Illinois, for religion may not have been the only reason Cowan invited JS to encourage Mormon settlement in that area. Cowan represented Henderson County residents who may have hoped to profit from Mormon migration into western Illinois. On 16 February, JS visited Shokokon in company with Cowan, Parley P. Pratt, and Orson Hyde, and on 20 February, JS purchased city lots from Robert McQueen. (Allaman, "Joseph Smith's Visits to Henderson County," 46–55; JS, Journal, 15, 16, and 17 Feb. 1843; Henderson Co., IL, Deed Records, vol. 1, pp. 312–313, microfilm 1,392,775, U.S. and Canada Record Collection, FHL.)

381. Possibly John Bair. (Nauvoo, IL, Tax list, district 3, 1842, p. 218, microfilm 7,706, U.S. and Canada Record Collection, FHL; JS History, vol. D-1, 1466.)

382. JS had been concerned about the operation of the Nauvoo post office since the previous fall and in November petitioned the United States postmaster general to replace Sidney Rigdon as postmaster. (JS, Journal, 8 Nov. 1842; see also 8 Sept. 1842, esp. 142n485 herein.)

383. The previous year Adams committed adultery while proselytizing in the East, thereby losing the confidence of church members in that region. Adams discussed his adultery and desire to repent in two letters to JS. Adams returned to Nauvoo by request, and at a meeting of the First Presidency and the Quorum of the Twelve on 27 May 1843 JS noted that Adams "had given satisfactions to him concerning the things whareof he was accused he had confessed all wharein he had done wrong & had asked for mercy & he had taken the right course to save himself that he woold now begin new in the church." (George J. Adams to JS, Nauvoo, IL, 11 Oct. 1842, JS Collection, CHL; George J. Adams, Boston, MA, to JS, Nauvoo, IL, 23 Feb. 1843, JS Collection, CHL; Quorum of the Twelve Apostles, Minutes, 10 Feb. and 27 May 1843; Woodruff, Journal, 27 May 1843.)

by the Ancient of days.³⁸⁴ sat with him on the 9. 10. & 11 days of June last.— & shall sit in council with ancient of Days on tuesday next— have had a mission from him to the 4 Quarters of the world. & have been have establishd the 12 stakes of Zion— I have visited them all but one in. the South. I have suffered much for 2 or 3 years— been without clothes & sufferd much I despise a theif but to clothe myself— I opened the store of Moses Smith on the eve of 23ᵈ of Janury— by bori[n]g into a bored [board] window & took out the goods present (several Hundrd peices). hid them in the cornfield. & carried them home from time to time in under the same roof with smith. No one knows any thing about the robbery but mys[e]lf— found the $50 bill among the goods. Mrs had a peice of cloth to make some frocks. Witnesses Harri[e]t Nurse.— Mary Olney— Isaac Chase——— Joseph Hadlock Mr Far [Winslow Farr]— Moses Smith.— Decision of court Mr Nurse be dischar[ge]d— & Olney be remand[e]d to prison for trial or bo[u]nd under $5.000 bonds [p. [179]] Olney stated that the church had never taught him to steal. or any such thing. Olney was cut off from the chu[r]ch some time Since³⁸⁵ [*12 lines blank*] [p. [180]]

11 February 1843 • Saturday

Saturday Feb— 11ᵗʰ 1843 City council assembled at 10 O 'clock A.M. 7 new councillors sworn in,³⁸⁶ When the Mayor came in and said he had been doing a good deed. had been conversing with Elder [Sidney] Rigdon— & he & his family were willing to be saved, good feelings prevaild.— & we have shaken hands togethr³⁸⁷

---

384. Latter-day Saints understood "the Ancient of Days" to be a reference to Adam. (Explanation, 19 May 1838, in JS, Journal, 19 May 1838, in *JSP*, J1:271 [D&C 116]; "The Ancient of Days," *Times and Seasons*, 15 May 1843, 4:204.)

385. Olney was disfellowshipped from the church on 17 March 1842 for "setting himself up as a prophet & revelator." Unable to pay bail after having been charged with larceny and burglary in the mayor's court, Olney was to be committed to the county jail to await trial by the circuit court. However, being a "large, powerful, athletic man," he escaped from the officers transporting him to jail. Olney gave himself up to Marshal Henry G. Sherwood two weeks later, on 25 February 1843. (Nauvoo High Council Minutes, 17 Mar. 1842; City of Nauvoo v. Olney [Nauvoo Mayor's Ct. 1843], Nauvoo Mayor's Court Docket Book, 45–50; "Effects of Apostacy," *Times and Seasons*, 1 Feb. 1843, 4:89; "Outrageous Theft," *The Wasp*, 15 Feb. 1843, [2]; JS, Journal, 25 Feb. 1843.)

386. Seven of the city councilors and aldermen elected 6 February 1843 were already serving in the positions they had been elected to. The other six—Orson Hyde, Sylvester Emmons, Benjamin Warrington, Daniel Spencer, George A. Smith, and Stephen Markham—were new to their respective positions and were presumably sworn in this day. The identity of the seventh "councillor" sworn in this day is unclear. (JS, Journal, 6 Feb. 1843; "City Election," *The Wasp*, 8 Feb. 1843, [2].)

387. Difficulties between JS and Rigdon were first recorded in JS's journal on 12 May 1842.

A. general Election of Petty officers took place.—³⁸⁸ prophecid to James Sloan Recorder— that it would be better for him 10 years hence not to Say any thing more about fees.——— Mayor Made his Inaugural Address— & ⟨in which he⟩ urged the necessity of the city council acting upon the principle of liberality & of relievi[n]g [p. [181]] the city f[r]om all unnecessary expences & burthens. Not to attempt to improve the city but enact such laws as will promote peace & good order. & the people will improve the city, capitalist will come in from all quarters & mills factories. & machinery of all kinds & buildings will arise on every hand this will become a great city. & prophecid that if the council would be liberal in their proceedings they would become rich.— & spoke at considerable length again[s]t the principle of pay for every little service rendered and espec[i]ally that of committe[e]s having extra pay.— [p. [182]] for services— & reproved the Judges of the late Election for not holding the poll open after 6 o clock when there were many wishing to vote.—³⁸⁹ Judges were Geo. W. Harris Daniel Spencer,— & _____ [Benjamin] Warrington— Dr [Robert D.] Foster took an active part in electioneering for the written opposition ticket. & obstructing the passage to the polls—— adjour[ne]d at 3. P.M. for 1 hour assembled at 4—— the subject of markettig [marketing] was introduc[e]d when Alderman [George W.] Harris spoke.³⁹⁰ B[righam] Young Harris again recomm[en]ding 2 houses for marketi[n]g. Hyrum Smith advocating the same. said he "there is old aunt Sabry [Sabra Granger]³⁹¹ she comes to Market with [p. [183]] horse & carriage. with her butter & we can accommodate old Aunt Sabry.— Mayor said if we began too large we shall do nothing. If the council will give me leave I will build a house a small one. at once. & the markett ought to be holden by the corporation if ⟨of⟩³⁹² the house, when built, will Support itself then we can go on the hill & build another or on [*illegible*]

---

388. On this date the city council elected a number of city officers, including James Sloan as recorder, William Clayton as treasurer, and Henry G. Sherwood as city marshal. (Nauvoo City Council Minute Book, 11 Feb. 1843, 159.)

389. An ordinance passed a month earlier stipulated that "the Judges of the Election may, if they shall deem it necessary, for the purpose of receiving the votes of all the electors wishing to vote; postpone the closing of the Polls, until twelve O Clock at night." According to Wilford Woodruff, the election was "a warm contest . . . esspecially in the evening." (Nauvoo City Council Minute Book, 14 Jan. 1843, 133; Woodruff, Journal, 6–11 Feb. 1843.)

390. George W. Harris was made an alderman on 30 October 1841. Although he is not identified as having been reelected in the 6 February 1843 election, he continued to serve in this position. ("City Election," *The Wasp*, 8 Feb. 1843, [2]; JS, Journal, 6 Feb. 1843; see also Nauvoo City Council attendance records, 11 Feb. 1843, Nauvoo, IL, Records, CHL.)

391. Granger was nearly forty-nine at the time. Helen Mar Whitney also referred to her as "Aunt Sabry Granger." (Helen Mar Whitney, "Travels beyond the Mississippi," *Woman's Exponent*, 1 Sept. 1884, 13:58.)

392. TEXT: Instead of "if ⟨of⟩", possibly "of ⟨if⟩".

[largr?]. Council should hold an influen[c]e over the prices in market so that the poor shall not be oppressd.³⁹³ the mechanic should not oppress the farmer. the upper part [p. [184]] of the town has no right to rival us—³⁹⁴ here on the bank of the river was where we fir[s]t pitched our tents where the sickness & deaths occured.— we have been the making of the upper part of the townn. we have given them the Temple. we began here & let the market go out from this part of the city. let the upper part of the town be marketed by the waggon till they can build a Market.— voted that a market house be built. that the committee on public improveme[n]t be requird to select a piece of grou[n]d for Market & the rise³⁹⁵ of grou[n]d on Main St Reported. [p. [185]] voted that it be left discretion[ar]y with the Mayor how large the market shall be.—³⁹⁶ [*9 lines blank*]

changing the furniture in the house to receive mother Smith. in the family. Young & [Willard] Richards wrote G[eorge] J. Adams to come to Nauvoo.—³⁹⁷ & silencd him, [p. [186]]

12 February 1843 • Sunday

Sunday feb 12, 1843.—— some 7 or 8 young men called to see me part of them from the city of N. York they treated me with the greatest respect I shewed them the fallacey of Mr [William] Millers data.³⁹⁸ concerni[n]g the Millnim [Millennium]³⁹⁹ & preachd them quite a sermon. shewed them, that

---

393. Ultimately, price regulation was not included in the provisions regulating the Main Street market. (Nauvoo City Council Minute Book, 25 Feb. 1843, 163–166.)

394. Nauvoo was built on land made uneven by a bluff rising above the floodplain about a mile inland from the bank of the Mississippi River. The first Nauvoo settlers located on the low ground closest to the river. As the town grew, it extended to the higher country inland on the bluff. At first it was intended that Main Street on the "flat" would be the commercial center of the city, but by 1843 the upper part of town on Mulholland Street became a rival commercial district. (Flanders, *Kingdom on the Mississippi,* 188–189; Leonard, *Nauvoo,* 143–148.)

395. TEXT: Possibly "size".

396. In addition to approving the construction of a market, the city council on this date determined that the location of the market would be on "Main Street, opposite or near to Ivin's brick House." Two weeks later, on 25 February, the city council passed "An Ordinance, concerning a Market on Main Street," explaining the physical design of the market and how its construction was to be financed. The ordinance also described how the market would function to regulate the sale of perishable commodities in the city during its hours of operation on Mondays, Wednesdays, and Fridays, "or every day except Sunday, to be regulated by the City Council." (Nauvoo City Council Minute Book, 11 and 25 Feb. 1843, 160, 163–166.)

397. Adams received Young and Richards's letter on 10 March 1843 and replied that he would "start immediately for Nauvoo." (George J. Adams, New York, to Brigham Young and Willard Richards, Nauvoo, IL, 10 Mar. 1843, Brigham Young Office Files, CHL; see also JS, Journal, 10 Feb. 1843.)

398. TEXT: Instead of "data", possibly "date".

399. Miller was a Baptist who maintained that a thorough examination of the books of Daniel and Revelation revealed that the second advent of Christ was imminent. He did not claim the gift of prophecy, merely that he had read the existing revelations and assigned a proper chronology to his eschatology.

the error is in the Bible or translation. & that Miller is in want of information The prophecies must be fulfilld sun be turnd into darkness & moon into black & many more things before Christ come.— [p. [187]]

13 February 1843 • Monday

Monday Feb 13^([th]) 1843— Elder [Sidney] Rigdon came in early in the morning & gave a brief history the 2^d visit ~~to~~ of the Presidency to Jackson Co Missouri.—⁴⁰⁰

Recited in German. & walkd out in the city with Elder [Orson] Hyde ⟨retur[ne]d at 12 o'cclock.—⟩ Elder Samuel Snider [Snyder] of Job ⟨creek⟩ branch gave ~~the~~ a bag of flour. hearing the presidint was in want also a dollar in cash from Sister Davis, of the same place.—⁴⁰¹ John C. Annis come in for council about ~~work~~ wood taken f[r]om Iowa.— & got it.⁴⁰² The Marshall⁴⁰³ came in and stated that one Ralston [William H. Rollosson]⁴⁰⁴ was trying to get the Post office. & Dr [Robert D.] Foster had [p. [188]] signed the Petition for the first, one— gave inst[r]uction concerning ~~1/8~~ bonding 1/8 of the lot north of his dwelling to John Oakley for $500. $ dow[n]. $100 in 3 month.

¼ 4 P.M. said he would go to printing office with W[illiam] W. Phelps.

evening at O. Hydes. with Bro Dixon from Salem Mss. said that those who come here having money and purchased without the chu[r]ch & without coun-

---

His message was accepted by thousands of premillennial Christians in the early 1840s. Miller began preaching in 1831 that the second advent of Christ would occur "in the year 1843 or before." His views became widely known after his publication of *Evidence from Scripture and History of the Second Coming of Christ, about the Year 1843; Exhibited in a Course of Lectures* (Troy, NY: Kemble and Hooper, 1836). As followers of Miller's interpretation of scripture grew in number, he was joined by several other prominent millennialists, including Joshua V. Himes, George Storrs, Josiah Litch, Henry Dana Ward, and Charles Fitch. (William Miller to Anna and Joseph Atwood, 31 May 1831, cited in Rowe, *God's Strange Work,* 96; Rowe, *God's Strange Work,* chaps. 4–7.)

400. The second journey of JS to Jackson County, Missouri, took place in spring 1832, for the purpose of organizing the management of church stores and printing projects, and sustaining church leaders. Rigdon gave his recollections to Willard Richards for the latter's work on JS's history. (Sidney Rigdon, Statement, [Feb. 1843], Historian's Office, JS History Documents, ca. 1839–1880, CHL.)

401. Goods and money were being sent to JS to help defray the legal and travel expenses he incurred in connection with his habeas corpus hearing in Springfield. Later in the month, the Quorum of the Twelve wrote letters to church members in various areas asking them to help supply JS and his family with necessities so that he could devote his time and efforts to church concerns. (See 245n280 herein; and JS, Journal, 18 Feb. 1843.)

402. Annis was a millwright in Nauvoo. (Nauvoo Masonic Lodge Minute Book, 16 June 1842; Nauvoo City Council Minute Book, 15 Mar. 1841, 16.)

403. Henry G. Sherwood.

404. Rollosson was a non-Mormon businessman in the Nauvoo area. (Gregg, *History of Hancock County, Illinois,* 938–939, 944–945.)

cil. must be cut of[f]— and many observations which aroused bro. Dixons feelings much[405]

 Copy— To the Hon Mr Bryant [John A. Bryan] 2ᵈ assᵗ P. M. [Post Master] General we your petitioners beg leave respectfully to submit that as an attempt is now ~~being made~~ by certain individuals being made. to place the Post office in this place into hands of William H. Rollinson [Rollosson] a strangir in our place. and one whose conduct since he came here, has been such as to forbid our having confidence in him. and we do hope. and pray. both for our sakes. and that. of the public. that he may not recive the appointme[n]t of Post Master in Nauvoo Ills. but that the present post master[406] may continue to hold the office— Bro J. Smith. If the foregoing can have a number of respectable subscribers I believe Rollison cannot get the office. I should like to have it so as to send it out on Thursdays[407] mail. Respˡʸ [Respectfully] Sidney Rigdon [p. [189]]

14 February 1843 • Tuesday

Tuesday Feb 14. 1843 read proof of some of the Book of covenants.[408] with W[illiam] W. Phelps. German Lesson. from 9½ to 11. A.M. Stoves removed from the Mayors office. to the smoke house— which is designed for the Mayors office till a new one can be built.—[409]

[410]Mr [John] Cowan arrived from Shokokon, much conversation with various individuals

sold Dr [Willard] Richards a cow.— [*5 lines blank*] [p. [190]]

---

 405. JS and others went into debt to purchase the land on which Nauvoo was built, with the hope that immigrating Saints would then purchase city lots from them to pay off the debt. Church leaders expected that people with money would purchase these lots to help pay off the debts they had contracted rather than buy lots from other speculators. (See Promissory notes, JS et al., to Horace Hotchkiss; JS et al. to John Gillett and Smith Tuttle, 12 Aug. 1839, JS Collection, CHL; Brigham Young et al., "An Epistle of the Twelve," *Times and Seasons,* 15 Oct. 1841, 2:567–570; JS, Journal, 13 Apr. 1843, p. 355 herein; and William Clayton, "Notice to Emigrants and Latter-day Saints Generally," *Nauvoo Neighbor,* 20 Dec. 1843, [3].)
 406. Sidney Rigdon.
 407. TEXT: Possibly "Shundays".
 408. JS and Wilford Woodruff commenced working on what would become the second edition of the Doctrine and Covenants on 30 January 1843. (Woodruff, Journal, 1–4 Feb. 1843; JS, Journal, 3 Feb. 1843.)
 409. The stove was moved from a large room in JS's house to an adjacent small brick building built as a smokehouse. The mayor's office was again moved the following month from the smokehouse to JS's red brick store. (Historian's Office, JS History, draft notes, 14 Feb. 1843; JS, Journal, 28 Mar. 1843.)
 410. TEXT: Ink from this point to the end of the entry matches ink in the following entry.

15 February 1843 • Wednesday

Wednesday Feb 15.[411] 1843 helped change the top plate of the office stove— after reading in the Alton paper about the Libellous letter written to Mr Bassett of Quincy about Judge [Nathaniel] Pope. [Justin] Butterfield & the Ladies attending the trial at Springfield[412] about ⟨1 o clock⟩ ~~noon~~ started for Skokokon with [John] Cowan. O[rson] Hyde— & P[arley] P. Pratt.— in sleighs.[413] previous to starting Wm Law. Gave 1 barrel. flour, 5 bushels Meal. and 10. bu of brann.— when we came on the prairie it was so cold I proposed [p. [191]] to Mr Cowan. and wait till the morrow. but he chose to go forward.— and we arrived safely at Mr Roses,[414] where we had supper. and gave long exposition of Millerism. slept with Mr Cowan,—

16 February 1843 • Thursday

Thursday Feb. 16. 1843 After breakfast. I started with Mr [John] Cowan— & Bro [Orson] Hyde & [Parley P.] Pratt started from Michael Cranes to go to Shokokon 5 miles. on the way Hyde & Pratt turnd over & Hyde hurt his hand, and their horse ran away & we brought ~~their~~ him back— we din[e]d at ⟨Mc.⟩Quinns [Robert McQueen's] [p. [192]] mills. & went[415] to Skokokon. & veiwd the place which is very desirable for a city. when we returnd to the place of Dining & 3 Elder Hyde prayd I preached to a large & attentive audience 2 hours f[r]om 19 Rev— 10 verse & shewed them that any man who denied his being a prop[h]et was not a prea[c]her of righteousness. they opened their eyes & appeard well pleased. & had a good effect. after meeting when we had retur[ne]d as far as Mc Quinns Mills. Mr Cowan turnd up to the fence &

---

411. TEXT: Possibly "13 15".

412. Published in the 18 January issue of the *Quincy Herald,* the "Libellous letter" was actually addressed to John H. Pettit, editor of that newspaper. The letter deplored JS's discharge from arrest on a writ of habeas corpus in Springfield earlier that month, charged Judge Nathaniel Pope and United States district attorney Justin Butterfield with failing to fulfill their official duties, and called into question the virtue of the ladies who had attended the hearing. While the editor of the *Alton Telegraph* condemned the letter as libelous, he expressed continuing contempt for JS. ("Joseph Smith the Mormon Prophet," *Quincy [IL] Herald,* 18 Jan. 1843, [2]; "The Calumniators Detected," *Alton [IL] Telegraph and Democratic Review,* 11 Feb. 1843, [2]; Notice, *Alton Telegraph and Democratic Review,* 18 Feb. 1843, [3]; "The *Quincy Herald,* Judge Pope, the Discharge of Joe Smith," *Alton Telegraph and Democratic Review,* 28 Jan. 1843, [2].)

413. Cowan visited JS five days earlier, requesting a "talented Mormn preacher" to move to Shokokon, where he would be at "liberty to invite as many Mormons to settle in that place as May please to so to do." (JS, Journal, 10 Feb. 1843.)

414. Probably Jeremiah Rose, one of the three original settlers of Quincy, Illinois. Rose was a member of the First Congregational Church of Quincy. In 1836, he moved to the area near Shokokon that would later become part of Henderson County. (Asbury, *Reminiscensces of Quincy, Illinois,* 25.)

415. TEXT: Possibly "west".

proposed to call. while waiting a mo[p. [193]]ment. Mr Cranes horse, (for he went with our company.) which was behind ran. and Jumped into our sleeigh as we Jumped out & thence over our horse. & the fence sleigh & all. fence 8 rails high. & bothe horses ran over lots. & through the woods clearing themselves from the sleighs. & had their frolic out witho[u]t Hurting themselves or riders,— it was truly a wonderful feat. & as wonderful a diliverace [deliverance] of the parties We took supper at Mr Cranes & I staid at Mr Roses. Dr Richards [Willard Richards] invited brethrn to come on Monday & pile up & chop wood. for th[e] Presidnt. [p. [194]]

17 February 1843 • Friday

Friday Feb— 17. 1843. ⟨& 18⟩ Mr [John] Cowan returnd with me to my house. where we arrivd about noon. and enjoyed myself by my own fire side with many of my fri[en]ds around me. Mr cowan proposed to give me 1/4 of city lots in Shokokon & 2 each to [Orson] Hyde & [Parley P.] Pratt.—[416]

18 February 1843 • Saturday

Saturday Feb. 18 1843.— about house & office. mostly some at ~~city~~ High council. in store. or Lodge Room. [Josiah] Ells on trial from Laharpe.[417] several called for council on law. one ⟨Chistophe[r] Dixon⟩ again[s]t Nauvoo house.— carlos granger called.— [p. [195]] Esqr [Calvin A.] Warren called. had hurt his horse. said it was not the first time he had missed it by not following Joseph's advice.— at dinner Joseph said. when the earth was sanctified & became like a sea of glass. it would be one g[r]eat urim & Thumim the Saints could look in it & see as they are seen.[418]

The 12 wrote a letter to the Saints in Laharpe to call for food for the Presidnt[419] [p. [196]]

---

416. On 20 February, Robert McQueen deeded to JS over thirty lots in Shokokon for $1,230. JS assigned power of attorney to Amasa Lyman to sell the land on his behalf. (Henderson Co., IL, Deed Records, vol. 1, pp. 312–313, microfilm 1,392,775, U.S. and Canada Record Collection, FHL; Power of attorney, JS to Amasa Lyman, Nauvoo, IL, 28 Feb. 1843, JS Collection, CHL; JS, Journal, 1 Mar. 1843.)

417. The La Harpe, Illinois, elders quorum decided to disfellowship Ells on charges of killing hogs that were not his, "lying about a settlement with James Dunn" and "calling him an old lying hy[p]ocrite," stealing Brother Griffith's potatoes, and "fraudu[le]ntly obtaining one hundred and twenty dollars from Br Huddleston." In response to his appeal to the Nauvoo high council on this date, Ells was acquitted of the charges. (Nauvoo High Council Minutes, 18 Feb. 1843.)

418. This language was echoed by JS on 2 April 1843. (Instruction, 2 Apr. 1843, in JS, Journal, p. 324 herein, and Clayton, Journal, p. 404 herein [D&C 130:8–9].)

419. The letter urged church members at La Harpe to help supply JS and his family with the necessities of life so he could devote his whole time to the spiritual affairs of the church. Similar letters were written to the Saints in Ramus, Lima, and Augusta. (Brigham Young, Nauvoo, IL, to "the church," La Harpe, IL, 18 Feb. 1843, draft, Brigham Young Office Files, CHL; Brigham Young, Nauvoo, IL, to

19 February 1843 • Sunday

Sunday Feb 19ᵗʰ 1843 from 9 A.M. to 1 P.M with ⟨High Council⟩ listening to the proof of a great Big nothing. in a case between Wilson Law. and [*blank*] [Moses] Nickerson— I who had been fighting some time p[r]evious I explaind the laws of the U. S. the Laws of Iowa & Illinois— shewd them that Nickesen had the oldest claim & best. right & left it for Law to say how much Nickesen should have. the parties shook hands in token of settlement of all diffculties.⁴²⁰ [p. [197]]

20 February 1843 • Monday

Monday morning Feb 20 about 70 of the brethren came together according to previous notice. and drawed and sawed & chopped. and split. & moved and piled a large lot of wood ⟨for the presidnt⟩. and the day was spent by them in much pleasantry & good humor & feeling. a white oak log 5 ft. 4 inches diameter was ⟨This tree was cut. & drawed by Joseph⟩ cut through with a cross cut saw in 4½ minutes by Hiram Da[y]ton & bro Tidwell from 9. to 11. reciting in German— from 11. to 12 [p. [198]] ⟨Snow. melted away so as to destroy sl[e]ighing.—⟩ in court, in brick store. on assumpsit Charles R. Dana— vs Wᵐ B. Brink—⁴²¹ adjour[ne]d for ten days.— Last night Arthur Mil[l]ikin had a quantity of books stolen and found them— at 3 this P.M. in Hyrum Smiths Hayloft Thomas Morgan & Robert Taylor. Morgan 15 ⟨Robert Taylor ~~16~~ 15⁴²² next april⟩ years old ⟨both members of the Chu[r]ch⟩. were arrested on suspicion in the foreno[o]n and on finding the books immediately went to trial befor the Mayor.— having had a brief examinati[o]n about nooon⁴²³ court adjournd till 10 tomorrow [p. [199]]

"the church," Ramus, IL, 23 Feb. 1843, draft, Brigham Young Office Files, CHL; Historian's Office, JS History, draft notes, 3 Mar. 1843; JS Journal, 24 Mar. 1843, p. 316 herein.)

420. The case, which according to the high council minutes lasted from 9:00 a.m. until midnight, revolved around title to an island in the Mississippi River. According to the minutes, Nickerson "put in money with Arthur Morrison" to purchase the island as part of Iowa's Half-Breed Tract, after which Morrison was to "make a deed to Nickerson." Morrison, however, "did not reserve the claim for Nickerson which he had purchased with Nickersons money" but rather sold the island to Law without informing Law of his earlier agreement. Complicating matters further, Nickerson had apparently settled on the island. Having understood from Isaac Galland that the Mississippi islands had not been included in the United States survey, JS argued that the islands were not part of the Half-Breed Tract at all but rather were "refused lands which the government did not see fit to do anything with" and that they "consequently were free plunder or belonged to the actual setler." (Nauvoo High Council Minutes, 19 Feb. 1843; JS, Journal, 6 Apr. 1843, p. 337 herein.)

421. This case was brought before JS on 2 March 1843. (See p. 280 herein.)

422. TEXT: Instead of "~~16~~ 15", possibly "~~16 17~~ 15".

423. TEXT: Possibly "noon the".

⟨while the court was in session 2 boys were seen fighting in the street. by Mills tavern. the mayor saw it. & ran over immediately & caught one of the boys (who had began ~~the~~ to fight with clubs) & stoppd him. & then, the other. and gave the bystande[r]s a lecture for not interfering in such cases.— & retur[ne]d to Court

No body is allowed to fight in this city but me, said the mayor—⟩
evening called at [[Heber C.] Kimball's][424]

⟨This day John Q. Adams presentd a petition to the house of Representative. signed by 51,863 citizens of Mass[ll.] praying Congress "to pass such acts and propose such amendme[n]ts to the constitution. as will separate the petitioners from all connection with ~~slavery~~ the institution of slavery."[425]———⟩

21 February 1843 • Tuesday

Tuesday February 21. 1843.[426] Mayors court. at the smoke house. 10 A.M. City of Nauvoo vs. Robert Taylor. & Thomas J. Morgan plad [pled] guilty. Taylor for Stealing— & Morgan for receiving— sentencd 6 months imprisonment in cartharge Jail.[427] 11 went to Temple. found Bro Hawes [Peter Haws] preaching about Nauvoo [p. [200]] house, Mr Wooworth [Lucien Woodworth]. spoke say something in vindicating my own character. commenced under peculiar circumstances.— have made all contra◊cts for Nauvoo house, was employed to build from the commencement. some brick on hand. most ready to start brick work one says "can you give me something to eat? I'll try. another says I will have my pay. "go to hell & get it." ⟨said I—⟩ I have set me down to a dry Johncake & cold water and the men who have workd with me no man shall go onto my povrty stricken foundation to build himself up. for I began it & will finish it, Not that public spirit here as in other cities dont deny revelation if the Temple and Nauvoo [p. [201]] house are not finished you must run— away.— when I have had a pou[n]d of meat or quart of meal I have divided

---

424. TEXT: Transliteration from Taylor shorthand: "k/q-m-b-l-s".

425. The minutes of the House of Representatives record that "as objections were made from all parts of the House, the petition was not presented." (*Congressional Globe*, 27th Cong., 3rd Sess., p. 317 [1843].)

426. TEXT: Possibly "~~1841~~ 1843".

427. While there were provisions for keeping convicted criminals in custody, there was no official jail in Nauvoo during JS's lifetime. Section 27 of the Nauvoo city charter stated that "the city council shall have power to provide for the punishment of offenders, by imprisonment in the county or city jail." Notwithstanding the sentence pronounced in this journal entry, on petition of the citizens of Nauvoo, JS directed that Taylor and Morgan work out their sentence on the city's highways. (An Act to Incorporate the City of Nauvoo [16 Dec. 1840], *Laws of the State of Illinois* [1840–1841], p. 57, sec. 27; Historian's Office, JS History, draft notes, 1 Mar. 1843; JS, Journal, 1 Mar. 1843.)

> Snow. melted away so as to destroy
> *sleighing.*—
> in court, in brick store, on
> assumpsit. Charles R. Dana
> vs. Wm. B. Brink — adjourd
> for ten days. — Last night
> Arthur Milliken had a
> quantity of books stolen
> and found them at 3 this
> P.M. in Hyrum Smiths
> Hayloft. Thomas Morgan
> & Robert Taylor *Robert Taylor* ^Martin^ 15 *next April*
> *both members of the Church*
> years old. were arrested
> on suspicion in the forenoon
> & on finding the books im-
> =mediately went to hear before
> the Mayor. — having had a
> brief examination about noon
> court adjourned till 10. Tomorow

Cancellations and insertions. Cancellations and insertions like the ones seen on this page appear throughout Joseph Smith's second Nauvoo (third Illinois) journal. Handwriting of Willard Richards. JS, Journal, Dec. 1842–June 1844, bk. 1, p. [199], JS Collection, Church History Library, Salt Lake City. (Photograph by Welden C. Andersen.)

Examples of significant insertions. Willard Richards inserted ten lines of text within the first five printed lines on the page and a shorter insertion in the middle of the page. This page also features an instance of shorthand (on the thirteenth handwritten line). Handwriting of Willard Richards. JS, Journal, Dec. 1842–June 1844, bk. 1, p. [200], JS Collection, Church History Library, Salt Lake City. (Photograph by Welden C. Andersen.)

with the workman.[428] (pretty good Doctrin for paganism said Joseph)[429] have had about 300 men on the Job— the best men in the world. those that have not complaind I want them to continue with me. & them who hate mormonism & every thing else that's good. I want them to get their pay & run away

Joseph says[430] well the pagan prophet has preached us a pretty good sermon thiss morni[n]g— to break off the yoke of oppressesion ⟨I dont know as I can better it much—⟩ and say what he is a mind to. [p. [202]]

~~for~~ that the pagans and the pagan prophetts to feel more our prosperity is curious. I am almost converted to his doctrine, "he has prophecied if these buildings go down it will curse the place." I verily know it is true. Let us build the templ. there may be some speculatins about Nauvoo house. say some— some say because we live on the hill we must build up this part on the hill.[431] does that coat fit you D^r [Robert D.] Foster? pretty well! put it on then. this is the way people swell like the ox or toad.

They'l come down under the hill among little folks brother Joseph how I love you— and get up opposition. & sing[432] names to strangers & scoundrels &c [p. [203]]

I want all men to feel for me. when I have shook the bush— & bore the burdn and if they do not—, I speak in[433] authority

in the name the Lord ⟨god⟩ he shall be damnd,— people on the flats are aggrandiz[i]ng themselves. by the Nauvoo house.

who laid the foundation of the Temple. Bro Joseph in the name of the Lord. not for his aggrandizement but for the good of the whole

Our speculators say our poor folk on the flat are down & keep them down. How the Nauvoo house cheats this man & that man— say the speculators. they are fools ought to hide their heads in a hollow punkin & never take it out.— [p. [204]]

the fir[s]t principle brought into consideratio[n] is aggrandizement. some think it unlawful— but it is lawful while he has a disposition to aggrandize all around him. false principle, to aggrandize at the expence of another. every thing God does is to aggrandize his kingdom

---

428. TEXT: Instead of "workman", possibly "workmen".

429. Woodworth, who was overseeing the construction of the Nauvoo House, was not a member of the church at this time. He referred to himself as the "Pagan Prophet." (Historian's Office, JS History, draft notes, 21 Feb. 1843; Woodruff, Journal, 21 Feb. 1843.)

430. TEXT: Possibly "say,".

431. Foster, Hiram Kimball, Daniel H. Wells, and other investors were promoting building projects on the hill near the temple, thereby drawing labor and resources away from the Nauvoo House project. (JS, Journal, 11 Feb. 1843; Flanders, *Kingdom on the Mississippi*, 185–189.)

432. TEXT: possibly "singn [sign]".

433. TEXT: Possibly "Possibly ~~of~~ in".

Nauvoo House. A revelation dated 19 January 1841 directed the church to build the Nauvoo House, which was to serve both as a residence for Joseph Smith and his family and as a hotel or boardinghouse. Joseph Smith declared that the construction of the Nauvoo House was as important as the construction of the Nauvoo temple. Following Smith's death, however, the Saints channeled their resources toward finishing the temple and left the Nauvoo House uncompleted. These two paintings by David Hyrum Smith show how far work on the Nauvoo House had progressed before the effort was abandoned, as well as the building's location on the bank of the Mississippi River. (Courtesy the Lynn and Lorene Smith family and Community of Christ.)

how does he lay the foundation? build a temple to my great name. and call the attention of the great. but where shall we lay our heads an old log cabin

I will whip Hiram Kimball & Esqr [Daniel H.] Wells and every body else over Dr Fosters head, instead of building the Nauvoo house build a great many little skeletons see Dr Fosters mammoth skeletons [p. [205]] of Dr Foster[434] rising all over town but there is no flesh on them. personal aggrandizement. dont care how many bones— somebody may come along & clothe them.— elephants. crocodiles &^c eaters. such as grog shop &c— card shops &c— those who live in glass houses should not throw stones. The building of N[auvoo] House is just as sacred in my view as the Temple.[435]

I want the Nauvo[o] House bui[l]t it must be built, our salvation depends upon it. When men have done what they can or will for the temple. let them do what they can for the Nauvoo House. We never can accomplish our work at the expence [p. [206]] of another. There is a great deal of murmuring in the church— about me, but I dont care any thing about it. I like to hear it thunder. to hear the saints grumbling.— the growling dog get the sorest head. If any man is poor and afflicted. let him come and tell of it.— & not complain— or grumble

finishing Nauvoo House like a man finihig [finishing] a fight. if he gives up he is killd— if he holds out a little longer he may live— a story. a man who will whip his wife is a coward. & fought with a man who had whippd wife.——— still remembrd he was whipped his wife. & whipped him till he cried enough.— hang on to the [p. [207]] Nauvoo house thus & you will build it. & you will be on Pisagah [Pisgah] & the gr[e]at men who come will pile their gold & silver till you are weary of receivng them. & if you are not careful will be lifted up & fall and they will cover up & cloak all your former sins— & hide a multitude of sins.[436] & shine forth fair as the sun &c[437]

those who have labord & cannot get your pay be patient, if you take the means which are set apart let him he will destroy themselves, [p. [208]]

if any man is hungry let him come to me & I will feed him at my table.

---

434. JS was playing on the name of Foster's "Mammoth Hotel," a three-story brick building under construction at the time on the northeast corner of Mulholland and Woodruff streets, just east of the Nauvoo temple site. (JS, Journal, 21 Jan. 1844, JS Collection, CHL; Cochran et al., *History of Hancock County, Illinois,* 441; Berrett, *Sacred Places,* 3:184.)

435. A 19 January 1841 revelation mandated the construction of the Nauvoo temple and the Nauvoo House. (Revelation, 19 Jan. 1841, in Doctrine and Covenants 103:9–27, 33–36, 1844 ed. [D&C 124:22–82, 111–122].)

436. See James 5:20.

437. See Song of Solomon 6:10; see also Revelation, Mar. 1829, in Doctrine and Covenants 32:3, 1835 ed. [D&C 5:14]; and Prayer, 27 Mar. 1836, in *Prayer, at the Dedication of the Lord's House,* 2 [D&C 109:73].

if any are hungry or naked dont take away the brick &c but come & tell. I will divide. & then if he is not satisfied I will ~~kill~~ kick his back side

there cannot be some fire without some smoke. well if the stories about Jose[ph] Smith are true. then the stories of J. C. Bennet. [John C. Bennett] are true about the Ladies of Nauvoo. Ladies that the Releif society was organized of those who are to be wifes to Jos Smith.[438] Ladies you know whithr it is true. no use of living among hogs without a snout. this biting an[d] devouri[n]g each other.[439] [p. [209]] for Gods sake stop it.

one thing more, political economy. our duty to concentrate ~~that~~ all our influence to make popular that which is sound & good. & unpopular that which is unsou[n]d Tis right ⟨politically⟩ for a man who has influe[n]ce to use it as well as for a man ~~to~~ who has no influ[en]ce to use his. from henceforth I will maintain all the influe[n]ce I can get. in relation to politics I will speak as a man in religion in authority. if a man lifts a dagger to kill me, I will lift my tongue.— when I last preached. heard such a [p. [210]] groani[n]g I thought of the paddy's. ell [eel] when he tried to kill him could not contrive any way so he put it [in] the water to drown him. and as he began to came[440] to— see said he what pain he is in how he wigles his tail.— the banks are failing & it is the privilige to say what a curency we want. gold & silver to build the Temple & Nauvoo house.[441] we want your old nose rings & finger rings & brass ket[t]les no longer. if you have old raggs—[442] watches. guns go & peddle them. & bring

---

438. JS here refers to the section titled "The Mormon Seraglio" in Bennett's recent attack on JS and the church. (Bennett, *History of the Saints,* 217–225.)

439. See Galatians 5:15.

440. TEXT: Possibly "come".

441. By 30 June 1842, well over one hundred banks in the United States had failed since the Panic of 1837. As demand for specie payments increased, Illinois's only chartered banks, the Bank of Illinois at Shawneetown, the Bank of Cairo, and the State Bank of Illinois, were forced to suspend specie payments on multiple occasions. By fall 1842, the notes of the State Bank were so devalued that the state treasury refused to accept them as payment for taxes. By February 1843, the state legislature passed acts requiring both the State Bank of Illinois and the Bank of Illinois at Shawneetown to cease operations and liquidate their assets, and in March 1843, the charter of the Bank of Cairo was repealed. In early 1842, JS wrote to Edward Hunter in the East: "The State Bank is down, and we cannot tell you what Bank would be safe a month hence, I would say that Gold and silver is the only safe money a man can keep these times, you can sell specie here for more premium, than you have to give, therefore there would be no loss, and it would be safe, The Bank you deposit in might fail before you had time to draw out again." (Dowrie, *Development of Banking in Illinois,* 104, 114–115, 124–126; Pease, *Frontier State,* 308–315; An Act to Diminish the State Debt, and Put the State Bank into Liquidation [24 Jan. 1843], An Act to Put the Bank of Illinois into Liquidation [25 Feb. 1843], and An Act to Repeal the Charter of the Bank of Illinois [4 Mar. 1843], *Laws of the State of Illinois* [1842–1843], pp. 21–30, 36–39; JS, Nauvoo, IL, to Edward Hunter, West Nantmeal, PA, 9 and 11 Mar. 1842, JS Collection, CHL.)

442. The term "rags" here may have referred to paper money, or perhaps to rags that could be used to produce paper. ("Rag," in *Oxford English Dictionary,* 8:105.)

the hard metal. if we will do this by popular opinion you will have a sound currency. [p. [211]] send home banks notes.— & take no paper money. & let every man write his neighbor before he starts to get gold and Silver.— I have contemplated these things a long time, but the time has not come till now. to speak till now.

I would not do as the Nauvoo House committee[443] has done. sell stock for an old stone house[444] where all the people who live die. & put that stock into a mans ha[n]ds to go east and purchace ~~goods~~ Rags to come here & build up Mamoth bones with.

as a political Man in the [p. [212]] name of Old Joe Smith I command the Nauvoo commitee not to sell a share in the N[auvoo] House without the Gold or Silver, excuse bro [John] Snider he was in England. when they sold stock for stone house.—[445] I leave it

the meeting was got up by N. Committe [Nauvoo House committee] the pagans. Roman Catholics. & Methodist & Baptist shall have peace in Nauvoo only they must be grou[n]d in Joe smiths mill.— I have been in their mill I was grou[n]d in Ohio. & [New] York States a presbyteri[a]n smut machine—[446] & last machine was in Missouri & last of all I have been th[r]ough Illinoiss smut machine & those [p. [213]] who come here must go th[r]ough my smut machine & that is my tongue,

Dr Foster remarked much good may grow out of a very little, and much good may come out of this. If any man accuses me of Exchanging N[auvoo] House] stock for Rags &c. I gave a $1000 to this house. & $50 to relief so[c]iety & some to Fulmer[447] to get stone to build Joseph house. & I ~~might~~ mean to build Joseph a house & you may build this. & I will help you I mean to profit this. & will divide the mammoth bones with you. I am guilty of all [p. [214]] I have been charged,— I have signed my ~~letter~~ name to a petition to have

---

443. George Miller, Lyman Wight, John Snider, and Peter Haws.
444. On 20 January 1841, Robert D. Foster contracted to purchase, over the course of several years, "the upper Stone House" from Hyrum Smith for $5,000. Foster sold the house to the Nauvoo House Association on 18 May 1842 for seventy-seven shares of stock at $50 per share. At the same time, Hyrum Smith sold his remaining "Interest in the upper Stone House" for nine $50 shares of stock. (Bond, Hyrum Smith to Robert D. Foster, 20 Jan. 1841, Nauvoo House Association, Records, CHL; Nauvoo House Association, Stock Book, [79]–[86].)
445. Snider, a member of the Nauvoo House Association, was on a mission to England from 26 March 1842 to 23 January 1843. (JS, Journal, 26 Mar. 1842 and 23 Jan. 1843.)
446. A machine for removing impurities from grain during the milling process. ("Smut," in *Oxford English Dictionary*, 9:294.)
447. Probably David Fullmer.

W[m] H. Rolinson [Rollosson] to have the Post Office.—[448] I did not know a petition for Joseph Smith.—[449]

Joseph[:] I thought I would make a coat. it dont fit the D[r]. ⟨only in the P[ost] office⟩ if ~~if~~ it does fit any one let the⟨m⟩ put it on.

The bones are skeletons[450] and as old Ezekiel said I command the flesh & the sinnews to come upon them. ⟨that they may be clothed.—⟩[451]

Blessing by Bro. P[arley] P. Pratt.— [p. [215]]

22 February 1843 • Wednesday

Wednesday Feb 22. 1843 9 a,m,[452] the President & Mr [John] Cowan came in the office. and soon after. Abel Owen presented a claim again[s]t Carter Cahoon & Company. & notes of Oliver Granger of about 700 dollars— for payment.[453] Joseph told him to burn the papers & he would help him. he gave the papers to Joseph. & Joseph gave him an order on on Mr Cowan for $15. for provisions,

Rode out about the city with Mr Cowan.

recited in German [p. [216]]

23 February 1843 • Thursday

Thursday Feb 23 1843.— recited in German— Rode out a few miles but did not get off my horse.— P.M. Mr [Walter] Bagby called to collect taxes Mr [William] Clayton ⟨was⟩ sent for & came to examine the books.— bro Dixon called to see the mayor about some lost or stolen property.

3½ P.M. the Mayor burned 23$— of city scrip on the stove[454] hearth & while burning said so may all uncurrent. & unsound money go down as ~~these~~

---

448. See JS, Journal, 13 Feb. 1843.

449. The previous November a petition was sent to United States postmaster general Charles A. Wickliffe requesting that JS replace Sidney Rigdon as Nauvoo postmaster. (JS, Journal, 8 Nov. 1842; 142n485 herein.)

450. TEXT: Possibly "skeleton".

451. See Ezekiel 37:7–8.

452. TEXT: "a,m" is triple underlined in original.

453. Church leaders in Kirtland, Ohio, created several mercantile organizations through which a variety of goods were purchased for the use of the Saints. Jared Carter, Reynolds Cahoon, and Hyrum Smith formed Carter, Cahoon, & Company, which dissolved when most church members left Ohio. JS sent Oliver Granger back to Kirtland to function as the agent for the church settling its financial affairs there. (Staker, *Hearken, O Ye People*, 441–444; 32n104 herein.)

454. TEXT: Possibly "stone".

this burns.—[455] said he would pay no taxes on Hotchkiss purchase[456] Amasa Lyman went to Shokokon to commence preaching.— this morning[457] [p. [217]]

24 February 1843 • Friday

Friday Feb 24. 1843. Rode out with Elder [Brigham] Young. dined at Mr. [*blank*] Rode to D^r [Robert D.] Fosters. had some conversation about the Post Office and other Similar matters.[458] Foster had some feeling on the occasion. returnd to the office, walkd away with Elder Young. at about 3 P.M. [*5 lines blank*] [p. [218]]

25 February 1843 • Saturday

Saturday Feb 25— 1843 Recivd a Gold watch—[459] A.M. in city council.—[460] P.M. 3. oclock met after adjournment. I have read the Constitution. & find my doubts. removed.— the constitution is not a law. but empowers the people to make laws.— constitution govern the lands of Iowa but is not a law for the people. constitution tells what shall not be lawful tender— Constitution section 10 this is not saying gold & silver shall be lawful tender— it only provid[e]s the states may make a law— to make gold and silver— lawful Tender. [p. [219]] the Ligislature have ceded up to us the privilige of enacting laws we stand in the same relation as the state.— This clause is for the Legislature, is not a law— for the people. diametrically contra[r]y to the constitution. this state have passed a

---

455. An ordinance was passed on 4 March 1843 making gold and silver the only lawful tender in Nauvoo. (Nauvoo City Council Minute Book, 4 Mar. 1843, 167; JS, Journal, 4 Mar. 1843, pp. 294, 295 herein.)

456. On 12 August 1839 JS, Hyrum Smith, and Sidney Rigdon contracted to purchase "upwards of five hundred acres" from Connecticut land speculators Horace Hotchkiss, John Gillett, and Smith Tuttle. By the terms of the contract, Hotchkiss and his partners continued to hold title to the land until they were paid in full, which had not happened by 1843. As title holders they, rather than JS, were responsible for paying the taxes on the land. (Brigham Young et al., "An Epistle of the Twelve," *Times and Seasons*, 15 Oct. 1841, 2:567–570; Horace Hotchkiss, Fair Haven, CT, to JS, Nauvoo, IL, 27 May 1842, JS Collection, CHL; JS, Journal, 5 Jan. 1843, p. 234 herein.)

457. On 10 February 1843 John Cowan requested that a Mormon "preacher" move to Shokokon. JS later gave power of attorney to Lyman to sell land in Shokokon, Illinois. Lyman also oversaw the survey of a town site and began building in the area. He and his family remained there until late June 1843. (JS, Journal, 10 Feb. and 1 Mar. 1843; "Amasa Lyman's History," *Deseret News*, 15 Sept. 1858, 122; see also JS, Journal, 17 Feb. 1843.)

458. Three days earlier JS publicly denounced Foster for supporting William Rollosson's bid for the position of Nauvoo postmaster and promoting his own construction projects that competed with the building of the Nauvoo House. (JS, Journal, 21 Feb. 1843, pp. 271–276 herein.)

459. Willard Richards later identified this watch as a gift of Samuel Brown. (Historian's Office, JS History, draft notes, 25 Feb. 1843.)

460. Two city ordinances were passed during this session, one of them an ordinance allowing for the construction of a market house. (Nauvoo City Council Minute Book, 25 Feb. 1843, 163–166; see also JS, Journal, 11 Feb. 1843.)

stay law. making it lawful ⟨to⟩ tender to property. and if we creat[e] no law. we must be govend [governed] by them.— shall we be such fools as to abide their laws. which are unconstitutional? No. we will make a law for Gold & Silver then[461] their law ceases & we can collect our debts.— "Powers not delegated to the states— or reservd fr[o]m the states" is constituti[o]nal,[462] [p. [220]]

congress. or constitution acknowledgd that the people have all power not reserved to itself) ⟨I am a Lawyer⟩ I am big Lawyer. & comprehnd heavn earth & hell— to bring forth knowledge which shall cover up all Lawyers & doctors—) this is the doctrine of the constitution so help me God.— the constitution is not Law to us— but provision to make laws, Where it provides that no one shall not be hinderd from worshipping God acording to his[463] own conscenc [conscience] is a law.— No legislatu[r]e can enact a law,— to prohibit constitution provid[e]s to regulate [p. [221]] bodies of men not individuals [Daniel H.] Wells objected to its taking effect immediatily. O[rson] Pratt amend[e]d to 1st June.— O[rson] Spencer— said he could have wished Dani[e]l Webster the Lion of the West East had heard the Lion of the west in the chair. unnecessary to wait. so said [Brigham] Young.— Ordinance Regulating the currency.)[464] before the Council.— [William W.] Phelps and [Willard] Richards were invited to give an opinion (by the Mayor) & did. in affirmative.— and left afterwa[r]d the Mayor gave another speech—

[Oliver] Olney came to to the Marshalls.[465] & was i◊◊◊◊d[466]

26 February 1843 • Sunday

Sunday March February 26 at home. with his mother who was with an affection of the Lungs. nursing with his own hands.

[Oliver] Olney carr[i]ed to Carthage [p. [222]]

---

461. TEXT: Possibly "there".

462. According to the tenth section of the first article of the United States Constitution, "No State shall . . . make any Thing but gold and silver Coin a Tender in Payment of Debts." JS probably referred to the "stay law" passed in Illinois the previous month, requiring a higher valuation of land when there was a forced sale of land for debt or taxes in depressed times. JS's statement regarding powers not delegated to the states is a paraphrase of the Tenth Amendment of the Constitution. (An Act Entitled "Act Regulating the Sale of Property on Judgments and Executions" [6 Jan. 1843], *Laws of the State of Illinois* [1842–1843], pp. 186–189.)

463. TEXT: Possibly "the his".

464. The debate centered on a proposed ordinance stipulating that "Gold and Silver Coin only be received as lawful tender" in payment of city taxes, fines, and debts, and that "City Scrip shall not hereafter be emitted as moneyed Currency." The ordinance passed on 4 March 1843. (Nauvoo City Council Minute Book, 4 Mar. 1843, 167; JS, Journal, 4 Mar. 1843, pp. 294, 295; see also 277n455 herein.)

465. Henry G. Sherwood.

466. Olney was charged with burglary and larceny two weeks earlier. (JS, Journal, 10 Feb. 1843.)

27 February 1843 • Monday

Monday Feb. 27— 1843 in house mostly with his mother who was sick— came in the office and signed a writ or search warrant for Bro Dixon to search— Fidlers[467] & John Eagles house for a box of shoes.—

28 February 1843 • Tuesday

Tuesday Feb 28— Mostly with his mother & family Mr. John Brassfield who helped Joseph to escape from the missourians came and spent the day and night.[468]

P.M. mother rather easier. To Elder [Orson] Hydes. to dinner at 4 o clock P,M.

notice in Chicago Express that W̅m̅ ⟨Hiram⟩ Redding had seen sign of the son of man.—[469] wrote Editor of Times & Seasons. for No 8. vol 4 that Reding had not seen the sign of the son of man. and he would not come in [18]43— &c see times & Seasons[470] [p. [223]]

1 March 1843 • Wednesday

Wednesday March 1. 1843 Recidted [Recited] in ~~Hebrew~~ German. in the office reviewing his valedi[c]tory. published in Times & Seasons No 7. Vol 4.—[471] went with Marshall[472] to Bro [William] Laws to get provision for the prisoners [Thomas] Morgan & [Robert] Taylor[473]

---

467. Possibly George or Henry Fidler. (Platt, *Nauvoo,* 41, 59.)

468. A reference to the escape of JS and his companions en route from Gallatin to Columbia, Missouri, in April 1839, after having spent more than four months in the jail at Liberty, Missouri. Brassfield was one of the guards who facilitated the escape with the sale of two horses. (Jessee, "Prison Experience," 33–34; Promissory note, JS to John Brassfield, 16 Apr. 1839, JS Collection, CHL.)

469. See Matthew 24:30. In addition to printing Redding's statement about seeing the sign of the Son of Man, William Brackett, the editor of the *Chicago Express,* made an explicit comparison between Redding and JS, suggesting, and then explaining, his conviction that "so far at least as revelations are concerned, we think Joe Smith has his match at last." ("St. Charles Patriot—Extra" and "Millerism in Illinois," *Chicago Express,* 7 Feb. 1843, [2], [3].)

470. In his letter to the editor, JS stated that Christ's second coming would not take place until prophecies of signs preceding the Second Coming were fulfilled. (JS, "Correspondence," *Times and Seasons,* 1 Mar. 1843, 4:113.)

471. Unable to fulfill "the arduous duties of the editorial department any longer," JS resigned as editor of the *Times and Seasons* at the completion of the newspaper's third volume, dated 15 October 1842, and appointed John Taylor in his place. This journal entry refers to a second valedictory castigating "the editors of the public journals" for their unfair treatment of JS in the press. (JS, "Valedictory," *Times and Seasons,* 15 Nov. 1842, 4:8; JS, "Correspondence," *Times and Seasons,* 15 Feb. 1843, 4:97–98.)

472. Henry G. Sherwood.

473. A week earlier, Morgan and Taylor pleaded guilty to theft and were sentenced to six months' imprisonment. "On petition of the Inhabitants of the City," however, JS decided that the prisoners "should work out their punishment on the highways of Nauvoo." (JS, Journal, 20 and 21 Feb. 1843, pp. 267, 268 herein; Historian's Office, JS History, draft notes, 1 Mar. 1843.)

Elder [Orson] Hyde called to get a horse this afternoon. Joseph orderd Ira[474] to get his best horse. and ~~let~~ Put on the Lieut Generals[475] saddle.— & let Elder Hyde ride the govenor on the Liutenants saddle.—[476]

Signed a power of attorney dated 28 February to Amasa [p. [224]] Lyman[477] to seell [sell] all the Lands in Henderson County deeded to me by Mr Mc. Quinn [Robert McQueen].—[478]

walked out

———— ☙ ————

Editorial Note

The following two journal entries—for 2 and 3 March 1843—deal almost exclusively with a medical malpractice suit that was tried in the Nauvoo mayor's court, over which JS presided. The case grew out of events that occurred on 22–24 October 1842 involving the plaintiff's pregnant wife, Margaret Kennedy Dana, and the defendant, Dr. William Brink, a Thomsonian physician. The plaintiff, Charles Dana, charged Dr. Brink, who had been called to treat a fever in Margaret Dana, with causing premature childbirth by misdiagnosis and unjustifiable practices that left Margaret's health impaired.[479] Willard Richards, a Thomsonian doctor himself,[480] devoted over forty pages of the journal to recording the arguments and testimony presented in the case—probably because of his professional interest in the medical details. Richards's notes of the trial, although disjointed at times, also illustrate how JS and his associates understood and applied the law.

———— ☙ ————

2 March 1843 • Thursday

Thursday march 2^d 1843 adjourned case of Charles Dana vs D^r[481] [William] Brink in assumpsit came up at 10 A.M. Before the Mayor at Masons. Hall.—[482]

---

474. Probably Ira Willis, whom JS's son Joseph Smith III remembered as "a man-of-all-work about the premises where we lived." (Mary Audentia Smith Anderson, "The Memoirs of President Joseph Smith," *Saints' Herald,* 25 Dec. 1934, 1637.)

475. JS.

476. JS purchased a horse on 11 July 1842 that he named "Jo Duncan," after the former governor of Illinois who was running again for the office in the 1842 election opposite Thomas Ford. (JS, Journal, 11 July 1842; Historian's Office, JS History, draft notes, 11 July 1842.)

477. Power of attorney, JS to Amasa Lyman, Nauvoo, IL, 28 Feb. 1843, JS Collection, CHL.

478. John Cowan offered land in Shokokon, Henderson County, to JS on 17 February 1843. On 20 February, McQueen deeded to JS over thirty lots in Shokokon for $1,230. (JS, Journal, 17 Feb. 1843; Henderson Co., IL, Deed Records, vol. 1, pp. 312–313, microfilm 1,392,775, U.S. and Canada Record Collection, FHL.)

479. See "Decision," *The Wasp,* 22 Mar. 1843, [2]–[3].

480. "History of Willard Richards," *Deseret News,* 23 June 1858, 73.

481. TEXT: The "r" in "D^r" is double underlined.

482. The upper room of JS's store. The case was called up ten days earlier but postponed until this date. (JS, Journal, 20 Feb. 1843.)

Orson Spencer side justice, [Onias] Skinner Esqr for Plaintive. claimed $99[483] failing to perform correctly as physic[i]an in treatment of Dana's wife,[484] complaint read. Witnesses D^r [Robert D.] Foster, D^r [John F.] Weld, Dr Bennet [Samuel Bennett]

Mrs [Patty Bartlett] Sessions[485] [p. [225]]

[Sidney] Rigdon, & marsh [William H. J. Marr] Esqr for defendant Rigdon objectod to certain witn[e]sses viz. the physicians.— enough to alarm Nauvoo. Enough to swear themselves into business and the other who is opposd out of business not the 20th time that attempt havve been made of this kind. Legislatures have taken it up.— came here professing Botanice. Physic[i]an.—[486] the other Boerhavein Physic[i]ans. came from ⟨Germany⟩ England to America.— to Dr Rush.[487] antipodes feet come togethr insted of ⟨their⟩ heads. they have ever[488] been crying out agai[n]st Botanic. & Botanic agai[n]st the othe[r]s. for Poyson.— if they [p. [226]] are permittd to witness this court is to decide between the practices.[489] the Legislatu[r]e and no court has attempted to

---

483. Illinois law limited the jurisdiction of justices of the peace in contract or "assumpsit" cases like this one to those where the debt or demand did not exceed one hundred dollars. (An Act concerning Justices of the Peace and Constables [3 Feb. 1827], *Revised Code of Laws, of Illinois* [1826–1827], pp. 259–260, sec. 1.)

484. Margaret Kennedy Dana.

485. In addition to Drs. Foster, Weld, and Bennett, and midwife Sessions, other witnesses at the trial included Dr. George R. Bostwick, Mary Deuel, Prudence Marks Miles, Jacob Shoemaker, Charles Higbee, and Margaret Kennedy Dana.

486. Thomsonian or "botanic" physicians like Brink believed all illness was caused by cold and that any treatment producing heat would aid in recovery. They used cayenne pepper, steam baths, and *Lobelia inflata* (a plant) to cause heavy sweating and vomiting. Foster, Weld, and Bennett, on the other hand, were "regular" physicians—doctors who had been educated at medical academies and universities and who believed that a hyperactive state of the arteries was the cause of disease. "Regular" doctors treated patients with an aggressive form of bloodletting and calomel purges. Brink's lawyers, Rigdon and Marr, objected to the testimony of Drs. Foster, Weld, and Bennett in this trial on the grounds that the testimony of practitioners of a competing school of thought not only could bias the court against Brink but could also prejudice the local citizens against Brink's professional practice. (Haller, *People's Doctors*, 40; Porter, *Greatest Benefit to Mankind*, 393; Whorton, *Nature Cures*, 28–31; "Medical Notice," *The Wasp*, 2 July 1842, [3]; see also "Thomsonianism," *Hagerstown [MD] Mail*, 27 May 1836, [2]; and "Calomel," *Tioga Eagle* [Wellsboro, PA], 17 Aug. 1842, [3].)

487. Eighteenth-century physician and professor Herman Boerhaave of Leiden University began a tradition of practical university education of medical students that was later adopted and altered by William Cullen, Scottish physician and professor at University of Edinburgh. Benjamin Rush trained as a physician under Cullen, adopting the idea of university education in medicine yet altering Cullen's philosophy of health and disease. Rush educated some three thousand medical students in his lectures at the newly founded University of Pennsylvania. Rigdon is using Boerhaave and Rush as symbols of pragmatic, university trained, "regular" physicians. (King, *Medical World*, 60–86; Porter, *Greatest Benefit to Mankind*, 246–247.)

488. TEXT: Possibly "even".

489. TEXT: Possibly "parties".

decide.— let them bring physi[ci]ans of the same school for witnesses, Mr Dana knew what practice the Do[c]tor was of and why not call phycns [physicians] of the same school—

your honor has once been tried on acount. of your r[e]ligion—— the physicas [physicians] mu[s]t testify accordi[n]g to their practice believi[n]g the other to be wrong.— if this order of things should prevail you would loose your head & I mine. [p. [227]]

Skinner replied. where a party claims interest he must establish. his claim. objection should be made before Placing virodirce [*voir dire*?],—[490] [*blank*] to settle this grand question interest. no witness can be obje[c]ted to on ground of inter[e]st unless the party must be a gainer or looser in the case, Bailor cannot be witness. no other ⟨kind⟩ interest can destroy testimony. if every witness was desirous to have the suit go on th[e]ir testimo[n]y would be valid

Evidenc Harrisns Dige[s]t. ⟨Page 1047—⟩[491] immediat inter[e]st in the suit. only.

Philips on Evidence 71.[492] Rule of Int &c [p. [228]] Baron Gilbert where there is a certain benefit at stake.— Watsons Reports 199 5 Wendell Repo[r]t. 55, 13 Mass 99 & 99.— Swanns Tractes[493] 59—[494] We defy the gentlemn to present any. difent [different] rule of law——

Marsh [Marr][:] not on the ground of definite inter[e]st we made the objctin [objection] we objct to witnesses on ground of incompetincy— of judging of a diff[er]ent practice.— this state has not decided which practice.— what makes them witneses. from knowledge of facts or experts.— were they present if so I have no objction. A should contract for building a boat.— C is caled to exami[n]e (who is a sail boat) [p. [229]] or brick house.— judgd by a carpenter. those who are of the same school are competent. those are experts who are of the practice with the prac◊ticee Def[e]ndant Judge [Sylvester] Emmons[495] asked leave to reply— objcted by Marsh [Marr]—— Opinion of

---

490. *Voir dire* (Old French for "to tell the truth") was a legal term used to refer to a hearing on the competence of jurors or witnesses, or sometimes to the oath to tell the truth, the meaning possibly used here. Skinner seems to be arguing that an objection to a witness must precede taking the oath. According to the published trial summary, "after the witnesses were sworn for the plaintiff, the defendants counsel raised an objection to them." ("Decision," *The Wasp*, 22 Mar. 1843, [2].)
491. Harrison, *Digest of All the Reported Cases,* 2:1047.
492. Phillipps and Amos, *Treatise on the Law of Evidence*, 1:71.
493. TEXT: Possibly "Treates" or "Treatis".
494. Ten Eyck v. Bill, 5 Wendell 55 (N.Y. Sup. Ct. 1830); Higginson v. Dall, 8 Tyng 98 (Mass. Sup. Jud. Ct. 1816); Swan, *Treatise on the Law,* 59.
495. Emmons served with Skinner as counsel for the plaintiff, Charles Dana. ("Petition," *The Wasp*, 22 Mar. 1843, [2].)

the court cannot tell whither they are competent or not till they give their testimony.

~~Mars~~ What is the rule of competen[c]y?

Mrs [Prudence Marks] Miles.— ~~called~~ some delicacy to be heard alone.— Rigdon requestd that witneses be examind alone,

Skinner[:] we shall look to the court

Marsh [Marr]— producd the law ~~for~~ and court orderd the house cleard.

Skinner. we design to shew certain [p. [230]] facts by witnesse[s] present & then to physic[i]ans to know whither they consider the treatment correect

Rigdon ⟨it is⟩ effort to secure to themselves the advantage we have conten[d]ed again[s]t.

⟨Physic[i]an[496]⟩ to give testimony on testimny they have not heard.— because the witness are examined apart. let us have this trial on the principle of common sense.— lady presentd to witness ce[r]tain things. & physi[ci]ans called to testify on that testimny as they are called one by one— & we object to any other course,— Ladies build a mud house & Doctors chink it.

Emmons— singular case. to requ[e]st witneses Doctors to withdraw. read section of Law [p. [231]] in Medical Men, & on science May witness— Philips on evidnce 1 836. 899.—[497]

objected to witness for which this court was adjond [adjourned] on the same prin[c]iple.

corrected by Rigdon—

Marsh [Marr] insisted on what the law of the state grants us.—

Court is of opinion it can do no harm to have witneses present.

Mr[s.] Miles pre[se]nt at Mrs [Margaret Kennedy] Dana's— on her sickness. had been sick severl weeks. did not know what it was, was ~~hurt~~ Injurd[498] by a fright present when Dr Brink came about noon [p. [232]] dont think she was in labor pains. did [not?] discover any symptoms of labor pains, did not stay but a minute or. two,— did not return till about 11. P.M. said he had given her smut rye.—[499] she said she was in pain,— we expected they were labor pains.

---

496. Possibly "Physicans".

497. Phillipps and Amos, *Treatise on the Law of Evidence*, 2:836. Page 836 of this, the fifth American edition, corresponds to page 899 of the eighth London edition.

498. TEXT: Instead of "~~hurt~~ Injurd", possibly "~~Injurd~~ hurt".

499. This was ergot, or *Claviceps purpurea*, a fungus that grows on rye, used to contract uterine muscles during labor and to minimize bleeding. Samuel Thomson strongly cautioned botanical or Thomsonian doctors against the use of ergot, reporting that it "destroys the elastic power of the muscles to such a degree, that they never regain their natural tone," and that "the consequence of such treatment often proves fatal." ("Ergot," in *Oxford English Dictionary*, 3:271; Thomson, *Narrative of the Life*, 188.)

Brink said her water had discharged & she would be dilverd [delivered] in a short time. child apperd to be pitchd one side. Mrs Dana did not know. the waters had discha[r]ged. Brink staid till morning, there when he introduc[e]d his hand hurt her. & begged to let her alone. and let have its own operation, on the bed used more violence than I thoght was necessa[r]y but not enough to ◊◊◊◊d[500] her out of her position I did not examine the woman dont know any thing about it. by Court[:] [p. [233]] you have been at such cases & know what is usual? yes— Mrs Dana was not expecting it for 10 days. dont recollect that Dr Brink said it was necessary to deliver her of the child on account of Diarehas or fever. but ~~was~~ sent for D^r to cure fever, &c, wasnt expetig [expecting] to be confind.— she was better when I went away in the morning. got easier and did not know when it would be. had not meddld with her since before day light. Monday P.M her water discharged she told me— from Saturday. went for Sister Sessions was in labor pains, deliv[er]ed some time monday night. had 4 living children[.] since she was confind [p. [234]] she told me she had not been free from pain, had had the piles— 3 or 4 weeks ago

obje[c]tion by ~~court~~ Marsh [Marr]. to the saying of the parties ~~of~~ Since the operation.

Rigdon. objected to the testim[o]ny of parties concernd.—

court is of opinion any injury the woman may have receivd may be made to appear by patient or any other testim[on]y

had not been free f[r]om pain sinc[e] her delivry 3 or 4 month ago. 11 o clock I expected she was going to be delivrd soon.— Mrs Sessions said Mrs Danas water had not escaped. dont know who told me.— she did not expect to be confined for 10 days.— [p. [235]]

court adjournd for one hour.—

3 o clock, opend court,

(Mary D[e]uel)— was present at Mrs Dana's sickness 24^(th.) october. was not there prior to Dr Brink[501] being there. was present with them.— she was lying on the bed apperig [appearing] in considrabl pain. not labor pains— I was called 11 at night, D^r [Brink] was there previous. was at my house after the syringe— to give her injecti[o]n[502] Mr Dana he thought the child had been dead 2 or 3 days. I told my sister she was not expecting to be sick 1 or 2 or 3 weeks.— I did not examine the patient. she said her period had not come yet. Mr Dana expected to have mother Session when she was confind.— called

---

500. TEXT: Possibly "crowd".
501. TEXT: Possibly "Brinks".
502. Prior to the introduction of hypodermic syringes, the term *injection* referred to an enema. Cayenne pepper and lobelia enemas were commonly used by Thomsonians to raise body temperature and aid natural body functions. (Whorton, *Nature Cures*, 29, 31.)

Brink [p. [236]] to give fever powders, Dr Brink thought it time for delivery. needed to be hurried. she begged of him to let her alone, youl Kill me.— D^r s[a]id he hurt her as little as he could. the child was turned. and must be turnd back.— He gave her smut rye. pepper & composition. & soked her feet— he though[t] she would be delive[re]d in 3 pains more there was no such pain as I ever saw before. Dr said he never was when[503] he was so sick before.— I thought he was not fit to be there.— 2 oclock. 3 more meansts before morning.— his operation was unusual under the circumstances, I insisted she would not get through with[o]ut some one of more experienc[e] [p. [237]] she was fixed on a seat for she could not lie so. but soon moved aright. & the Dr sat down and commencd. operati[n]g by his hand.— she begged him to let go. & he said he could not somethi[n]g would go back. next day she was perfectly easy— & went to sleep. Dr was there, said nothi[n]g sister session was present.— since the birth she says it is the cause of all her difficu[l]ty. & piles.— has 5 or 6 children before. had no such symptms, Dr said it was necessary to keep up the irritations to create pain

(Marr) cross examiatin [examination]. 1st visit 11 sat night. I expressd disapprobation, in an 1½ hour. to Si[s]ter Mil[e]s I think the pains were from the [p. [238]] medicine— It might have been a cutting[504] hors [hers?] painss.[505] indepentdt [independent] of Med[icine]— I did not examine. a day or two before. she told me she did not expe[c]t to be confind for 3 or 4 [weeks].— women may be decived 2. 3. or even 4 weekss.— could not say he entered the Os [*Os tincae*]—[506] had no pains after Dr Brink left he was calld away in the night, betwe[e]n 2 oclock & daylight.— I proposed to have some one called. he opposed.— he proposed to call vienna [Jacques],— she appears to be weak, bearing down,

(By Court) was it unusual for physic[i]an to treat patient as Brink did?

I[t] is unusual.— I have Dr Bennet [Samuel Bennett] of this town operatee. & Botanic physic[i]ans in other places— [p. [239]]

have had no great experince say 50 or 60 cases. never saw Similar treatment from Botanic practice.— if the chi[l]d is born in 3 pains more. it will be something I never experncd [experienced]

(Mrs Session) sunday mornig I was called.— by Mr Dana.— say Dr Brink is at my house I calld him yesterday to cool the bowels. & still the f[e]ver & he says she is going to be confined. and the women are dissatisfied.— went

---

503. TEXT: Possibly "where".
504. TEXT: Possibly "clotting".
505. That is, a cutting that caused her pains.
506. *Os tincae* is an archaic medical term referring to "the lower or outer orifice of the utero-cervical canal." ("Os," in *Oxford English Dictionary*, 7:217.)

Dr Brink shook hands and held on. we have a difficult case— the membrane is broken the waters have escaped. the child is turnd. I sent for you to turn the child. because my hand is swoll[en] [p. [240]] I prepard and sat down to her. I said D^r what have you giv?⁵⁰⁷ Nervine raspbery cayinane.—⁵⁰⁸ I said Did I understa[n]d you the water had escaped? yes— understa[n]d you the child was [w]rong and must be turnd? yes.— it was a fair presentat[io]n? I̶ Did I underad [understand] you the child was Dead? yes.— I had my finger on the childs head. & felt pulsation.— the waters have not gatherd tis a fair presntation. your child is a live.— as I run my my finger round (s̶p̶o̶t̶ ⟨open⟩ as large as a tea cup near the) ⟨the⟩ childs head ⟨reached the ear.⟩— a ruptu[r]e.— when was you hurt. with my last child. if ever.— had no Labor pains.— had no pains [p. [241]] but such as appeard wind. I got up. sat down to talk with the D^r— about a pati[e]nt he had Doctord and said it had been Dead 3 weeks when I took it the skin was fair and I think it had just died.— Dr went to Wash.— I asked Mrs Dana what the Dr gave her. she said Ergot.— He came to me for it last week— when I moved her onto her bed I found mark of the ruptures on the under clothes. fresh blood.— D^r retur[ne]d— & asked me what is the cause of her pain. last night? that Ergot you gave her. curse the Doctors. if y̶o̶u̶ ⟨a D^r⟩ should do so by me I would kill him if I could.— I gave him a figure— [p. [242]] never undertake to get a nut out of the burr till it is ripe and it will fall out. the Dr went away— now said I. we have deliv[er]ed the Dr. I will go home & when you get ready— send for me:

I went home & when I got there I made a minute of my visit. that I found Dr Brink had [not?] operated according to nature right or reason. sunday P.M. I took a living child. and as I had told her the waters had broke when I got there.

Mr Dana stated to Dr Brink, I never had my feelings wrought up so in all my children. as last night.— D^r you know I did not call you here to officiate in such a capacity. Dr Brink said he only gave her 11 grains Ergot.— [p. [243]]

(D[e]uel) not the same bed but bedding was the same——

Blood was of differnet appernce [appearance] than what is usual. as though it came from the ruptures, 3 places she would twinge never saw such relaxation ⟨as there⟩ was— mouth of womb about as large as common size teacup.— Bro Dana. requested me to call. I did & she said she had not been well.— thought Brink hurt her,— could not hold her water. ⟨Brink⟩ gave her two injection himself which she thoght was the cause of it. they wer very hot could hardly

---

507. TEXT: Instead of "giv", possibly "givn".

508. Cayenne pepper (*Capsicum annuum*), which botanical or Thomsonian doctors used to promote perspiration. (Haller, *People's Doctors*, 21, 26.)

get up stairs, weak in her back. I have atten[d]ed 30 years in the profession, never witnessed such an operation before. child was [p. [244]] born after midnight we called it tuesday morning I asked her if her true time had come? she said she thought 3 or 4 weeks— but was certain 10 or 12 days.— on one garment where the blood was it appeard as though some one had wiped a hand or the fingers. it appeard of a fresh bloody texture— as Pubis was turned up towards the back said Dr Brink

(Mrs Dana) sworn.

(Marr.) objected to the ~~testify~~ testimony of a wife in civil suit.

(Rigdon) would not obje[c]t. if the defendant can be admitted. poor rule if ~~the~~ ⟨it⟩ will not work both ways.— [p. [245]] Philips on evidence, ⟨evidence admitted⟩[509]

(Mrs Dana) in the morning as Dr Brink was first called. to give me somethi[n]g to allay my fever. steeped something & gave me which increasd my pain— staid in the P.M. & got the syringe and adminsterd which appeard to me all peppr. what he sta[ye]d all night. what for I dont know— it was a mere[510] imposition administ[er]ed as other witnesss stated which created pain every time I took them. I refer to the injecti[o]ns of pepper in the first instances which gave me pain. afterwa[r]ds the drinks. I told him my time was not for 3 or 4 [p. [246]] weeks that every thing was wrong ~~with~~ that an inflamation had taken place in my bowels which had killed the child & I must have help immediately or I could not live there was nothing unnatural before he commenced. & I so insistd to him, the fresh blood was from no other than from his treatment.— easier after he desisted. no laber pains till monday 7 childrn— nevr sufferd so wokup trembling bering ~~down~~ bearing down. never had those symptoms before. not ben able to do any thing since. have not been free from pain since.— [p. [247]] no other cause to attribute the pain but Brinks— treatme[n]t.

⟨Cou[r]t Did Brink take an usual[511] corse?⟩

Bring [Brink] took an unusual ~~affect~~ cours Brink. placed his head on my bowels and exerted his strength in other ways which gave me great pain.

(Mr [Jacob] Shoemaker) Mr Dana asked me to go down to Mr Brinks— I went as a neighbor 3 times before we found him at home. Mr Dana made his

---

509. See Phillipps and Amos, *Treatise on the Law of Evidence,* 1:40–41, 158–159. JS reviewed the relevant passage in Blackstone's *Commentaries on the Laws of England* that evening, which he used to support his decision to allow Margaret Kennedy Dana to testify. (JS, Journal, 2 Mar. 1843, p. 289 herein; Decision," *The Wasp,* 22 Mar. 1843, [3]; Blackstone, *Commentaries,* 1:355–366.)

510. TEXT: Possibly "more".

511. TEXT: Possibly "unu[sua]l".

propositi[o]n to leave it to men[512] or 3 men, Mr Brink told him he he would not make any settleme[n]t what he had done he had done right— I gave her Ergot & [p. [248]] cayenne pepper. and othr medic[i]nes mentiond— said he had done nothi[n]g but what any physic[i]an would do. acknowledged what th[e]y told him about her time.

(D[r] Bennett.) to explain as matter of science on testimony. already given Philips on evidence 259,[513]

Court is willing to give its opinion is not bound to know. D[r] Brink is a Botanical D[r].— or the other to be mineral—[514] court will hear men of good character.

the[515] When Dr is called to a pregnant woman to adminstr for dyestry [dysentery] & & she says her time is not for 3 or 4 [weeks] [p. [249]] would be justifid in giving any thing to produce delivry? No. diffrnc [difference] in Labor pains[516] & others?[517] under certain combinati[o]ns.— Ergot is not good— from 15 to 30. grains a specific effect on the Uterus. to expel the contents of the uterus. to produce delivery.— under the circumstances would a person be justified in inse[r]ting the hand? if every thing is natural ⟨it⟩ would be uncalled for— such deliv[er]y f[r]om the impression I have no circumstances existing existed to warra[n]t the proceding.— the introdu[c]tion of the hand. altogethe[r] unnecasarily. [p. [250]] introduction of the hand is unnecess[ar]y to ascertain the situati[o]n of the foetus. would be productive of great pain if done roughly or unskillfully, perfmd [performed]

after labor pains have existed some time. mouth of the womb will enlarge.— in this case by violenc[e] I would think.— it would not be Justifiable to force open the womb— might be lascerated or rupturd, such lac[e]ration might be discoverd, such treatmnt would be likely to produce the effects proved no reason why physic[i]an sho[u]ld conclude the child was dead— & use means to produce delivery. could not be justified in case.

adjord [adjourned] to 10 tomorrow m[o]rning [p. [251]]

---

512. TEXT: Possibly "man".
513. Phillipps and Amos, *Treatise on the Law of Evidence*, 1:234.
514. Thomsonian physicians derisively referred to regular physicians as "mineral doctors" because of their use of mercury, arsenic, iron, and other minerals or mineral-like substances in treating disease. (See, for example, "Report of Wilson Thomson," *Thomsonian Recorder* [Columbus, OH], 26 Oct. 1833, 24; "Dr. Crookshank and the Cholera," *Thomsonian Recorder* [Columbus, OH], 13 Sept. 1834, 397.)
515. TEXT: Possibly "her" or "then".
516. TEXT: Possibly "pain".
517. TEXT: Instead of "others", possibly "attedsn".

evening in company with [William W.] Phelps & [Willard] Richards in the middle room. looking out of Blackstone[518] on evidenc[e] of wife for husband.[519] &c.—

3 March 1843 • Friday

Friday March 3ᵈ— 1843.— Court opened at 10— according to adjournment.—

⟨Dr Bennet [Samuel Bennett]⟩ should there be an obliquity of the womb a gentle action may be justfiable. the exertion in this case I think the exertion ~~would~~ ⟨was⟩ ~~be~~ unjustifiable.

could nto [not] be a falling back of the womb— at that stage of pregnancy. and if there was a midwife would easily dectect it. [p. [252]] a delivery at such time would be calculated to injur the womb common cases requi[r]e no help what was done was unnecesry mouth of the womb will be open ~~in~~ by Regular pain. not be opend as in this case witho[u]t force.— ⟨force⟩ would injure the parts. ⟨injuries⟩ reasonably refered to to the force. if things were[520] wrong as stated by the Dr. woman would be likely to know it first. (Law read by Court. Swans Treaties 63)[521]

(Court) what do you know Dʳ Bennet. about this case? mouth womb open. before labor pains— & lacerated suppose it had been [p. [253]] hurt. fresh blood & rupture, by force— to combat the fever &c ⟨woman⟩ would be the fi[r]st to know if she was in labor. Medical men will never attempt examination witho[u]t cause.— then not necessa[r]y to insert the hand. to ascertain presentation. (cross)

have known mouth womb to be elastic. so as easily to be prest open. Ergot acts upon the womb to contract it so the child would press open the mouth. at intervals of the pain there is a relaxation when the finger might be inserted. This dilation was from. the intrusion of the hand. [p. [254]] no uncommon thing to have blood pass in fir[s]t stages of labor. when (os tinc[a]e) is dilated.

---

518. TEXT: Possibly "Blackstones". Blackstone's *Commentaries on the Laws of England* states that when a man and woman are married, the contract makes them "one person in law." Blackstone, citing a legal maxim that persons should not be witnesses in their own case, argued that husbands and wives generally "are not allowed to be evidence for, or against, each other." Blackstone also states, however, that "in cases of evident necessity, where the fact is presumed to be particularly within the wife's knowledge, there is an exception to the general rule. Thus, a wife may be a witness on the prosecution of her husband for an offence committed against her person." JS used this latter quotation in his decision to support his ruling that Margaret Kennedy Dana could testify in her husband's suit. (Blackstone, *Commentaries*, 1:355–366, esp. 364n46; "Decision," *The Wasp*, 22 Mar. 1843, [2]–[3].)

519. TEXT: Instead of "husband", possibly "husbands".

520. TEXT: Possibly "~~was~~ were".

521. Swan, *Treatise on the Law*, 63.

not 1/2 cases where blood passes— much blood might or might or might not flow from the ruptures. ⟨could not have occured before the fright⟩ a woman of Mrs Session [Patty Bartlett Sessions] experinc [experience] would know as well as a physician. 11 grains of Ergot would not produce any great effect in absence of labor pains. where the womb was rupturd & the head of the child pressing— mouth opend by force.— womb would not contract again.— parturition scarcely happens when acute disease is going on— fresh wound red blook [blood]. 1st [first] stages partu[p. [255]]rition darker.

(Dr [John F.] Weld)[522] no necessity for physic[i]an to interfere at all. highly criminal rupturs might have been made. ruptures caused by violence, sometime, duties of physic[i]an to let her alone. force deleterious.— what was done might produce laceration of the os uteri & inflamatin [inflammation] & varios things such as wer mentind [mentioned] by witness

No precise time for womb to open

saw nothing to justify the course pursud. much to condemn—

have conversd with Mrs [Margaret Kennedy] Dana. within a week. (Philips on Evidinc) 202) (Harrisons Digest 1037.) [p. [256]]

⟨⟨1st⟩ (Philips on evidence ⟨160 ⟨En⟩ 171⟩ 152)

(Harisns[523] Digest. 2ᵈ vol 1031)

(190 Phips Dige[s]t)

361 Blackstone[524]⟩

I felt there was a little overbearance particilarly because the was young, young[525] perhaps in court matters. than in knowledge and as Lawyers know a great deal & are very wise. I will put them to the trouble of finding the Quotation any thing the wife may have said will be receivd in evidence

(Weld) would attribute the injur[i]es to the violence used. complained of the bearing down of the womb— never knew mouth of the womb to dilatate without Labor pains.— Ergot specific effect is on uterus to contract [p. [257]] 15 to 20 grains common dose.—[526] ⟨i⟩ dont know as 11 grains would produce

---

522. Weld was born in Vermont in 1808 and moved to Illinois as early as 1837. A graduate of Dartmouth College, he was a "regular" physician. Although not a Mormon, he was active in Nauvoo public meetings. He advertised his services in Nauvoo as a "Practitioner in Medicine, Surgery, & Obstetrics." Weld was the surgeon of the First Cohort of the Nauvoo Legion. ("Dr. J. F. Weld," *The Wasp*, 14 Jan. 1842, [4]; "Death of Dr. John F. Weld," *Deseret Weekly*, 20 Aug. 1892, 276.)

523. TEXT: Possibly "Harrisn".

524. Phillipps and Amos, *Treatise on the Law of Evidence*, 1:202; Harrison, *Digest of All the Reported Cases*, 2:1037; Phillipps and Amos, *Treatise on the Law of Evidence*, 1:152, 160; Harrison, *Digest of All the Reported Cases*, 2:1031; Phillipps and Amos, *Treatise on the Law of Evidence*, 1:190; Blackstone, *Commentaries*, 1:361.

525. TEXT: Possibly "youngr".

526. TEXT: Instead of "dose", possibly "doses".

abortion.— never gave but in one case.— were I called in such a case I would wait and see. what the consquences would be—[527] have seen this appearance of blood without harse [harsh] treatment. been in practice 7 years

(Dr [Robert D.] Foster) sayings of patient index to treatment. if things were wrong that would be first known to the mother. duty of physician to let her alone.—

os. tinc[a]e— dillated by ergot. capable for to introduce even finger.— punching the woman by the head might weaken some of the inter[p. [258]]nal organs, causes. that have ben stated here before. of if the hand had been pressed[528] the bone of the pelvis. ⟨the foetus⟩ it would have been expelled before 24. or 48 hours if he the[529] had hand [hand had?] not passed[530] do not considr the injury could have been sustaind in the womb.— Ergot Same as Dr Weld.— 11 grains would be inert.— a free use of Ergot might destroy the tone of the womb.— do not consider it possible that the os-tinsee [Os tincae] should have been opened thus by inserting the hand & rupt[ur]ing the womb. without producing birth sooner than it was

adjournd 1 hour ½ 1 pm 1 o clock adjournd for 1½ hour (Philips on Evide[n]ce 151.)[531] [p. [259]]

3 oclock court opened.

(Dr Higby [Charles Higbee])[532] effects unavoidably follow introducing the hand or any instrume[n]t in the mouth of the womb. so as to displace the membrane. would be birth in from 24. to 36 hours or more sometimes

(council for plaintiff closed)

⟨defence⟩ 1st general character of the Defendant as practitioner. 2d— rebutting testim[o]ny

(Dr ⟨Geo— R.⟩ Bostwick)[533] practiced 24. years had 2300 cases of obstetrics. rather difficu[l]t to tell the amount of inju[r]y & when & by whom.— have known premature labor prorducd [produced] by Diarhaea when I had no othe[r] cause to attribute it to. have seen peter Wiliams wife [p. [260]] complete dilation of the os uteri. have seen frequent dilations without pain— then close

---

527. TEXT: Instead of "—", possibly "I".
528. TEXT: Possibly "passed".
529. TEXT: Instead of "he the", possibly "the he".
530. TEXT: Possibly "forrcd".
531. Phillipps and Amos, *Treatise on the Law of Evidence,* 1:151.
532. Higbee was a graduate of the University of Pennsylvania and therefore a "regular" physician. He advertised his services in Nauvoo as "more especially in diseases of women and children." ("Dr. Charles Higbee," *The Wasp,* 22 Mar. 1843, [4].)
533. Bostwick was a physician and resident of Fort Madison, Iowa Territory. ("Wm. Law as He Is!," *Nauvoo Neighbor,* 25 Sept. 1844, [2]; "Melancholy," *Milwaukie Daily Sentinel,* 3 Feb. 1846, [2]; Bassett, *Buffalo County, Nebraska,* 2:110.)

and go their time— and close again.— if there is sufficnt ~~contractile~~ ⟨dilateing⟩ powers. in the neck of the womb ergot may be given as freee as flour. its effect is on the top of the womb— also stops Hermorage of the womb.— if dilated by force I should expect immediate delivery in a few hours. 5 or 6 hours it might 30 hours if a weak system. if 3 ruptures so large I should think it would poduc [produce] more blood. I look for a fontanells when the head is presentd. never knew a finger inserted to the ear. in such cases prese[n]ted to court uterus in [p. [261]] plate. might wait 6 or 7 hours if there was nothing peculiar. before giving Ergot. bearing down. from passage child. hurt. &c fright produces abortion. I concur with Dr Foster. about inserting the finger would give some mild purgative in such cases. In case of fever I have found the child dead when the mother did not know it have seen water discharge 3 times in one case 1½ hour I bur[s]t[534] one myself— I would rather manage a Dozen such Ladies to manage than give my opinion in this case.— inserting finger as Mrs Sessions did is uncalled for and cruel[535] [p. [262]]

court ruled that testimony to prove defendents general character was illegal & would not be heard.—[536]

Dr Bennet said he had no intrest in this suit. had practiced medicne ~~medicine~~ in this place but never charged a cent receivd a cent ⟨n⟩or[537] have any book account.

(Dr [Harvey] Tate) objected by court[538]

adjournd from 5 To 7 oclock

---

534. TEXT: Possibly "bust".
535. TEXT: Possibly "evil".
536. Phillipps's *Treatise on the Law of Evidence* states that "the character of the parties to a civil suit affords, in general, such a weak and vague inference as to the truth of points in issue between them, that it is not usual to admit evidence of this description." The published version of the trial in *The Wasp* describes defense witness Charles Ivins being rejected by the court because the reason he was being called was to testify concerning the defendant's character. (Phillipps and Amos, *Treatise on the Law of Evidence*, 1:443; "Decision," *The Wasp*, 22 Mar. 1843, [2]–[3].)
537. TEXT: Possibly "nor".
538. Tate was born in Miami County, Ohio, in 1810, possibly in the village of West Milton. A graduate of the Medical College of Ohio in 1840, he was a "regular" physician. Tate advertised his medical services in Nauvoo as especially for female patients with cases of "Prolapsus Uteri and Hernia or Rupture" and published several articles on inflammation and disease in *The Wasp*. It is not known why JS objected to Tate's testimony. Although Tate was not allowed to testify in the initial trial, he was one of the witnesses summoned for Brink's appeal to the municipal court in April 1843. (Martin, *History of Cass County*, 2:767; Perrin, *History of Cass County Illinois*, 84; Entry for Harvey Tate, 1841, Nauvoo Temple, Record of Baptisms for the Dead, vol. A, p. 160; "Elder's Conference," *Times and Seasons*, 1 Apr. 1843, 4:157–159; "H. Tate, M.D.," *The Wasp*, 3 Dec. 1842, [3]; Harvey Tate, "Remarks on Inflamation," *The Wasp*, 31 Dec. 1842, [2]; Harvey Tate, Letter to the editor, *The Wasp*, 1 Feb. 1843, [2]–[3]; Harvey Tate, "Letter Third— On Inflammation," *The Wasp*, 22 Feb. 1843, [2]–[3]; Harvey Tate, "Letter Fourth," *The Wasp*, 5 Apr. 1843, [1]; Subpoena, 4 Apr. 1843, Dana v. Brink [Nauvoo Mun. Ct. 1843], Nauvoo, IL, Records, CHL.)

7 court open—

in the interim called at Br Durphy's his wife⁵³⁹ sick

also Bishop Whitnys [Newel K. Whitney's]. with Dr Rich^ds [Willard Richards]——— ⟨5 loaded teams arrivd with provision from Ramus———⟩⁵⁴⁰

Plea of Mr [Onias] Skinner for Plaintiffe [p. [263]]

1. [William] Brink. not called to ~~her~~ confinement

2^d— No bus[in]ess to undertake delivery

3 was told labor pains not come on

4 said child was dead

5 pretended every thing was wrong

6 pronouncd waters gathrd & broke

7 injections so hot ⟨as to put her in g[rea]t Pain———⟩

8 deni[e]d giving Ergot

9 used violence

10 introduced hi[s]⁵⁴¹ hand

11 made 3 ruptures

12 extreme violenc[e]. when implored to let her alone (Swans Treatise 429)⁵⁴² Fraud)

4 minutes before 8. [William H. J.] Marr commenced his plea, (Statute of Illinois 405)⁵⁴³

amount of Damage in $ & cents [p. [264]]

22 minutes past 8. Esqr [Sidney] Rigdon commenced his plea (united states dispensatory.⁵⁴⁴

28 minutes past 9 Esqr [Sylvester] Emmons commenced his plea. (Swans Treaties 240 contract)⁵⁴⁵ 10¼ o'clock closed

adjournd to next friday 10 oclock to give its decision fr[o]m this stand.⁵⁴⁶

---

539. Probably Elizabeth Davis Durfee, wife of Jabez Durfee and a friend of JS and Emma Smith.

540. On 23 February 1843, the Quorum of the Twelve, over the signature of Brigham Young, wrote to church members in Ramus, Illinois, urging them to send provisions for the use of JS and his family so JS could devote more time to the "spiritual interest" of the church. The five teamloads of provisions that arrived on 3 March were part of the response. A similar request for assistance appears in the earlier JS journal entry for 18 February 1843. (Brigham Young, Nauvoo, IL, to "the church," Ramus, IL, 23 Feb. 1843, draft, Brigham Young Office Files, CHL.)

541. TEXT: Possibly "he".

542. Swan, *Treatise on the Law*, 429.

543. An Act concerning Justices of the Peace and Constables [3 Feb. 1827], *Public and General Statute Laws of the State of Illinois* [1834–1837], p. 405, sec. 9.

544. George B. Wood and Franklin Bache, *The Dispensatory of the United States* (Philadelphia: Grigg and Elliot, 1839).

545. Swan, *Treatise on the Law*, 240.

546. On 10 March 1843, JS delivered his written opinion in favor of the plaintiff, Charles Dana. (JS, Journal, 10 Mar. 1843; "Decision," *The Wasp*, 22 Mar. 1843, [2]–[3].)

had 1 hours interview at home with W[illiam] W Phelps after court. concerning. Trial

Mother Smith better[547]

F [*5 lines blank*] [p. [265]]

4 March 1843 • Saturday

~~Friday~~ ⟨Saturday⟩ March 4. 1843 9 A.M. Brother Benjamin Johnson. and the brethren from Ramus, who came ~~from~~ for to bring provisions ⟨corn. Pork. oats flour— wheat.— as per Bill⟩ at the house.— agreed to go with Hiram [Hyrum Smith] to Ramus one week to day—[548] Bro John[son] wanted to know. if they might build a meeting house in Ramus out of chu[r]ch property. Joseph. said the property of the church should be disposed of as the church said it was for them to decide not him . . .—

There is a wheel. this is the Hub we will drive the fir[s]t spoke in Ramus 2^d— Laharpe. 3^d Shokokon. 4. Lima that is 1/2 the wheel. the other half is over the river we will let that [p. [266]] alone at present. we will call the saints from Iowa to these spokes then ~~sold~~ send elders over & convert the whole.— It is like a bank. they will not discount, because they have plenty of speciee. we will draw ~~the~~ th[e]ir speciee. then they will discount our paper. (call for our elders.)—

9½ called at the office & gave instructions concerning making out the decision of court

10 o clock. opened city council prayer B. Geo A. Smith.— Bill regulating currency read.[549] the Legislature of Illinois have long been trying to repeal the Charter of Nauvoo.— upon which the mayor made some [p. [267]] as he had done on former occasions[550] to shew the council & others that that the Legislature cannot repeal a charter where there is no repealing clause.—[551] upon which he read a letter from James Arlington Bennet to confirm his decision.—

---

547. JS's mother, Lucy Mack Smith, had been ill since 26 February. (JS, Journal, 26 Feb. 1843.)

548. Actually, JS went to Ramus with Brigham Young. (JS, Journal, 11 Mar. 1843.)

549. The bill resulted in an ordinance passed later this day stating that "Gold and Silver Coin only be received as lawful tender in payment of City Taxes, and of debts, and also of fines imposed under the Ordinances of the City" and that "City Scrip shall not hereafter be emitted as moneyed Currency." This ordinance was discussed on 25 February 1843. (Nauvoo City Council Minute Book, 4 Mar. 1843, 167; JS, Journal, 25 Feb. 1843.)

550. On his trip to Springfield, JS argued that the Illinois state legislature could not repeal the Nauvoo charter. (JS, Journal, 28 and 31 Dec. 1842, pp. 196, 205 herein.)

551. The previous day, the Illinois House of Representatives, by a vote of 58 to 33, passed a bill repealing provisions of the Nauvoo charter, among which were those pertaining to habeas corpus. The state senate, however, failed to act on the measure before the close of the legislative session on 6 March 1843. (*Journal of the House of Representatives . . . of Illinois*, 3 Mar. 1843, 527–528; "House of Representatives," *The Wasp*, 15 Mar. 1843, [2].)

Letter Dated Arlington House Feb 1.st. 1843.—⁵⁵² spoke against [Alexander] Maᶜkenzie's murdering those boys. [Philip] Spencer &c— as stated in Arlingtons letter.— called it murder. the boys had the malary [malaria] on the coast of Africa & did not know what they did.——⁵⁵³

In debate on the bill. Geo A Smith thought imprisonme[n]t better than hanging.

Mayor said he was opposed to hanging if a man kill anothe[r] shoot him [p. [268]] or cut his throat. spilling his blood on the ground and let the smoke thereof ascend up to God. and if I ever have the privilige of Making a law on this point I will have it so.—

In reply to councillors who though[t] it impolitic to stop circulating uncurrent Bank notes <u>at once</u>⁵⁵⁴

Mayor said ~~it~~ ⟨he⟩ would use a figure. and talk like a father to his children.— if you want to kill a serpent. don't cut off his head for fear he will bite you. but cut off his tail piece by piece & perhaps you wont get bit. so with ~~the~~ this bill— if paper currency is an evil [p. [269]] put it down at once. ~~the~~ Stop the circulation at once.— when councillors get up here let them talk sense. Great God where is common sense & reason? is there none in the Earth? why have the kanker lingering. to sap our life.— get a 5.$ bill can get nothing with it. dare not touch it any one, because it is a [t u r d].⁵⁵⁵ shovel it out then. I wish you had my soul long enough to know how good it feels.—— It is <u>expedient</u> when you strike at an enemy, strike the most deadly blow, possible.— ([Orson] Hyde asked what the [p. [270]] editor would do) Mayor said advertise in the next paper to your agents to send you gold & silver. as we take no paper here.⁵⁵⁶

---

552. This letter from Bennet to JS dated 1 February 1843 has not been located.

553. Reference is made to an incident aboard the United States brig *Somers,* commanded by Mackenzie in fall 1842. After Mackenzie fulfilled orders that took him to the coast of Africa, he returned to the United States via St. Thomas, when he was confronted with mutiny by members of his crew. On 1 December, with the recommendation of the senior officers on board the ship, Mackenzie had the three prime suspects—Philip Spencer, Samuel Cromwell, and Elisha Small—executed. (See "Naval Court of Inquiry—Mutiny on Board the Somers," *Daily National Intelligencer* [Washington DC], 2 Jan. 1843, [3]; "Mutiny on Board the Somers," *Daily National Intelligencer,* 3 Jan. 1843, [2]–[3]; "Horrible Mutiny!!," *The Wasp,* 14 Jan. 1843, [3]; and "Somers Mutiny," *The Wasp,* 22 Feb. 1843, [1]–[2].)

554. A week earlier, some members of the city council opposed eliminating the use of city scrip immediately. (See JS, Journal, 25 Feb. 1843.)

555. TEXT: Possibly "[t u r d y]", with no period following. Transliteration from Taylor shorthand: "t [*vowel*] r d"; possibly "t [*vowel*] r d [*vowel*]".

556. The next issue of *The Wasp* cited the ordinance regulating currency and recommended that citizens with "a large amount" of paper money "send it back to the banks that issued it, and get a substance, instead of a shadow." ("An Ordinance Regulating the Currency," *The Wasp,* 8 Mar. 1843, [3]; Editorial, *The Wasp,* 8 Mar. 1843, [2].)

Prisoners may be kept in the city as safe as in the ~~city~~ Prison of the state. by chaining to a block, with, a guard. & labor in blacksmith shops or any where else,— & never have a prisoner sent out of the city. for imprisonme[n]t.— Bills passed to stop circulation of paper currency in the city. punish counterfeiting &c . . . by unanimous vote.—

Dr Samuel Bennet [Bennett] chosen Alderman.[557]

A[lbert] P. Rockwood. fire warden for 1st ward. [p. [271]]

Elijah Fordham. firewarden: 2d ward

Charles C. Rich. firewarden 3d ward

⟨voted.⟩ opened an alley— north & South through block 126— 1½ P.M adjournd to next regular meeting.[558]

dined. about 3 P.M. cold. clear. repaird to office with. O[rson] Spencer

Proverb— For a man to be a great man, he must not dwell upon small things; though he may <u>enjoy</u> them. spoken ~~a~~ while entering the office— Explanati[o]n a prophet cannot be a scribe. &c . . .

Joseph said to Dr [Willard] Richards there is one thing you fail in as historian the naming or noticing surrounding objects. [p. [272]] weather &c the weather is extremely cold & freezing and has been almost continually since October. there was a breaking up of the ice in the River in Februa[r]y so that Boats passd from St Louis to Quincy— and the falls were clear so that boats passd from Montrose to Keokuk. but the river has not been cleard yet f[r]om ~~the~~ [Esaias] Edwards Brick house[559] & upwa[r]ds— & the breth[re]n have brought a multitude of wood on the ice from the opposite shore and the islands. hundreds of cords per day. ~~Feb 2~~ ground clear except a little ice. [p. [273]]

⟨Brought in by Hyrum Smith,⟩ "Christian soldier Jan 7th 1843" "41st article of Court Martial laws." "No such sentence (that of Death) shall be carried into execution until <u>confirmed</u> by the president of the Unitd States; or if the trial take place <u>out</u> of the United States, until it be <u>confirmed</u> by the <u>commander</u>

---

557. Stephen Markham, one of the four aldermen elected in February, resigned from his position because he was elected without his knowledge. On 25 February 1843, the same day the city council accepted Markham's resignation, they appointed Wilson Law in his place. Then on 4 March Bennett was appointed in Law's place, Law "having declined to act." ("City Election," *The Wasp*, 8 Feb. 1843, [2]; Nauvoo City Council Minute Book, 25 Feb. and 4 Mar. 1843, 167–168.)

558. The council actions mentioned in the journal entry appear in the Nauvoo City Council minutes. (Nauvoo City Council Minute Book, 4 Mar. 1843, 167–169.)

559. Edwards's home on block 111, lot 2, was located on the east bank of the Mississippi River at the head of the Des Moines rapids. (Nauvoo Books of Assessment, Fourth Ward, 1842, p. 4, Nauvoo, IL, Records, CHL; Nauvoo, IL, Tax list, district 3, 1842, p. 228, microfilm 7,706, U.S. and Canada Record Collection, FHL.)

of the <u>Fleet or Squadron</u>,— Capt M[ackenzie] does not rank as commander of the two latter."⁵⁶⁰

Joseph. "They'l Hang Ma͡ckenzie, or, imprison ~~them~~, ⟨Him⟩ or break Him of his office")⁵⁶¹

The Battle of Gog and Magog is after the Millenium,⁵⁶² The[y] [p. [274]] were command[ed] to come up to Jerusalem to worship in the Millenium.—⁵⁶³

continued to write on decision of court⁵⁶⁴ till 4½ o clock— then called at Bro [Jabez] Durphy's— to see sick—⁵⁶⁵

~~Wood Worths~~ ⟨[Woodworths]⁵⁶⁶⟩ & Whitneys— [and Kimballs]⁵⁶⁷ [*10 lines blank*] [p. [275]]

5 March 1843 • Sunday

Sunday March 5ᵗʰ 1843 ⟨taking care of Mother all day.⟩⁵⁶⁸ [*14 lines blank*] [p. [276]]

6 March 1843 • Monday

Monday March 6[ᵗʰ] 1843 read Elder [George J.] Adams letter in the "Bee"— Boston. also another communicati[o]n showing the progress of ~~his~~ truth in Boston.—⁵⁶⁹ 9 o clock— called at office. told Dʳ Richds [Willard Richards] to answer. or communtee⁵⁷⁰ to the Bee.—⁵⁷¹ recited in German at the

---

560. "The Somers Mutiny," *Christian Soldier,* 27 Jan. 1843, 91; Maltby, *Treatise on Courts Martial,* 265.

561. At a subsequent naval court of inquiry, Commander Alexander Mackenzie was cleared of any wrongdoing; that court's decision was later confirmed by the president of the United States. ([Sumner], "Mutiny of the *Somers,*" 223–225; McFarland, *Sea Dangers,* 205.)

562. See Revelation 20:8.

563. See Zechariah 14:16–19.

564. In the *Dana v. Brink* case.

565. Probably Elizabeth Davis Durfee. (JS, Journal, 3 Mar. 1843, p. 293 herein.)

566. TEXT: Possibly "[Woodworth's]". Transliteration from Taylor shorthand: "w-d-w-r-th-s".

567. TEXT: Possibly "[and Kimball's]". Transliteration from Taylor shorthand: "n k/q-m-b-l-s". The shorthand symbol for *n* is also used to represent the word *and*. (Taylor, *Universal System of Stenography,* plate 1.) JS was "married or sealed" to Emily Partridge by Heber C. Kimball at Kimball's home on the evening of 4 March 1843. (Emily Dow Partridge Young, Affidavit, Salt Lake Co., Utah Territory, 1 May 1869, in Joseph F. Smith, Affidavits about Celestial Marriage, 1:11; Young, Diary and Reminscences, [315]–[317].)

568. TEXT: Ink in this insertion matches ink in entries for 7–10 March.

569. A copy of Adams's article from the *Boston Weekly Bee*, titled "A Short Sketch of the Rise, Progress and Faith, of the Latter Day Saints, or Mormons," and a statement by a convert to the church who signed his name H. R. were published in the *Times and Seasons*. ("What Do the Mormons Believe," *Times and Seasons,* 15 Mar. 1843, 4:141–143; "H.R.," Letter to the editor, *Times and Seasons,* 15 Mar. 1843, 4:143–144.)

570. TEXT: Possibly "commented".

571. Eleven days later Richards began writing a series of letters under the pseudonym "Viator" to be published in the *Boston Daily Bee,* the first of which bears the date 17 March 1843 and was read to JS that

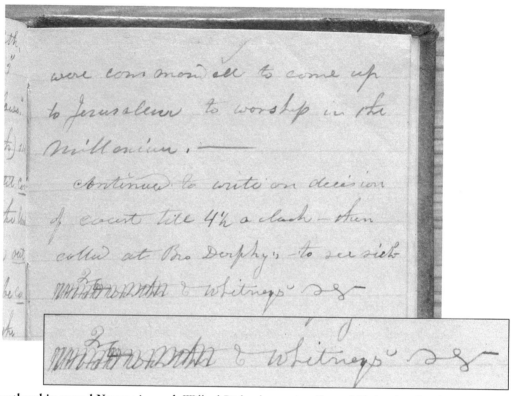

Shorthand in second Nauvoo journal. Willard Richards occasionally used Taylor shorthand to inscribe single words or short passages as he kept Joseph Smith's journal. Handwriting of Willard Richards. JS, Journal, Dec. 1842–June 1844, bk. 1, p. [275], JS Collection, Church History Library, Salt Lake City. (Photograph by Welden C. Andersen.)

hou[s]e.— called at office for paper— after Dinner lay down to rest.— toward evening rode out

this evening presented a grand display of burning prairie on the bank of the river opposite Nauvoo.— east wind through the day. cold thawed a little ~~during~~ in middle the day.— [p. [277]]

7 March 1843 • Tuesday

Tuesday March 7.ᵗʰ· at the office at 9 A.M. heard read decision of court.⁵⁷² gave an order on Lot⁵⁷³ for corn to Bro. Allen. sister Sayres [Ruth Sayers] called to exchange notes hers for Dr [William W.] Rust;s— at office before dinner conversing on medicine. after dinner signed several deeds.⁵⁷⁴ Bro [William] Clayton present to settle—⁵⁷⁵ Brother Manhard⁵⁷⁶ brought & gave 2 loads of corn & 1. hog— to Presidit [President] from. Iowa.—⁵⁷⁷ rec[k]oned with Theodore Turl[e]y. who enquired what was wisdom concerning a brewery in this place?⁵⁷⁸ rec[k]oned with Dym[p. [278]]ic [Dimick] Huntington,⁵⁷⁹ East wind. through the day 3 o clock rain commencd. informed [William W.] Phelps & [Willard] Richards they might bond themselves at dinner (Clayton began to settle with the brethrn about Lots at mayors office)

---

day. (JS, Journal, 17 Mar. 1843, esp. 312n644 herein; compare Willard Richards [Viator, pseud.], Nauvoo, IL, 17 Mar. 1843, Letter to the editor, *Boston Daily Bee*, 12 Apr. 1843, [2]; and "Truthiana," 1843, draft, CHL.)

572. JS delivered the official decision in the case of *Dana v. Brink* on 10 March, as recorded in the JS journal entry for that date.

573. Possibly a reference to Cornelius Lott, who managed JS's farm outside Nauvoo.

574. Some of these deeds were with Gilbert Gouldsmith, George Hampton, and Dimick Huntington. (Hancock Co., IL, Deed Records, vol. 19-O, pp. 280–281, microfilm 954,601, U.S. and Canada Record Collection, FHL; Deed, JS [Trustee-in-trust] to George Hampton, Hancock Co., IL, 7 Mar. 1843, Nauvoo Restoration, Incorporated, Collection, CHL; Hancock Co., IL, Deed Records, vol. N, pp. 45–46, microfilm 954,600, U.S. and Canada Record Collection, FHL.)

575. As Nauvoo city treasurer and one of JS's clerks, Clayton spent much of his time regulating Nauvoo land transactions. (Nauvoo City Council Minute Book, 11 Feb. 1843, 159; William Clayton, Affidavit, Salt Lake City, Utah Territory, 16 Feb. 1874, p. [1], in Joseph F. Smith, Affidavits about Celestial Marriage, CHL.)

576. Possibly William Manhard, who is mentioned in JS's journal entry for 3 February 1843.

577. Members of the Quorum of the Twelve wrote letters asking that provisions be sent to JS so that he and his family could be provided for while his time was devoted to the operation of the church. (JS, Journal, 18 Feb. 1843.)

578. Three days later, JS said he "had no objection" to Turley's proposed brewery. (See JS, Journal, 10 Mar. 1843.)

579. TEXT: Beginning with the comma following "Huntington", black ink commences. The black ink matches the ink color of the following entry.

8 March 1843 • Wednesday

Wednesday March 8th 1843 Suddenly in the night wind changed to NW. extremely cold this morn very plesat [pleasant]. & clear— much floating ice in the river.— at the office 8 oclock signed some writing concerni[n]g the Ligion—[580] after Dinner in office ⟨Mr [John] Cowan came in—⟩ wrote a letter[581] to [Emma][582] conver[s]ed with the Prussian[583] abo[u]t Military tactics. recond [reckoned] with [William] Ford.—[584] 5 o clock cloudy.— Rode out with cowan.— [p. [279]]

9 March 1843 • Thursday

Thursday march 9th. 1843. this morning received another No of the Bee containing minutes of conference in Boston &c— Read decision of court in Dana vs Brink

Mr [John] Cowan took court papers[585] & Butterfilds [Justin Butterfield's] opinion[586] to go to Govr. of Iowa to have him recall the Mo. writ.[587]

---

580. Nauvoo Legion.

581. JS's letter to Emma of this date has not been located.

582. TEXT: Transliteration from Taylor shorthand: "[*vowel*]-mm-[*vowel*]". The second character, *m*, has an enlarged loop, which in Taylor shorthand represents two *m* sounds. Richards may have been thinking of the longhand spelling of "Emma" when he inscribed the enlarged *m*. Later in the journal Richards again apparently departed from Taylor shorthand rules to more closely follow longhand style by enlarging characters in order to represent them as capital letters. (Taylor, *Universal System of Stenography*, 35–36; JS, Journal, 12 June and 5 Nov. 1843, JS Collection, CHL.)

583. Probably Alexander Neibaur, born 8 January 1808 in Ehrenbreitstein. This area became part of the Prussian empire following the Napoloeonic Wars. ("General Record of the 5th Quorum," vol. 1, p. 10.)

584. William Clayton wrote of the day's events: "At Prest Josephs Office. Walked with him to look at some lots &c settled with Wm Ford." (Clayton, Journal, 8 Mar. 1843.)

585. William Clayton copied the official court papers after hearing Judge Nathaniel Pope's decision on 6 January 1843. (JS, Journal, 6 Jan. 1843.)

586. Perhaps a reference to a lengthy letter Butterfield wrote to Sidney Rigdon on 20 October 1842 regarding the legality of JS's arrest and the attempted extradition to Missouri. Alternatively, Willard Richards may have meant Nathaniel Pope's opinion, or official decision, at the habeas corpus hearing in Springfield. (Justin Butterfield, Chicago, IL, to Sidney Rigdon, [Nauvoo, IL], 20 Oct. 1842, copy, Sidney Rigdon, Collection, CHL; "Circuit Court of the United States for the District of Illinois," *Sangamo Journal* [Springfield, IL], 19 Jan. 1843, [1].)

587. By providing Iowa Territory governor John Chambers with copies of these documents, JS hoped to persuade Chambers to recall a writ previously issued in Iowa on requisition of the Missouri governor for JS's arrest. The trip was successful; Chambers wrote a letter to Cowan on 10 March stating that although a warrant had been issued it was returned unserved and that he would not issue another warrant unless the governor of Missouri sent a new requisition. Unaware of Chambers's response, JS remarked on 6 April 1843 that the "Govr of Iowa has granted a writ. for me. on affidav[i]t of [Lilburn W.] Boggs.— he still holds that writ as a cudgel over my head." (John Chambers, Burlington, Iowa Territory, to John Cowan, 10 Mar. 1843, JS Office Papers, CHL; JS, Journal, 6 Apr. 1843, p. 335 herein.)

12 o clock called with a letter concerning land of Hotchkiss. read decision. read papers.— Bro [William W.] Phelps you shall know law. and understa[n]d law and you shall be a lawyer in Israel and the time shall come when I shall not need say thus & thus is the law for you [p. [280]] shall know. the Law.—

William O. clark gave a load of corn Bro Sanford Porter a hog, issued attahmet [attachment] for Peter Haws agai[ns]t. Artemus Johnson,—[588] ([William] Clayton in office)

(sleet & rain through the day) and evening)

10 March 1843 • Friday

Friday March 10.th 1843 clear & cold,— read the decission in office with O[rson] Spencer

at 10 repaired to the Hall over the store[589] and 10 ⟨15[590] past⟩ commencd the decision— in case of Dana vs Brink.[591] "that the Plaintiff recover his bill[592] $99 & costs."—[593] (the whole included 12 pages written matter" after decision [p. [281]] court referred to the threat of the Defendant council. adrsing[594] [addressing] court. as attempting to intimidate &c, council explain satisfactorily.— also court referred to what Dr [William] Brink had said since trial that his he had not a fair chance. his witn[es]ses were not allowed, repelld by court.[595]

2 after-noon, Mayor come in office, when Daniel Sherwood 14 years old, was brought up on suspic[i]on of stealing a watch from the house of Geo

---

588. In cases of debt less than fifty dollars, when the defendant was either hiding or resisting arrest, a justice of the peace could issue a writ of attachment that would give the constable authority to seize the defendant's property to the amount to satisfy the debt. (An Act to Regulate Proceedings by Attachment before Justices of the Peace [27 Feb. 1837], *Laws of the State of Illinois* [1836–1837], pp. 12–13, secs. 1–2.)

589. That is, JS's red brick store.

590. TEXT: Or "25".

591. "Decision," *The Wasp*, 22 Mar. 1843, [2]–[3].

592. Dr. William Brink charged Charles Dana ten dollars for his medical services, though Dana apparently refused to pay the bill prior to the trial.*a* Brink had repeatedly advertised his medical services as carrying the guarantee of "no cure no pay."*b* Brink "filed an account . . . for the services rendered plaintiff's wife on the 22d and 23d of October, 1842, of $10.00" during the course of the trial, but JS refused to "allow this account as a set off," citing contract law that prevented medical practitioners from collecting fees for services in cases of "gross carelessness or unskillfulness."*c* (*a*. JS, Journal, 2 Mar. 1843, p. 288 herein. *b*. "Medical Notice," *The Wasp*, 2 July 1842, [3]. *c*. "Decision," *The Wasp*, 22 Mar. 1843, [3].)

593. The court awarded Charles Dana the full amount he sought (ninety-nine dollars), which was also essentially the maximum amount allowed by law. According to the notice of appeal from the mayor's court, court costs totaled $11.59½. (Notice of appeal, 31 Mar. 1843, Dana v. Brink [Nauvoo Mun. Ct. 1843], Nauvoo, IL, Records, CHL; see also JS, Journal, 2 Mar. 1843, pp. 280–281 herein; and 281n483 herein.)

594. TEXT: Instead of "adrsing", possibly "ordering".

595. Possibly a reference to the court's refusal to allow Charles Ivins to testify as a character witness for Brink. ("Decision," *The Wasp*, 22 Mar. 1843, [2]–[3].)

Nelson.— (No positive testimony— appearing against him) Mayor ordered his father to take take him home and try him if he found the boy guilty to whip him severly. for he is too young to imprison or whip.— [p. [282]]

⟨Mayor ordered Wood worth [Lucien Woodworth] to fix a room in the Nauvoo. house— with a large stone in the center to chain the boys to— & chain them till their time is out.—⟩⁵⁹⁶

as Thomas Morgan went out wishd to speak with Mayor, said he had been told by several that Joseph had taught that it was right to steal,— ⟨viz⟩ O. P. [Orrin Porter] Rockwell David ⟨B.⟩ Smith. & James smith which was the means of drawing Thomas into the practice of stealing.— David Smith once attempted to shoot me. the gun did not go and he was so mad that he though [threw?] down the gun & broke the stock,— it was my gun.— he was carrying to rest me.— after the attempt we stopped to rest, & refresh, when unknown to him. I removed the priming from the gun & pistols. wet the touch holes & made him carry them all home with me. & row⁵⁹⁷ me across the river from [p. [283]] Montrose. Joseph decided that that he had no objection⁵⁹⁸ to having a brewery— put up. by Theodore Turl[e]y.⁵⁹⁹

    Proverb—
As finest steel doth show a brighter polish
The more you rub the same;
E'en so, in love, rebuke will ne'er demolish
A wise man's goodly name.

ordered a search warrant for Wᵐ Law. for tools &c stolen. & believd to be in the house of Danl Sherwood.

when in Kirtland I saw. Elder [Reynolds] Cahoons boy steal a cucumber. put it in his pocket. I told Cahoon of it. at the same time his boy came up and denied it saying he had an apple. let it fall [p. [284]] and picked it up. there said Cahoon I did not beleive he stole it.—— his boys drove their cows among mine while the women were milking. to endanger their safety.— & I rebuked him and threatened him and made him confess in public next day. this was about the time of the commencmet [commencement] of building Temple in

---

596. Robert Taylor and Thomas Morgan were sentenced to six months' imprisonment in Carthage Jail but served their time in Nauvoo. (JS, Journal, 21 Feb. and 1 Mar. 1843, pp. 268, 279 herein.)
597. TEXT: Possibly "saw".
598. TEXT: Or "objections".
599. Three days earlier Turley asked JS if a brewery should be built in Nauvoo. (JS, Journal, 7 Mar. 1843.)

Kirtland.——[600] Signed the Warrant. said he should not send decision of Court to press without a petition.[601]

Ordered an execution for [Charles] Dana ~~to attach~~ again[s]t Brink.— and signed——

Dana swore he feared Brink would abscond or place his prope[r]ty out of reach.—[602] [p. [285]] [*page [286] blank*]

Book 2 (First Part), 10 March–30 April 1843

Editorial Note

The second book of Willard Richards's JS journal begins at 4:00 p.m. on 10 March 1843—the events of the earlier part of the day having been recorded in the first memorandum book—and continues through July 1843. This second book details JS's involvement in numerous civic, legal, and ecclesiastical affairs and contains several accounts of his teachings. These accounts include comments made to Orson Hyde on 2 April that were later canonized; lengthy discourses delivered at the April 1843 "special Conference" of the Church; practical instructions given to newly arrived immigrants on 13 April; a discourse on resurrection given on 16 April; and instructions given to several members of the Quorum of the Twelve on 19 April. Only the first part of Richards's second book, from 10 March through 30 April, is presented here; the remainder will be published in the third volume of

---

600. Construction of the temple in Kirtland began in the summer of 1833, at which time Reynolds Cahoon's three younger sons were Pulaski, Daniel, and Andrew, ages twelve or thirteen, eleven, and eight, respectively. (Shurtleff and Cahoon, *Reynolds Cahoon*, 78.)

601. A petition of this date signed by Alpheus Cutler, Reynolds Cahoon, Peter Haws, Hyrum Smith, and forty others urged JS to publish his decision in the case of *Dana v. Brink*. "By so doing," they wrote, "we believe many will receive information, genuine in its place, and very important to husbands and wives." The petition and decision were published on 22 March 1843 in *The Wasp*.

602. In April Brink appealed the 10 March decision before the Nauvoo Municipal Court, which determined that the municipal court had no jurisdiction in the case. Brink appealed again before the Hancock County Circuit Court in May 1843. No judgment was rendered until the May 1844 session, however, when a jury upheld JS's decision but reduced the judgment from ninety-nine to seventy-five dollars. The court was unable to collect, and in September 1844 Dana filed a declaration demanding that the judgment and damages be collected. The case was continued for several terms of court thereafter without result. Finally, in October 1846, the court approved a motion that "this suit be dismissed at the plaintiff's costs." Dana may have settled privately with Brink and/or Moses Smith and Jonah R. Ball, who as cosigners on the bond required for appeal were legally obligated to pay if Brink did not. (JS, Journal, 19 Apr. 1843, p. 364 herein; Dana v. Brink [Nauvoo Mun. Ct. 1843], Nauvoo Municipal Court Docket Book, 53–54; Declaration, Sept. 1844, Dana v. Brink [Hancock Co. Cir. Ct. 1844], Hancock Co., IL, Circuit Court, Civil and Criminal Files, box 21, microfilm 1,521,366, U.S. and Canada Record Collection, FHL; Appeal, 23 May 1844, and Scifa, 19 Oct. 1846, Dana v. Brink [Hancock Co. Cir. Ct. 1844], Hancock Co., IL, Circuit Court Records, vol. D, pp. 114, 455, microfilm 947,496, U.S. and Canada Record Collection, FHL.)

Second of four memorandum books. The second book of "President Joseph Smith's Journal" covers the period from 10 March to 14 July 1843. Volume 2 of the Journals series of *The Joseph Smith Papers* reproduces the journal entries through April 1843. JS, Journal, Dec. 1842–June 1844, bk. 2, JS Collection, Church History Library, Salt Lake City. (Photograph by Welden C. Andersen.)

the Journals series of *The Joseph Smith Papers,* along with the journal contained in Richards's third and fourth memorandum books.

———— ☙ ————

10 March 1843 • Friday (continued)

Friday March 10th 1843

4. P.M. Bro Norton claimed 2 trying squares,⁶⁰³ Wm Law, 1 Padlock: David grant 1. shirt:— of property found by the marshall on warrant Just issued—⁶⁰⁴ a bit stock⁶⁰⁵ and smoothing plane & 3 or 4 other little tools were presented on this case.— Mayor present.— clear and cold.— ⟨10 minutes before 7— I Willard [Richards]⟩

~~Saturday March 11.th.~~

⟨W.⟩ Richards, discovered a stream of light in the South West quarter of the heavens.— the pencil rays of light ⟨were⟩ in the form of a broad sword. with the hilt downward. the blade raised, pointing from the west south west [p. 1] raised ~~at~~ to an angle of— 45 degrees, from the horizon. and extending nearly ⟨or within 2 or 3 degre[e]s⟩ to the Zenith of the degree where the sign appeard. this sign gradually disappeard from 7½ oclock and at 9 had Entirely disappeared.⁶⁰⁶

11 March 1843 • Saturday

Saturday March 11th. So cold last night as to freeze water in the warmest rooms in the city. river fillid with anchor ice—⁶⁰⁷ 8½ o clock. in the office Joseph said he had tea with his breakfast. his wife asked him if [it] was good.— he said if it was a little stronger he should like it better, when Mother [Lydia Dibble] Granger remarked, [p. 2]

---

603. "Try squares" consist of two straight edges secured at right angles to each other used for testing whether work (such as woodwork) is square. ("Try," in *Oxford English Dictionary,* 11:438.)

604. The warrant was issued earlier in the day to search for stolen tools and other articles in Daniel Sherwood's house. (JS, Journal, 10 Mar. 1843, p. 302 herein.)

605. A brace or handle in which a drilling or boring bit is secured. ("Bit," in *Oxford English Dictionary,* 1:881.)

606. An article in *The Wasp* a few weeks later identified the "stream of light" in the heavens as a comet and incorrectly suggested it was the reappearance of a comet that was seen in 1264 and 1556. The comet referred to in the entry, identified as the "Great March Comet of 1843," or C/1843 D1, was neither the 1264 nor the 1556 comet. This 1843 comet was documented from February to April and at its most brilliant "had outshone any comet seen in the preceding seven centuries," possibly reaching a brightness more than sixty times that of the full moon. ("The Comet," *The Wasp,* 19 Apr. 1843, [1]; Kronk, *Cometography,* 1:309–311; 2:129–137; Bortle, "Great Comets in History," 45–46.)

607. Ice that forms on the bottom of a river. ("Anchor," in *Oxford English Dictionary,* 1:312.)

"It is so strong, and good, ⟨I should think it would answer—⟩
Both for drink, and food,"——

A dream, then related, Night before last I dreamed that a⟨n⟩ ⟨old⟩ man came to me ⟨and said⟩ there was a mob force coming upon him, and he was likely to loose his life, that I was Liut [Lieutenant] General and had the command of a large force. and I was also a patriot and disposed to protect the innocent & unoffinding. & wanted I should assist him.

I told him I wanted some written documents to show the facts that they are the aggressors, & I would raise a force sufficent for his protection, that I would call out the [Nauvoo] Legion,— He turned to go from me. but turned again and [p. 3] said to me. "I have any amount of men at my command and will put them under your command."[608]

The words of Joseph— while conver[s]ing about the sign in the heavens last Evening.— So ⟨As⟩ sure as there is a God who sits enthroned in the heavens. & so ⟨as⟩ sure as he ever spoke by me. so sure there will be a speedy and bloody war, and the broad sword seen last evening is the sure sign therof—[609]

about 9 A.M. Joseph & Brigham [Young] started for Ramus,

It is reported in the papers. that the workmen. employed on the General [p. 4] Pratte"[610] (which was burned and sunk last fall. near Memphis,) in the missisippi)) with a diving bell on the third of Janu[a]ry. found the wreck in about 24 ft water in that night was an earth quake.[611] next day the wreck had disapperd. no trace could be found, and the water was from 100 to 120 feet deep.— & for about 100 feet. no bottom, a bar was discove[re]d where previous was deep water.——[612]

[613]Joseph & Brigham had a pleasant and delightful ride. and arrived at Bro

---

608. JS related the same dream three weeks later, between meetings at a conference in Ramus, Illinois, on 2 April 1843, and Orson Hyde provided an interpretation. (JS, Journal, 2 Apr. 1843, p. 324 herein; see also Clayton, Journal, 2 Apr. 1843, p. 405 herein.)

609. On 25 December 1832, JS predicted wars that would begin with a rebellion in South Carolina. (Revelation, 25 Dec. 1832, in Revelation Book 1, p. 157, in *JSP*, MRB:291 [D&C 87].)

610. The steamship *General Pratte* had some 520 passengers—most of them German immigrants—on board when it caught fire and was destroyed 23 November 1842. All of the passengers apparently survived. ("The Burning of the Gen. Pratt," *Pennsylvania Inquirer and National Gazette* [Philadelphia], 12 Dec. 1842, [2]; "Steamboat Burnt," *New-Orleans Bee*, 29 Nov. 1842, [2].)

611. On 4 January 1843 a magnitude 6.3 earthquake occurred with an epicenter near Memphis, Tennessee, causing severe damage to several buildings in the area. The quake was felt from the seacoast of Georgia to Rhode Island and from Indiana to Mississippi. (Stover and Coffman, *Seismicity of the United States*, 68.)

612. See "A Hole in the Mississippi," *Philadelphia North American and Daily Advertiser*, 11 Feb. 1843, [2]; News item, *Racine (Wisconsin Territory) Advocate*, 22 Feb. 1843, [2].

613. TEXT: The remainder of this entry is written in a different brown ink, which matches that of the

Mc.Clary's [William McCleary's] in Ramus. 15 minutes before 4. P.M.— at Benjamin Johnsons[614] to lodge while they staid in Ramus.— in the eve Joseph pulled up Bro Mors [Justus A. Morse]. with one hand pulling sticks.—[615] [p. 5]

12 March 1843 • Sunday

Sunday March 12th. Joseph preachd 14 John— in my fathers house are many mansions[616] &. found the brethren well and in good spirits had a very pleasant visit P.M.

Brigham [Young] preacchd [preached].

13 March 1843 • Monday

Monday March 13th. throwed the bully of Ramus wrestling.—[617] 2 P.M. held church meeting. Appointed Almon Babbitt Presiding Elder of Ramus by unanimous voice of the church, in the evening held a meeting for blessing children. 27 blessed. [p. 6]

mercury 3 degrees below zero at sun rise in Nauvoo. It is said by many the sword was seen in the heavens last eve again. It is said in the papers that iron filings & sulphur have fallen in form of snow storm. in Missouri. in five counties.—[618] This day heard that the Quincy Institute was burned last week. 3 or 4 tracks were followed in the light snow from the institute to the middle of the river which was frozen over[619]

Mr Ivins. arrived at Nauvoo and stated that [Orrin] Porter Rockwell came with him from New Jersey to St Louis when[620] Porter was taken by advertisem[en]t [p. 7] Saturday March 5. & put in St Louis Jail.[621] New meeting house

---

following entry.

614. TEXT: Or "Johnson.".

615. Morse was remembered as the strongest man in Ramus. (Historian's Office, JS History, draft notes, 11 Mar. 1843.)

616. See John 14:2.

617. According to the draft notes used to compile JS's history, this was William Wall, "the most expert wrestler of Ramus." (Historian's Office, JS History, draft notes, 13 Mar. 1843.)

618. As the time proposed by William Miller for the second coming of Christ drew near, newspaper reports of iron filings falling through the air and other "wonderful signs and tokens" heralding the imminent return of Christ to the earth proliferated. (See "Signs and Tokens," *Republican Compiler* [Gettysburg, PA], 13 Mar. 1843, [2]; and 262n399 herein.)

619. The "Mission Institute" near Quincy, Illinois, provided a college-level education for "any who may wish to preach the Gospel, either at home or abroad." Less openly, it also served as a center of abolitionism, whose members would reportedly "decoy the slaves from their masters in Missouri and run them off" to Illinois. The fire reported here by Willard Richards consumed the chapel of the institute the night of 7–8 March 1843 and was presumably set by Missourians in retaliation for the institute's abolitionist activities. (Nelson, *Appeal to the Church,* 18; "Incendiary," *Quincy [IL] Whig,* 15 Mar. 1843, [2].)

620. TEXT: Possibly "where".

621. Rockwell was charged with the May 1842 attempted murder of Missouri's former governor

lately dedicated ~~to~~ in.⁶²² Quincy— & the dedication sermon was all against the Mormons.—⁶²³ Elder O[rson] Hyde has gone down there to preach. & the Mormons say they ⟨would be glad to have their new meeting house⟩ ~~want their Meeting house. &c for~~ Elder Hyde to preach in.——⁶²⁴

14 March 1843 • Tuesday

Tuesday March 14ᵗʰ· Joseph & Brigham [Young] returnd abo[u]t 4. P.M. had a severe, cold, ride,— ⟨This evening. appeared a large circle round the moon. similar to what is frequently seen but larger.—⁶²⁵ (See page 11)⁶²⁶⟩ [p. 8]

15 March 1843 • Wednesday

Wednesday March 15ᵗʰ Dictated letter to G[eorge] J. Adams— read letter from [Justin] Butterfield⁶²⁷ & Arlington Bennett [James Arlington Bennet].—⁶²⁸

Lilburn W. Boggs. Ivins's report confused the date Rockwell was arrested in St. Louis, as 5 March 1843 fell on a Sunday rather than Saturday. Other sources for the date of Rockwell's arrest are contradictory. The draft notes of the JS History, as well as a later statement by Rockwell himself copied into JS's multivolume manuscript history of the church, date the arrest to Saturday, 4 March 1843, while the *Missouri Republican* reported it as taking place on Sunday, 5 March. Richard Blennerhassett's 7 March 1843 letter to Newel K. Whitney dates the arrest to 6 March 1843. Advertisements for the apprehension of JS and Rockwell appeared in the *Sangamo Journal, Alton Telegraph and Democratic Review,* and other Illinois newspapers. (JS, Journal, 8 Aug. 1842; Historian's Office, JS History, draft notes, 4 Mar. 1843; JS History, vol. E-1, 1827; News item, *Daily Missouri Republican* [St. Louis], 17 Mar. 1843; Richard Blennerhassett, St. Louis, MO, to Newel K. Whitney, Nauvoo, IL, 7 Mar. 1843, Newel K. Whitney, Papers, BYU; "Four Hundred Dollars Reward!," *Sangamo Journal* [Springfield, IL], 7 Oct. 1842, [2]; Notice, *Alton [IL] Telegraph and Democratic Review,* 1 Oct. 1842, [2].)

622. TEXT: Instead of "~~to~~ in", possibly "~~for to~~ in" or "~~to~~ for".

623. William Carter preached the sermon at the dedication of the Congregational church in Quincy on 1 March 1843. The minutes of the meeting do not give details of the sermon's content. (First Union Congregational Church, Quincy, IL, Church records, vol. 2, p. 30, microfilm 960,879, U.S. and Canada Record Collection, FHL.)

624. Hyde returned from his brief mission to Quincy two weeks later. (JS, Journal, 30 Mar. 1843.)

625. Wilford Woodruff described the phenomenon in detail: "At about half past seven oclock in the evening the sword which had made its appearen[c]e for several evenings past moved up near the moon & formed itself into a large ring round the moon two Balls immediately appeared in the ring opposite of each other sumthing in the form of sundogs annother half ring is hung from those Balls sumthing in the shape of a horse shoe extending outside of the first ring with one line runing through the centre of the moon." (Woodruff, Journal, 14 Mar. 1843.)

626. A reference to manuscript page 11 of this document—that is, of Willard Richards's second memorandum book. (Observations in the Night Sky, 14 Mar. 1843, p. 310 herein.)

627. JS responded to Butterfield by 19 March. (See 313n652 herein.)

628. In this letter, Bennet referred to the "peculiar distressed situation" about which JS had written him earlier—a reference, presumably, to John C. Bennett's recent threats to have JS arrested on charges dating back to the Missouri conflict of 1838–1839. James Arlington Bennet recounted to JS the steps he had taken to thwart Bennett's designs and assured JS that any effort to prosecute JS would be unsuccessful. Bennet also noted that John C. Bennett's book attacking the Mormons was a failure, and he castigated *New York Herald* editor James Gordon Bennett, who continued to "make sport" of JS in the pages

Signed Deeds for. sister [Lydia Dibble] granger. & [Mary Bailey] Smith. & Alreed [Reuben W. Allred].[629]

Spent the day mostly in the office.

gave the following name to the "Wasp" enlarged. as is contemplated
"The Nauvoo Neighbor"
"Our Motto, the saints singularity"
"Is unity. liberty. Charity."[630]

Joseph. prophecied in the name of the Lord Jesus Christ. that [Orrin] Porter Rockwell will get away from the Missourians,[631]

told Hawes [Peter Haws] he must curtail his boys or they will get into State Prison.[632] [p. 9]

Dream.— last night dreamed of swimming in a river of pure water clear as crystal, over a school of fish. of the largest ⟨size⟩ I ever saw. they were directly under my belly— I was astonished & felt afraid they might drown me or do me injury. they were the largest I ever saw.—

conversed much about Porter. wishing the boy well. [*6 lines blank*] [p. 10]

---

of his paper. JS responded two days after receiving the letter. (James Arlington Bennet, Arlington House, Long Island, NY, to JS, Nauvoo, IL, 20 Feb. 1843, JS Materials, CCLA; JS, Journal, 18 Jan. and 17 Mar. 1843.)

629. Nauvoo Registry of Deeds, Record of Deeds, bk. A, pp. 187–188; bk. B, pp. 42–43; Indenture, JS (Trustee-in-trust) to Lydia Dibble Granger, Hancock Co., IL, 15 Mar. 1843, Henry E. Huntington Library, San Marino, CA.

630. An announcement declared *The Wasp* was to be discontinued with the 19 April issue, its size doubled, and its title changed to *Nauvoo Neighbor*. The final issue of *The Wasp* was the 26 April 1843 issue, and the inaugural issue of the *Nauvoo Neighbor*, edited by John Taylor, appeared on 3 May 1843. Under the nameplate, the newspaper regularly printed the phrases approved by JS: "OUR MOTTO—THE SAINTS' SINGULARITY—IS UNITY, LIBERTY, CHARITY." The change of names may be partly attributable to the fact that James Arlington Bennet did not like *The Wasp* as a name for the paper. "Mildness should characterise every thing that comes from Nauvoo," he wrote to JS, "and even a name . . . has much influence on one side or the other." ("Prospectus of a Weekly Newspaper, Called the Nauvoo Neighbor," *The Wasp*, 5 Apr. 1843, [1]; James Arlington Bennet to JS, 16 Aug. 1842, pp. 136–137 herein.)

631. Rockwell was arrested in St. Louis in early March 1843 for the attempted murder of Missouri's former governor Lilburn W. Boggs. Ultimately Rockwell was not indicted for shooting Boggs, but he was indicted for attempting to escape while the grand jury at Independence, Missouri, investigated the charges against him. The case was transferred to the Fifth Judicial Circuit with Austin A. King presiding as judge and Alexander Doniphan serving as Rockwell's court-appointed attorney. The trial was held 11 December 1843; the jury convicted Rockwell of jailbreaking and sentenced him to five minutes' imprisonment. Rockwell was released on 13 December and arrived in Nauvoo on 25 December 1843. (JS, Journal, 13 Mar. 1843; see also 307n621 herein; Smith, "Mormon Troubles in Missouri," 249–251; and JS, Journal, 25 Dec. 1843, JS Collection, CHL.)

632. Haws's sons Alpheus and Albert were seventeen and twelve years old, respectively. (Black, *Early Members of the Reorganized Church*, 3:376.)

Observations in the Night Sky, Initial Diagram • 14 March 1843

⁶³³⟨Tuesday march 14⁽ᵗʰ⁾ 1843⁶³⁴⟩ [*drawing of atmospheric phenomenon consisting of circles labeled A through D keyed to explanations*]

A. a large circle seen round the moon on the evening of this day & dark shades within the circle & around the moon which is the darkest spot in the centre—

C. This circle was visible this evening about 8. o cl'k and continued through the evening. the parhelion on this circle, B.B. were brightest as also the circle C. about 1/4 before 9 o clock, the circle & parhelion were very brilliant & grew paler. by nine o clock.— Description of W[illiam] W. Phelps.

D. an additional circles seen about 9. ock by. Joseph. ⟨&⟩ the whole diagram as then seen and described by the prophet.

[D.] This circle is a mistake⁶³⁵

Dʳ R[obert] D. Foster. states that at 11. o clock there were an an innumerable Nº— of circles interwoven as above. around the moon.

The whole designed to represent as one of the signs of the times, "A Union of Power, & combination of the Nations." says Joseph.

not correct.—

See page 17 [p. 11]

16 March 1843 • Thursday

⁶³⁶Thursday March 16ᵗʰ· 1843 9 A.M. in the office. read a piece on Mormonism in "Uncle Sam" Feb 18ᵗʰ· written by reporter of the paper.—⁶³⁷ & conversed with Hiram [Hyrum Smith] Dʳ [Robert D.] Foster. & many others,—

17 March 1843 • Friday

Friday March 17⁽ᵗʰ⁾ 1843 a part of the fore noon in the office— & the remainder at home. P.M. settled with Father [Asahel] Perry gave him a deed of 80 acres of land & city lot & prophecied that it wo[u]ld not be 6 mo before he could sell it for cash⁶³⁸ [p. 12]

---

633. TEXT: Blue ink commences.
634. A corrected diagram drawn by Richards appears on manuscript page 17.
635. TEXT: A rectangle is inscribed around this sentence.
636. TEXT: Brown ink commences.
637. Probably the weekly newspaper by that name printed in Boston and published by George H. Williams and Henry L. Williams.
638. As trustee-in-trust for the church, JS signed two deeds to Perry: one for $800 on eighty acres in Hancock County, and one for $1,000 on a city lot in Nauvoo. (Hancock Co., IL, Deed Records, vol. L, pp. 245–246, microfilm 954,599, U.S. and Canada Record Collection, FHL; Nauvoo Registry of Deeds, Record of Deeds, bk. A, pp. 197–198.)

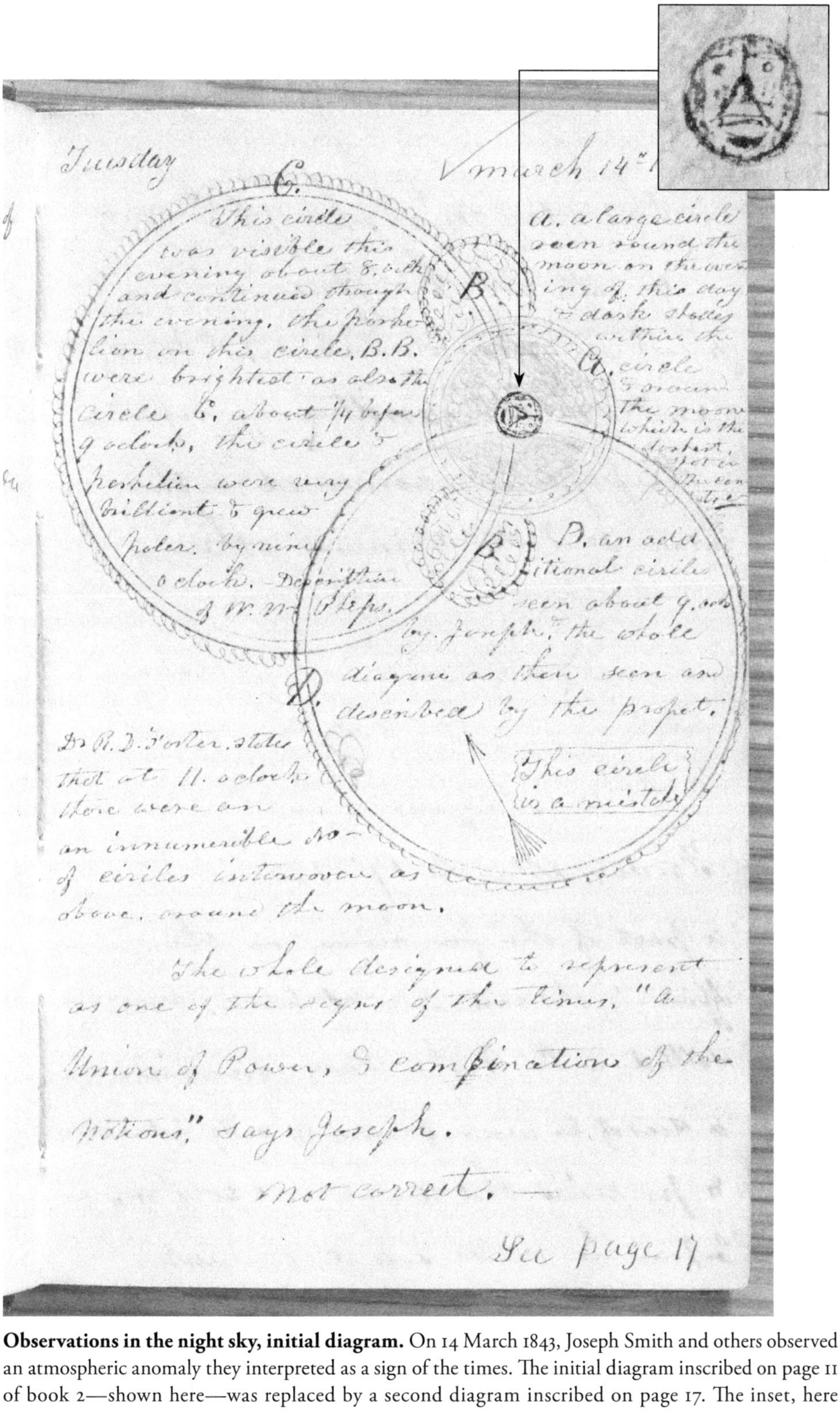

Observations in the night sky, initial diagram. On 14 March 1843, Joseph Smith and others observed an atmospheric anomaly they interpreted as a sign of the times. The initial diagram inscribed on page 11 of book 2—shown here—was replaced by a second diagram inscribed on page 17. The inset, here rotated ninety degrees, is a representation of the "man in the moon." Handwriting of Willard Richards. JS, Journal, Dec. 1842–June 1844, bk. 2, p. 11, JS Collection, Church History Library, Salt Lake City. (Photograph by Welden C. Andersen.)

[639]4 o'clock P.M. N[ewel] K. Whitney brought in a letter from R[ichard] S. Blennerhassett esqr <u>St. Louis</u> conce[r]ning [Orrin] Porter Rockwell. Dated Ma[r]ch 7.[640] saying Porter was arrested the the day previos[641] and wishing instruction.—[642] Read and dictated answer.—[643] heard read letters No 1. Boston Bee. by Viator.[644] and his own to [James] Arlington Bennet.[645]

2 P.M. walked out with 4 or 5 ladi[e]s towa[r]ds the Store.—[646] went into. Holmes.

a report is circulated that that new indictments have been found in Mo. again[s]t Joseph. Hyrum [Smith]. & some 100. others on the old. subject.[647] & John C. Bennet[t] is going to do so and so.— [p. 13]

---

639. TEXT: Blue ink commences.
640. Richard Blennerhassett, St. Louis, MO, to Newel K. Whitney, Nauvoo, IL, 7 Mar. 1843, Newel K. Whitney, Papers, BYU.
641. Other sources identify either 4 or 5 March 1843 as the date for Rockwell's arrest. (JS, Journal, 13 Mar. 1843; 307n621 herein.)
642. A 14 March letter from Joseph Wood, a Mormon lawyer at Bonhomme, Missouri, clarified that upon his visiting St. Louis on a criminal case, he learned that one of his "brethren" was in the local jail charged with the attempted murder of former Missouri governor Lilburn W. Boggs. Wood visited the jail, and Rockwell requested legal counsel, whereupon Wood promised to defend him and engaged Blennerhassett to assist in the case. (Joseph Wood, Bonhomme, MO, to JS et al., Nauvoo, IL, 14 Mar. 1843, JS Collection, CHL.)
643. In his response, JS requested that Blennerhassett work to delay Rockwell's trial until additional legal counsel could be retained and that Blennerhassett keep Rockwell's friends in Nauvoo informed of the case's developments. ([JS], Nauvoo, IL, to Richard Blennerhassett, St. Louis, MO, 17 Mar. 1843, draft, on verso of "Truthiana," 1843, draft, CHL.)
644. The first of a series of nine letters to the *Boston Daily Bee*. Willard Richards was the author of the letters, with possible input from JS, who ten days earlier requested that Richards write to the *Bee*. The series, signed "Viator," was written in the style of a traveler who visited Nauvoo and reported his impressions of JS and Mormonism. The draft versions of the letters include a series title, "Truthiana," which did not appear in the published versions. It is unclear whether the ninth letter from "Viator" was published in the *Bee*, but the eighth and ninth letters were later published in the *Times and Seasons*. Willard Richards's letters of 17 and 24 March 1843; 1, 8, 15, and 22 April 1843; and 17 and 26 July 1843 were printed in the 12, 18, and 28 April 1843; 11, 20, and 22 May 1843; and 5 and 19 August 1843 issues of the *Boston Daily Bee*. Drafts of the 17 and 26 July 1843 and the 18 August 1843 letters are in William W. Phelps's handwriting and contain corrections that were included in the published versions. (Richards, Journal, 19 and 26 Mar. 1843; 1, 9, 15, and 27 Apr. 1843; 17 July 1843; 19 Aug. 1843; JS, Journal, 6 Mar. 1843; "Truthiana," 1843, draft, CHL; "From the Boston Bee," *Times and Seasons*, 1 Sept. 1843, 305–307.)
645. JS's letter to Bennet was a response to Bennet's letter dated 20 February 1843. In his letter, JS thanked Bennet for his concern and celebrated his discharge from arrest in Springfield. (JS, Nauvoo, IL, to James Arlington Bennet, Arlington House, Long Island, NY, 17 Mar. 1843, photocopy, JS Collection, CHL; see also 308n628 herein.)
646. JS and Emma Smith, together with Eliza R. Snow, a Mrs. Allred, Elizabeth Davis Durfee, and others, attended the closing of Snow's school. (Eliza R. Snow, Journal, 17 Mar. 1843.)
647. Judge Nathaniel Pope's decision in January 1843 prevented JS's extradition to Missouri to face the charge of being an accessory in the shooting of former Missouri governor Lilburn W. Boggs. John C. Bennett and others then sought to have JS extradited to Missouri on earlier charges, including treason, stemming from his alleged criminal participation in the 1838 "Mormon War" in Caldwell and Daviess

18 March 1843 • Saturday

Saturday⁶⁴⁸ March ~~19th~~ ⟨18th⟩ 1843. Most of the fore noon in the office in cheerful conversation. closed ~~his~~ Letter to Arlington Bennett [James Arlington Bennet].⁶⁴⁹ laid down on the writing table with ⟨back of th[e]⟩ head on Law Books, Saying write & tell the world I accknowlidge myself a very great lawyer. I am going study law & this is the way I study. and ~~went~~ fell asleep. & went to snoring. ⁶⁵⁰this was about noon. In the after-noon rode out. & about 4 took a game ~~of~~ at ball east of main street. [p. 14]

19 March 1843 • Sunday

Sunday March ~~20th~~ ⟨19th.⟩ Rode with Emma to the farm⁶⁵¹ returnd about 11. A.M.—

at home the remainder of the day

D[imick] Huntington started for. Chicago with letter to. [Justin] Butterfield. concerning. O. P. [Orrin Porter] Rockwell⁶⁵² [*10 lines blank*] [p. 15]

20 March 1843 • Monday

Monday March ~~21st~~ ⟨20st⟩ 1843. Rode to Hiram Kimball's— with Mrs. [Margaret Lawrence] Butterfield, about a deed.

Rec[k]oned with R[obert] D. Foster, and give Foster a note to balance. all demands Foster took the acknowled[g]ement of about 20 deeds. of the Trustee to sundry individuals.⁶⁵³ and left the office about 3 o'clock,

---

counties in Missouri.*a* The indictment was handed down at the June 1843 term of the Daviess County Circuit Court, which initiated what was ultimately an unsuccessful extradition attempt later that year.*b* JS's enemies made a similar attempt—also unsuccessful—to extradite him to Missouri in 1841.*c* (*a.* John C. Bennett, Springfield, IL, to Sidney Rigdon and Orson Pratt, Nauvoo, IL, 10 Jan. 1843, Sidney Rigdon, Collection, CHL. *b.* Indictment, June 1843, State of Missouri v. JS for Treason [Daviess Co. Cir. Ct. 1843], Western Americana Collection, Beinecke Rare Book and Manuscript Library, Yale University, New Haven, CT. *c.* "The Late Proceedings," *Times and Seasons,* 15 June 1841, 2:447–449.)

648. TEXT: Beginning with the first "a" in "Saturday", brown ink commences.

649. JS had begun the letter by the previous day, as indicated by the 17 March journal entry.

650. TEXT: Blue ink commences.

651. JS's farm to the east of Nauvoo.

652. In the letter, JS asked Butterfield to take charge of the defense of "friend Porter," who was arrested in early March for the attempted murder of former Missouri governor Lilburn W. Boggs. Ultimately Alexander Doniphan represented Rockwell before the Fifth Judicial Circuit. Huntington returned to Nauvoo on 2 April 1843. (JS, Nauvoo, IL, to Justin Butterfield, [Chicago, IL], 18 Mar. 1843, copy, JS Collection, CHL; see also 309n631 and 323n694 herein.)

653. Records have been located of nine deeds involving JS as trustee that Foster officially acknowledged as justice of the peace. The "sundry individuals" included Willard and Jennetta Richards, Dimick Huntington, Gilbert Gouldsmith, George C. Hampton, John Tidwell, Elizabeth Davis Durfee, Reuben W. Allred, Mary Bailey Smith, and Asahel Perry. (Indenture, Willard and Jennetta Richards to JS [Trustee-in-trust], 23 Feb. 1843, JS Collection, CHL; Hancock Co., IL, Deed Records, vol. L,

This evening from 7 to 9 was seen ⟨by Bro [Peter] Haws. & othe[r]s⟩ in the heavens a dark stripe of considerable width passing over our zenith, dark as the darkest clouds.[654] [p. 16]

Observations in the Night Sky, Corrected Diagram • 14 March 1843

⟨Tuesday⟩ ⟨March 14. 1843⟩ [*drawing of atmospheric phenomenon showing intersecting circles with accompanying descriptions*][655]

This circle was similar to the one around the moon in appearance. but larger.

A.A. Parhelion, visible from 8 to 9 o clock— P.M. when it was seen by Joseph and this diagram was drawn from his description

This space was darker than other parts of the horizon

Moon

Circle such as is frequently seen.

The outer part of parhelion was much more brilliant than the inner.

The above is a diagram of one of the signs of the times designed to represent. "A union of power and combination of Nations" says Joseph.

Dr R[obert] D. Foster, says that at 11. oclock the circles interwoven around the moon were innumerable. [p. 17]

21 March 1843 • Tuesday

[656]Tuesday March 22ᵈ ⟨21ˢᵗ⟩—1843 called at the office about 9. & wrote an order.— and took leave for Shokokon,—[657] cold west— wind as it has been for a week. cold, freezing water in the houses [*11 lines blank*] [p. 18]

22 March 1843 • Wednesday

Wednesday March 23 22— [*16 lines blank*] [p. 19]

---

pp. 245–246, microfilm 954,599, U.S. and Canada Record Collection, FHL; Nauvoo Registry of Deeds, Record of Deeds, bk. A, pp. 197–198, 219–220; bk. B, pp. 1, 42–43, 250–251.)

654. In his description of the dark band in the sky that appeared throughout the week, Wilford Woodruff recorded that "the light that has been represented as a sword has made its appearance for several nights past in the same place & also on the opposite of the horizen has been seem A black streak about the size of the light one, while one is as black as darkness the other has considerable of the appearance of the blaze of a Comet." (Woodruff, Journal, 20–25 Mar. 1843.)

655. Richards's original diagram appears on manuscript page 11.

656. TEXT: Brown ink commences.

657. Willard Richards, who was keeping JS's journal, remained in Nauvoo. William Clayton indicated in his own journal that JS set out for Shokokon, Illinois, with Clayton but that they parted company that day, Clayton going on to Shokokon and then meeting up with JS on the return trip on 24 March. (Clayton, Journal, 21, 22, 23, and 24 Mar. 1843.)

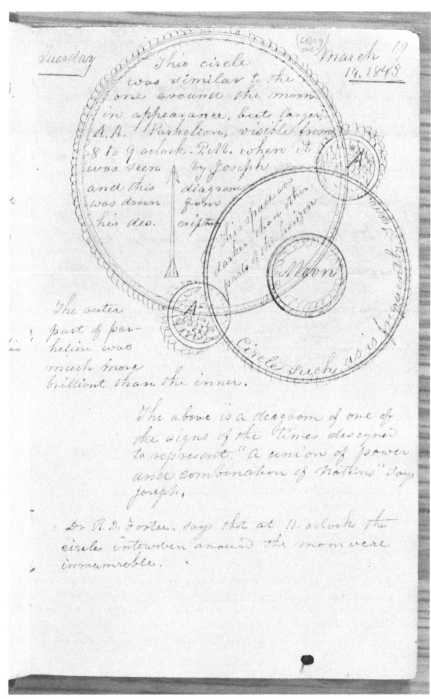

Observations in the night sky, corrected diagram. On 14 March 1843, Joseph Smith and others observed an atmospheric phenomenon they interpreted as a sign of the times. The initial diagram inscribed on page 11 of book 2 was replaced by a second diagram—shown here—inscribed on page 17. Handwriting of Willard Richards. JS, Journal, Dec. 1842–June 1844, bk. 2, p. 17, JS Collection, Church History Library, Salt Lake City. (Photograph by Welden C. Andersen.)

23 March 1843 • Thursday

Thursday March 24 ⟨23ᵈ⟩ ⟨7½— A.M.⟩ mercury 1. Deg below zero at sunrise [*drawing of sun with parhelia*]

⁶⁵⁸Semicircle Near the Zenith. [p. 20]

Sun

Parhelion. appearance of the Sun. March 23ᵈ. at 1843. at 7½ o'clock A.M.

Parhelion. The colors of the circles, were of the hue of the rainbow, only brighter⁶⁵⁹ [p. 21] [*page [22] blank*]

24 March 1843 • Friday

⁶⁶⁰Friday March 24. 1843 [*5 lines blank*] ⁶⁶¹having been out west. arrived at home about one or two occlock

⁶⁶²1 Loaded team came in from Augu[s]ta with provision—⁶⁶³ & two from Lima this evening⁶⁶⁴ [p. [23]]

25 March 1843 • Saturday

Saturday March 25. 1843 In the office at 8 o clock. heard a report from Hyrum [Smith] concerning theives, as given by Z. [Wilson]⁶⁶⁵ and directed. a proclamation to be published offering secur[i]ty to all who will divulge their secrets,—⁶⁶⁶

---

658. TEXT: Blue ink commences.

659. Strange sights in the sky were widely reported about this time. Orson Pratt, in an article in the *Times and Seasons,* identified the phenomena as parhelia. (JS, Journal, 10, 14, and 20 Mar. 1843; Orson Pratt, "Halos and Parhelia," *Times and Seasons,* 1 Apr. 1843, 4:151–152.)

660. TEXT: Brown ink commences.

661. TEXT: Blue ink commences.

662. TEXT: Brown ink commences.

663. TEXT: Instead of "provision", possibly "provisions".

664. Members of the Quorum of the Twelve previously wrote letters to the branches of the church in Ramus, Augusta, Lima, and La Harpe requesting provisions for JS and his family so JS could devote his time to the needs of the church. (JS, Journal, 18 Feb. 1843; Historian's Office, JS History, draft notes, 3 Mar. 1843; Brigham Young, Nauvoo, IL, to "the church," Ramus, IL, 23 Feb. 1843, draft; Brigham Young, Nauvoo, IL, to "the church," La Harpe, IL, 18 Feb. 1843, draft, Brigham Young Office Files, CHL.)

665. TEXT: Transliteration from Taylor shorthand: "w-l-s-n".

666. In the proclamation, JS as mayor noted the reported existence of a "band of desperadoes, bound by oaths of secrecy, under severe penalties in case any member of the combination divulges their plans of stealing and conveying properties from station to station, up and down the Mississippi and other routes." Having heard that some members of the group would not provide legal authorities with information about the criminals for fear of retaliation, JS promised to "grant and ensure protection against all personal mob violence, to each and every citizen of this city" who would provide him with the names of those who were in any way involved with the thieves. (JS, "Proclamation," *The Wasp,* 29 Mar. 1843, [3].)

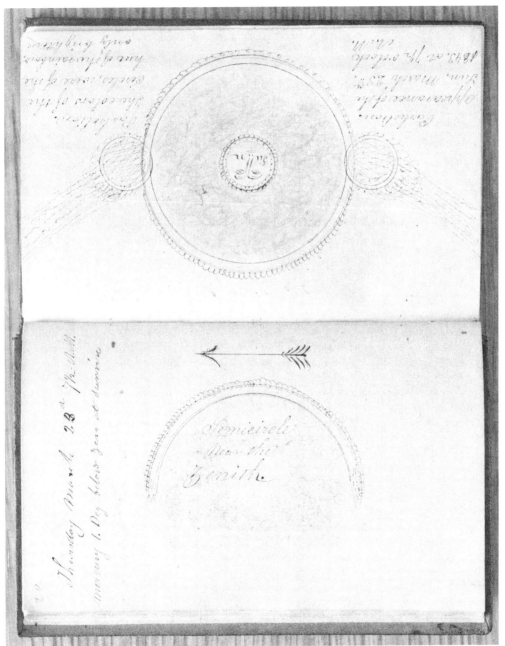

Parhelia. On the morning of 23 March 1843, Willard Richards observed rings around and near the sun, which he depicted in Joseph Smith's journal. Handwriting of Willard Richards. JS, Journal, Dec. 1842–June 1844, bk. 2, pp. 20–21, JS Collection, Church History Library, Salt Lake City. (Photograph by Welden C. Andersen.)

Received a letter from A[braham] Jonas requesting the use of a cannon to celebrate ⟨the creation of⟩ the New. County of Marquetts and answerd it that he might have it.—[667]

also Rec[d.] Letter from Senator [Richard] Young contain[i]ng a bond for 1/4 Section of Land from Welch [John C. Walsh]—[668]

9 Baptizd Esqr Miflin of Philadilphia [p. [24]]

10 orderd a writ agai[n]st A. Fields for disorderly conduct.—[669]

& gave E[benezer] Robinson an order on T. [John Taylor] & Woodruf [Wilford Woodruff] for papers $16.—[670]

A. Fields was brought in about noon drunk or pretending to be so and was ordered to be put in irons till sober, he abused all present by his drunken appeara[n]ce.

has been out in the city dined at 2 o clock.—

"Awful Gale" says St Louis Gazette, within the last 6 weeks 154 vissels were wrecked on the coast of England & 190 lives lost;— on the coast of Ireland 5 vessels & 134 lives; on the coast of Scotland 17 vissels 39 lives; on the coast on of france 4 vessels.— & 100 lives. value of vessel & cargoes roughly estimated £825,000.—[671] [p. [25]]

---

667. Contrary to what the entry states, Jonas, a resident of Columbus, Illinois, was requesting the cannon to celebrate the fact that the proposed county of Marquette would not be created—and to irritate the residents of Quincy as well. At the time, citizens of Quincy were agitating that Adams County, home to both Quincy and Columbus, be split into two counties, Adams and Marquette. Residents of Columbus, which was to be in the new Marquette County if the plan were approved, opposed the move. Residents of Quincy fired off a cannon every time favorable news was received from Springfield regarding the creation of the new county—a gesture Columbus residents found offensive. The state legislature approved the new county, but as Jonas pointed out in his letter, its organization depended "on the people electing County officers—on the 1st Monday in April." Jonas wrote that those living in the proposed county "have determined not to Organize—nor elect officers—consequently the law will be inoperative." Residents in the new county finally elected a state representative in 1846, although two years later the county (renamed "Highland" by this time) was merged with Adams County. (Abraham Jonas, Columbus, IL, to JS, Nauvoo, IL, 21 Mar. 1843, JS Collection, CHL; JS, Nauvoo, IL, to Abraham Jonas, Columbus, IL, 25 Mar. 1843, Newel K. Whitney, Papers, BYU; Collins and Perry, *Past and Present of the City of Quincy and Adams County, Illinois,* 94–95; An Act to Change the Name of the County of Marquette . . . [27 Feb. 1847], *Laws of the State of Illinois* [1846–1847], pp. 38–41.)

668. JS was in the process of purchasing the northwest quarter of Section[8, Township 6 North, Range 8 West from Walsh for $2,500. Young was acting as a liaison between JS and Walsh during the transaction. (JS per William Clayton, Nauvoo, IL, to Richard M. Young, Washington DC, 23 Dec. 1842; JS per William Clayton, Nauvoo, IL, to Richard M. Young, Washington DC, 9 Feb. 1843, Newel K. Whitney, Papers, BYU.)

669. Fields was tried two days later, as reported in the following journal entry for 27 March.

670. Taylor and Woodruff were leasing the printing office that published the *Times and Seasons* and *The Wasp* from JS, who purchased it from Ebenezer Robinson the previous year. (JS, Journal, 4 Feb. and 2 Dec. 1842.)

671. The report Willard Richards found in the *St. Louis Gazette* appears to have been originally

26 March 1843 • Sunday

⁶⁷²Sunday March 26ᵗʰ· at home all day. [*15 lines blank*] [p. [26]]

27 March 1843 • Monday

Monday March 27. 1843.— Dictated a letter to Esquire [Sidney] Rigdon shewing that he beleived said Rigdon was concernd with J. C. Bennet [John C. Bennett] Geo. W. Robinson. & Jar[e]d Carter, & unless satisfa[c]tion was made should withdraw fellowship. & bring him before conference. Letter was presented by W[illard] Richards.⁶⁷³

11. court assembled over the store to try A. Field. for drunkenness & abusing his wife. Fined $10. costs & bail $50. for 6 months to keep the peacee. [p. [27]]

28 March 1843 • Tuesday

Tuesday March 28 removed the office from the Smoke house to the Presidents officce over the Counting room in the Store.—⁶⁷⁴ [*12 lines blank*] [p. [28]]

29 March 1843 • Wednesday

Wednesday March 29. Sat on trial with orson Spencer. on case of Dʳ [Robert D.] Foster.⁶⁷⁵ Judgment agai[n]st Foster. R̶e̶m̶o̶v̶e̶d̶ ̶f̶r̶o̶m̶ ̶S̶m̶o̶k̶e̶ ̶h̶o̶u̶s̶e̶ ̶t̶o̶ ̶o̶f̶f̶i̶c̶e̶ ̶o̶v̶e̶r̶ ̶t̶h̶e̶ ̶s̶t̶o̶r̶e̶.̶ [*illegible*]⁶⁷⁶ [*11 lines blank*] [p. [29]]

---

published as "The Late Awful Gale," *Times* (London), 10 Feb. 1843, 8.

672. TEXT: Blue ink commences.

673. JS charged Rigdon with practicing "secret plottings" and "decception" against JS and the church and being involved in the "abominable practices" of Bennett, Robinson, and Carter, with specific reference to Rigdon's conduct as postmaster. In his reply, Rigdon denied the charges against him and sought a reconciliation with JS. Difficulties between the two persisted, however, with JS again raising the issue of Rigdon's fellowship in the church in August and October 1843. (JS, Nauvoo, IL, to Sidney Rigdon, Nauvoo, IL, 27 Mar. 1843, copy, JS Collection, CHL; Sidney Rigdon to JS, Nauvoo, IL, 27 Mar. 1843, JS Collection, CHL; JS, Journal, 13 Aug. 1843, JS Collection, CHL; "Minutes of a Special Conference," *Times and Seasons*, 15 Sept. 1843, 4:329–332; see also JS, Journal, 29 Aug. and 8 Nov. 1842; 18 Jan. 1843, pp. 123, 167–168, 245–246 herein.)

674. The mayor's office was moved from JS's house to the smokehouse on 14 February, as noted in JS's journal entry for that date.

675. According to the draft notes used to compile JS's history, this was a "case of debt." (Historian's Office, JS History, draft notes, 29 Mar. 1843.)

676. Possibly "t̶o̶his".

30 March 1843 • Thursday

[677]Thursday March 30 ⟨1843⟩ 9 A.M. came [678]and gave inst[r]uctions to have Brinks [William Brink's] bond returnd to him if it was delayed till after 10. o clock[679]

Called at 11. brought in N[ew] York Herald. reported March 11.— that the Isla[n]d of antigua was destroyd by an earthquake on the 8[th] of Feb. & Nevis & [St.] Kitts were considerably injured.[680]

Andrew. L. Lamoreaux paid $73 for W[m.] Henry [Henrie]. on Temple.

Dr Brink brought in a new Bond. which the Mayor rejected as informal.

told Charles Ivins he might improve his share of the Ferry one year [p. [30]] told Charles Ivins unless he considerd Dr Brink good for heavy damages, he was foolish to go his bonds.—[681]

[682]New. York Herald of the 11th of March published the vision in Poetry &c Miss [Eliza R.] Snows. festival song. &c.—[683]

[684]Brinks Case ⟨took⟩ appeal from Mayor's Court To the municipal to be tried 10th April. 10. A.M.[685]

[686]1½ P.M was called to sit as Justice, with Alderman [George W.] Harris, on case of Webb & Rigby, ~~on~~ for forcible entry and detainer. during trial esqr.

---

677. TEXT: Brown ink commences.

678. TEXT: Blue ink commences.

679. Appeal was allowed from a justice of the peace court within twenty days of decision, which JS gave at the 10:00 a.m. session of the mayor's court on 10 March 1843. As part of the appeal, the appellant was required to give a bond within this period to cover court costs. Brink's bond was deemed "informal" in that it was not presented until after 11:00 a.m., which exceeded, by an hour or more, the twenty days allowed for reception of the bond. The law provided for a "reasonable" extension, however, if a bond was rejected for "informality or insufficiency," and later in the day JS allowed Brink's appeal to go forward. (JS, Journal, 10 Mar. 1843; An Act concerning Justices of the Peace and Constables [3 Feb. 1827], *Revised Code of Laws, of Illinois* [1826–1827], p. 268, sec. 31; William Brink et al., Bond, 29 Mar. 1843, Dana v. Brink [Nauvoo Mayor's Ct. 1843], JS Collection, CHL.)

680. "Another Island Destroyed by an Earthquake," *New York Herald,* 11 Mar. 1843, [1].

681. Ivins had signed Brink's bond as surety. (William Brink et al., Bond, 29 Mar. 1843, Dana v. Brink [Nauvoo Mayor's Ct. 1843], JS Collection, CHL.)

682. TEXT: Brown ink commences.

683. It was the 8 March issue of the *New York Herald* that published Snow's "Jubilee Song," which was sung at a feast on 18 January 1843 celebrating JS's discharge in the case of the attempted murder of former Missouri governor Lilburn W. Boggs. Also in this issue of the *New York Herald* was the poetic rendition of JS's 16 February 1832 vision (now D&C 76) and an excerpt of a letter from Orson Hyde. Snow's song, the poetic "Vision," and Hyde's letter were first published in the 1 February 1843 issue of the *Times and Seasons.* (JS, Journal, 18 Jan. 1843; "Highly Important and Curious from Nauvoo," *New York Herald,* 8 Mar. 1843, [2]; *Times and Seasons,* 1 Feb. 1843, 4:81–85, 90–91, 96.)

684. TEXT: Blue ink commences.

685. The appeal was considered on 19 April 1843, when it was determined that the municipal court had no jurisdiction in the case. (JS, Journal, 19 Apr. 1843, p. 364 herein.)

686. TEXT: Brown ink commences.

[Onias] Skinner [fined?] 10 dollars for contempt of court ~~on~~ for insulting a witness. & cheeckd [checked] said Skinner in his plea. & threatend to fine him $10 [p. [31]] more for Contempt of Court.[687] but lett him off on submission &c trial closed about one Friday Morning Jury of 12 men.—

Elder [Orson] Hyde returnd from Quincy having deliverd 10 Lectures & baptized 3 persons[688] [*10 lines blank*] [p. [32]]

31 March 1843 • Friday

Friday March 31. 1843. 10 A.M Opened Mayords [Mayor's] Court for Trial of Amos Lower for assau[l]ting John H. Burghardt after hearing the testimony. find. Defenda[n]t $,10:— [*3, possibly 4, unidentified symbols*] [*11 lines blank*] [p. [33]]

Editorial Note

Willard Richards, who was keeping JS's journal at this time, did not accompany JS on his four-day trip to Ramus, Illinois, from 1 to 4 April 1843. Richards evidently reconstructed JS's activities and teachings during this time for JS's journal from the journal of William Clayton, who accompanied JS to Ramus, and from conversations with others who made the trip. As an important primary source for Richards's information about JS's activities between 1 and 4 April, Clayton's journal entries for these dates are provided in full in Appendix 2.

---

1 April 1843 • Saturday

Saturday April 1. 1843 called at the office with Mr [William] Clayton. about 10. A.M. for the "Law, of the Lord,"[689] & about noon & heard read Truthiana Nº 3.—[690] very warm and pleasant.

[691]2 P. M. started with. Wᵐ Clayton. O[rson] Hyde. & J. B. Backenston [Jacob B. Backenstos] for Ramus— arrivd abouut 6½. very muddy. very

---

687. TEXT: Beginning with the period following "Court", blue ink commences.
688. Hyde went to Quincy earlier in the month to preach. (JS, Journal, 13 Mar. 1843.)
689. The large record book containing copies of revelations, financial donations, and JS's journal entries from 13 Dec. 1841 to 20 Dec. 1842.
690. The third in a series of nine letters written by Willard Richards under the pseudonym "Viator" to the *Boston Daily Bee*. This third *Bee* installment continues a JS sermon on the prodigal son begun in the second letter, offers a description of JS, and praises the character of the Latter-day Saints. (Willard Richards [Viator, pseud.], Nauvoo, IL, 1 Apr. 1843, Letter to the editor, *Boston Daily Bee*, 28 Apr. 1843, [2]; see also "Truthiana," 1843, draft, CHL; and 312n644 herein.)
691. TEXT: Brown ink commences.

Friday March 31. 1843.
*10 A.M. Opened Mayors court for trial of Amos Lower for shooting John H. Burghardt. after hearing the testimony. find Defendat $10 — *

Unidentified symbols. The journal entry for 31 March 1843 ends with several unidentified characters. Handwriting of Willard Richards. JS, Journal, Dec. 1842–June 1844, bk. 2, p. [33], JS Collection, Church History Library, Salt Lake City. (Photograph by Welden C. Andersen.)

Joyfully receivd by Bro Benjamin F. Johnson— J. B. Backenston. was with me continually. [*6 lines blank*] [p. [34]]

2 April 1843 • Sunday

[692]Sunday April 2. 1843 Missouri St. Louis Republican Ma[r]ch 24 says. at Point Petre. [Pointe-à-Pitre] W. I. [West Indies] islands 2000 . . . ran together in the public square. the earth opend and swallowed ~~them up~~ the whole mass.[693]

Wind N.E. snow fell several inches but melted more or less.—

D[imick] Huntington returnd from chicago.—[694]

after breakfast called on Sister Sophronia [Smith McCleary]—

10 A. M.— to meeting. Elder [Orson] Hyde Preached 1 epistle John 1. chap ist 3 verses— when he shall appear we shall be like. him[695] &c. he will appear on a white horse.— as a warrior,[696] & may be we shall have some of the same spirit.— our god is a warrior.— John. 14.23— it is our privilege to have the father & son dwelling in our hearts. &c [p. [35]]

[697]Cloudy. earth 1/2 covered with snow

[698]Elder Hyde remarked that he read in one of the newspapers— conceng [concerning] the passage of an act in one of the eastern states ~~for~~ to prohibit the citizens fr[o]m killing crows. bec[a]use they eat up all the filth & carrion from of[f] the earth.— thusly[699] tending to preserve the hea[l]th of the people. but offer them a peice of clean fresh meat & a crow will not touch it for he has no appitite for it. he had often thought that there was a very great resemblance between the pri[e]sts of the day & these crows. for they were continually picking up all the dirt & filth & meanness of the mormons.— feasting on it if it

---

692. TEXT: Blue ink commences.
693. "Earthquake in the West Indies," *Daily Missouri Republican* (St. Louis), 22 Mar. 1843, [2]. Additional accounts of the 8 February 1843 earthquake that devastated Pointe-à-Pitre on the island of Guadeloupe in the West Indies were published in the *Times and Seasons* and *The Wasp*. ("More Particulars of the Earthquake at Gaudalope," *Times and Seasons*, 15 Apr. 1843, 4:172–174; 1 May 1843, 4:178–179; "Earthquake in the West Indies," *The Wasp*, 12 Apr. 1843, [2].)
694. JS had sent Huntington to Chicago two weeks earlier with a letter to Justin Butterfield, requesting Butterfield's help in Orrin Porter Rockwell's legal defense. (JS, Journal, 19 Mar. 1843; JS, Nauvoo, IL, to Justin Butterfield, [Chicago, IL], 18 Mar. 1843, copy, JS Collection, CHL.)
TEXT: Beginning with the dash following "chicago.", brown ink commences.
695. See 1 John 3:2.
696. See Revelation 19:11.
697. TEXT: Blue ink commences. Richards's heading on this page, "Monday April 3d 1843", written in blue ink, was partially overwritten with "Sunday" and "2d" using brown ink.
698. TEXT: Brown ink commences.
699. TEXT: Possibly "thereby".

was[700] a precious morsel. but offer them any good and salutary ⟨from⟩ among— the mormns they have no appitite & will turn away from it

I think for the same reason the Legislature lets the crows live we ought to let the priests live gather ~~up~~ & eat up all the filth & rubbish from the mormon people that they may be healthy. [p. [36]]

[701]dined at Sophronia's soon as ~~he~~ we arrived.— Elder Hyde I am going to offer some corrections to you. Elder H. repli[e]d— they shall be thankfully recieved.—[702] When he shall appear we shall see him as he is. we shall see that he is a man like ourselves.—[703] And that same sociality. which exists amogt [amongst] us here. will exist amo[n]g us there only it will be coupled with eternl glory which glory we do not now enjoy.

14 John 23.— the appearing of the father and of the Son in that verse is a personal. appearance.— to say that the father and the Son dwells in [p. [37]] a mans heart is an old Sectarian notion. and is not correct.

There ~~is~~ are no angels who administer to this earth but who belong ~~to~~ or have belongd to this earth. The angels do not reside on a planet like this earth. but they reside in the presence of God— but on a Globe like a sea of glass. & fire. "sea of glass before the throne.— &c."[704] where all things are manif[e]st past present & to come,—

The place where God resides is a great Urim And Thumim.

This earth in its sanctifid & immortal state. will be a Urim & Thummim for all things below it in the scale of creation. but not above it.— [p. [38]]

related the Dream. written on page 3d Book ⟨B⟩[705]

Interpretati[o]n By O. Hyde— old man.— Govermnt of these Unitd States, who will be invaded by a foriegn foe. probably England. U. S. Goverment will call on Gen Smith to defend probably all this western territory and offer him any am[ou]nt of men he shall desire & put them under his command.

I prophecy in the Name of the Lord God that the commenceme[n]t of bloodshed as preparat[o]ry to the coming of the son of man. will commenc[e] in South Carolina.— (it probably may arise through the slave trade.)— this

---

700. TEXT: Possibly "were".

701. TEXT: Richards's heading on this page, "Tuesday April 4[th] 1843", written in blue ink, was canceled by strikethrough using brown ink.

702. Portions of William Clayton's and Willard Richards's accounts of JS's teachings of 2 April 1843 were later canonized (D&C 130).

703. See 1 John 3:2.

704. See Revelation 4:6.

705. A reference to JS's dream recorded in this journal, on manuscript page 3 of Willard Richards's second memorandum book. (JS, Journal, 11 Mar. 1843.)

~~the~~ a voice declard to me. while I was praying earne[s]tly on the subje[c]t 25 December 1832.—⁷⁰⁶ [p. [39]]

I earnestly desird to know concern[in]g the coming of the Son of Man & prayed. when— a voice said to me, Joseph, my, son, if thou livest until thou art 85 years old thou shalt see the facce of the son of man. therefore let this suffice & trouble me no more on this matter.—⁷⁰⁷

1. P. M. attended meeting.

Joseph read 5.ᵗʰ chapter of ~~Johns~~ revelation, referring particularly to the 6[ᵗʰ] verse. shewing from that. the a[c]tual existenc[e] of beasts in heaven probable those were beasts which had lived on another planet. than our's—

God never made use of the figure of a beast to represent the kingdom of heaven.— Beasts. 7 eyes Pr[i]esthood.— [p. [40]]

this is the fi[r]st time I have ever taken a text in Revelati[o]n.— and if the young elders would let such things alone it would be far⁷⁰⁸ better.— then corrected Elder Hyde as in private.—

supped at Bro [Benjamin] Johnson's.— expected to sta[r]t for Carthage, but bad weather prevntd [prevented] called another meeti[n]g. by bell.— read Rev[elation]— between Meeti[n]gs with Elder Hyde & expou[n]ding.— during this time several came in & expressd fear that I had come in contact with⁷⁰⁹ the old scripture

Meeting 7. eve resumd the subjct of the beast.— shewed very plainly that Johns vision was very different from Daniels Prophecy— one refering to things ex[is]ting in heaven. the other a figure of things ~~on the~~ which are on the earth.—⁷¹⁰ [p. [41]]

whatever principle of inteligence we attain unto in this life. it will rise with us in the revalatin [revelation],⁷¹¹ and if a person gains more knowledge and intelignce. through his obedience & diligence. than another he will have so much the advantage in the world to come—

---

706. JS's 25 December 1832 revelation on war, which mentions the rebellion of South Carolina, is found in Revelation Book 1, p. 157, in *JSP,* MRB:291 [D&C 87].

707. JS retold this experience in a special conference of the church four days later and added the conclusions he reached about the meaning of the message he received. (JS, Journal, 6 Apr. 1843, p. 338 herein.)

708. TEXT: Possibly "for".

709. "Come in contact with" was an idiom for "contradict" or "disagree." ("Contact," in *Oxford English Dictionary,* 2:889.)

710. See Revelation 4–5; and Daniel 7–8.

711. For "revalatin," the William Clayton journal has "resurrection." (Clayton, Journal, 2 Apr. 1843, p. 404 herein.)

There is a law irrevocably decreed in heaven. before the foundation of the world upon which all blessings are predicated and when we obtain a blessing it is by obedi[e]nce to the law upon which that blessing is predicated.

again revertd to Elders Hyde mistake. &c the Father has a body of flesh & bones as tangible as mans[712] [p. [42]] the Son also, but the Holy Ghost is a personage of spirit.— and a person cannot have the personage ⟨of the H G. [Holy Ghost]⟩ in his heart he may recive the gift of the holy Ghost. it may descend upon him but not to tarry with him.—

What is the meaning of the scriptures. he that is faithful over a few thi[n]gs shall be made ruler over many? & he that is faithful over many shall be made ruler over many more?

What is the mea[n]ing of the Parable of the 10 talents?[713] [blank] Also [blank] conversation with Nicodemus. except a man be born of water & of the spi[ri]t.—[714]

I shall not tell you?—

Closed by flagellating the audience [p. [43]] for their fears.— & calld upon Elder Hyde to get up. & fulfil his covenant to preach 3/4 of an hour.— otherwise I will give you a good whipping.—

Elder Hyde arose & said Brothe[r]s & Sisters I feel as though all had been Said that can be said. I can say nothing but bless you.—

To B. F. Johnsons—— one[715] the 144000 seald[716] are the pri[e]sts who are appointed to administer in the daily sacrifice.— [6 lines blank] [p. [44]]

3 April 1843 • Monday

Monday April 3ᵈ 1843 Millers's [William Miller's] Day of Judgment has arrived. but. tis too. pleas[a]nt. for false prophets.—[717]

---

712. TEXT: Possibly "ours mans".
713. See Matthew 25:14–30; and Luke 19:11–27.
714. See John 3:1–5.
715. TEXT: Possibly "are".
716. See Revelation 7:3–4; 14:1.
717. Though Miller affirmed many times that he had never set a precise date for the second coming of Christ, many "Millerites" predicted specific days. One of the most widely anticipated and reported dates was 23 April 1843. George Storrs, however, a prominent Millerite preacher and publisher from New York, was involved in a controversy that led many Millerites to believe 3 April 1843 was the date of the Second Coming. The *Christian Secretary* reported that Storrs had set 3 April as the precise date in lectures given in Hartford, Connecticut, because it coincided with the day of the Crucifixion. The Millerite newspaper the *Signs of the Times* repudiated the idea that any date had been fixed by Miller and after interviewing Storrs denied that the latter had ever fixed 3 April as the day of the advent. The *Christian Secretary* refused to retract, stating that not only had witnesses heard Storrs's affirmation but that 3 April was a widespread belief among Millerites in the area. The view that 3 April was the date affixed by many Millerites was evident in Moses Stuart's book on interpreting biblical prophecy, which referred

I Dined at Joel Johnsons on a big Turkey. 2. P.M— startd for carthage arrived at 4. P.M.⁷¹⁸ staid at J[acob] B. Backenstos's.—— even[in]g reading ⟨Book of⟩ Revelati[o]n with Elder [Orson] Hyde & conversing with esqr Backman [George Bachman].— [*7 lines blank*] [p. [45]]

4 April 1843 • Tuesday

April 4— Tuesday Spent 5 hours preaching to Esqr Backman [George Bachman].— Chauncey Robinson [Robison], & the Backenstoses.— Backman "said almost thou persuadst me to be a christian.—"⁷¹⁹

2 P.M. left. arrived at Nauvo[o] 5, P.M. [*10 lines blank*] [p. [46]]

5 April 1843 • Wednesday

Wednesday April 5. 1843— attend Muenicepal Courts— for people vs. Hoops.— on Habeus corpus.— after hearing the testim[o]ny they were discharged⁷²⁰ Johnathan Hoops gave me recept for $50. in lands in Iowa. dated Sept 2ᵈ— 1840.— [*9 lines blank*] [p. [47]]

---

to Millerites as "the men of April 3d." JS evidently accepted 3 April as the common Millerite designation for the Second Advent, a supposition possibly conveyed to him two months earlier through his conversation on Millerism with a group of "young men" from New York City. (Doan, *Miller Heresy, Millennialism, and American Culture,* 47–48; "The Time of the End," *Christian Secretary,* 13 Jan. 1843, [3]; "The Christian Secretary of Hartford," *Christian Secretary,* 27 Jan. 1843, [3]; "The Time of the End," *Signs of the Times,* 4 Jan. 1843, 121; Notice, *Signs of the Times,* 18 Jan. 1843, 141; see also "Spring," *Vermont Chronicle* [Bellows Falls], 5 Apr. 1843, 55; Stuart, *Hints on the Interpretation of Prophecy,* 173; and JS, Journal, 12 Feb. 1843.)

718. JS and his companions may have stopped at Carthage, Illinois, to search the records there for any evidence that Horace Hotchkiss and John Gillett had been legally able to sell the several hundred acres of land JS, Sidney Rigdon, and Hyrum Smith had contracted to purchase from them in August 1839. Chauncey Robison, Hancock County recorder, wrote JS in March that he had found record of a deed Hotchkiss and Gillett had executed in 1836, conveying the lands they owned in Commerce to another party. "I have not yet discovered on Record any Deed of power of Attorney authorizing the said Hotchkiss and Gillett to convey the said Lands," Robison wrote JS, "and am doubtful whether their Conveyance to you and your Brother & S Rigdon is valid." Robison had recommended that JS "send some Competent person" to make a thorough search of the records in Carthage for some evidence that Hotchkiss and Gillett had authority to make the sale. The evening's "business at the Court house" to which William Clayton refers in his journal may have included the recommended search. (Clayton, Journal, 3 Apr. 1843, p. 405 herein; Brigham Young et al., "An Epistle of the Twelve," *Times and Seasons,* 15 Oct. 1841, 2:568; Chauncey Robison, Carthage, IL, to [JS], 8 Mar. 1843, Newel K. Whitney, Papers, BYU.)

719. King Agrippa's response to the apostle Paul, as recorded in Acts 26:28.

720. JS, chief justice of the Nauvoo Municipal Court, presided over this habeas corpus hearing in the case of *State of Illinois v. Hoopes and Hoopes.* According to the court record, Jonathan Hoopes and Lewis Hoopes "did on the first day of April last . . . enter the Premises of Samuel Driggs in a riotous & tumultuous manner and forcibly turned the Deponent [Betsyann Driggs] out of the House, and with noise & force of Arms and by bringing a Horse in the House did seriously frighten the [deponent] and drive her out of the House, thereby committing a riot against the peace and good Order of the Citizens of Illinois." After hearing several witnesses on both sides of the case, "the Court Adjudged that the Prisoners be and are acquitted of the charges, and Ordered that they be released & dis[c]harged therefrom." (State

Drawing of Nauvoo temple. Circa 1841–1846. The temple's cornerstones were laid 6 April 1841. On 28 October 1842 workmen completed laying a temporary floor on which church members could hold meetings, and by 6 April 1843 the walls were between four and twelve feet high. The building was not completed until May 1846, almost two years after Joseph Smith's death. (Church History Library, Salt Lake City.)

6 April 1843 • Thursday

Thursday, April 6,ᵗʰ 1843 The first day of the Jubilee,⁷²¹ of the church of Jesus Christ of Latter day Saints. a special Conference⁷²² assembled ~~of~~ on the platform of the temple. or ⟨rough⟩ floor of the basement, at 10. o clock A.M.— the sun shone clearly. & was very warm & pleasant. scarce a speeck of snow ~~was~~ ⟨is⟩ to be seen ⟨except on the north side of Zarahemla Hill. is considerable⟩ but the ice was about 2 feet deep in the river west of the temple & north of that point; & south ⟨of that⟩ the channel is clear of ice,— the walls of the temple are from 4. to 12 feet above the floor. of the conference.—

President Joseph was detained by a court ~~between in an action between~~ [p. [48]] widow [Mercy Fielding] Thompson. vs. sister & Bro Dixon (from Salem) in assumpsit. & President B[righam] Young. ~~took~~ had charge of the meeting. & during the absence of President Joseph.— Quorum of the Twelve present. H[eber] C. Kimball O[rson] Pratt. W[ilford] Woodruff— John Taylor— Geo A Smith. W[illard] Richards. ~~O. Hyde.~~ 1/2 past 11. o clock—

Amasa Lyman ~~Present.~~ Prayed, after a hymn was sung by the quire [choir]. & O. Pratt read the 3ᵈ· chap. of 2ᵈ Epis[t]le of Peter. & preached on the subject of the resurrection—

10 ⟨mi[nutes]⟩ before ~~H.~~ ⟨12⟩ President⁷²³ Joseph Smith & Elder [Sidney] Rigdon and O[rson] Hyde arrived.— the floor was about 3/4 covered. with listeners— [p. [49]] 12 o clock— O. Pratt gave way & Joseph. rose to state the object of the meeting. It is my object to ascertain the stanig [standing] of the first presidency. (as I have been instructed⁷²⁴) I present myself for trial, I shall next present my councillors for trial.— 3ᵈ to take into consideration the sending out of the twelve ⟨or some porti[o]n of them⟩ or some body else to get means to build ~~the~~ up Nauvoo. House— ~~& temple~~

---

of Illinois v. Hoopes and Hoopes [Nauvoo Mun. Ct. 1843], Nauvoo Municipal Court Docket Book, 51–52.)

721. The anniversary of the organization of the church on 6 April 1830. Wilford Woodruff noted that the term *Jubilee* was used because this anniversary marked the "commen[c]ement of the fourteenth year of the church"—an apparent reference to, and adaptation of, the seven-year sabbatical cycle outlined in the Old Testament. (Woodruff, Journal, 6 Apr. 1843; Leviticus 25:1–17.)

722. The conference was not termed a "general conference" because JS had directed in October 1841 that there would not be another "general conference" of the church until the Nauvoo temple was completed. Portions of the proceedings of the conference were published in the *Times and Seasons*, and significant reports of some of the sermons can be found in General Church Minutes. ("Special Conference," *Times and Seasons*, 1 May 1843, 4:180–185; "The Ancient of Days," *Times and Seasons*, 15 May 1843, 4:204; "A Discourse," *Times and Seasons*, 1 June 1843, 4:218–220; "A Discourse Delivered by Elder Joshua Grant," *Times and Seasons*, 15 June 1843, 4:236–238; General Church Minutes, 6–7 Apr. 1843; see also Clayton, Journal, 6 Apr. 1843; and 19n52 herein.)

723. TEXT: Possibly "~~Presant~~ President".

724. TEXT: Possibly "indicted".

4— Elders will have the privelige of appeals from the differce conferences to this if there are any such cases.— It is important that this conference [p. [50]] give importance to the N[auvoo] House. as a prejudice exists against the Nauvoo. House in favor of the Lords House———[725]

There is no place where men of wealth & character & influence can go to repose thimselves. and it is neccessary we should have such a place.

Are you satisfied with the first presedincy, so far as I am concerned, or will you choose another? If I have done any thing to injure my character in the sight of men & angels— or men & women. come forward tell of it. & if not ever after hold your peace. [p. [51]]

President B. Young arose & nominatd Joseph Smith to contin[u]e as ~~our~~ the Presdent. ⟨of the church⟩ Orson Hyde 2$^{\underline{dd}}$ it.— Voted unanimously— Such a show of hands was never seen before in the church.— Joseph retur[ne]d his thanks——— to the assembly. & said he would serve them according to the best of his ability.

⟨next president Joseph⟩ Brought forward Elder Rigdon for trial. Br Young nominated Elder Rigdon. to continue. 2$^{\underline{d}}$ by O. Hyde Elder Rigdon. spoke, ⟨the⟩ last conferce [conference] I have had previlige of attenedd [attending] was at the Laying of the corner Stone of this house.[726] & I have had no health,— and been connected with circumstances [p. [52]] the most forbidding. which doubtless has producd some feeling——— I have never had a doubt of the work ... my feelings concerning Bennet [John C. Bennett] were always the same, & told my family to guard that fellow. for some time he will make a rupture among this people.— had so little confidence. I always felt myself at his difiance.— I was once theatend [threatened] by warren Parish, ⟨if I would not coincide with his words.⟩ I have just such a threatnig [threatening] letter from. J. C. Bennet. that if I did not turn my course. I should feel the force of his power.— there is an increase ⟨of my⟩ of hea[l]th & strength. & I desire to serve you in any way it is possible for me to do. If any one has any feelings I hope they will express them.— [p. [53]]

Dymick Huntingtn [Dimick Huntington] asked concrning Rigdons. stating that Bennet was a gentleman & had nothing again[s]t him. ⟨Some time since.⟩ Rigdon recollects nothing or little about the conversations.— thinks Dimick Mistaken Dimicks knows he was not.—

---

725. Six weeks before this April conference, JS made similar comments about the importance of building the Nauvoo House. (JS, Journal, 21 Feb. 1843, p. 273 herein.)

726. The cornerstone of the Nauvoo temple was laid on 6 April 1841. ("Communication," *Times and Seasons*, 15 Apr. 1841, 2:380–383.)

Rigdon. ⟨said,⟩ Bennet never offerd any abuse to my family.— ⟨& at⟩ at that time ~~he~~ I had never been familiar with him.— Dymick[:] I have no private pique agai[n]st Elder Rigdon.—

voted, (~~in general~~) ⟨almost unanimous⟩ that Elder Rigdon retaind his standing.—

⟨Joseph presentd Wm Law for trial.⟩ Moved by. B. Young. 2^d By Heber Kimball ~~that Wm Law.~~ & voted that Wm Law— retain his standing.—

Voted unanimously that Hyrum. Smith retain his offices[727] as Patriarch. &c.—[728] [p. [54]]

Hyrum said the Lord bless the people.

& Elder Rigdon said so too.—

⟨Joseph said I do not know any thing agai[n]st the twelve, if I did I would presnt them for trial.⟩

It is not right that all the burden of the Nauvoo House should rest on a few individuals—

and ⟨we⟩ will now consider the prepriety of sending the twelve to[729] collect means for the Nauvoo House.—

there has been too great latitude in individuals for the building of the Temple to the exclusion of the Nauvoo house.

It. has been reportd that the—— twelve have wages $2.00 per day for ~~their services~~ ⟨I never heard— this till recently. & I do not believe I have never known their having any thing⟩ I go in for binding up the twelve,[730] &

Let this confrence institute an order to this end [p. [55]] ⟨&⟩ let no man pay money or stock into the hands of the twelves except the ~~payee~~ payer transmit the account immediately to the Trustee's in trust. & no man else. ⟨but the twelve⟩ have authority to act as agents for the Temple & Nauvoo House.———[731]

---

727. TEXT: Possibly "office".

728. The same revelation that designated Hyrum Smith as patriarch also appointed him as "a prophet and a seer and a revelator" to the church, to "act in concert" with JS, who would "shew unto him the keys whereby he may ask and receive, and be crowned with the same blessing, and glory, and honor, and priesthood, and gifts of the priesthood, that once were put upon him that was my servant Oliver Cowdery." (Revelation, 19 Jan. 1841, in Doctrine and Covenants 103:29, 1844 ed. [D&C 124:94–95].)

729. TEXT: Possibly "also to".

730. That is, each of the Twelve would sign bonds for faithful collection and delivery of funds to JS as trustee-in-trust for the church. (See "Special Conference," *Times and Seasons*, 1 May 1843, 4:180–185.)

731. While the conference approved JS's proposal that only the Twelve be authorized to collect funds for the temple and Nauvoo House, JS later authorized several other men to serve as collecting agents as well. (See Bond, Peter Haws and Shadrach Roundy to JS, 31 May 1843, JS Collection, CHL; Letter of recommendation for James Brown, 31 May 1843, copy, JS Collection, CHL; Letter of attorney, JS et al. to Amos Fielding, 13 Mar. 1844, copy, JS Collection, CHL.)

I will mention one case— he is a good man. that's man's name is Russel [Samuel M. Russell]. he had been East on bussines[s] for his brothe[r].⁷³² & took money belonging to the temple. & put it in the bag with his brothers money. 2 or three days after ⟨his return⟩ he called on his brother, for the money. but his brother thought he had paid out too much money— & he would keep the [p. [56]] chu[r]ch money.— ⟨to make good his own⟩ I called to see Russel [Daniel Russell] about the money. and he treated me so politely I concluded he never meant to pay—⁷³³ Bro Russel [Samuel Russell]. said, ⟨that⟩ his brother said he should not be out of money again.— There was $20. of the chu[r]ch money, & some dried apple for the Prest.⁷³⁴

I propose that ~~your~~ you send moneys for the temple by the twelve some or all; or some agent of your choosing & if you send by others & the money is lost, tis lost to yourselves. I cannot be responsible for it.

It is wrong for the church to make a bridge of my nose⁷³⁵ in appropriati[n]g chu[r]ch funds.—— The incorporation requ[ire]d of me securietis [securities].— which were lodged in the proper hands—⁷³⁶ [p. [57]]

Temple committee ~~have~~ are bound to me in ⟨the sum⟩ $2,000— & the chu[r]ch is running to them ⟨with funds⟩ every day— & I am not responsible for it.

so long as you consider me worthy to hold this office. it is your duty to attend to the legal forms belonging— to the business.— My desire is, ⟨that⟩ the conference minutes go forth, to inform all bra[n]ches of the order of doing

---

732. Daniel Russell.

733. According to the conference minutes kept by William Clayton, Daniel Russell stated that he had not known there were church funds in the money bag and that he had spent all of the money. (General Church Minutes, 6 Apr. 1843; compare "Special Conference," *Times and Seasons*, 1 May 1843, 4:182; and JS History, vol. D-1, 1514–1515.)

734. The published minutes of the conference clarify that Samuel Russell spoke up from the congregation and stated that his brother was not out of money and that his brother still had the twenty dollars that had been donated to the church, along with some dried fruit that had been sent along for the president. ("Special Conference," *Times and Seasons*, 1 May 1843, 4:182; JS History, vol. D-1, 1514–1515.)

735. An idiom meaning "to pass over or disregard a person." JS's point was that people donating money to the temple should not bypass him, as trustee-in-trust for the church, by giving funds directly to the temple committee. In December 1841 JS had made a similar point, forbidding the temple committee from receiving funds for building the temple unless those funds were directed to JS and recorded by the temple recorder. ("Nose," in *Oxford English Dictionary*, 7:216; JS, Journal, 11, 13 Dec. 1841, p. 15 herein.)

736. The "incorporation" to which JS is referring is a reference to his compliance with an Illinois statute authorizing religious societies to elect or appoint a trustee or trustees to hold property for the society. Following the procedure outlined in the statute, a special conference of the church elected JS "sole Trustee in Trust for the Church" on 30 January 1841. JS made a certificate of the action on 2 February 1841, which was attested by Justice of the Peace Daniel H. Wells on 3 February 1841 and subsequently filed in the Hancock County recorder's office. (An Act concerning Religious Societies [6 Feb. 1835], *Laws of the State of Illinois* [1834–1835], pp. 147–149; Appointment, 2 Feb. 1841, copy, JS Collection, CHL.)

business. & the twelve be appointd to this spicial mission of collecting funds for the Nauvoo House.—[737]

when I went to the white House at Washigtn [Washington]. ⟨&⟩ presented Letters from Thomas Carlin. [Martin] Van Buren. said ⟨Thos Carlin. Thos Carlin⟩ whos Thos Carlin?— I erred in spirit,— & ⟨I⟩ confess my mistake, in being angry with Martin Van Buren [p. [58]] for saying Thos Carlin is nobody.— let it be recorded on earth and in heaven that I am clear of this sin.—[738]

There has been complaints again[s]t the Temple Committee.— for appropriati[n]g the chu[r]ch funds to the benefit of their own children. to the neglect of others who need assistanc[e] more than they do.—

I have ⟨the⟩ complaint, by Wm Clayton. Wm. Clayton called. Says I have to say to the confernce. I am not so fully prepreded [prepared] to ~~present~~ substantiate the proof as I could wish—

I am able to prove that partiality used to a great extent. [p. [59]] I am able to prove by the books that [Reynolds] Cahoon & Higby [Elias Higbee] have used property for their own families— to the exclusion of others.—— ⟨Joseph said⟩ Let the. trial of the Committee be deferrd to another day— ⟨then let⟩ the Lion & unicorn— come together— day after tomorrow. Mr Clayton can have the privelige of bringing his books. to the trial.—[739]

~~Voted that the~~ Moved and Seconded & voted that the twelve be appointed a committe[e] to receive & gather funds to build the Nauvoo House. [*blank*] with this proviso, that the twelve ~~and~~ give bonds ~~to~~ for good delivery. to trustee in trustee.— & ~~payee~~ payer make immediate report to the trustee in trust.—[740] Bro W[illiam] W. Phelps proposd that the twelve give duplicate receipt's. [p. [60]]

President Young. remarked he should never give reciepts for cash. ⟨except such as he put in his own pocket for his own use.⟩ but wished this speculation

---

737. The minutes of this portion of the conference, including the discussion and decision about the Twelve serving as authorized collection agents for the temple and Nauvoo House, were published in the *Times and Seasons*. Pursuant to this decision, the Twelve met with JS on 19 April 1843 to organize themselves for a mission to the East to collect funds for the Nauvoo House. ("Special Conference," *Times and Seasons*, 1 May 1843, 4:180–185; JS, Journal, 19 Apr. 1843, pp. 365–367 herein.)

738. JS met with United States president Van Buren in Washington DC on 29 November 1839 in an unsuccessful effort to obtain compensation for the Saints' losses in the Missouri expulsion. The published conference minutes show that this digression in JS's discourse followed his comment that the temple committee was "nobody" to be collecting funds for the temple. (JS and Elias Higbee, Washington DC, to Hyrum Smith et al., [Nauvoo, IL], 5 Dec. 1839, in JS Letterbook 2, pp. 85–88; "Special Conference," *Times and Seasons*, 1 May 1843, 4:182.)

739. Clayton presented his charges against the temple committee on 7 April rather than 8 April. (JS, Journal, 7 Apr. 1843, p. 340 herein.)

740. JS.

to stop.— & asked ~~when~~ if any one knew any thing against any one of the twelve, any dishonesty. I know of one who is not.—

~~Joseph~~ ⟨And referred to muzzling the ox that treadetheth out the corn.—⟩[741]

Joseph Said, I will answer Bro Brigham,— let the twelve spend the time belonging to the temple for to collect funds— and the remainder of the time they may labor for their support.—[742]

The idea of not muzzling the ox that treadeth out the corn— is a good old quaker song.—[743] I have never taken the first farthing of church funds for my [p. [61]] own use. till I have first consulted the proper author[i]ties.— & when there was no quorum of the twelve or high priests I have asked the temple Committee who had ~~not~~ no business with it.— Elder [Alpheus] Cutler said it was so.— Let this conference stop all agents in collecting funds, except the twelve.———[744]

1½— P.M. hym by Quoir.— 12— 2 P.M dismissed by prayer O. Hyde— for 1. ⟨hour⟩

[745]3½ Hyrum commenced by observing that he had some communication. to make before Joseph came, & would read from the wasp. last number.—[746] a man who formerly belonged to the Church. reveald to me there are a band of men & some [p. [62]] strong in the faith of the Doctrine of Latter Day Saints. & some who do not belong to the chu[r]ch, ⟨were bound ~~to~~ by secret oaths &c⟩ that it is right to steal from any one who does not belong to the church if they gave 1/4 part to the temple. if they did not remain stedfast— they ripped open th[e]ir bowels & gave them to the cat fish.— & they are the very gadianton robbers[747] of the last days.— then ⟨read⟩ his own affidavit. as reprinted in the "Wasp," dated 26. Nov 1841 ⟨& the⟩ doings of the conference at Ramus. &

---

741. See Deuteronomy 25:4; 1 Corinthians 9:1–11; and 1 Timothy 5:17–18.

742. Young apparently felt that the responsibility of the Twelve to collect funds for the temple and Nauvoo House would require so much of their time that they would not be able to support their families, and therefore they should be allowed to use some of the donations for this purpose. Two weeks later, JS assured the Twelve their needs would be met through goods he received for the Nauvoo House. (See "Special Conference," *Times and Seasons*, 1 May 1843, 4:180–185; JS, Journal, 19 Apr. 1843, p. 367 herein.)

743. TEXT: Or "songs". Quakers referenced 1 Corinthians 9:9 to support their belief that ministers of the gospel should receive enough to supply their needs from individuals who heard and accepted their preaching rather than through an indiscriminate, state-supported collection of funds. (See, for example, *Confession of Faith*, 14–15; [Fox], *To the Protector and Parliament of England*, 30–34.)

744. JS later authorized others to collect funds for the temple. (See 331n731 herein.)

745. TEXT: Blue ink commences, with revisions in brown ink.

746. The 29 March 1843 issue of *The Wasp*.

747. An organization of murderous thieves in the Book of Mormon. (See Book of Mormon, 1840 ed., 399–400, 412 [Helaman 2:4; 6:18].)

proclamation ⟨or declarati[o]n of⟩ of the twelve ⟨&⟩ affidavit of Joseph.—⁷⁴⁸ These This ⟨t⟩ said the theif or ⟨theives⟩ ⟨have been compared to⟩ confessor refers to the little foxes— the presidency &c are the great foxes— & they told. ⟨us ⟨me⟩ this was the interpretation given. the preaching from the ⟨stand.—⟩ by the theives⟩

David Holman. James Dunn. confessed [p. [63]] ⟨to me when they lived in my house that⟩ they had stolen from the world, I told him to get out of my house. the Dunn ⟨David Holman⟩ lifted his hand to heaven & swore if I would forgive him he would never do so again. he went to Montrose. & stole & run away to Nauvoo, f[o]und a barrel of flour on the bank. just deliverd from a steam boat. stole the flour went to Keokuk & sold it. saying he had pickd up the barrel in the ⟨river⟩ & as it was likely a little damaged he would take $2.00. got his pay & went his way.

made made many observations. to the Saints. on stealing.—

Joseph followed. I want the Elders to make hono[ra]ble proclamati[o]n abroad [p. [64]] what the feelings of the presidency are,— I despise a theif above ground. He would betray me ⟨if he could get the oppetinity [opportunity]⟩ if I were the biggest rogue in the world, he would steal my horse when I wanted to run away. ⟨then⟩ read pr[o]clamatin [proclamation] of the Mayor on stealing. dated 25. day March 1843.— "Wasp." No. 48[th]—⁷⁴⁹ many observati[o]n confirmatory & said, enough Said. for this conference on this Subject.—

Elders had have a privilige to appeal from any decision of a branch. to know if they shall retain their office or membership—

necessary I explain concerni[n]g Keokuk it is known that the Govr of Iowa has granted a writ. for me. on affidav[i]t [p. [65]] of [Lilburn W.] Boggs.— he still holds that writ as a cudgel over my head. (U. S. Atttorney told me all writs issued thus were legally dead.)—⁷⁵⁰ I said that is a stumper & I will shew them a trick the Devil never did. ⟨that is⟩ leave them. every man who wishes to out

---

748. In the statement of the Quorum of the Twelve and in the affidavits that Hyrum Smith read, JS, Hyrum Smith, and the Twelve condemned the growing problem of theft in and around Nauvoo and denied involvement with thieves. The article about the conference at Ramus reported the excommunication of five men for "Larceny, &c." ("Thieves! Robbers!! Villains!!!," *The Wasp*, 29 Mar. 1843, [2]–[3].)

749. JS, "Proclamation," *The Wasp*, 29 Mar. 1843, [3]; "Special Conference," *Times and Seasons*, 1 May 1843, 4:184; see also JS, Journal, 25 Mar. 1843.

750. After the United States Circuit Court for the District of Illinois discharged JS from the extradition order in the Boggs case, appeals were made to Iowa governor John Chambers to dismiss a similar writ he had issued. Chambers reported in a letter on 10 March that his warrant had been returned unserved and that he would not issue another unless the governor of Missouri ordered a new requisition. (JS, Journal, 9 Mar. 1843, esp. 300n587 herein; John Chambers, Burlington, Iowa Territory, to John Cowan, 10 Mar. 1843, JS Office Papers, CHL.)

economically. with regard to futurity.— let them come over here[751] as soon as they can settle their affairs without sacrifice let them come & we will protect them & let that governme[n]t know that we don't like to be imposed upon.—

about the first of August 1842 Mr [Jacob] Remick came to my house. put on a long face. said he was in distress. about to loose $1400 for ⟨a debt of⟩ 300 at sheriffs [p. [66]] sale. ⟨said he the⟩ sale takes place to-morrow.— I have money in St Louis . . .— next morning he called. I did not like the looks of him. ⟨but thought I⟩ he is a stranger. I have been a stranger, &. better loose 200 than be guilty of sin of ingratitude. took his note. on demand. ⟨the⟩ day I was taken I asked him from [for?] the money.— you ought to have it ⟨said he but⟩ I have not got my mony from St Louis.— I have a curious plan in my mind. I will give you a quit claim deed of the land you bought of [Isaac] Galland & ⟨your notes to⟩ Gallands notes which I have as his agent" I, said Joseph, have not asked you for your property. & would not give a snap. ⟨for it.⟩— but I will accept your offer. but want my money— ⟨Said he I will give you deed.⟩ (1/2 my land in the) [p. [67]] state.) ⟨&⟩ he gave me deeds. & I got them recorded.—[752] he calld for some more favors. & I let him have some cloths— ⟨to the amount of⟩ 6 or 7 hundrd dollars. I have offerd this land to many, who if they would go to settle there but nobody will go.—[753] ⟨I agre[e]d⟩ if I found he owned as much as he pretended I would give my influence to build up Keokuk. J. G. Remick. ⟨is his name he has got almost⟩ most $1100 ⟨from me,⟩ he looks exactly like a woodchuck, & talks like a woodchuck on a stump with a chaw of tobacco. ⟨in his mouth.⟩ he tried to git his hands to steal a stove from near my stove[754] & carry it off on the boat raft,[755] he is a thief.— My advice is, [p. [68]] if they choose, ⟨to⟩ come away from Keokuk. and not go there more. I am not so much of a christian as many suppose I am. when a man undertakes to ride me. I am apt to thud[756] ⟨kick⟩ him off & ride him.—

I would'nt b[u]y property in the Iowa. I considerd it stooping to accept it a ⟨as a⟩ gift.—

⟨I wish to speak of the⟩ ——— 1/2 breed lands opposite this. city. 1/2 breed land.— 1/2 breed land.— and every man there who is not 1/2 breed had better

---

751. That is, leave Iowa for Illinois.
752. The transaction occurred 14 September 1842. (JS, Journal, 14 Sept. 1842, p. 153 herein.)
753. In September 1842, JS counseled John Smith, Daniel C. Davis, and Wilford Woodruff to move to Keokuk, Iowa Territory. (JS, Journal, 15 Sept. 1842; and 157n530 herein.)
754. TEXT: Possibly "store".
755. TEXT: Instead of "boat raft", possibly "Craft ⟨raft⟩".
756. TEXT: Possibly "throw".

come away.⁷⁵⁷ & in a little time we will call them all 1/2 breed.— I wish we could swap some of our 1/2 breeds here for ⟨the 1/2 breeds who⟩ lives there. I will give you a key, if any ⟨one⟩ will growls tomorrow you will know him to be a 1/2 breed.— [p. [69]] My opinion is the Legislature have done well in giving the best tittle to settlers. & squatter.— Those who have deeds to those islands⁷⁵⁸ from the chancery of Iowa. have as good titles as any, but the settlers under ⟨the⟩ Laws of Iowa. Legislature & chancery of Iowa. ⟨are⟩ at variance.

I believe it a fine⁷⁵⁹ of swindli[n]g ~~from~~ by. court of Chancery.—

Dr Galland said those Islands dont belong to any body, ⟨they were⟩ throon [thrown] out of U.S. survey.— hence no man had a claim, ⟨& it was⟩ so considerd; when I came here.—

my advice to the Mormons, who have deed & possessions, ⟨is⟩ fight it out. you who have no deeds or possessi[o]ns, let them [p. [70]] alone.— touch not a stick of their timber.—

Deeds given by court of chancery. warrents & defends again[s]t all unlawful claims.— It is a 1/2 breed, it an anomaly, without form & void, a nondescript. if they have your note. let them come here & sue you then you can carry up your case to the highest court.— so long as the <u>Laws</u> have a shadow of tittle, it is not right for the Mormons to go & carry away the wood In the name of the Lord God, I forbid any man from using any observati[o]ns of mine, to rob— the land of wood.——

Moses Martin has ~~had~~ been tried & had fellowship withdrawn ⟨by the chu[r]ch⟩ at ~~Keokuk.~~ Nashville [Iowa Territory] [p. [71]]

⟨The question has been asked⟩

can a member not belonging to the chu[r]ch⁷⁶⁰ bring a member before the high council, for trial? I answer No! I ask no jurisdiction. ⟨in religious matters⟩ I merely give my opinion when asked. If there was any feelings at Naashville because I gave my opniones [opinions], there is no occasion for it. I only advice the breth[r]en to come from Iowa, & they may do as they please. ⟨about coming.⟩ If I had not actually got into this work, & been called of God, I would back out . . . but I cannot back out,— I have no doubt of the truth. were I going to prophecy. I would procpesy [prophesy] the end will not come in 1844.

---

757. JS's counsel to church members to "come away" from the half-breed lands in Lee County, Iowa, reflects the confused condition of the area's land titles after years of rampant speculation, poor record keeping, and ineffective court and legislative decisions. (Flanders, *Kingdom on the Mississippi*, 28–29, 36–37.)

758. Islands in the Mississippi River between Nauvoo, Illinois, and Montrose, Iowa.

759. TEXT: Or "piece".

760. That is, a branch of the church, or congregation.

or 5— or 6. or 40 years ~~more~~ [p. [72]] there are those of the rising generation who shall not taste death till christ come.

⟨I was once praying earnestly upon this subject. and a voice said unto me.⟩ My son, if thou livest till thou art 85 years of age, thou shalt see the face of the son of man. . . . ⟨I was left to draw my own conclusions concerni[n]g this &,⟩ I took the liberty to conclude that if I did live till that time ~~Jesus~~ ⟨he⟩ would make his appearance.— ⟨but I do not say whether he will make his appeara[n]ce, or I shall go where he is.—⟩[761]

I prophecy in the name of the Lord God.— & let it be written. ⟨that the⟩ Son of Man will not come in the heavns till I am 85. years old

48 years hence or about 1890.—

⟨then Red⟩ 14 Rev— 6 verse another angel [p. [73]] fly in the midst of heaven; for the hour of his Judgmnt is come.— to exterminati[o]n— from the commenceme[n]t. commence when angel commences preachi[n]g this. gospel ⟨1 day— 1000 years—[762]⟩. 1000 year as 1 day.—[763] 41. yrs 8 months.— only 6 years from the voice, saying, if thou live till thou art 85,— ⟨years old &c⟩

Hosea 6th chapter after 2 days &c,[764] 2520 years which— bri[n]gs it to 1890.— [John] Taylor says 45 years according ⟨to⟩— bible recokoning.

the coming of the Son of man never will be, never can be till the judgm[en]ts spoken of for this ⟨hour⟩ are poured out, ⟨which Jud[g]ments are commenced.—⟩

Paul says ye are th[e] children of the light & not of the darkness, that that day [p. [74]] should not overtake us as a theif in the night.—[765] it is not the design of the Almighty to come upon the Earth & crush it, & grind it to powder.— he will reveal it to his servants the prophets.[766] ⟨O what wondrous wise men there are going about & braying ~~like~~[767]⟩ (other[s] talk like an ass. cry

⟨O, lord, where—⟩ Joe Smith.— Joe Smith.— ~~&c~~ ⟨whare—⟩ ⟨O.⟩ away up on the top of the top less throne aha. ⟨&c—⟩

Jerusalem— ⟨must be⟩ rebuilt. ⟨Judah return. must return⟩ & the timple— water come out from under the temple— the ⟨waters of the⟩ dead sea be heald.— ⟨it will take⟩ some time to build the walls & the temple. &c & all ⟨this must be done before—⟩

---

761. JS related this experience four days earlier in Ramus, Illinois, where it was recorded by William Clayton. (Instruction, 2 Apr. 1843, in JS, Journal, p. 325 herein, and Clayton, Journal, pp. 403–404 herein [D&C 130:15].)

762. TEXT: Instead of "years", possibly "year".

763. See 2 Peter 3:8.

764. See Hosea 6:2.

765. See 1 Thessalonians 5:2, 4–5.

766. See Amos 3:7.

767. TEXT: Possibly "~~like an~~".

Son of Man ⟨will make his appence [appearance]⟩. wars & rumours of wars. signs in the heavens above on the earth beneath— sun turnd into [p. [75]] darkness. moon to blood. earthquakes in divers places, oceans heaving beyond their bounds.—[768] ⟨then⟩ one grand sign of the Son of the son of man in heaven.— but what will the world. do? they will say it is a planet. a comet. &c— conseq[u]ently the son of man will come as the sign of coming of the son of man. ⟨is⟩ as the light of the morni[n]g cometh out of the East.—[769] 10. minutes before 6[th]— Singing. praye[r] by. W. W. Phelps adjurnd [adjourned] to 10 A.M. tomorrow. [770]Sister Richards[771] requstd [requested] prayer for her health [p. [76]]

7 April 1843 • Friday

Friday April 7[th] 1843— assembled at 10. according to adjourn[m]ent

President [William] Marks. presentd the requ[e]st of Sister Van Hymon— Milane Webb.— Sister Dodds—— ⟨for⟩ th[e] prayers of the Conference. Singing by Quoir.— President ⟨Joseph⟩ rather hoarse from Speaking so long yesterday. said he would use the boys lungs to day.—

prayer by O[rson] Hyde— appeals from the Elders were then called for. Elder. [Pelatiah] Brown arose. said Elder [Benjamin] Winchester calld for his licence but he did not give it.[772] Set down Said the president. . . . B[righam] young prisiding; Jedidiah [Jedediah] M, Grant. was voted should go to Philadelphia and preside there.

also Joshua. Grant. Go to Cincinatie to preside. . . . [p. [77]]

voted that Peletiah Brown go to the village of Palmyra. in the State of N. york. & build up a church. . . .

Bro Brown— signified his willingness to go any where the conferenc[e] shall direct.

Singing by Quoir.—

---

768. TEXT: Instead of "bounds", possibly "bounds".

769. In this summary of events that are to precede the second coming of Christ, JS referenced numerous passages of scripture from the Old and New Testaments, as well as from his own revelations. (See especially Ezekiel 47:1–12; Matthew 24:6–7, 27–30; and Revelation, 27 and 28 Dec. 1832, in Doctrine and Covenants 7:24–25, 1844 ed. [D&C 88:87, 90].)

770. TEXT: Brown ink commences, matching ink in following entry.

771. Jennetta Richards Richards.

772. The previous month Brown was called before the high council for his involvement in a personal conflict and for "teaching false doctrine," at least part of which apparently involved his interpretation of the four beasts mentioned in Revelation 5:8. (Nauvoo High Council Minutes, 19 Mar. 1843; see also JS, Journal, 8 Apr. 1843, pp. 345–347 herein.)

Templee committee were called up for trial.⁷⁷³ at 11. o'clock. ⟨Wᵐ Clayton said.⟩ some may expect I am going to be a means of a downfall. of the Temple committee. tis not so. but I design to shew they have been partial.⁷⁷⁴

Elder Higby [Elias Higbee] has over run the amount allowed by trustees about 1/4.— pretty much all elder Higby's son has receivd in money & store pay.— Higbys son has had nothing deducted [p. [78]] for his tenth.

Elder [Reynolds] Cahoon.

Wᵐ· S. Cahoon [William F. Cahoon] has paid all his tenth

the others of Cahoons sons have had nothing to their credit in tenth.

the committee have had a great amou[n]t of store pay.—

one man who is laboring continually wanted 25 cts. in store when his family were sick.— Higby said he could not have it.

Wᵐ S. Cahoon⁷⁷⁵ was never appointed a boss— over the cutting shop.— but was requsted to keep an amou[n]t of labor in the shop.— during the last 6 months very little has been brought into to the committee. [p. [79]]

there are certain individuals in this city who are watching every man who has any thing to give the temple.— to get it from him— & pay for the same in his labor.—

Elder [Alpheus] Cutler— said he did not know of any wrong. if any one would shew it he would make it right.— <u>voted. Clear, unanimisly</u>

Elder [Reynolds] Cahoon. said this is not an unexpectd matter at all. to be called up. I do not want you to think I am perfect

some how or other. since Elder cutler ~~has~~ went up into the pine country.⁷⁷⁶ I have from some cause been placed very peculiar circumstances, . . . ⟨I think I never⟩ was placed in so tight a screw since I was born. been screwed to the back bone.— [p. [80]]

---

773. Clayton's complaint against the temple committee had been mentioned the previous day, but the trial was postponed to allow Clayton more time to present his evidence. As the journal entry indicates, the temple committee's responsibilities included managing the temple store—stocked through the donations of church members—where those working to build the temple could obtain provisions in exchange for their labor. The temple committee had been accused of mismanagement on at least two earlier occasions. (JS, Journal, 1 Oct. 1842; 28 Nov. 1842; 6 Apr. 1843, pp. 159–160, 169–170, 333 herein; "Baptism for the Dead," *Times and Seasons,* 15 Dec. 1841, 3:625–627.)

774. Clayton began assisting Willard Richards in recording donations for the temple on 14 February 1842 and replaced Richards as temple recorder on 3 September 1842. (Clayton, History of the Nauvoo Temple, 18, 31.)

775. "Wᵐ S. Cahoon" is evidently an error. In the draft notes of JS's manuscript history, the name of his brother Pulaski Cahoon is substituted. William was a carpenter, while Pulaski was a stonecutter as the journal entry implies. (Historian's Office, JS History, draft notes, 7 Apr. 1843; Nauvoo Masonic Lodge Minute Book, 17 Mar. and 16 June 1842.)

776. Cutler spent the winter of 1841–1842 in Wisconsin cutting timber for use in Nauvoo. (Nauvoo High Council Minutes, 22 Sept. 1841 and 30 July 1842.)

The Marshall brought up a man for disorderly. conduct. Mayor fined him $5,⁰⁰ or go out of the crouwd.— ~~The~~

⟨[Reynolds] Cahoon said:—⟩

The better people have ~~been~~ known my proceedings. the better they have liked them.—

when. President Smith had goods last summer we had better property. goods would not bye corn without some cash.— instead of horses &ᶜ, we took store pay.— I have dealt out meal & flour to the hands to the last ounce when I had not a morsel of bread meal or flour in my house; if the Trustee.⁷⁷⁷ Bro Hyrum [Smith]. or the twelve or ⟨all⟩ ~~any~~ will examine & see if I have too much it shall go freely.— [p. [81]] I call upon all the brethren if they have any thing. to bring it forward & have it adjusted.

<u>Hyrum</u>. Said he felt it his duty to defend the committe[e] so far as he could. he wo[u]ld as soon go to hell as be a committee. . . . but to make a comparison for the temple committee. a little boy came in & said he saw an elephant on a tree. & the people did not beleive it. & they looked and it was only an owl.—

[Reynolds] Cahoon said when Bro Cutler was gone. Higbee keept the books, & we have found as many mistakes again[s]t Bro Higby, as ~~&~~ in his favor . . . . voted unanimously clear in his favor—— [p. [82]]

Elder Higby— said ~~he~~ ⟨I⟩ ~~was~~ am not afraid or ashamed to appear before you.—

when I keept the books. I had much other business— & made some mistakes.— my house was built out of a lot I bot of Hiram Kimball &c &ᶜ & not much of it from the Temple.— voted in favor of Elder Higbee.— unanimously.—

President Joseph. statd that the business of the confernce had closed. & the rem[ai]nder of the confernce would be devoted to instruction⁷⁷⁸—— it is an insult to the meeting to ~~have~~ people run out of meeting ⟨Just⟩ before we close. if they must go let them go 1/2 an hour before. No Gentleman will go out of meeting Just at close. [p. [83]]

Singing by Choir, 12½— adjond [adjourned] till 2 o clock.— prayer— by B. Young.— [*15 lines blank*] [p. [84]]

2½ ⟨25 mi—s mi[nute]s⟩ P.M. Singing, & prayer by B. Young opened the confernce— Elder O[rson] Pratt. read 7 chapter Daniel. ~~from~~ 9[th] verse.— &ᶜ,

The 2ᵈ advent of the Son of God is a subject which occupies the attention of the people. of this day. the Latter day Saints belive he will come at least 1000

---

777. JS.
778. TEXT: Possibly "instructions".

years before the final consummation.— Millerit[e]s belive he will make his 2ᵈ advent in a few months,⁷⁷⁹ but they will find themselves mistaken. . . .

mistaken as they are good will coome out of the investigation. it will arouse the attention of multitudes to ~~an~~ the⁷⁸⁰ faccts⁷⁸¹ as they exist or will open the minds of the people to the truth when it shall be proclaimed by the elders of Israel. . . . They belive that the stone is not to strike the image on [p. [85]] his feet⁷⁸² till⁷⁸³ the 2ᵈ advent. & a king~~dom~~ will come direct from heaven.—⁷⁸⁴ we belive god will not destroy the kingdoms of the earth till. he has set ⟨up⟩ his own kingdom.

Do Millerites look for more revalation? No! they raise the midnight cry⁷⁸⁵ but does not tell the people what to do. Latter D[ay] S[aints] ⟨are the⟩ most reasonable.— & the most inteleget [intelligent] of any people on the face of the whole earth.— I have tried ⟨them⟩ 13 years.— ⟨I had as⟩ lives worship a horrs [horse] or a stump as a God who gives no instruction to his people.

Ancient of Days.— one came to the Ancient of Days—⁷⁸⁶ Many suppose this was the son. after jud[g]ment. sat son of man comes to Ancient of Days. [p. [86]] the most Ancient man of God that lived in days. else he could not have been the Ancient of Days. Father Adam is to come, and organize a great Council to prepare for the coming of the 2ᵈ advent—⁷⁸⁷ Jesus comes to the Ancient of Days⁷⁸⁸

⟨we beleive in. . . .⟩ Miracls. & they do not.— Angels— ⟨will come ⟨a[nd]⟩ the⟩ heavens ⟨will be⟩ opened send fo[r]th Angels.— to prepare the earth for Christs 2ᵈ Coming

one man thinks he is authorizd to call on men to repent. &c— I defy any one to scan⁷⁸⁹ the errors of any genraations. without revelations.

---

779. Millerites believed the second coming of Jesus Christ would take place sometime around 1843. (See 262n399 and 326n717 herein.)
780. TEXT: Instead of "an the", possibly "~~on~~ the" or "~~or~~ the".
781. TEXT: Possibly "~~hours~~ faccts".
782. See Daniel 2:34.
783. TEXT: Possibly "~~at till~~".
784. William Miller, "Mr. Miller's Reply to Cambell, Smith, and Others, on the Little Horn in Daniel's Fourth Kingdom," *Signs of the Times*, 20 Mar. 1840, 1–2.
785. *The Midnight Cry* was one of the Millerite periodicals edited by Joshua V. Himes. It took its name from Christ's parable in Matthew 25:6, in which "at midnight there was a cry made" informing the ten virgins that the bridegroom was coming.
786. See Daniel 7:13.
787. See Explanation, 19 May 1838, in JS, Journal, 19 May 1838, in *JSP*, J1:271 [D&C 116].
788. This portion of Orson Pratt's address was published as "The Ancient of Days," *Times and Seasons*, 15 May 1843, 4:204.
789. TEXT: Possibly "score".

Resurrection. . . . ⟨of the body is denyed⟩ by many because it is contrary to the law⟨s⟩ of nature. because. flesh & bones are constantly changing— completely oncee⁷⁹⁰ in 7 or 10 years. . . . if this is [p. [87]] true a man in 70 years would have matter enough for 10 diffint [different] bodies. objectors says this resurrection cannot be true. for if so. men would be quarreling which body belong[s] to himself & othe[r]s.—

who shall have the best right to it. I do not beleive that more than 3/4 of our bodies is composed of animal organizati[o]n.⁷⁹¹ but is purely vegetable, hence through all the 70 years a man will have one or two parts. which will be the same original.— if he receives the matter ~~if of the is~~ ⟨was⟩ in possession of 50 years before he died— he ~~is~~ has the same bady [body].—

the people liviing ~~in~~ ⟨a⟩ the house. are the occupants of the house. & the house [p. [88]] though repaired all though [through?] its diff[er]ent parts & from time to time even to new timbers throughout, yet. it is said to be the same house still—

while the choir was singing— Prest. Joseph remarked. to Elder [Sidney] Rigdon this day is a Millinium. it ~~as~~ is a millenium within these walls there is nothing but peace ⟨nothing to be seen from the stand, but the heads & bodies of the congregation, as they stood on the walls. & covered the walls & the floor it was one mass. of Saints or people. to speak was literally speaking to the people. for there was nothing else to be seen,⟩

25 past 3. Elder W$^{m.}$⁷⁹² Smith.

said he had no doubt but that many who were baptizd by John enjoyd much of the religion of Jesus.— but when he came. there was more light.— and unless they followd it. the light that they had received became darkness. If the sects have any power it is only such as they have usurped from the Pope [p. [89]] no man has authority except he be sent.— while bewildering clouds spread their glooming wings over our horizons & the Almighty sits in the heavens⁷⁹³ laughi[n]g at our ignorance, ⟨the⟩ Midnight cry. ⟨is raisd &⟩ what shall I cry? all tables are b[e]come unclean.— what shall I cry? they have ~~changed~~, tragessd [transgressed] ⟨the laws. changed ordinances⟩ broken the everlasting covenant?—⁷⁹⁴ what,— How shall retain my darling religion.— again[s]t this "new light" or mormonism.—⁷⁹⁵ I have about as much religion as others, but I have not got so much but what I Might recivee a little more, &

---

790. TEXT: Possibly "new".
791. TEXT: Instead of "organizatin", possibly "organizatins".
792. TEXT: The "m" in W$^{m.}$ is double underlined.
793. TEXT: Possibly "heaven".
794. See Isaiah 24:5.
795. TEXT: Instead of "mormonism", possibly "mormonish".

when I pray for more light & God bestows it. I will not say as the poor Negro.— [p. [90]]

Negro who prayed behind the stone wall if what he said was not true. he hoped the stone wall would fall on him. ⟨when⟩ some one pushed a stone on his head. & poor negro cried out I did not mean what I said—

so with sectarians. about Rev[elations] & healings.

said had had a conversation[796] with a Reverend presbytiran. who asked me what I. beleived I told him. we beleivd the gospel as preachd by the ancints apostles. & to leave the fi[r]st principles & go on to perfection.[797] o said the ~~priest~~ Revd Presbyter[ia]n. that means leaving their dead works.— but said I how can I leave the fi[r]st principls before I embrace them? O said ⟨he⟩ these are some of the mysteries of the kingdom. we know but little about them tis no more use to argue with you than[798] a stump [p. [91]]

unfurl the golden banner.—

we will stay in Sodom till— we are burned. we will stay in Jerusalem till the Romans come & burn the temple of the Great God. for if we escape the calamities it will prove we are not true.—

⟨⟨the ice started down stream.— of considerable dimensions— west of the stand or temple. up nearly opposite the old Post office building.⟩⟩ [p. [92]]

1/4 [to] 5. ⟨P.⟩ Joseph said to complete the subject of Bro Pratts. I thought it a glorious subject with one ~~additional idea~~ ⟨addition⟩

their is no fundamental principle belonging to a human System that ~~never~~ goes into another— ⟨in this world. or the world to come.—⟩ the principle of Mr Pratt was correct. I care not what the theories of ~~men~~ ⟨man⟩ are—

we have the testimony that God will raise us up & he has power to do it.— If any one supposes— that any part of our bodies. that is the fundame[n]tal parts thereof, ever goes into another body ~~the~~[799] is mistaken.— 5— Choir sung.—[800] & ⟨Notice that Bro Joseph. will preach tomorow morni[n]g at 10——⟩ prayer. by. Elder ~~Rigdon~~ ⟨[John] Taylor⟩. [p. [93]] [*page [94] blank*]

8 April 1843 • Saturday

[801]Prayer by Elder [John] Taylor—

3 requ[e]sts.[802]

---

796. TEXT: Possibly "conversatins".
797. See Hebrews 6:1.
798. TEXT: Possibly "other".
799. TEXT: Possibly "⟨t⟩he".
800. TEXT: Possibly "sang".
801. TEXT: Blue ink commences.
802. For other significant sources on JS's 8 April 1843 sermon, see William Clayton's two reports, the

1st that all who have faith will pray Lord to calm the wind. for as it is now. I can not speak.

2 that the Lord will strength⟨en⟩ my Lungs—

3ᵈ that I may have the Holy Ghost.

The subject whicch I shall sp[e]ak from ⟨is⟩ the, beasts spoken of by John.—[803] I have seldom spoken from ⟨the revelati[o]ns⟩ & I do it now to do away division & not that the knowledge is so much needed.—

knowledge is necessary to prevent division although it may puff up it does away suspince [suspense]——

in knowledge is power, hence [p. [95]] God[804] knows how to subject all beings he has power— over all.

should not have called up this subject if it had not been for this old white head before. Father [Pelatiah] Brown.——— I did not like the old man being called up. ⟨before the High council.⟩— for erring in doctrine.——— why I feel so good to have the privelige of thinki[n]g & believing as I please.

they undertook to correct him there Whether they did or not I dont care[805] Rev— 5 chap. 8 verse.—

Father Brown had been to work & confounded all christendom, that these were figure John saw in heavn to represent the different kingdoms of God on earth. [p. [96]] he put down sectarianism, & so far so good.——— but I could not help laughing that God should take a figure of a beast to repr[e]sent his kingdom consisting of ⟨Men⟩. . . . To take a lesser figure to represnt a gr[e]ater, old white head you missed it that time. By figure of Beasts God represented the kingdoms of the world.— Bear. Lion &c represe[n]ted the kingdoms. of the world, Says Daniel.[806] ⟨for⟩

I refer to the prophets, to qualify my observations. to keep out of the wasp nests or young elders,

The things John[807] ~~say~~ saw had no allusion to the day of Adam Enoch Abraham or Jesus— only as clearly specified & set forth to John. I saw that that which [p. [97]] was lying in futurity. Rev 1.1.— read ⟨is⟩ key to the whole subject

---

second of which was an amalgamation of Willard Richards's report here with his own report. ("Minutes of a Sermon of Joseph Smith," and "April 8ᵗʰ 1843 Wᵐ Clayton's Report of Joseph's Sermon of This Date," JS Collection, CHL.)

803. See Revelation 4–6; 7:11; 14:3; 15:7; 19:4.

804. TEXT: Or "Gods".

805. For the charges brought against Brown in the high council, see 339n772 herein.

806. See Daniel 7:3–7, 17.

807. TEXT: Possibly "~~of~~ John".

4. beasts. & 24 Elders which was out of every nation— ⟨it is⟩ great stuffing, to stuff all nations into 4 beasts & 24 Elders things which ⟨he⟩[808] saw had no allusions to what had been.— but what must shortly come to pass.— Rev is one of the plain[e]st. books god ever caused to be written—

what John saw he saw in heaven— ⟨that which the⟩ the prophet Saw, in vision, ⟨was⟩ on earth, ⟨and⟩ in Hebrew, ⟨it⟩ is a Latitude & Longitude compar[e]d with English version

they saw <u>figurs</u> of beasts.— they why, Dani[e]l did not say ⟨see⟩ a[809] lion & a bear. he saw an image like unto a bear:— in every [p. [98]] place.— John saw. the actual beast itself. ⟨it was⟩ to let John know that beasts existed there & not to represent figurs of things on the[810] Earth.—— ⟨The⟩ prophets always had interpretati[o]ns of the[i]r[811] visions &c

God always holds himself respons[i]ble to give revelati[o]ns of his visions & ⟨if⟩ he does it not. we are not responsible.—

speculators need not fear they shall be condemnd. if God has given no Rev[elation]

How do you prove John saw visions Beasts in heaven? 5 ⟨C[hapter]⟩ 11 ⟨v—⟩ Revelation.— 13 verse every creature. which was in heaven and on the Earth

I John saw all beasts &c in heaven. for I expect he saw the beasts of ⟨a⟩ 1000 forms ⟨from⟩ 10,000 worlds like this.— the grand secret was to tell what [p. [99]] was[812] in heaven.— God will gratify himself with all these animals. . . .

says one I cannot beleive in salvati[o]n of bea[s]ts.— I suppose God could underst[a]nd the beasts &c, in certain worlds— the 4 beasts, were angels there. dont know where they came from; ⟨they were inteligent⟩ inteligent.—

⟨but my⟩ Darling religion, says, ⟨they⟩ meant something beside beast.— then the 24 elders must mean something else:— 4 beasts meant[813] Buonpart [Bonaparte] & Cyrus. &c— then the 24 elders ment[814] the kingdoms of the Beasts.— It is all as flat as a pancake

what do ⟨you⟩ use such flat & vulger ⟨expressions. for⟩ being a prophet? because the old women understa[n]d it, they make [p. [100]] pancakes.— the whole argument is flat, & I dont know of any thing bette[r] to repr[e]sent.— the argument.—

---

808. John the Revelator.
809. TEXT: Possibly "I a".
810. TEXT: Possibly "this".
811. TEXT: Possibly "the".
812. TEXT: Possibly "the was" or "he was".
813. TEXT: Possibly "must".
814. TEXT: Possibly "must".

there is no revelation any where to shew that the beasts meant any thing but beasts

O ye Elders of Israel hearken to my voice & when ye are sent into the world to preach. tell those things you are sent to tell. declare the first principles, & let mysteries alone lest you be overthrown.—

Father Brown when you go to palmyrar [Palmyra][815] say nothi[n]g about the 4 B[e]asts Danl. 12 13 . . . ⟨C.⟩ 2. verse—[816] ⟨some say⟩ Deadly wound.— ⟨means⟩ Nebuchadnezzar.— Constantine.— & the catholic [p. [101]] now for the wasp nest.— priests. & Dragon for Devil they have translated beast in heaven— it was not to rep[res]ent beast on heaven— it was an angel in heaven. who has power in the last days to do a work.——— all the world wonderd after the beast:— ⟨&⟩ if the beast was all the world. how could the world wonderd after the beast? When the old devil shall give power to to the beast to do all his mighty work all the wo[r]ld will wonder—

who is able to make war with the beast?[817] says the inhabita[n]ts of the earth.— if it means[818] the kin[g]doms of the world it dont mean the kingdoms [p. [102]] of the Saints.— who is able to make war with my gr[e]at big self.— The Dragon.— we may interpret it.— & it is sometimes Apolyel.—[819] 9 verse 12 chap—[820] key word.— independent beasts. abstract from the human family.— (25 minutes past 11. lungs faild— the wind blew briskly.)— I said more than I ⟨ever⟩ did before except once at Ramus. & then the little ⟨upstarts ⟨fellows⟩ stufferd[821] me like a cock⟩. cock turkey— ⟨with the prop[h]ecies of Daniels—⟩ and crammed it down my throat. with their fingerss—[822]

after singing[,] 27— to 12 John Taylor commenced. saying I did not know but I might say someth[i]ng but since the prophet has got [p. [103]] through I find there is nothing left but the tail.— Elder Taylor says— if you write it down we are all fools it will not be ⟨very⟩ far from the mark"——— No man in the church knows any thing but what He has been told.—

---

815. The previous day Brown was appointed to "build up a church" in Palmyra, New York. (JS, Journal, 7 Apr. 1843, p. 339 herein.)
816. See Revelation 13:2–3.
817. See Revelation 13:4.
818. TEXT: Possibly "mean".
819. "Apollyon," the angel of the bottomless pit in Revelation 9:11. In Greek, *Apollyon* means "destroyer."
820. See Revelation 12:9.
821. TEXT: Possibly "stuffed".
822. JS may have been referring to his recent trip to Ramus, where he made similar comments about the beasts in Daniel and Revelation. (JS, Journal, 2 Apr. 1843, p. 325 herein.)

he had never said much about Bea[s]ts &c in his preaching & when he had, he had done it to attract attention & keep the people from running after a greater fool than himself.

Daniel saw an image of Gold &c Iron. Clay &c.— the prop[h]et explained. thou Nebuchadnezzar— art the ~~kindom~~ head— &c[823]

12. ten minutes choir sung. Elder [Orson] Hyde prayed— adjond [adjourned] till 2 o clock.— [p. [104]]

⟨12.— o clock noon—⟩ Strong west wind. & the ice is floating down the Missisippi. (~~to~~ Seen from the stand.)

2.26 minutes. meeting open by singing the wind was so high from the N. West that the speaker changed his position from the stand on the East end of the temple walls to a temporary (& momentary) stand near the west end,— the day ~~was~~ is warm (& pleasant. except strong wind)

Prayr by Elder Cahoon.— Singing.—

⟨12 ⟨mi[nutes]⟩— 3—⟩ Elder Taylor— resumed th[e] subject where he adjour[ne]d in the forenoon Little horn[824] was the Pope some say— Pope of Rome prevaild against the saints or chu[r]ch—— whence the Chu[r]ch of England [p. [105]] Presbyterin. Methodist &c— put the chu[r]ch of Rome in the place of the Devil & ~~then~~ When they find out the old Lady is their mother, they dont like the relationship

mentiond the 10 kingdoms or the toes.

while in the days of these kings or some of them. the God of heaven should set up a kingdom ~~which~~ which should never end.[825] I am not going to say

with regard to the littl stone, when ~~when~~ this kingdom will be set up. but it will be a kingdom. & the saints will take & possess it. & it will be a kingdom on earth not in heaven.— not Methodist. not Presbyt[er]ian or babtist I was going to say the church of Rome comes the [p. [106]] nearest. to a kingdom. of any of them. Not. Millerites. they expect. thee [826]coming of christ is like lightning.[827] whereas the kingdom is like a little stone cut out of the mountain without hands—[828] 3:20— Singing Choir.—

Elder O. Hyde said it was 3 years since I met with you & was set apart to a foreign mission by you.—[829]

---

823. See Daniel 2:31–38.
824. See Daniel 7:8.
825. See Daniel 2:44.
826. TEXT: Brown ink commences.
827. See, for example, Miller, *Evidence from Scripture*, 75; and Storrs, *Bible Examiner*, 11.
828. See Daniel 2:34.
829. In April 1840, Hyde and John E. Page were called on a mission to Europe and Jerusalem to

Mat. 24 chapter. in part read. conce[r]ning the temple—[830] Jesus acted very unchristian like. & uncharitable. and meddld with other peoples property. took a scourge of small cords & drove them out of the temple.[831] the german bible says there shall not be one stone left upon another that shall not be broken.—[832] [p. [107]]

Compard the Gifts in the church to the ~~gifts~~ ⟨golden⟩ ~~in the chu[r]ches~~ vessels of the temple which Nebuchadnazzar or some other nezzar took away.— where are they? in. Babylon.[833] wrapped up in a napkin.— give me so much money & I will give you so much Gospel— say the Sectarian priests.

> There is now and then one,
> Like the gleaning of grapes when vintage is done[834]

he[835] compard the Mormons to the rough stone. which could not be made to fit any where & would be thrown away— so with the Mormons the[y] will not ~~for~~ fit any way or where, but Must [p. [108]] be cast out. by all soci[e]ties, & yet at last they will come out head of the heap— the saints shall possess the kingdom[836]

I have been in the four quarters of the world among 14 or 15 diff[er]ent languages & people— & they all agree that some great event is coming. close at hand is coming. what has produced this impression? the true light that light that lighteth every man that cometh into the world.—[837] it is like the press that presses the paper on to the whole type at once. & God is the press-man.

when this gospel has been prea[c]hed to all nations. the hour of his judgmnt is come.—[838]

good bye 5— 5 singing.[839] & prayer. Taylor [p. [109]] [*page [110] blank*]

---

meet with Jewish leaders. Hyde, who completed the mission alone, returned to Nauvoo 7 December 1842. (JS, Journal, 7 Dec. 1842; 49n181 herein.)

830. See Matthew 24:1–2.
831. See John 2:13–15.
832. Orson Hyde referred to the German translation of the same passage of scripture while giving a sermon at the Illinois capitol building in Springfield, Illinois. (See JS, Journal, 1 Jan. 1843, p. 208 herein.)
833. See 2 Chronicles 36:7.
834. See Isaiah 24:13.
835. Orson Hyde.
836. See Psalm 118:22; Daniel 7:18.
837. See John 1:9.
838. See Revelation 14:6–7.
839. TEXT: Beginning with the period following "singing", blue ink commences.

9 April 1843 • Sunday

Sunday April 9: 10— 25 A M. Meeting opend by singing ⟨"spirit of God &c"⟩ at Temple stand

Prayer by William Smith. Singing

Joseph remarkd that some might have expectd him to preach but. his breast[840] & lungs wo[u]ld not admit. Joshua Grant. will occupy the stand a while followd by. Amasa Lym[a]n[841] [*10 lines blank*] [p. [111]]

10 April 1843 • Monday

Monday April 10. ~~1842~~ 1843 Elders conference commenced at the Temple at. 10 o clock A. M.—[842] [*14 lines blank*] [p. [112]]

11 April 1843 • Tuesday

Tuesday April 11. 1843. called at office. 11 A.M.— & 1. P.M. to give some inst[r]uctions to have an order made out for W[illiam] W. Phelps to get a note out of the Bank at St Louis. and started after Wm Clayton to find the date of the note[843]

some raine. & wind.— conference adgund [adjourned]. till tomorrow 10 A.M. [*7 lines blank*] [p. [113]]

---

840. TEXT: Possibly "heart".
841. Grant spoke on preaching the gospel throughout the world, and Lyman spoke about the Book of Mormon and the need for revelation to all of God's children. ("A Discourse," *Times and Seasons,* 15 June 1843, 4:236–238; "A Discourse," *Times and Seasons,* 1 June 1843, 4:218–220.)
842. This conference of elders was called "for the purpose of carrying out the Suggestions of President Joseph Smith at the Special Conference 3 days previous, 'that the Elders would be sent out to preach, by the Counsel of the Twelve.'" Brigham Young called and conducted the meeting, and although many of the Twelve and others were present, the minutes of the meeting do not note JS's presence. (General Church Minutes, 10 and 12 Apr. 1843.)
843. This may refer to the note listed in JS's "Inventory of Property"—prepared for his December 1842 bankruptcy hearing—held by the Bank of Missouri at St. Louis and payable to JS, Hyrum Smith, George Miller, and Peter Haws, for $4,866.38. Charles B. Street, Marvin B. Street, and Robert F. Smith were the signers of the note. By means of this note the two Streets had acquired a five-sixths interest in the steamboat *Nauvoo,* which had been purchased from the United States 10 September 1840 by Haws, with JS, Hyrum Smith, Henry Miller, and George Miller standing as surety for Haws's promissory note. Following the wreck of the *Nauvoo* later in the fall, however, the Streets refused to make good their note, upon which they still owed some $4,000. Efforts by JS and others to collect the unpaid balance on the Streets' note ended when the circuit court dismissed their suit—initiated 7 February 1844—in May 1846. ("Inventory of Property," in Letter to John W. Woods, Nauvoo, IL, ca. 7 Aug. [1842], JS Collection, CHL; Oaks and Bentley, "Joseph Smith and Legal Process," 737–741; see also 177n588 herein.)

12 April 1843 • Wednesday

Wednesday April 12[th] 1843 9 A.M.— in conve[r]sation with Mr Gillet [John Gillett]. concerning Hotchkiss purchase.—[844] Mr Jackson present Gave a certificate. (writtn by Elder [Orson] Hyde.) to Wm Weeks to carry out the designs & archeticture of the temple, in Nauvoo.[845]

Conferenc[e] of Eldrs commenced at 10— & closed at 12^{20}⁄$_{60}$ having ordained about 22 elders. & appointed about 118 to diff[er]ent Missions in U S. & Canida[846] & restord Almon Babbitt to fellowship.[847] &c &c. See Minutes of the quorum of the twelve.—[848]

befor the Conf[er]ence closed the Steamer Amaranth appeard in ⟨X⟩[849] [p. [114]] ⟪(notice was given at close of the confernc [conference] for the emigrants[850] to meet at the stand tomorrow morn[in]g 10. to hear inst[r]uction)⟫ ⟨X⟩ sight of the Temple. Coming up the River. & about nooon. landed her passengers at the wharf opposite the old Post Office. building— about 240 of the saints from England in char[g]e of Elder Lorenzo Snow who has ben

---

844. The conversation may have included a discussion about the recently discovered record of a deed Horace Hotchkiss and Gillett had executed in 1836, calling into question the validity of their land sale to church leaders in 1839. Other topics may have included the payment of taxes on the Hotchkiss purchase and renegotiating the contract between the church and the Hotchkiss partnership—the latter taking place three months later when William Clayton "settled with [Smith] Tuttle and Gillett for the Hotchkiss tract by giving back the land into their hands & they giving J[S] a Bond for a Deed for 50 lots." (327n718 herein; JS, Journal, 23 Feb. 1843; Flanders, *Kingdom on the Mississippi*, 173–174; Clayton, Journal, 7 July 1843; see also Hancock Co., IL, Bonds and Mortgages, 7 July 1843, vol. 1, pp. 500–501, microfilm 954,776, U.S. and Canada Record Collection, FHL.)

845. The certificate was given "in consequence of misunderstanding on the part of the temple committee, & their interference with the business of the architect [William Weeks]" with the instruction "that no person or persons shall interfere with him, or his plans, in the building of the Temple." Weeks's general plans for the temple were the only ones JS accepted of the "several plans or draughts . . . made by several individuals" in about October 1840. (Historian's Office, JS History, draft notes, 12 Apr. 1843; Clayton, History of the Nauvoo Temple, 3–4.)

846. The elders conference began on 10 April. Elders were assigned to over seventy locations in the United States and Canada and were instructed to provide for the temporal needs of their families before leaving on their missions. (JS, Journal, 10 Apr. 1843; 350n842 herein; General Church Minutes, 10 Apr. 1843.)

847. Babbitt, who had been "enticing" members of the church "to stop in places not appointed for the gathering," was disfellowshipped from the church 2 October 1841 for having "taught doctrine contrary to the revelations of God and detrimental to the interest of the church." On 13 March 1843, under JS's direction, Babbitt was appointed presiding elder at Ramus, Illinois. ("Minutes of a Conference," *Times and Seasons*, 15 Oct. 1841, 2:577; JS, Journal, 13 Mar. 1843; General Church Minutes, 10 Apr. 1843.)

848. Detailed minutes of the 10–12 April 1843 elders conference are in General Church Minutes, 10–12 Apr. 1843.

849. Richards completed this sentence near the top of the following manuscript page, where he inserted another large "X" to identify where the sentence resumes.

850. TEXT: Possibly "imigrants".

prea[c]hing in England 2 or 3 years.⁸⁵¹ Joseph & Emma— were present & a large Company of the brethren & sister. ready to greet their friends on their arrival. after unloding ⟨Saints⟩. the Amaranth proceded up the river. this is the fi[r]st boat up this season.

Bro Snow & Co— left Liverpool in January.⁸⁵² [p. [115]]

About 5. P.M. The Steamer "Maid of Iowa.["] hauled up at the Nauvoo House Landing. & discharged about 200 saints. In charge of Elders P[arley] P. Pratt & Levi Richards.— these had been detain at St Louis. Alton &ᶜ— through the Winter. having come out of Liverpool in the fall.———⁸⁵³ Capt [Dan] Jones of the "Maid of Iowa["] was baptizd a few weeks since. Joseph was presnt at the landing & the first to boa[r]d the steamer, & appea[re]d melted in tenderness when he met sister [Mary Ann Frost] Pratt. (who had been to England with Parley) & her little daugter only 3 or 4 days old.—⁸⁵⁴ the "Maid ⟨of Iow[a]—"⟩ it was 11 days coming from St Louis. [p. [116]] detain by ice, &ᶜ.—

Joseph was very busy the P.M & eve[n]ing among the brethrn. shaking hands & conversing freely. till about 9 o clock— & rejoiced to meet so many of the saints & in such good health & fine spirits equal to any that had ever come in Nauvoo. [*9 lines blank*] [p. [117]] [*pages [118]–[119] blank*]

13 April 1843 • Thursday

Thursday April 13 1843 Trial of Brink. vs. Dana⁸⁵⁵ came up at 10 o clock AM. but was adjound [adjourned] to Wednesday next. 9. A.M.—

---

851. Snow arrived in Liverpool on 22 October 1840. (Lorenzo Snow, London, England, to "Dear and Highly Respected Aunt," 16 Feb. 1841, in Snow, *Biography and Family Record of Lorenzo Snow,* 50.)

852. Snow reported that he "started the sixteenth of January from Liverpool 1843 destined for New Orleans." (Lorenzo Snow, Journal, 65.)

853. The Saints on the *Maid of Iowa* were the first of about eight hundred British converts who left Liverpool between 17 September and 29 October 1842 in four different ships. They were forced to pass the winter south of Nauvoo because of ice on the upper Mississippi. (Pratt, *Autobiography,* chap. 41; Woods, *Gathering to Nauvoo,* 153.)

854. Mary Ann Frost Pratt, wife of Parley P. Pratt, a member of the Quorum of the Twelve Apostles, had been in England since October 1840. There, Parley Pratt, who had arrived there in April 1840, edited the *Millennial Star* and helped supervise church emigration and publications. Returning to America with British converts, he and his family landed in New Orleans in early January 1843. He left his family at Chester, Illinois, and continued alone on horseback to Nauvoo. Sometime later he returned for his family and accompanied them and British converts to Nauvoo, where they arrived on 12 April 1843. The baby daughter was Susan Pratt, born 5 April 1843 en route to Nauvoo. (Pratt, *Autobiography,* 332–333, 335–336, 343; "Autobiographical Sketch of Mary Ann Stearns Winter," *Relief Society Magazine,* [Oct. 1916]: 574–577.)

855. Charles Dana sued Dr. William Brink in the Nauvoo mayor's court for injuring his expectant wife through misdiagnosis and unjustifiable medical procedures. After a two-day trial in March 1843, the mayor's court ruled "that the plaintiff recover . . . his bill, ninety-nine dollars and costs." Brink appealed to the Nauvoo Municipal Court, which on this date postponed the hearing until 19 April 1843. (JS,

at 10. ⟨A.M.⟩ the Emigrants & a great multitude of others assembld at the temple— when after Singing by the choir. & prayer by Elder [Heber C.] Kimball, Joseph addressed the assembly & said [*8 lines blank*] [p. [120]]

I most heartily congratulate you on your safe arrival— at Nauvoo. & your safe deliverance from all the dangers & diffcultis you have had to encou[n]ter

but you must not think your tribulations. are ended.—

I shall not address you on doctrin but concerni[n]g your temporal welfare

inasmuch as you have come up here assaying to keep the Comma[n]dments ⟨of God⟩ I pronou[n]ce the blessings of heaven ⟨& earth⟩ upon you. & inasmuch as will ⟨follow⟩ counsel. & act wisely. & do right [p. [121]] these blessings shall rest upon you so far as I have power ~~of~~ ⟨with⟩ God to seal them up[o]n you

I am you[r] servnt. & it is only through the Holy Ghost. that I can do you good. God is able to do his own work.

we do not present ourselves ⟨before you⟩ as any thing but your humble servnts. willing to ~~be spent~~ spend & be spent in your ~~servant~~ services.

we shall dwell on your temperal welware [welfare]. on this occasion. In the 1st place. where a crowd is flocking from all parts of the world of diffrt [different] minds; religion; &c, ⟨there will be some⟩ who do not live up to the Commandm[en]ts. ⟨there will be⟩— & designing characters, [p. [122]] who would turn you aside & lead you astray.— specuators who would get away your property. therefore it is necessary we should have an order here, ⟨&⟩ when emigra[n]ts arrive to instruct. them concerning these things.

If the heads of the church ~~had~~ have laid the foundati[o]ns ⟨of this place, & have had the trouble ~~of~~⟩ & of doing what has been done— are they not better qualifid to tell you how to lay out your money & than those who have had no interest— &c

Some start on the revelati[o]ns[856] to come here. & get turned away & loose all, & then come, and enter their complaints, ⟨to us⟩ when it is too late to do any thing for them [p. [123]]

the object of this meeting is to tell you these things & then if you ⟨will pursue the same cou[r]ses you must bear the consequence. There are sev[er]al objects in your coming here———⟩ one objct has been to bring you from. Sectarian bondage another. from National bondage. where you can be planted in a fertile soil, We have brought you into a free government. not that you are to consider yourselves outlaws. by free governme[n]t, we do not mean that a

---

Journal, 2–3 and 10 Mar. 1843; 19 Apr. 1843, pp. 280–294, 301, 363–364 herein; "Decision," *The Wasp*, 22 Mar. 1843, [2]–[3]; Dana v. Brink [Nauvoo Mun. Ct. 1843], Nauvoo Municipal Court Docket Book, 53–54.)

856. TEXT: Instead of "revelatins", possibly "revelatin".

man has a right to steal ⟨rob⟩. &c ⟨but free⟩ from Bondage. taxation— oppression. free in every thing if he conduct himself hone[s]tly & circumspe[c]tly with his n[e]ighbor, free in a spiritual capacity.— [p. [124]]

This is the place that is appointed for the oracles of God to be revealed. If you have any darkness you have only to ask & the dar[k]ness is removed. tis not necessary that miracles should be ⟨wrought⟩ to remove darkness Miracles are the fruits of faith. "how shall we believe on him on ⟨of⟩ whom ⟨&c⟩[857] &c we have not heard.⟩

I.E. inasmuch as I have received knowledge before I God may correct ⟨the scriptur by me if he choose⟩

faith comes by hearing the word of God.[858] ⟨& not faith by hearing & hearing by the word &c⟩ If a man has not faith enough to do one thing he may do another, ⟨if he cannot remove a Mountain he may heal the Sick.⟩ where faith is there will be some of the fruits. all gift & powed ⟨which were⟩ out ⟨poured⟩ out from heaven were poured out on [p. [125]] the heads of those who had faith. You must have a oneness of heart in all things, You shall be satisfied one way or the other with us before you have done with us.— ⟨there are a⟩ great many old huts here ⟨but they⟩ are all new. our city is not 6 or 700 years ⟨old⟩ as ⟨those⟩ you come from, it is only a 4 year old not ⟨a⟩ 4 year old not ⟨but⟩ 3 year old. ⟨we⟩ comncd [commenced] building 3 years last fall. ⟨there⟩ few old setlers—[859] I got away fro[m] my keepers ⟨in Missouri⟩ & ran & came on these shore[s],[860] & found 4 or 500 families & ⟨I⟩ went to work to get meat & flour folks were not afraid to trust. me. I went to work & bought all this region of country:— ⟨& I cried⟩ Lord what will thou have me to do? ⟨& the answr was⟩ build up a city [p. [126]] ⟨&⟩ call my saints to this place:[861] & our hea[r]ts leaped with joy to see you coming here. We have been praying for you all winter, from the bottom of hearts, We are glad to see you—

---

857. See Romans 10:14.

858. See Romans 10:17.

859. Willard Richards described the pre-Mormon lowlands of the Nauvoo peninsula as a wetland with dense undergrowth and containing less than a dozen houses. JS moved to an existing log house 10 May 1839, and sometime around 11 June 1839 Theodore Turley built another house—the first house built in the area by a Latter-day Saint. On 15 October 1839, the JS journal noted "quite a number of families moving in." (Historian's Office, JS History, draft notes, 11 June and 10 May 1839; JS, Journal, 10 May and 15 Oct. 1839, in *JSP*, J1:338, 353.)

860. On 16 April 1839, JS and his companions were allowed to escape from their custody while traveling to Columbia, Missouri, for trial on charges stemming from the "Mormon War." Six days later, on 22 April 1839, JS crossed the Mississippi River to Quincy, Illinois. (JS, Journal, 16 and 22 Apr. 1839, in *JSP*, J1:336.)

861. As early as 24 April 1839, at a meeting over which JS presided, it was "resolved—That the advice of this conference to the Brethren in general is . . . move on to the north (to Commerce, Illinois) as soon as they possibly can." (General Church Minutes, 24 Apr. 1839.)

we are poor— & cannot do by you as we would. but will do all we can.—

'Tis not to be expected that all can locate in the city.— there are ~~are~~ some who have money & will ⟨build— &⟩ hire. others, those who cannot purchase. lots can go out in the country.— the farmers wants your labors.— no industrious man[862] need suffer in this land.—

the claims of the poor ⟨on us⟩ are such that [p. [127]] we have claim ~~of~~ ⟨on⟩ your good feelings for your money. to help the poor. & the chu[r]ch debts ⟨also have their dem[a]nds to⟩— save the credit of the church. this credit has been obtain to help the poor. & keep them from starvation. &c— those who purchase church lands. & pay for it, this shall be their sacrifice,[863]

Men of 50. & 100.000 dollars, who were robbed ⟨of every thing⟩ in the State of Mo. are laboring in this city for a morsel ⟨of bread.⟩. ⟨& there are those⟩ who must have starved but for the providence of God through me. If any man[864] say here is land. or there is land. beleive it— not.— we can beat all our competitors in lands. price. & every [p. [128]] think [thing], ⟨we have the⟩ high[e]st pricees. best lands. & do the most good with. th[e] money. ⟨we get.⟩ ⟨our system⟩ ~~it~~ is a real smut machine a bolting[865] machine.—[866] & all the ⟨shorts⟩ brann & smut. runs away & all the flour remains with us.—

suppose I sell you land for $10. per acre & I gave 3. 4. 5 per acre . . . then you are speculating ⟨says one,⟩ yes, I will tell you how. I buy others lands & give them to the widow & the fatherless,———

---

862. TEXT: Possibly "men".
863. By the end of the year, a "Notice to Emigrants and Latter-day Saints Generally" was appearing in the *Nauvoo Neighbor* over the signature of William Clayton, who assisted the trustee in the sale of Church lands: "I feel it my duty to say to the bretheren generally, and especially those who are emigrating to this place, that there is in the hands of the Trustee in Trust, a large quantity of lands, both in the city and adjoining Townships in this county, which is for sale—some of which belongs to the church and is designed for the benefit of the poor, and also to liquidate debts owing by the church, for which the Trustee in Trust is responsible. Some also is land which has been consecrated for the building of the temple, and some for the Nauvoo House. If the brethren who move in here and want an inheritance will buy their lands from the Trustee in Trust, they will thereby benefit the poor, the Temple and the Nauvoo House, and even then only be doing that which is their duty and which I know, by considerable experience, will be vastly for their benefit and satisfaction in days to come. Let all the brethren therefore, when they move into Nauvoo, consult President Joseph Smith the Trustee &c, and purchase their lands of him, and I am bold to say that God will bless them and will hereafter be glad they did so. We hold ourselves ready at any time to wait upon the brethren and show them the lands belonging to the church and Temple &c., and can be found any day either at President Joseph Smith's Bar Room or the Temple Recorder's Office, at the Temple. W. CLAYTON, CLERK. Nauvoo, Dec. 16, 1843." (William Clayton, "Notice to Emigrants and Latter-day Saints Generally," *Nauvoo Neighbor*, 20 Dec. 1843, [3]; original paragraph breaks ignored.)
864. TEXT: Possibly "men".
865. TEXT: Possibly "beating".
866. Machines for removing husks and impurities from grain during the milling process.

If ~~they these~~ ⟨the⟩ speculators run again[s]t me they run again[s]t the buckler of Jehovah.— God did not send me up as he did Joshua, in former days God sent [p. [129]] his servnts to fight, but in the last days he has promised to fight the battle himself.[867]

God will deal with you himself. & will bless or curse you as you do behave your selves. I speak to you as one having authority.[868] that you may know when it come & that you may have faith. & know that God has sent me.

⟨The lower part of the town is the most healt[h]y,⟩[869] In ⟨th[e]⟩ upper part of the town the Merchants will say I am partial— &c but The lower part of the town is much the most healthy. I tell you in the name of the Lord.— I have been out in all parts of the city. att all times of night to learn these thi[n]gs. [p. [130]]

The Doctors in this region dont know much; & the lawyers, ⟨when I spoke about them—⟩ began to say we will ~~known~~ renounce you. on the stand.— but they dont come up & I take the libe[r]ty to say what I ~~care~~ have a mind to about. them.

Doctors wont tell you <u>where</u> to go to be well. they want to kill. or cure you to get Your money.———

Calomel Doctor will give you calomel to cure a sliver in the big toe

& does not stop to know ~~if~~ whether the stomach is empty or not.— ⟨& calomel on an empty stomach will kill the patient.⟩[870]

& the Lobelia doctors will do the same.[871]

point me out a patient & I will [p. [131]] tell you whether calomel or Lobelia will kill ~~kill~~ ⟨him⟩ or not. if you give it, The river Missisippi is healthy. unless they drink, it. & it is more healthy then the spring water— dig wells from 15 to 30 feet. and it will be healthy.

---

867. See Revelation, 6 Aug. 1833, in Doctrine and Covenants 86:6, 1844 ed. [D&C 98:37]; and Revelation, 22 June 1834, in Doctrine and Covenants 102:3, 1844 ed. [D&C 105:14].

868. See Mark 1:22; and Matthew 7:29.

869. Mosquito-borne malaria was common during the summer months in Nauvoo, although drainage ditches eventually alleviated the problem somewhat. (Rollins et al., "Transforming Swampland into Nauvoo," 125–157.)

870. JS's assertion here may have been based on an experience in his own family: Lucy Mack Smith believed that the death of JS's older brother Alvin in November 1823 resulted from a "heavy dose" of calomel "lodged in his stomach." (Lucy Mack Smith, History, 1844–1845, bk. 4, [3].)

871. "Regular" physicians often used calomel, a mercury chloride compound, in their treatment of patients, especially as an emetic. Thomsonian or botanic physicians decried the use of calomel and instead treated their patients with lobelia. JS here identified the competing medical philosophies by their characteristic use of these two prescriptions. ("Calomel," *Thomsonian Recorder* [Columbus, OH], 19 July 1834, 330; see also 281n486 herein.)

There are many sloughs on th[e] Islands. f[r]om ⟨whence⟩ Miasma arises in the summer, and is blown[872] over the upper part of the city.— but it does not extend over the lower part of the city.—[873]

all those pers[o]ns who are not used to liv[i]ng on a river, or lake or large pond of water— I do not want you should stay on the banks of the river. [p. [132]] get away to the lower part of the city. back on the hill . . . where you can get. good— well water.—

if you feel any inconvenince take some mild physic. 2 or 3 times & then some good bitters— if you cant get any thing else take a little salts. & Cyanne [cayenne] pepper— if you cant get salt take pecoria.—[874] or gnaw down a butter-nut tree, ⟨eat some⟩ boneset, ⟨or⟩ hoarhound.[875]

Those who have ~~may~~ money come to me & I will let you have lands & those who have not money if they look as well as I do I will give you advice that will do you[876] good 12¼— I bless you in the name of Jesus Chit [Christ] Amen [p. [133]]

Hyrum [Smith]. made remarks concerning the proppets [prophets]. every report in circulation not congenial to good understanding, is false.— false as the dark regions of hell.— closed 12²⁵⁄₆₀

Joseph gave notice that Bro Garder wantd 2 or 300 hands— ditching—[877] a good job.—

Singing by choir.— Bro Thompson requests prayers.— closed. by Prayr O[rson] Pratt

After Meeting.— Many of the Saints repaird to the landing. of the Nauvoo House. as the "Maid of Iowa" arrived (during the Meeting.) from Keokuk where it went last ~~light~~ Night after the freight which it left to get over the Rapids.— Joseph was among them till about 3 o clock & then when the boat left walked away with [p. [134]] bro [Heber C.] Kimball. [*16 lines blank*] [p. [135]]

---

872. TEXT: Possibly "~~blown~~ ⟨flown⟩".

873. "Miasma" in the early nineteenth century referred to poorly defined "infecting substances floating in the air; the effluvia of any putrefying bodies, rising and floating in the atmosphere." Miasma was generally considered noxious. ("Miasma," in *American Dictionary*, 529.)

874. Possibly a phonetic approximation of, or colloquialism for, "ipecacuanha" (a plant).

875. Bitters, epsom salt, cayenne pepper, ipecacuanha, boneset, horehound, lobelia, and the butter-nut tree were herbs, plants, and other agents used medicinally.

876. TEXT: Possibly "your".

877. The ditches were to drain the low-lying areas of Nauvoo. (See 356n869 herein.)

14 April 1843 • Friday

Friday April 14[th] 1843 Went out to the farm. & beyond and sold 20 acres of land, and returnd

Started to go again and on the Side hill. broke the carriage & retu[r]ned home. [*10 lines blank*] [p. [136]] [*page [137] blank*]

15 April 1843 • Saturday

Saturday April 15, attended court martial at his house. gave instructi[o]ns to have an notice written to John F. cowan.[878] of Shokokon appointing him his aiddecamp. as Leut [Lieutenant]. Gen,

4⟨.5⟩ P.M. rode out with emma.— [*10 lines blank*] [p. [138]]

16 April 1843 • Sunday

Sunday morning April 16. 1843 Meeting at the Temple. A.M. 10. o ck

Joseph read Bro [Parley P.] Pratts letters to the Editor[879] of "T[imes] & Seasons" concrning the death of Lorenzo Barn[e]s.[880] ⟨& remarked he read it because it was so appropriate to all who had died in the faith.—⟩ Almost all who have fallen in these last days, in the church, have fallen in a strange land, this is a strange land. to tho[s]e who have come from a distance.

we should cultivate sympathy for the afflicted. among us.

If there is a place on earth. where men should cultivate this spirit & pour in the oil & wine ⟨in the bosom of the afflicted⟩ it is this place.

⟨and this spirit is manifest here—⟩ and although he is a stranger ⟨& afflicted.⟩ when he arrives, he finds. a brother— & friend ready to administer to his necessities.— [p. [139]]

another remark, I would esteem it one of the greatest blessings, if I am to be afflicted in this world, to have my lot cast where I can find breth[r]en[881] & friends all arou[n]d me, ⟨but⟩ this is not. ⟨thing. I referred to is ⟨it⟩ is⟩ to have

---

878. In February 1843 Cowan had requested "a talented Mormn preacher" to move to Shokokon and to invite "as many Mormons to settle in that place as May please to so to do." JS signed Cowan's appointment as one of his aides-de-camp in the Nauvoo Legion on 18 April 1843. (JS, Journal, 10 Feb. and 18 Apr. 1843.)

879. TEXT: Possibly "Editors".

880. "Correspondence," *Times and Seasons*, 1 Apr. 1843, 4:148–149. Pratt had learned of the death of Barnes at St. Louis and wrote Wilford Woodruff and John Taylor, editor of the *Times and Seasons*, on 1 April from Alton, Illinois. Thirty-year-old Barnes died of the "quick consumption" 20 December 1842 in Bradford, England, while presiding over the Bradford Conference. A former member of Zion's Camp in 1834 and a dedicated missionary, Barnes was identified as "the first gospel messenger from Nauvoo who has found a grave in a foreign land." (Editorial, *LDS Millennial Star*, Jan. 1843, 3:159; "Letter from Elder Woodruff," *Times and Seasons*, 15 May 1845, 6:907–908.)

881. TEXT: Possibly "brothers" or "brother".

the privilige of having our dead buri[e]d on the land where god has appointd to gather his saints together,— & where there will be nothing but saints, where they may have the privelige of laying their bodies where ⟨the⟩ Son will make his appearance. & where they may hear the. sound of the trump that shall call them forth, to behold him, that in the morn of the resurrecti[o]n, they may come forth in a body. & come right up out of their graves. & strike hands ⟨immediately⟩ in eternal glory. ⟨& felicity rather⟩ than to be [p. [140]] scattered thousands of miles apart. There is something good. & sacred to me— ⟨in this thing.⟩ the place where a man is buried has been sacred to me.— ⟨this subjct is made mention of—⟩ In Book of Mormon & Scriptures. & ⟨to⟩ the aborigines ⟨regard⟩ the burying places of the⟨ir⟩ fathers as ⟨is⟩ more sacred that than any thing else.

When I. heard of the death of our beloved bro ⟨Barns it would not have affected me so much⟩ if I had the opp[o]rtunity of burying him in the land of Zion. I beleive, those who have buried their friends here their condition is enviable. Look at Joseph in Egypt how he required his friends to bury him in the tomb of his fathers,— see the expence & great company — & ⟨which attended the⟩ embalming. ⟨&c ⟨and⟩ the going up of the great company. to his burial.⟩[882]

It has always been considird a g[r]eat curse not to obtain an honorable buryal. ⟨& one of the gratest curses the anci[e]nt prophets could put on any one was. that he man should go without a burial.⟩[883] [p. [141]]

I have said, father, I desire to be burid here, & before I go home, but if ⟨this is not thy will⟩ not may I return, or find Some kind friend to bring me back, & gather my friends, who have fallen in foreign lands, & bring them up hither, that we may may all lie[884] together.—

I will tell you what I[885] want. if tomorrow I shall be calld to lay in yonder tombs. in the morning of the resurrecti[o]n, let me strike hand⟨s⟩ with my father, & cry, my father, & he will say my son, my Son,— as soon as the rock rends. & before we come out of our graves.[886]

& may we contemplate these things so? [p. [142]] yes, if we learn how to live & how to die [blank]. when we lie down we contemplat how we may rise up in the morni[n]g and ⟨it is⟩ pleasing for friends to lie down together locked

---

882. While the last request and reburial of the patriarch Joseph supports JS's point, JS is actually describing the last request and burial of Joseph's father, Jacob, in the tomb of his fathers. (See Exodus 13:19; Joshua 24:32; and Genesis 49:29–32; 50:2–13, 25.)

883. See, for example, Isaiah 14:19–20.

884. TEXT: Possibly "live ⟨lie⟩".

885. TEXT: Possibly "at ⟨I⟩".

886. JS expressed similar sentiments in a journal entry he dictated the previous summer while in hiding. (JS, Journal, 23 Aug. 1842, p. 117 herein.)

in the arms of love, to sleep, & wake in each others embrace ⟨& renew their conversation.⟩

would you think it strange that I relate what I have seen in vision in relation.— this intere[s]ting theme.

Those who have died in Jesus christ, may expect to enter in to all that fruition of Joy when they come forth. which they have possessed here, [p. [143]]

so plain was the vision I actually saw men, before they had ascend[e]d from the tomb, as though they were getti[n]g up slowly, they tooke[887] each othe[r] by the hand & it was my father & my Son. my mother & my daughter. ⟨my brother & my sister⟩ & when the voice calls, suppose I am laid by the side of my fathe[r].— what would be the first Joy of my heart? where is my fathr. my mother. my sister. they are by my side ⟨I embrace them. & they me.⟩

It is my meditati[o]n all the day & more than my meat & drink to know how I shall make the saints of God to comprehe[n]d the visions[888] that roll like ⟨an⟩ overflowing surge; to ⟨before⟩ my ~~vision~~ ⟨mind⟩. [p. [144]]

O how I wo[u]ld delight to bring before you things which you never thought of. but poverty. & the cares of the world prevent. but I am glad I have the privilige of communicati[n]g to you some things, which if grasped closely a will be a help to you when the clouds ⟨are⟩ gath[eri]ng. & the storms ⟨are⟩ ready——— to bu[r]st up[o]n you like peals of thunder, lay hold of these things & let not you[r] knees tremble, ⟨nor your hearts faint.⟩ what can Earthequakes ~~do~~. wars. & tornados do? nothing.— all your losses will be made up to you in the resurrecti[o]n provi[d]ed you continue faithful

by the vision of the almighty I have seen it.— [p. [145]] more painful to me the thoughts of annihilation & than death. if I had no expectation of seeing my mother Broth[ers] ~~&~~ Sisters & fri[e]nds again my heart would burst in a moment. & I should go down to my grave. The expectati[o]n of seeing my f[r]iends in the morni[n]g of the resurrection cheers my soul. and make be bear up aginst the evils of life. it ~~it~~ is like their taking a long journey. & on their return we meet them with increasd joy.

God has reveald his son from the heavens. & the doctrine of the resurrection also. & we have a knowledge that those we bury here. God bring them up again. clothed upon, &[889] quckend [quickened] by the spirit [p. [146]] of the great god. & what mattereth it whether we lay them down, or we lay down with them. when we can ~~live~~ keep them no longer

---

887. TEXT: Possibly "~~take~~ ⟨tooke⟩".
888. TEXT: Possibly "~~wisdom~~ ⟨visions⟩" or "[*illegible*] ⟨visions⟩".
889. TEXT: Possibly "&⟨c⟩".

then let them sink down; like a ship in the storm. the mighty anchor holds the storm so let those[890] thuths [truths] sink down in our hearts. that we may even here begin to enjoy.[891] that which shall be in full hereafter.

Hosanna. Hosanna. Hosanna, to Almighty god that rays of light begin to bu[r]st fo[r]th upon us even now.

I cannot find words to express myself I am not learnd. but I have as good feelings as any man. O that I had the [p. [147]] the language of the archangel to express my feelings[892] once to my frends. but I never expect to

when othe[r]s regoice I regoice. when I they mourn I would mourn—

to Marcellus Bates. let me admi[ni]ster comfort, you shall soon have the company of your[893] companion in a wo[r]ld of glory—[894] & the frends of Bro. Barns.— & all the saints who are mourning, this has been a warning voice to us all. to be sober— & diligent— & lay aside mirth & vanity. & folly.—— & be prepard to die tomorrow . . . (preached abo[u]t 2 hours) [p. [148]]

⟨Erastus⟩ Snow. said he was a boa[r]der with Pret. J., Smith the fi[r]st week he was in Nauvoo. helped carry the chain for the surveyor & lay out the fir[s]t farms. has been absent. 2½ years.—[895] 5— 12—) (P[reache]d about 1, h[our].)

Prop[he]t Joseph said as president of this house I forbid any man's leaving this house ju[s]t as we are going to close the meeting. he is no gentleman who will do it. I dont care who it comes from— if it were from the King of England. I forbid it.—[896]

singing. & prayer ⟨by Elder [John] Taylor.⟩ [5 lines blank] [p. [149]] [page 150 blank]

17 April 1843 • Monday

Monday April 17. 1843— [16 lines blank] [p. [151]]

[897]This day a letter was received at the Nauvoo Post office. Sidney Rigd[o]n Post M[aster].— of which the following is a copy

---

890. TEXT: Possibly "these".
891. TEXT: Instead of "enjoy", possibly "enj[oy]ing".
892. TEXT: Possibly "feeling," or "feeling.".
893. TEXT: Or "you".
894. Bates's twenty-year-old wife, Jenette Pratt Bates, died of consumption sometime during the week ending Friday, 10 February 1843. ("Reports of Deaths," *The Wasp*, 22 Feb. 1843, [3].)
895. Snow and his wife, Artimesia Beman Snow, left Nauvoo 7 November 1840 to serve a mission in the eastern states. Snow left his wife and two children in Salem, Massachusetts, and arrived in Nauvoo 11 April 1843 to visit with church leaders and family members, after which he returned to the East. (Erastus Snow, Journal, 1838–1840, 94–97; 1841–1847, 40.)
896. Ten days earlier, JS made similar remarks about leaving meetings early. (JS, Journal, 7 Apr. 1843, p. 341 herein.)
897. TEXT: Brown ink commences.

Washington D.C. April 1. ~~1844~~ 1843

Sir—

The government of the Un[ited] States need your service no longer. You will deliver all your accounts to this office, sealed and addressed, to the Post Master General. as the Post Of[fice] at Nauvoo, Ill, is hereby abolished. the President of the Uni Sts [United States] having Directed it so

Respe[c]tfully your Most Ob^t Serv^{t,}
Charles A. Wic[k]liffe[898]

You will receive your letters &c at any P.O. you direct C.A.W. Superscripti[o]n.

By order of J[ohn] Tyler Pre. of. the. U.S.

Navoo Post Office Ill.[899] [p. [152]]

⟨rain last night— green grass begins to be seen⟩

[900]April 17. Monday—

walked out in the city. with Claytn [William Clayton]. called on brother [John] Taylor. handed him the letter purporting to be from the Attorney Gen of the U State and gave him instr[u]ctions abo[u]t it.[901]

looked at Several lots. calld at Samuel Bennet[t']s. to make arrangeme[n]ts to leave that hou[s]e, above the old bur[y]ing ground.— retu[rne]d home. had convesatin [conversation] with Erastus Snow.[902] Receivd 50 Gold Sovreigns[903] of P[arley] P. Pratt for the templ & Nauvoo House

---

898. The United States postmaster general, 1841–1845.

899. According to William Clayton, Sidney Rigdon "foolishly supposed [this letter] genuine and neglected to do his duty on that account He started for Carthage to learn some thing more about it and was met by Mr Hamilton an old Mail contracter who satisfied E[lde]r Rigdon that it was all a hoax, and he returned home. On thursday the Mail arrived as usual and there is no evidence but it is merely another attempt to disturb our peace by designing men." (Clayton, Journal, 23 Apr. 1843.)

900. TEXT: Blue ink commences.

901. JS received a hoax letter the previous evening purporting to be from United States attorney general Hugh S. Legaré ordering JS to deliver himself to the governor of Illinois "in order to be tried before the Supreme Court of the U. S. next term" on the charge of "high treason." (Clayton, Journal, 17 and 23 Apr. 1843; "Hugh Legaré," Washington DC, to JS, Nauvoo, IL, 31 Mar. 1843, JS Collection, CHL.)

902. Snow had left his family in Salem, Massachusetts, where he was serving a mission, for a brief visit to Nauvoo. Snow later reported that during his stay in Nauvoo, JS told him about "baptism for the dead and marriage for eternity" and that the Lord was now "requiring his chosen and proved servants to take unto themselves wives." According to Snow, JS "introduced several of those who had been sealed to himself and others of the first elders of the Church." ("Autobiography of Erastus Snow," 107–110.)

903. A British gold coin first issued in 1817 valued at one pound or twenty shillings. In 1842, Congress set the value of one pound at $4.84 for government transactions, meaning that the £50 donation was worth about $242. (An Act to Regulate the Value to Be Affixed to the Pound Sterling by the Treasury Department [27 July 1842], in *Public Statutes at Large*, 27th Cong., 2nd Sess., chap. 66, p. 496.)

5½ P.M. calld at the printing office. retu[rne]d home & listind to the reading of a synopsis of his sermon of last sabbath.— [p. [153]]

18 April 1843 • Tuesday

Tuesday, Morning April 18,ᵗʰ· 9. A.M. at home. signed an⁹⁰⁴ appointment. to John F. Cowan as his aid ⟨decamp⟩ in the Nauvoo Legion.⁹⁰⁵ conversed with cowan— &ᶜ. & went ~~into~~ onto the prairie,— (Twelve met a[t] presidents office)⁹⁰⁶ sold 130 acres of land to the English Brethren.⁹⁰⁷ signd ~~an~~ transcript of his Docket Thomson M. [Mercy Fielding Thompson] vs Dixon—⁹⁰⁸ 3, P,M.

⁹⁰⁹⟨in the evening had a talk with⟩ A ⟨the⟩ deligation of the [*blank*] Indians,⁹¹⁰ who complained of having th[e]ir cattle & horses &c stolen & they were much troubled & wanted to know what they should do. they had borne their greivances patie[n]tly.—⁹¹¹ [p. [154]]

19 April 1843 • Wednesday

Wednesday April 19ᵗʰ· 1843 at the office at 9 o'clock. waiting for the assembling of the Municiepel Court. in Case of Dana Versus Brink or Brink vs. Dana. appealed case—⁹¹²

---

904. TEXT: Possibly "on".
905. Three days earlier JS gave instructions to notify Cowan of this appointment. (JS, Journal, 15 Apr. 1843.)
906. Wilford Woodruff reported that the Quorum of the Twelve gathered to confer with JS on this date, but "President Smith not being Presant the conference adjourned untill next day." (Woodruff, Journal, 18 Apr. 1843.)
907. Possibly the southeast quarter of Section 25, Township 7 North, Range 8 West, at least part of which was sold to "sundry English brethren" on 19 April 1843. (Trustees Land Book B, 17 and 19 Apr. 1843, 17–18; Deed, JS [Trustee-in-trust] to Thomas Hamonds et al., [17 Apr. 1843], Nauvoo Restoration, Incorporated, Collection, CHL.)
908. JS heard this case on 6 April 1843. (JS, Journal, 6 Apr. 1843, p. 329 herein.)
909. TEXT: Brown ink commences.
910. William Clayton noted that the delegation consisted of three "Indian Chiefs." The draft notes of JS's history identify the Indians as members of the Potawatomi tribe, as did the "Mr. Hitchcock" who evidently served as interpreter. (Clayton, Journal, 18 Apr. 1843; Historian's Office, JS History, draft notes, 18 Apr. 1843; Henry King, Keokuk, Iowa Territory, to John Chambers, Burlington, Iowa Territory, 14 July 1843, in U.S. Bureau of Indian Affairs, Letters Received by the Office of Indian Affairs.)
911. The three Potawatomi chiefs were reportedly "dissatisfied with the white people bordering on their lands" and, having heard that JS could talk to the "Great Spirit," came seeking his advice about how to deal with them. They also "wanted to know if Smith would give them any assistance in case of an outbreak on the frontier" and told him that "they had smoked the pipe with ten tribes who had agreed to defend each other to the last extremity." JS replied that "he could give them no assistance, that his hands were tied by the U. S. but that he could sympathize with them" and advised them to "be friendly to the neighbouring tribes, and pray a great deal to the G[reat] Spirit." (Henry King, Keokuk, Iowa Territory, to John Chambers, Burlington, Iowa Territory, 14 July 1843, in U.S. Bureau of Indian Affairs, Letters Received by the Office of Indian Affairs.)
912. Charles Dana sued Dr. William Brink in the Nauvoo mayor's court for injuring his expectant

[913]12½ Mayors Court[914] opened. original papers called for.— Clerk— ([James] Sloan) enqird [enquired] if the execution would would issue from this court? Sit down said the mayor & attend to your own business— if any thing is wanted I will tell you time enough— [William H. J.] Marr Esqr[915] opend the case. &c. moved this case be dismissd for want of Jurisdiction in the cou[r]t below,[916] & read from pag[e] 400. Statutes Ill.—[917] case of Tort not assumpsit.— Mayors court no jurisdiction. Chitty's pl[e]adings— 88 138.[918] what Assumpsit is. &c Blackston[e] Com[mentaries]— [p. [155]] vol 2ᵈ pages 122. 157. 161. 163.[919]

Defndnts[920] council [*blank*] read Lieghs Nisi Prius. 199. 550[921] margin— [Wililam] Brinks counsil[922] stated th[e]ir[923] appeal was contrary to thei[r][924] council.

after the court had decided that the mayor had Jurisdiction. but this court[925] had not. dismissd.[926] Mayor stated that a legal bond was not presented till. after the 20 days had Expired.—[927]

after adjournmnt. while conver[s]ing with Dʳ Brink & Esqr Marr. Joseph said he had been called to thousands of cases in sickness & he had never faild

---

wife through misdiagnosis and unjustifiable medical procedures. After a two-day trial in March 1843, the mayor's court ruled "that the plaintiff recover . . . his bill, ninety-nine dollars and costs." (Dana v. Brink [Nauvoo Mun. Ct. 1843], Nauvoo Municipal Court Docket Book, 53–54; JS, Journal, 2, 3 and 10 Mar. 1843; "Decision," *The Wasp,* 22 Mar. 1843, [3].)

913. TEXT: Blue ink commences.

914. Actually the Nauvoo Municipal Court.

915. Attorney for William Brink.

916. That is, the mayor's court, which originally heard the *Dana v. Brink* case.

917. Marr probably read from Jonathan Scammon's compilation of *The Public and General Statute Laws of the State of Illinois,* in which the jurisdiction of justices of the peace is discussed on page 402 rather than page 400 (Chicago: Stephen F. Gale, 1839).

918. Probably a later edition of Joseph Chitty's *A Practical Treatise on Pleading,* first published in the United States in 1809.

919. Blackstone, *Commentaries,* 2:91, 127–128, 130–131, 132.

920. Probably referring to Charles Dana, who was the respondent, not a defendant, in this appeal. (Dana v. Brink [Nauvoo Mun. Ct. 1843], Nauvoo Municipal Court Docket Book, 53.)

921. Leigh, *Abridgment of the Law of Nisi Prius,* 1:198–199, 549–550.

922. William H. J. Marr.

923. TEXT: Possibly "this".

924. TEXT: Possibly "this".

925. The Nauvoo Municipal Court. The Nauvoo charter gave the mayor's court the same civil and criminal jurisdiction as justice of the peace courts but limited appeals to the municipal court to cases "arising under the city ordinances." Brink's appeal did not meet this criterion. (An Act to Incorporate the City of Nauvoo [16 Dec. 1840], *Laws of the State of Illinois* [1840–1841], p. 55, secs. 16–17.)

926. Brink later appealed to the Hancock County Circuit Court, which eventually reduced the judgment to seventy-five dollars. (See 303n602 herein.)

927. Illinois law required that appeal from a justice of the peace court be made within twenty days of the decision, with the appeal attended by a bond covering court costs. (See 320n679 herein.)

of ~~administerd~~ administ[er]ing comfort, where the patient had thrown themself unreservedly on him and the reason was he never prescribed any that would injure the patient if it did him no good.— I have lost a fathe[r] brothe[r] [p. [156]] & child because. in my anxiety I have depended more on the jud[g]ment of other men than my own, while I have raised up others who were lower than they were.

I will here remark (& by the[928] bye I will say that man who stands there (pointing to Levi Richa[r]ds) is the best physic[i]an I have ever been acquainted with. & I say it hone[s]tly.)[929] people will seldom die with disease provided we know it seasonably. & treat it mildly. pat[i]ently. & perseveri[n]gly. & do not use harsh means. It is like the Irishmans digging down the mountain. he does not put his shoulder to it to push it over but puts it in his wheell barrow & carries it away day after day. & day after day. [p. [157]] and perseveres & the whole mountain is removed, so we should persevere in the use of simple remedies. (& not push again[s]t the constitution of the pati[e]nt.) day after day & the disease will be removed & the pati[e]nt saved. It is better to <u>save</u> the life of a man than to <u>raise</u> one from the dead. 1 P.M. to Dinner

[930]returned to the office soon after— & had conversation with 3 gentlemen introduced by Geo A. Smith,

3. P.M. in the presidendents office; B[righam] Young Wm Smith, P[arley] P. Pratt. O[rson] Pratt. W[ilford] Woodruff— J[ohn] Taylor. Geo a Smith. W Richds [Willard Richards].—

Joseph said. to the Twelve.—[931]

Go in the name of the Lord God & tell [p. [158]] [Lucien] Woodworth to put the hands onto the Nauvoo House & begin the work. & be patient till means can be provided.—[932]

call on the inhabitants of Nauvoo. & get them to bring in their means, then Go to Laharpe & serve them the same.

Thus commence your career,

---

928. TEXT: Possibly "then".
929. Like his brother Willard Richards, Levi Richards was a Thomsonian doctor. JS credited Levi for helping to save his life from a severe illness in June 1837. (JS History, vol. B-1, 762.)
930. TEXT: Brown ink commences.
931. In this meeting, Woodruff noted, JS directed the Quorum of the Twelve Apostles "to take a mission in the East to obtain means to build the Nauvoo house as we were appointed so to do by the Conference." Willard Richards evidently created this journal account of the meeting from minutes he kept during the meeting. (Woodruff, Journal, 19 Apr. 1843; see also JS, Journal, 6 Apr. 1843, p. 333 herein; Quorum of the Twelve Apostles, Minutes, 19 Apr. 1843.)
932. Woodworth, who was overseeing construction of the Nauvoo House, earlier recounted the difficulties he faced keeping workmen on the project with insufficient funds and supplies. (JS, Journal, 21 Feb. 1843, pp. 268–271 herein.)

Brigham Young. July 1845. As president of the Quorum of the Twelve Apostles, Young worked closely with Joseph Smith in directing the affairs of the church during the Nauvoo years. In this painting by Seal Van Sickle, Young is holding a book titled "Law of the Lord," the volume in which Joseph Smith's first Nauvoo journal was kept. The other two books on the table are the Bible and the Book of Mormon. (Courtesy Pioneer Memorial Museum, International Society Daughters of Utah Pioneers, Salt Lake City.)

And never stand still till the Master appear, for it is necessary the house should be done.

Out of the stock that is handed me. you shall have as you have need. for the laborer is worthy of his hire.[933]

I hereby command the hands to go to work on the house trusting in the Lord. Tell Woodworth to put them on & he shall be backed up with it.— You must get cash, [p. [159]] property, lands, horses, cattle &c, & flour, corn wheat &c. the grain can be grou[n]d at this mill. If you can get hands onto the house it will give such an impetus to the work, it will never stop till it is completed. Let the twelve keep together. you will do more good to keep together, not travel together. but. meet in conference alternately from place to— place & associate together, & not be fou[n]d more than 200 miles apart— Thus travel from Maine here till they make a perfect highway from for the Saints, from here to maine.

It is better for you to be togethe[r]. for it is difficult for a man to have strength of Lungs & health to be instant in season & out of season.— under all circumstances & you can [p. [160]] assist each other, & when you go & spend. a day or two in a place you will find it as it is with [William] miller.[934] they will gather together in great companies.

If 12 men cannot build that house they are poor tools.

President Young asked if the Twelve should go to England? Said Joseph.—

No. I dont want the Twelve to go to England this year. I have sent them to England & they have broke the ice ⟨& done well⟩ & now I want to send some of the Elders & try them. I will not I designate who.[935] Lorenzo Snow may stay at home till he gets rested.[936]

The twelve must travel to Save their lives. I feel all the veins & Stratas necessary for [p. [161]] the twelve to move in to save their lives

You can never make any thing out of Benjamin Winchester. if you take him out of the channel he wants to be in.[937]

---

933. See Luke 10:7. JS's assurance that the needs of apostles would be met through goods he received answered an earlier concern of Brigham Young's. (See 334n742 herein.)

934. Miller was a Baptist who claimed that the second coming of Christ would occur around 1843. (See 262n399 herein.)

935. The minutes of the meeting, also kept by Willard Richards, read, "I will not designate. where [they] should go." (Quorum of the Twelve Apostles, Minutes, 19 Apr. 1843.)

936. Snow had recently returned to Nauvoo after serving a mission in England for almost three years. (JS, Journal, 12 Apr. 1843.)

937. Winchester was a successful but controversial and divisive missionary, writer, and local church leader in the Philadelphia area. On 16 May 1842 the Quorum of the Twelve published a notice informing church members that Winchester was "silenced from preaching . . . for not obeying the instruction which he received from the Presidency" during a visit he made to Nauvoo. In July 1842, he was "restored to his

Send Samuel James to England.⁹³⁸ thus saith the Lord, also. Reuben Hedlock. he's a heavenly messenger whereever he goes.⁹³⁹ [*blank*] need not be in a hurry. send these two. & when you think of some one else send them.

John Taylor. I believe you can do more good in the editorial department⁹⁴⁰ than preaching. he can write for thousands to read while he can preach to but few. We have no one else we can trust the paper with. & hardly with you. you suffer the paper to come out with so many mistakes. [p. [162]]

⟨Parley may stay at home & build his house.⟩⁹⁴¹

Bro Geo. A. Smith. I dont know how I can help him to a living. but to go. put on a long face & make them doe [dole?] over to him if he will go his lungs will hold out. the Lord will give him a good pair of lungs yet.—⁹⁴²

Woodruff can be spared from the printing office,⁹⁴³ if you both stay you will die.⁹⁴⁴

Orson Pratt. I want him to go.

---

former fellowship and standing," but church leaders at the same time counseled him to leave Philadelphia. However, Winchester remained in the Philadelphia area, and local leaders continued to complain to leaders in Nauvoo about his activities. ("Notice," *Times and Seasons,* 16 May 1842, 3:798; "Notice," *Times and Seasons,* 15 July 1842, 3:862; Peter Hess, Philadephia, PA, to Hyrum Smith et al., [Nauvoo, IL], 16 Feb. 1843, photocopy, JS Collection, CHL; Whittaker, "East of Nauvoo," 31–83.)

938. James was called on a mission to Scott County, Illinois, ten weeks later. (General Church Minutes, 3 July 1843.)

939. The minutes of the meeting, kept by Willard Richards, say Hedlock "has a heavnly messenger wherever he goes." (Quorum of the Twelve Apostles, Minutes, 19 Apr. 1843.)

940. That is, as editor of the *Times and Seasons.* (See 279n471 herein.)

941. Pratt and his family arrived in Nauvoo on 12 April 1843 after his mission to England. Initially without a home of their own, the family lived for a time in "one small room" that served as "kitchen parlour, dining room, bedroom, & publick office." (Parley P. Pratt, Nauvoo, IL, to John Van Cott, Canaan Four Corners, NY, 7 May 1843, CHL; see also 352n854 herein.)

942. Probably refers to George A. Smith's health problems, which included coughing or spitting up blood on occasion. On 14 July 1843, George A. Smith wrote to his wife, Bathsheba Bigler Smith, from Cincinnati that he had "Not Ben troubled With Bleeding" on this mission, but then noted in an 18 September letter that he "spit some Blood" when speaking in Boylston Hall to one thousand people. (George A. Smith, Cincinnati, OH, to Bathsheba Bigler Smith, Nauvoo, IL, 14 July 1843; George A. Smith, Boston, MA, to Bathsheba Bigler Smith, Nauvoo, IL, 18 Sept. 1843, George Albert Smith, Papers, CHL.)

943. Woodruff had overseen the business aspects of the printing office when the Quorum of the Twelve first purchased the office from Ebenezer Robinson in early February 1842. Woodruff continued to work in the office after JS turned the editorship over to John Taylor in November 1842, at which time Woodruff was identified with Taylor as a printer and publisher of the paper. (JS, Journal, 4 Feb. 1842; Woodruff, Journal, 19 Feb. 1842; Masthead, *Times and Seasons,* 15 Nov. 1842, 4:16.)

944. TEXT: Possibly "d̶i̶e̶ ⟨dis⟩" or "dis". George A. Smith, who was present at this meeting, is apparently responsible for expanding this to "disagree" in draft material for the "History of Joseph Smith" published in early Mormon newspapers. (See Historian's Office, JS History, draft notes, 19 Apr. 1843; George A. Smith, Great Salt Lake City, Utah Territory, to Wilford Woodruff, 21 Apr. 1856, in Historian's Office, Historical Record Book, 218–221; Jessee, "Writing of Joseph Smith's History," 441.)

Bro Brigham asked if he should go? Yes, Go. I want John E. Page. to be called away from pittsburgh. send a good elder to take his place.⁹⁴⁵

Orson Hyde can go. & travel.—

You will all go to Boston.⁹⁴⁶

I want Elder Richards to continue in the history [p. [163]] at present. perhaps he will have to travel some to save his life. The History is going out by little & little in the papers & cutting its way.⁹⁴⁷ so that when it is completed it will not raise a persecution again[s]t us.

When Lyman Wight comes home I intend to send him right back again.⁹⁴⁸

Wᵐ Smith is going east with his sick wife.⁹⁴⁹

I want you to cast up a highway for the saints from here to maine.

[Heber C.] Kimball will travel.

Dont be scart about the temple. dont say any thing against it. but make all men know your mission is to build the Nauvoo House. [p. [164]]

It is not necessary that Joshua Grant should be ordained a high Priest. he is to[o] young. he is one of Zebedee Coltrins children, & has got into Zebedee's spirit. & Jedediah [Grant] also.⁹⁵⁰ & they clip 1/2 their words. & I intend to

---

945. Page was called to serve in Pittsburgh at the 7 April 1842 conference of the church. ("Conference Minutes," *Times and Seasons*, 15 Apr. 1842, 3:761–763.)

946. On this mission, eight members of the Quorum of the Twelve—Brigham Young, Heber C. Kimball, Parley P. Pratt, Orson Pratt, Orson Hyde, John E. Page, Wilford Woodruff, and George A. Smith—held a conference in Boston on 9–11 September 1843. Most had traveled there in groups and held smaller conferences between early July and early September in many locations, including New York, Philadelphia, Cincinnati, and Pittsburgh. (JS History, vol. E-1, 1716–1733; Woodruff, Journal, 7 July–10 Sept. 1843; George A. Smith to Bathsheba Bigler Smith, Nauvoo, IL, 14 and 21 July 1843; 2, 14, and 30 Aug. 1843; 10 and 18 Sept. 1843, George Albert Smith, Papers, CHL.)

947. Richards took over compiling and writing JS's history on 1 December 1842. The first installment of the history had been published in the 15 March 1842 issue of the *Times and Seasons*. By 15 April 1843 an additional twenty-five installments—one in each issue of the paper since the 15 March 1842 issue—had been published, bringing the published history up to the arrival of Oliver Cowdery, Parley P. Pratt, and other missionaries in Kirtland, Ohio, in the fall of 1830. (JS, Journal, 1 Dec. 1842; 171n566 herein; "History of Joseph Smith," *Times and Seasons*, 15 Mar. 1842, 3:726–728; 15 Apr. 1843, 4:172.)

948. Wight was in Kirtland at the time. He left the Kirtland area 13 May 1843 for Nauvoo, where he arrived 16 June 1843. ("Minutes of a Conference," *Times and Seasons*, 1 Aug. 1843, 4:282–286; Wight, *Address by Way of an Abridged Account*, 4; Lyman Wight, Mountain Valley, TX, to Wilford Woodruff, [Salt Lake City, Utah Territory], 24 Aug. 1857, p. 12, Historian's Office, Histories of the Twelve, ca. 1858–1880, CHL.)

949. William Smith's wife, Caroline Grant Smith, began suffering from dropsy, or edema, shortly after her arrival in Illinois in 1839. In 1843 she and William moved to Philadelphia, where she underwent treatment by a doctor "Celebrated for the Cure of Dropsy." Caroline died in May 1845. ("Funeral of Mrs. Caroline Smith," *Times and Seasons*, 1 June 1845, 6:918–920; William Smith, [Philadelphia, PA], to JS, Nauvoo, IL, 28 Oct. 1843, JS Collection, CHL.)

950. Jedediah and Joshua Grant held the office of seventy in the Melchizedek Priesthood. (Young, *History of the Organization of the Seventies*, 2–3.)

heal them of it.—[951] If a highpriet [high priest] comes along and goes to snub. him. let him knock his teeth down his throat &^c^. &^c^—

You shall make a monstrous wake as you go.

[William] Clayton, tell the temple committee to put hands on that house (Diagonal corner f[r]om the Brick Store) to finish it ~~forthwith.~~ right off. the Lord hath need of other houses as well as a temple.[952]

If I can sell $10,000 of property this spring. I will meet you at any confrence in [p. [165]] Maine, or any confernce where you are and stay as long as it is wisdom.

Take [*blank*] Zundall [John Jacob Zundel] & [*blank*] [*blank*] Messer [Frederick Moeser] & tell them never to drink a drop of ale, or wine ⟨or any spirit⟩ only that which flows right out from the presence of God. & send them to Germany.[953] & when you meet with an Arab. send him to Arabia, when you find an Italian send him to Italy. & a french man to France. or an Indian that is suitable. send him among the Indians. & this & that man send them. to the diff[er]ent places where they belong.— send sombody to Central America. To Spanish [p. [166]] America & dont let a single corner of the earth go without a mission.

Write to Oliver Cowdery. & ask him if he has not eat husks long enough:[954] if he is not [*illegible*][955] ready to return & go up to Jerusalem, Orson Hyde hath need of him.[956] (A letter was written & signed by the me[m]bers of the Quorum present)[957]

---

951. The edited report of the discourse contained in JS's manuscript history clarifies JS's statements about Jedediah Grant, Joshua Grant, and Zebedee Coltrin: "It is not necessary that Jedediah and Joshua Grant should be ordained High Priests, in order to preside they are too young; they have got into Zebedee Coltrin's habit of clipping half their words, and I intend to break them of it." (JS History, vol. D-1, 1539.)

952. JS's new home, the "Nauvoo Mansion," on the corner of Main and Water streets in Nauvoo. The building was to serve as a hotel as well as JS's home. He moved into the home about 31 August 1843 and opened it as a hotel on 3 October 1843. (JS, Journal, 31 Aug. and 15 Sept. 1843; "Pleasure Party, and Dinner at 'Nauvoo Mansion,'" *Nauvoo Neighbor,* 4 Oct. 1843, [4].)

953. Neither man served a mission to Germany at this time.

954. See Luke 15:16. Cowdery, one of the Three Witnesses to the Book of Mormon, had been excommunicated from the church in 1838 and was living in Tiffin, Ohio. Prior to JS's request that members of the Quorum of the Twelve write to Cowdery, Phineas Young, who kept in contact with Cowdery, had written to Brigham Young and Willard Richards that Cowdery's "heart is still with his old friends" and that Phineas believed Cowdery "would be with them in person . . . soon" if misunderstandings were resolved. (JS, Journal, 12 Apr. 1838, in *JSP,* J1:251–255; Phineas Young to Brigham Young and Willard Richards, 14 Dec. 1842, Brigham Young Office Files, CHL.)

955. TEXT: Possibly "not" or "mst".

956. Hyde returned from a mission to Europe and Jerusalem in December 1842. (JS, Journal, 7 Dec. 1842.)

957. In their letter, dated 19 April 1843, the Twelve told Cowdery that they "thought perhaps our old, long esteemed friend might by this time have felt his lonely solitary situation . . . & that he might have a

Joseph went home about 4½ P.M.
Voted that W. Richards procure a good book for the records of the Twelve.—
Voted that O. Hyde & W. Richards take charge of the book & bring up the records.— ad^d. [adjourned] Monday next. 1. P.M. [p. [167]] [*page [168] blank*]

20 April 1843 • Thursday

Thursday April 20^[th] 1843 out on the prairie with [William] Clayton
P.M. settled with Manhard—[958]
listined to the proof of the Elders Confere[n]ce.[959] [*11 lines blank*] [p. [169]]

21 April 1843 • Friday

Friday April 21. officer Drill[960] [*14 lines blank*] [p. [170]] [*page [171] blank*]

22 April 1843 • Saturday

Saturday April 22. The Cohorts of the Legion were ~~on~~ in exercise this day.[961] & Liut [Lieutenant] Gen— J.— Smith's Staff[962] came out by his invitation. & spent the day in riding exercising or organizing. & in council or court. Martial to ascertan to what staff ~~the~~ Robert D. Foster, Surgeon Gen. Hugh Mc.Fall. adgutant gen, Daniel H. Wells Commiss[a]ry Gen. & Leona[r]d Soby Quarter Ma[s]ter. Gen, belonged[963] [*6 lines blank*] [p. [172]] [*page [173] blank*]

---

disposition to return." If such was the case, they assured him, "your brethren are ready to receive you." Cowdery responded to the Twelve's invitation—which was not mailed from Nauvoo until 10 December 1843—on 25 December 1843, briefly alluding to "ambitious and wicked men" whose false charges had resulted in his excommunication. Assuring the Twelve that "I entertain no unkindly feelings toward you, or either of you," Cowdery quietly passed over their invitation to return to the church at that time; he later returned to the church and was rebaptized in 1848. (Brigham Young et al., Nauvoo, IL, to Oliver Cowdery, 19 Apr. 1843, copy, Luna Eunice Caroline Young Thatcher, Collection, CHL; Oliver Cowdery to the Quorum of the Twelve Apostles, 25 Dec. 1843, Brigham Young Office Files, CHL.)

958. Clayton's journal for this date reads, "P.M at the pres. endeavoring to settle with Manhards went on foot through the City to shew them lots." (Clayton, Journal, 20 Apr. 1843.)

959. The elders conference was held ten days earlier. The minutes of the conference were published in "Elder's Conference," *Times and Seasons*, 1 Apr. 1843, 4:157–159.

960. According to the second section of the Nauvoo Legion court-martial's "Ordinance No. 3," an officer drill was to be held on the day before the cohort parades, which were to be held on the fourth Saturday of April. (Nauvoo Legion Minute Book, 3 Aug. 1842, 23.)

961. The legion consisted of two "cohorts," the first made up of "horse troops" and the second of infantry. Each cohort was commanded by a brigadier general. Each cohort was to parade on the fourth Saturday of April. (Nauvoo Legion Minute Book, 3 Feb. 1841, 2–3; 3 Aug. 1842, 23.)

962. See Nauvoo Legion Officers, p. 514 herein.

963. Foster, McFall, Wells, and Soby had been members of the staff of John C. Bennett, who was replaced by Wilson Law as major general of the Nauvoo Legion on 13 August 1842.

23 April 1843 • Sunday

⁹⁶⁴Sunday April 23ᵈ 1843. 9 to 10 A.M. at home. with elder [Orson] Hyde heard read thuiana [Truthiana]. N°·, 6,— ⟨objected to its being printed it was too strong meat⟩⁹⁶⁵ and ⟨heard read⟩ minutes of special conference which were not explicit enough &— said he would ~~write~~ dictate them over again.—⁹⁶⁶

11. o'clock meeting at temple Stand. B[righam] Young. Parley [P. Pratt]. & O[rson] Pratt. O[rson] Hyde Geo. A Smith. W[illard] Richards. O. Hyde prayed. B Young. preached 24 past 11. Text. Salvation. Twelve commencd their mission to build the ~~Temple~~ ⁹⁶⁷Nauvoo— House.⁹⁶⁸ ⟨for th[e]⟩ salvation of chu[r]ch it was necessa[r]y thes[e] public buildings should be erected. &ᶜ

P.M. P. P. Pratt addressd the assembly. concrnig [concerning] the city as it was 3 years ago. & as it is. his disappontmet [disappointment] at finding greater [p. [174]] improvements than he anticipated. more brick houses &ᶜ.⁹⁶⁹ Elder [Peter] Haws— spake concerni[n]g the pine country & called for 25 hands to go up thither.⁹⁷⁰ &c. also the N[auvoo] House. Elder Hyde followed. & Elder Brigham Young inst[r]ucted the laborers on the N. House to commence next morning.—⁹⁷¹ beg food of their neighbors, ~~is~~ to commence if necessary. &

---

964. TEXT: Blue ink commences.

965. Willard Richards's first draft of his sixth "Truthiana" letter focused on the Nauvoo Legion, casting Nauvoo and the Saints in a militaristic light many residents of Illinois would have found offensive. Richards rewrote the letter four days later, changing the emphasis to building the Nauvoo House and the strong cooperative ethic of converts immigrating to Nauvoo. ("Truthiana," 1843, draft, CHL; Richards, Journal, 27 Apr. 1843; Willard Richards [Viator, pseud.], Nauvoo, IL, 22 Apr. 1843, Letter to the editor, *Boston Daily Bee,* 22 May 1843, [2]; see also 312n644 herein.)

966. The "special conference" was the conference that began on 6 April 1843. Whether JS again dictated the minutes of the 6–9 April 1843 special conference is unclear. In addition to the account of the conference recorded in JS's journal and the published account in the *Times and Seasons,* four sets of minutes, differing in various ways, are contained in General Church Minutes. (JS, Journal, 6–9 Apr. 1843, pp. 329–350 herein; 329n722 herein.)

967. TEXT: Brown ink commences.

968. Pursuant to the decision of the special conference held on 6 April 1843, JS on 19 April directed the Quorum of the Twelve to go on a mission to collect funds for building the Nauvoo House. (JS, Journal, 6 and 19 Apr. 1843, pp. 334, 365–367 herein; "Special Conference," *Times and Seasons,* 1 May 1843, 4:182–183; see also 369n946 herein.)

969. Pratt had left the Nauvoo area for his first English mission on 29 August 1839 and returned on 7 February 1843—an absence of almost three and a half years. (Pratt, *Autobiography,* chaps. 36–41; Clayton, Journal, 7 Feb. 1843.)

970. Haws, a member of the Nauvoo House Association, had been involved with the church's lumber mills in Wisconsin since 1841, when he and Alpheus Cutler of the temple committee were appointed to "take a company of laborers . . . and enter into the business of lumbering." Two companies of laborers, many with families, went to the "pine country" during summer 1843. (George Miller, St. James, MI, to "Dear Brother," 26 June 1855, *Northern Islander,* 16 Aug. 1855, [3]–[4]; George Miller, St. James, MI, to "Dear Brother," 27 June 1855, *Northern Islander,* 23 Aug. 1855, [1]–[2]; JS, Journal, 21 July 1843, JS Collection, CHL; see also 68n274 herein.)

971. Four days earlier, JS instructed the Quorum of the Twelve to direct Lucien Woodworth to put

requested families to bored [board] hand[s] till means could be procur[e]d. [*7 lines blank*] [p. [175]] [*page [176] blank*]

24 April 1843 • Monday

April 24— Monday ⟨A M.⟩ rode out with his children.

The twelve met at Preside[n]ts J Smiths of 1. P.M. see minutes⁹⁷² [*13 lines blank*] [p. [177]]

25 April 1843 • Tuesday

Tuesday Morning 25 April 9 A.[M.] called at the office a few moments, and heard the report of the proceedings of the 12. the day previous [*10 lines blank*]

3 ⟨o clock⟩ & 15 minuts. rain fell in torrents & wind blew. so dark for 15 minutes could not see to write. considerable hail fell. wind N.W.— land coverd with water. [p. [178]]

26 April 1843 • Wednesday

Wednesday April 26— [*15 lines blank*]
squally. & cool some rain.— [p. [179]]

27 April 1843 • Thursday

Thursday april 27⁽ᵗʰ⁾ 1843 Court. Johnathan Ford. proved a Stolen horse.— See Mayors Docket,⁹⁷³ ~~very pleasant but cool.~~ [*12 lines blank*]
very pleasant, but cool [p. [180]]

28 April 1843 • Friday

Friday April 28⁽ᵗʰ⁾ 9 A.M. at his yard in front of the house. converig [conversing] with a gentle man & giving driectins [directions] to the boys about removing the house banking [*12 lines blank*] [p. [181]]

---

laborers to work on the Nauvoo House. (JS, Journal, 19 Apr. 1843, p. 365 herein.)

972. Seven apostles—Brigham Young, Heber C. Kimball, Orson Hyde, John Taylor, George A. Smith, Willard Richards, and Wilford Woodruff—were present. The apostles voted that "all the Twelve, go to Augusta, Iowa Territory, to spend the next Sabbath. & devise some means to secure the property" that had recently been purchased near the Nauvoo House. The minutes also show that the quorum met again at 5:00 p.m. at Taylor's house, where they voted that Lucien Woodworth be requested to furnish them with a draft of plans for the Nauvoo House. (Quorum of the Twelve Apostles, Minutes, 24 Apr. 1843.)

973. This docket has not been located. It may refer to a continuation of the mayor's court docket generated by John C. Bennett and James Sloan that ends in February 1843.

29 April 1843 • Saturday

Saturday April 29. 1843[974] [*16 lines blank*] [p. [182]]

30 April 1843 • Sunday

Sunday April 30th 1843 10 A.M. Trial before the First presidency— Present Joseph Smith. councellors W[m.] Law & Sidney Rigdon, ~~Anson Matthews vs.~~ Graham Coltrin ⟨vs. Anson Matthews [Mathews]⟩ 12 noon adgoud [adjourned] 1 hour.— ~~Bro John Taylor took minutes in the P.M.~~

⟨appeal from High Council.⟩ On complaint. 1st, For a failure in refusing to perform according to contract respecting the sale of a piece of Land. by him sold to me.

2[d.] for transferring his property in a way to enable him to bid defiance to the result & force of Law. to compel him to evade the aforesaid contract, [p. [183]] thereby wronging me out of my ~~Right~~ Just claim to the same, & also for lying. &[c], &[c], Nauvo[o] March 20th 1843[975]

adgourd [adjourned] from 12 to 1½ o clock. P;M.

witnesses for Plaintiff.— [Henry G.] Sherwood, N[ewman] G. Blodget, Zebedee Coltrin Father coltrin,—[976] Witness for Difendant. [977]⟨2 affidavits— of Geo Reals,⟩[978] Mrs Matthews.[979] Bro Bowitt,[980] Samuel Thompson. Richard Slater,—

---

974. William Clayton recorded that JS "rode out to Prarie" this day in company with himself (Clayton), William Smith, Samuel Smith, and John Topham. (Clayton, Journal, 29 Apr. 1843.)

975. On 20 March 1843, Coltrin charged Mathews and his wife, Elizabeth Burgess Mathews, with unchristian conduct, asserting that Mathews had refused to fulfill a contract "respecting the sale of a piece of Land" to Coltrin and that he had transferred his property in such a way that Coltrin was unable to claim it. In a trial held before the Nauvoo high council on 14 April 1843, Coltrin "admitted" to the first charge but denied the second, after which the high council decided Coltrin's complaint was "sustained in substance" and directed Mathews to abide by the decision or be disfellowshipped. Mathews appealed the case to the First Presidency, asserting that he had not fully understood the charges against him and had not been prepared with suitable witnesses; that he had been deprived of an important witness when the trial was moved to a place other than that originally appointed; and that Coltrin and his witnesses had given "partial and unjust testimony denying positive facts" that Mathews could prove. (Nauvoo High Council Minutes, 14 Apr. 1843; Anson Mathews, "Appeal No. 1," Nauvoo High Council Papers, CHL.)

976. John Coltrin, father of Graham Coltrin and Zebedee Coltrin.

977. TEXT: The caret for the following insertion appears at the beginning of a line, before "dant" in "Difendant".

978. A possible reference to two statements (rather than formal affidavits) by Reals supporting Mathews's claims. Official minutes of the trial identify these statements as "George Reels testimony." (George Reals, Statements, Nauvoo High Council Papers, CHL; "Trial before the First Presidency," 30 Apr. 1843, p. 5, JS Collection, CHL.)

979. Elizabeth Burgess Mathews.

980. Spelled "Browit" in the First Presidency minutes of this trial. Possibly Daniel Browett, a convert from England. ("Trial before the First Presidency," 30 Apr. 1843, p. 4, JS Collection, CHL; Quorum of the Twelve Apostles, Minutes, 11 Feb. 1841; Record of Seventies, bk. B, 47, 113.)

Decision of Court is that the charges are not sustained. (See Minutes on file)⁹⁸¹

adjournd to next Sunday— 2 oclock P.M. [p. [184]]

B[righam] Young H[eber] C Kimball. W[ilford] Woodruff & Geo. A Smith. & Joseph You[n]g were at Augusta & Iowa— and held meeting⁹⁸² [*13 lines blank*] [p. [185]]

[*The second and final part of this journal will appear in* Journals, Volume 3]

---

981. "Trial before the First Presidency," 30 Apr. 1843, JS Collection, CHL.

982. Six days earlier, on 24 April 1843, members of the Twelve voted to spend Sunday, 30 April, in Augusta. According to Woodruff, Peter Haws accompanied the five men mentioned in the journal. Woodruff reported that they "held a conference at Augusta" and "preached the Nauvoo House & many Promised to assist in building it." (372n971 herein; Woodruff, Journal, 29 and 30 Apr. 1843.)

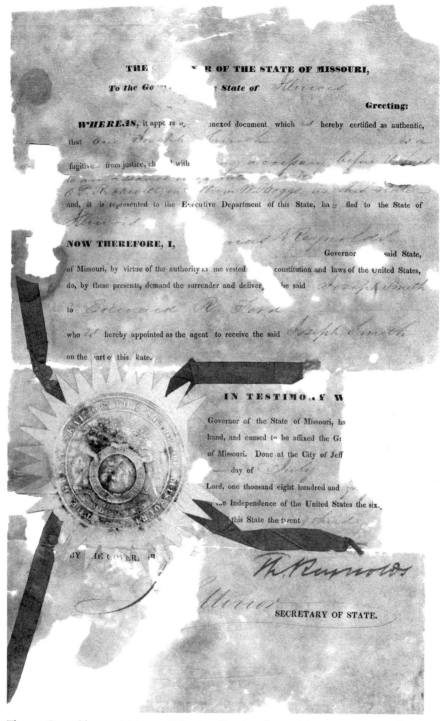

Thomas Reynolds, requisition. 22 July 1842. Based on former Missouri governor Lilburn W. Boggs's affidavit stating that Joseph Smith had been complicit in an attempt made on Boggs's life on 6 May 1842, Missouri governor Thomas Reynolds issued a requisition to Illinois governor Thomas Carlin, demanding that Smith be extradited to Missouri for trial. This extradition attempt ended with Illinois governor Thomas Ford's 6 January 1843 order discharging Joseph Smith. (Courtesy Abraham Lincoln Presidential Library, Springfield, IL.)

APPENDIX 1: MISSOURI EXTRADITION ATTEMPT, 1842–1843, SELECTED DOCUMENTS

Introduction

On 6 May 1842, former Missouri governor Lilburn W. Boggs was shot at his home in Independence, Missouri. Boggs's injuries were serious but not fatal. The ensuing criminal investigation focused first on a silversmith named Tompkins.[1] However, early insinuations about a possible Mormon involvement soon gained greater traction after John C. Bennett, the former mayor of Nauvoo, Illinois, published reports alleging that JS's associate Orrin Porter Rockwell, who was in Independence at the time of the assassination attempt, committed the crime at the express direction of JS. While no direct evidence implicated either Rockwell or JS, animosity was known to exist between the accused men and Boggs because Boggs had played a pivotal role in the expulsion of the Mormons from Missouri in 1838.

In an affidavit dated 20 July 1842, Boggs stated that based on "evidence and information now in his possession," he believed JS was an accessory before the fact in orchestrating the assassination attempt. Based on that affidavit, Missouri governor Thomas Reynolds issued a requisition on 22 July 1842 for the extradition of JS from Illinois to Missouri, claiming he was a fugitive from justice.[2] Illinois governor Thomas Carlin then issued an arrest warrant for JS based on Reynolds's requisition. JS was arrested in Nauvoo on 8 August 1842 and immediately petitioned for a writ of habeas corpus. The Nauvoo Municipal Court granted the writ and ordered JS to appear before it for a hearing on the arrest. The arresting officer, uncertain as to the legality of the municipal court's actions, returned the writ and arrest warrant to Carlin, thereby necessitating the release of JS. Governor Carlin disputed the effort to review the arrest, claiming that the municipal court lacked legal authority to rule on the warrant. On 20 September 1842, Governor Carlin increased his efforts to comply with Missouri's extradition request by issuing a proclamation

---

1. McLaws, "Attempted Assassination," 53–55.
2. This requisition began the second of three attempts (1840–1841, 1842–1843, and 1843) to extradite JS to Missouri.

offering a reward to any citizen for the capture of JS, who had gone into hiding to avoid arrest.

In August 1842, Thomas Ford, a lawyer and former associate justice of the Illinois Supreme Court, was elected Illinois governor, replacing Thomas Carlin. Following this change in administration, a delegation representing JS traveled from Nauvoo to Springfield in early December to determine Governor Ford's disposition regarding the extradition efforts. Meeting with several prominent attorneys, judges, and politicians, including Ford, the delegation concluded that should JS appear in Springfield, the entire situation could be resolved satisfactorily. The delegation also met with Justin Butterfield, the United States attorney for the district of Illinois, and retained him to represent JS in the matter.

Accompanied by a few close colleagues, JS left for Springfield on 27 December 1842 and arrived on 30 December. Upon JS's arrival, Butterfield recommended filing a new petition for a writ of habeas corpus in federal court before Judge Nathaniel Pope. As the petition needed to be based on an arrest and as the original arrest warrant was not immediately available, the following day (Saturday, 31 December 1842) Butterfield filed a petition for a new arrest warrant. Governor Ford issued the new arrest warrant the same day, and Butterfield filed a petition for a writ of habeas corpus. Pope granted and issued the writ, set bail at $4,000, and scheduled the hearing on the writ for the following Monday, 2 January 1843.

On Monday morning, JS (represented by Butterfield) and the state of Illinois (represented by Illinois attorney general Josiah Lamborn) appeared before Judge Pope. Lamborn asked for a continuance to prepare for the hearing on the writ. Pope granted the request and moved the hearing to Wednesday, 4 January 1843.

At the hearing, Lamborn, speaking first, made two substantive arguments: First, the case should be dismissed because the federal court lacked jurisdiction to rule on the arrest warrant and underlying requisition as these matters were governed by the state. Second, no factual inquiry was appropriate and the court should consider only any procedural irregularities in the extradition pleadings. Butterfield and his associate counsel, Benjamin Edwards, countered that a matter of extradition arising between two states was inherently, perhaps exclusively, a federal issue as contemplated by the United States Constitution. Second, Butterfield argued that it was appropriate for the court to examine both the legal sufficiency and the accuracy of the facts underlying the extradition request. This argument included an attack on the admissibility of Boggs's affidavit and proffered additional affidavits rebutting the facts alleged by Boggs. These affidavits were submitted to establish that JS could not be considered a fugitive from Missouri justice because he was in Nauvoo when the assassination attempt occurred.

The following day, Judge Pope announced his opinion from the bench. He ruled that the federal court had jurisdiction over the proceedings as conferred on it by the United States Constitution. Pope then addressed the merits of the case, ruling that he did not need to determine the admissibility of the affidavits submitted by JS, his colleagues, and others, as the Boggs affidavit itself was insufficient to support the requisition. Pope found Boggs's allegations to be both opinion and conclusions of law, neither of which were admissible factual contentions. Finally, the Boggs affidavit failed to aver that JS had actually fled from the state, a prerequisite to his being classified as a fugitive; Missouri governor Reynolds's inclusion of such an allegation in the requisition did not remedy this defect. Based on these findings, Judge Pope ordered the discharge of JS.

Relying in part on the notes that Willard Richards had taken throughout the proceedings, Pope prepared a written opinion of his 5 January ruling. This opinion was first published on 16 January 1843 in the *Times and Seasons;* soon after, it was published in the Springfield newspaper *Sangamo Journal,* as well as in various other newspapers, including the Nauvoo newspaper *The Wasp.* The official version of Judge Pope's opinion was first published in McLean's *Reports* in 1847.[3]

Documents

1. Lilburn W. Boggs, Affidavit, 20 July 1842
2. Thomas Reynolds, Requisition, 22 July 1842
3. Thomas Carlin, Proclamation, 20 September 1842
4. Joseph Smith, Petition for New Arrest Warrant, 31 December 1842
5. Arrest Warrant, 31 December 1842
6. Joseph Smith, Petition for Writ of Habeas Corpus, 31 December 1842
7. Writ of Habeas Corpus, 31 December 1842
8. Joseph Smith, Affidavit, 2 January 1843
9. Wilson Law and Others, Affidavit, 4 January 1843
10. Jacob B. Backenstos and Stephen A. Douglas, Affidavit, 4 January 1843
11. Court Ruling, 5 January 1843
12. Thomas Ford, Order Discharging Joseph Smith, 6 January 1843

---

1. Lilburn W. Boggs, Affidavit, 20 July 1842

Lilburn W. Boggs, Affidavit, [Jackson County, MO], 20 July 1842; handwriting probably of Samuel Weston; signature of Lilburn W. Boggs; one page; JS Extradition Records, 1839–1843, Abraham Lincoln Presidential Library, Springfield, IL. Includes endorsements on verso.

[4]State of Missouri
County of Jackson

[Th]is day Personally Appeared before [me] [Sam]uel Weston a Justice of the peace within and for the County of Jackson the Subscriber Lilburn W Boggs who being Duly sworn Doeth Depose and say that on the night of the Sixth day of May 184[2] while sitting in his Dwelling in the Town of I[nde]pendence

---

3. A comparison of the earlier published versions with the McLean version shows no substantive differences.

4. TEXT: Portions of text in this document are obscured by a ribbon or are missing because of page tears. All supplied text in this transcript comes from a copy of the affidavit inscribed by William Clayton and housed in JS Collection, CHL.

in the County of Jackson he was Sho[t] [wit]h intent to kill and that his life was Despaired of for several days an[d] that he beleives and has good reason to beleive from Evidence and information now [in] his possession that Joseph Smith Com[mo]nly [cal]led the Mormon Prophet was Accessary before the fact of the intended Murder and that the said Joseph Smith is a Citizen or resident of the State of Illinois and the said Deponient hereby Applyes to the Governor of the State of Missouri to make a Demand [on] the Governor of the State of Illinois to Deliver the said Joseph Smith Com[m]only Called the Mormon prophet to some person Autherised to receive and Convey him to the State and County aforesaid there to be dealt with according to Law

Lilburn W Boggs

Sworn to and Subscribed
before me this 20th d[a]y of
July 1842 Samuel Weston JP [p. [1]]
5⟨Demand of the Gov. of
Mo. for Joseph Smith
a fugitive from justice
[*1/4 page blank*]
Warr[an]t issued Augt. 2nd. 1842
[*1/2 page blank*]
Filed Aug [*page torn*] 1842⟩ [p. [2]]

2. Thomas Reynolds, Requisition, 22 July 1842

Thomas Reynolds, Requisition, Jefferson City, MO, to Thomas Carlin, 22 July 1842; printed form with handwriting of an unidentified scribe; signatures of Thomas Reynolds and James L. Minor; one page; JS Extradition Records, 1839–1843, Abraham Lincoln Presidential Library, Springfield, IL.

6THE GOV[ERNO]R OF THE STATE OF MISSOURI,
To the Gove[rnor of th]e State of ⟨Illinois⟩7

Greeting:

WHEREAS, it appe[a]rs by the [an]nexed document, which ⟨is⟩ hereby certified as authentic, that ⟨one Joseph Smith is a⟩ fugitive from justice, ch[arged] with ⟨[bei]ng accessary, before the fact to an assault [with] int[ent] to K[ill, made by one] O P. Rockwell on [Li]lburn W. Boggs, in this State—⟩

---

5. TEXT: The verso page is inscribed in landscape orientation.
6. TEXT: Portions of text in this document are missing because of page tears or are obscured by a ribbon or by the seal that appears after the second paragraph. All supplied text in this transcript comes from a copy of the requisition inscribed by William Clayton and housed in JS Collection, CHL.
7. TEXT: Text appearing in angle brackets in this transcript represents handwritten inscriptions on the printed requisition form.

and, it is represented to the Executive Department of this State, ha⟨s⟩ fled to the State of ⟨Illinois⟩

NOW THEREFORE, I, ⟨[Tho]mas Reynolds⟩ Governor [of the] said State, of Missouri, by virtue of the authority in me vested [by the] constitution and laws of the United States, do, by these presents, demand the surrender and deliver[y] [of] [t]he said ⟨Joseph Smith⟩ to ⟨Edward R. Ford⟩ who ⟨is⟩ hereby appointed as the agent to receive the said ⟨Joseph Smith⟩ on the [p]art o[f] this State.

[*seal*][8]

IN TESTIMONY W[HEREOF, I]

Governor of the State of Missouri, ha[ve hereunto set my] hand, and caused to be affixed the Gr[eat Seal of State] of Missouri. Done at the City of Jeff[erson this]— day of ⟨July⟩ [in the year of our] Lord, one thousand eight hundred and fo[rty two,] o[f] [th]e Independence of the United States the six[ty-seventh and of] this State the twent⟨y third⟩

BY THE GOVERNOR, ⟨Th. Reynolds⟩

⟨J[as L.] Minor⟩ SECRETARY OF STATE.

3. Thomas Carlin, Proclamation, 20 September 1842

Thomas Carlin, "Proclamation," 20 Sept. 1842, published in Illinois Register *(Springfield), vol. 7, no. 32 (new series vol. 4, no. 9), 30 Sept. 1842, p. [3]; edited by William Walters and George R. Weber. The microfilm copy of the text excerpted herein was filmed by the Department of Photographic Reproductions, University of Chicago Library, Chicago, IL, 1968.*

PROCLAMATION.

EXECUTIVE DEPARTMENT, ILL.,
September 20th, 1842.

WHEREAS, a requisition has been made upon me, as the executive of this State, by the Governor of the State of Missouri, for the apprehension and surrender of O. P. Rockwell who is charged with the crime of shooting Lilburn W. Boggs with intent to kill, in the County of Jackson and State of Missouri on the night of the Sixth day of May A D. 1842. And whereas, a demand has also been made by the Governor of Missouri upon me for the apprehension and surrender of Joseph Smith (commonly called the Mormon Prophet) who is charged with the crime of being accessory to the shooting of said Boggs at the time and place aforesaid, with intent to kill.

---

8. TEXT: Official seal of the state of Missouri.

And whereas in obedience to the Constitution and Laws of the United States, and of this State, executive [w]arrants⁹ have been issued, and the said Rockwell and Smith arrested as fugitives from justice from the State of Missouri.

And whereas, the said Rockwell and Smith resisted the laws by refusing to go with the officers who had them in custody as fugitives from justice, and escaped from the custody of said officers.

Now, therefore, I, Thomas Carlin, Governor of the State of Illinois, in conformity to an act entitled "An act concerning fugitives from justice," approved January 6, 1827, do offer a reward of two hundred dollars to any person or persons, for the apprehension and delivery of each, or either of the above named fugitives from justice, viz: O. P. Rockwell and Joseph Smith, to the custody of James M Pitman and Thomas C. King, or to the sheriff of Adams county at the city of Quincy.

In testimony whereof, I have hereunto set my hand, and caused the great seal of State to be affixed the day and date above mentioned.

[L.S]¹⁰

By the Governor,

THO. CARLIN.

Lyman Trumbull, Sec. of State.

The Fulton Advocate, Quincy Herald, Galena Sentinel, and Rockford Pilot, will copy the above 2 weeks.

9–2w–$3.

4. Joseph Smith, Petition for New Arrest Warrant, 31 December 1842

JS, [Springfield, IL], Petition to Thomas Ford, [Springfield, IL], 31 Dec. 1842; handwriting of Justin Butterfield; signature of JS; two pages; JS Extradition Records, 1839–1843, Abraham Lincoln Presidential Library, Springfield, IL. Includes endorsements.

/¹¹To his excel[*page torn*]cy

¹²To his excellency Thomas F[or]d
Governor of the State of Illinois

---

9. Omitted letter "w" supplied from another copy of the item.
10. "L.S" is an abbreviation for *locus sigilli,* Latin for "location of the seal."
11. TEXT: Justin Butterfield handwriting begins.
12. TEXT: Portions of text in this document are missing because of page tears. All supplied text in this transcript comes from a copy of the petition written in an unidentified hand and housed in JS Collection, CHL.

the Petition of Joseph Smith Respectfully showeth that he has come to Springfield for the purpose of being arrested upon the warrant issued against him by Governor Carlin upon the requesitin of the Govenor of Missouri: and suing out a habeas Corpus to test the validity of the arrest and the p[ower] of the Governor to surrender him up to the authorities of Missouri in this case— he is informed that the persons who [h]ave the said warra[n]t have been duly directed by the Secretary of State to place the same in the hands of the Sheriff of Sangamon Conty [in] order that your petitioner might be arrested thereon but that the said direction has not been complied with— and that the said warrant is [n]ow at Quincy in this State— your petitioner therefore respectfully request that another or an alias warrant may be issued upon the said requisition an[d] deliver[ed] to said person in this City to be served in order that your Petitioner may [p.[1]] test the right of the Executive of this State to surrender your Petition to the Executive of Missouri upon the said requisition, by habeas corpus upon petitioner makes this request for the sole pupose of having this question settled by the Judicial Tribunal it being expessly undertood that he waive none of his legal rights in making this request,

Joseph [S]mith

dated Dcmbr 3[1], 1842
/¹³⟨1842
/¹⁴Let a warrant issue
as within prayed f[or]
directed to /¹⁵the Shff of
Sangamon County
Thomas Ford
/¹⁶Filed Dec. 31. 1842⟩ [p. [2]]

5. Arrest Warrant, 31 December 1842

Arrest Warrant, Thomas Ford, [Springfield, IL], to William F. Elkin, Springfield, IL, 31 Dec. 1842; handwriting of William Trumbull and probably William F. Elkin; signatures of Thomas Ford, Lyman Trumbull, and William F. Elkin; two pages; JS Extradition Records, 1839–1843, Abraham Lincoln Presidential Library, Springfield, IL.

---

13. TEXT: Justin Butterfield handwriting ends; unidentified begins. Remainder of document is written sideways, as if the page was turned ninety degrees clockwise.
14. TEXT: Unidentified handwriting ends; Justin Butterfield begins.
15. TEXT: Justin Butterfield handwriting ends; Thomas Ford begins.
16. TEXT: Thomas Ford handwriting ends; unidentified begins.

/¹⁷The people of the state of Illinois To the sheriff of Sangamon County Greeting:

Whereas it has been made known to me by the Executive Authority of the state of Missouri that one Joseph Smith stands charged by the affidavit of Lilburn W Boggs made on the 20th day of July 1842 at the County of Jackson in the state of Missouri before Samuel Weston a justice of the peace within and for the County of Jackson aforesaid, with being accessary before the fact to an assault with intent to kill made by one O P. Rockwell on Lilburn W Boggs on the night of the sixth day of May AD 184[2] at the County of Jackson in said state [of Missouri] and that the said Joseph Smith has fled [from the] Justice of said state and taken reffuge in [the] [S]tate of Illinois.

Now therefore, I Thomas F[ord] Governor of the state of Illinois pursuant t[o] [t]he constitution and laws of the United States a[nd] of this state, do hereby command you to arre[st] [and] apprehend the said Joseph Smith if [he be found] within the limits of the state aforesaid and cause him to be safely kept and delivered to the custody of Edward R Ford who has been duly Constituted the agent of the said state of Missouri to receive said fugitive from the Justic of said state, he paying all fees and charges for the arrest and apprehension of said Joseph Smith and make due return to the Executive Department of this state the manner in which this writ may be executed

In testimony whereof I have hereunto set my hand and caused the Great seal of [p.[l]] state to be affixed. Done at the City of Springfield this 31st day of December in the year of our Lord one thousand Eight hundred and forty two and of the Independence of the United States the Sixty seventh

[seal]¹⁸

By the Governor

/¹⁹Thomas Ford

/²⁰Lyman Trumbull,
Secretary of state

/²¹Executed this writ immediately after receiving it, by arresting and taking into my Custody the within named Joseph Smith— and soon thereafter and on the ◊◊me day, to wit, the 31st day of December 1842 was servd with a writ of <u>Habe</u>[page torn] <u>Corpus</u>, issued by the Circuit Court of the United

---

17. TEXT: William Trumbull handwriting begins. Portions of text are missing because of damage to the document. All supplied text in this transcript comes from a copy of the first portion of the arrest warrant, inscribed by William Clayton and housed in JS Collection, CHL.

18. TEXT: Embossed imprint of official seal of the state of Illinois.

19. TEXT: William Trumbull handwriting ends; Thomas Ford begins.

20. TEXT: Thomas Ford handwriting ends; Lyman Trumbull begins.

21. TEXT: Lyman Trumbull handwriting ends; unidentified begins—probably William F. Elkin.

St[*page torn*]es for the district of Illinois, Commanding me to shew by what authority I held the said Joseph Smith in Custody— to which [*page torn*] of Habeas Corpus, I returned that I detained the said Joseph Smith by virtue of the within Warrant— And thereupon the said Circuit Court took into its custody the said Joseph Smith and appointed the 4th. day of January 1843 for the hearing of said Cause—

And afterwards to wit: the 4th. day of January 1843 said cause was heard by said Circuit Court, and the said Joseph ⟨Smith⟩ discharged from the arrest of this writ— all of which will more fully appear by reference to the Records of said United States Circuit Court

William F. Elkin Shff S.C.

January 6th. 1843. [p.[2]]

6. Joseph Smith, Petition for Writ of Habeas Corpus, 31 December 1842

JS, Petition to the United States Circuit Court for the District of Illinois, Springfield, IL, 31 Dec. 1842; reference copy; handwriting of William Clayton; two pages; JS Collection, CHL.

To the Honorable the Circuit Court of the United States for the District of Illinois

The petition of Joseph Smith respectfully sheweth that he has been arrested and is detained in custody by William F. Elkin Sheriff of Sangamon County upon a Warrant issued by the Governor of the State of Illinois upon the requisition of the Governor of Missouri as a fugitive from justice a copy of the said Warrant and the requisition and the affidavit upon which the same was issued is hereto annexed. And your petitioner is also arrested by Wilson Law and by him also held and detained in custody (jointly with the said Sheriff of Sangamon County) upon a proclamation issued by the Governor of the State of Illinois a copy of which proclamation is hereunto annexed.— Your Petitioner prays that a writ of Habeas Corpus may be issued by this Court directed to the said William F. Elkin and Wilson Law commanding them forthwith and without delay to bring your Petitioner before this Honorable Court to abide such order and direction as the said Court may make in the premises. Your Petitioner states that he is arrested and detained as aforesaid under color of a law of the United States and that his arrest and detention is illegal and in violation of law, and without the authority of law, in this, that your Petitioner is not a fugitive from justice nor has he fled from the State of Missouri. [p. [1]] And your Petitioner as in duty bound will ever pray——

Joseph Smith. [p. [2]]

7. Writ of Habeas Corpus, 31 December 1842

Writ of Habeas Corpus, Roger Taney to William F. Elkin and Wilson Law, 31 Dec. 1842; reference copy; handwriting of William Clayton; two pages; JS Collection, CHL.

The United States of America
To William F. Elkin Sheriff of Sangamon County State of Illinois & Wilson Law

Greeting— We command you, that you do forthwith, without excuse or delay, bring or cause to be brought, before the Circuit Court of the United States for the District of Illinois; at the District Court Room in the City of Springfield· the body of Joseph Smith, by whatever name or addition he is known or called, and who is unlawfully detained in your custody, as it is said, with the day, and cause of his caption and detention; then & there to perform and abide such order and direction as the said Court shall make in that behalf. And hereof make due return, under the penalty of what the law directs.

Witness Roger B. Taney chief Justice of the Supreme Court of the United States at Springfield in the District of Illinois this 31 day of December A.D. 1842 & of our Indepence the 67. year.— James F. Owings clk

L.S.[22] [p. [1]]

And afterwards on the said 31$^{st.}$ day of December aforesaid the said writ of Habeas Corpus was returned, with returns endorsed thereon in the words and figures following

I William F. Elkin Sheriff of Sangamon County do hereby return to the within writ that the within named Joseph Smith is in my custody by virtue of a Warrant issued by the Governor of the State of Illinois upon the requisition of the Governor of the State of Missouri made on the affidavit of L. W. Boggs and a copy of the said Warrant requisition and affidavit is hereunto annexed

dated December 31. 1842

W$^{m.}$ F Elkin Shff. S. C.
Illinois

I Wilson Law do return to the within writ that the said Joseph Smith is in my custody by virtue of an arrest made by me of his body under and by virtue of a proclamation of the Gov. of the State of Illinois a copy whereof is hereunto annexed

dated December 31. 1842

Wilson Law

---

22. TEXT: "L.S." (*locus sigilli,* Latin for "location of the seal") is inscribed in larger handwriting within a hand-drawn representation of a seal.

The return to the within writ of Habeas Corpus appears by the foregoing returns and the schedule hereunto annexed, and the body of said Joseph Smith is in Court

December 31. 1842

Wm. Paentiss[23]
U. S. Marshall
Dis^{t.} of Ills [p. [2]]

8. Joseph Smith, Affidavit, 2 January 1843

JS, Affidavit, [Springfield, IL], 2 Jan. 1843; reference copy; handwriting of William Clayton; one page; JS Collection, CHL.

Circuit Court of the United
States District of Illinois
In the matter
of
Joseph Smith upon Habeas Corpus

Joseph Smith being brought up on Habeas Corpus before this Court comes and denies the matter. set forth in the return to the same in this, that he is not a fugitive from the justice of the State of Missouri; but alledges[24] and is ready to prove that he was not in the State of Missouri at the time of the commission of the alledged crime set forth in the affidavit of L. M. Boggs, nor had he been in said State for more than three years previous to that time, nor has he been in that State since that time— but on the contrary at the time the said alledged assault was made upon the said Boggs as set forth in said Affidavit the said Smith was at Nauvoo in the County of Hancock in the State of Illinois, and that he has not fled from the justice of the State of Missouri and taken refuge in the State of Illinois, as is most untruly stated in the warrant upon which he is arrested. and that the matter set forth in the requisition of the Governor of Missouri and in the said Warrant are not supported by oath

Joseph Smith

State of Illinois Ss. Joseph Smith being duly sworn saith that the matter and things set forth in the foregoing statement are true.

Joseph Smith

Sworn and subscribed to before me this 2nd. day of Jany 1843
James F. Owings Clk

---

23. William Prentiss.
24. TEXT: Possibly "alleages".

9. Wilson Law and Others, Affidavit, 4 January 1843

Wilson Law, Henry G. Sherwood, Theodore Turley, Shadrack Roundy, Willard Richards, William Clayton, John Taylor, William Marks, and Lorin Walker, Affidavit, [Springfield, IL], 4 Jan. 1843; reference copy; handwriting of Willard Richards and James F. Owings; two pages; JS Collection, CHL.

/²⁵Circuit Court of the United States. District of Illinois——

In the matter of Joseph Smith upon Habeus Corpus }

District of Illinois— Wilson Law, Henry G. Sherwood, Theodore Turley, Shadrach Roundy, and Willard Richards & William Clayton & Hiram Smith being duly sworn say that they know that Joseph Smith was in Nauvoo, in the county of Hancock, in the state of Illinois during the whole of the sixth & seventh days of May last; That on the sixth day of May Aforesaid the said Smith attended an officer drill at Nauvoo from Ten Oclock in the forenoon to about four o'clock in the afternoon at which drill the said Joseph Smith was present: And these deponents Hiram Smith, Willard Richards, Henry G. Sherwood, & John Taylor ⟨and William Clayton——⟩ were with the said Smith, at Nauvoo aforesaid during the evening of the sixth day of May last & sat with said ~~Smith~~ Joseph Smith in Nauvoo Lodge from Six until nine oclock. of said evening;—

and these deponents. Hiram Smith, Willard Richards, & William Marks were with the Said Smith at his dwelling house, in Nauvoo, on and during the evening of the fifth day of May last. & conversed with him;— and ~~these~~ ⟨all⟩ of the deponents aforesaid do say that on the seventh day of May aforesaid the Said Smith reviewed the Nauvoo Legion, & was present with the said Legion all that day, in the presence of many thousand peopl◊, and it would have been impossible for the said Joseph Smith to have been at any place in the State of Missouri, at any time, on or between the sixth & seventh days of May aforesaid; and these deponents Willard Richards William Clayton, Hiram Smith. & Lorin Walker say that they have seen & conversed with the said [p. [1]] Smith at Nauvoo aforesaid. ~~every day~~ ⟨daily⟩ from the Tenth of February last until the first of July last and know that he has not been absent from said city of Nauvoo. at any time, during that time, long enough to have been in the

---

25. TEXT: Willard Richards handwriting begins.

State of Missouri.— that Jackson county in the State of Missouri, is about three hundred miles from Nauvoo

Wilson Law
Henry G. Sherwood
Theodore Turley
Shadrach Roundy—
Willard Richards—
William Clayton
~~Hyrum Smith~~—
John Taylor
William Marks
Lorin Walker

/[26]Sworn to and subscribed in Open Court this 4[th.] Jan. 1843—
Owings Clk
/[27]James H. ~~Judge~~ Ralston
J. N. Morris[28]
Almeron Wheat—
Geo C. Dixon
J. B. Backenstos—
stephn A ~~Judge~~— Duglass—
Jacob Davis— [p. [2]]

10. Jacob B. Backenstos and Stephen A. Douglas, Affidavit, 4 January 1843

Jacob B. Backenstos and Stephen A. Douglas, [Springfield, IL], Affidavit, 4 Jan. 1843; reference copy; handwriting of William Clayton; one page; JS Collection, CHL.

Circuit Court of the United
States, District of Illinois

In the matter
of
Joseph Smith upon
Habeas Corpus

---

26. TEXT: Willard Richards handwriting ends; James F. Owings begins.
27. TEXT: James F. Owings handwriting ends; Willard Richards begins. This line and the six following it are written sideways across the page beneath Owings's inscription, as if the page was turned ninety degrees counterclockwise; this entire section is crossed out with a large X.
28. Isaac Newton Morris.

District of Illinois Ss. Stephen A. Douglas James H. Ralston, Almeron Wheat, J. B. Backenstos, being duly sw[o]rn each for himself says that he were at Nauvoo, in the County of Hancock in this State, on the seventh day of May last, that they saw Joseph Smith on that day reviewing the Nauvoo Legion at that place, in the presence of several thousand persons

J. B. Backenstos
Stephen A. Douglas

Sworn to & subscribed in open Court this 4$^{th.}$ Jany 1843
Jas F. Owings Clk

11. Court Ruling, 5 January 1843

John McLean, Reports of Cases Argued and Decided in the Circuit Court of the United States, for the Seventh Circuit; *Cincinnati, OH: Derby, Bradley & Co., 1847; vol. 3, pp. 121–139; includes typeset signature marks.*

CIRCUIT COURT OF THE UNITED STATES.
ILLINOIS—DECEMBER TERM, 1842.
BEFORE THE HONORABLE NATHANIEL POPE.

The following case was decided by Judge Pope, the district judge. Judge McLean does not attend the winter term in Illinois.

EX PARTE JOSEPH SMITH, (THE MORMON PROPHET,) ON HABEAS CORPUS.

J. Butterfield & B. S. Edwards, counsel for Smith.

J. Lamborn, attorney general, for the state of Illinois.

THIS case came before the court upon a return to a writ of *habeas corpus,* which was issued by this court on the 31st of December, 1842, upon a petition for a *habeas corpus* on the relation of Joseph Smith, setting forth that he was arrested and in custody of William F. Elkin, sheriff of Sangamon county, upon a warrant issued by the governor of the state of Illinois, upon a requisition of the governor of the state of Missouri, demanding him to be delivered up to the governor of Missouri, as a fugitive from justice; that his arrest, as aforesaid, was under color of a law of the [p. [121]] United States, and was without the authority of law in this, that he was not a fugitive from justice, nor had he fled from the state of Missouri.

Afterwards, on the same day, the sheriff of Sangamon county returned upon the said *habeas corpus,* that he detained the said Joseph Smith in custody, by virtue of a warrant issued by the governor of the state of Illinois, upon the requisition of the governor of the state of Missouri, made on the affidavit of Lilburn W. Boggs. Copies of the said affidavit, requisition and warrant were annexed to the said return in the words and figures following:

"State of Missouri, } ss.
County of Jackson,

This day personally appeared before me, Samuel Weston, a justice of the peace within and for the county of Jackson, the subscriber, Lilburn W. Boggs, who, being duly sworn, doth depose and say, that on the night of the 6th day of May, 1842, while sitting in his dwelling in the town of Independence, in the county of Jackson, he was shot with intent to kill, and that his life was despaired of for several days; and that he believes, and has good reason to believe, from evidence and information now in his possession, that Joseph Smith, commonly called the Mormon Prophet, was accessory before the fact of the intended murder; and that the said Joseph Smith is a citizen or resident of the state of Illinois; and the said deponent hereby applies to the governor of the state of Missouri to make a demand on the governor of the state of Illinois, to deliver the said Joseph Smith, commonly called the Mormon Prophet, to some person authorised to receive and convey him to the state and county aforesaid, there to be dealt with according to law.

LILBURN W. BOGGS.

Sworn to and subscribed before me, this 20th day of July, 1842.

SAMUEL WESTON, J. P." [p. 122]

"The Governor of the State of Missouri,
To the Governor of the State of Illinois—GREETING.

Whereas, It appears by the annexed document, which is hereby certified to be authentic, that one Joseph Smith is a fugitive from justice, charged with being accessory before the fact to an assault with intent to kill, made by one O. P. Rockwell, on Lilburn W. Boggs, in this state, and it is represented to the executive department of this state, has fled to the state of Illinois:

Now, therefore, I, Thomas Reynolds, governor of the said state of Missouri, by virtue of the authority in me vested by the constitution and laws of the United States, do by these presents demand the surrender and delivery of the said Joseph Smith to Edward R. Ford, who is hereby appointed as the agent to receive the said Joseph Smith, on the part of this state.

In testimony," &c.

"The People of the State of Illinois,
To the Sheriff of Sangamon County—GREETING.

Whereas, It has been made known to me by the Executive authority of the state of Missouri, that one Joseph Smith stands charged by the affidavit of one Lilburn W. Boggs, made on the 20th day of July, 1842, at the county of Jackson, in the state of Missouri, before Samuel Weston, a justice of the peace, within and for the county of Jackson aforesaid, with being accessory before the fact to an assault with an intent to kill, made by one O. P. Rockwell, on

Lilburn W. Boggs, on the night of the 6th day of May, 1842, at the county of Jackson, in said state of Missouri, and that the said Joseph Smith has fled from the justice of said state, and taken refuge in the state of Illinois:

Now, therefore, I, Thomas Ford, governor of the state of Illinois, pursuant to the constitution and laws of the United States, and of this state, do hereby command you to arrest [p. 123] and apprehend the said Joseph Smith, if he be found within the limits of the state aforesaid, and cause him to be safely kept and delivered to the custody of Edward R. Ford, who has been duly constituted the agent of the said state of Missouri, to receive said fugitive from the justice of said state, he paying all fees and charges for the arrest and apprehension of said Joseph Smith, and make due return to the executive department of this state, the manner in which this writ may be executed.

"In testimony whereof," &c.

The case was set for hearing on the 4th day of January, 1843, on which day Josiah Lamborn, attorney general of the state of Illinois, appeared, and moved to dismiss the proceedings, and filed the following objection to the jurisdiction of the court, viz:

"1st. The arrest and detention of Smith was not under or by color of authority of the United States, or of any officers of the United States, but under and by color of authority of the state of Illinois, by the officers of Illinois.

"2d. When a fugitive from justice is arrested by authority of the governor of any state, upon the requisition of the governor of another state, the courts of justice neither state nor federal, have any authority or jurisdiction to inquire into any facts behind the writ."

The counsel of the said Joseph Smith then offered to read in evidence affidavits of several persons, showing conclusively that the said Joseph Smith was at Nauvoo, in the county of Hancock and state of Illinois, on the whole of the 6th and 7th days of May, in the year 1842, and on the evenings of those days, more than three hundred miles distant from Jackson county, in the state of Missouri, where it is alleged that the said Boggs was shot, and that he had not been in the state of Missouri at any time between the 10th day of February and the 1st day of July, 1842, the said per[p. 124]sons having been with him during the whole of that period. That on the 6th day of May aforesaid, he attended an officers' drill at Nauvoo aforesaid, in the presence of a large number of people, and on the 7th day of May aforesaid he reviewed the Nauvoo Legion in presence of many thousand people.

The reading of these affidavits was objected to by the attorney general of the state of Illinois, on the ground that it was not competent for Smith to impeach or contradict the return to the *habeas corpus*. It was contended by the counsel of the said Smith, 1st. That he had a right to prove that the return was untrue. 2d. That the said affidavits did not contradict the said return, as there was no averment under oath in said return that the said Smith was in Missouri at the time of the commission of the alleged crime, or had fled from the justice of that state. The court decided that the said affidavits should be read in evidence, subject to all objections; and they were read accordingly.

The cause was argued by J. Butterfield and B. S. Edwards, for Smith, and by Josiah Lamborn, attorney general of the state of Illinois, contra.

J. Butterfield, counsel for Smith, made the following points:—

1. This court has jurisdiction.

The requisition purports on its face to be made, and the warrant to be issued, under the Constitution and laws of the United States, regulating the surrender of fugitives from justice.—2d sec. 4th article Const. U. S.—1st sec. of the act of Congress of 12th Feb. 1793.

When a person's rights are invaded under a law of the United States, he has no remedy except in the courts of the United States—2d sec. 3d article Const. U. S. 12th Wend. 325. 16 Peters, 543.

The whole power in relation to the delivering up of fugi[p. 125]tives from justice and labor, has been delegated to the United States, and Congress have regulated the manner and form in which it shall be exercised. The power is exclusive. The state Legislatures have no right to interfere, and if they do, their acts are void.—2d and 3d clause of 2d sec. 4th article Constitution United States—2d vol. laws United States, 331. 16 Peters 617–18, 623. 4th Wheaton's Rep. 122, 193. 12 Wend. 312.

All courts of the United States are authorised to issue writs of *habeas corpus* when the prisoner is confined under or by color of authority of the United States—Act of Congress of Sept. 24th, 1789, sec, 14, 2d Condensed 33. 3d Cranch, 447. 3d Peters, 193.

2. The return to the *habeas corpus* is not certain and sufficient to warrant the arrest and transportation of Smith.

In all cases on *habeas corpus* previous to indictment, the court will look into the depositions before the magistrate, and though the commitment be full and in form, yet if the testimony prove no crime, the court will discharge *ex parte*. Tayler 5th, Cowen 50.

The affidavit of Boggs does not show that Smith was charged with any crime committed by him in Missouri, nor that he was a fugitive from justice.

If the commitment be for a matter for which by law the prisoner is not liable to be punished, the court must discharge him. 3 Bac. 434.

The Executive of this state has no jurisdiction over the person of Smith to transport him to Missouri, unless he has fled from that state.

3. The prisoner has a right to prove facts not repugnant to the return, and even to go behind the return and contradict it, unless committed under a *judgment* of a court of competent jurisdiction. 3d Bacon, 435, 438. 3 Peters, 202. Gale's Rev. Laws of Ills. 323. [p. 126]

The testimony introduced by Smith at the hearing, showing conclusively that he was not a fugitive from justice, is not repugnant to the return.

J. Lamborn, attorney general of the state of Illinois, in support of the points made by him, cited 2d Condensed Rep. 37; Gordon's Digest, 73; Gale's Statutes of Illinois, 318; Conkling, 85; 9th Wendell, 212.

And afterwards, on the 5th day of January, 1843, Judge Pope delivered the following

OPINION.

The importance of this case, and the consequences which may flow from an erroneous precedent, affecting the lives and liberties of our citizens, have impelled the court to bestow upon it the most anxious consideration. The able arguments of the counsel for the respective parties, have been of great assistance in the examination of the important question arising in this cause.

When the patriots and wise men who framed our constitution were in anxious deliberation to form a perfect union among the states of the confederacy, two great sources of discord presented themselves to their consideration; *the commerce between the states, and fugitives from justice and labor.* The border collisions in other countries had been seen to be a fruitful source of war and bloodshed, and most wisely did the Constitution confer upon the National Government, the regulation of those matters, because of its exemption from the excited passions awakened by conflicts between neighboring states, and its ability alone to adopt a uniform rule, and establish uniform laws among all the states in those cases.

This case presents the important question arising under the constitution and laws of the United States, whether a citizen of the state of Illinois can be transported from his [p. 127] own state to the state of Missouri, to be there tried for a crime, which, if he ever committed, was committed in the state of Illinois; whether he can be transported to Missouri, as a fugitive from justice, when he has never fled from that state.

Joseph Smith is before the court, on *habeas corpus,* directed to the sheriff of Sangamon county, state of Illinois. The return shows that he is in custody under a warrant from the executive of Illinois, professedly issued in pursuance of the Constitution and laws of the United States, and of the state of Illinois, ordering said Smith to be delivered to the agent of the executive of Missouri, who had demanded him as a fugitive from justice, under the 2d section, 4th article of the constitution of the United States, and the act of Congress passed to carry into effect that article. The article is in these words, viz: "A person charged in any state with treason, felony, or other crime, who shall flee from justice and be found in another state, shall on demand of the executive authority of the state, from which he fled, be delivered up to be removed to the state having jurisdiction of the crime." The act of Congress made to carry into effect this article, directs that the demand be made on the executive of the state where the offender is found, and prescribes the proof to support the demand, viz: indictment or affidavit.

The court deemed it respectful to inform the governor and attorney general of the state of Illinois, of the action upon the *habeas corpus*. On the day appointed for the hearing, the attorney general of the state of Illinois appeared, and denied the jurisdiction of the court to grant the *habeas corpus*.

1st. Because the warrant was not issued under color or by authority of the United States, but by the state of Illinois.

2d. Because no *habeas corpus* can issue in this case from either the federal or state courts, to inquire into facts [p. 128] behind the writ. In support of the first point, a law of Illinois was read, declaring that whenever the executive of any other state shall demand of the executive of this state, any person as a fugitive from justice, and shall have complied with the requisition of the act of Congress, in that case made and provided, it shall be the *duty* of the executive of this state to issue his warrant to apprehend the said fugitive, &c. It would seem that this act does not purport to confer any additional power upon the executive of this state, independent of the power conferred by the constitution and laws of the United States, but to make it the *duty* of the executive to obey and carry into effect the act of Congress. The warrant on its face purports to be issued in pursuance of the constitution and laws of the United States, as well as of the state of Illinois. To maintain the position that this warrant was not issued under color or by authority of the laws of the United States, it must be proved that the United States could not confer the power on the executive of Illinois. Because if Congress could and did confer it, no act of Illinois could take it away, for the reason that the constitution, and laws of the United States, passed in pursuance of it, and treaties, are the supreme law of the land; and the judges in every state shall be bound thereby, any thing in the constitution or laws of any state to the contrary notwithstanding. This is enough to dispose of that point. If the legislature of Illinois, as is probable, intended to make it the *duty* of the governor to exercise the power granted by Congress, and no more, the executive would be acting by authority of the United States. It may be that the legislature of Illinois, appreciating the importance of the proper execution of those laws, and doubting whether the governor could be punished for refusing to carry them into effect, deemed it prudent to impose it as a duty, the neglect of which would expose him to impeachment. If it intended more, the law [p. 129] is unconstitutional and void. 16 Peters, 617. *Prigg* v. *Pennsylvania.*

In supporting the second point, the attorney general seemed to urge that there was greater sanctity in a warrant issued by the governor, than by an inferior officer. The court cannot assent to this distinction. This is a government of laws, which prescribes a rule of action, as obligatory upon the governor as upon the most obscure officer. The character and purposes of the *habeas corpus* are greatly misunderstood by those who suppose that it does not review the acts of an executive functionary. All who are familiar with English history, must know that it was extorted from an arbitrary monarch, and that it was hailed as a second *magna charta,* and that it was to protect the subject from arbitrary imprisonment by the king and his minions, which brought into existence that great palladium of liberty in the latter part of the reign of Charles the Second. It was indeed a magnificent achievement over arbitrary power. Magna Charta established the principles of liberty; the *habeas corpus* protected them. It matters not how great or obscure the prisoner, how great or obscure the prisonkeeper, this munificent writ, wielded by an independent judge, reaches all. It penetrates alike the royal towers and the local prisons, from the garret to the secret recesses of the dungeon. All doors fly open at its command, and the shackles fall from the limbs of prisoners of state as readily as from those committed by subordinate officers. The warrant of the king and his secretary of state could claim no more exemption from that searching inquiry, "The cause of his caption and detention," than a warrant granted by a justice of the peace. It is contended that the United States is a government of granted powers, and that no department of it can exercise powers not granted. This is true. But the grant is to be found in the 2d section of the 3d article of the Constitution of the United States: [p. 130] "The judicial power shall extend to all cases in law, or equity, arising under this constitution, the laws of the United States, and treaties made and which shall be made under their authority."

The matter under consideration presents *a case* arising under the 2d section, 4th article of the Constitution of the United States, and the act of Congress of February 12th, 1793, to carry it into effect. The judiciary act of 1789 confers on this court (indeed on all the courts of the United States,) power to issue the writ of *habeas corpus,* when a person is confined "under color of or by the authority of the United States." Smith is in custody under color of, and by authority of the 2d section, 4th article of the Constitution of the United States. As to the instrument employed or authorised to carry into effect that article of the Constitution (as he derives from it the authority to issue the warrant,) he must be regarded as acting by the authority of the United States. The power is not official in the governor, but personal. It might have been granted to any one else by name, but considerations of convenience and policy recommended the selection of the executive, who never dies. The citizens of the states are citizens of the United States; hence the United States are as much bound to afford them protection in their sphere, as the states are in theirs.

This court has jurisdiction. Whether the state courts have jurisdiction or not, this court is not called upon to decide.

The return of the sheriff shows that he has arrested and now holds in custody Joseph Smith, in virtue of a warrant issued by the governor of Illinois, under the 2d section of the 4th article of the Constitution of the United States, relative to fugitives from justice, and the act of Congress passed to carry it into effect. The article of the constitution does not designate the person upon whom the demand [p. 131] for the fugitive shall be made; nor does it prescribe the proof upon which he shall act. But Congress has done so. The proof is "an indictment or affidavit," to be certified by the governor demanding. The return brings before the court the warrant, the demand and the affidavit. The material part of the latter is in these words, viz:—"Lilburn W. Boggs, who being duly sworn, doth depose and say, that on the night of the 6th day of May, 1842, while sitting in his dwelling in the town of Independence, in the county of Jackson, he was shot with intent to kill; and that his life was despaired of for several days, and that he believes, and has good reason to believe, from evidence and information now in his possession, that Joseph Smith, commonly called the Mormon prophet, was accessary before the fact of the intended murder, and that the said Joseph Smith is a citizen or a resident of the state of Illinois."

This affidavit is certified by the governor of Missouri to be authentic. The affidavit being thus verified, furnished the only evidence upon which the governor of Illinois could act. Smith presented affidavits proving that he was not in Missouri at the date of the shooting of Boggs. This testimony was objected to by the attorney general of Illinois, on the ground that the court could not look behind the return. The court deems it unnecessary to decide that point, inasmuch as it thinks Smith entitled to his discharge for defect in the affidavit. To authorise the arrest in this case, the affidavit should have stated distinctly, 1st. That Smith had committed a crime. 2d. That he committed it in Missouri.

It must appear that he fled from Missouri, to authorise the governor of Missouri to demand him, as none other than the governor of the state from which he *fled,* can make the demand. He could not have fled from justice, unless he committed a crime, which does not appear. It must appear that the crime was committed in Missouri, to warrant [p. 132] the governor of Illinois in ordering him to be sent to Missouri for trial. The 2d section, 4th article, declares, he "shall be removed to the state having jurisdiction of the crime."

As it is not charged that the crime was committed by Smith in Missouri, the governor of Illinois could not cause him to be removed to that state, unless it can be maintained that the state of Missouri can entertain jurisdiction of crimes committed in other states. The affirmative of this proposition was taken in the argument with a zeal indicating sincerity. But no adjudged case or dictum was adduced in support of it. The court conceives that none can be. Let it be tested by principle.

Man in a state of nature is a sovereign, with all the prerogatives of king, lords and commons. He may declare war and make peace, and, as nations often do who "feel power and forget right," may oppress, rob and subjugate his weaker and unoffending neighbors. He unites in his person the legislative, judicial and executive power—"can do no wrong," because there is none to hold him to account. But when he unites himself with a community, he lays down all the prerogatives of sovereign, (except self-defence,) and becomes a subject. He owes obedience to its laws and the judgments of its tribunals, which he is supposed to have participated in establishing, either directly or indirectly. He surrenders, also, the right of self-redress. In consideration of all which, he is entitled to the aegis of that community to defend him from wrongs. He takes upon himself no allegiance to any other community, so owes it no obedience, and therefore cannot disobey it. None other than his own sovereign can prescribe a rule of action to him. Each sovereign regulates the conduct of its subjects, and they may be punished upon the assumption that they know the rule and have consented to be governed by it. It would be a gross violation of the social compact, [p. 133] if the state were to deliver up one of its citizens to be tried and punished by a foreign state, to which he owes no allegiance, and whose laws were never binding on him. No state can or will do it.

In the absence of the constitutional provision, the state of Missouri would stand on this subject in the same relation to the state of Illinois, that Spain does to England. In this particular, the states are independent of each other. A criminal, fugitive from the one state to the other, could not be claimed as of right to be given up. It is most true, as mentioned by writers on the laws of nations, that every state is responsible to its neighbors for the conduct of its citizens, so far as their conduct violates the principles of good neighborhood. So it is among private individuals.— But for this, the inviolability of territory, or private dwelling, could not be maintained. This obligation creates the right, and makes it the duty of the state to impose such restraints upon the citizen, as the occasion demands. It was in the performance of this duty, that the United States passed laws to restrain citizens of the United States from setting on foot and fitting out military expeditions against their neighbors. While the violators of this law kept themselves within the United States, their conduct was cognizable in the courts of the United States, and not of the offended state, even if the means provided had assisted in the invasion of the foreign state. A demand by the injured state upon the United States for the offenders, whose operations were in their own country, would be answered, that the United States' laws alone could act upon them, and that, as a good neighbor, it would punish them.

It is the duty of the state of Illinois to make it criminal in one of its citizens to aid, abet, counsel, or advise, any person to commit a crime in her sister state. Any one violating the law would be amenable to the laws of Illinois, executed by its own tribunals. Those of Missouri could [p. 134] have no agency in his conviction and punishment. But if he shall go into Missouri, he owes obedience to her laws, and is liable before her courts, to be tried and punished for any crime he may commit there; and a plea that he was a citizen of another state, would not avail him. If he escape, he may be surrendered to Missouri for trial. But when the offence is perpetrated in Illinois, the only right of Missouri is, to insist that Illinois compel her citizens to forbear to annoy her. This she has a right to expect. For the neglect of it, nations go to war and violate territory.

The court must hold that where a necessary fact is not stated in the affidavit, it does not exist. It is not averred that Smith was accessary before the fact, in the state of Missouri, nor that he committed a crime in Missouri: therefore, he did not commit the crime in Missouri—did not flee from Missouri to avoid punishment.

Again, the affidavit charges the shooting on the 6th of May, in the county of Jackson, and state of Missouri, "that he believes and has good reason to believe, from evidence and information now (then) in his possession, that Joseph Smith was accessary before the fact, and is a resident or citizen of Illinois."

There are several objections to this. Mr. Boggs having the "evidence and information in his possession," should have incorporated it in the affidavit, to enable the court to judge of their sufficiency to support his "belief." Again, he swears to a legal conclusion, when he says that Smith was *accessary before the fact*. What acts constitute a man an accessary is a question of law, and not always of easy solution. Mr. Boggs' opinion, then, is not authority. He should have given the facts. He should have shown that they were committed in Missouri, to enable the court to test them by the laws of Missouri, to see if they amounted to a crime. Again, the affidavit is fatally defective in this, that Boggs swears to his *belief.* [p. 135]

The language in the constitution is, "charged with felony, or other crime." Is the constitution satisfied with a *charge* upon suspicion? It is to be regretted that no American adjudged case has been cited to guide the court in expounding this article. Language is ever interpreted by the subject matter. If the object were to arrest a man near home, and there were fears of escape if the movement to detain him for examination were known, the word *charged* might warrant the issuing of a capias on *suspicion*. Rudyard, (reported in Skin.) 676, was committed to Newgate for refusing to give bail for his good behavior, and was brought before the common pleas on *habeas corpus*. The return was, that he had been complained of for exciting the subjects to disobedience of the laws against *seditious conventicles,* and upon examination they found *cause* to suspect him. Vaughan, chief justice, "*Tyrrel and Archer* v. *Wild,* held the return insufficient—1st. because it did not appear but that he might abet frequenters of conventicles in the way the law allows; 2d. to say that he was complained of, or was examined, is no proof of his guilt; and then to say that he had cause to suspect him, is too cautious; for who can tell what they count a cause of *suspicion,* and how can that ever be tried? At this rate they would have arbitrary power, upon their own allegation, to commit whom they pleased."

From this case, it appears that *suspicion* does not warrant a commitment, and that all legal intendments are to avail the prisoner. That the return is to be most strictly construed in favor of liberty. If suspicion in the foregoing case did not warrant a commitment in London by its officers, of a citizen of London, might not the objection be urged with greater force against a commitment of a citizen of our state, to be transported to another, on *suspicion?* No case can arise demanding a more searching scrutiny into the evidence, than in cases arising under this part of [p. 136] the constitution of the United States. It is proposed to deprive a freeman of his liberty—to deliver him into the custody of strangers, to be transported to a foreign state, to be arraigned for trial before a foreign tribunal, governed by laws unknown to him—separated from his friends, his family and his witnesses, unknown and unknowing. Had he an immaculate character, it would not avail him with strangers. Such a spectacle is appalling enough to challenge the strictest analysis.

The framers of the constitution were not insensible of the importance of courts possessing the confidence of the parties. They therefore provided that citizens of the different states might resort to the federal courts in civil causes. How much more important that the criminal have confidence in his judge and jury? Therefore, before the *capias* is issued, the officers should see that the case is made out to warrant it.

Again, Boggs was shot on the 6th of May. The affidavit was made on the 20th of July following. Here was time for inquiry, which would confirm into certainty or dissipate his suspicions. He had time to collect facts to be laid before a grand jury, or be incorporated in his affidavit. The court is bound to assume that this would have been the course of Mr. Boggs, but that his suspicions were light and unsatisfactory.

The affidavit is insufficient—1st. because it is not positive; 2d. because it charges no crime; 3d. it charges no crime committed in the state of Missouri. Therefore, he did not flee from the justice of the state of Missouri, nor has he taken refuge in the state of Illinois.

The proceedings in this affair, from the affidavit to the arrest, afford a lesson to governors and judges, whose action may hereafter be invoked in cases of this character.

The affidavit simply says that the affiant was shot with intent to kill, and he believes that Smith was accessory [p. 137] before the fact to the intended murder, and is a citizen or resident of the state of Illinois. It is not said who shot him, or that the person was unknown.

The governor of Missouri, in his demand, calls Smith a fugitive from justice, charged with being accessary before the fact to an assault with intent to kill, made by one O. P. Rockwell, on Lilburn W. Boggs, in this state (Missouri). This governor expressly refers to the affidavit as his authority for that statement. Boggs, in his affidavit, does not call Smith a *fugitive from justice,* nor does he state a fact from which the governor had a right to infer it. Neither does the name of O. P. Rockwell appear in the affidavit, nor does Boggs say Smith *fled.* Yet the governor says he *fled* to the state of Illinois. But Boggs only says he is a *citizen* or *resident* of the state of Illinois.

The governor of Illinois, responding to the demand of the executive of Missouri for the arrest of Smith, issues his warrant for the arrest of Smith, reciting that—"whereas, Joseph Smith stands charged, by the affidavit of Lilburn W. Boggs, with being accessary before the fact to an assault with intent to kill, made by one O. P. Rockwell, on Lilburn W. Boggs, on the night of the 6th day of May, 1842, at the county of Jackson, in the said state of Missouri, and that the said Joseph Smith has fled from the justice of said state, and taken refuge in the state of Illinois."

Those facts do not appear by the affidavit of Boggs. On the contrary, it does not assert that Smith was accessary to O. P. Rockwell, nor that he had *fled from* the *justice of the state of Missouri, and taken refuge in the state of Illinois.*

The court can alone regard the *facts* set forth in the affidavit of Boggs, as having any legal existence. The mis-recitals and over-statements in the requisition and warrant, are not supported by oath, and cannot be received as evidence to deprive a citizen of his liberty, and transport [p. 138] him to a foreign state for trial. For these reasons, Smith must be discharged.

At the request of J. Butterfield, counsel for Smith, it is proper to state, in justice to the present executive of the state of Illinois, Governor Ford, that it was admitted on the argument, that the warrant which originally issued upon the said requisition, was issued by his predecessor; that when Smith came to Springfield to surrender himself up upon that warrant, it was in the hands of the person to whom it had been issued at Quincy in this state; and that the present warrant, which is a copy of the former one, was issued at the request of Smith, to enable him to test its legality by writ of *habeas corpus*.

Let an order be entered that Smith be discharged from his arrest. [p. 139]

12. Thomas Ford, Order Discharging Joseph Smith, 6 January 1843

Thomas Ford, Order, 6 Jan. 1843; handwriting and signature of Thomas Ford; one page; JS Collection, CHL.

I do hereby certify that I have inspected the foregoing record, and that there is now no further cause for arresting or detaining Joseph Smith therein named by virtue of any proclamation or executive warrant heretofore issued by the Governor of this state and that since the judgment of the Circuit Court of the United States for the District of Illinois all such proclamations and warrants are inoperative and void Witness my hand and seal[29] at Springfield this 6th day of Jany 1843[30]

Thomas Ford
Gov of Ill

---

29. TEXT: No seal is present; however, there is residue, apparently from an adhesive wafer, at the end of the document where a seal apparently once was affixed.

30. TEXT: A broken piece of what appears to be sealing wax is attached above Ford's signature.

APPENDIX 2: WILLIAM CLAYTON, JOURNAL EXCERPT, 1–4 APRIL 1843

Source Note

William Clayton, Journal excerpt, 1–4 Apr. 1843; handwriting of William Clayton; ten pages; in William Clayton, Journals, 3 vols., Nov. 1842–Jan. 1846, CHL. Includes redactions and use marks.

Historical Introduction

William Clayton's personal journal from 1–4 April 1843 served as a source for JS's journal entries for those dates. Clayton accompanied JS on a trip from Nauvoo to Ramus, Illinois, and kept detailed notes of JS's activities and teachings, while Willard Richards, JS's journal keeper, remained in Nauvoo. Richards evidently later composed JS's journal entries for these dates from Clayton's journal and from conversations he had with those who made the trip. As an important primary source for Richards's information about JS's activities at this time, Clayton's journal entries for 1–4 April are reproduced here in full.

---

1 April 1843 • Saturday

Sat 1ˢᵗ· A. M at the Office. Pres. Joseph called for me to go with him to Ramus. about 2 o clock we started O[rson] Hyde & J[acob] B. Backenstos went with us [p. [65]] the roads were very muddy. we arrived about 6½ o clock, and were very joyfully received, we slept at Benj. F. Johnsons.

2 April 1843 • Sunday

Sunday 2— Heard E[lde]r Orson Hyde preach ⟨on 1 Epistle of John 1 chap— 1, 2. 3 verses⟩ ~~on~~ in the A. M. dined at sister [Sophronia Smith] McCleary's Pres. Josephs sister. P. M. Joseph preached on Revelations chap. 5. he called on me to open the meeting. He also preachd on the same subject in the evening. During the day President Joseph made the following remarks on doctrine. "I was once praying very earnestly to know ~~to~~ the time of the comeing of the son of man when I heard a voice repeat the following 'Joseph my son, if thou livest untill thou art 85 years old thou shalt see the face of the son of man, therefore let this suffice and trouble me no more on this matter.' [p. 66] I was left thus without being able to decide wether this coming referred to the beginning of the Millenium, or to some previous appearing, or wether I should die and thus see his face. I believe the coming of the son of man will not be any sooner than that time" In correct⟨ing⟩ two points in E[lde]r Hydes discourse he observed as follows, "The meaning of that passage where it reads 'when he shall appear we shall be like him for we shall see him as he is' is this, When the saviour appears we shall see that he is a man like unto ourselves, and that same sociality which exists amongst us here will exist among us then[1] only it will be coupled with eternal glory which we do not enjoy now. [p. 67] Also The appearing of the father and the son in John c 14 v 23 is a personal appearing, and the idea that they will dwell in a mans heart is a sectarian doctrine and is false"

In answer to a question which I proposed to him as follows, 'Is not the reckoning of Gods time, Angels time, prophets time & mans time according to the planet on which they reside he answered Yes "But there is no Angel ministers to this earth only what either does belong or has belonged to this earth And the Angels do not reside on a planet like our earth but they dwell with God and the planet where he dwells is like crystal, and like a sea of glass before the throne. This is the great Urim & Thummim whereon all things [p. 68] are manifest both things past, present & future and are continually before the Lord. The Urim & Thummim is a small representation of this globe. The earth when it is purified will be made like unto crystal and will be a Urim & Thummim whereby all things pertaining to an inferior kingdom, or all kingdoms of a lower order will manifest to those who dwell on it. And this earth will be with Christ Then the white stone mentioned in Rev. c 2 v 17 is the Urim & Thummim whereby all things pertaining to an higher order of kingdoms even all kingdoms will be made known and ~~the~~ a[2] white stone is given to each of those who come into ~~this~~ the celestial kingdom, whereon is a new name [p. 69] written which no man knoweth save he that receiveth it. The new name is the key word.

Whatever principal of intelligence we obtain in this life will rise with us in the resurrection: and if a person gains more knowledge in this life through his diligence & obedience than another, he will have so much the advantage in the world to come. There is a law irrevocably decreed in heaven before the foundations of this world upon which all blessings are predicated; and when we

---

1. TEXT: Possibly "there".
2. TEXT: Instead of "~~the~~ a", possibly "a ~~the~~".

obtain any blessing from God, it is by obedience to that law upon which it is predicated.

The Holy Ghost is a personage, and a person cannot have the personage [p. 70] of the H. G. in his heart. A man may receive the gifts of the H. G, and the H. G. may descend upon a man but not to tarry with him.["]

He also related the following dream "I dreamed that a silver-headed old man came to me and said he was invaded by a gang of robbers, who were plundering his neighbors and threatening destruction to all his subjects. He had heard that I always sought to defend the oppressed, and he had come to see if the General would call out his Legion and protect him, and he had come to hear with his own ears what answer I would give him. I answered, if you will make out the papers and shew that you are not the aggressor I will call out the Legion [p. 71] and defend you while I have a man to stand by me. The old man then turned to go away. When he got a little distance he turned suddenly round and said I must call out the Legion and go and he would have the papers ready when I arrived, and says he I have any amount of men which you can have under your command.["]

E[lde]r Hyde gave the this interpretation "The old man represents the government of these United States who will be invaded by a foreign foe, probably England. The U. S. government will call on you to defend probably all this Western Territory, and will offer you any amount of men you may need for that purpose.["] [p. 72]

Once when Pres.^{t} Joseph was praying earnestly to know concerning the wars which are to preceed the coming of the son of man, he heard a voice proclaim that the first outbreak of general bloodshed would commence at South Carolina— see Revelation

The sealing of the 144000 was the number of priests who should be anointed to administer in the daily sacrifice &c.

During pres.^{t} Joseph's remarks he said their was a nice distinction between the vision which John saw as spoken of in Revelations & the vision which Daniel saw. the former relating <u>only</u> to things as they actually existed in heaven— the latter being a figure representing things on the earth. God never made use of the figure [p. 73] of a beast to represent the kingdom of heaven— when they were made use of it was to represent an apostate church.

We slept at B. F. Johnsons [Benjamin F. Johnson's].

3 April 1843 • Monday

⟨Monday 3$^{rd.}$⟩ About 2 o clock we left Ramus for Carthage. We arrived about 4 at Mr [Jacob B.] Backenstos's. After supper I went to do some business at the Court house. I slept in company with the Sheriff in the Court house.

4 April 1843 • Tuesday

Tuesday 4— Spent the forenoon hearing pres. J. talk to Mr Backman [George Bachman] who seemed disposed to believe the truth. We left Carthage about 2 and arrived at home[3] about 5½.

---

3. TEXT: Possibly "house".

REFERENCE MATERIAL

Chronology for the Years 1839–1843

This brief chronology is designed as a reference tool for situating any particular journal entry or range of entries among the principal events of JS's life. It includes major journeys, births and deaths of immediate family members, selected revelations and discourses, developments in ecclesiastical organization, and other significant incidents. JS's plural marriages are not included; readers seeking information on women mentioned in this volume for whom there is sound documentary evidence that they were married or sealed to JS should consult the Biographical Directory (pages 439–504 herein). Readers wishing to conduct further research into events in JS's life may consult the documented chronology posted on the Joseph Smith Papers website.

1839

November		First issue of *Times and Seasons* published, with Ebenezer Robinson and Don Carlos Smith as editors, Commerce, Illinois.
	28	Arrived in Washington DC to present to United States government a petition seeking redress for Saints' losses incurred during expulsion from Missouri.

1840

March	early	Returned to Commerce from Washington DC.
April	6	At Commerce, appointed Orson Hyde and John E. Page to meet with Jewish leaders in London, Amsterdam, Constantinople, Jerusalem, and elsewhere.
	21	United States postmaster general officially changed name of Commerce post office to Nauvoo.
June	13	Son Don Carlos Smith born, Nauvoo.
July	14	Wrote from Nauvoo to Saints in Crooked Creek branch (Ramus, Illinois) approving organization of a stake there.
August	8	Wrote from Nauvoo to John C. Bennett, of Wayne County, Illinois, inviting him to visit Nauvoo.
	15	While preaching funeral sermon for Colonel Seymour Brunson, introduced doctrine of proxy baptism for deceased persons, Nauvoo.
	31	Announced plans to erect a temple, Nauvoo.
September	1	Missouri governor Lilburn W. Boggs initiated extradition proceedings against JS and others stemming from charges from the 1838 conflict in Missouri by sending requisition to Illinois governor Thomas Carlin, Independence, Jackson County, Missouri.
	14	Father, Joseph Smith Sr., died at age sixty-nine, Nauvoo.

| October | 15 | Dictated letter from Nauvoo to apostles on missions to Great Britain, agreeing to their request to return in spring. |

1841

January	19	Revelation regarding Nauvoo temple, Nauvoo House, and priesthood appointments, Nauvoo.
	30	At special church conference, elected sole trustee-in-trust for church, Nauvoo.
February	1	Charter for city of Nauvoo (approved by Illinois legislature and governor in December 1840) took effect, and first general elections held; John C. Bennett elected mayor, Nauvoo.
	3	At meeting organizing city council, presented bills concerning University of Nauvoo and Nauvoo Legion and sworn in as member of city council, Nauvoo.
	4	Attended court-martial organizing Nauvoo Legion; elected lieutenant general of Nauvoo Legion, Nauvoo.
	23	At Springfield, Illinois, Governor Thomas Carlin approved articles of incorporation for Nauvoo House Association, a corporation established to gather funds for and supervise construction of Nauvoo House.
March	ca. 26	Revelation at Nauvoo directing Saints to settle in Lee County, Iowa Territory.
April	6	Supervised laying of Nauvoo temple cornerstones and attended military parade celebrating eleventh anniversary of church, Nauvoo.
	7	John C. Bennett named assistant president in First Presidency "until President Rigdon's health should be restored," Nauvoo.
June	5	Arrested at Bear Creek, Illinois, based on requisition that former Missouri governor Lilburn W. Boggs issued to Illinois governor Thomas Carlin to extradite JS as a fugitive from justice; obtained writ of habeas corpus at Quincy, Illinois.
	7	Departed Quincy for hearing in Monmouth, Illinois.
	10	Judge Stephen A. Douglas ruled arrest warrant invalid and discharged JS, Monmouth.
August	7	Brother Don Carlos Smith died at age twenty-five, Nauvoo.
	12	Met with group of Indians and discussed promises made concerning them in Book of Mormon, Nauvoo.
	15	Son Don Carlos Smith died at age fourteen months, Nauvoo.
	16	Called "special conference of the Church" to elevate the Quorum of the Twelve Apostles "to stand in their place next to the First Presidency," Nauvoo.
	27	Clerk Robert B. Thompson died, Nauvoo.
October	2	Laid southeast cornerstone of Nauvoo House and placed original Book of Mormon manuscript and other items inside, Nauvoo.

	3	Instructed Saints to discontinue proxy baptisms for dead until they could be performed in temple, Nauvoo.
November	8	Attended dedication of wooden baptismal font built in basement of Nauvoo temple, Nauvoo.
	21	First proxy baptisms for dead in Nauvoo temple performed in temple font, Nauvoo.
December	5	Began proofreading new edition of Book of Mormon prior to its being stereotyped, Nauvoo.
	13	Appointed Willard Richards recorder for Nauvoo temple and scribe for private office of JS; Richards began writing in JS's journal, which would continue almost daily until week of JS's death, Nauvoo.

1842

January	5	Opened red brick store for business, Nauvoo.
February	4	Church closed contract to purchase printing office of Ebenezer Robinson, Nauvoo.
	6	Unnamed son born and died, Nauvoo.
	15	Publication of first issue of *Times and Seasons* listing JS as editor; JS later claimed no responsibility for content of this issue, Nauvoo.
	24	Authorized Ebenezer Robinson to use stereotype plates to make another impression of Book of Mormon and print fifteen hundred copies, Nauvoo.
March	1	*Times and Seasons* published JS's letter to John Wentworth, which outlined church's history and foundational beliefs, Nauvoo.
		Book of Abraham excerpt with facsimile 1 published in *Times and Seasons,* Nauvoo.
	15	Officiated as Grand Chaplain at installation of Nauvoo Masonic Lodge; admitted as member of lodge, Nauvoo.
		Additional Book of Abraham excerpt with facsimile 2 published in *Times and Seasons.*
	17	Organized Female Relief Society of Nauvoo and appointed his wife Emma Smith as president, Nauvoo.
April	16	First issue of the *The Wasp* published, with William Smith as editor, Nauvoo.
May	4	Presented sacred ceremonies and instructions known as "endowment" to Hyrum Smith, Brigham Young, and others in upper room of red brick store, Nauvoo.
	6	Former Missouri governor Lilburn W. Boggs shot and seriously wounded, Independence, Missouri.
	11	With other church leaders, excommunicated John C. Bennett.
	14	Word of attempted assassination of Lilburn W. Boggs reached Nauvoo.

	16	Facsimile 3 of Book of Abraham published in *Times and Seasons*, Nauvoo.
June	15	*Times and Seasons* published announcement (dated 11 May 1842) that First Presidency and other church leaders had withdrawn hand of fellowship from John C. Bennett, Nauvoo.
	19	Elected mayor by city council, replacing John C. Bennett, who had resigned; Hyrum Smith elected vice mayor, Nauvoo.
	30	William Clayton began keeping JS's journal, replacing Willard Richards, who was preparing to leave for Massachusetts to bring his family to Nauvoo.
July	1	*Times and Seasons* published JS's lengthy exposé of John C. Bennett, Nauvoo.
	8	*Sangamo Journal* published first of John C. Bennett's seven letters attacking JS and the church, Springfield.
	22	Missouri governor Thomas Reynolds issued requisition to Illinois governor Thomas Carlin to extradite JS and Orrin Porter Rockwell in connection with shooting of Lilburn W. Boggs, Jefferson City.
	27	Illinois governor Thomas Carlin reported receiving petitions on JS's behalf from Nauvoo citizens, Quincy.
August	8	Arrested on charge of being accessory in shooting of Lilburn W. Boggs, Nauvoo. Nauvoo Municipal Court issued writ of habeas corpus; JS remained in Nauvoo while officers took writ and arrest warrant to Quincy seeking Governor Thomas Carlin's advice.
	by 10	Went into hiding to avoid arrest; in and out of hiding for about four months, Nauvoo and surrounding area.
	17	In Nauvoo, Emma Smith wrote first of two letters to Illinois governor Thomas Carlin, requesting that he end proceedings to extradite JS to Missouri.
September	1, 7	Wrote two letters while in hiding that instructed Saints on proxy baptism for deceased persons and church record keeping, Nauvoo.
	20	Governor Thomas Carlin issued proclamation for JS's arrest.
October	30	Church members attended first Sabbath meeting held in unfinished Nauvoo temple; JS too ill to attend service, Nauvoo.
November	15	Resigned as editor of *Times and Seasons;* replaced by John Taylor, Nauvoo.
December	1	Appointed Willard Richards to write history of church with William W. Phelps, Nauvoo.
	2	From Nauvoo, sent delegation to newly elected Illinois governor Thomas Ford to discuss dismissing outstanding warrant for his arrest.
	9–20	William Clayton, Willard Richards, and others traveled from Nauvoo to Springfield in unsuccessful effort to discharge JS's debts through bankruptcy.

	21	Appointed Willard Richards his private secretary; Richards replaced William Clayton as keeper of JS's journal, Nauvoo.
	26	Arrested in Nauvoo by friend Wilson Law on charge of being accessory in shooting of Lilburn W. Boggs for purpose of safely conveying JS to Springfield for habeas corpus hearing.

1843

January	4, 5	Appeared in federal court for habeas corpus hearing; Judge Nathaniel Pope ruled that Lilburn W. Boggs's affidavit, upon which Missouri writ of extradition was based, was defective and that JS should be discharged from arrest, Springfield.
	6	Illinois governor Thomas Ford signed order discharging JS from arrest and declaring previous proclamation and arrest warrants for JS void, Springfield.
	10	Arrived in Nauvoo from Springfield.
February	6	Reelected mayor in second biennial Nauvoo city election, Nauvoo.
	21	Spoke on need to build both temple and Nauvoo House, Nauvoo.
March	27	Sent letter to Sidney Rigdon expressing suspicions that Rigdon was colluding with persons working against church; received letter from Rigdon denying involvement with apostates, Nauvoo.
April	2	Discoursed on nature of God, destiny of earth, war, obedience, and Second Coming, Ramus, Illinois.
	6	At special conference, church voted to appoint Quorum of the Twelve as agents who were authorized to collect funds for Nauvoo temple and Nauvoo House, Nauvoo.

Geographical Directory

This directory provides geographical descriptions of most of the places mentioned in this volume of *The Joseph Smith Papers*. It includes towns and villages, counties and states, and landforms and waterways, except for nonspecific or unidentifiable references such as "prairie." It includes many specific structures mentioned in the journals, such as stores and offices. It also includes some institutions that moved from place to place, such as the printing office.

Each place is listed with a complete political location and, in most cases, with grid coordinates for one or more reference maps (pages 427–437 herein) on which the place appears. Many entries also include information such as municipal history, population, and distinctive natural environments, as well as details more particular to the significance of the place within JS's journals between December 1841 and April 1843. Unless otherwise noted, all places were within the United States of America in the early 1840s. Spellings of the time period have been used for proper nouns. "LDS church" refers to the church established by JS in 1830 and later known as the Church of Jesus Christ of Latter-day Saints.

Readers wishing to conduct further research may consult the documented geographical directory posted on the Joseph Smith Papers website.

Adam-ondi-Ahman, Grand River Township, Daviess County, Missouri. Map 2: D-2. JS announced area as gathering place for Saints, May 1838. Because of Missouri difficulties, town almost completely abandoned by 20 Nov. 1838.

Adams County, Illinois. Map 3: D-1; Map 6: G-2.

Alton, Madison County, Illinois. Map 3: E-2. Incorporated as town, 1833. Incorporated as city, 1837. Population in 1840 about 2,300. Population in 1845 about 2,600. Terminus of National Road. Important shipping port on Mississippi River. Several ferry crossings based in Alton during 1840s.

American House, Springfield, Sangamon County, Illinois. Not mapped. One of the largest hotels in Illinois. Built by Elijah Iles, 1838, on southeast corner of Sixth and Adams streets.

Arlington House, Flatbush, Kings County, New York. Not mapped. Residence of James Arlington Bennet, a correspondent of JS. Bennet was proprietor and architect of house.

Augusta, Des Moines County, Iowa Territory (now state). Map 6: A-3. Located ten miles southwest of Burlington on Skunk River. Settled 1833. After being expelled from Missouri, Latter-day Saints moved to Commerce (later Nauvoo), Illinois, and surrounding areas, including Augusta. Lyman Wight settled there after leaving Missouri in 1839 and converted many to LDS church. Population in 1841 about 50. Mormon population in 1843 about 84. LDS branch discontinued, 1844, and Saints were counseled to move to Nauvoo.

Beardstown, Cass County, Illinois. MAP 3: C-2. Settled 1819. Important ferry crossing on Illinois River. Shipping outlet for goods produced in surrounding counties, including Sangamon. Incorporated as town, 1837.

Boston, Suffolk County, Massachusetts. MAP 1: B-6. Founded 1630. Incorporated as city, 1822. Population in 1840 about 93,400. By 1843, fourteen branches of LDS church with hundreds of members had been established in Boston area.

Brick store, Nauvoo, Hancock County, Illinois. See "Store [JS's red brick store]."

Brooklyn, Schuyler County, Illinois. MAP 3: C-2.

Burlington, Burlington Township, Des Moines County, Iowa Territory (now state). MAP 1: B-2; MAP 2: C-3. Settled 1832. Incorporated as town, 1837. Capital of Wisconsin Territory, 1837; capital of Iowa Territory, 1838–1841. Population in 1836 about 500. Population in 1838 about 1,000. Population in 1844 about 2,000. Population in 1855 about 11,000.

Canada. MAP 1: A-4. In late eighteenth and early nineteenth centuries, Americans and British subjects used term *Canada* in reference to British colonies of Upper Canada and Lower Canada in North America. Former territory of Canada divided into Upper Canada and Lower Canada, 1791; reunited, 1841. Boundaries corresponded roughly to present-day Ontario (Upper Canada) and Quebec (Lower Canada), with exception of unclear western boundary. Many Saints who were baptized into LDS church in Canada emigrated to Mormon communities in U.S. By early 1840s, over 2,000 people in Canada had converted to Mormonism and at least thirty-six branches of church were located between Lambton Co., Upper Canada, and Prince Edward Island.

Carthage, Hancock County, Illinois. MAP 1: B-2; MAP 2: C-3; MAP 3: C-1; MAP 6: D-4. Settled 1831. Hancock Co. seat, 1833. Incorporated as town, 1837. Population in 1837 about 350. Population in 1845 about 280. Location of Hancock Co. courthouse and of two-story jail where JS and Hyrum Smith were murdered on 27 June 1844.

Cass County, Illinois. MAP 3: D-2.

Chicago, Cook County, Illinois. MAP 1: B-3; MAP 2: C-5; MAP 3: B-5. Incorporated as city, 1837. Population in 1840 about 4,500. Population in Dec. 1844 about 10,900. Two elders, one priest, one deacon, and twenty-two lay members of LDS church located in Chicago, 1841. Twenty-five church members located in Chicago with one hundred additional church members located between Chicago and Peoria, Illinois, 1845.

Commerce (now Nauvoo), Hancock County, Illinois. MAP 4: C-5; MAP 8: C-2. See "Nauvoo."

Committee house, Nauvoo, Hancock County, Illinois. NOT MAPPED. Small brick office near site of Nauvoo temple. Meeting place where temple committee conducted business related to building Nauvoo temple.

Court (Circuit Court of the United States for the District of Illinois), Springfield, Sangamon County, Illinois. NOT MAPPED. Located on second floor of Tinsley building, across the square from old state capitol. Location of JS's habeas corpus hearing, Jan. 1843.

Des Moines River, Missouri and Iowa Territories. MAP 2: C-2; MAP 4: E-1; MAP 6: D-1.

Farm (JS's), Hancock County, Illinois. MAP 7: D-7. Nearly one hundred sixty acres located about three miles east of Nauvoo on south side of Old Road to Carthage. By 1842, Cornelius P. Lott and wife, Permelia, managed the farm.

Farmington, Lee County, Iowa Territory (now state). MAP 2: C-3.

Far West, Rockford Township, Caldwell County, Missouri. MAP 1: C-2; MAP 2: D-1. Laid out Aug. 1836. Had 150 houses by 1838. During Mormon period, population as high as about 3,000 to 5,000. JS's home from 14 Mar. 1838 until 31 Oct. 1838. As church headquarters, was center of Mormon activity in Missouri. Site where Saints surrendered and Missouri militia took JS and other leaders prisoner, late Oct. and early Nov. 1838, after Missouri governor Lilburn W. Boggs issued order to exterminate Saints or drive them from state. Leaders were sent to jail, and remaining Saints were forced to leave state.

Fountain Green, Hancock County, Illinois. MAP 6: C-5. Area settled by Ute Perkins, 1826. Originally named Lick Grove, then Horse Lick Grove. Post office established, 1833. Name changed to Fountain Green, 1835. Platted, May 1835. Several area residents joined LDS church, 1839. Other Latter-day Saints settled among earlier inhabitants, 1840. Population in 1845 about 43. Church members sold most of their property, by Nov. 1845, in preparation to leave Illinois.

Galena, Jo Daviess County, Illinois. MAP 3: A-2. Jo Daviess Co. seat. Originally known as "the Point" and still referred to as such after laid out and named Galena in 1826. Principal town in lead mine country. Population in 1840 about 1,800. Population in 1845 about 4,000. Several Saints worked in town's lead mines while Nauvoo temple was being built.

Geneva, Scott County, Illinois. MAP 3: D-2.

"Grove," Commerce (now Nauvoo), Hancock County, Nauvoo, Illinois. MAP 9: D-4. Before Nauvoo temple was completed, large meetings were often held outdoors in three groves located near temple. Groves had stands for speakers and often served as sites for religious, social, and political gatherings. Grove most commonly used for public meetings located directly west of Nauvoo temple site. Two other groves located south and northeast, respectively, of temple. See also "Stand."

Half-Breed Tract, Lee County, Iowa Territory (now state). MAP 4: D-2. About 119,000 acres of land located between Mississippi and Des Moines rivers and south of site of Fort Madison. In 1824, U.S. Congress set the land aside for children of American Indians who had intermarried with whites. Act passed, 1834, relinquishing Congress's revisionary right and allowing "half-breeds" to sell the land. New York Land Company, with Isaac Galland as one of five trustees, purchased much of reservation, 1836. Galland also purchased half-breed land under his name; offered to sell LDS church half-breed land, 1838. Church agents Oliver Granger and Vinson Knight purchased about 15,400 acres of Half-Breed Tract from Galland, 1839. Land partitioned, 1841. JS encouraged Saints to abandon Half-Breed Tract, Apr. 1843, though many remained there.

Hancock County, Illinois. MAP 3: C-1; MAP 4: E-5; MAP 6. Formed from Pike Co., 1825. Attached to Adams Co. until Sept. 1829, when Hancock Co. became populous enough to organize own government. Described in 1837 as predominantly prairie and "deficient in timber." Population in 1835 about 3,200. Population in 1840 about 10,000. Population in 1845 about 22,600. Early settlers mainly from middle and southern states. Included Commerce (later Nauvoo), where Latter-day Saints eventually reestablished themselves, 1839–1846, following expulsion from Missouri in 1838. Saints also settled in several other communities throughout Hancock Co. JS and Hyrum Smith were murdered at jail at county seat, Carthage, 27 June 1844.

Hiram Township, Portage County, Ohio. Map 1: B-4. Established 1816. Population in 1830 about 520. JS revised Bible, dictated several revelations, and decided to publish collection of revelations in Hiram Township. Mob of local residents tarred and feathered JS and Sydney Rigdon, Mar. 1832.

Hotchkiss Purchase, Commerce (now Nauvoo), Hancock County, Illinois. Map 5: C-4. Four hundred acres that included part of Commerce (later Nauvoo). LDS church purchased land for about $114,500 in Aug. 1839. One of three major land purchases by church in Commerce.

Illinois. Map 1: B-3; Map 2: C-4; Map 3. Organized as U.S. territory, 1787. Admitted as state, 1818. Population in 1840 about 479,000. Population in 1845 about 662,000. Plentiful, inexpensive land attracted settlers from northern and southern states. Following expulsion from Missouri, Mormons gathered in Quincy, Springfield, and other areas, winter 1838–1839. Church purchased land around Commerce (later Nauvoo), May 1839, and most Saints settled there. Mormons became politically dominant in the area because of rapid immigration, leading to tension between Mormons and local residents. JS and Hyrum Smith were murdered, 27 June 1844, in jail at Carthage, Hancock Co. Saints forcibly expelled from Nauvoo, 1846, and began westward migration to present-day Utah.

Illinois River, Illinois. Map 2: C-4; Map 3: C-3.

Independence, Blue Township, Jackson County, Missouri. Map 1: C-2; Map 2: D-1. Settled 1827. Jackson Co. seat. JS revelation of July 1831 designated Independence as "the center place" of "Zion," where Saints were to gather and build temple. Mob violence erupted, July 1833, as increasing numbers of Saints entered Missouri. Earlier settlers forcibly expelled Saints from county by Nov. 1833. See also "Jackson County" and "Zion."

Iowa Territory (now state). Map 4: B-2; Map 6: A-1; Map 7: B-2. Area acquired by U.S. in Louisiana Purchase, 1803. First major white settlements, ca. 1833. Organized as territory containing all present-day Iowa, much of present-day Minnesota, and parts of North and South Dakota, 1838. Population in 1840 about 43,100. Population in 1844 over 75,000. Population in 1846 about 102,400. Admitted as state, 1846. After expulsion from Missouri in 1838–1839, many Latter-day Saints found refuge in eastern Iowa Territory, especially near Montrose, Lee Co.

Islands, Mississippi River. Map 7: D-2. Two tree-covered islands located in Mississippi River between Nauvoo, Illinois, and Montrose, Iowa Territory. Source of wood for the Saints. JS found shelter on islands, summer 1842, when Missouri and Illinois authorities sought to extradite him to Missouri.

Jackson County, Missouri. Not mapped. Settled 1808. Organized 1826. Population in 1836 about 4,500. Population in 1840 about 7,600. Latter-day Saints first entered Jackson Co., Jan. 1831. Mormon population in summer 1833 about 1,200. In July 1833, mob violence erupted as increasing numbers of Saints entered Missouri. Earlier settlers forcibly expelled Saints from county by Nov. 1833. JS led group of Saints on Camp of Israel expedition in failed effort to redeem Mormon lands in Jackson Co., summer 1834. See also "Independence" and "Zion."

Jerusalem, Palestine, Pachalic of Damascus, Syria, Ottoman Empire. NOT MAPPED. Population in 1840 about 13,000. Visited by apostle Orson Hyde, Oct. 1841, and dedicated by Hyde for return of the Jews, 24 Oct. 1841.

Job's Creek (now Baptist Creek), Hancock County, Illinois. MAP 6: C-6. Creek that runs through Hancock and McDonough counties. Branch of LDS church located near Job's Creek.

Keokuk, Jackson Township, Lee County, Iowa Territory (now state). MAP 1: B-2; MAP 2: C-3; MAP 3: C-1; MAP 6: D-2. Located near confluence of Mississippi and Des Moines rivers. First settled, 1820. Fur trading post opened there, 1828. Named Keokuk after Meskwaki Indian chief, 1829. Platted 1837. Population in 1841 about 150. Population in 1846 about 500. Incorporated 1847. After expulsion from Missouri in 1838–1839, many Saints located temporarily in Keokuk, where they found employment and acquired land. Keokuk branch of church had thirteen members by Aug. 1841. Vigilance committee demanded removal of several Mormon families, late 1843.

Kirtland, Kirtland Township, Geauga County (now in Lake County), Ohio. MAP 1: B-4. Settled 1810. Township organized, 1817. Visited by Mormon missionaries, 1830. Population of Kirtland Township in 1831 about 70 Latter-day Saints and 1,100 others. Population in 1838 about 2,000 Latter-day Saints and 1,200 others. Population in 1839 about 100 Latter-day Saints and 1,500 others. Church membership grew quickly, and Kirtland community became headquarters of church as well as JS's home, 1831. Under threats from dissidents and outside antagonists, JS and other church leaders fled Kirtland, early 1838. Other loyal Saints followed. By spring 1841, Kirtland branch membership increased to about 300–400 because of missionary work and included about 100 English converts. Kirtland stake reorganized, fall 1841. Saints made further organized efforts to leave Kirtland, 1843–summer 1845, but many Saints remained. Kirtland temple used for church meetings through 1845; afterward used for social, educational, political, and business purposes.

La Harpe, Hancock County, Illinois. MAP 6: B-5. Settled as Franklin, 1830. Platted and renamed La Harpe, 1836. Mormon immigration and missionary work led to creation of LDS church branch, 1841. Population in 1845 about 330.

Lancaster, Lancaster Precinct (now in Philadelphia Township), Morgan County (now in Cass County), Illinois. MAP 3: D-2. Laid out by John Dutch, May 1837. Dutch built and operated a tavern there known as "Halfway House" because located halfway between Beardstown, Cass Co., and Springfield, Sangamon Co. (on route JS and others traveled to and from Springfield). Town vacated, by 1843.

Lee County, Iowa Territory (now state). MAP 3: C-1; MAP 6: A-2. Organized 1836. First permanent settlement, 1820. Population in 1840 about 6,100. Population in 1844 about 10,300. Population in 1846 about 12,900. After expulsion from Missouri in 1838–1839, many Saints found refuge in eastern Iowa Territory, especially near Montrose, Lee Co. Saints purchased about 20,000 acres of Half-Breed Tract in Lee Co., 1839. Iowa stake organized, Oct. 1839. Later renamed Zarahemla stake. By Aug. 1841, stake had 683 members in eight branches. Stake dissolved, Jan. 1842. See also "Half-Breed Tract," "Keokuk," "Montrose," and "Zarahemla."

Lima, Adams County, Illinois. Map 1: B-2; Map 3: C-1; Map 6: F-2. Settled 1833. Post office established, 1836. Many Mormons who had been expelled from Missouri settled in Lima. Town had between ten and twelve houses, by 1843. Population in 1850 about 900. Considered an important settlement by church leaders; however, most Saints in area settled about 2½ miles northeast in Yelrome (Morley's Settlement), Hancock Co. Lima stake organized, Oct. 1840. Church conference held in Lima, 23 Sept. 1841, with 424 members from Lima area present. Saints abandoned area, 1845.

Liverpool, Lancashire (now in Merseyside County), England. Not mapped. Chief port in England during nineteenth century. First Mormon missionaries arrived in Liverpool, July 1837. Became center of Latter-day Saint immigration to U.S.

Macedonia, Hancock County, Illinois. Map 6: D-5. See "Ramus."

Maine. Map 1: A-7. Admitted as state, 1820. Population in 1840 about 501,800. First visited by Mormon missionaries, 1832. Branches of church located in Farmington and Saco by 1834. Wilford Woodruff and others arrived in 1837 and converted many, particularly on Fox Islands.

Marquette County (now part of Adams County), Illinois. Not mapped. To counter 1840 movement to relocate Adams Co. seat from Quincy to Columbus, community leaders in Quincy used their influence with Illinois legislature to divide off eastern townships of Adams Co. to form Marquette Co., 1843. Citizens of Marquette Co. refused to organize county government until after exhausting legal appeals. They elected a representative to Illinois legislature, 1846; this legislator succeeded in changing county name to Highland, 1847, and in dissolving Marquette Co. back into Adams Co. with acceptance of state constitution, 1848.

Masonic hall, Nauvoo, Hancock County, Illinois. Illinois lodge Grand Master Abraham Jonas granted dispensation to organize Nauvoo lodge, 15 Oct. 1841. Nauvoo lodge organized, Dec. 1841, and installed, Mar. 1842. Prior to dedication of Masonic hall on Main Street in Apr. 1844, Nauvoo lodge met in a variety of locations. Meetings to organize lodge on 29 and 30 Dec. 1841 were held in Hyrum Smith's office (Map 9: F-2). Many lodge meetings, particularly in 1842, were held on upper floor of JS's red brick store (Map 9: F-2) in large room, frequently referred to as "lodge room." By Apr. 1844, and possibly as early as Jan. 1843, Nauvoo lodge met on upper floor of Henry Miller's home (Map 9: E-3). Alexander Mills's tavern (Map 9: E-3) was referred to as "Alexander Mills's Masonic Hall Tavern," but no known evidence indicates that Nauvoo lodge used tavern for regular meetings—only for informal gatherings. Cornerstone for Masonic hall (not mapped) laid at corner of Main and White streets, June 1843; building dedicated, Apr. 1844.

Massachusetts. Map 1: B-6. Mormon missionaries baptized converts and organized two small branches of church in Massachusetts, 1832. Population in 1840 about 737,700. By 1843, Massachusetts had fourteen branches of church.

Memphis, Shelby County, Tennessee. Map 1: C-2.

Mentor Township, Geauga County (now in Lake County), Ohio. Map 1: B-4.

Michigan. Map 1: A-3, B-3.

Mississippi River. Map 2: D-3; Map 3: F-3; Map 6: B-2. Stretches 2,340 miles from Minnesota to Gulf of Mexico. Major travel route for commerce and Saints immigrating to Nauvoo, Illinois. At least four landings in Nauvoo: Nauvoo House Landing, Lower Stone House (or Ferryboat) Landing, Kimball Landing, and Upper Stone House Landing.

Missouri. Map 1: C-2; Map 2: E-2; Map 3: F-1. Area acquired by U.S. in Louisiana Purchase, 1803. Established as territory, 1812. Thousands immigrated, mainly from South. Missouri Compromise, 1820, allowed Missouri into Union as slave state, 1821. Population in 1836 about 244,000. Population in 1840 about 380,000. Population in 1844 about 510,500. Many Mormons migrated to Missouri, especially to Far West, Caldwell Co. JS moved to Far West, which became new church headquarters, 1838. Regional and cultural differences caused tension and eventually violence. Conflict in Daviess and Carroll counties escalated to point that Missouri governor Lilburn W. Boggs issued order to exterminate Saints or drive them from state. JS taken prisoner by Missouri militia, late 1838, and incarcerated through winter in jail at Liberty, Clay Co., while Saints driven from state. JS allowed to escape, Apr. 1839. Three separate attempts to extradite JS to Missouri failed, 1840–1841, 1842–1843, and 1843. First and third extradition attempts based on Mormon-Missouri conflict; second based on alleged complicity in attempt to assassinate former Missouri governor Lilburn W. Boggs.

Montrose, Lee County, Iowa Territory (now state). Map 3: C-1; Map 6: C-2; Map 7: D-2. Settled by Louis-Honoré Tesson, 1796–1803. Captain James White established ferryboat between Illinois and Iowa Territory that lightered over Des Moines Rapids, 1832. U.S. government purchased land from White and established Fort Des Moines, 1834. Fort abandoned and town surveyed, 1837. Became important port with Mississippi River to the east and Des Moines River to the west. Several Latter-day Saints settled in Montrose Township after being driven from Missouri, 1838–1839, because of availability of shelter at fort. Church membership grew rapidly from immigration. Montrose town incorporated, 1857.

Nashville (now Galland), Montrose Township, Lee County, Iowa Territory (now state). Map 6: C-2. Settled by Isaac Galland, 1829. Laid out and incorporated, 1841, but charter was never adopted.

Nauvoo, Hancock County, Illinois. Map 1: B-2; Map 2: C-3; Map 3: C-1; Map 6: C-2; Map 7: D-3; Map 8; Map 9. Principal gathering place for the Saints following expulsion from Missouri. Beginning 1839, church purchased lands in earlier settlements of Commerce and Commerce City, as well as surrounding areas. With post office designation change in Apr. 1840, area was officially named Nauvoo. Lower portion of Nauvoo known as "the Flats," where JS's home, Nauvoo House, and red brick store were located. "The flats" were located along bank of Mississippi River, several feet above high-water mark, and extended eastward about one mile; ground described as gradually sloping upward to area known as "the Bluff," where ground again rose sixty to seventy feet to site where Latter-day Saints designated temple block. After ascent, ground was level and continued into prairie. JS often preached and attended meetings at "Hill," located near temple. Four riverboat landing sites were established at Nauvoo: Upper Stone House Landing, Kimball Landing, Lower Stone House (or Ferryboat) Landing, and Nauvoo House (Main Street) Landing. Incorporated as city when Illinois granted Nauvoo a charter, 1840. City charter secured powers, including authority to establish Nauvoo Legion and University of Nauvoo, and called for a mayor, four aldermen, and nine councilmen to serve in municipal government. Number of aldermen could change as city's population grew. Served as church headquarters, 1839–1846. Construction on Nauvoo temple began, 1841, but was not completed until after JS's death. Cornerstone of Nauvoo House laid, Oct. 1841. JS introduced many principles and institutions in Nauvoo, including plurality of gods, celestial marriage, temple endowments, proxy rituals for dead, Relief Society, "Holy Order," and Council of Fifty. Tension developed between Nauvoo Saints and neighbors in Hancock and surrounding counties. After JS was murdered on 27 June 1844, Latter-day Saints in Nauvoo, under leadership of Brigham Young, finished temple, received endowments, and crossed Mississippi River in 1846 en route to Salt Lake Valley. Emma Smith and other Saints remained in Nauvoo, which reverted to a small town.

Nauvoo House, Nauvoo, Hancock County, Illinois. MAP 9: F-3. JS revelation instructed Saints to build boardinghouse for travelers and immigrants, Jan. 1841. Construction of building funded by shares of stock sold for fifty dollars each. Cornerstone of Nauvoo House laid, Oct. 1841, but building was never finished. Emma Smith's second husband, Lewis C. Bidamon, removed part of the structure and built a house on portion of existing foundation.

Nauvoo House Landing, Nauvoo, Hancock County, Illinois. NOT MAPPED. Located on south end of Main Street, near Nauvoo House and JS's homestead. Popular docking place for steamers carrying immigrants from British Isles. Boats that used the landing included *Maid of Iowa, Mermaid,* and *Osprey.*

Nauvoo post office, Nauvoo, Hancock County, Illinois. MAP 9: E-3. First post office in area known as Venus, 1830–1834. Changed to Commerce. On 21 Apr. 1840, renamed Nauvoo post office and George W. Robinson appointed postmaster. Robinson operated post office in Lower Stone House and lived there with father-in-law Sidney Rigdon. Rigdon appointed postmaster, 24 Feb. 1841. Robinson and Rigdon moved to a new house, which became the post office, on corner of Main and Sidney streets.

New Jersey. MAP 1: C-6.

New Orleans, Orleans Parish, Louisiana. NOT MAPPED. Acquired by U.S. in Louisiana Purchase, 1803. Population in 1840 about 102,200. Port of New Orleans important to import and export of trade, including trade on Mississippi River, which reached Nauvoo. Many British Saints traveled through New Orleans while immigrating to Illinois.

New store. See "Store [JS's red brick store]."

New York (state). MAP 1: B-5. Admitted as state, 1788. Population in 1835 about 2,200,000. Population in 1840 about 2,400,000. Heavy European immigration to U.S. through harbor of New York City. Canals, particularly Erie Canal (completed 1825), escalated inland commercial activity. Smith family lived in New York, 1816–1831. Church organized in Fayette Township, 1830. About 400 members of church in western New York, late 1840.

New York City, New York County, New York. MAP 1: B-6. Incorporated 1665. Harbor contributed to dramatic economic and population growth. Largest city in U.S. by 1790. Population of New York Co. in 1830 about 200,000; population in 1840 about 310,000. Parley P. Pratt and others performed early missionary work in New York City.

LDS church branch met in Columbia Hall on Grand Street, 1839. Branches also organized in Brooklyn and Long Island. Mormon population in late 1840 about 200.

Office, Nauvoo, Hancock County, Illinois. MAP 9: F-3. Term usually applies to JS's private office, which was located at various places during JS's lifetime, including his home and a smokehouse on his property. Moved to second floor of JS's red brick store, Mar. 1841. Served as church headquarters. Location where JS kept his sacred writings and translated Book of Abraham. Prior to completion of Nauvoo temple, office used in part of endowment ceremonies. "Office" may also refer to temple recorder's office or registrar's office. Church recorder Willard Richards shared JS's office in red brick store until Nov. 1842, when temple recorder's office moved to a new small brick building near temple. JS also assigned Willard Richards to record transfer of land deeds and to receive tithes; thus, location of registrar's office is same as recorder's office.

Ohio. MAP 1: B-4. Admitted as state, 1803. Population in 1830 about 940,000. Population in 1840 about 1,500,000. Mormon missionaries preached in Western Reserve of northeastern Ohio, Oct. 1830. JS revelation declared "the Ohio" to be first formal gathering place of newly organized church. JS's home and church headquarters, 1831–1838. Most Saints left Ohio and immigrated to Missouri, 1838.

Old burying ground, Nauvoo, Hancock County, Illinois. MAP 9: D-4. One-half acre cemetery located at junction of Durphy and White streets. Predated Latter-day Saints' arrival to Commerce (later Nauvoo) and was replaced as main city cemetery, June 1842, by "old pioneer burying ground," located outside city on Carthage Road.

Palmyra Township, Wayne County, New York. MAP 1: B-5. First permanent white settlement, ca. 1789. Population in 1830 about 3,400. Joseph Smith Sr. family lived in or near Palmyra, 1816–1830. JS had 5,000 copies of Book of Mormon printed at E. B. Grandin printing office on Main Street in Palmyra village, 1829–1830. Smith family left Palmyra Township, late 1830.

Parade ground, Nauvoo, Hancock County, Illinois. MAP 9: D-2. Nauvoo Legion had several parade grounds, including ones located on Carthage Road and on public square. Most frequently used parade ground from 1840 to Apr. 1843 was located west of Main Street.

Paris, Edgar County, Illinois. MAP 2: D-5; MAP 3: D-5.

Philadelphia, Philadelphia County, Pennsylvania. MAP 1: C-6. Founded as Quaker settlement by William Penn, 1681. Population in 1840 about 258,000. Population in 1850 about 409,000. Orson Pratt among first Mormon missionaries to preach in Philadelphia, 1835. City had about 100 members of church, 1839; about 890 members, by 1841.

Pine country, Crawford County (now in Jackson County), Wisconsin Territory (now state). MAP 2: A-3. Also known as "pinery." Area near Black River where lumbering operation was established to provide timber for construction of Nauvoo temple, Nauvoo House, and other public buildings. Four mills were established on Black River: three near Black River Falls and one at junction of Roaring Creek and Black River. Mills abandoned, early 1844.

Pittsburgh, Allegheny County, Pennsylvania. MAP 1: B-5.

Pleasant Vale Township, Pike County, Illinois. MAP 3: D-1. Settled by 1823. Post office established, 1827. New Canton, only city in township, founded 2 Apr. 1835. Population of settlement later bolstered by Mormon immigration. Pleasant Vale stake organized, by Mar. 1841; stake discontinued, 24 May 1841. Between one hundred and two hundred members of Pleasant Vale church branch, led by branch president William Draper, built house of worship in northwest part of township, Dec. 1841.

Plymouth, Hancock County, Illinois. MAP 3: C-2; MAP 6: E-6. Settled 1831. Surveyed and post office established, 1836. In 1840, population within three miles of Plymouth about 800. Population in 1845 about 56. Village where members of JS's family lived. JS's sister Katherine Smith Salisbury lived with her husband in Plymouth, 1839. JS's brother William Smith moved to a farm there, 1839. William Smith owned tavern on public square that his brother Samuel Smith came to manage in 1842. JS stayed in Plymouth, 27 Dec. 1842, while traveling to Springfield, Illinois, to stand trial.

Post office, Nauvoo, Hancock County, Illinois. See "Nauvoo post office."

Prairie du Chien, Crawford County, Wisconsin Territory (now state). MAP 2: B-3.

Printing office, Nauvoo, Hancock County, Illinois. MAP 9: F-2. Located at four different places from 1839–1846: cellar of warehouse on bank of Mississippi River, 1839; frame building on northeast corner of Water and Bain streets, 1839–1841; newly built printing establishment on northwest corner of Water and Bain streets, 1841–1845; and part of three-building complex on northwest corner of Main and Kimball streets, 1845–1846. Sold by Ebenezer Robinson to JS, Feb. 1842. Leased by JS to John Taylor and Wilford Woodruff, Dec. 1842. Published third and fourth editions of Book of Mormon, four editions of Doctrine and Covenants, and newspapers *Times and Seasons, The Wasp,* and *Nauvoo Neighbor.* JS conducted business at printing office.

Quincy, Adams County, Illinois. MAP 1: C-2; MAP 2: D-3; MAP 3: D-1. Incorporated as town, 1834. Incorporated as city, 1840. Population in 1840 about 2,300. Population in 1845 about 4,000. Adams Co. seat. Important manufacturing and shipping center because of river port. Mormon exiles from Missouri, including JS's family, found refuge in Quincy area, winter 1838–1839. Many church leaders excommunicated at church conference held in Quincy, Mar. 1839. JS arrived in Quincy after escape from imprisonment, late Apr. 1839. Church conference to approve Iowa Territory purchases and mission of the Twelve to Europe held in Quincy, May 1839. Quincy stake organized, Oct. 1840; stake discontinued, spring 1841, and branch organized. Branch continued until Mormons left Illinois in 1846. Residence of Illinois governor Thomas Carlin. After murder of JS, 1844, leading citizens (later known as Quincy Committee) of Adams Co. met to find a way to end growing hostilities between Saints and other residents.

Ramus (now Webster), Hancock County, Illinois. MAP 6: D-5. Founded, 1839–1840, by group of Mormons after expulsion from Missouri. Town platted, 1840. Incorporated as Macedonia, Mar. 1843. Population in 1845 about 380. Post office established, 1844. Location of Crooked Creek branch. Branch membership reached 400–500. Stake organized, July 1840; stake discontinued and reorganized as branch, Dec. 1841. Location of one of first meetinghouses built by Saints. Most Mormons left by Apr. 1846; some remained until 1850. Renamed Webster, 1847.

Red brick store. See "Store [JS's red brick store]."

Rushville, Schuyler County, Illinois. Map 3: C-2. Settled 1826 and called Rushton. Schuyler Co. seat, Mar. 1826. Name changed to Rushville, Apr. 1826. Incorporated as town, May 1831. Population in 1837 about 1,200. Additional charter granted, 1839.

Salem, Essex County, Massachusetts. Map 1: B-6.

Sangamon County, Illinois. Map 3: D-3. Area settled 1817. Formed 30 Jan. 1821. Population in 1840 about 15,200. Population in 1845 about 18,700.

Seneca County, New York. Not mapped. Formed 1804. Population in 1830 about 21,000. LDS church organized in Fayette Township, 6 Apr. 1830.

Shokokon, Henderson County, Illinois. Map 2: C-3; Map 3: C-1; Map 6: A-4. Located on bank of Mississippi River. Laid out by Robert McQueen, 1836. Location for landing rafts of lumber cut in Wisconsin Territory forests. Population never exceeded 300. Saints owned land near Shokokon, by Feb. 1843. JS visited with interest in making area LDS settlement, Feb. 1843.

Smokehouse, Nauvoo, Hancock County, Illinois. Map 9: F-3. Located in yard immediately northwest of JS's house and used temporarily for mayor's office and mayor's court.

Springfield, Sangamon County, Illinois. Map 1: C-3; Map 2: D-4; Map 3: D-3. Settled 1818. Incorporated as town, 1832. Became state capital, 1837. Incorporated as city, 1840. Sangamon Co. seat. Population in 1840 about 1,600. Population in 1843 about 2,600. Stake organized, Nov. 1840; discontinued, May 1841; branch organized, Jan. 1842. After arrested on charge of being accessory in attempt to assassinate former Missouri governor Lilburn W. Boggs, JS traveled to Springfield, late Dec. 1842, for habeas corpus hearing before federal judge Nathaniel Pope. After hearing in early Jan. 1843, JS was discharged.

"Stand," Nauvoo, Hancock County, Illinois. Term usually refers to a speaker's stand located in one of three "groves" where JS and others often spoke. JS also preached at temple stand, a temporary structure built at various times on the east, west, and south walls of unfinished Nauvoo temple. See also "Grove."

St. Louis, St. Louis County, Missouri. Map 1: C-2; Map 2: D-3; Map 3: E-2. Founded by French fur trader, 1764. Acquired by U.S. in Louisiana Purchase, 1803. Incorporated as town, 1809; incorporated as city, 1822. Population in 1840 about 16,500. Population in 1844 about 28,400. Population in 1845 about 35,900. Important trade center because of its location on Mississippi River and its proximity to Ohio, Missouri, and Illinois rivers.

Store [JS's red brick store], Nauvoo, Hancock County, Illinois. Map 9: F-2. Completed 1841. Opened for business, 5 Jan. 1842. Owned by JS but managed mostly by others. First floor housed JS's general store and Bishop Newel K. Whitney's office, which served as tithing office. Second floor contained JS's private office, where he kept and translated sacred writings (such as Book of Abraham) and organized Council of Fifty. Large upper room, also on second floor, was used as an assembly room, which at various times served as a school, Masonic lodge, and meeting place for priesthood quorums, Nauvoo temple and Nauvoo House committees, Nauvoo Legion, city and state officials, and Relief Society. In upper room, Relief Society was organized, 17 Mar. 1842, and JS introduced endowment to nine individuals, 4–5 May 1842. Some University of Nauvoo classes held in upper room. Nauvoo city court and mayor's court also convened in upper room. Location of state political convention that nominated JS as candidate for U.S. president, 17 May 1844. See also "Masonic hall" and "Office."

Temple, Kirtland, Kirtland Township, Geauga County (now in Lake County), Ohio. NOT MAPPED. Cornerstone laid, 23 July 1833. Dedicated, 27 Mar. 1836.

Temple, Nauvoo, Hancock County, Illinois. MAP 9: D-4. JS revelation of Jan. 1841 commanded Saints to build a temple and a hotel (Nauvoo House). Cornerstone laid, 6 Apr. 1841. Saints volunteered labor, money, and other resources for temple construction. Construction led by committee, which included Reynolds Cahoon, Alpheus Cutler, and Elias Higbee. Basement with wooden baptismal font completed, fall 1841. Baptisms for dead, previously performed in Mississippi River, performed in temple baptismal font. Work to complete temple continued after murder of JS in 1844. Wooden font taken down, by Jan. 1845. By Dec. 1845, enough work in attic rooms was completed to initiate ordinances. New stone baptismal font completed, ca. Jan. 1846. About 5,500 people received endowments, Dec. 1845–Feb. 1846. Dedicated, 30 Apr. 1846. First floor had offices and an assembly hall; second floor was similar; third floor (attic) had offices, dressing rooms, and endowment rooms. Temple also served as multipurpose meeting place where Sunday services and general conferences were held. Fire destroyed interior, roof, and tower, Oct. 1848; tornado destroyed exterior walls, May 1850. See also "Baptism," in Glossary.

Terre Haute, Harrison Township, Vigo County, Indiana. MAP 2: D-5; MAP 3: D-5.

Theatre, Springfield, Sangamon County, Illinois. NOT MAPPED. Located directly south of American House. William P. Hastings was manager of theatre.

Union County, Illinois. MAP 3: F-3.

United States of America. MAP 1. Population in 1805 about 6,000,000; population in 1830 almost 13,000,000; population in 1844 about 20,000,000.

Van Buren County, Iowa Territory (now state). MAP 3: C-1.

Virginia. MAP 1: C-4.

Virginia, Cass County, Illinois. MAP 3: D-2.

Warren, Hancock County, Illinois. MAP 6: E-1. Platted on school section no. 16, one mile south of Warsaw, by July 1841. Willard Richards moved to Warsaw to sell lots in Warren, Sept. 1841. Joseph Fielding brought company of 204 British Saints immigrating to U.S. to Warren vicinity to purchase lots and settle, Nov. 1841. Antagonism from Warsaw residents prompted First Presidency to request British Saints move to Nauvoo, Dec. 1841. Town never established.

Warsaw, Hancock County, Illinois. MAP 3: C-1; MAP 6: D-1. Located at foot of Des Moines Rapids of Mississippi River at site of three military forts: Fort Johnson (1814), Cantonment Davis (1815–1818), and Fort Edwards (1818–1824). First settlers participated in fur trade. Important trade and shipping center for farms in Hancock, McDonough, and Adams counties. Post office established, 1833. Laid out, 1834. Incorporated as town, 1837. Population in 1845 about 470. Thomas Sharp, a local newspaper editor, helped found anti-Mormon political party. Five of the nine men indicted for murdering JS and Hyrum Smith were from Warsaw.

Washington, District of Columbia. MAP 1: C-5. Created as district for seat of U.S. federal government by acts of Congress in 1790 and 1791. Headquarters of executive, legislative, and judicial branches of U.S. government. Population in 1840 about 23,400. JS visited

Washington DC, 1839, seeking redress and compensation for losses suffered by Saints during expulsion from Missouri, but President Martin Van Buren refused assistance. Missionaries visited, 1841 and 1843.

Wiggins's (Ebenezer Wiggins's) farm, Hancock County, Illinois. MAP 6: C-2; MAP 7: C-5.

Woodland (JS's), Hancock County, Illinois. MAP 6: D-2.

Zarahemla, Montrose Township, Lee County, Iowa Territory (now state). MAP 6: C-1; MAP 7: D-1. Settled about one mile west of Mississippi River, ca. May 1839. By Oct. 1839, enough Saints were in Lee Co. that Iowa stake was organized. By Aug. 1841, stake name changed to Zarahemla, as advised by JS revelation. Stake had 750 members in eight branches. Stake discontinued, Jan. 1842. See also "Montrose."

Zion. NOT MAPPED. Term used by early Latter-day Saints both as name for God's people generally and for a particular place where God's people dwell. JS revelation of July 1831 designated Jackson Co., Missouri, as primary area where Saints were to gather and "the place for the city of Zion." JS dictated several revelations about Zion and her "redemption," meaning the reinstatement of the Saints to their lands in Jackson Co. As Saints were driven to Clay Co. and then moved further northward to Caldwell Co., Missouri, the geography of Zion expanded. In 1840, after Saints were driven from Missouri and established headquarters in Illinois, JS declared Zion was entire American continent and any place Saints gathered. See also "Independence" and "Jackson County" in this directory; and "Zion" in Glossary.

Maps

The following nine maps show nearly every town and city mentioned in this volume of *The Joseph Smith Papers,* along with other features and boundaries, as they existed during the period indicated on each map.

To locate a particular place on these maps, consult the Geographical Directory in this volume. The directory provides grid coordinates and other information for each place.

1. Volume Overview
2. Regional Overview, 1842–1843
3. Illinois, 30 April 1843
4. Church Land Purchases: Lee County, Iowa Territory, and Hancock County, Illinois, April–August 1839
5. Church Land Purchases: Commerce, Illinois, and Vicinity, 1839
6. Hancock County, Illinois, 1842–1843
7. Nauvoo and Surrounding Area, 30 April 1843
8. Nauvoo Plats, Blocks, and Lots, 30 April 1843
9. Nauvoo, Illinois, 30 April 1843

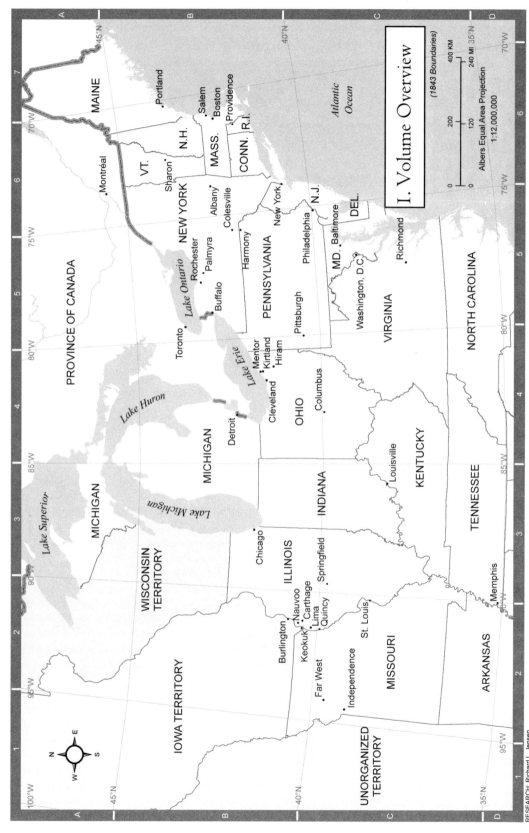

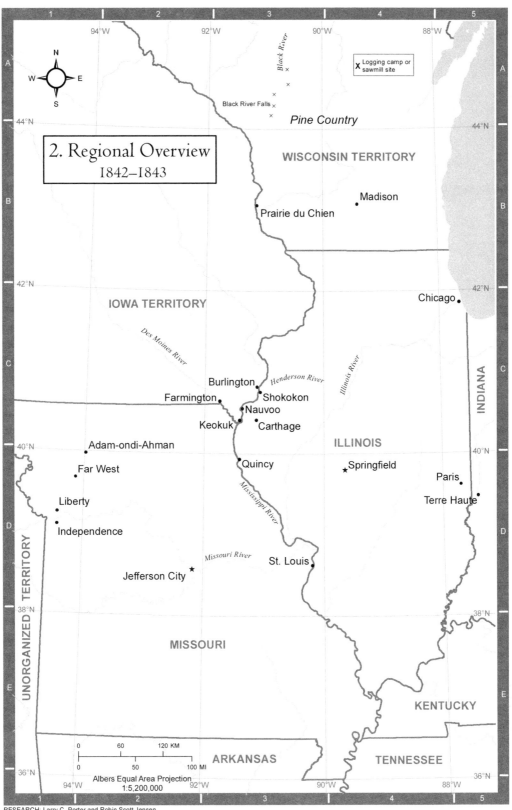

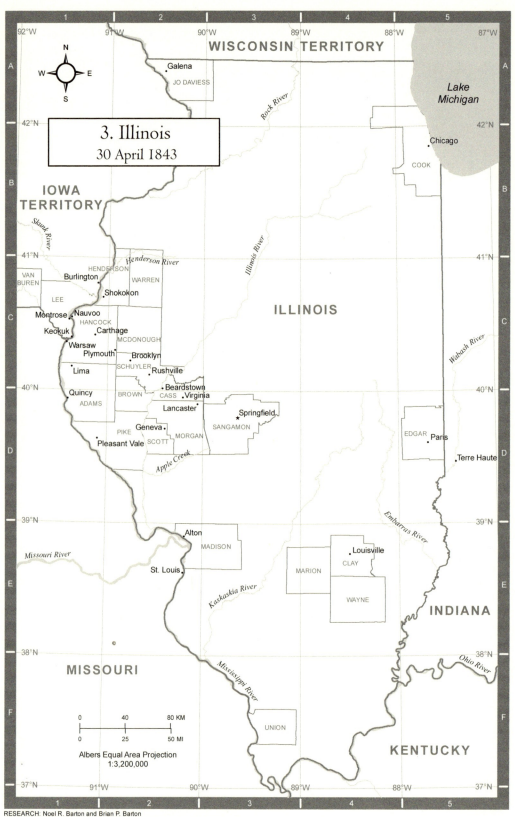

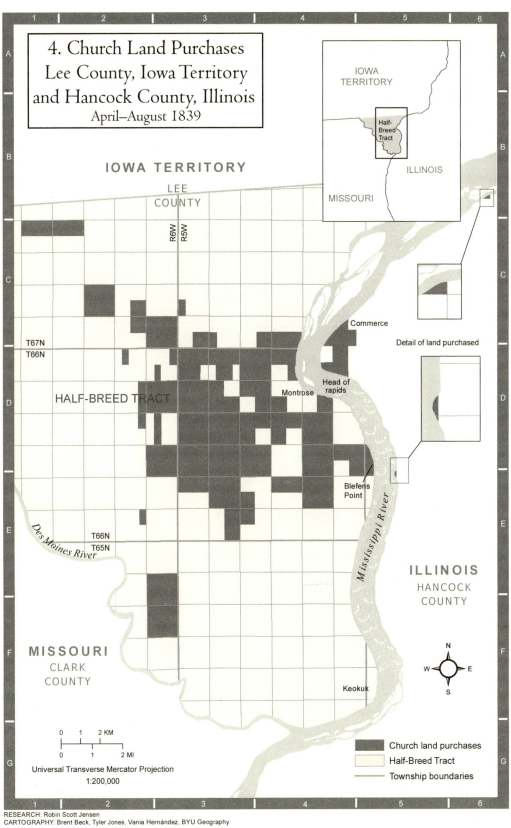

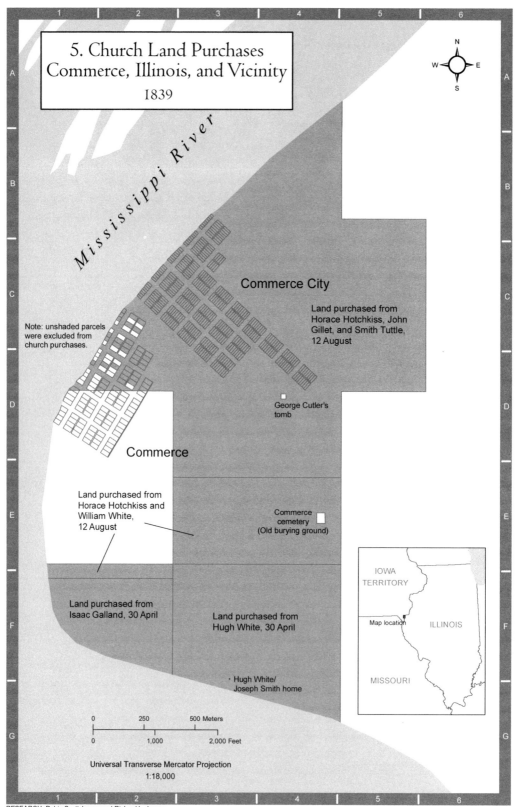

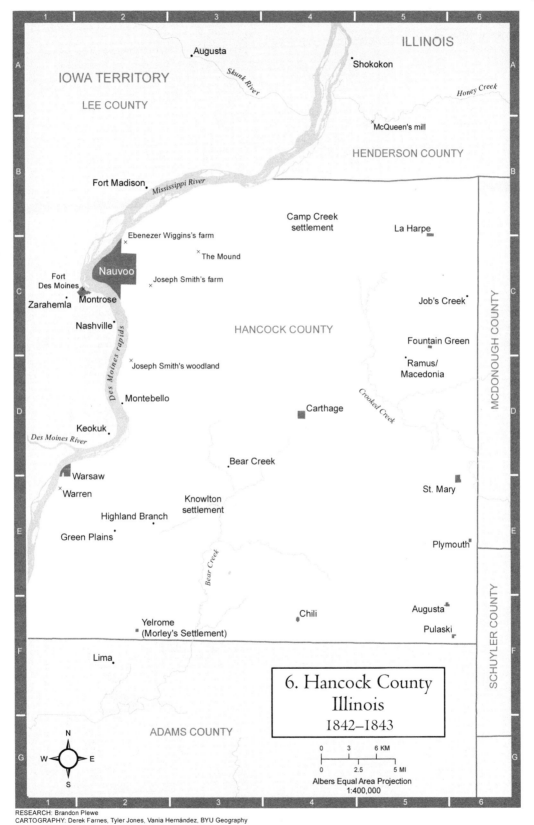

6. Hancock County Illinois 1842–1843

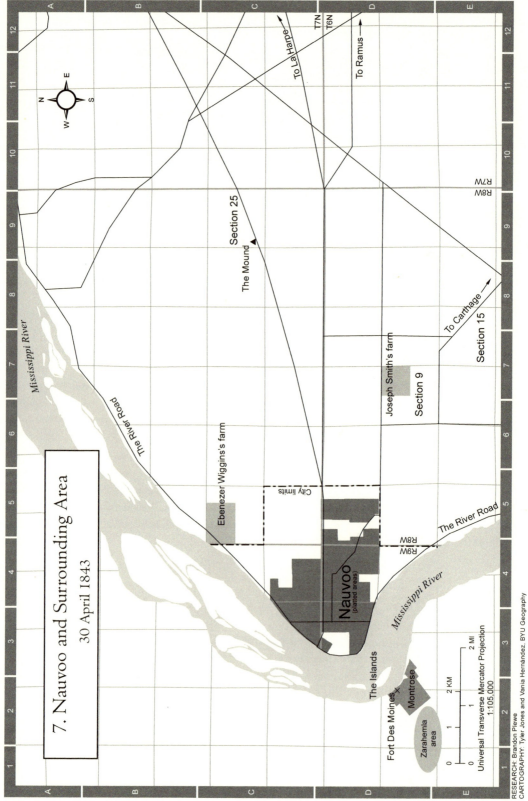

7. Nauvoo and Surrounding Area
30 April 1843

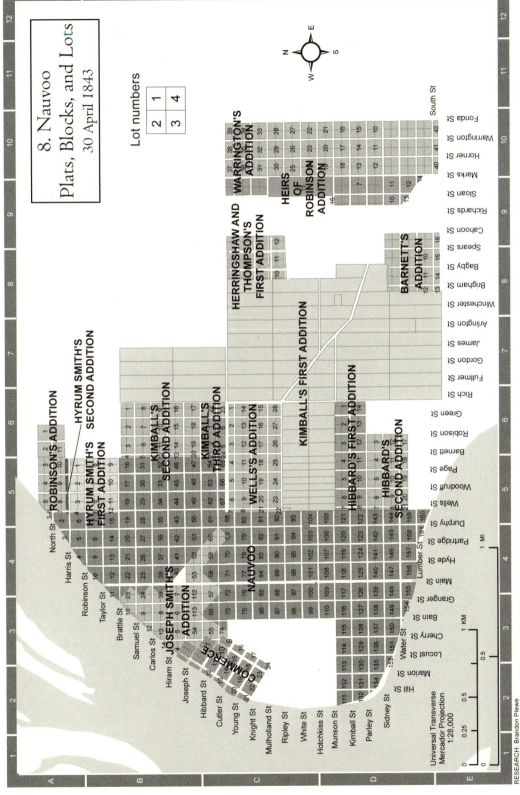

Nauvoo, Illinois
30 April 1843

Selected Properties and Residences

1. Albert Perry Rockwood
2. Upper stone house
3. Amos Davis store/lumberyard
4. Amos Davis home/tavern
5. Hiram Kimball
6. Orson Spencer
7. Orson Pratt
8. Parley P. Pratt
9. Samuel Bennett
10. Francis Higbee/Elias Higbee
11. Edward Hunter
12. Grove/stand
13. Temple
14. Robert D. Foster Mammoth Hotel
15. Frederick Moeser grocery
16. David Yearsley
17. Nauvoo Legion parade ground
18. Old burying ground
19. Orson Hyde
20. William Clayton
21. Wilford Woodruff
22. Heber C. Kimball
23. Esaias Edwards
24. James Sloan
25. Lucien Woodworth
26. Brigham Young
27. Sylvester Stoddard
28. John Taylor
29. Wilson Law
30. Alexander Mills Masonic Hall Tavern
31. Henry Miller
32. William and Wilson Law mills
33. Sidney Rigdon home/post office
34. Printing office
35. Hyrum Smith
36. William Marks
37. William Law
38. Theodore Turley/blacksmith shop
39. Elizabeth Davis Durfee
40. Hyrum Smith office
41. Peter Haws
42. JS store
43. JS home/office/smokehouse
44. Nauvoo House
45. Davidson Hibbard

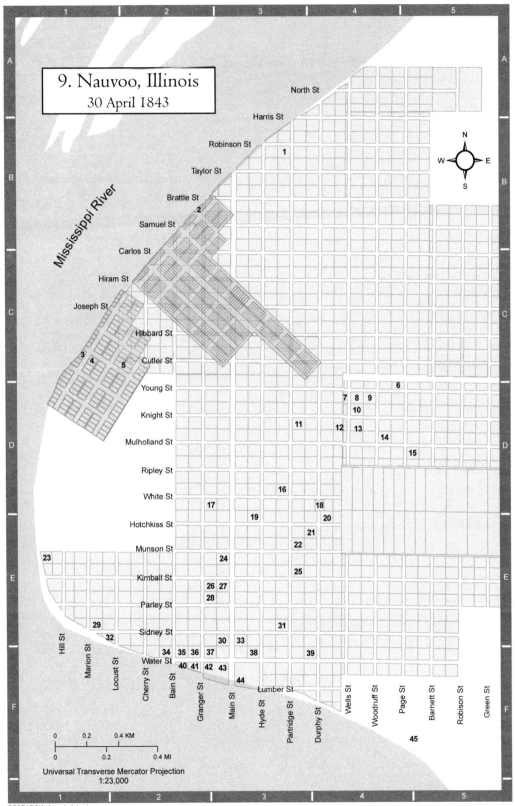

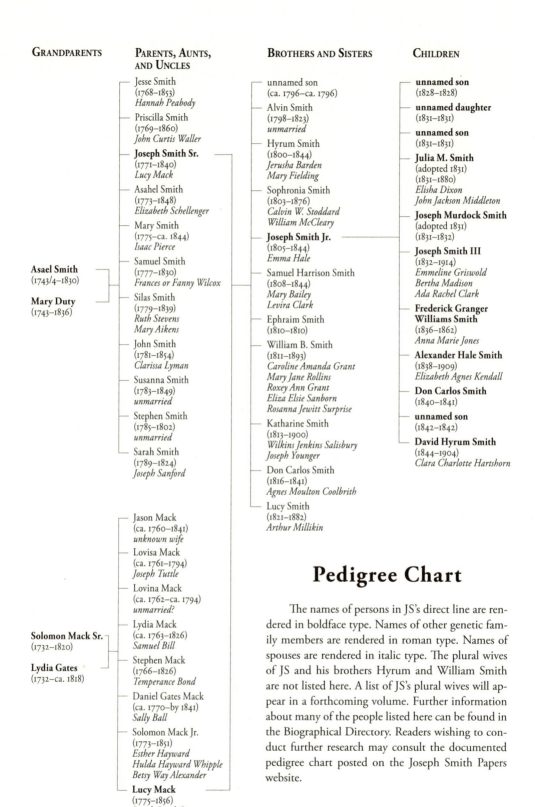

Pedigree Chart

The names of persons in JS's direct line are rendered in boldface type. Names of other genetic family members are rendered in roman type. Names of spouses are rendered in italic type. The plural wives of JS and his brothers Hyrum and William Smith are not listed here. A list of JS's plural wives will appear in a forthcoming volume. Further information about many of the people listed here can be found in the Biographical Directory. Readers wishing to conduct further research may consult the documented pedigree chart posted on the Joseph Smith Papers website.

Biographical Directory

This register contains brief biographical sketches for most of the persons mentioned in this volume. These persons include church leaders, members of JS's family, people JS encountered on his travels, and acquaintances. The directory also includes information about the scribes of documents in this volume.

The biographical entries identify persons by complete name (correctly spelled), birth and death dates, and additional information, such as parentage and birth place, migrations and places of residence, dates of marriage and names of spouses, occupation and denominational affiliation, religious and civic positions, and place of death. Occupations listed in an entry may not be comprehensive. Key figures with major significance to JS's activities receive the fullest biographical sketches. Others receive much briefer descriptions, often with less data than is available. Because unverified and sometimes incorrect data has been recirculated for decades, professional genealogists on the staff of the Joseph Smith Papers Project have utilized original sources whenever possible.

Entries for women are generally listed under their final married names, with appropriate cross-references under maiden names or earlier married names. Partial names in the text, such as "Mr. Angels," are not included in this directory when research could not determine the full name. In some cases, a footnote in the text provides possible identifications. The online index to this volume can often lead the reader to helpful information.

Women who appear in this directory for whom there is significant documentary evidence that they were married or sealed to JS during his lifetime are identified as having been married or sealed to JS. Given the variable and often problematic nature of the sources involved, the editors have made these identifications using, when possible, the terminology employed in the sources themselves. The editors have also indicated in some instances that a marriage or sealing to JS appears possible from available evidence but is by no means certain. Furthermore, the editors have not identified as plural wives of JS several women who have been listed by some scholars as plural wives; in these cases, the editors felt that evidence was too ambiguous and circumstantial to warrant even a provisional note in this directory. A more comprehensive discussion of the women who have been identified as JS's plural wives, as well as an analysis of the sources behind these identifications, will appear in a forthcoming publication of this series. That analysis may result in a reevaluation of identifications noted here.

Locations that are noted include city or town, county, and state, when identified, for the first mention of a locale in each sketch. The counties and states of a handful of well-known cities have been omitted. "LDS church" refers to the Church of Jesus Christ of Latter-day Saints. "RLDS church" refers to the church known originally as the New Organization and subsequently as the Reorganized Church of Jesus Christ of Latter Day Saints (1860–2001) and the Community of Christ (2001 to the present).

Even the fullest entries in this directory provide, of necessity, only a bare skeleton of a person's life. Readers wishing to conduct further research may consult the documented biographical directory posted on the Joseph Smith Papers website.

Adams, George Washington Joshua (1811–11 May 1880), tailor, actor, clergyman. Born in Oxford, Sussex Co., New Jersey. Lived in Boston during 1820s and 1830s. Became Methodist lay preacher. Married Caroline. Moved to New York City, before 1840. Baptized into LDS church, Feb. 1840, in New York City. Ordained an elder by Parley P. Pratt, Mar. 1840, in New York City. Served mission to New York City, 1840. Served mission to England, 1841–1842. Ordained a high priest, 6 Apr. 1841, in Manchester, Lancashire, England. Continued missionary activities in Boston and elsewhere in Massachusetts, 1842. Visited JS, 7 Sept. 1842, at Nauvoo, Hancock Co., Illinois. Returned to Boston, by Jan. 1843. Moved to Nauvoo, spring 1843. Appointed to serve mission to Russia, 1 June 1843; mission unfulfilled. Appointed to serve mission to raise funds for construction of Nauvoo temple, June 1843. Appointed to serve mission to Lee Co., Illinois, 3 July 1843, to disabuse public mind concerning JS's arrest. Returned to Nauvoo, spring 1844. Appointed to notify Quorum of the Twelve of murder of JS, 30 June 1844. Disfellowshipped and excommunicated, Apr. 1845. Appointed counselor to James J. Strang in Strang's Church of Jesus Christ of Latter Day Saints, 8 Aug. 1849. Crowned Strangite king, 8 July 1850, at Beaver Island, Michilimackinac Co., Michigan. Excommunicated from Strangite movement, by 13 Oct. 1850. Became Campbellite preacher, late 1850s. Organized Church of the Messiah, Jan. 1861, in Springfield, Hampden Co., Massachusetts. Moved to Indian River, Washington Co., Maine, 1861. Led colony of followers from Maine to Jaffa, Palestine, Aug. 1865; colony failed. Moved to England, June 1868. Moved to Philadelphia, 1870. Died in Philadelphia.

Adams, James (24 Jan. 1783–11 Aug. 1843), lawyer, judge, insurance agent, land speculator. Born at Simsbury, Hartford Co., Connecticut. Son of Parmenio Adams and Chloe. In New York militia, served as ensign, 1805; as lieutenant; as captain, 1807, and as major, 1811–1816. Married Harriet Denton, ca. 1809. Moved to Oswego Co., New York. Served in War of 1812. Served as brigadier general in Forty-Eighth Infantry Brigade, 1818–1820. Settled at Springfield, Sangamon Co., Illinois, 1821. Elected justice of the peace, 1823, at Springfield. Served with Illinois militia in Winnebago War, 1827, and in Black Hawk War, 1831–1832. Baptized into LDS church, by 1840, at Springfield. Deputy Grand Master of second Grand Masonic Lodge of Illinois. Regent of University of Nauvoo, 1840. Worshipful Master of Springfield Masonic Lodge, 1841. Probate judge, 1841, at Springfield. Ordained a high priest by Hyrum Smith, 2 Oct. 1841, at Nauvoo, Hancock Co., Illinois. Served as branch president, 1842, at Springfield. Ordained a patriarch by JS. Elected probate judge of Hancock Co., by 1843. Died at Nauvoo.

Adams, John Quincy (11 July 1767–23 Feb. 1848), lawyer, diplomat, politician. Born in Braintree (later in Quincy), Suffolk Co., Massachusetts. Son of John Adams and Abigail Smith. Lived alternately in Braintree and Boston, from 1772. Studied law at Harvard University. Married Louisa Catherine Johnson, 26 July 1797, in London. President of U.S., 1824–1828. Moved to Quincy, 1829. Served as U.S. representative from Massachusetts, 1831–1848; championed civil liberties and opposed slavery. Died in Washington DC.

Aldrich, Mark (22 Jan. 1802–21 Sept. 1873), furrier, postmaster, land developer, merchant, politician. Born in Washington Co. (later in Warren Co.), New York. Son of Artemas Aldrich and Huldah Chamberlain. Moved to Hadley Township, Saratoga Co., New York, by Aug. 1810. Moved to Luzerne Township, Warren Co., by Aug. 1820. Married Margaret Wilkinson, 1829. Moved to St. Louis, 1829; to Point, unorganized U.S. territory (later in Keokuk, Lee Co., Iowa Territory), 2 July 1829; and to Fort Edwards (later in Warsaw), Hancock Co., Illinois, 1832. Served as first postmaster of Warsaw, 1834–1838. Elected Hancock Co. representative in Illinois legislature, 1836, 1838. Implicated in murder of JS, 1844. Moved to California, 1850; to Tucson, Doña Ana Co., New Mexico Territory (later in Arizona), 1855. Served in council of Arizona territorial legislature, 1864, 1866, and 1873. Died in Tucson.

Babbitt, Almon (9 Oct. 1812–Sept. 1856), postmaster, editor, attorney. Born at Cheshire, Berkshire Co., Massachusetts. Son of Ira Babbitt and Nancy Crosier. Baptized into LDS church, ca. 1830. Located in Amherst, Lorain Co., Ohio, July 1831. Served mission to New York, fall 1831. Served mission to Pomfret, Chautauque Co., New York, fall 1833. Married Julia Ann Johnson, 23 Nov. 1833, in Kirtland, Geauga Co., Ohio. Participated in Camp of Israel expedition to Missouri, 1834. Appointed member of First Quorum of the Seventy, Feb. 1835. Served mission to Upper Canada, 1837–1838. Led company of Canadian Latter-day Saints to Missouri, 1838. Appointed to gather reports and publications circulated against LDS church, 4 May 1839, at Quincy, Adams Co., Illinois. Appointed president of Kirtland stake, 3 Oct. 1840, at Nauvoo, Hancock Co., Illinois. Disfellowshipped, 1841. Moved to Ramus (later Webster), Hancock Co. Attended church conference, restored to fellowship, and appointed presiding elder of Ramus, 1843. Appointed commander of Ramus militia. Elected to Illinois legislature, representing Hancock Co., 1844. Member of Council of Fifty. Appointed one of five trustees responsible for financial and temporal affairs in Nauvoo, 1846. Appointed postmaster of Nauvoo, 1846. Participated in battle at Nauvoo and signed surrender treaty, Sept. 1846. Migrated to Salt Lake Valley, 1849. Elected delegate to U.S. Congress for provisional state of Deseret, 5 July 1849. Disfellowshipped, 1849, 1851. Appointed secretary of Utah Territory, 1852. Excommunicated, May 1854. Was killed at Ash Hollow, Garden Co., Nebraska Territory.

Backenstos, Jacob B. (8 Oct. 1811–25 Sept. 1857), merchant, sheriff, soldier, politician, land speculator. Born at Lower Paxton, Dauphin Co., Pennsylvania. Son of Jacob Backenstos and Margaretha Theis. Member of Lutheran Reformed Church. Married Sarah Lavina Lee, niece of Robert E. Lee, 15 Dec. 1835, at Sangamon Co., Illinois. Friend of JS and Latter-day Saints, but never joined LDS church. Commissioned aide-de-camp to major general in Nauvoo Legion, Mar. 1842. Moved to Carthage, Hancock Co., Illinois, by early 1842. Member of Nauvoo Masonic Lodge. Served as clerk of Hancock Co. circuit court, 1843–1845. Served as Hancock Co. representative in Illinois legislature, Aug. 1844–Mar. 1845. Served as Hancock Co. sheriff, 1845–1846. Served in Mexican War. Moved to Oregon City, Clackamas Co., Oregon Territory, ca. Nov. 1849. Moved to Portland, Multnomah Co., Oregon Territory, by May 1857. Drowned in Willamette River, Multnomah Co.

Baker, Edward Dickinson (24 Feb. 1811–21 Oct. 1861), lawyer, politician, soldier. Born in London. Son of Edward Baker and Lucy Dickinson. Moved to Philadelphia, 1815; to New Harmony, Posey Co., Indiana, 1825; and to Belleville, St. Clair Co., Illinois, by

1826. Married Mary Ann Foss Lee, 27 Apr. 1831, in Greene Co., Illinois. Converted to Reformed or Christian Church (Campbellite) faith, ca. 1831. Served in Black Hawk War, 1832. Moved to Springfield, Sangamon Co., Illinois, 1835. Served as Sangamon Co. representative in Illinois legislature, 1837–1840. Served as state senator, 1840–1844. Against Illinois governor Thomas Ford's wishes, negotiated in Missouri with fugitive members of mob that killed JS to return to Illinois for trial, Sept. 1844; represented two of the accused at bail hearing, Oct. 1844, in Illinois. Served as U.S. representative from Springfield district, 1845–1846; resigned to accept commission as colonel of Illinois Fourth Regiment in Mexican War. Moved to Galena, Jo Daviess Co., Illinois, 1848. Served as U.S. representative from Galena district, 1849–1850. Moved to San Francisco, by 1852. Served as U.S. representative from California, 1859–1860. Moved to Salem, Marion Co., Oregon, 1860. Served as state senator, 1860–1861; resigned to join Union army in Civil War. Was killed at Battle of Ball's Bluff, near Leesburg, Loudoun Co., Virginia.

Benbow, John (1 Apr. 1800–12 May 1874), farmer. Born in Grendon Warren, Herefordshire, England. Son of Thomas Benbow and Anne Jones. Married Jane Holmes, 16 Oct. 1826, in Worcester, Worcestershire, England. Christened Anglican. Later joined United Brethren. Baptized into LDS church by Wilford Woodruff, 6 Mar. 1840, at Hill Farm, near Castle Frome, Herefordshire, England. Ordained an elder, by 21 June 1840. Given charge of church at Fromes Hill, Herefordshire, 1840. Immigrated to Nauvoo, Hancock Co., Illinois, 1840; paid passage for other Latter-day Saints to immigrate as well. Settled near area known as "The Mound," Hancock Co. Ordained a high priest by Hyrum Smith, 2 Feb. 1842, in Nauvoo. Appointed captain of fifty in Brigham Young's pioneer company, 1848. Arrived in Salt Lake Valley, 20 Sept. 1848. A founder of South Cottonwood (later Murray, Salt Lake Co., Utah Territory), 1848. Died in South Cottonwood.

Bennet, James Arlington (21 Dec. 1788–25 Dec. 1863), attorney, newspaper publisher, educator, author. Born in New York. Married first Sophia, ca. 1811. Served as third and later second lieutenant in First U.S. Artillery, 1 Aug. 1813–14 Oct. 1814. Published *American System of Practical Book-keeping*, 1824, with subsequent editions printed until 1855. Lived in New Utrecht/Gravesend, Kings Co., New York, by 1830. Published *Brooklyn Advocate* and *Nassau Gazette*, 1832–1836. Awarded honorary doctor of laws degree, 22 Apr. 1842, from University of Nauvoo. Appointed inspector general of Nauvoo Legion, Apr. 1842. Founded Arlington Academy, 1843, at New Utrecht. Baptized into LDS church by Brigham Young, 30 Aug. 1843, at Coney Island, Kings Co. Invited to run for U.S. vice presidency as JS's running mate, 1843; invitation withdrawn because of misunderstanding regarding Bennet's supposed birth in Ireland. Married second Julia Helen Berkeley, 30 Dec. 1851. Lived with Margaret Curtin, 1852–1863. Died in Brooklyn, Kings Co.

Bennett, James Gordon (1 Sept. 1795–1 June 1872), journalist, newspaper owner. Born at Newmill, Keith, Banffshire, Scotland. Catholic. Moved to Aberdeen, Aberdeenshire, Scotland, ca. 1815, and to Halifax, Halifax Co., Nova Scotia, 1819. Moved to Boston; to New York, ca. 1822; to Charleston, South Carolina, ca. 1822; to New York City, 1823; to Washington DC, 1827; back to New York City, 1829; to Philadelphia, 1832; and back to New York City, 1833. Founder of *New York Herald*, 1835. Married Henrietta Agnes Crean, 6 June 1840, at New York City. Lauded by JS for his evenhanded reporting on LDS doctrines and people. Appointed to rank of brigadier general in Nauvoo Legion, May 1842.

Awarded "freedom of the city" of Nauvoo and honorary doctor of laws degree from University of Nauvoo, 21 Aug. 1842. Died at New York City.

Bennett, John Cook (3 Aug. 1804–5 Aug. 1867), physician, minister, poultry breeder. Born at Fairhaven, Bristol Co., Massachusetts. Son of John Bennett and Abigail Cook. Moved to Marietta, Washington Co., Ohio, 1808; to Massachusetts, 1812; and back to Marietta, 1822. Married first Mary A. Barker, 9 Jan. 1826, at Marietta. Joined Pickaway Masonic Lodge, ca. 1827, in Circleville, Pickaway Co., Ohio. Methodist; later affiliated with Christian Disciple (Campbellite) faith. Acquainted with JS through Sidney Rigdon from early 1830s. Moved to Wheeling, Ohio Co., Virginia (later in West Virginia), 1831. Charged with lying and other misconduct by Pickaway Masonic Lodge, 1834. Moved to Fairfield, Wayne Co., Illinois, 1838. Commissioned brigadier general of Second Division in Illinois militia, 1839. Moved to Nauvoo, Hancock Co., Illinois, 1840. Baptized into LDS church, Sept. 1840, at Nauvoo. Helped draft and secure Nauvoo Charter, 1840. Served as quartermaster general in Illinois militia, 1840–1842. Elected major general and inspector general in Nauvoo Legion, Feb. 1841. Served as assistant president in First Presidency, 1841–1842; mayor of Nauvoo, 1841–1842; chancellor of University of Nauvoo, 1841–1842; and master in chancery of Hancock Co., 1841–1842. Grand Secretary of Nauvoo Masonic Lodge, 1841. Excommunicated for adultery, 11 May 1842. Cashiered from Nauvoo Legion, June 1842. Expelled from Nauvoo Masonic Lodge, 1842. After disaffection from church, publicly accused JS of committing adultery, attempting murder, and planning the 6 May 1842 attempt to kill former Missouri governor Lilburn W. Boggs. Urged Missouri and Illinois officials to renew 1838 charge of treason against JS, which resulted in JS's arrest in June 1843. Moved back to Fairfield, before Mar. 1843. Married second Sarah Ryder, 28 Mar. 1843, at Plymouth, Plymouth Co., Massachusetts. Briefly associated with George M. Hinkle's movement, The Church of Jesus Christ, the Bride, the Lamb's Wife, 1843, at Moscow, Muscatine Co., Iowa Territory; with Sidney Rigdon, 1844, at Nauvoo; and with James J. Strang's Church of Jesus Christ of Latter Day Saints at Voree, Racine Co., Wisconsin, as general-in-chief, 1846. Excommunicated from Strangite movement, 1847. Moved to Plymouth, 1847; to Great Falls, Strafford Co., New Hampshire, 1851; to Des Moines, Polk Co., Iowa, 1853; and to Polk City, Polk Co., 1856. Died at Polk City.

Bennett, Samuel C. (ca. 1810–May 1893), market inspector, barometer manufacturer, physician. Born in England. Married Selina. Baptized into LDS church, by 1839, in U.S. Ordained an elder, 23 Dec. 1839, in Philadelphia. Served as presiding elder, 1840, in Philadelphia. Served as branch president, 1840, in Cincinnati. Trustee of University of Nauvoo, 1841, in Nauvoo, Hancock Co., Illinois. Nauvoo city alderman, 1843–1845. Excommunicated, by Oct. 1844, in Nauvoo. Ordained an apostle in Sidney Rigdon's Church of Christ, 1845. Served as an apostle in James J. Strang's Church of Jesus Christ of Latter Day Saints, 1846–1853. Lived in Michilimackinac Co., Michigan, by 1850; in Allegheny (later in Pittsburgh), Allegheny Co., Pennsylvania, by 1860; and in Cuyahoga Co., Ohio, by 1870. Died in Cuyahoga Co.

Bishop, Francis Gladden (19 June 1809–30 Nov. 1864), watchmaker, minister. Born at Livonia, Ontario Co., New York. Son of Isaac Gates Bishop and Mary Hyde. Served as minister in Freewill Baptist Church, by 1831. Baptized into LDS church and ordained an elder, 2 July 1832, in Olean Point (later Olean), Cattaraugus Co., New York. Engaged in extensive missionary work from North Carolina to Upper Canada, 1833–1840. Moved to Kirtland, Geauga Co., Ohio, by 1836. Ordained a seventy, Feb. 1836, in Kirtland. Appointed secretary of church conference held in Rochester, Columbiana Co., Ohio, 28 Oct. 1837. Moved to Nauvoo, Hancock Co., Illinois, by 1842. Excommunicated, 11 Mar. 1842, in Nauvoo. Organized schismatic movement called "Kingdom of God," 1842. Lived at Kirtland, 1850. Participated in eight religious movements, 1847–ca. 1860. Moved to Council Bluffs, Pottawattamie Co., Iowa, by Mar. 1853. Moved to Cincinnati, by Apr. 1855. Appointed Indian agent for Utah Territory, spring 1858; maintained a residence in Little Sioux, Harrison Co., Iowa, until 1860. Resided in Denver and Golden City, Jefferson Co., Colorado, early 1860s. Moved to Salt Lake City, after Mar. 1864. Died in Salt Lake City.

Bogart, Samuel (2 Apr. 1797–11 Mar. 1861), preacher, military officer, farmer. Born in Carter Co., Tennessee. Son of Cornelius Bogart and Elizabeth Moffett. Served in War of 1812. Married Rachel Hammer, 19 May 1818, in Washington Co., Tennessee. Moved to Illinois and became Methodist minister. Served as commissioner in Schuyler Co., Illinois. Served as major in Black Hawk War, 1832. Located at Ray Co., Missouri, mid-1830s. Captain of company of mounted volunteers from Ray Co. during Mormon War, 1838; contended with Mormon militia at Battle of Crooked River near Ray Co., 25 Oct. 1838. Appointed to arrest Mormons who participated in Battle of Crooked River and to summon witnesses for court hearing at Richmond, Ray Co. Elected judge, Nov. 1839, at Caldwell Co., Missouri. Shot and killed opponent's nephew, Beatty Hines, during election-day argument. Fled to escape prosecution; settled in Washington Co., Republic of Texas, 1839. Moved to what later became Collin Co., Republic of Texas, 1845. Elected to Texas legislature, 1847, 1849, 1851, and 1859. Likely died near McKinney, Collin Co.

Boggs, Lilburn W. (14 Dec. 1796–14 Mar. 1860), bookkeeper, bank cashier, merchant, Indian agent and trader, lawyer, doctor, postmaster, politician. Born at Lexington, Fayette Co., Kentucky. Son of John M. Boggs and Martha Oliver. Served in War of 1812. Moved to St. Louis, ca. 1816, and engaged in business. Married first Julia Ann Bent, July 1817, at St. Louis. Moved to Franklin, Howard Co., Missouri, 1817; to Fort Osage, Howard Co., ca. 1818; to St. Louis, 1820; and back to Fort Osage, spring 1821. Married second Panthea Grant Boone, July 1823. Moved to Harmony Mission (Indian mission for Great Osage Nation; later near Papinville, Bates Co.), Missouri, by 1824. Located at Independence, Jackson Co., Missouri, 1826; elected to state senate on Democratic ticket, 1826, 1828. Elected lieutenant governor, 1832. Became governor upon resignation of predecessor, Daniel Dunklin, 1836, and served through 1840. Moved to Jefferson City, Cole Co., Missouri, 1836. Authorized 1838 expulsion of Mormons from Missouri under what was termed his "extermination order." Returned to Independence, before 1842. Severely wounded by assassin, 6 May 1842; accused JS of complicity with Orrin Porter Rockwell in perpetrating the crime. Returned to Jefferson City, 1842. Served in state senate, 1842–1846. Moved to Cass Co., Missouri, by 1843; returned to Independence, by 1845. Migrated to Sonoma, Mexico (later in Sonoma Co., California), 1846. In 1852, moved to Napa Valley, Napa Co., California, where he died.

Boynton, John Farnham (20 Sept. 1811–20 Oct. 1890), merchant, lecturer, scientist, inventor. Born at East Bradford (later Groveland), Essex Co., Massachusetts. Son of Eliphalet Boynton and Susanna Nichols. Baptized into LDS church by JS, Sept. 1832, at

Kirtland, Geauga Co., Ohio. Ordained an elder by Sidney Rigdon, 1832. Served missions to Pennsylvania, 1832, with Zebedee Coltrin; to Maine, 1833–1834; and to Painesville, Geauga Co., Ohio, Nov. 1834, with William E. McLellin. Ordained member of Quorum of the Twelve, Feb. 1835, in Kirtland. Served mission to eastern states and Canada with Quorum of the Twelve. Married first to Susannah (Susan) Lowell by JS, 20 Jan. 1836, at Kirtland. Dissented over handling of temporal matters associated with Kirtland Safety Society; disfellowshipped from Quorum of the Twelve, 3 Sept. 1837. Reinstated to church and membership in Quorum of the Twelve, 10 Sept. 1837. Excommunicated, 1837. Visited JS in Nauvoo, Hancock Co., Illinois, Sept. 1842. Settled at Syracuse, Onondaga Co., New York, ca. 1851. Wife died, 7 Aug. 1859. Assisted in running boundary line between U.S. and Mexico. Married second Caroline Foster Harriman, 20 Jan. 1883. Died at Syracuse.

Brink, William Bicking (1810–4 Feb. 1884), physician, cooper. Born in Pennsylvania. Married first Amelia. Practiced Thomsonian medicine. Defendant in malpractice lawsuit, 1843, at Nauvoo, Hancock Co., Illinois. Baptized into LDS church, by Apr. 1843. Ordained an elder, 10 Apr. 1843, at Nauvoo. Served mission to Pennsylvania, 1843. Lived at St. Louis, by 1850; at Freeburg, St. Clair Co., Illinois, by 1860; and at Los Angeles Co., California, by 1870. Married second Elizabeth Sayres, 2 June 1870, at Los Angeles. Moved to Bakersfield, Kern Co., California, by 1872. Died at Bakersfield.

Brooks, Lester (5 Nov. 1802–22 July 1878), stove plate molder. Born in Lanesborough, Berkshire Co., Massachusetts. Son of Sheldon Brooks and Sarah Noble. Moved to Pittsfield, Berkshire Co., before 1820; to Waterville, Oneida Co., New York, by 1828; and to Kirtland, Geauga Co., Ohio, by 1837. Baptized into LDS church. Ordained an elder, before Apr. 1837. Moved to Missouri, 1838. Returned to Kirtland, late 1839. Resided in Madison, Lake Co., Ohio, 1840. Appointed counselor in Kirtland stake presidency, 22 May 1841. Ordained a high priest, before 1845. Appointed by Brigham Young to preside over branch of church in Ohio, 1845. Presumably disaffected from church. Served mission to England for James J. Strang's Church of Jesus Christ of Latter Day Saints, 1846. Moved to Buffalo, Erie Co., New York, by 1850. Died at Buffalo.

Brown, Uriah (ca. 1784–after 1850), laborer, inventor. Born in Connecticut. Married Mary Perry, 3 Dec. 1805, in Nantucket, Nantucket Co., Massachusetts. Moved to Rushville, Schuyler Co., Illinois, by Dec. 1842. One of three non-Mormon members of Council of Fifty, 1844. Lived at Pottawattamie Co., Iowa, 1850.

Burdick, Thomas (17 Nov. 1795–6 Nov. 1877), farmer, teacher, judge, postmaster, clerk, civil servant. Born at Canajoharie, Montgomery Co., New York. Son of Gideon Burdick and Catherine Robertson. Married Anna Higley, 1828, at Jamestown, Chautauque Co., New York. Baptized into LDS church and moved to Kirtland, Geauga Co., Ohio, by Oct. 1834. Ordained an elder, by Jan. 1836. Appointed church clerk to record membership licenses, 24 Feb. 1836. Appointed elders quorum treasurer, 9 Nov. 1836. Appointed member of Kirtland high council, 7 Nov. 1837. Appointed bishop of Kirtland, 22 May 1841. Moved to Burlington, Des Moines Co., Iowa Territory, 1845. Moved to what became Council Bluffs, Pottawattamie Co., Iowa Territory, 1846. Located at San Bernardino, San Bernardino Co., California, 1853. Settled at San Gabriel Township, Los Angeles Co., California, winter 1853–1854. Died at Los Angeles Co.

Butterfield, Justin (1790–Oct. 1855), teacher, lawyer. Born in Keene, Cheshire Co., New Hampshire. Ca. 1810, moved to Watertown, Jefferson Co., New York, where he taught school and studied law. Admitted to bar, 1812, at Watertown. Practiced law in Adams, Jefferson Co., and Sackets Harbor, Jefferson Co. Married Elizabeth Pierce, ca. 1814, in Sackets Harbor. Moved to Hounsfield, Jefferson Co., by 1820; to New Orleans; back to Watertown, 1826; and to Chicago, 1835. An original trustee of Rush Medical College, Mar. 1837. District attorney of Illinois, 1841–1844. As U.S. attorney, instructed to resist JS's bankruptcy petition, 1842, and negotiated proposed settlement. Represented JS, Dec. 1842–Jan. 1843, at Springfield, Sangamon Co., Illinois, when Missouri authorities attempted to extradite JS to be charged as accessory in attempt to kill former governor Lilburn W. Boggs. Partner in law firm of Butterfield & Collins, as early as 1843, in Chicago. Died in Chicago.

Cahoon, Reynolds (30 Apr. 1790–29 Apr. 1861), farmer, tanner, builder. Born at Cambridge, Washington Co., New York. Son of William Cahoon Jr. and Mehitable Hodges. Married Thirza Stiles, 11 Dec. 1810. Moved to Western Reserve, 1811. Located at Harpersfield, Ashtabula Co., Ohio. Served in War of 1812. Moved near Kirtland, Geauga Co., Ohio, 1825. Baptized into LDS church by Parley P. Pratt, 12 Oct. 1830. Ordained an elder by Sidney Rigdon and a high priest by JS, 4 June 1831. Appointed counselor to Bishop Newel K. Whitney at Kirtland, 10 Feb. 1832. Appointed to serve mission with David W. Patten to Warsaw, Wyoming Co., New York, 23 Mar. 1833. Member of committee to oversee building of Kirtland temple. Member of Kirtland stake presidency. Moved to Missouri; arrived 7 June 1838. Appointed counselor to stake president at Adam-ondi-Ahman, Daviess Co., Missouri, 28 June 1838. Located in Iowa Territory following exodus from Missouri. Appointed counselor in Iowa stake, Lee Co., Iowa Territory, 1839. Appointed guard in Nauvoo Legion, Mar. 1841. Served on building committee for Nauvoo temple. Member of Nauvoo Masonic Lodge. Member of Council of Fifty, 11 Mar. 1844. Resided at Winter Quarters, unorganized U.S. territory (later in Omaha, Douglas Co., Nebraska), 1846. Migrated to Salt Lake Valley, 1848. Died in Salt Lake City.

Carlin, Thomas (18 July 1789–14 Feb. 1852), ferry owner, farmer, sheriff, politician. Born in Fayette Co., Kentucky. Son of Thomas Carlin and Elizabeth Evans. Baptist. Moved to Missouri, by 1803. Moved to Illinois, by 1812. Served in War of 1812. Married Rebecca Hewitt, 13 Dec. 1814, in Madison Co., Illinois. Moved to Greene Co., Illinois, 1818. Appointed first sheriff of Greene Co., 1821. Served as state senator, 1824–1828. Donated land for construction of public buildings in Carrollton, Greene Co. Served in Black Hawk War as captain of spy battalion in Illinois Mounted Volunteers, 1832. Appointed receiver of public monies by U.S. president Andrew Jackson, 1834, in Quincy, Adams Co., Illinois. Affiliated with Church of Christ in Quincy. Served as governor of Illinois, 1838–1842. Issued warrant for arrest of JS for involvement in attempt to kill former Missouri governor Lilburn W. Boggs, 1842. Returned to Carrollton, 1842. Elected state representative, 1849. Died near Carrollton.

Carter, Jared (14 June 1801–6 July 1849). Born at Killingworth, Middlesex Co., Connecticut. Son of Gideon Carter and Johanna Sims. Moved to Benson, Rutland Co., Vermont, after Apr. 1807. Married Lydia Ames, 20 Sept. 1823, at Benson. Moved to Chenango, Broome Co., New York, by Jan. 1831. Baptized into LDS church by Hyrum Smith, 20 Feb. 1831, in Colesville, Broome Co. Moved with Colesville branch to Thompson,

Geauga Co., Ohio, May 1831. Ordained a priest, June 1831. Ordained an elder, Sept. 1831. Appointed to serve missions to eastern U.S., 22 Sept. 1831 and Mar. 1832. Left to serve mission to Michigan, Dec. 1832. Appointed to serve mission to eastern U.S., Mar. 1833. Ordained a high priest, by May 1833. Appointed to obtain funds for Elders School, 4 May 1833. Member of Kirtland temple building committee, 1833. Appointed to first Kirtland high council, 17 Feb. 1834. Appointed to serve mission to Upper Canada, 20 Feb. 1834. Labored on Kirtland temple. Shareholder of Kirtland Safety Society, Jan. 1837. Appointed president of Kirtland high council, 9 Sept. 1837. Removed family to Far West, Caldwell Co., Missouri, 1837. Appointed member of Far West high council, 3 Mar. 1838. Moved from Far West to Commerce (later Nauvoo), Hancock Co., Illinois, 1839. Member of Nauvoo Masonic Lodge. Affiliated with James J. Strang's Church of Jesus Christ of Latter Day Saints, 1846. Excommunicated from Strangite movement, 8 Nov. 1846. Returned to LDS church. By June 1849, moved to DeKalb Co., Illinois, where he died.

Chambers, John (6 Oct. 1780–21 Sept. 1852), lawyer, politician. Born at Bromley Bridge (later Burnt Mills), Somerset Co., New Jersey. Son of Rowland Chambers and Phoebe Mullican. Lived at Mason Co., Kentucky, 1794–1841. Married first Margaret Taylor, 16 June 1803, at Mason Co. Married second Hannah Lee Taylor, 29 Oct. 1807, at Washington Co., Maryland. Enlisted in Kentucky militia, 1811. Served as Kentucky state representative, 1812, 1815. Served in War of 1812 as aide-de-camp to William Henry Harrison at Battle of the Thames, 1813. Served as judge in court of appeals, 1825–1827; as U.S. representative from Kentucky, 1828–1829, 1835–1839; and as Kentucky state representative, 1830, 1831. Served as governor of Iowa Territory, 1841–1845, while living at Burlington, Des Moines Co., Iowa Territory. Lived at Mason Co., 1845–1852. Died at Paris, Bourbon Co., Kentucky.

Clark, John Bullock (17 Apr. 1802–29 Oct. 1885), lawyer, politician. Born at Madison Co., Kentucky. Moved to Howard Co., Missouri, 1818. Practiced law in Fayette, Howard Co., beginning 1824. Clerk of Howard Co. courts, 1824–1834. Appointed brigadier general in Missouri militia, 1830. Appointed major general in Missouri militia. Appointed to command Missouri militia operations against Mormon forces, 27 Oct. 1838; arrived in Far West, Caldwell Co., Missouri, 4 Nov. 1838, after Mormons had surrendered. Insisted Mormons leave Missouri; transported Mormon prisoners to Richmond, where they underwent a preliminary hearing. Member of Missouri House of Representatives, 1850–1851. Member of U.S. House of Representatives, 1857–1861. Died at Fayette.

Clark, Sylvia Porter Sessions (31 July 1818–12 Apr. 1882). Born in Newry, Oxford Co., Maine. Daughter of David Sessions and Patty Bartlett. Moved to Far West, Caldwell Co., Missouri, Nov. 1837. Married Windsor Palmer Lyon, Mar. 1838, in Far West. Moved to Nauvoo, Hancock Co., Illinois, by Feb. 1841. Possibly "married or sealed" to JS, 8 Feb. 1842. Moved to Iowa City, Johnson Co., Iowa Territory, June 1846. Married Ezekiel Clark, 5 Feb. 1850, in Iowa City. Migrated to Salt Lake City, 4 Aug. 1854. Moved to Bountiful, Davis Co., Utah Territory, by June 1860. Died at Bountiful.

Clayton, William (17 July 1814–4 Dec. 1879), bookkeeper, clerk. Born at Charock Moss, Penwortham, Lancashire, England. Son of Thomas Clayton and Ann Critchley. Married Ruth Moon, 9 Oct. 1836, at Penwortham. Baptized into LDS church by Heber C. Kimball, 21 Oct. 1837, in River Ribble, Lancashire. Ordained a priest, Dec. 1837, in

Lancashire. Ordained a high priest by Heber C. Kimball and Orson Hyde, 1 Apr. 1838, at Preston, Lancashire. Served as second counselor in British mission presidency, 1838–1840. Immigrated to Nauvoo, Hancock Co., Illinois, 1840. Served as clerk of high council in Iowa Territory, 1841. Member of Nauvoo Masonic Lodge. Served as recorder and scribe to JS, 1842–1844, at Nauvoo. Appointed secretary of Masonic lodge, city treasurer, and temple recorder, Sept. 1842, at Nauvoo. Participated in plural marriage during JS's lifetime. Clerk of first company of pioneers to Utah, Apr.–Aug. 1847. Wrote and published *Latter-day Saint Emigrants' Guide,* 1847–1848. Died at Salt Lake City.

Cleminson (Clemenson), John James (28 Dec. 1798–28 Dec. 1879), farmer, teacher, cabinet maker, carpenter, clerk. Born at Lancaster, Lancashire, England. Migrated to St. John's, New Brunswick (later in Canada), 1812. Moved to Louisville, Jefferson Co., Kentucky, 1818. Moved to Lexington, Lillard Co., Missouri, by 1823. Married Lydia Lightner, 5 Jan. 1823, at Lillard Co., Missouri. Baptized into LDS church and moved to Far West, Caldwell Co., Missouri, by 1837. Elected Caldwell Co. clerk and circuit clerk, 1837. Testified against church leaders, Sept. 1837. Testified against JS at hearing in Richmond, Ray Co., Missouri, Nov. 1838. Moved to Rockport, Caldwell Co., by June 1840. Lived at Montrose, Lee Co., Iowa Territory, by Mar. 1842. Wrote to JS seeking reconciliation, May 1842. Ordained a high priest, 31 Jan. 1846. Lived at New Town, Monterey Co., California, 1852. Moved to San Bernardino, Los Angeles Co., California, 1852. By June 1860, lived at El Monte, Los Angeles Co., where he died.

Coltrin, Zebedee (7 Sept. 1804–21 July 1887). Born at Ovid, Seneca Co., New York. Son of John Coltrin and Sarah Graham. Belonged to Methodist church. Married Julia Ann Jennings, before 1828. Baptized into LDS church by Solomon Hancock, 9 Jan. 1831, at Strongsville, Cuyahoga Co., Ohio. Ordained an elder by John Whitmer, 21 Jan. 1831. Served mission to Missouri with Levi Hancock, summer 1831. Ordained a high priest by Hyrum Smith and Reynolds Cahoon, July 1832, at Kirtland, Geauga Co., Ohio. Appointed to serve mission with John Murdock to Thompson, Geauga Co., Ohio, and eastern states, 23 Mar. 1833. Appointed to serve mission with Henry Harriman to Canada, 20 Feb. 1834. Participated in Camp of Israel expedition to Missouri, 1834. Appointed a president of First Quorum of the Seventy, 28 Feb. 1835, at Kirtland. Reassigned from Seventy to high priests quorum, 6 Apr. 1837. Located at Commerce (later Nauvoo), Hancock Co., Illinois, 1839, but soon after moved to Kirtland. Wife died, 1841. Appointed second counselor to Almon W. Babbitt in Kirtland stake, 22 May 1841. Received into Nauvoo stake high priests quorum, 4 June 1843. Migrated to Salt Lake Valley with Brigham Young pioneer company, 1847. Settled at Spanish Fork, Utah Co., Utah Territory, 1852. Died at Spanish Fork.

Cowan, John F. (25 Apr. 1781–7 Nov. 1853), farmer. Born near Harpers Ferry, Berkeley Co., Virginia (later in West Virginia). Son of James Cowan Sr. and Mary Russell. Moved near Lebanon, Hamilton Co., Ohio, Nov. 1800. Married first Miss Sewell, ca. 1801. Married second Sarah French, ca. 1819. Lived at Turtle Creek, Warren Co., Ohio, Aug. 1820. Moved to Indiana, Aug. 1828. Moved to Bald Bluff, Henderson Co., Illinois, 1836. Traveled to Washington DC and Baltimore and met with U.S. president John Tyler, urging him to provide JS with a U.S. Army commission, 1844. Died in Bald Bluff.

Cowdery, Oliver (3 Oct. 1806–3 Mar. 1850), clerk, teacher, justice of the peace, lawyer, newspaper editor. Born at Wells, Rutland Co., Vermont. Son of William Cowdery and

Rebecca Fuller. Raised Congregationalist. Moved to western New York and clerked at a store, ca. 1825–1828. Taught term as local schoolmaster at Manchester, Ontario Co., New York, 1828–1829. Assisted JS as principal scribe in translation of Book of Mormon, 1829. With JS, was baptized and received Aaronic and Melchizedek priesthoods, 1829. Moved to Fayette, Seneca Co., New York, and was one of the Three Witnesses of the Book of Mormon, June 1829. Helped oversee printing of Book of Mormon by E. B. Grandin, 1829–1830. Among six original members of LDS church, 6 Apr. 1830. Led missionaries through Ohio and to Missouri, 1830–1831. With John Whitmer, left Ohio to take revelations to Missouri for publication, Nov. 1831. Assisted William W. Phelps in conducting church's printing operations at Jackson Co., Missouri, 1832–1833. Married Elizabeth Ann Whitmer, 18 Dec. 1832, in Kaw Township, Jackson Co. Edited *The Evening and the Morning Star,* 1833. Moved to Kirtland, Geauga Co., Ohio, ca. 1833. Member of United Firm, Literary Firm, and Kirtland high council. Appointed assistant president of church, 5 Dec. 1834. Edited Kirtland continuation of *The Evening and the Morning Star,* under modified title *Evening and Morning Star,* 1835–1836. Edited *LDS Messenger and Advocate,* 1834–1835, 1836–1837, and *Northern Times,* 1835. Served as church recorder, 1830–1831, 1835–1837. Elected justice of the peace in Kirtland, 1837. Moved to Far West, Caldwell Co., Missouri, 1837. Excommunicated, 1838. Returned to Kirtland, 1838, and briefly practiced law. Moved to Tiffin, Seneca Co., Ohio, where he continued law practice and held political offices, 1840–1847. Attended Methodist Protestant Church at Tiffin. Moved to Elkhorn, Walworth Co., Wisconsin Territory, 1847. Ran unsuccessfully for Wisconsin State Assembly, 1848. Coeditor of *Walworth County Democrat,* 1848. Requested and received readmission to LDS church, 1848, at Kanesville, Pottawattamie Co., Iowa. Died at Richmond, Ray Co., Missouri.

Cowles, Austin (3 May 1792–15 Jan. 1872), wheelwright, farmer, teacher, minister, millwright, miller, merchant. Born in Brookfield, Orange Co., Vermont. Son of Timothy Cowles and Abigail Woodworth. Moved to Unadilla, Otsego Co., New York, by 1810. Married first Phebe Wilbur, 14 Jan. 1813, in Unadilla. Minister of Methodist Episcopal Church. Moved to Friendship, Allegany Co., New York, 1819. Moved to Bolivar, Allegany Co., Feb. 1820. Served as inspector of common schools and town clerk, 1825, at Bolivar. Married second Irene H. Elliott, 21 Oct. 1827, in Amity, Allegany Co. Moved to Franklinville, Cattaraugus Co., New York, by June 1830. Baptized into LDS church, 1832, in New York. Received elder's license, 28 Sept. 1836, in Kirtland, Geauga Co., Ohio. Moved to Kirtland, ca. 1837. Moved to Hancock Co., Illinois, by 1840. Elected supervisor of streets, Feb. 1841, at Nauvoo. Appointed to Nauvoo high council, 6 Feb. 1841. Appointed counselor to Nauvoo stake president William Marks, Mar. 1841. Served mission to New Hampshire and Massachusetts, 1841. Member of Nauvoo Masonic Lodge. Excommunicated. Appointed counselor to William Law by LDS dissenters, Apr. 1844. Moved to Burlington, Des Moines Co., Iowa Territory, May 1844. Published affidavit against plural marriage in *Nauvoo Expositor,* June 1844. Moved to Hampton, Rock Island Co., Illinois, by Aug. 1844. Appointed to high priests quorum presidency in Sidney Rigdon's Church of Christ, Apr. 1845, in Pittsburgh. Returned to Kirtland and affiliated with James Brewster's Church of Christ; excommunicated, Sept. 1849. Moved to Sycamore, De Kalb Co., Illinois, 1850; to Fulton, Whiteside Co., Illinois, by June 1850; and to Hamilton Township, Decatur Co.,

Iowa, 1854. Affiliated with RLDS church at Hamilton Township. Died in Hamilton Township.

Crane, Michael Quiggle (15 May 1787–7 Nov. 1847), farmer, land speculator. Born in what later became Wayne Township, Lycoming Co., Pennsylvania. Son of George Washington Crane and Catherine Quiggle. Married first Ann Pfouts, ca. 1815, possibly in Lycoming Co. Married second Maria Covenhoven, 10 Oct. 1831, in Nippenose Township, Lycoming Co. Moved to Warren Co. (later in Henderson Co.), Illinois, ca. 1836, and settled in Lomax Township, Henderson Co., 1840. Owned part interest in sawmill in Wisconsin; leased interest to Latter-day Saints for preparing lumber for construction of Nauvoo temple, 1841. Served as Henderson Co. commissioner, 1842–1845. Hosted JS and large party that freed JS from arrest, 1843, in Lomax Township. Buried in Crane Cemetery, Lomax Township.

Cutler, Alpheus (29 Feb. 1784–10 June 1864), stonemason. Born in Plainfield, Cheshire Co., New Hampshire. Son of Knight Cutler and Elizabeth Boyd. Married Lois Lathrop, 17 Nov. 1808, in Lebanon, Grafton Co., New Hampshire. Moved to Upper Lisle, Broome Co., New York, ca. 1808. Served in War of 1812. Moved to Chautauque Co., New York, after 1814, and settled in Hanover, Chautauque Co., by 1830. Baptized into LDS church by David W. Patten, 20 Jan. 1833, in Chautauque Co. Moved to Kirtland, Geauga Co., Ohio, 1834. Labored on Kirtland temple. Member of Kirtland high council, 1835. Ordained an elder by Alvah Beman, 28 Jan. 1836, in Kirtland. Ordained a high priest by JS, 29 Apr. 1836, in Kirtland. Moved near Richmond, Ray Co., Missouri, 1836; to Caldwell Co., Missouri, 1838; and to Commerce (later Nauvoo), Hancock Co., Illinois, by summer 1839. Appointed member of temple construction committee, 1840, in Nauvoo. Appointed guard in Nauvoo Legion, Mar. 1841. Served mission to Wisconsin Territory, 1841–1842, to obtain lumber for construction of Nauvoo temple. Member of Nauvoo high council, 1841–1846. Member of Nauvoo Masonic Lodge. Appointed to Council of Fifty, 1844. Appointed by JS to serve mission to Indians, before June 1844, at Nauvoo. Led third company of Latter-day Saints to leave Nauvoo and chose site of Winter Quarters, unorganized U.S. territory (later in Omaha, Douglas Co., Nebraska), for the Saints, 1846. Established town of Manti (later near Shenandoah), Fremont Co., Iowa, 1850. Excommunicated, 20 Apr. 1851. Established Church of Jesus Christ (Cutlerite), 19 Sept. 1853, in Fremont Co. Lived at Fisher, Fremont Co., 1860. Died in Manti.

Dana, Charles Root (8 Nov. 1802–7 Aug. 1868), mason, farmer. Born in Schenectady, Albany Co., New York. Son of Francis Dana and Huldah Root. Married Margaret Kennedy Lusk, ca. 1827, in Lowville, Lewis Co., New York. Moved to Hammond, St. Lawrence Co., New York, ca. 1829. Baptized into LDS church by James Blakesley, 18 Apr. 1839. Ordained an elder by James Blakesley, 1839, in Hammond. Served mission, 1839–1840. Moved to Nauvoo, Hancock Co., Illinois, 1841. Preached in Pittsburgh, 1842. Crane operator during construction of Nauvoo temple. Ordained a high priest, by 1845. Moved to Mount Pisgah, Clarke Co., Iowa Territory, ca. 1846. Served missions to eastern U.S. to raise funds to help poor Latter-day Saints move west, 1847, 1848–1849. Migrated to Ogden, Weber Co., Utah Territory, 1850. Served as Utah territorial legislator, 1852. Died in Ogden.

Dana, Margaret Kennedy (1 Apr. 1807–15 June 1850). Born at Argyle, Washington Co., New York. Daughter of Alexander Kennedy and Sybil Cannon. Married first Mr. Lusk, ca. 1825. Married second Charles Root Dana, ca. 1827, in Lowville, Lewis Co., New York. Moved to Hammond, St. Lawrence Co., New York, ca. 1829. Baptized into LDS church by James Blakesley, 18 Apr. 1839. Moved to Nauvoo, Hancock Co., Illinois, 1841. Removed to Mount Pisgah, Clarke Co., Iowa Territory, ca. 1846. Died about twenty-four miles west of Missouri River in present-day Nebraska while immigrating to Utah Territory.

Davis, Amos (20 Sept. 1814–22 Mar. 1872), merchant, farmer. Born in Hopkinton, Rockingham Co., New Hampshire. Son of Wells Davis and Mary. Moved to Commerce (later Nauvoo), Hancock Co., Illinois, 1836. Married first Elvira Hibard, 1 Jan. 1837, in Hancock Co. Baptized into LDS church, Apr. 1840. Instructed in JS revelation to buy stock for building Nauvoo House, 19 Jan. 1841. Member of Nauvoo Masonic Lodge. JS involved in lawsuits against Davis, 1842–1843, in Nauvoo. Moved to Winter Quarters, unorganized U.S. territory (later in Omaha, Douglas Co., Nebraska), winter 1846. Returned to Illinois. Sued church trustees for debt, 1847, in Nauvoo. Married second Catharine Cormack, 26 July 1848, in Hancock Co. Married third Harriet S. Andrews, 27 Jan. 1850, in Hancock Co. Married fourth Mary Jane Isenberger, 12 Apr. 1866, in Hancock Co. Died in Appanoose Township, Hancock Co.

Davis, Jacob Cunningham (16 Sept. 1820–25 Dec. 1883), lawyer, farmer, politician. Born near Staunton, Augusta Co., Virginia. Son of William C. Davis and Sarah (Sallie) Van Lear. Lived at Augusta Co., 1830. Moved to Warsaw, Hancock Co., Illinois, by 1838. Served as Illinois circuit clerk, 1841–1843. Served as state senator, 1842–1848. Captain of Warsaw militia rifle company, 1844. Among those indicted and subsequently acquitted for murders of JS and Hyrum Smith. Served as Illinois state senator, 1850–1856. Married Judith P. Mitchell Foree, 9 Dec. 1852, in Clark Co., Missouri. Served as U.S. representative from Illinois, 1856–1857. Moved to Clark Co., by 1857. Died in Alexandria, Clark Co.

Decker, Isaac (29 Dec. 1799–14 June 1873), farmer, carpenter. Born in Columbia Co., New York. Son of Peter Decker and Hanna Snooks. Moved to Phelps, Ontario Co., New York, by Aug. 1820. Married first Harriet Page Wheeler, 1820, in Phelps. Moved to Freedom, Cattaraugus Co., New York. Moved to New Portage, Medina Co., Ohio, where baptized into LDS church. Received elder's license, 23 May 1836, in Kirtland, Geauga Co., Ohio. Moved to Kirtland, by fall 1837. Donated his wealth to church while in Kirtland. Moved to Daviess Co., Missouri, late 1837; to Far West, Caldwell Co., Missouri, 1838; to Quincy, Adams Co., Illinois; to Winchester, Scott Co., Illinois, by 1840; and to Nauvoo, Hancock Co., Illinois, 1841. Member of Nauvoo Masonic Lodge. Divorced wife, before 1843, in Nauvoo. Ordained a high priest, before 24 Dec. 1845. Moved to Salt Lake City, 1847. Married second Delight Day. Moved to Midway, Wasatch Co., Utah Territory, by 1870. Moved to Salt Lake City, after 1870. Died in Salt Lake City.

Derby, Erastus H. (14 Sept. 1810–3 Dec. 1890), tailor, carpenter, farmer, joiner. Born in Hawley, Hampshire Co., Massachusetts. Son of Edward Darby and Ruth Phoebe Hitchcock. Moved to Ohio, by 1834. Married Ruhamah Burnham Knowlton, 10 Aug. 1834, in Carthage, Hamilton Co., Ohio. Moved to Hancock Co., Illinois, soon thereafter. Baptized into LDS church, early 1840, in Hancock Co. Moved to Nauvoo, Hancock Co., by 1842. Member of Nauvoo Masonic Lodge. Served as a scribe for JS's journal, Aug. 1842. Traveled to Missouri to ask Governor Thomas Reynolds to remit arrest warrant for JS. Ordained a seventy. Moved to Pottawattamie Co., Iowa, by 1850; to Ohio, by late 1850;

to Chicago, by 1855; and to Williams Co., Ohio, by 1860. Fought in Civil War. Moved to Le Sueur, Le Sueur Co., Minnesota, 1872. Died in Le Sueur.

Dixon, George C. (1810–25 July 1871), lawyer. Born in England. Immigrated to New York, 1835. Married Henrietta C. C. Gourgas. Moved to Quincy, Adams Co., Illinois, by 1840. Coauthor of articles of association for St. John's Episcopal Church, 1850, at Keokuk, Lee Co., Iowa. Died at Keokuk.

Doniphan, Alexander William (9 July 1808–8 Aug. 1887), lawyer, military general, insurance/bank executive. Born near Maysville, Mason Co., Kentucky. Son of Joseph Doniphan and Ann Smith. Father died in 1813; sent to live with older brother George, 1815, in Augusta, Bracken Co., Kentucky. Attended Augusta College, 1822–1826. Studied law in office of jurist Martin Marshall, in Augusta. Passed Kentucky and Ohio bar examinations, 1829. Located at St. Louis, Mar. 1830. Moved to Lexington, Lafayette Co., Missouri, and opened law office there, 1830. Moved to Liberty, Clay Co., Missouri, 1833. Employed as legal counsel by Latter-day Saints during their expulsion from Jackson Co., Missouri, 1833. Elected to Missouri General Assembly representing Clay Co., 1836, 1840, and 1854. Married Elizabeth Jane Thornton, 21 Dec. 1837. Appointed brigadier general in state militia. Intervened to prevent execution of JS and other church leaders at Far West, Caldwell Co., Missouri, Nov. 1838. Again represented JS and others in courts, 1838–1839. Served in Mexican War, 1846–1847. Returned to Liberty. Moved to St. Louis, 1863. Moved to Richmond, Ray Co., Missouri, ca. 1869. Died at Richmond.

Douglas, Stephen Arnold (23 Apr. 1813–3 June 1861), lawyer, politician. Born at Brandon, Rutland Co., Vermont. Son of Stephen Arnold Douglass and Sarah Fisk. Moved to Ontario Co., New York, 1830. Moved to Jacksonville, Morgan Co., Illinois, 1833. Served as attorney general of Illinois, 1835–1836. Served as state representative, 1836–1841; moved to Springfield, Sangamon Co., Illinois, 1837. Served as registrar of land office, 1837–1839, at Springfield. Served as Illinois secretary of state, 1840–1841, at Springfield. Moved to Quincy, Adams Co., Illinois, 1841. Served as state supreme court justice, 1841–1842. Served as U.S. representative, 1843–1847. Married first Martha Denny Martin, 1847, at Rockingham Co., North Carolina. Moved to Chicago, 1847. Served as U.S. senator, 1847–1861. Married second Adèle Cutts, 20 Nov. 1856, at Washington DC. Died at Chicago.

Draper, William, Jr. (24 Apr. 1807–28 May 1886), farmer, shoemaker, miller, merchant. Born at Richmond Township, Frontenac Co., Midland District (later in Greater Napanee, Lennox and Addington Co., Ontario), Upper Canada. Son of William Draper Sr. and Lydia Lathrop. Married Elizabeth Staker, 1825, in Kingston, Frontenac Co. Moved to Loughborough Township, Frontenac Co. Baptized into LDS church, 20 Mar. 1833, in Loughborough Township. Ordained a priest by Brigham Young, June 1833, in Loughborough Township. Moved to Kirtland, Geauga Co., Ohio, Sept. 1834. Served missions to Canada, 1835, 1836. Began serving mission to Morgan Co., Illinois, 16 Apr. 1838. Moved to Huntsville, Randolph Co., Missouri, June 1838. Moved to Caldwell Co., Missouri, Aug. 1838. Ordained a high priest by Don Carlos Smith, 1838. Moved to Pike Co., Illinois, Mar. 1839. Moved to Green Plains (later in Warsaw), Hancock Co., Illinois, spring 1843. Moved back to Pike Co., Oct. 1845. Appointed bishop at what became Council Bluffs, Pottawattamie Co., Iowa Territory, May 1846. Migrated to Salt Lake City, 1849. Moved to

Millcreek and South Willow Creek (later Draper), Great Salt Lake Co., Utah Territory, 1850. Moved to Sanpete Co., Utah Territory, early 1865. Died at Freedom, Sanpete Co.

Dudley, Julius (1804–17 Nov. 1875), vessel trade manager, tannery operator, surveyor, farmer. Born in Killingworth, Middlesex Co., Connecticut, 1804. Married Jerusha Stevens, 15 Oct. 1829, in Killingworth. Served as brigadier general in Connecticut state militia. Served as Connecticut state representative from East Berlin, Hartford Co. Moved to Franklin, Somerset Co., New Jersey, by 1850; to Westfield, Richmond Co., New York, by 1860; and to Berlin, Hartford Co., by 1870. Died in Berlin.

Duncan, Joseph (22 Feb. 1794–15 Jan. 1844), soldier, politician. Born at Paris, Bourbon Co., Kentucky. Son of Joseph Duncan and Anna Maria McLaughlin. Presbyterian. Served in War of 1812. Moved to Kaskaskia, Randolph Co., Illinois, 1818. Moved to Jackson Co., Illinois, by 1819. Served as justice of the peace, 1821–1823, in Jackson Co. Served as major general in Illinois militia, beginning 1822. State senator from Jackson Co., 1824–1826. Served as U.S. representative from Illinois, 1827–1834. Married Elizabeth Caldwell Smith, 13 May 1828, at Washington DC. Moved to Jacksonville, Morgan Co., Illinois. Served in Black Hawk War, 1831. Governor of Illinois, 1834–1838. Campaigned again for governor, 1842, on anti-Mormon platform; lost to Thomas Ford. Died at Jacksonville.

Dunham, Jonathan (14 Jan. 1800–28 July 1845), soldier, police captain. Born in Paris, Oneida Co., New York. Son of Jonathan Dunham. Married Mary Kendall. Moved to Rushford, Allegany Co., New York, by 1830. Baptized into LDS church and ordained an elder, by 1836. Served mission to New York, 1836. Ordained a seventy by Joseph Young, 20 Dec. 1836, in Kirtland, Geauga Co., Ohio. Served mission to Indians in New York, 1837. Camp engineer for Kirtland Camp, 1838. Moved to Adam-ondi-Ahman, Daviess Co., Missouri, 1838. Leader in Missouri Mormon militia, 1838. Moved to Kirtland, ca. 1838. Served missions to Indiana, Pennsylvania, and New York, 1839. Served mission to Indians in present-day Kansas, 1840. Moved to Nauvoo, Hancock Co., Illinois, by 1841. Member of Nauvoo Masonic Lodge. Colonel in Nauvoo Legion, 1842. Construction superintendent for Nauvoo Legion arsenal, 1843. Served mission to Indians in Missouri, 1843. In Nauvoo, appointed captain of police, 1843; wharf master, 1844; and acting major general of Nauvoo Legion, 1844. Among those arrested for destruction of *Nauvoo Expositor* press, June 1844. Escorted bodies of JS and Hyrum into Nauvoo, June 1844. Appointed brigadier general in Nauvoo Legion. Appointed to Council of Fifty, 1845, in Nauvoo. Died in Newton Co., Missouri, while serving mission.

Durfee (Durphy), Elizabeth Davis. See Lott, Elizabeth Davis.

Durfee (Durphy), Jabez (23 Dec. 1791–Apr. 1867), carpenter, millwright. Born in Tiverton, Newport Co., Rhode Island. Son of Perry Durfee and Annie Salisbury. Married first Electa Cranston, ca. 1811, in Tiverton. Moved to Lenox, Madison Co., New York, by 1820. Moved to New London, Huron Co., Ohio, before 1830. Baptized into LDS church, before 1833. Assisted building temple in Kirtland, Geauga Co., Ohio. Moved to Jackson Co., Missouri, by 1833. Married second Elizabeth Davis Goldsmith Brackenbury, 3 Mar. 1834, in Clay Co., Missouri. Moved to Far West, Missouri, ca. 1835. Ordained an elder, 29 Apr. 1836, in Kirtland. Moved to Daviess Co., Missouri, Dec. 1837; to Quincy, Adams Co., Illinois, 1838; and to Commerce (later Nauvoo), Hancock Co., Illinois, 1839. Labored on Nauvoo temple. Ordained a high priest, Dec. 1845, in Nauvoo. Married third Magdalena

Pickle, 21 Jan. 1846, in Nauvoo. Moved to Council Bluffs, Pottawattamie Co., Iowa, before 1850. Excommunicated at Council Bluffs, 1850. Moved to Fisher, Fremont Co., Iowa, by June 1860. Married fourth Sarah, before 1860. Moved to White Cloud, Mills Co., Iowa. Died at White Cloud.

Dutch, John (7 Oct. 1775–25 Apr. 1850), sea captain, land speculator, hotelier, merchant. Born in Salem, Essex Co., Massachusetts. Son of John Dutch and Fanny Jones. Lived at Salem, 1798. Married Hannah Batchelder, 29 Apr. 1798, in Beverly, Essex Co., Massachusetts. Moved to Boston, by 1820. Operated an inn, 1820–1822, in Boston. Wife died, 1828. Moved to Morgan Co., Illinois, by 1837. Laid out town of Lancaster, Lancaster Precinct, Morgan Co. (later in Philadelphia Township, Cass Co.), Illinois, May 1837. In Lancaster, built and operated hotel known as "Halfway House" because located halfway between Beardstown, Cass Co., Illinois, and Springfield, Sangamon Co., Illinois. Died in Virginia, Cass Co.

Edwards, Benjamin Stephenson (13 June 1818–4 Feb. 1886), lawyer, judge. Born at Edwardsville, Madison Co., Illinois. Son of Ninian Edwards and Elvira Lane. Moved to Belleville, St. Clair Co., Illinois, 1824. Graduated from Yale, 1838, in New Haven, New Haven Co., Connecticut. Admitted to Illinois bar, 1839. Married Helen Kissam Dodge, 13 Aug. 1839. Moved to Springfield, Sangamon Co., Illinois, by June 1840. Acted as a defense attorney in JS's extradition case, 1843. Served as delegate to Illinois constitutional convention, 1862. Elected circuit court judge, 1869, in Springfield. Served as president of Illinois State Bar Association. Died at Springfield.

Ellis, Nancy Rigdon (8 Dec. 1822–1 Nov. 1887). Born in Pittsburgh or in Friendship, Allegany Co., New York. Daughter of Sidney Rigdon and Phebe Brooks. Moved to Bainbridge, Geauga Co., Ohio, 1826. Moved to Mentor, Geauga Co., 1827. Baptized into LDS church, likely ca. Nov. 1830, in Ohio. Moved to Kirtland, Geauga Co., 1831; to Hiram, Portage Co., Ohio, 1831; back to Kirtland, by 1833; to Salem, Essex Co., Massachusetts, 1836; back to Kirtland, 1837; to Far West, Caldwell Co., Missouri, 1838; and to Commerce (later Nauvoo), Hancock Co., Illinois, 1839. Moved to Pittsburgh, 1844. Married Robert Ellis, 13 Sept. 1846. Died in Pittsburgh.

Ells, Josiah (4 Mar. 1806–15 Oct. 1885), blacksmith, gunsmith, preacher. Born in Lewes, Sussex Co., England. Son of Thomas Ells and Hannah Smart. Joined Methodist church, 1826. Married Eliza L. Campion, 25 Mar. 1828, in Leicester, Leicester Co., England. Immigrated to Philadelphia, 1831. Moved to Monmouth Co., New Jersey, 1835. Baptized into LDS church by Benjamin Winchester, 1 Oct. 1838, in Upper Freehold Township, Monmouth Co. Ordained an elder, Dec. 1838. Served as presiding elder in local branch, beginning Dec. 1838. Moved to Nauvoo, Hancock Co., Illinois, Apr. 1840. Appointed lieutenant colonel in Nauvoo Legion, 3 July 1841. Member of Nauvoo Masonic Lodge. Attempted to rescue JS from his arrest in Lee Co., Illinois, June 1843. Disfellowshipped, 3 Nov. 1844. Ordained an apostle in Sidney Rigdon's Church of Christ, Apr. 1845. Moved to Pittsburgh, by June 1850. Joined RLDS church, by Apr. 1865. Ordained an apostle in RLDS church, 6 Apr. 1865, in Plano, Kendall Co., Illinois. Moved to Allegheny (later in Pittsburgh), Allegheny Co., Pennsylvania, by June 1870. Moved to West Wheeling, Belmont Co., Ohio, by June 1880. Died in Wheeling, Ohio Co., West Virginia.

Emmons, Sylvester (28 Feb. 1808–15 Nov. 1881), lawyer, newspaper publisher. Born in Readington Township, Hunterdon Co., New Jersey. Son of Abraham Emmons and Margaret Vlerebome. Moved to Philadelphia, 1831. Moved to Illinois, 1840. Admitted to bar in Hancock Co., Illinois, May 1843. Member of Nauvoo City Council, 1843–1844. Editor of *Nauvoo Expositor,* 1844. Moved to Beardstown, Cass Co., Illinois, 1844. Edited *Beardstown Gazette,* 1844–1852. Married Elizabeth Miller, 21 Dec. 1847, in Cass Co. Died in Beardstown.

Enos, Salome Paddock (12 Mar. 1791–25 Oct. 1877), hotelier. Born in Woodstock, Windsor Co., Vermont. Daughter of Gaius Paddock and Mary Wood. Married Pascal Paoli Enos, 4 Sept. 1815, in Woodstock. Moved to Cincinnati, 1815; to St. Charles, St. Charles Co., Missouri, 1816; to St. Louis, 1817; to Six Mile (later Granite City), Madison Co., Illinois, 1820; and to Springfield, Sangamon Co., Illinois, 1823. Husband died, 1832. Hostess to many notable people, including JS, in Springfield, 1840–1860. Died in Springfield.

Fielding, Amos (16 July 1792–5 Aug. 1875), butcher, farmer, match maker, surveyor. Born in Lancashire, England. Son of Matthew Fielding and Mary Cooper. Christened Anglican. Immigrated to U.S., 1811; returned to Lancashire, by 1829. Married Mary Haydock, 28 June 1829, in Eccleston, Lancashire. Baptized into LDS church and ordained an elder, fall 1837. Resided in Liverpool, Lancashire, 1841. Served as church agent in Liverpool. Led group of Latter-day Saints to Nauvoo, Hancock Co., Illinois, 1842. Member of Nauvoo Masonic Lodge. Member of Council of Fifty. Migrated to Salt Lake City, 1854. Died in Salt Lake City.

Fielding, Joseph (26 Mar. 1797–19 Dec. 1863), farmer. Born at Honeydon, Bedfordshire, England. Son of John Fielding and Rachel Ibbotson. Immigrated to Upper Canada, 1832. Baptized into LDS church by Parley P. Pratt, 21 May 1836, in Black Creek, Charleton Settlement (near Toronto), Upper Canada. Moved to Toronto, Mar. 1837. Ordained a priest by Parley P. Pratt, Apr. 1837, near Toronto. Moved to Kirtland, Geauga Co., Ohio, May 1837. Served mission to Preston, Lancashire, England, 1837–1840. Ordained an elder by Heber C. Kimball, 29 Oct. 1837, at Preston. Ordained a high priest by Heber C. Kimball, 1 Apr. 1838, at Preston. Served as mission president, 1838–1840. Married Hannah Greenwood, 11 June 1838, at Preston. Led group of Latter-day Saints to Nauvoo, Hancock Co., Illinois, 1841. Member of Nauvoo Masonic Lodge. Moved to Winter Quarters, unorganized U.S. territory (later in Omaha, Douglas Co., Nebraska), 1846; to Salt Lake City, 1848; and to Millcreek, Great Salt Lake Co., Utah Territory, by 1850. Died at Millcreek.

Ford, Edward R. (1774–after 1850), law enforcement officer. Born in South Carolina. Married Susanna. Moved to Lewiston (near present-day New Florence), Montgomery Co., Missouri, by 1830. Moved to Lindsey, Benton Co., Missouri, by 1840. Missouri state agent commissioned to arrest JS for complicity in attempt to kill former governor Lilburn W. Boggs, 1842. Moved to Boone Co., Missouri, by 1850.

Ford, Thomas (5 Dec. 1800–3 Nov. 1850), newspaperman, lawyer, politician, judge, author. Born in Uniontown, Fayette Co., Pennsylvania. Son of Robert Ford and Elizabeth Logue Forquer. Moved to St. Louis, 1804; to New Design (later American Bottom), Randolph Co., Illinois, 1804; to Lexington, Fayette Co., Kentucky, 1819; back to St. Louis, 1824; and to Edwardsville, Madison Co., Illinois, 1825. Married Frances Hambaugh, 12 June 1828. Moved to Galena, Jo Daviess Co., Illinois, 1829. Served as state attorney for

Illinois's Fifth Judicial Circuit, 1829–1835; as judge of Illinois's Sixth Judicial Circuit, 1835–1837; as judge of Chicago municipal court, 1837–1839; and as judge of Illinois's Ninth Judicial Circuit, 1839–1841. Judge of Illinois Supreme Court, 1841–1842. Governor of Illinois, 1842–1846. Promised protection to JS when JS was jailed in Carthage, Hancock Co., Illinois. Addressed citizens of Nauvoo, Hancock Co., on evening JS was murdered, 27 June 1844. Revoked Nauvoo charter, Jan. 1845. Moved to Peoria, Peoria Co., Illinois, 1847. Wrote *A History of Illinois*, published posthumously in 1854. Died in Peoria.

Foster, Lucian Rose (12 Nov. 1806–19 Mar. 1876), photographer, accountant, bookkeeper, clerk. Born in New Marlboro, Berkshire Co., Massachusetts. Son of Nathaniel Foster and Polly Case. Married first Harriet Eliza Burr. Married second Mary Ann Graham. Baptized into LDS church, by Dec. 1840. Appointed clerk of church conference at New York City, 4 Dec. 1840. Served as branch president, 1841–1844, in New York City. Served as clerk of church conference, 1843, in New York City. Moved to Nauvoo, Hancock Co., Illinois, 1844. Member of Nauvoo Masonic Lodge. Served as member of central correspondence committee for JS presidential campaign, 1844. Member of Council of Fifty, 1845–1846. Married third Ann Mariah Still, before 1846. Moved back to New York, ca. 1846. Excommunicated, 1846, in New York. Affiliated with Sidney Rigdon's Church of Christ. Affiliated with James J. Strang's Church of Jesus Christ of Latter Day Saints, 1846–1849. Married fourth Eliza Leeman Ulrich, before 1870. Moved to Brooklyn, Kings Co., New York, by 1870. Died in Salt Lake City.

Foster, Robert D. (14 Mar. 1811–1 Feb. 1878), physician, land speculator. Born in Braunston, Northamptonshire, England. Son of John Foster and Jane Knibb. Married Sarah Phinney, 18 July 1837, at Medina Co., Ohio. Baptized into LDS church, before Oct. 1839. Ordained an elder, Oct. 1839, in Nauvoo, Hancock Co., Illinois. Instructed in JS revelation to buy stock for building Nauvoo House, 19 Jan. 1841. Appointed surgeon general in Nauvoo Legion, Mar. 1841. Regent of University of Nauvoo, 1841–1844. Member of Nauvoo Masonic Lodge. Appointed to serve mission to Tioga Co., New York, 10 Apr. 1843. Excommunicated, 18 Apr. 1844, in Nauvoo. Cashiered from Nauvoo Legion, May 1844. Publisher of *Nauvoo Expositor*. Appointed apostle in William Law's schismatic church, and actively worked against JS until JS's death. Identified by Willard Richards as member of mob that killed JS and Hyrum Smith, 1844, at Carthage, Hancock Co. Moved to Canandaigua, Ontario Co., New York, by 1850. Moved to Loda, Iroquois Co., Illinois, by 1859. Died in Loda.

Fuller, Amos Botsford (26 Mar. 1810–29 Mar. 1853), blacksmith, farmer. Born at Stockholm, St. Lawrence Co., New York. Son of Luther Fuller and Lorena (Lovina) Mitchell. Married Esther Victoria Smith, cousin of JS, 8 Mar. 1832, at Stockholm. Baptized into LDS church, 17 Feb. 1836, at Kirtland, Geauga Co., Ohio. Received elder's license, 29 Oct. 1836, at Kirtland. Ordained a seventy by Zebedee Coltrin, 3 Jan. 1837, at Kirtland. Moved to Kirtland, by 1837. Served missions to New York, New Hampshire, Vermont, and Ohio, 1837–1838. Moved to Nashville (later Galland), Lee Co., Iowa Territory, by 1840. Appointed to serve mission to Chicago, 1842. Appointed to serve mission to Vermont, 1843. Moved to Voree, Racine Co., Wisconsin Territory, 1846. Affiliated with James J. Strang's Church of Jesus Christ of Latter Day Saints, 1846–1847; excommunicated, 1847, at Voree. Moved to Des Moines, Polk Co., Iowa, by 1850. Died at Des Moines.

Fullmer, David (7 July 1803–21 Oct. 1879), teacher, merchant, farmer. Born in Chillisquaque Township, Northumberland Co., Pennsylvania. Son of Peter Fullmer and Susannah Zerfoss. Moved to Huntington Township, Luzerne Co., Pennsylvania, by 1820. Married Rhoda Ann Marvin, 18 Sept. 1831, in Union Township, Luzerne Co. Moved to Jefferson Township, Richland Co., Ohio, 1835. Baptized into LDS church by Henry G. Sherwood, 16 Sept. 1836, in Ohio. Ordained an elder by Reuben Hedlock, 23 Feb. 1837, in Kirtland, Geauga Co., Ohio. Moved to Caldwell Co., Missouri, 1837; to Daviess Co., Missouri, 1838; and to Commerce (later Nauvoo), Hancock Co., Illinois, 1839. Ordained a high priest, Oct. 1839. Appointed to Nauvoo high council, 1839. Member of Nauvoo Masonic Lodge. Served mission to Michigan, 1844. Member of Nauvoo City Council; when city charter revoked, appointed to new town council, 1845. Member of Council of Fifty. Moved to Iowa Territory as captain of one hundred emigrant families, 1846. Moved to Garden Grove, Decatur Co., Iowa, 1847. Moved to Winter Quarters, unorganized U.S. territory (later in Omaha, Douglas Co., Nebraska), 1847. Moved to Salt Lake City, 1848. Served in legislature of provisional state of Deseret, 1849, and then of Utah Territory. Died in Salt Lake City.

Galland, Isaac (15 May 1791–27 Sept. 1858), merchant, postmaster, land speculator, doctor. Born at Somerset Co., Pennsylvania. Son of Matthew Galland and Hannah Fenno. Married first Nancy Harris, 22 Mar. 1811, in Madison Co., Ohio. Married second Margaret Knight, by 1816. Moved to Washington Co., Indiana, by 1816. Located at Owen Co., Indiana, by 1820, and at Edgar Co., Illinois, shortly after 1820. Moved to Horselick Grove (later in Hancock Co.), Illinois, 1824. Married third Hannah Kinney, 5 Oct. 1826. Moved to Oquawka, Henderson Co., Illinois, 1827. Established settlement of Nashville on west bank of Mississippi River, in unorganized U.S. territory, where he practiced medicine, established trading post, and founded first school in what later became Iowa Territory. Moved family to Fort Edwards (later Warsaw), Hancock Co., Illinois, 1832. Served as colonel in Black Hawk War, 1832. Married fourth Elizabeth Wilcox, 25 Apr. 1833. Platted original town of Keokuk, Lee Co., Wisconsin Territory (later in Iowa), 1837. Moved to Commerce (later Nauvoo), Hancock Co., winter 1838–1839. Purchased land in Half-Breed Tract in Lee Co. and sold some nineteen thousand acres of it to Latter-day Saints, 1839. Also sold properties in Commerce to Latter-day Saints. Baptized into LDS church and ordained an elder by JS, 3 July 1839. Instructed in JS revelation to buy stock for building Nauvoo House, 19 Jan. 1841. Acted as authorized agent for church in settling certain land transactions involving property exchanges by eastern Latter-day Saints moving to Nauvoo. Withdrew from church activity, ca. 1842. Resident of Keokuk, Lee Co., Iowa Territory, 1842–1853. Moved to Sacramento, Sacramento Co., California, 1853; eventually settled in Petaluma, Sonoma Co., California. Moved to Fort Madison, Lee Co., 1856. Died at Fort Madison.

Gillet, Truman, Jr. (21 May 1811–after 1850), farmer. Born in Schuyler, Herkimer Co., New York. Son of Truman Gillet and Phebe Doty. Moved to Newport, by 1820. Moved to Williamstown, Oswego Co., New York, by 1830. Married Fidelia Teal, before 1832, in New York. Baptized into LDS church. Moved to Ohio, by 1836. Ordained an elder, 14 June 1836, in Kirtland, Geauga Co., Ohio. Moved to Hancock Co., Illinois, by 1840. Served missions to New York, 1840, and to Iowa Territory, 1841. Disfellowshipped and reinstated, 1841. Member of Nauvoo Masonic Lodge. Served mission to New York, 1843.

Appointed to serve missions to Illinois and New York, 1843. Ordained a seventy, by 1846. Moved to Platte Township, Andrew Co., Missouri, by 1850.

Granger, Carlos (15 June 1790–after 1850), wainwright. Born in Suffield, Hartford Co., Connecticut. Son of Bildad Granger and Hannah Caulkin. Married Sarah Stiles, 31 May 1813. Moved to Painesville, Geauga Co., Ohio, by 1820. Described himself as "friendly" to Mormons. Moved to Clay Co., Missouri, by 1834. Moved to Nauvoo, Hancock Co., Illinois, by 1840. Signed petition to U.S. Congress, 1843, requesting redress for Missouri grievances. Moved to Missouri, by 1847. Lived in Schuyler Co., Missouri, by 1850.

Granger, Gilbert (14 Oct. 1814–25 Aug. 1850). Born in Phelps, Ontario Co., New York. Son of Oliver Granger and Lydia Dibble. Moved to Kirtland, Geauga Co., Ohio, 1833. Married first Alice Marble, 20 June 1838, in Cuyahoga Co., Ohio. Married second Susan Bristol Williams, 24 May 1849. Traveled to California during gold rush, 1849. Died near American River in California.

Granger, Oliver (7 Feb. 1794–23/25 Aug. 1841), sheriff, church agent. Born at Phelps, Ontario Co., New York. Son of Pierce Granger and Clarissa Trumble. Married Lydia Dibble, 8 Sept. 1813, at Phelps. Member of Methodist church and licensed exhorter. Sheriff of Ontario Co. and colonel in militia. Nearly blind from 1827 onward. Lived at Phelps, 1830. Baptized into LDS church and ordained an elder by Brigham and Joseph Young, ca. 1832–1833, at Sodus, Wayne Co., New York. Moved to Kirtland, Geauga Co., Ohio, 1833. Served mission to eastern states with Samuel Newcomb. Ordained a high priest, 29 Apr. 1836, at Kirtland. Served mission to New York with John P. Greene, spring 1836. Appointed to Kirtland high council, 8 Oct. 1837. Appointed to settle JS's business affairs in Kirtland, 1838. Left Kirtland for Far West, Caldwell Co., Missouri, June 1838, possibly to confer regarding JS's Kirtland business affairs. Directed in July 1838 revelation to move to Far West. Returned to Kirtland to settle his and JS's affairs and move family to Far West. Left Kirtland for Far West in Oct. 1838 with family, but turned back by mob in Missouri and returned to Kirtland. Following Mormon exodus from Missouri, moved from Kirtland to Commerce (later Nauvoo), Hancock Co., Illinois, spring 1839. Acted as agent in securing lands in Lee Co., Iowa Territory, 1839. Appointed to preside over church in Kirtland, 4 May 1839. Died at Kirtland.

Granger, Sabra (17 Feb. 1794–1849), nurse. Born in Chesterfield, Cheshire Co., New Hampshire. Daughter of Eldad Granger and Sarah Holmes. Moved to Westmoreland, Cheshire Co., by 1800. Baptized into LDS church, 26 June 1832. Moved to Kirtland, Geauga Co., Ohio, by 1836. Member of Kirtland Safety Society, 1837. Married John Gribble, Dec. 1837, in Geauga Co. Moved to Far West, Caldwell Co., Missouri, with Kirtland Camp, 1838. Moved to Nauvoo, Hancock Co., Illinois, by 1842. Separated from husband and resumed maiden name, 1845, in Nauvoo. Lived with Newel K. Whitney family in Winter Quarters, unorganized U.S. territory (later in Omaha, Douglas Co., Nebraska), by 1847.

Grant, Jedediah Morgan (21 Feb. 1816–1 Dec. 1856), farmer. Born in Union, Broome Co., New York. Son of Joshua Grant and Athalia Howard. Lived in Springwater, Ontario Co., New York, 1820. Lived in Naples, Ontario Co., 1830. Baptized into LDS church by John F. Boynton, 21 Mar. 1833. Participated in Camp of Israel expedition to Missouri, 1834. Moved to Kirtland, Geauga Co., Ohio, 1834. Ordained an elder, 1834.

Labored on Kirtland temple, 1835–1836. Ordained a seventy by JS, 28 Feb. 1835, in Kirtland. Served a mission with Harvey Stanley, 1835. Served missions to New York, 13 Apr. 1836–6 Mar. 1837, and to North Carolina, June 1837. Moved to Far West, Caldwell Co., Missouri, 9 Oct.–12 Nov. 1838. Expelled from Missouri; moved with father's family to Knox Co., Illinois, 25 Dec. 1838. Appointed to serve mission to Virginia and North Carolina. Presided over branch in Philadelphia, June 1843–Mar. 1844. Began serving mission, 9 May 1844, with Wilford Woodruff and George A. Smith; recalled to Nauvoo, before June 1844. Married Caroline Van Dyke, 2 July 1844, in Nauvoo, Hancock Co., Illinois. Returned to Philadelphia and presided over church there, July 1844–May 1845. Moved to Winter Quarters, unorganized U.S. territory (later in Omaha, Douglas Co., Nebraska), Feb. 1846. Appointed captain of company of immigrating Latter-day Saints and moved to Salt Lake City, June–Oct. 1847. Elected Speaker of the House in Utah territorial legislature, 13 Dec. 1852, in Salt Lake City. Ordained an apostle, 1854, in Salt Lake City. Served as second counselor to Brigham Young in First Presidency, 1854–1856. Died in Salt Lake City.

Greene, John Portineus (3 Sept. 1793–10 Sept. 1844), farmer, shoemaker, printer, publisher. Born at Herkimer, Herkimer Co., New York. Son of John Coddington Greene and Anna Chapman. Married first Brigham Young's sister Rhoda Young, 11 Feb. 1813. Moved to Aurelius, Cayuga Co., New York, 1814; to Brownsville, Ontario Co., New York, 1819; to Watertown, Jefferson Co., New York, 1821; and to Mentz, Cayuga Co., 1826. Member of Methodist Episcopal Church; later, member of Methodist Reformed Church. A founder of Methodist Protestant Church, 1828. Moved to Conesus, Livingston Co., New York, 1829. Moved to Mendon, Monroe Co., New York, by 1832. Baptized into LDS church by Eleazer Miller, Apr. 1832, at Mendon; ordained an elder by Eleazer Miller shortly after. Organized branch of church at Warsaw, Genesee Co., New York, 1832. Moved to Kirtland, Geauga Co., Ohio, Oct. 1832. Appointed to preside over branch in Parkman, Geauga Co., spring 1833. Returned to Kirtland, fall 1833. Ordained a high priest and left to serve mission to eastern U.S., 16 Sept. 1833. Left to serve mission to western New York and Canada, 25 Feb. 1834. Served mission to eastern U.S., 1835. Served mission to Ohio to raise funds for Kirtland temple, Mar. 1836. Left to serve mission to New York, 13 July 1836. Member of Kirtland high council. Left to serve mission to Canada, 16 Nov. 1837. Moved to Far West, Caldwell Co., Missouri, 1838. Member of Caldwell Co. militia. Participated in Battle of Crooked River, near Ray Co., Missouri, 25 Oct. 1838. Moved to Quincy, Adams Co., Illinois, Nov. 1838. Served mission to Ohio, Pennsylvania, and New York, 1839. Moved to Nauvoo, Hancock Co., Illinois, spring 1840. Member of Nauvoo City Council, 1841–1843. Married second Mary Eliza Nelson, 6 Dec. 1841, in Nauvoo. Member of Nauvoo Masonic Lodge. Served mission to Ohio and New York, Aug. 1842. Elected Nauvoo city marshal, Dec. 1843. Assessor and collector of Nauvoo Fourth Ward. Carried out orders of JS and city council to suppress *Nauvoo Expositor* press, 10 June 1844. Died at Nauvoo.

Hackleton, Samuel (22 Dec. 1804–6 July 1848), farmer, trader. Born in Marblehead, Essex Co., Massachusetts. Son of John Hackleton and Mary. Moved to Jay, Oxford Co., Maine, by 1828; to Fulton Co., Illinois, by June 1830; and back to Marblehead, 1831. Served as state representative from Fulton Co., 1832. Fought in war between U.S. and Sac and Fox Indian nations, 1832. Served as state representative from Fulton Co., 1834; as Illinois presidential elector, 1836; as state senator, 1836–1840; as state representative, 1842; and as Speaker of the House in Illinois legislature, 1842. Served in Mexican War, 1847. Killed in battle at Santa Fe Co. in area that later became New Mexico.

Harris, George Washington (1 Apr. 1780–1857), jeweler. Born at Lanesboro, Berkshire Co., Massachusetts. Son of James Harris and Diana (Margaret) Burton. Married first Elizabeth, ca. 1800. Married second Margaret, who died in 1828. Moved to Batavia, Genesee Co., New York, by 1830. Married third Lucinda Pendleton, 30 Nov. 1830, at Batavia. Moved to Terre Haute, Vigo Co., Indiana, where baptized into LDS church by Orson Pratt, 1834. Moved to Far West, Missouri, by 1836. Appointed to Far West high council, 1838. Owned land at Adam-ondi-Ahman, Daviess Co., Missouri, 1838. Moved to Illinois, by 1839. Appointed to high council in Commerce (later Nauvoo), Hancock Co., Illinois, 6 Oct. 1839. Nauvoo city alderman, 1841–1845. President of Nauvoo Coach and Carriage Manufacturing Association. Started west with Mormon exodus from Nauvoo, 1846. Bishop and member of high council at what became Council Bluffs, Pottawattamie Co., Iowa Territory, 1846. Died at Council Bluffs.

Hatch, Jeremiah (25 Sept. 1766–23 May 1851), laborer, farmer. Born in Dutchess Co., New York. Son of Nathaniel Hatch and Axcez Parmalee. Moved to Topsfield, Essex Co., Massachusetts, by 13 May 1782. Served in American Revolution as a fifer, 1782. Married Elizabeth Haight, 23 Nov. 1789, in Ferrisburgh, Addison Co., Vermont. Moved to Lincoln, Addison Co., by 1820. Moved to Bristol, Addison Co., by 15 July 1828. Baptized into LDS church by Pelatiah Brown, Nov. 1840, in Lincoln. Moved to Nauvoo, Hancock Co., Illinois, by 23 Dec. 1842. Ordained a high priest by Hyrum Smith, 9 Apr. 1843, in Nauvoo. Moved to Pottawattamie Co., Iowa, by 1850. Died in Pleasant Grove (later near Council Bluffs), Pottawattamie Co., Iowa.

Haws, Peter (17 Feb. 1796–1862), farmer, miller, businessman. Born in Leeds Co., Johnstown District (later in Ontario), Upper Canada. Son of Edward Haws and Polly. Married Charlotte Harrington. Baptized into LDS church. Moved to Kirtland, Geauga Co., Ohio. Served mission with Erastus Snow to Illinois, 1839. Moved to Illinois, ca. 1839. Alternate on Nauvoo high council, 1840–1841. Member of Nauvoo House Association. Ordained a high priest, 18 Dec. 1841, in Nauvoo. Member of Nauvoo Masonic Lodge. Served mission with Amasa Lyman to raise funds for construction of Nauvoo temple and Nauvoo House, 1843. Served mission with George Miller to Mississippi and Alabama, Sept.–Oct. 1843. Member of Council of Fifty. Moved to what became Council Bluffs, Pottawattamie Co., Iowa Territory, 1846. Visited Lyman Wight's colony in Texas, 1848. Returned to Council Bluffs. Excommunicated, 1849, in Council Bluffs. Moved to area near Humboldt River in Lovelock Valley, Carson Co., Utah Territory (later in Nevada Territory), by 1854. Moved to California, by 1855. Died in California.

Hedlock, Reuben (1809–5 July 1869), printer, carpenter, journeyman. Born in U.S. Married first Susan Wheeler, 1827. Married second Lydia Fox. Baptized into LDS church, by 1836. Moved to Kirtland, Geauga Co., Ohio, and ordained an elder, by 1836. Appointed counselor to Alvah Beman in presidency of elders quorum in Kirtland, 25 Jan. 1836. Ordained a seventy, before 20 Sept. 1837. Appointed president of elders quorum, 27 Nov. 1837, after Beman's death. Moved to Missouri with Kirtland Camp, 1838; to Far West, Caldwell Co., Missouri, before 1839; and to Quincy, Adams Co., Illinois, Apr. 1839. Settled family in Commerce (later Nauvoo), Hancock Co., Illinois, Sept. 1839. Left to serve mission to England, Sept. 1839; arrived in Liverpool, 6 Apr. 1840, and returned, Apr. 1841. Ordained a high priest, 3 Oct. 1841, in Nauvoo. Member of Nauvoo Masonic Lodge. Presided over British mission, Oct. 1843–Jan. 1845, Jan.–July 1846. Disfellowshipped, 16 July 1846. Excommunicated, 17 Oct. 1846, at Manchester, Lancashire, England. Married third Mary A., by 1851. Lived in Marylebone, London, England, 1851, and in Croydon, Sussex Co., England, 1861. Died at Gravesend, Kent Co., England.

Helm, Meredith (2 Mar. 1802–9 Mar. 1866), farmer, physician. Born in Williamsport, Washington Co., Maryland. Married Elizabeth Orondorff, 17 Oct. 1825, at Washington Co. Graduated from Baltimore Medical College. Worshipful Master of Friendship Masonic Lodge, 1827, at Williamsport. Moved to Springfield, Sangamon Co., Illinois, 1834. Grand Master of Grand Masonic Lodge of Illinois, 1842–1843, at Springfield. Member of Board of Health, 1843, at Springfield. Lifted brief suspension of dispensation for Nauvoo Masonic Lodge and allowed new lodges, Nov. 1842. Resigned from Masonry, July 1844. Died in Springfield.

Hibbard (Hibard), Davidson (Davison) (9 Sept. 1786–11 Sept. 1852), farmer. Born in Brookfield, Orange Co., Vermont. Son of Roger Hibbard and Sarah Davidson. Married Sarah Tilton, 1816. Moved to area in Massachusetts that later became Maine, by 17 Apr. 1816. Lived at Morgan Co., Illinois, by 2 Aug. 1824. Commissioned captain in Twenty-First Regiment of Illinois militia, 12 Jan. 1826. Appointed justice of the peace, 1827. Moved to Hancock Co., Illinois, 1829. Elected coroner of Hancock Co., 1832. Elected justice of the peace, 1835. Moved to Nauvoo, Hancock Co., by 1842. Member of Nauvoo Masonic Lodge. Died in Nauvoo.

Higbee, Charles (1807/1808–24 Oct. 1844), doctor. Born in Trenton, Mercer Co., New Jersey. Son of Charles Higbee. Graduated from University of Pennsylvania. Married Caroline Howell, ca. 1834, in Philadelphia. Practiced medicine in Cincinnati, 1834–1842. Moved to Nauvoo, Hancock Co., Illinois, by 1843. Died in Cincinnati.

Higbee, Chauncey Lawson (7 Sept. 1821–7 Dec. 1884), lawyer, banker, politician, judge. Born in Tate Township, Clermont Co., Ohio. Son of Elias Higbee and Sarah Elizabeth Ward. Lived in Fulton, Hamilton Co., Ohio, 1830. Baptized into LDS church, 1832. Moved to Jackson Co., Missouri, 1833; to Clay Co., Missouri, 1833; and to what became Caldwell Co., Missouri, 1836. Located at Quincy, Adams Co., Illinois, 1839. Moved to Nauvoo, Hancock Co., Illinois, by 1842. Appointed aide-de-camp to major general John C. Bennett in Nauvoo Legion, Nov. 1841. Excommunicated, 24 May 1842, in Nauvoo. Editor of *Nauvoo Expositor,* 1844. Identified by Willard Richards as member of mob that killed JS and Hyrum Smith, 27 June 1844, at Carthage, Hancock Co. Moved to Griggsville, Pike Co., Illinois, 1844. Moved to Pittsfield, Pike Co., 1847. Married Julia M. White, 14 Feb. 1854, in Adams Co. Served in Illinois legislature, 1854. Served as state senator, 1858–1861. Died in Pittsfield.

Higbee, Elias (23 Oct. 1795–8 June 1843), clerk, judge, surveyor. Born at Galloway, Gloucester Co., New Jersey. Son of Isaac Higbee and Sophia Somers. Moved to Clermont Co., Ohio, 1803. Married Sarah Elizabeth Ward, 10 Sept. 1818, in Tate Township, Clermont Co. Lived at Tate Township, 1820. Located at Fulton, Hamilton Co., Ohio, 1830. Baptized into LDS church, summer 1832, at Jackson Co., Missouri. Ordained an elder by Isaac Higbee, 20 Feb. 1833, at Cincinnati. Migrated to Jackson Co., Apr. 1833. Driven from

Jackson Co. into Clay Co., Missouri, Nov. 1833. Ordained a high priest by Orson Pratt, 7 Aug. 1834, in Clay Co. Served mission to Missouri, Illinois, Indiana, and Ohio, 1835. Labored on Kirtland temple. Returned to Clay Co. Member of Clay Co. high council, 1836. Moved to what became Caldwell Co., Missouri, spring 1836. Presiding judge of Caldwell Co. Appointed to high council in Far West, Caldwell Co., 1837. With John Corrill, appointed church historian, 6 Apr. 1838, at Far West. Participated in Battle of Crooked River, near Ray Co., Missouri, 25 Oct. 1838. Fled Missouri; located at Quincy, Adams Co., Illinois, 1839. Member of committee that investigated lands offered for sale by Isaac Galland, 1839. Settled at Commerce (later Nauvoo), Hancock Co., Illinois, 1839. Traveled to Washington DC with JS to seek redress for Missouri grievances, Oct. 1839–Mar. 1840. Appointed member of Nauvoo temple committee, 6 Oct. 1840. Appointed guard in Nauvoo Legion, Mar. 1841. Member of Nauvoo Masonic Lodge. Died at Nauvoo.

Higbee, Francis Marion (1820–after 1850), attorney, merchant. Born in Tate, Clermont Co., Ohio. Son of Elias Higbee and Sarah Elizabeth Ward. Moved to Fulton, Hamilton Co., Ohio, by 1830. Baptized into LDS church, 1832. Moved to Jackson Co., Missouri, 1833; to Kirtland, Geauga Co., Ohio, 1835; and back to Missouri, 1836. Arraigned with JS in Richmond, Ray Co., Missouri, 11 Nov. 1838; released from jail, by 29 Nov. 1838. Moved to Illinois, early 1839. Lived in Hancock Co., Illinois, 1840. Member of Masonic lodge in Nauvoo, Hancock Co. Appointed aide-de-camp to major general in Nauvoo Legion, June 1842, at Nauvoo. Located at Pleasant Hill, Pike Co., Illinois, Nov. 1842. Returned to Nauvoo, summer 1843. Excommunicated, 18 May 1844, in Nauvoo. Publisher of *Nauvoo Expositor,* 1844. Lived at Pontoosuc, Hancock Co., 27 June 1844. Formed a new church with other LDS apostates. Identified by Willard Richards and Jacob B. Backenstos as member of mob that killed JS and Hyrum Smith, 1844, at Carthage, Hancock Co. Resided in Hancock Co., 1850.

Hinkle, George M. (13 Nov. 1801–Nov. 1861), merchant, physician, publisher, minister, farmer. Born in Jefferson Co., Kentucky. Son of Michael Hinkle and Nancy Higgins. Married first Sarah Ann Starkey. Baptized into LDS church, 1832. Moved to Far West, Caldwell Co., Missouri. Served on high councils at Clay Co., Missouri, and Caldwell Co., 1836–1838. Commissioned colonel in Missouri state militia. During Missouri conflict in 1838, directed defense of De Witt, Carroll Co., Missouri, and commanded Mormon militia defending Far West. While assisting in negotiation of truce between state militia and Latter-day Saints at Far West, surrendered church leaders to General Samuel Lucas. Excommunicated, 17 Mar. 1839, at Quincy, Adams Co., Illinois. Moved to Duncan Prairie, Mercer Co., Illinois, 1839. Organized religious society named The Church of Jesus Christ, the Bride, the Lamb's Wife at Moscow, Muscatine Co., Iowa Territory, 24 June 1840. Affiliated briefly with Sidney Rigdon and Church of Christ, 1845. Moved to Iowa Territory, by Dec. 1845. Wife died, 1 Dec. 1845. Returned to Mercer Co., by June 1850. Married second Mary Loman Hartman. Moved to Decatur Co., Iowa, by 1852. Moved to Adair Co., Iowa. Served in Civil War, 1861. Died at Decatur, Decatur Co.

Hollister, David Sprague (4 June 1808–after 3 Oct. 1851), merchant, steamboat owner and captain, speculator. Born in Middleburgh, Schoharie Co., New York. Son of Stephen Hollister and Anna Sprague. Moved to Newark, Licking Co., Ohio, ca. 1829. Married Mary Ann Wilson, Oct. 1831, in Utica, Licking Co. Moved to Granville, Licking

Co., by 1834; to Milwaukee, 1835–1836; to Quincy, Adams Co., Illinois, 1842; and to Nauvoo, Hancock Co., Illinois. Baptized into LDS church, by Mar. 1842. Received elder's license, 17 Mar. 1842, in Nauvoo. Member of Nauvoo Masonic Lodge. Ordained a high priest, 7 Sept. 1844, in Nauvoo. Member of Council of Fifty, 1844. Served mission to Baltimore, 1844. Moved to Philadelphia, by 1848. Moved to Washington Township, Licking Co., by 1850. Died in California.

Hotchkiss, Horace Rowe (15 Apr. 1799–21 Apr. 1849), merchant, land speculator. Born in East Haven, New Haven Co., Connecticut. Son of Heman Hotchkiss and Elizabeth Rowe. Moved to New Haven, New Haven Co., by 1815. Married Charlotte Austin Street, 22 Feb. 1824, in East Haven. Purchased land in and around Commerce (later Nauvoo), Hancock Co., Illinois, 1836; sold the land to JS and other church leaders, 1839, for development of Nauvoo. Died in New Haven.

Howe, Eber Dudley (9 June 1798–10 Nov. 1885), newspaper editor and publisher, farmer, wool manufacturer. Born at Clifton Park, Saratoga Co., New York. Son of Samuel William Howe and Mabel Dudley. Moved with family to Ovid, Seneca Co., New York, 1804. Located at Niagara District (later in Ontario), Upper Canada, 1811. Enlisted with New York Volunteers in War of 1812 at Batavia, Genesee Co., New York, 1814. Worked for *Buffalo Gazette,* ca. 1816, at Buffalo, Erie Co., New York. Assisted in publishing *Chautauqua Gazette,* 1817–1818, at Fredonia, Chautauque Co., New York. Worked for *Erie Gazette,* Sept. 1817, at Erie, Erie Co., Pennsylvania. Cofounded and published *Cleveland Herald,* 1819–1821, at Cleveland. Moved to Painesville, Geauga Co., Ohio, spring 1822; founded and published *Painesville Telegraph,* beginning 1822. Married Sophia Hull of Clarence, Erie Co., June 1823. An abolitionist, his house was a station on the Underground Railroad to assist runaway slaves. Published anti-Mormon articles in *Painesville Telegraph* from 1831 until 1835, when he sold paper to his brother Asahel Howe. Published anti-Mormon book *Mormonism Unvailed,* 1834; with Doctor Philastus Hurlbut, advanced the Rigdon-Spaulding theory of the origin of the Book of Mormon. Involved in agriculture, 1840, at Concord Township, Lake Co., Ohio. Died at Painesville.

Hunter, Edward (22 June 1793–16 Oct. 1883), farmer, currier, surveyor, merchant. Born at Newtown Township, Delaware Co., Pennsylvania. Son of Edward Hunter and Hannah Maris. Volunteer cavalryman in Delaware Co. militia, 1822–1829. Served as Delaware Co. commissioner, 1823–1826. Moved to West Nantmeal Township (later Wallace Township), Chester Co., Pennsylvania, 1827. Married Ann Standley, 30 Sept. 1830, at Chester Co. Baptized into LDS church by Orson Hyde, 8 Oct. 1840, at West Nantmeal Township. Moved to Nauvoo, Hancock Co., Illinois, 1841. Appointed herald and armor bearer in Nauvoo Legion, Sept. 1841. Member of Nauvoo Masonic Lodge. Housed JS secretly, Sept. 1842. Regent of University of Nauvoo, 1842–1844. Member of Nauvoo City Council. Served as bishop of Nauvoo Fifth Ward, 1844–1846. Served as bodyguard to JS. Following murder of JS in Carthage, Hancock Co., 1844, escorted bodies of JS and Hyrum Smith into Nauvoo and helped bury them privately. Ordained a high priest by Brigham Young, before Nov. 1844, at Nauvoo. Moved to Winter Quarters, unorganized U.S. territory (later in Omaha, Douglas Co., Nebraska), 1846. Migrated to Salt Lake City, 1847. Served as presiding bishop of church, 1851–1883. Died at Salt Lake City.

Huntington, Dimick Baker (26 May 1808–1 Feb. 1879), farmer, blacksmith, shoemaker, constable, coroner, deputy sheriff, Indian interpreter. Born at Watertown, Jefferson Co., New York. Son of William Huntington and Zina Baker. Married Fannie Maria Allen, 28 Apr. 1830. Baptized into LDS church, 1 Aug. 1835. Ordained an elder at Kirtland, Geauga Co., Ohio. Constable at Caldwell Co., Missouri, and later deputy sheriff. Participated in Battle of Crooked River, near Ray Co., Missouri, 25 Oct. 1838. Served as constable at Nauvoo, Hancock Co., Illinois. Drum major in Nauvoo Legion band, 1841. Appointed Nauvoo city marshal, 1841. Member of Nauvoo Masonic Lodge. Served as coroner, 1842–ca. 1846, in Nauvoo. Arrested for destruction of *Nauvoo Expositor* press, 1844. Arrived in Salt Lake Valley, July 1847. Ordained a high priest in Salt Lake City. Helped establish settlements in Utah and Sanpete counties. Served as interpreter in meetings between Indian tribes and settlers. Died at Salt Lake City.

Hurlbut, Doctor Philastus (3 Feb. 1809–16 June 1883), clergyman, farmer. Born at Chittenden Co., Vermont. "Doctor" was his given name. Preacher for Methodist Episcopal Church in Jamestown, Chautauque Co., New York. Baptized into LDS church, 1832/1833, at Jamestown. Ordained an elder by Sidney Rigdon, 18 Mar. 1833. Appointed to serve mission to East with Daniel Copley, 19 Mar. 1833. Excommunicated, June 1833. Married Maria Sheldon Woodbury, 29 Apr. 1834, in Ashtabula Co., Ohio. Employed by citizens of Geauga Co., Ohio, to collect information about Smith family and origin of Book of Mormon. Findings were published in Eber D. Howe's *Mormonism Unvailed*, 1834. Arrested for allegedly threatening JS's life, 1834, and ordered to enter into recognizance to keep the peace. Moved to Gerard Township, Erie Co., Pennsylvania, 1834/1835. With Eber Howe, advanced the Rigdon-Spaulding theory of the origin of the Book of Mormon. Located at Gibsonburg, Sandusky Co., Ohio, 1836/1837. Joined Salem United Brethren Church in Gibsonburg; ordained an elder in that church, ca. 1846. Appointed member of board of trustees of Otterbein College, 1847, in Westerville, Franklin Co., Ohio. Suspended permanently from ministry, 1852. Died at Madison Township, Sandusky Co.

Hyde, Marinda Nancy Johnson (28 June 1815–24 Mar. 1886). Born in Pomfret, Windsor Co., Vermont. Daughter of John Johnson and Alice (Elsa) Jacob. Baptized into LDS church, Apr. 1831, in Hiram, Portage Co., Ohio. Moved to Kirtland, Geauga Co., Ohio, 1833. Married Orson Hyde, 4 Sept. 1834, in Kirtland. Moved to Far West, Caldwell Co., Missouri, 1838. Lived in Missouri, 1838–1839. Moved to Nauvoo, Hancock Co., Illinois. "Married or sealed" to JS, Apr. 1842 or May 1843. Moved to Pottawattamie Co., Iowa Territory, 1846. Migrated to Salt Lake City, 1852. Divorced husband, Apr. 1870, in Sanpete Co., Utah Territory. Died in Salt Lake City.

Hyde, Orson (8 Jan. 1805–28 Nov. 1878), laborer, clerk, storekeeper, teacher, editor, businessman, lawyer, judge. Born at Oxford, New Haven Co., Connecticut. Son of Nathan Hyde and Sally Thorpe. Moved to Derby, New Haven Co., 1812. Moved to Kirtland, Geauga Co., Ohio, 1818. Joined Methodist church, ca. 1827. Later affiliated with Reformed Baptists (later Disciples of Christ or Campbellites). Baptized into LDS church by Sidney Rigdon and ordained an elder by JS and Sidney Rigdon, 30 Oct. 1831, at Kirtland. Ordained a high priest by JS and appointed to serve mission to Ohio, Nov. 1831, in Orange, Cuyahoga Co., Ohio. Baptized many during proselytizing mission with Samuel H. Smith to eastern states, 1832. Appointed clerk to church presidency, 1833. Appointed to serve mission to

Jackson Co., Missouri, summer 1833. Served mission to Pennsylvania and New York, winter and spring 1834. Member of Kirtland high council, 1834. Participated in Camp of Israel expedition to Missouri, 1834. Married to Marinda Nancy Johnson by Sidney Rigdon, 4 Sept. 1834, at Kirtland. Ordained member of Quorum of the Twelve by Oliver Cowdery, David Whitmer, and Martin Harris, 15 Feb. 1835, in Kirtland. Served mission to western New York and Upper Canada, 1836. Served mission to England with Heber C. Kimball, 1837–1838. Moved to Far West, Caldwell Co., Missouri, summer 1838. Sided with dissenters against JS, 1838. Lived in Missouri, 1838–1839. Removed from Quorum of the Twelve, 4 May 1839. Restored to Quorum of the Twelve, 27 June 1839, at Commerce (later Nauvoo), Hancock Co., Illinois. Served mission to Palestine to dedicate land for gathering of Israel, 1840–1842. Member of Nauvoo Masonic Lodge, 1842. Member of Nauvoo City Council, 1843–1845. Participated in plural marriage during JS's lifetime. Departed Nauvoo during exodus to the West, mid-May 1846. Served mission to Great Britain, 1846–1847. Presided over Latter-day Saints in Iowa before migrating to Utah Territory. Appointed president of Quorum of the Twelve, 1847. Published *Frontier Guardian* at Kanesville (later Council Bluffs), Pottawattamie Co., Iowa, 1849–1852. Migrated to Utah Territory, 1852. Appointed associate judge of U.S. Supreme Court for Utah Territory, 1852. Elected to Utah territorial legislature, 27 Nov. 1852, 1858. Presided over church in Carson Co., Utah Territory (later in Nevada Territory), 1855–1856. Served colonizing mission to Sanpete Co., Utah Territory, by 1860; presided as ecclesiastical authority there, 1860–1877. Died at Spring City, Sanpete Co.

Ivins, Charles (16 Apr. 1799–29 Jan. 1875), merchant, hotelier, ferry owner, farmer. Born in Burlington Co., New Jersey. Son of Israel Ivins and Margaret Woodward. Married Elizabeth Lippencott Shinn, 1 May 1823, in Burlington Co. Moved to Monmouth Co., New Jersey, before 1840. Baptized into LDS church, by Feb. 1840, in New Jersey. Moved to Nauvoo, Hancock Co., Illinois, spring 1841. Member of Nauvoo Masonic Lodge. Moved to La Harpe, Hancock Co. Excommunicated, 18 May 1844. Publisher of *Nauvoo Expositor*, 1844. Involved with mob that murdered JS and Hyrum Smith on 27 June 1844. Moved to Keokuk, Lee Co., Iowa Territory, by 1845. Died at Keokuk.

Ivins, James (22 Mar. 1797–3 Apr. 1877), farmer. Born in Upper Freehold Township, Monmouth Co., New Jersey. Son of Israel Ivins and Margaret Woodward. Married Mary Schenk. Presumably baptized into LDS church. Moved to Nauvoo, Hancock Co., Illinois, by 1842. Member of Nauvoo Masonic Lodge. Left church in Nauvoo. Moved to Keokuk, Lee Co., Iowa Territory, by 1846. Moved to Landis Township (later in Vineland), Cumberland Co., New Jersey, by 1870. Likely died in Landis Township.

Johnson, Benjamin F. (28 July 1818–18 Nov. 1905), brickmaker, merchant, tavern keeper, leatherworker, farmer, nurseryman, beekeeper. Born at Pomfret, Chautauque Co., New York. Son of Ezekiel Johnson and Julia Hills. Moved to Kirtland, Geauga Co., Ohio, 1833. Baptized into LDS church by Lyman E. Johnson, spring 1835, at Kirtland. Moved to Adam-ondi-Ahman, Daviess Co., Missouri, 1838. Ordained an elder by Heber C. Kimball, 10 Mar. 1839, at Far West, Caldwell Co., Missouri. Moved to Springfield, Sangamon Co., Illinois, 1839. Served missions to eastern states and Upper Canada, 1840–1842. Married Melissa Bloomfield LeBaron, 25 Dec. 1841, at Kirtland. Settled at Ramus (later Webster), Hancock Co., Illinois, 1842. Member of Masonic lodge in Nauvoo, Hancock Co. Served as business agent for JS, 1842–1844. Appointed to Council of Fifty, 1843, at Nauvoo. Ordained a high priest by John Smith, 1843, at Ramus. Moved to Nauvoo, 1845; to Bonaparte, Van Buren Co., Iowa Territory, 1846; and to Salt Lake City, 1848. Moved to Summit Creek (later Santaquin), Utah Co., Utah Territory, 1851. Served in Utah territorial legislature, 1855–1867. Delegate to constitutional convention, 1856, at Salt Lake City. Moved to Spring Lake, Utah Co., 1862. Moved to Tempe, Maricopa Co., Arizona Territory, 1882. Moved to Colonia Díaz, Chihuahua, Mexico, 1890. Moved to Mesa, Maricopa Co., 1892. Died at Mesa.

Johnson, Joel Hills (23 Mar. 1802–24 Sept. 1882), miller, farmer, merchant. Born at Grafton, Worcester Co., Massachusetts. Son of Ezekiel Johnson and Julia Hills. Moved to Newport, Campbell Co., Kentucky, 1813. Moved to Pomfret, Chautauque Co., New York, 1815. Baptized into Baptist church, 1825, at Forestville, Chautauque Co. Married first Anna P. Johnson, 2 Nov. 1826, at Canadaway (later Fredonia), Chautauque Co. Moved to Amherst, Lorain Co., Ohio, 1830. Baptized into LDS church by Sylvester Smith, 1 June 1831, at Amherst. Ordained a teacher, 24 Aug. 1831, at Amherst; an elder, 20 Sept. 1831, at Amherst; and a high priest, 25 Oct. 1831, at Orange, Cuyahoga Co., Ohio. President of Amherst branch, 1831. Served mission to New York, Jan. 1832. Moved to Kirtland, Geauga Co., Ohio, 1833. Labored on Kirtland temple. Served mission to southeastern Ohio. Ordained a seventy. Helped organize Kirtland Camp migration to Missouri, 1838. Moved to Carthage, Hancock Co., Illinois, Jan. 1839; settled on west branch of Crooked Creek (eight miles from Carthage), 18 Feb. 1840. Appointed president of Crooked Creek stake, 1840. Married second Susan Bryant, 20 Oct. 1840, at Hancock Co. Moved to Ramus (later Webster), Hancock Co., Nov. 1840. Married third Janet Fife, 25 Oct. 1845. Moved to Knox Co., Illinois, June 1846. Migrated to Salt Lake City, 6 May 1848–19 Oct. 1848. Elected member of House of Representatives for provisional state of Deseret, 1849. Moved to what later became Iron Co., Utah Territory, 15 May 1850; to Florence, Douglas Co., Nebraska Territory, 1858; and to southern Utah Territory, 1861. Died in Kane Co., Utah Territory.

Johnson, Joseph Ellis (28 Apr. 1817–17 Dec. 1882), teacher, postmaster, newspaper editor, druggist, farmer, horticulturist, merchant. Born in Pomfret, Chautauque Co., New York. Son of Ezekiel Johnson and Julia Hills. Baptized into LDS church, ca. 1833. Labored on temple, 1833, in Kirtland, Geauga Co., Ohio. Taught school in Springfield, Sangamon Co., Illinois, 1839. Married Harriet Snider, ca. Aug. 1840, at Hancock Co., Illinois. Served as postmaster, 1840, in Ramus (later Macedonia), Hancock Co. Taught school, 1843, in Macedonia (later Webster). Served as church recorder and secretary to patriarch John Smith. Ordained an elder, by 1846. Moved to Kanesville (later Council Bluffs), Pottawattamie Co., Iowa, 1848. Member of Iowa legislature, 1852. Moved to Utah Territory, 1861. Member of Utah territorial legislature, 1862. Left to serve colonizing mission to southern Arizona Territory, 1882. Died in Tempe, Maricopa Co., Arizona Territory.

Johnson, Luke (3 Nov. 1807–8 Dec. 1861), farmer, teacher, doctor. Born at Pomfret, Windsor Co., Vermont. Son of John Johnson and Elsa Jacobs. Lived at Hiram, Portage Co., Ohio, when baptized into LDS church by JS, 10 May 1831. Ordained a priest by Christian Whitmer shortly after baptism. Ordained an elder, by Oct. 1831. Ordained a high priest, 25 Oct. 1831. Served missions to Ohio, Pennsylvania, Virginia, and Kentucky, 1831–1833. Married first Susan Harminda Poteet, 1 Nov. 1833, in Cabell Co., Virginia (later in West Virginia). Appointed to high council, 17 Feb. 1834, at Kirtland, Geauga Co., Ohio.

Participated in Camp of Israel expedition to Missouri, 1834. Member of Quorum of the Twelve, 1835–1837. Served mission to eastern states, 1835, and to New York and Upper Canada, 1836. Constable in Kirtland. Disfellowshipped, 3 Sept. 1837. Reinstated to church and membership in Quorum of the Twelve, 10 Sept. 1837. Excommunicated, 1838. Taught school in Virginia and also studied medicine, which he practiced at Kirtland. Rebaptized into LDS church by Orson Hyde, 8 Mar. 1846, at Nauvoo, Hancock Co, Illinois. Wife died, 1846. Married second America Morgan Clark, Mar. 1847. Member of Brigham Young pioneer company to Salt Lake Valley, 1847. Moved to St. John, Tooele Co., Utah Territory, 1858. Bishop at St. John. Died at Salt Lake City.

Jonas, Abraham (12 Sept. 1801–8 June 1864), auctioneer, merchant, newspaper publisher, lawyer. Born in Exeter, Devonshire, England. Son of Benjamin Jonas and Annie Ezekial. Jewish. Immigrated to U.S.; settled in Cincinnati, ca. 1819. Married first Lucy Orah Seixas, before 1825, probably in Cincinnati. Moved to Williamstown, Grant Co., Kentucky, 1825. Served in Kentucky legislature, 1828–1833. Married second Louisa Block, 11 Oct. 1829. Grand Master of Grand Masonic Lodge of Kentucky, 1833–1834. Moved to Columbus, Adams Co., Illinois, 1836. Moved to Quincy, Adams Co., 1838. Founded newspaper *Columbus Advocate,* 1840. Organized second Grand Masonic Lodge of Illinois, 1840; served as Grand Master, 1840–1842. Instrumental in establishment of Nauvoo Masonic Lodge and advancement of JS in Masonry, 1842. Served in Illinois legislature, 1843–1844. Died in Quincy.

Jones, Dan (4 Aug. 1811–3 Jan. 1862), steamboat owner and captain, farmer, mayor. Born in Flintshire, Wales. Son of Thomas Jones and Ruth. Married Jane Melling, 3 Jan. 1837, in Denbigh, Denbighshire, Wales. Immigrated to U.S., ca. 1840. Moved to Nauvoo, Hancock Co., Illinois, after 1840. Baptized into LDS church, Jan. 1843. Member of Nauvoo Masonic Lodge. Operated a steamboat between Nauvoo and Montrose, Lee Co., Iowa Territory, 1843. Served mission to Wales, 1844–1849. Moved to provisional state of Deseret, 1849. Moved to Manti, Sanpete Co., Utah Territory, by 1850. Presided over Wales mission, 1852–1855. Moved to Provo, Utah Co., Utah Territory, by 1860. Died in Provo.

Kilbourn(e), David Wells (12 Apr. 1803–24 Apr. 1876), merchant, land agent, postmaster, lawyer, railroad executive. Born in Marlborough, Hartford Co., Connecticut. Son of David Kilbourn(e) and Lydia Welles. Member of Presbyterian church. Married Harriet Rice in Albany, Albany Co., New York, 28 June 1827. Settled in New York City. Moved to Des Moines Co., Wisconsin Territory (later Lee Co., Iowa Territory), fall 1836. Represented New York Land Company at Fort Des Moines, Lee Co., purchasing and selling land in Half-Breed Tract. Laid out town of Keokuk, Lee Co., June 1837. Platted town of Montrose, Lee Co., 1837, and established a general store with his brother Edward. Appointed postmaster of Montrose, 1839. Unsuccessful Whig candidate for Iowa Territorial Council, 1840, 1841. In 1843, moved to Fort Madison, Lee Co., where he continued working for New York Land Company. Delegate from Iowa at National Whig Convention in Baltimore, 1852. Moved to Keokuk, 1852. Died in New York City.

Kilbourn(e), Edward (22 Jan. 1814–3 Feb. 1878), merchant, land speculator, gas manufacturer, railroad operator. Born at Marlborough, Hartford Co., Connecticut. Son of David Kilbourn(e) and Lydia Welles. Moved to Lee Co., Iowa Territory, by 1839. In partnership with his brother David, established a general store, 1839, at Montrose, Lee Co. Married

Caroline Amelia Foote, 26 July 1843, at Lake Co., Ohio. Lived at Keokuk, Lee Co., by 1850. Died at Keokuk.

Kimball, Heber Chase (14 June 1801–22 June 1868), blacksmith, potter. Born at Sheldon, Franklin Co., Vermont. Son of Solomon Farnham Kimball and Anna Spaulding. Married Vilate Murray, 22 Nov. 1822, at Mendon, Monroe Co., New York. Member of Baptist church at Mendon, 1831. Baptized into LDS church by Alpheus Gifford, 15 Apr. 1832, at Mendon. Ordained an elder by Joseph Young, 1832. Moved to Kirtland, Geauga Co., Ohio, 1833. Participated in Camp of Israel expedition to Missouri, 1834. Ordained member of Quorum of the Twelve, 1835. Served mission to the East with Quorum of the Twelve, 1835. Presided over first Latter-day Saint missionaries to British Isles, 1837–1838. Moved from Kirtland to Far West, Caldwell Co., Missouri, 1838. Worked closely with Brigham Young and others in supervising removal of Latter-day Saints from Missouri, 1838–1839. Present at Far West temple site, 26 Apr. 1839, when members of Quorum of the Twelve formally began their missionary assignment to British Isles. In removing from Missouri, initially located at Quincy, Adams Co., Illinois, and then Commerce (later Nauvoo), Hancock Co., Illinois, May 1839. Served mission with Quorum of the Twelve to British Isles, 1839–1841. Member of Nauvoo City Council, 1841–1845. Member of Nauvoo Masonic Lodge. Participated in plural marriage during JS's lifetime. Served mission to eastern states, 1843. Labored on Nauvoo temple. Joined exodus from Illinois into Iowa Territory, Feb. 1846. Member of Brigham Young pioneer company to Salt Lake Valley; arrived July 1847. Sustained as first counselor to Brigham Young in First Presidency at what became Council Bluffs, Pottawattamie Co., Iowa, 27 Dec. 1847. Elected lieutenant governor in provisional state of Deseret. Served in Utah territorial legislature. Died at Salt Lake City.

Kimball, Hiram S. (31 May 1806–27 Apr. 1863), merchant, iron foundry operator, mail carrier. Born in West Fairlee, Orange Co., Vermont. Son of Phineas Kimball and Abigail. Moved to Commerce (later Nauvoo), Hancock Co., Illinois, 1833, and established several stores. Married Sarah M. Granger, 23 Sept. 1840, in Kirtland, Geauga Co., Ohio; returned to Nauvoo three weeks later. Member of Nauvoo Masonic Lodge. Appointed assistant adjutant general in Nauvoo Legion, 3 June 1842. Nauvoo city alderman, 1841–1843. Baptized into LDS church by Eli Maginn, 20 July 1843, in Nauvoo. Ordained a high priest, by 17 Jan. 1846. Operated Nauvoo iron foundry, by 1846. Wounded in Battle of Nauvoo, Sept. 1846. Moved to Utah Territory, 1850. Died en route to serve mission to Sandwich Islands when ship's boiler exploded.

Kimball, Sarah Ann Whitney (22 Mar. 1825–4 Sept. 1873). Born in Kirtland, Geauga Co., Ohio. Daughter of Newel K. Whitney and Elizabeth Ann Smith. Moved to Hancock Co., Illinois, by 1840. Member of Nauvoo Fourth Ward, 1842. "Married or sealed" to JS "for time and eternity," 27 July 1842, in Nauvoo, Hancock Co. Married Joseph C. Kingsbury, 29 Apr. 1843, in Nauvoo. Married Heber C. Kimball as a plural wife. Moved to Salt Lake City, 1848. Died in Salt Lake City.

King, Austin Augustus (21 Sept. 1802–22 Apr. 1870), attorney, judge, politician, farmer. Born at Sullivan Co., Tennessee. Son of Walter King and Nancy Sevier. Married first Nancy Harris Roberts, 13 May 1828, at Jackson, Madison Co., Tennessee. In 1830, moved to Missouri, where he practiced law at Columbia, Boone Co. Served as colonel in Black Hawk War, 1832. Elected to state legislature as Jacksonian Democrat from Boone

Co., 1834, 1836. In 1837, removed to Richmond, Ray Co., Missouri, where he received appointment as circuit judge in northwestern Missouri by Governor Lilburn W. Boggs. Between 1837 and 1848, served as judge of Missouri's Fifth Judicial Circuit, consisting of counties of Clinton, Ray, Caldwell, Clay, Daviess, Carroll, and Livingston. In Nov. 1838, presided at preliminary hearing of JS and other Mormons at Richmond; committed them to jail pending trials to be held Mar. 1839. Governor of Missouri, 1848–1852. Married second Martha Anthony Woodson, 10 Aug. 1858, in Kingston, Caldwell Co. Represented Missouri in U.S. Congress, 1863–1865. Died at St. Louis. Buried in Richmond.

King, Thomas C. (25 July 1806–17 Apr. 1854), merchant. Born in Virginia. Lived at Quincy, Adams Co., Illinois, by Jan. 1832. Served as constable, beginning Aug. 1835. Married Juliett Ann McDade, 9 June 1836, in Adams Co. Served as Adams Co. coroner, by Aug. 1836. Served as fireman, by 1839, at Quincy. Member of Bodley Masonic Lodge in Quincy, 1840. Served as undersheriff of Quincy, by Aug. 1842. Listed as Junior Warden in Bodley lodge, 3 June 1842. With Edward Ford and James Pitman, attempted to arrest JS for complicity in attempt to kill former Missouri governor Lilburn W. Boggs, 8 Aug. 1842, in Nauvoo. Died at Quincy.

Knight, Joseph, Jr. (21 June 1808–3 Nov. 1866), miller, carder, millwright. Born at Halifax, Windham Co., Vermont. Son of Joseph Knight Sr. and Polly Peck. Moved to Jericho (later Bainbridge), Chenango Co., New York, ca. 1809. Moved to Windsor (later in Colesville), Broome Co., New York, 1811. Became acquainted with JS when Knight's father hired JS, 1826. Baptized into LDS church by Oliver Cowdery, 28 June 1830, at Colesville. Moved with Colesville branch to Thompson, Geauga Co., Ohio, May 1831; moved to Kaw Township, Jackson Co., Missouri, July 1831. Married Betsey Covert, 22 Mar. 1832, at Kirtland, Geauga Co. Moved to Clay Co., Missouri, 1833; to Far West, Caldwell Co., Missouri, 1837; to Lima, Adams Co., Illinois, 1839; to Nauvoo, Hancock Co., Illinois, 1840; and to La Harpe, Hancock Co. Ordained a priest at La Harpe. Moved back to Nauvoo, 1844. Captain in emigrant company traveling through Iowa Territory, 1846. Moved to what became Council Bluffs, Pottawattamie Co., Iowa Territory, 1846. Migrated to Salt Lake City, 1850. Died at Salt Lake City.

Knight, Joseph, Sr. (3 Nov. 1772–2 Feb. 1847), farmer, miller. Born at Oakham, Worcester Co., Massachusetts. Son of Benjamin Knight and Sarah Crouch. Lived at Marlboro, Windham Co., Vermont, by 1780. Married first Polly Peck, 1795, at Windham Co. Moved to Bainbridge, Chenango Co., New York, 1809. Moved to Windsor (later in Colesville), Broome Co., New York, 1811. Universalist. Hired JS, 1826. Present at Smith family farm when JS retrieved gold plates, 1827, at Manchester, Ontario Co., New York. Baptized into LDS church by Oliver Cowdery, 28 June 1830, at Colesville. Moved with Colesville branch to Thompson, Geauga Co., Ohio, 1831; moved to Kaw Township, Jackson Co., Missouri, July 1831. Married second Phebe Crosby Peck, by Oct. 1833, in Missouri. Lived at Liberty, Clay Co., Missouri, by 1834. Moved to Nauvoo, Hancock Co., Illinois, by 1840. Ordained a high priest, ca. Sept. 1844, at Nauvoo. Member of Nauvoo Masonic Lodge. Died at Mount Pisgah, Clarke Co., Iowa.

Knight, Newel (13 Sept. 1800–11 Jan. 1847), miller, merchant. Born at Marlborough, Windham Co., Vermont. Son of Joseph Knight Sr. and Polly Peck. Moved to Bainbridge, Chenango Co., New York, ca. 1809. Moved to Windsor (later in Colesville), Broome Co.,

New York, 1811. Married first Sally Coburn, 7 June 1825. Became acquainted with JS when Knight's father hired JS, 1826. Baptized into LDS church by David Whitmer, last week of May 1830, in Seneca Co., New York. Ordained a priest, 26 Sept. 1830. Branch president who led Colesville branch from Broome Co. to Thompson, Geauga Co., Ohio, May 1831. Ordained an elder, before June 1831. Moved again with Colesville branch moved to Kaw Township, Jackson Co., Missouri, July 1831. Ordained a high priest, by July 1832. Expelled from Jackson Co. and moved to Clay Co., Missouri, 1833. Appointed member of Clay Co. high council, July 1834. Wife died, Sept. 1834. Lived at Kirtland, Geauga Co., Ohio, spring 1835–spring 1836. Married second to Lydia Goldthwaite Bailey by JS, 24 Nov. 1835, at Kirtland. Lived at Clay Co., 1836. Member of high council at Far West, Caldwell Co., Missouri, 1837–1838. Left Missouri during exodus and moved to Commerce (later Nauvoo), Hancock Co., Illinois, 1839. Member of Commerce high council, 1839–1845. Left Nauvoo, 1846. Died in present-day northern Nebraska.

Knight, Vinson (14 Mar. 1804–31 July 1842), farmer, druggist, school warden. Born at Norwich, Hampshire Co., Massachusetts. Son of Rudolphus Knight and Rispah (Rizpah) Lee. Married Martha McBride, 14 Mar. 1826. Moved to Perrysburg, Cattaraugus Co., New York, by Mar. 1834. Owned farm at Perrysburg when baptized into LDS church, spring 1834. Moved to Kirtland, Geauga Co., Ohio, by Dec. 1835. Ordained an elder, 2 Jan. 1836. Ordained a high priest and appointed counselor to Bishop Newel K. Whitney, 13 Jan. 1836, at Kirtland. Appointed township clerk, 1837. Member of Kirtland Safety Society, Jan. 1837. Served mission, 1837. Moved to Far West, Caldwell Co., Missouri, by Nov. 1837. Appointed to Far West high council, 6 Nov. 1837. Located at Adam-ondi-Ahman, Daviess Co., Missouri, summer 1838. Appointed acting bishop at Adam-ondi-Ahman, 28 June 1838. Exiled from Missouri; located at Quincy, Adams Co., Illinois, 1839. Church land agent; with others purchased approximately 19,000 acres of Half-Breed Tract in Lee Co., Iowa Territory, from Isaac Galland, and about 190 acres in Hancock Co., Illinois, from Galland and from Hugh White, 1839. Appointed bishop in Commerce (later Nauvoo), Hancock Co., 4 May 1839. Appointed bishop of Lower Ward at Commerce, 5 Oct. 1839. Instructed in JS revelation to buy stock for building Nauvoo House, 19 Jan. 1841. Appointed presiding bishop of church, 19 Jan. 1841. Member of Nauvoo City Council, 1841–1842. Served as warden of Nauvoo common schools and member of Nauvoo University building committee, 1841–1842. Appointed guard in Nauvoo Legion, Mar. 1841. Member of Nauvoo Masonic Lodge. Died at Nauvoo.

Lamborn, Josiah (31 Jan. 1809–31 Mar. 1847), lawyer. Born in Chester Co., Pennsylvania. Son of Samuel Lamborn and Mary McGinnis. Moved to Columbia Township, Hamilton Co., Ohio, 1811; to Washington Co., Kentucky; to Springfield, Sangamon Co., Illinois, 1832; and to Jacksonville, Morgan Co., Illinois, by 1834. Married Marie Therese Allen, 27 Apr. 1837, in St. Louis. Practiced law in Illinois. Served as attorney general of Illinois, 1840–1843, in Springfield. Represented Illinois in opposing JS's habeas corpus petition, Jan. 1843, in Springfield. A prosecuting attorney in trial of those indicted for murdering JS and Hyrum Smith, 1845, but did not appear at trial. Died in White Hall, Greene Co., Illinois.

Law, William (8 Sept. 1809–12/19 Jan. 1892), merchant, millwright, physician. Born in Co. Tyrone, Ireland. Son of Richard Law and Ann Hunter. Immigrated to U.S. and settled in Springfield Township, Mercer Co., Pennsylvania, by 1820. Moved to Delaware Township, Mercer Co., by 1830. Moved to Churchville, Chinguacousy Township, York Co. (later in Ontario), Upper Canada, by 1833. Married Jane Silverthorn, 11 June 1833, in York. Baptized into LDS church, 1836. Ordained an elder by Parley P. Pratt, 24 Apr. 1837. Served as presiding elder of Churchville branch, 1837–1838. Moved to Georgetown (later Sheakleyville), Mercer Co., by 1838. Moved to Commerce (later Nauvoo), Hancock Co., Illinois, 1839. Instructed in JS revelation to buy stock for building Nauvoo House, 19 Jan. 1841. Served as counselor in First Presidency, 1841–1844, in Nauvoo. Served mission to Philadelphia, 1841. Appointed aide-de-camp to lieutenant general in Nauvoo Legion, Mar. 1841. Member of Nauvoo City Council, 1841–1843. Member of Nauvoo Masonic Lodge. Removed from First Presidency, by Jan. 1844; excommunicated, 18 Apr. 1844, in Nauvoo. Appointed by LDS dissenters to replace JS as president of church; eventually organized new church, 1844. Publisher of *Nauvoo Expositor*, 1844. Moved to Burlington, Des Moines Co., Iowa Territory, June 1844; to Hampton, Rock Island Co., Illinois, by Oct. 1844; and to Jo Daviess Co., Illinois, by 1847. Lived at Findley Township, Mercer Co., 1850; in Apple River, Jo Daviess Co., by 1860; and in Shullsburg, Lafayette Co., Wisconsin, by 1870. Died in Shullsburg.

Law, Wilson (26 Feb. 1806–15 Oct. 1876), merchant, millwright, land speculator, farmer. Born in Ireland. Son of Richard Law and Ann Hunter. Immigrated to U.S. and settled in Springfield Township, Mercer Co., Pennsylvania, by 1820. Moved to Delaware Township, Mercer Co., by 1830. Moved to Commerce (later Nauvoo), Hancock Co., Illinois, 1839. Baptized into LDS church and ordained an elder, in Nauvoo. Member of Nauvoo City Council, 1841–1843. Elected brigadier general in Nauvoo Legion, Feb. 1841, and then major general, Aug. 1842. Member of Nauvoo Masonic Lodge. Married first to Elizabeth F. Sikes by JS, 25 Dec. 1842, in Nauvoo. Served mission to Ohio, 1843. Excommunicated, 18 Apr. 1844, in Nauvoo. With his brother William and LDS church dissenters, organized new church, 1844. Publisher of *Nauvoo Expositor*, 1844. Moved to Burlington, Des Moines Co., Iowa Territory, June 1844. Moved to Hampton, Rock Island Co., Illinois, by Oct. 1844. Lived in Delaware Township, Mercer Co., by 1850. Married second Eliza Sowash, 13 Jan. 1853, in Jefferson Township, Mercer Co. Moved to Gratiot, Lafayette Co., Wisconsin, by 1860. Moved to Shullsburg, Lafayette Co., by 1870. Died in Shullsburg.

Leal, Clark (10 Aug. 1805–21 Apr. 1845), farmer. Born in Kortright, Delaware Co., New York. Son of Alexander Leal and Lydia Rose. Married Jane McClaughry, 16 Dec. 1830. Moved to Fountain Green, Hancock Co., Illinois, 1837. Served as school treasurer in Fountain Green. Died in Fountain Green.

Lott, Cornelius P. (27 Sept. 1798–6 July 1850), farmer. Born in New York City. Son of Peter Lott and Mary Jane Smiley. Married Permelia Darrow, 27 Apr. 1823, in Bridgewater Township, Susquehanna Co., Pennsylvania. Lived in Bridgewater Township, 1830. Baptized into LDS church, before 1834. Moved to Kirtland, Geauga Co., Ohio, by 1836. Received elder's license, 1 Aug. 1836, in Kirtland. Moved to Daviess Co., Missouri, by 1838. Moved to Pike Co., Illinois, by June 1840. Managed JS's farm in Nauvoo, Hancock Co., Illinois. Member of Nauvoo Masonic Lodge. Ordained a high priest, 22 Jan. 1845, in Nauvoo. Left

Illinois, by Aug. 1846. Migrated to what later became Utah Territory, Sept. 1847. Died at Salt Lake City.

Lott, Elizabeth Davis (11 Mar. 1791–16 Dec. 1876). Born in Riverhead, Suffolk Co., New York. Daughter of Gilbert Davis and Abigail Reeve. Christened Presbyterian. Moved to Southold, Suffolk Co., by 1810. Married first Gilbert Goldsmith, 13 Apr. 1811, in Cutchogue, Suffolk Co. Joined Methodist church. Married second Joseph Blanchett Brackenbury, after 1815. Moved to Newton Township, Kings Co., New York, by Nov. 1820. Moved to New London, Huron Co., Ohio, 1824. Baptized into LDS church by John Carl, 10 Apr. 1831. Moved to Big Blue settlement, Jackson Co., Missouri, 1832. Married third Jabez Durfee (Durphy), 3 Mar. 1834, in Clay Co., Missouri. Moved to Far West, Missouri, ca. 1835; to Daviess Co., Missouri, Dec. 1837; to Quincy, Adams Co., Illinois, 1838; and to Commerce (later Nauvoo), Hancock Co., Illinois, 1839. Present with Emma Smith in Nauvoo when JS's body was brought from Carthage, Hancock Co., June 1844. Married fourth Cornelius P. Lott as a plural wife, 22 Jan. 1846, in Nauvoo. Moved to Winter Quarters, unorganized U.S. territory (later in Omaha, Douglas Co., Nebraska), 1846; back to Quincy; to Pike Co., Illinois, by 1850; to Salt Lake City, 1855; to De Kalb Co., Missouri, 1857; back to Salt Lake City, 1858; to Washington, De Kalb Co., Missouri, by 1860; to Denver, 1862; to San Bernardino, San Bernardino Co., California, 1865; back to Salt Lake City, 1868; and to White Cloud, Doniphan Co., Kansas, by 1870. Baptized into RLDS church, by 1870. Died in White Cloud.

Lucas, Samuel D. (19 July 1799–23 Feb. 1868), store owner, recorder of deeds. Born at Washington Co., Kentucky. Son of Samuel Lucas Sr. Married Theresa Bartlett Allen, 10 Nov. 1823, in Harrison Co., Kentucky. Member of Presbyterian church. Lived at Independence, Jackson Co., Missouri, by 1827. Jackson Co. court justice, 1831. Secretary of citizens committee that met to negotiate departure of Latter-day Saints from Jackson Co., July 1833, in Independence. Major general in Missouri militia; in absence of designated commander, John B. Clark, led militia forces and confronted Mormon forces near Far West, Caldwell Co., Missouri, Oct. 1838. Disbanded Mormon forces, took JS and other Mormon leaders prisoner, and escorted them to Independence before Clark arrived. County clerk, 1842, and clerk of circuit court, 1848, in Jackson Co. Died in Independence.

Lyman, Amasa Mason (30 Mar. 1813–4 Feb. 1877), boatman, gunsmith, farmer. Born at Lyman, Grafton Co., New Hampshire. Son of Boswell Lyman and Martha Mason. Baptized into LDS church by Lyman E. Johnson, 27 Apr. 1832. Moved to Hiram, Portage Co., Ohio, June 1832. Ordained an elder by JS and Frederick G. Williams, 23 Aug. 1832, at Hiram. Left to serve mission to southern Ohio and Virginia, 24 Aug. 1832. Left to serve mission to New York and New Hampshire, 21 Mar. 1833. Ordained a high priest by Lyman E. Johnson and Orson Pratt, 11 Dec. 1833, in Elk Creek, Otsego Co., New York. Participated in Camp of Israel expedition to Missouri, 1834. Ordained a seventy by JS, Oliver Cowdery, and Sidney Rigdon, ca. Mar. 1835. Married Maria Louisa Tanner, 10 June 1835, at Kirtland, Geauga Co., Ohio. Served mission to New York, spring 1836. Charter member of Kirtland Safety Society, 1837. Moved to Far West, Caldwell Co., Missouri, 1837; to McDonough Co., Illinois, winter 1839–1840; to Lee Co., Iowa Territory, spring 1840; and to Nauvoo, Hancock Co., Illinois, spring 1841. Served mission to northern Illinois and Wisconsin Territory, 1841. Appointed to serve mission to raise funds for construction of Nauvoo temple and Nauvoo

House, Oct. 1841. Served mission to Tennessee, spring 1842. Member of Nauvoo Masonic Lodge. Member of Nauvoo City Council, 1842–1843. Ordained member of Quorum of the Twelve, 20 Aug. 1842, at Nauvoo. Elected a regent of University of Nauvoo, 20 Aug. 1842. Served mission to southern Illinois, 1842. Served colonizing mission to Shokokon, Henderson Co., Illinois, Feb.–June 1843; returned to Nauvoo, summer 1843. Counselor in First Presidency, 1843–1844. Moved to Winter Quarters, unorganized U.S. territory (later in Omaha, Douglas Co., Nebraska), 1846. Captain of wagon companies to Salt Lake Valley, 1847, 1848. Appointed to establish colony of San Bernardino, Los Angeles Co., California, 1851. Migrated to Salt Lake Valley, 1858. President of European mission, 1860–1862. Moved to Fillmore, Millard Co., Utah Territory, 1862. Deprived of apostleship, 6 Oct. 1867, and excommunicated, 12 May 1870. President of Godbeite Church of Zion, 1870. Died at Fillmore.

Lyon, Sylvia Porter Sessions. See Clark, Sylvia Porter Sessions.

Lyon, Windsor Palmer (8 Feb. 1809–Jan. 1849), physician, druggist, merchant. Born at Orwell, Addison Co., Vermont. Son of Aaron Child Lyon and Roxana Palmer. Baptized into LDS church, 1832, in New York. Lived at Willoughby, Cuyahoga Co., Ohio, 1835–1836, where he owned a store. Owned land in Far West, Missouri, 1836. Married Sylvia Porter Sessions, Mar. 1838, at Far West. Moved to Hancock Co., Illinois, by Feb. 1841. Lived in Nauvoo Fourth Ward, 1842, at Nauvoo, Hancock Co. Appointed aide-de-camp to major general in Nauvoo Legion, June 1842. Opened drug and variety store at Nauvoo. Ordained a high priest, by 3 Feb. 1846. Moved to Johnson Co., Iowa Territory, by Nov. 1846. Resided at Iowa City, Johnson Co., 1848. Died at Iowa City.

Mack, Temperance Bond (8 Sept. 1771–15 Sept. 1850). Born in Gilsum, Cheshire Co., New Hampshire. Daughter of Stephen Bond and Mary Yemmons. Married Stephen Mack, 1788, in Gilsum. Moved to Tunbridge, Orange Co., Vermont. Moved to Norwich, Orange Co., 1816; to Detroit, by 1822; and to Pontiac, Oakland Co., Michigan Territory, 1823. Husband died, 1826. Presumably baptized into LDS church. Moved to Kirtland, Geauga Co., Ohio; to Far West, Caldwell Co., Missouri, by 30 Dec. 1838; to Nauvoo, Hancock Co., Illinois, by Sept. 1841; back to Pontiac, 1844; back to Nauvoo, by 1845; to what became Council Bluffs, Pottawattamie Co., Iowa Territory, 1846; and to Winter Quarters, unorganized U.S. territory (later in Omaha, Douglas Co., Nebraska), 1846. Arrived in Salt Lake City, 20 Sept. 1848. Died at Salt Lake City.

Mackenzie, Alexander (6 Apr. 1803–13 Sept. 1848), author, naval officer. Born in New York City. Son of John Slidell and Margery Mackenzie. Joined U.S. Navy as midshipman, ca. 1815; promoted to lieutenant, 1825, and to commander, 1841. Wrote several books based on his travels as a naval officer. Married Catherine Alexander Robinson, 1 Oct. 1835, in New York City. Changed surname from Slidell to Mackenzie, 1837, to honor wishes of maternal uncle. As commander of U.S. ship *Somers,* uncovered a mutiny plot and hanged two of its organizers, 1842. Moved to Mount Pleasant, Westchester Co., New York, after 1835. Died near Tarrytown, Westchester Co.

Marcy, William Learned (12 Dec. 1786–4 July 1857), lawyer, politician. Born at Sturbridge (later Southbridge), Worcester Co., Massachusetts. Son of Jedediah Marcy and Ruth Larned. Moved to Woodstock, Windham Co., Connecticut, 1804; to Newport, Newport Co., Rhode Island, 1805; to Providence, Providence Co., Rhode Island, 1806; and to Troy, Rensselaer Co., New York, 1808. Married Dolly Newell, 27 Sept. 1812, at Sturbridge. Served as Troy city recorder, 1816–1818, 1821–1823. Served as adjutant general of New York, 1821–1823, at Troy. Moved to Albany, Albany Co., New York, and served as state comptroller, 1823–1829. Married Cornelia Knower, 29 Apr. 1824, at Guilderland, Albany Co. Served as state supreme court justice, 1829–1831, at Albany; as U.S. senator and chairman of committee on judiciary, 1831–1833, at Washington DC; and as governor of New York, 1833–1838, at Albany. Served as U.S. secretary of war, 1845–1849, and as U.S. secretary of state, 1853–1857, at Washington DC. Died at Ballston Spa, Saratoga Co., New York.

Markham, Stephen (9 Feb. 1800–10 Mar. 1878), carpenter, farmer, stock raiser. Born at Rush (later Avon), Ontario Co., New York. Son of David Markham and Dinah Merry. Moved to Mentor, Geauga Co., Ohio, 1809. Moved to Unionville, Geauga Co., 1810. Married Hannah Hogaboom, before 1824. Moved to Chester, Geauga Co., by July 1824. Baptized into LDS church by Abel Lamb, July 1837, at Kirtland, Geauga Co. Led company of sixty Latter-day Saints to Far West, Caldwell Co., Missouri, 1838. Appointed member of committee at Far West to supervise removal of Latter-day Saints from Missouri, Jan. 1839. Escorted family of JS from Far West to Quincy, Adams Co., Illinois, Feb. 1839. Returned to Far West and assisted in disposal of Mormon properties. Moved to Nauvoo, Hancock Co., Illinois, before 1841. Commissioned captain in Nauvoo Legion, 1 Feb. 1841. Appointed counselor to Nauvoo priests quorum president Samuel Rolfe, 21 Mar. 1841. Elected lieutenant colonel in Nauvoo Legion, 1 May 1841. Member of Nauvoo Masonic Lodge. Elected Nauvoo city alderman, 8 Feb. 1843. Ordained an elder, Apr. 1843, in Nauvoo. Sent to serve mission to Berlin, Huron Co., Ohio, Apr. 1843. Appointed to serve mission to Illinois, 15 Apr. 1844. Ordained a high priest, 7 Oct. 1844, in Nauvoo. Captain in Brigham Young pioneer company migrating to Salt Lake Valley, 1847. Returned to Winter Quarters, unorganized U.S. territory (later in Omaha, Douglas Co., Nebraska), Aug. 1847. Settled in Davis Co., Utah Territory, 1850. Served colonizing mission to southern Utah Co., Utah Territory, 1851, and helped settle towns of Spanish Fork, Utah Co., and Palmyra, Utah Co. Served colonizing mission to Fort Supply, near present-day Green River, Wyoming. Returned to Spanish Fork, Sept. 1857. Died at Spanish Fork.

Marks, William (15 Nov. 1792–22 May 1872), farmer, printer, publisher, postmaster. Born at Rutland, Rutland Co., Vermont. Son of Cornell (Cornwall) Marks and Sarah Goodrich. Married first Rosannah R. Robinson, 2 May 1813. Lived at Portage, Allegany Co., New York, where he was baptized into LDS church, by Apr. 1835. Ordained a priest, by 3 Apr. 1835. Ordained an elder, by 3 June 1836. Moved to Kirtland, Geauga Co., Ohio, by Sept. 1837. Appointed member of Kirtland high council, 3 Sept. 1837, and agent to Bishop Newel K. Whitney, 17 Sept. 1837. President of Kirtland stake, 1838. While at Kirtland, appointed stake president at Far West, Caldwell Co., Missouri, 8 July 1838. Did not reach Far West before expulsion of Latter-day Saints from Missouri. Located with Latter-day Saints at Quincy, Adams Co., Illinois, 1839. Appointed president of stake in Commerce (later Nauvoo), Hancock Co., Illinois, 5 Oct. 1839. Instructed in JS revelation to buy stock for building Nauvoo House, 19 Jan. 1841. Nauvoo city alderman, 1841–1843. Appointed a regent of University of Nauvoo, 3 Feb. 1841. Appointed guard in Nauvoo Legion, Mar. 1841. Member of Nauvoo Masonic Lodge. Member of Council of Fifty, 1844. Aligned himself with leadership claims of Sidney Rigdon following death of JS, 1844.

Counselor to James J. Strang, 6 Mar. 1846. Located at Shabbona, DeKalb Co., Illinois, by June 1850. Affiliated with Charles B. Thompson, 1852–1853, and John E. Page, 1855, in leadership of new religious movements. Baptized into RLDS church, 10 June 1859, at Amboy, Lee Co., Illinois. Ordained a counselor in RLDS church presidency, 8 Apr. 1863. Married second Julia A. Muir, 5 Sept. 1866, in Shabbona. Moved to Little Rock, Kendall Co., Illinois, by June 1870. Died at Plano, Kendall Co.

Maxcy, James (17 Nov. 1791–20 Sept. 1878), deputy sheriff, city marshal, constable. Born in Prince Edward Co., Virginia. Son of Joel Maxcy and Susan Davis. Moved to Warren Co., Kentucky, ca. 1798. Served in War of 1812. Married Mariah Cook, 30 June 1815, at Warren Co., Kentucky. Lived in Bowling Green, Warren Co., 1820. Moved to Springfield, Sangamon Co., Illinois, 1834. Elected Tyler of Masonic lodge, 20 Apr. 1839, at Springfield. Served as deputy sheriff of Sangamon Co., by 1841. Died in Sangamon Co.

McCleary, Sophronia Smith (16 May 1803–22 July 1876). Born at Tunbridge, Orange Co., Vermont. Daughter of Joseph Smith Sr. and Lucy Mack. Moved to Lebanon, Grafton Co., New Hampshire, 1811. Migrated with family from Norwich, Windsor Co., Vermont, to Palmyra, Ontario Co., New York, 1816–Jan. 1817. Joined Presbyterian church, ca. 1820. Married first Calvin W. Stoddard, 30 Dec. 1827, at Palmyra, Wayne Co., New York. Lived at Macedon, Wayne Co., 1830. Lived at Kirtland, Geauga Co., Ohio, by 1832. Husband died, 1836. Married second William McCleary, 11 Feb. 1838, at Kirtland. Left Ohio for Far West, Caldwell Co., Missouri, May 1838. Fled to Illinois, Feb. 1839. Lived at Macedonia (later Webster), Hancock Co., Illinois, 1843. Lived at Tennessee, McDonough Co., Illinois, 1860. Received into RLDS church, 8 Apr. 1873. Died at Fountain Green, Hancock Co.

McCleary, William (9 Oct. 1793–ca. 1847). Born at Rupert, Bennington Co., Vermont. Married Sophronia Smith Stoddard, 11 Feb. 1838, at Kirtland, Geauga Co., Ohio. Ordained an elder in LDS church by Reuben Hedlock, 26 Feb. 1838, at Kirtland. Left Ohio for Far West, Caldwell Co., Missouri, May 1838. Fled to Illinois, Feb. 1839. Lived at Macedonia (later Webster), Hancock Co., Illinois, when appointed to conduct election for board of trustees for that community, 3 Mar. 1843. Ordained a high priest, 8 Oct. 1844, at Nauvoo, Hancock Co. Built wagons in Nauvoo in preparation for Mormon exodus in 1846 but apparently remained in Illinois.

McCoy, Isaac (13 June 1784–21 June 1846), preacher, surveyor, secretary, author, wheelwright. Born near Uniontown, Fayette Co., Pennsylvania. Son of William McCoy and Elizabeth. Moved to North Bend, Northwest Territory (later in Hamilton Co., Ohio), 1789, and to Jefferson Co., Kentucky, 1789. Moved to Shelby Co., Kentucky, by Mar. 1801. Baptized into Baptist church. Married Christiana Polk, 6 Oct. 1803, in Shelby Co. Moved to Vincennes, Knox Co., Indiana Territory, 1804. Moved to Clark Co., Indiana Territory, and received license to preach, 11 July 1807, from Silver Creek Baptist Church. Moved to area north of Vincennes, 1808. Ordained a minister in Maria Creek Baptist Church, 13 Oct. 1810. Moved to Wayne Township, Randolph Co., Indiana, May 1820. Moved to Niles, Michigan Territory, Oct. 1821. Established Carey Mission for Ottawa and Miami Indian tribes, at Niles. Founded Thomas Station Indian Mission, 1823, near Grand Rapids, Kent Co., Michigan. Appointed member of government commission to arrange transfer of Ottawa and Miami Indians to the West, 1828. Moved to Lexington, Lafayette Co., Missouri,

Aug. 1829. Lived at Howard Co., Missouri, by June 1830. Lived at Jackson Co., Missouri, by June 1840. Appointed corresponding secretary and general agent of American Indian Mission Association, 1842. Moved to Louisville, Jefferson Co., Kentucky, 1842. Died in Louisville.

McFall, Hugh (ca. 1798–after 1860), carpenter. Born in Pennsylvania. Married Elizabeth. Moved to Ohio, by 1834. Moved to Illinois, by 1839. Lived at Hancock Co., Illinois, 1840. Appointed adjutant general in Nauvoo Legion, 9 Mar. 1841. Member of Nauvoo City Council, 1841–1842. Moved to Mississippi, by 1848. Lived at Noxubee Co., Mississippi, by 1850.

McQueen, Robert (8 Aug. 1808–13 Dec. 1886), miller, miner, farmer. Born in New York City. Moved to Warren Co. (later Henderson Co.), Illinois, by 1836. Cofounded Shokokon, Warren Co., with Charles A. Smith. Elected justice of the peace in Warren Co., 1838. Married Mary P. Crane, 6 Oct. 1842, in Henderson Co. Moved to Yuba Co., California, by 1850; lived at Parks Bar and Long Bar (later areas near Sicard Flat), Yuba Co. Settled in Tammany Hollow, Nez Perce Co., Idaho Territory, by 1880. Died in Nez Perce Co.

Miles, Prudence Marks (1 May 1795–9 Feb. 1852). Born in Pawlet, Rutland Co., Vermont. Daughter of Cornwall Marks and Sarah. Married first Josiah Browd Prescot, 24 Aug. 1814, in Pawlet. Married second Samuel Miles, 19 May 1825, in Pawlet. Moved to Genesee Co., New York, by 1826. Moved to Freedom, Cattaraugus Co., New York, by 1830. Baptized into LDS church, winter 1833–1834, in Cattaraugus Co. Moved to New Portage, Medina Co., Ohio, 1835; near Far West, Caldwell Co., Missouri, May 1836; to Lima, Adams Co., Illinois, by 1839; and to Commerce (later Nauvoo), Hancock Co., Illinois, fall 1839. Migrated to Salt Lake Valley, by Oct. 1849. Died in Salt Lake City.

Miller, George (25 Nov. 1794–after July 1856), carpenter, mill operator, lumber dealer, steamboat owner. Born near Stanardsville, Orange Co., Virginia. Son of John Miller and Margaret Pfeiffer. Moved to Augusta Co., Virginia, 1798; to Madison Co., Kentucky, 1806; to Boone Co., Kentucky, 1808; back to Madison Co., ca. May 1813; to Lexington, Fayette Co., Kentucky, ca. 1813; to Cincinnati, spring 1815; to Baltimore, 1816; and to Charlottesville, Albemarle Co., Virginia, 1817. Married Mary C. Fry, 25 June 1822, in Madison Co., Virginia. Moved to Illinois, 1831. Mason. Baptized into LDS church by John Taylor, 10/12 Aug. 1839. Moved to Lee Co., Iowa Territory, 1839. Moved to Nauvoo, Hancock Co., Illinois, 1840. Ordained a high priest by JS, Hyrum Smith, and Newel Knight, before Sept. 1840, in Nauvoo. Served mission to Iowa Territory and Illinois, 1840–1841. Member of Nauvoo House Association. Member of Nauvoo Legion, 1841; appointed brigadier general, Sept. 1842. Served mission to Kentucky, 1841–1842. Member of Nauvoo Masonic Lodge. President of high priests, 1842, in Nauvoo. When JS was accused of ordering assassination of former Missouri governor Lilburn W. Boggs, Miller wrote letter to Missouri governor Thomas Reynolds, 4 Sept. 1842, in defense of JS's character. Served mission to Wisconsin pineries on Black River, Wisconsin Territory, 1842–1843, to procure lumber for Nauvoo temple and Nauvoo House. Commissioned brigadier general in Nauvoo Legion, 27 Apr. 1843. Served mission to Mississippi and Alabama, 1843. Served mission to pineries in Wisconsin Territory, 1843–1844. Presiding bishop and member of Council of Fifty, 1844. Served mission to Kentucky to campaign for JS as president, 1844. Trustee-in-trust for church following JS's death, 1844. President of high priests, 1844. Member of

Nauvoo City Council, 1845. Moved to what became Council Bluffs, Pottawattamie Co., Iowa Territory, 1846; to Tahlequah, Cherokee Co., Indian Territory (later in Oklahoma), 1847; and to Pedernales (near Fredericksburg), Gillespie Co., Texas, 1848. Briefly associated with Lyman Wight. Moved to Austin, Travis Co., Texas, 1848. Excommunicated, 3 Dec. 1848. Moved to Voree, Racine Co., Wisconsin, 1850, to join followers of James J. Strang's Church of Jesus Christ of Latter Day Saints. Moved with Strangites to Beaver Island, Mackinac Co., Michigan, 1851. Moved to Marengo, McHenry Co., Illinois. Died in Marengo.

Miller, William (15 Feb. 1782–20 Dec. 1849), farmer, author, military officer, preacher. Born in Pittsfield, Berkshire Co., Massachusetts. Son of William Miller and Paulina Phelps. Moved to Hampton, Washington Co., New York, 1786. Moved to Poultney, Rutland Co., Vermont, 1803. Married Lucy Phelps Smith, 29 June 1803. Elected sheriff, 1809, in Poultney. Commissioned a lieutenant in Vermont militia, 21 July 1810. Served in War of 1812. Returned to Hampton, 1815. Elected Hampton town supervisor, 1821, 1829, and 1832. Licensed as Baptist minister, Sept. 1833, by Low Hampton Baptist Church. Elected justice of the peace in Washington Co., 1835. Founded Advent faith (later Seventh-day Adventist Church), 1845. Died in Hampton.

Millikin, Arthur (9 May 1817–23 Apr. 1882), clerk, saddler, laborer, baggage master, city weigher. Born at Saco, York Co., Maine. Son of Edward Millikin and Hannah Andrews. Baptized into LDS church, ca. 1835. Moved to Kirtland, Geauga Co., Ohio, by 1837. Moved to Missouri, 1838. Served as drummer boy at Battle of Crooked River, 1838. Moved to Nauvoo, Hancock Co., Illinois. Married JS's sister Lucy Smith, 4 June 1840, at Nauvoo. Appointed second lieutenant in Nauvoo Legion, Apr. 1841. Member of Nauvoo Masonic Lodge. Supported James J. Strang as successor to JS, 1846, at Nauvoo. Moved to Knoxville, Knox Co., Illinois; to Hancock Co., 1850; and to Colchester area, McDonough Co., Illinois, by 1860. Received into RLDS church, 8 Apr. 1873. Died at Colchester.

Moeser, Frederick Henry (21 Aug. 1805–1853), merchant, baker, butcher. Born in Germany. Son of Johan Georg Moeser and Anna Margaret Appel. Immigrated to Pittsburgh, before 1835. Married first Magdalena Zundel, before Feb. 1835. Moved to Beaver Co., Pennsylvania, by Oct. 1836. Moved to Ohio, 1836. Baptized into LDS church, by 1839. Moved to Missouri, by 1839; to Quincy, Adams Co., Illinois, by June 1840; and to Nauvoo, Hancock Co., Illinois, by 1842. Received elder's license, 26 Jan. 1842, in Nauvoo. Member of Nauvoo Masonic Lodge. Appointed by JS to serve mission to Germany, 19 Apr. 1843. Ordained a seventy, by 3 Jan. 1846. Left LDS church. Moved to St. Louis, 1846–1847. Returned to Hancock Co. and married second Elizabeth Backlosh, 22 Sept. 1848. Died in Warsaw, Hancock Co.

Moffet, Levi (10 May 1800–31 Mar. 1857), miller, merchant. Born in Oppenheim, Montgomery Co., New York. Son of John Moffet and Abigail Swift. Moved to Trumbull Co., Ohio, by 1820. Married first Elizabeth Keck, 29 Jan. 1824, in Trumbull Co. Led group of settlers to Des Moines Co., Michigan Territory (later in Iowa Territory), 1835. Established town of Augusta and built Iowa Territory's first carding mill in Des Moines Co. Built passenger steamboat *Maid of Iowa*. Wife died, 29 Mar. 1838. Married second Antoinette Chauvin, 17 June 1840. Became one of first officers of Hiram Masonic Lodge, 25 Apr. 1844, in Augusta. Died in Augusta.

Morley, Isaac (11 Mar. 1786–24 June 1865), farmer, cooper, merchant, postmaster. Born at Montague, Hampshire Co., Massachusetts. Son of Thomas Morley and Editha (Edith) Marsh. Family affiliated with Presbyterian church. Moved to Kirtland, Geauga Co., Ohio, before 1812. Married Lucy Gunn, June 1812, at Montague; immediately returned to Kirtland. Served in War of 1812 as private and captain in Ohio militia. Elected trustee of Kirtland, 1818. Baptized into Reformed Baptist (later Disciples of Christ or Campbellite) faith by Sidney Rigdon, 1828. Baptized into LDS church by Parley P. Pratt, 15 Nov. 1830. Latter-day Saints migrating from New York settled on his farm at Kirtland, 1831. Ordained a high priest by Lyman Wight, 4 June 1831. Counselor to Bishop Edward Partridge at Kirtland, 1831, and in Missouri, 1831–1838. Lived at Independence, Jackson Co., Missouri, 1831. Appointed to set in order branches of church in Missouri, 3 Dec. 1832. Appointed bishop, 25 June 1833. Driven from Jackson Co. into Clay Co., Missouri, Nov. 1833. Member of Missouri high council, by 19 Dec. 1833. Left to serve mission to eastern states with Edward Partridge, 17 Feb. 1835. Returned to Missouri and moved family to Far West, Missouri, Apr. 1836. Ordained a patriarch by JS, Sidney Rigdon, and Hyrum Smith, 7 Nov. 1837. Moved to Hancock Co., Illinois, 1839; founded Yelrome (Morley's Settlement), where he served as bishop. Appointed president of stake at Lima, Adams Co., Illinois, 22 Oct. 1840. Member of Masonic lodge in Nauvoo, Hancock Co. Moved to Winter Quarters, unorganized U.S. territory (later in Omaha, Douglas Co., Nebraska), 1846. Migrated to Salt Lake Valley, 1848. Elected senator of provisional state of Deseret, 12 Mar. 1849. Led initial settlement of Latter-day Saints at Sanpete Valley, unorganized U.S. territory (later in Sanpete Co., Utah Territory), 28 Oct. 1849, and presided at Manti, Sanpete Co., 1849–1853. Member of Utah territorial legislature, 1851–1857. Died at North Bend (later Fairview), Sanpete Co.

Morris, Isaac Newton (22 Jan. 1812–29 Oct. 1879), lawyer, newspaper editor, politician, farmer, railroad owner and commissioner. Born in Bethel, Clermont Co., Ohio. Son of Thomas Morris and Rachel Davis. Moved to Oxford, Butler Co., Ohio, before 1835. Moved to Warsaw, Hancock Co., Illinois, 1836. Married Mary Ann Robbins, 1837. Moved to Quincy, Adams Co., Illinois, 1838. Editor of *Quincy Argus* (later *Quincy Herald*), 1839. Declined appointment as secretary of state for Illinois, 1840. Assisted Latter-day Saints seeking refuge from Missouri expulsion. President of Illinois and Michigan Canal Company. In Carthage, Hancock Co., Illinois, chaired convention to negotiate removal of Saints from Nauvoo, Hancock Co. Democrat. Served as state representative, 1846–1848. Represented Illinois in U.S. Congress, 1857–1861. Died in Quincy.

Noble, Joseph Bates (14 Jan. 1810–17 Aug. 1900), farmer, miller, stockman. Born in Egremont, Berkshire Co., Massachusetts. Son of Ezekiel Noble and Theodotia Bates. Moved to Penfield, Monroe Co., New York, 1815. Moved to Bloomfield, Ontario Co., New York, ca. 1828. Baptized into LDS church, 1832. Participated in Camp of Israel expedition to Missouri, 1834. Moved to Kirtland, Geauga Co., Ohio, by 1834. Married Mary Adeline Beman, 11 Sept. 1834, in New York. Appointed member of First Quorum of the Seventy, 1835. Received elder's license, 7 Apr. 1836, at Kirtland. Served mission to southern Ohio, 1836–1838. Moved to Far West, Caldwell Co., Missouri, 1838. Moved to Montrose, Lee Co., Iowa Territory, 1839. Served as counselor to Bishop Elias Smith in Montrose. Moved to Nauvoo, Hancock Co., Illinois, 1841. Served as bishop in Nauvoo Fifth Ward, beginning

1841. Commissioned second lieutenant in Iowa territorial militia, beginning 1841. Member of Nauvoo Masonic Lodge. Appointed quartermaster sergeant in Nauvoo Legion, 3 June 1842. Participated in plural marriage during JS's lifetime. Migrated to Salt Lake Valley, 1847. Resided in Bountiful, Davis Co., Utah Territory. Moved to Montpelier, Bear Lake Co., Idaho, by 1900. Died at Wardboro, Bear Lake Co.

Olney, Oliver H. (11 Aug. 1796–ca. 1845), wool manufacturer, farmer. Born at Eastford, Windham Co., Connecticut. Son of Ezekiel Olney and Lydia Brown. Married first Alice (Elsa) Johnson, daughter of John Johnson and Elsa Jacobs, 14 Sept. 1820, at Hiram, Portage Co., Ohio. President of Kirtland teachers quorum, 1836. Ordained a seventy by Hazen Aldrich, 20 Dec. 1836, at Kirtland, Geauga Co., Ohio. Driven out of De Witt, Carroll Co., Missouri, into Caldwell Co., Missouri, 1838. Wife died, 1841. Excommunicated, 1842, at Nauvoo, Hancock Co., Illinois. Printed anti-Mormon tract titled *The Absurdities of Mormonism Portrayed,* spring 1843. Married second Phebe Wheeler, 19 Oct. 1843, at Nauvoo. In St. Louis, published exposé on polygamy titled *Spiritual Wifery at Nauvoo Exposed,* 1845.

Owen, Thomas Harvey (25 June 1797–27 Feb. 1880), farmer, stockman, ferryboat owner, religious professor, clergyman. Born in Buncombe Co., North Carolina. Son of Mosby Owen. Moved to Frankfort Township, Franklin Co., Illinois, 1816. Married Mary Paine Wren, 18 Apr. 1818. Moved six miles east of Carthage, Hancock Co., Illinois, 1831. Represented Hancock Co. in Illinois House of Representatives, 1834–1836, 1842–1844. Represented Hancock Co. in Illinois Senate, 1836–1838. Appointed postmaster at DeKalb, Hancock Co., 1839. Appointed elisor in trial of those accused of murdering JS and Hyrum Smith, 1845. Moved to Nauvoo, Hancock Co., 1846, and appointed postmaster. Moved to California, 1849–1850. Moved to Solano Co., California. Elected to California legislature, 1852. Moved to Zem Zem, Lake Co., California, 1867; to Coyote Valley, Lake Co., by June 1870; and to Santa Rosa, Sonoma Co., California, 1876. Died in Santa Rosa.

Page, John Edward (25 Feb. 1799–14 Oct. 1867). Born at Trenton, Oneida Co., New York. Son of Ebenezer Page and Rachel Hill. Married first Betsey Thompson, 1831, in Huron Co., Ohio. Baptized into LDS church by Emer Harris, 18 Aug. 1833, at Brownhelm, Lorain Co., Ohio. Ordained an elder by Ebenezer Page, Sept. 1833, at Florence, Erie Co., Ohio. Married second Lavona Stephens, 26 Dec. 1833, in Huron Co. Moved to Kirtland, Geauga Co., Ohio, 1835. Proselytized in Upper Canada, 1836–1837, and led company of converts from Upper Canada to Missouri, 1838. Located at De Witt, Carroll Co., Missouri, and then Far West, Caldwell Co., Missouri, 1838. Ordained member of Quorum of the Twelve, 19 Dec. 1838, at Far West. Married third Mary Judd, ca. Jan. 1839. Moved to Warsaw, Hancock Co., Illinois, 1839. With others of the Twelve, returned to Far West to fulfill revelatory directive, 26 Apr. 1839. Preached in eastern U.S., 1841–1842. Member of Masonic lodge in Nauvoo, Hancock Co. Presided over church in Pittsburgh, 1843. Published *The Gospel Light,* 1843–1844. Served mission to Washington DC, 1843–1844. Removed from Quorum of the Twelve, 9 Jan. 1846. Excommunicated, 26 June 1846. Supported James J. Strang's claim as successor to JS. Editor of Church of Jesus Christ of Latter Day Saint (Strangite) newspaper *Zion's Reveille,* 1847. Affiliated with faction led by James C. Brewster, 1849. Moved to Walworth Co., Wisconsin, by 1850. Held own religious services with

William Marks and other friends, by 1855. Joined Church of Christ (Hedrickites), Nov. 1862. Died near Sycamore, De Kalb Co., Illinois.

Parker, John Davis (22 Nov. 1799–26 Feb. 1891), farmer, wainwright. Born in Saratoga, Saratoga Co., New York. Son of Abel Parker and Mary Davis. Served in War of 1812 as teamster in General John E. Wool's company, 1813–1814. Married Harriet Sherwood. Moved to Galway, Saratoga Co., by 1830. Baptized into LDS church by Stephen Burnett, May 1832. Participated in Camp of Israel expedition to Missouri, 1834. Ordained a seventy by JS, 28 Feb. 1835, in Kirtland, Geauga Co., Ohio. Moved to Commerce (later Nauvoo), Hancock Co., Illinois, 1839. Member of Nauvoo Legion, 1841. Served mission to New Orleans, 1841–1842. Member of Nauvoo Masonic Lodge. Deputy sheriff of Hancock Co., 1843–1844. Member of Council of Fifty, 1844–1882. Ordained a high priest. Moved to what became Council Bluffs, Pottawattamie Co., Iowa Territory, 1846. Migrated to Centerville, Davis Co., Utah Territory, 1852. Moved to Kanarra (later Kanarraville), Kane Co., Utah Territory, 1866. Died in Kanarra.

Parry, Patty Bartlett (4 Feb. 1795–14 Dec. 1892), midwife. Born in Newry, York Co., Maine. Daughter of Enoch Bartlett and Anna Hall. Married David Sessions, 29 June 1812, in Bethel, Oxford Co., Maine. Lived in Newry. Moved to Andover, Oxford Co., by 1820. Baptized into Methodist church. Baptized into LDS church, summer 1834, in Maine. Moved to Far West, Missouri, 1836. Moved to Hancock Co., Illinois, by 1840. "Married or sealed" to JS "for time and all eternity," 9 Mar. 1842. Moved to Winter Quarters, unorganized U.S. territory (later in Omaha, Douglas Co., Nebraska), 1846. Migrated to Salt Lake City, 1847. Married John Parry, 14 Dec. 1851, in Salt Lake City. Moved to Cache Co., Utah Territory, by 1856; to Salt Lake City, by 1860; and to Bountiful, Davis Co., Utah Territory, 1872. Died in Bountiful.

Patten, David Wyman (14 Nov. 1799–25 Oct. 1838), farmer. Born in Vermont. Son of Benoni Patten and Edith Cole. Moved to Theresa, Oneida Co., New York, as a young child. Moved to Dundee, Monroe Co., Michigan, as a youth. Married Phoebe Ann Babcock, 1828, in Dundee. Affiliated with the Methodists. Baptized into LDS church by his brother John Patten, 15 June 1832, at Fairplay, Greene Co., Indiana, and ordained an elder by Elisha Groves, 17 June 1832. Served mission to Michigan Territory, 1832. Ordained a high priest by Hyrum Smith, 2 Sept. 1832. Served mission to eastern states, 1832–1833. Moved family from Michigan Territory to Florence, Erie Co., Ohio, 1833. With William Pratt, carried dispatches from JS to church leaders in Clay Co., Missouri, Dec. 1833. Served mission to southern U.S. with Warren F. Parrish, 1834–1835. Ordained member of Quorum of the Twelve, 15 Feb. 1835, at Kirtland, Geauga Co., Ohio. Served mission to Tennessee, spring 1835. With the Twelve, served mission to eastern states, summer 1835. Moved from Kirtland to Far West, Missouri, 1836. Member of presidency pro tempore of church in Far West, 1838. Captain of local militia in Caldwell Co., Missouri. Mortally wounded during Battle of Crooked River, near Ray Co., Missouri, 25 Oct. 1838. Died near Far West.

Phelps, William Wines (17 Feb. 1792–7 Mar. 1872), writer, teacher, printer, newspaper editor, publisher, postmaster, lawyer. Born at Hanover, Morris Co., New Jersey. Son of Enon Phelps and Mehitabel Goldsmith. Moved to Homer, Cortland Co., New York, 1800. Married Sally Waterman, 28 Apr. 1815, in Smyrna, Chenango Co., New York. Editor of *Western Courier*. Moved to Wooster, Wayne Co., Ohio, by 3 July 1819. Returned to

Homer, by Nov. 1821. Moved to Trumansburg, Tompkins Co., New York, 1823. Edited Anti-Masonic newspaper *Lake Light.* Moved to Canandaigua, Ontario Co., New York, Apr. 1828, and there published Anti-Masonic newspaper *Ontario Phoenix.* Obtained copy of Book of Mormon, 1830. Met JS, 24 Dec. 1830. Migrated to Kirtland, Geauga Co., Ohio, 1831. Baptized into LDS church, 16 June 1831, at Kirtland. Ordained an elder by JS, June 1831, at Kirtland. Appointed church printer, 20 July 1831. Ordained a high priest, 1831. Moved to Jackson Co., Missouri, late 1831. Became editor of *The Evening and the Morning Star* and *Upper Missouri Advertiser,* published 1832–1833 at Independence, Jackson Co. Published Book of Commandments, but most copies destroyed by mob action when printing office razed, 20 July 1833. Exiled from Jackson Co. to Clay Co., Missouri, Nov. 1833. Appointed counselor/assistant president to David Whitmer, president of church in Missouri, 3 July 1834. Returned to Kirtland and served as JS's scribe. Helped compile Doctrine and Covenants and first Latter-day Saint hymnal, 1835, at Kirtland. Prolific writer of hymns. Appointed to draft rules and regulations for Kirtland temple, 13 Jan. 1836. Returned from Kirtland to Clay Co., where he resumed duties with Missouri presidency, 1836. Appointed postmaster, 27 May 1837, at Far West, Caldwell Co., Missouri. Excommunicated, 17 Mar. 1838. Moved to Dayton, Montgomery Co., Ohio, before Mar. 1840. Reconciled with church, July 1840; rebaptized into LDS church, 1841. Returned to Kirtland, by May 1841. Appointed to serve mission to eastern U.S., 23 May 1841. Appointed recorder of church licenses, 2 Oct. 1841, in Kirtland. Moved to Nauvoo, Hancock Co., Illinois, by Dec. 1841. Acted as clerk to JS and assisted John Taylor in editing *Times and Seasons* and *Nauvoo Neighbor.* Assisted Willard Richards in writing JS's history, by Jan. 1843. Elected fire warden, 11 Feb. 1843. Elected to Nauvoo City Council, early 1844. Member of Council of Fifty, by 11 Mar. 1844. Migrated to Salt Lake Valley, 1848. Served as counselor to Parley P. Pratt on exploration mission to southern Utah Territory, Nov. 1849. Admitted to Utah territorial bar, 1851. Member of Utah territorial legislative assembly, 1851–1857. Died at Salt Lake City.

Pickett, Agnes Moulton Coolbrith (11 July 1811–26 Dec. 1876). Born at Scarborough, Cumberland Co., Maine. Daughter of Joseph Coolbrith and Mary Hasty Foss. Moved to Boston, by 1832. Baptized into LDS church, 1832, at Boston. Moved to Kirtland, Geauga Co., Ohio, summer 1833. Married Don Carlos Smith, 30 July 1835, at Kirtland. Moved to Norton, Summit Co., Ohio, by 1838. Moved to Missouri, summer 1838. Soon afterward located at Millport, Daviess Co., Missouri, near Adam-ondi-Ahman. Moved to Commerce (later Nauvoo), Hancock Co., Illinois, late summer 1839. Husband died, 7 Aug. 1841. Possibly married JS as a plural wife. Moved to St. Louis and married William Pickett, 1846. Migrated to Weber Co., Utah Territory, by 1850. Moved to California, 1852. Lived at Marysville, Yuba Co.; San Francisco; San Bernardino, San Bernardino Co.; Los Angeles; and Oakland, Alameda Co., California. Died at Oakland.

Pitman, James M. (5 Nov. 1813–24 Feb. 1879), lumber dealer, real estate broker, housing contractor, railroad director, prison warden. Born at St. Charles Co., Missouri. Son of Richard Berry Pittman and Lucinda Hutchings. Adhered to Quaker faith. Moved to Quincy, Adams Co., Illinois, 1835. Served as constable, 1842, at Quincy. With Edward Ford and Thomas King, attempted to arrest JS for complicity in attempt to kill former Missouri governor Lilburn W. Boggs, 8 Aug. 1842, at Nauvoo, Hancock Co., Illinois. Served as sheriff, 1844–1848, at Adams Co. Married Mary McDade, 11 Sept. 1845, at Adams

Co. Represented Adams Co. in state legislature, 1851–1854. Moved to Santa Clara Co., California, by 1879. Died at Santa Clara Co.

Pope, Nathaniel (5 Jan. 1784–22 Jan. 1850), lawyer, judge. Born at present-day Louisville, Jefferson Co., Kentucky. Son of William Pope and Penelope Edwards. Graduated from Transylvania University, 1806, at Lexington, Fayette Co., Kentucky. Moved to St. Genevieve, St. Genevieve District, Louisiana Territory (later in St. Genevieve Co., Missouri). Married Lucretia Backus, 1808. Moved to Kaskaskia, Randolph Co., Illinois Territory, 1809. Served as secretary of Illinois Territory, 7 Mar. 1809–17 Dec. 1816; as territorial delegate to U.S. Congress, 18 Dec. 1817–4 Dec. 1818; and as registrar of land office at Edwardsville, Madison Co., Illinois Territory, 30 Nov. 1818–3 Mar. 1819. Labored to have Illinois Territory admitted as a state, 1818. Served as U.S. district judge for Illinois, 1819–1850. Presided over JS's habeas corpus hearing, Jan. 1843, in Springfield. Moved to Alton, Madison Co., by 1845. Died at St. Louis.

Pope, William (Oct. 1813–May 1855), court clerk. Born in Kaskaskia, Randolph Co., Illinois Territory. Son of Nathaniel Pope and Lucretia Backus. Married Eliza Douglass. Moved to Springfield, Sangamon Co., Illinois, by June 1850. Served as clerk of circuit court, 1850. Died at St. Louis.

Powers, Stephen Willard (ca. 1815–ca. Sept. 1851), lawyer. Born in Ohio. Lived at Cuyahoga Falls, Portage Co., Ohio, before 1840. Married first the daughter of a Mrs. Bush, by 1840. Moved to North Akron, Summit Co., Ohio, by June 1840. Moved to Keokuk, Lee Co., Iowa Territory, by Aug. 1842. Practiced law at Keokuk. Married second Mary Hayden, 16 Aug. 1848, in Keokuk. Died in Keokuk.

Pratt, Orson (19 Sept. 1811–3 Oct. 1881), farmer, writer, teacher, merchant, surveyor, editor, publisher. Born at Hartford, Washington Co., New York. Son of Jared Pratt and Charity Dickinson. Moved to New Lebanon, Columbia Co., New York, 1814; to Canaan, Columbia Co., fall 1823; to Hurl Gate, Queens Co., New York, spring 1825; and to New York City, spring 1826. Returned to Hurl Gate, fall 1826, and to Canaan, spring 1827. Moved to Lorain Co., Ohio, fall 1827; to Chagrin (later Willoughby), Cuyahoga Co., Ohio, spring 1828; and to Connecticut, fall 1828. Returned to Hurl Gate, winter 1828–1829, and to Canaan, spring 1829. Baptized into LDS church by Parley P. Pratt, 19 Sept. 1830, at Canaan. Ordained an elder by JS, 1 Dec. 1830, in Fayette, Seneca Co., New York, and appointed to serve mission to Colesville, Broome Co., New York. With Samuel H. Smith, traveled from New York to Kirtland, Geauga Co., Ohio; arrived on 27 Feb. 1831. Served mission to Missouri, summer 1831. Moved to Hiram, Portage Co., Ohio, Dec. 1831. Ordained a high priest by Sidney Rigdon, 2 Feb. 1832, in Hiram. Served mission with Lyman E. Johnson to the East from Kirtland, Feb. 1832. Participated in Camp of Israel expedition to Missouri, 1834. Ordained member of Quorum of the Twelve by David Whitmer and Oliver Cowdery, 26 Apr. 1835, at Kirtland. Married Sarah Marinda Bates, 4 July 1836, at Henderson, Jefferson Co., New York. Served mission to Upper Canada, 1836. Served mission to Great Britain with other members of Quorum of the Twelve, 1839–1841. Member of city council, 1841–1845, in Nauvoo, Hancock Co., Illinois. Member of Nauvoo Masonic Lodge. Excommunicated, 20 Aug. 1842, at Nauvoo. Rebaptized into LDS church, 20 Jan. 1843, and ordained to his former office in Quorum of the Twelve. Moved to what became Council Bluffs, Pottawattamie Co., Iowa Territory, 1846. Entered Salt Lake Valley with

Mormon pioneers, 1847. Presided over church in Great Britain, 1848. Member of Utah territorial legislature. Appointed church historian, 1874. Died at Salt Lake City.

Pratt, Parley Parker (12 Apr. 1807–13 May 1857), farmer, editor, publisher, teacher, school administrator, legislator, explorer, author. Born at Burlington, Otsego Co., New York. Son of Jared Pratt and Charity Dickinson. Traveled west with brother to acquire land, 1823. Affiliated with Baptist church at age eighteen. Lived in Ohio, 1826–1827. Married first Thankful Halsey, 9 Sept. 1827, at Canaan, Columbia Co., New York. Proselytized to Reformed Baptist (later Disciples of Christ or Campbellite) faith by Sidney Rigdon, 1829. Baptized into LDS church and ordained an elder by Oliver Cowdery, 1 Sept. 1830, at Seneca Lake, Seneca Co., New York. Served mission to unorganized Indian Territory and Missouri with Oliver Cowdery and others, 1830–1831. Stopped at Kirtland, Geauga Co., Ohio, and vicinity en route; missionaries baptized some 130 individuals. Returned to Kirtland, 3 Apr. 1831. Ordained a high priest by Lyman Wight, 4 June 1831. Served mission to western U.S., 7 June 1831–May 1832. Moved to Jackson Co., Missouri, summer 1832. Appointed president of Elders School in Independence, Jackson Co. Left to serve mission to eastern U.S., Mar. 1834. Participated in Camp of Israel expedition to Missouri, 1834. Moved to Kirtland, Oct. 1834. Ordained member of Quorum of the Twelve, 21 Feb. 1835. Served mission to eastern U.S., spring 1835–28 Aug. 1835. Served mission to Canada, Apr.–June 1836. Shareholder of Kirtland Safety Society, 1837. Wife died, 25 Mar. 1837. Married second Mary Ann Frost Stearns, 14 May 1837, at Kirtland. Left to serve mission to New York City, July 1837. Moved to Far West, Caldwell Co., Missouri, Apr. 1838. First lieutenant in Missouri state militia, 1838. Participated in Battle of Crooked River, near Ray Co., Missouri, 25 Oct. 1838. Jailed at Richmond, Ray Co., and Columbia, Boone Co., Missouri, 1838–1839. Reunited with family, 11 July 1839, in Illinois. Served mission to England, 1839–1842. Edited first number of *LDS Millennial Star* published in Manchester, England, 27 May 1840. President of British mission, 1841–1842. Arrived at Nauvoo, Hancock Co., Illinois, 7 Feb. 1843. Member of Nauvoo Masonic Lodge. Participated in plural marriage during JS's lifetime. Directed affairs of church in New York City, 1844–1845. Moved to Mount Pisgah, Clarke Co., Iowa Territory, 14 Feb. 1846. Left to serve mission to England, 31 July 1846. Arrived at Winter Quarters, unorganized U.S. territory (later in Omaha, Douglas Co., Nebraska), 8 Apr. 1847. Arrived in Salt Lake Valley, 28 Sept. 1847. Led exploration party into southern Utah Territory, Nov. 1849–Feb. 1850. Served mission to Chile, 16 Mar. 1851–18 Oct. 1852. Served mission to eastern U.S., beginning Sept. 1856. Murdered at Van Buren, Crawford Co., Arkansas.

Pratt, Sarah Marinda Bates (5 Feb. 1817–25 Dec. 1888), seamstress. Born in Henderson, Jefferson Co., New York. Daughter of Cyrus Bates and Lydia Harrington. Baptized into LDS church by Orson Pratt, 18 June 1835, near Sackets Harbor, Jefferson Co. Married Orson Pratt, 4 July 1836, in Henderson. Moved to Kirtland, Geauga Co., Ohio, 1836. Resided in New York City, 1838–1839. Moved to Commerce (later Nauvoo), Hancock Co., Illinois, 1839. Served mission with husband to eastern states, 1843. With John C. Bennett, accused JS of moral improprieties, 1842. Presumably excommunicated with husband, 20 Aug. 1842; rebaptized into LDS church, 20 Jan. 1843. Moved to what became Council Bluffs, Pottawattamie Co., Iowa Territory, 1846. Moved to Liverpool, Lancashire, England, 1848, when husband was appointed to preside over church in Great Britain.

Migrated to Salt Lake City, 1851. Moved to St. George, Washington Co., Utah Territory, 1862. Moved back to Salt Lake City, 1864. Excommunicated, 4 Oct. 1874, in Salt Lake City. Died in Salt Lake City.

Prentiss, William (1801–23 Dec. 1852), farmer, U.S. marshall. Born in Kentucky. Moved to Washington DC. Married first Maria Stribling Brown, 18 June 1829, in Washington DC. Wife died, 13 Mar. 1831, in Washington DC. Married second Sarah Ann. Moved to New York, by 1833; to New Orleans, by 1836; and to Sangamon Co., Illinois, by 1840. Secretary of Board of Public Works in Illinois. Served as U.S. marshall for northern district of Illinois, 1841–1844. Moved to Shelby Co., Illinois, by 1850. Likely died in Shelby Co.

Ralston, James Harvey (12 Oct. 1807–9 May 1864), soldier, lawyer, judge, politician. Born in Bourbon Co., Kentucky. Son of John Ralston and Elizabeth Neely. Served in Black Hawk War, 1832. Married first Jane S. Alexander, 1833, in Quincy, Adams Co., Illinois. Member of Illinois House of Representatives, 1836–1838. Circuit judge, 1837. Member of Illinois Senate, 1840–1844. Served in Mexican War as captain and assistant quartermaster, 26 June 1846–3 Mar. 1849. Wife died, 1847. Moved to California, by 1850. Member of California's first state senate. Married second Harriet N. Jackson, 20 Oct. 1853, in New York City. Moved to Utah Territory (later in Nevada Territory), ca. 1860; lived at Austin, Lander Co., Nevada Territory, by 1863. Died near Austin.

Redding, Hiram (6 Sept. 1811–before 3 Aug. 1846), farmer. Born in Gilsum, Cheshire Co., New Hampshire. Son of Thomas Redding and Prudence Bill. Married Miranda Mead, 31 Dec. 1836. Moved to Ogle Co., Illinois, before 1843. Died in Ogle Co.

Remick, Jacob Gilman (17 Mar. 1798–June 1860), lawyer. Born in Tamworth, Strafford Co., New Hampshire. Son of William Remick and Abigail Gilman. Moved to Industry, Kennebec Co., Maine, 1805. Married Hannah Shaw, 3 Feb. 1824, in Industry. Moved to Bangor, Penobscot Co., Maine, by 1840; to Galveston, Galveston Co., Texas, by 1850; and to Stillwater, Washington Co., Minnesota, by 1860. Died in Washington Co.

Reynolds, Thomas (12 Mar. 1796–9 Feb. 1844), attorney, politician, judge. Born at Mason Co. (later Bracken Co.), Kentucky. Son of Nathaniel Reynolds and Catherine Vernon. Admitted to Kentucky bar, 1817. Moved to Illinois, by 1818. Served as clerk of Illinois House of Representatives, 1818–1822. Served as chief justice of Illinois Supreme Court, 1822–1825. Married Eliza W. Young, 2 Sept. 1823, in Fayette Co., Kentucky. Served as representative in and speaker of Illinois House of Representatives, 1826–1828. Moved to Fayette, Howard Co., Missouri, ca. 1829. Served as representative in and speaker of Missouri House of Representatives, 1832–1834; as judge of Second Judicial District of Missouri, 1837–1840; and as governor of Missouri, 1840–1844. Committed suicide in Jefferson City, Cole Co., Missouri.

Richards, Franklin Dewey (2 Apr. 1821–9 Dec. 1899), carpenter, businessman, newspaper editor. Born at Richmond, Berkshire Co., Massachusetts. Son of Phinehas Richards and Wealthy Dewey. Raised Congregationalist. Baptized into LDS church by Phinehas Richards, 3 June 1838, at Richmond. Moved to Missouri, 1838. Moved to Quincy, Adams Co., Illinois, 1839. Ordained a seventy by Joseph Young, 9 Apr. 1840, at Nauvoo, Hancock Co., Illinois. Served mission to northern Indiana, 1840–1841. Served mission to Ohio, 1841–1842. Member of Nauvoo Masonic Lodge. Married Jane Snyder, 18 Dec. 1842, at Job Creek, Hancock Co. Ordained a high priest by Brigham Young, 17 May 1844, at Nauvoo. Participated in plural marriage during JS's lifetime. Served mission to England, 1844; recalled at New York because of death of JS. Served mission to Michigan to raise funds for construction of Nauvoo temple, 1845. Served as assistant to church clerk, 1845–1846, at Nauvoo. Served mission to British Isles, 1846–1848. Presided over British mission, 1847. Migrated to Salt Lake City, 1848. Ordained an apostle by Heber C. Kimball, 12 Feb. 1849, at Salt Lake City. Member of Utah territorial legislature, periodically from 1852 to 1875. Presided over British mission, 1851–1852, 1854–1856, and 1867–1868. Moved to Ogden, Weber Co., Utah Territory, 1869. Served as assistant church historian. Served as church historian, 1889–1899. President of Quorum of the Twelve, 1898–1899. Died at Ogden.

Richards, Willard (24 June 1804–11 Mar. 1854), teacher, lecturer, doctor, clerk, printer, editor, postmaster. Born at Hopkinton, Middlesex Co., Massachusetts. Son of Joseph Richards and Rhoda Howe. Moved to Richmond, Berkshire Co., Massachusetts, 1813. Moved to Chatham, Columbia Co., New York, by Nov. 1820; returned to Richmond, by Nov. 1821. Moved to Nassau, Rensselaer Co., New York, by 6 Apr. 1823. Traveled through New England, giving lectures on scientific subjects for several years, beginning 1827. Practiced medicine at Thomsonian infirmary, beginning 1834, in Boston. Moved to Holliston, Middlesex Co., 1835. Moved to Kirtland, Geauga Co., Ohio, by Dec. 1836. Baptized into LDS church by Brigham Young, 31 Dec. 1836, in Kirtland. Appointed to serve mission to eastern U.S., 13 Mar. 1837. Served mission to England, 1837–1841. Married Jennetta Richards, 24 Sept. 1838, in Walker Ford, Chaigley, Lancashire, England. Ordained member of Quorum of the Twelve, 14 Apr. 1840, at Preston, Lancashire. Moved to Nauvoo, Hancock Co., Illinois. Moved to Warsaw, Hancock Co., 31 Aug. 1841; returned to Nauvoo, 1841. Before death of JS, completed personal history of JS up to Aug. 1838. Member of Nauvoo City Council, 1841–1843. Appointed recorder for Nauvoo temple and JS's scribe, 13 Dec. 1841. Member of Nauvoo Masonic Lodge. Appointed JS's private secretary, Dec. 1842; church historian, ca. Dec. 1842; church recorder, 30 July 1843; Nauvoo city recorder, Aug. 1843; and clerk of municipal court. Participated in plural marriage during JS's lifetime. With JS in jail in Carthage, Hancock Co., when JS and Hyrum Smith were murdered. Moved to Winter Quarters, unorganized U.S. territory (later in Omaha, Douglas Co., Nebraska), 1846. Migrated to Salt Lake Valley and returned to Winter Quarters, 1847. Appointed second counselor to Brigham Young in church presidency, 27 Dec. 1847, at what became Council Bluffs, Pottawattamie Co., Iowa. Returned to Salt Lake Valley and appointed secretary and president of legislative council for provisional state of Deseret. Secretary of Utah Territory, postmaster of Salt Lake City, and editor of *Deseret News*. Died at Salt Lake City.

Rigdon, Nancy. See Ellis, Nancy Rigdon.

Rigdon, Sidney (19 Feb. 1793–14 July 1876), tanner, farmer, minister. Born at St. Clair, Allegheny Co., Pennsylvania. Son of William Rigdon and Nancy Gallaher. In 1817, joined United Baptists. Preached at Warren, Trumbull Co., Ohio, and vicinity, 1819–1821. Married Phebe Brook, 12 June 1820, at Warren. Minister of First Baptist Church of Pittsburgh, 1821–1824. Later joined Reformed Baptist (later Disciples of Christ or Campbellite) movement and became influential preacher. Moved to Bainbridge, Geauga

Co., Ohio, 1826. Moved to Mentor, Geauga Co., 1827. Introduced to Mormonism by his former proselyte to Reformed Baptist faith, Parley P. Pratt, who was en route with Oliver Cowdery and others on mission to unorganized Indian Territory. Baptized into LDS church by Oliver Cowdery, Nov. 1830. Scribe for JS, 1830. Ordained a high priest by Lyman Wight, 4 June 1831, in Kirtland, Geauga Co. Moved to Hiram, Portage Co., Ohio, 1831. Counselor/assistant president in church presidency, 1832–1844. Accompanied JS to Upper Canada on proselytizing mission and helped keep JS's diary during trip, 1833. Arrived at Far West, Caldwell Co., Missouri, from Kirtland, 4 Apr. 1838. With JS in jail at Liberty, Clay Co., Missouri, Nov. 1838–Feb. 1839. After release, found refuge at Quincy, Adams Co., Illinois. Accompanied JS to Washington DC to seek redress for Missouri grievances, 1839–1840. Member of city council in Nauvoo, Hancock Co., Illinois, 1841. Appointed postmaster of Nauvoo, 24 Feb. 1841. Member of Nauvoo Masonic Lodge. Claimed right to lead church after death of JS; excommunicated, 1844. Moved to Pittsburgh to lead schismatic Church of Jesus Christ of Latter Day Saints, 1844; name of church changed to Church of Christ, 1845. Located near Greencastle, Antrim Township, Franklin Co., Pennsylvania, May 1846. Removed to Friendship, Allegany Co., New York, where he died.

Robinson, Ebenezer (25 May 1816–11 Mar. 1891), printer, editor, publisher. Born at Floyd (near Rome), Oneida Co., New York. Son of Nathan Robinson and Mary Brown. Moved to Utica, Oneida Co., ca. 1831, and learned printing trade at *Utica Observer.* Moved to Ravenna, Portage Co., Ohio, Aug. 1833, and worked as compositor on *Ohio Star.* Moved to Kirtland, Geauga Co., Ohio, May 1835, and worked in printing office. Baptized into LDS church by JS, 16 Oct. 1835. Married first Angelina (Angeline) Eliza Works, 13 Dec. 1835, at Kirtland. Ordained an elder, 29 Apr. 1836, and a seventy, 20 Dec. 1836. Served mission to Richland Co., Ohio, June–July 1836, and shortly after served mission to New York. Moved to Far West, Caldwell Co., Missouri, spring 1837. Assisted with publication of *Elders' Journal,* summer 1838. Church clerk, and recorder and clerk of Missouri high council, 1838. Member of Far West high council, Dec. 1838. Justice of the peace, 1839. When driven from Missouri, moved to Quincy, Adams Co., Illinois, and worked on *Quincy Whig,* 1839. Became publisher, coeditor, and editor of *Times and Seasons,* 1839–1842, at Commerce (later Nauvoo), Hancock Co., Illinois. Member of Nauvoo Masonic Lodge. Justice of the peace in Hancock Co., by 1842. Served mission to New York, 1843. Moved to Pittsburgh, June 1844. Affiliated with Sidney Rigdon and served as his counselor. In May 1846, moved to Greencastle, Franklin Co., Pennsylvania, where he edited Rigdonite *Messenger and Advocate of the Church of Christ.* Moved to Decatur Co., Iowa, Apr. 1855. Baptized into RLDS church by William W. Blair, 29 Apr. 1863, at Pleasanton, Hamilton Township, Decatur Co. Wife died, 1880. Married second Martha A. Cunningham, 5 Feb. 1885. Affiliated with David Whitmer's Church of Christ, 1888. Edited Whitmerite periodical *The Return,* 1889–1891. Died at Davis City, Decatur Co.

Robinson, George W. (14 May 1814–10 Feb. 1878), clerk, postmaster, merchant, clothier, miller, banker. Born at Pawlet, Rutland Co., Vermont. Baptized into LDS church and moved to Kirtland, Geauga Co., Ohio, by 1836. Clerk and recorder for Kirtland high council, beginning Jan. 1836. Married Athalia Rigdon, oldest daughter of Sidney Rigdon, fall 1836, in Salem, Essex Co., Massachusetts. In Sept. 1837, appointed general church recorder to replace Oliver Cowdery. Moved to Far West, Caldwell Co., Missouri, 28 Mar.

1838. Sustained as general church recorder and clerk to First Presidency at Far West, Apr. 1838. Imprisoned with JS and other church leaders in Missouri, Nov. 1838. Ordained a seventy, before May 1839. Moved to Quincy, Adams Co., Illinois, winter 1839. Moved to Commerce (later Nauvoo), Hancock Co., Illinois, before 1840. Appointed first postmaster at Nauvoo, Apr. 1840. Member of Nauvoo Masonic Lodge. Left LDS church, by July 1842. Moved to Cuba, Allegany Co., New York, by 1846. Affiliated with Sidney Rigdon's Church of Christ as an apostle. Moved to Friendship, Allegany Co., 1847. Charter member of Masonic lodge in that community. Founder and president of First National Bank, 1 Feb. 1864. Died at Friendship.

Robison, Chauncey (27 Mar. 1805–4 Nov. 1891), clerk, postmaster, farmer. Born in Oneida Co., New York. Son of Charles Robison and Jerusha Rebecca Kellogg. Moved to Hancock Co., Illinois, 1829. Registrar in land office in Quincy, Adams Co., Illinois. Moved to Carthage, Hancock Co., 1837. Hancock Co. recorder, 1839–1847. Married Hannah D. Hughes, 1841, in Carthage. Member of Nauvoo Masonic Lodge; secretary of Hancock Lodge, 1843, in Carthage. Hancock Co. school commissioner, 1844–1845. Postmaster at Carthage. Moved to Louisiana, 1847. Moved to Nauvoo, Hancock Co., by 1848. Mayor of Nauvoo, 1849–1850. Moved to Appanoose Township, Hancock Co., 1850. Moved to Topeka, Shawnee Co., Kansas, 1888. Died in Topeka.

Rockwell, Orrin Porter (28 June 1813–9 June 1878), ferry operator, herdsman, farmer. Born in Belchertown, Hampshire Co., Massachusetts. Son of Orin Rockwell and Sarah Witt. Moved to Farmington (later in Manchester), Ontario Co., New York, 1817. Neighbor to JS. Baptized into LDS church, 1830, in Ontario Co. Moved to Ohio and then to Big Blue settlement, Kaw Township, Jackson Co., Missouri, 1831. Married first Luana Beebe, 2 Feb. 1832, in Jackson Co. Moved to Clay Co., Missouri. Moved to Far West, Caldwell Co., Missouri, by 1838. Ordained a deacon, 6 July 1838, in Far West. Traveled to Washington DC with JS to seek redress for Missouri grievances, Oct. 1839–Mar. 1840. Moved to Hancock Co., Illinois, by 1840. Member of Nauvoo Masonic Lodge. Imprisoned in Missouri, Mar. 1843, on suspicion of attempting to kill former Missouri governor Lilburn W. Boggs. Grand jury declined to indict him on that charge; released Dec. 1843 after serving five-minute sentence for jailbreak. Ordained a high priest, before 5 Jan. 1846. Migrated with Brigham Young pioneer company to Salt Lake Valley, 1847. Married second Mary Ann Neff; wife died, 28 Sept. 1866. Married third Christine Olsen. Died in Salt Lake City.

Rockwood, Albert Perry (5 June 1805–25 Nov. 1879), stonecutter, merchant, prison warden. Born in Holliston, Middlesex Co., Massachusetts. Son of Luther Rockwood and Ruth Perry. Married Nancy Haven, 4 Apr. 1827. Baptized into LDS church by Brigham Young, 25 July 1837, in Kirtland, Geauga Co., Ohio. Moved to Ohio. Returned to Massachusetts, May 1838. Moved to Far West, Caldwell Co., Missouri, July 1838. Ordained a seventy by Joseph Young, 5 Jan. 1839. Moved to Quincy, Adams Co., Illinois, 10 Jan. 1839. Moved to Nauvoo, Hancock Co., Illinois, by 1841. Captain in Illinois militia, by Feb. 1841. Appointed drill officer in Nauvoo Legion, 9 Mar. 1841. Member of Nauvoo Masonic Lodge. Served as commander of JS's lifeguards, 1843. Served as general in Nauvoo Legion. Appointed a president of First Quorum of the Seventy, Dec. 1845. Migrated to Salt Lake City, 1847. Served as member of Utah territorial legislature, 1851–1879. Died in Salt Lake City.

Rogers, David (27 May 1807–26 Apr. 1884), artist, portrait painter. Born in Cold Spring Harbor, Suffolk Co., New York. Son of Jacob Rogers and Elisabeth Bunce. Moved to New York City, by 1827. Married first Catherine, ca. 1831. Baptized into LDS church, by 1841. Ordained an elder, 29 Nov. 1841, in New York City. Painted portraits of JS and Emma Smith, Sept. 1842. Appointed secretary of church conference in New York City, 4 Sept. 1844. Appointed presiding elder in New York City, Feb. 1847. Excommunicated, fall 1847. Moved to Huntington, Suffolk Co., between 1858 and 1860. Married second Maria, before June 1880. Moved to Cold Spring Harbor, by June 1880. Died at Cold Spring Harbor.

Roundy, Shadrach (1 Jan. 1789–4 July 1872), merchant. Born at Rockingham, Windham Co., Vermont. Son of Uriah Roundy and Lucretia Needham. Married Betsy Quimby, 22 June 1814, at Rockingham. Lived at Spafford, Onondaga Co., New York. Member of Freewill Baptist Church in Spafford. There are two versions of story of his baptism into LDS church: first, that he sought out JS at Fayette, Seneca Co., New York, and was baptized by JS following their first interview, winter 1830–1831 (reportedly 23 Jan. 1831); second, that William E. McLellin baptized him, as reported in McLellin's journal entry for 30 Jan. 1832. Ordained an elder by Orson Hyde and Samuel H. Smith, 16 May 1832. Lived at Elk Creek, Erie Co., Pennsylvania, 1833. Moved to Willoughby, Cuyahoga Co., Ohio, by 1834. Member of the Seventy, 1836. Migrated to Far West, Caldwell Co., Missouri. Located at Warsaw, Hancock Co., Illinois, 1839. Moved to Nauvoo, Hancock Co., 1840. Commissioned aide-de-camp in Nauvoo Legion, Apr. 1841. Member of a bishopric in Nauvoo, 1841. Member of Nauvoo Masonic Lodge. Joined Nauvoo police force, 1843. Ordained a high priest, by 25 Dec. 1845. Bishop of Winter Quarters Fifth Ward, at Winter Quarters, unorganized U.S. territory (later in Omaha, Douglas Co., Nebraska). Member of Brigham Young pioneer company, arriving in Salt Lake Valley July 1847. Bishop of Salt Lake Sixteenth Ward, 1849–1856. Died at Salt Lake City.

Salisbury, Katharine Smith. See Younger, Katharine Smith.

Sayers, Edward (9 Feb. 1800–17 July 1861), horticulturalist. Born in Canterbury, Kent Co., England. Son of Edward Sayers and Mary. Married Ruth D. Vose, 23 Jan. 1841, in St. Louis. Purchased land in Nauvoo, Hancock Co., Illinois, from JS and Emma Smith, 19 May 1841. Moved to Nauvoo, before 1842. JS hid at Sayers's home, Aug. 1842, to avoid arrest for his alleged complicity in attempt to kill former Missouri governor Lilburn W. Boggs. Migrated to Utah Territory with Silas Richards's pioneer company, summer 1849. Lived at Salt Lake City for remainder of life.

Scammon, Jonathan Young (27 June 1812–17 Mar. 1890), lawyer, banker, newspaper publisher, philanthropist. Born at Whitefield, Lincoln Co., Maine. Son of Eliakim Scammon and Joanna Young. Educated in Kennebec Co., Maine, and Lincoln Co. Moved to Chicago, 1835. Served as deputy clerk of Cook Co., Illinois, circuit court, 1835–1836. Appointed attorney for State Bank of Illinois, 1837. Created charter for Chicago public school system, 1837. Married first Mary Ann Haven Dearborn, July 1837, at Bath, Sagadahoc Co., Maine. Served as school board member and reporter for Illinois Supreme Court, 1839–1845. Founded Chicago Society of the New Jerusalem (Swedenborgian), 1843. Served on editorial board of *Chicago Daily Journal,* 1844. Served as city alderman, 1845. Served as state senator, 1860–1861. Married second Maria Sheldon Wright, 5 Dec. 1867. Died at Chicago.

Sessions, Patty Bartlett. See Parry, Patty Bartlett.

Sharp, Thomas Coke (25 Sept. 1818–9 Apr. 1894), teacher, lawyer, newspaper editor and publisher. Born in Mount Holly, Burlington Co., New Jersey. Son of Solomon Sharp and Jemima Budd. Lived at Smyrna, Kent Co., Delaware, June 1830. Moved to Carlisle, Cumberland Co., Pennsylvania, 1835. Graduated from Dickinson College, 1840, in Carlisle. Admitted to Cumberland Co. bar, 14 Apr. 1840. Moved to Quincy, Adams Co., Illinois, July 1840. Moved to Warsaw, Hancock Co., Illinois, Sept. 1840. Edited *Western World* (later *Warsaw Signal*), 1840–1842, 1844–1846. Attended cornerstone-laying ceremony for Nauvoo temple, 1841, at invitation of JS. Married first Hannah G. Wilcox, 6 Sept. 1842. Indicted for murder of JS and Hyrum Smith, 1844; acquitted. Moved to Carthage, Hancock Co., Dec. 1865. Married second Anna E. Hewitt, 25 Nov. 1880, in Hannibal, Marion Co., Missouri. Died in Carthage.

Sheldon, Crawford Bernon (5 Oct. 1799–11 Mar. 1859), merchant. Son of Job Sheldon and Joanna Crawford Trippe. Moved to Lyndon, Caledonia Co., Vermont, by May 1800; to Warwick, Kent Co., Rhode Island, by Aug. 1810; and to New Milford, Litchfield Co., Connecticut, by May 1816. Married Abigail Maxson, 4 Jan. 1820. By 1828, moved to Delaware Co., New York, and served as county clerk. Lived at Delhi, Delaware Co., by 1830. Died at Delhi.

Sherwood, Henry Garlick (20 Apr. 1785–24 Nov. 1867), carpenter, surveyor. Born at Kingsbury, Washington Co., New York. Son of Newcomb Sherwood and a woman whose maiden name was Tolman (first name unidentified). Married first Jane J. McManagal (McMangle) of Glasgow, Lanark, Scotland, ca. 1824. Lived at Bolton, Warren Co., New York, 1830. Baptized into LDS church, by Aug. 1832. Ordained an elder by Jared and Simeon Carter, Aug. 1832. Moved to Kirtland, Geauga Co., Ohio, ca. 1834. Appointed to Kirtland high council, by 17 Aug. 1835. Married second Marcia Abbott, ca. 1835, in Windham Co., Vermont. Served mission to Ohio, Kentucky, and Tennessee, 1836. Migrated to Missouri; located at De Witt, Carroll Co., and then Daviess Co., 1838. Member of committee at Far West, Caldwell Co., Missouri, to supervise removal of Latter-day Saints from Missouri, Apr. 1839. Exiled from Missouri and located at Commerce (later Nauvoo), Hancock Co., Illinois, 1839. Member of Commerce high council, 6 Oct. 1839. Instructed in JS revelation to buy stock for building Nauvoo House, 19 Jan. 1841. Nauvoo city marshal, 1841–1843. Appointed guard in Nauvoo Legion, Mar. 1841. Member of Nauvoo Masonic Lodge. Member of Brigham Young pioneer company to Salt Lake Valley, 1847. Served colonizing mission to San Bernardino, Los Angeles Co., California, 1852. Returned to Utah Territory, 1855. Became disaffected with church and removed from high priests quorum, 27 Feb. 1856. Returned to San Bernardino, where he died.

Skinner, Onias Childs (22 July 1817–4 Feb. 1877), sailor, teacher, preacher, farmer, lawyer, railroad president. Born in Floyd, Oneida Co., New York. Son of Onias Skinner and Tirza. Moved to Whitestown, Oneida Co., by 1830; to Peoria Co., Illinois, 1836; and to Greenville, Darke Co., Ohio, 1838. Deputy marshal of Darke Co., 1840. Moved to Carthage, Hancock Co., Illinois, 1842. Moved to Quincy, Adams Co., Illinois, 1844. Leader of anti-Mormon movement in Warsaw, Hancock Co., 1844. Served as aide-de-camp to Illinois governor Thomas Ford, 1844. Served as special counsel for prosecution in JS's preliminary hearing on charge of treason, June 1844. Served as counsel for defense at trial for those accused of murdering JS, 1844. Married first Adaline McCormas Dorsey, 15 July 1845, in

Darke Co. State legislator, 1848–1849. Judge for Illinois Supreme Court, 1855–1858. Married second Sarah Wilton. Married third Helen Mar Cooley, 14 Jan. 1864, in Adams Co. Died in Quincy.

Sloan, James (28 Oct. 1792–24 Oct. 1886), city recorder, notary public, attorney, judge, farmer. Born in Donaghmore, Co. Tyrone, Ireland. Son of Alexander Sloan and Anne. Married Mary Magill. Baptized into LDS church. Ordained an elder, 28 Oct. 1837, in Columbiana Co., Ohio. Ordained a high priest, 18 Feb. 1838, in Columbiana Co. Moved to Daviess Co., Missouri, by 1838; to Quincy, Adams Co., Illinois; and to Commerce (later Nauvoo), Hancock Co., Illinois, by 1840. City recorder and clerk of municipal court, 1841–1843. Appointed war secretary in Nauvoo Legion, Mar. 1841. Elected church clerk, 2 Oct. 1841, in Nauvoo. Member of Nauvoo Masonic Lodge. Clerk of high priests quorum and war secretary of Nauvoo Legion, 1842, in Nauvoo. Elected notary public, 26 Sept. 1842, and city recorder, 11 Feb. 1843, in Nauvoo. Served mission to Ireland, 1843. Served as district clerk of Pottawattamie Co., Iowa, 1848–1851. Moved to Sacramento Co., California, by 1860. Joined RLDS church, by 1876. Died in Sacramento, Sacramento Co.

Slocum, John Jay (25 May 1803–12 May 1863), clergyman, publisher, college and newspaper founder. Born in Pittstown, Rensselaer Co., New York. Son of John Slocum and Phebe Slade. Attended Andover, Yale, and Princeton theological seminaries. Ordained a Presbyterian minister, 1834. Ministerial duties took him throughout midwestern and northeastern U.S. Credited with naming town of Lake Forest, Lake Co., Illinois, mid-1850s. Cofounded Lake Forest College. Moved to Kalamazoo, Kalamazoo Co., Michigan, by 1857. Moved to New York City, by 1860, and founded religious newspaper *New York World*. Moved to Lansing, Ingham Co., Michigan. Died at Lansing.

Smith, Agnes Moulton Coolbrith. See Pickett, Agnes Moulton Coolbrith.

Smith, Alvin (11 Feb. 1798–19 Nov. 1823), farmer, carpenter. Born at Tunbridge, Orange Co., Vermont. Son of Joseph Smith Sr. and Lucy Mack. Moved to Randolph, Orange Co., 1802; returned to Tunbridge. Moved to Royalton, Windsor Co., Vermont, and to Sharon, Windsor Co., by Dec. 1805; returned to Tunbridge, by Mar. 1808. Returned to Royalton, by Mar. 1810. Moved to Lebanon, Grafton Co., New Hampshire, 1811; to Norwich, Windsor Co., Vermont, 1813; and to Palmyra, Ontario Co., New York, 1816–Jan. 1817. Played prominent role in family economy, working to pay for 99.5-acre farm at Farmington (later Manchester), Ontario Co., jointly articled for with his father, 1820. Supervised construction of Smiths' frame home in Manchester. Supporter of JS's claims of heavenly manifestations. Experienced severe stomach cramps, perhaps caused by appendicitis, 15 Nov. 1823. Situation was apparently complicated by overdose of calomel. Died at Palmyra.

Smith, Don Carlos (25 Mar. 1816–7 Aug. 1841), farmer, printer, editor. Born at Norwich, Windsor Co., Vermont. Son of Joseph Smith Sr. and Lucy Mack. Moved to Palmyra, Ontario Co., New York, 1816–Jan. 1817. Moved to Farmington (later Manchester), Ontario Co., 1818. Baptized into LDS church by David Whitmer, ca. 9 June 1830, at Seneca Lake, Seneca Co., New York. Accompanied his father on mission to Asael Smith family in St. Lawrence Co., New York, Aug. 1830. Migrated from Seneca Falls, Seneca Co., to Kirtland, Geauga Co., Ohio, with Lucy Mack Smith company of Fayette, Seneca Co., branch members, May 1831. Employed by Kirtland printing shop under Oliver Cowdery, fall 1833. Married Agnes Moulton Coolbrith, 30 July 1835, at Kirtland. Ordained a high priest and appointed president of Kirtland high priests quorum, 15 Jan. 1836. Served mission to Pennsylvania and New York, 1836. Continued working in Kirtland printing shop, including involvement with *Elders' Journal.* Moved to New Portage, Medina Co., Ohio, Dec. 1837. Served mission to Virginia, Pennsylvania, and Ohio, spring 1838. Left Ohio for Far West, Caldwell Co., Missouri, May 1838. Served mission to Kentucky and Tennessee, 1838. Expelled from Far West, Feb. 1839; moved to Quincy, Adams Co., Illinois. Lived at Macomb, McDonough Co., Illinois, and then moved to Commerce (later Nauvoo), Hancock Co., Illinois, 1839. President of high priests in Commerce, 1839. Editor and publisher of *Times and Seasons,* with Ebenezer Robinson, 1839–1841, at Nauvoo. Elected member of Nauvoo City Council, 1 Feb. 1841. Appointed a regent of University of Nauvoo, 3 Feb. 1841. Elected brigadier general in Nauvoo Legion, 5 Feb. 1841. Died at Nauvoo.

Smith, Emma Hale (10 July 1804–30 Apr. 1879), clerk, scribe, editor, author, boarding house operator, clothier. Born at Harmony, Susquehanna Co., Pennsylvania. Daughter of Isaac Hale and Elizabeth Lewis. Member of Methodist church at Harmony. Married first to JS by Zachariah Tarble, 18 Jan. 1827, at South Bainbridge, Chenango Co., New York. Assisted JS as scribe during translation of Book of Mormon at Harmony, 1828, and joined him during completion of translation at Peter Whitmer Sr. farm, Fayette, Seneca Co., New York. Baptized into LDS church by Oliver Cowdery, 28 June 1830, at Colesville, Broome Co., New York. Migrated from New York to Kirtland, Geauga Co., Ohio, Jan.–Feb. 1831. Lived at John Johnson home at Hiram, Portage Co., Ohio, while JS worked on revision of Bible, 1831–1832. Edited *A Collection of Sacred Hymns, for the Church of the Latter Day Saints,* published 1835, at Kirtland. Fled Ohio persecution for Far West, Caldwell Co., Missouri, Jan.–Mar. 1838. Exiled from Missouri, Feb. 1839; located near Quincy, Adams Co., Illinois. Moved to Commerce (later Nauvoo), Hancock Co., Illinois, 10 May 1839. Appointed president of Female Relief Society at Nauvoo, 17 Mar. 1842. Fled to Fulton, Fulton Co., Illinois, Sept. 1846–Feb. 1847, then returned to Nauvoo. Married second Lewis Crum Bidamon, 23 Dec. 1847, at Nauvoo. Affiliated with RLDS church, 1860. Died at Nauvoo.

Smith, George Albert (26 June 1817–1 Sept. 1875). Born at Potsdam, St. Lawrence Co., New York. Son of John Smith and Clarissa Lyman. Baptized into LDS church by Joseph H. Wakefield, 10 Sept. 1832, at Potsdam. Moved to Kirtland, Geauga Co., Ohio, 1833. Labored on Kirtland temple. Participated in Camp of Israel expedition to Missouri, 1834. Appointed member of First Quorum of the Seventy, 1 Mar. 1835, at Kirtland. Served mission to eastern states with Lyman Smith, 1835. Served mission to Ohio, 1836. Arrived at Far West, Caldwell Co., Missouri, from Kirtland, 16 June 1838, and soon located at Adam-ondi-Ahman, Daviess Co., Missouri. Member of Adam-ondi-Ahman high council, 1838. In exodus from Missouri, located north of Quincy, Adams Co., Illinois. Ordained member of Quorum of the Twelve, 26 Apr. 1839, at Far West. Served mission to England, 1839–1841. Moved to Nauvoo, Hancock Co., Illinois, 1841. Married to Bathsheba W. Bigler by Don Carlos Smith, 25 July 1841, at Nauvoo. Moved to Zarahemla, Lee Co., Iowa Territory, 1841. Member of Nauvoo Masonic Lodge. Member of Nauvoo City Council, 1842–1843. Nauvoo city alderman, 1843–1844. Member of Brigham Young pioneer company that journeyed to Salt Lake Valley, 1847. Appointed church historian and recorder, 1854. Member of Utah territorial supreme court, 1855. First counselor to Brigham Young in church presidency, 1868. Died at Salt Lake City.

Smith, Hyrum (9 Feb. 1800–27 June 1844), farmer, cooper. Born at Tunbridge, Orange Co., Vermont. Son of Joseph Smith Sr. and Lucy Mack. Moved to Randolph, Orange Co., 1802; to Tunbridge, 1803; to Royalton, Windsor Co., Vermont, May 1804; to Sharon, Windsor Co., Aug. 1804; to Tunbridge, 1807; to Royalton, 1808; to Lebanon, Grafton Co., New Hampshire, 1811; to Norwich, Windsor Co., 1813; and to Palmyra, Ontario Co., New York, 1816–Jan. 1817. Member of Western Presbyterian Church of Palmyra, 1824. Lived at Palmyra, 1817–1825. Lived at Manchester, Ontario Co., 1825–1826. Married first Jerusha Barden, 2 Nov. 1826, at Manchester. Returned to Palmyra, 1826. Baptized by JS, June 1829, at Seneca Lake, Seneca Co., New York. One of the Eight Witnesses of the Book of Mormon, June 1829. Assisted in arrangements for publication of Book of Mormon, 1829–1830, at Palmyra. Among six original members of LDS church, 6 Apr. 1830. Presided over Colesville, Broome Co., New York, branch, 1830–1831. Migrated to Kirtland, Geauga Co., Ohio, 1831. Ordained a high priest by JS, 4 June 1831. Member of committee to supervise construction of Kirtland temple, 1833–1836. Participated in Camp of Israel expedition to Missouri, 1834. Appointed to Kirtland high council, 24 Sept. 1834. Sustained as assistant counselor in presidency of church, 3 Sept. 1837. Appointed counselor in First Presidency, 7 Nov. 1837. Married second Mary Fielding, 24 Dec. 1837, at Kirtland. Imprisoned at Liberty, Clay Co., Missouri, with his brother JS, 1838–1839. Allowed to escape, 16 Apr. 1839, while en route from trial in Gallatin, Daviess Co., Missouri, during change of venue to Columbia, Boone Co., Missouri. Arrived at Quincy, Adams Co., Illinois, 22 Apr. 1839. In JS revelation dated 19 Jan. 1841, instructed to buy stock for building Nauvoo House, appointed patriarch of church, released as counselor in First Presidency, and appointed a prophet, seer, and revelator in First Presidency. Functioned as an associate president with JS (though term "associate president" was not used at the time to describe his office or role). Elected to Nauvoo City Council, 1 Feb. 1841. Appointed chaplain in Nauvoo Legion, Mar. 1841. Member of Nauvoo Masonic Lodge. Vice mayor of Nauvoo, 1842–1843. Appointed to replace Elias Higbee as member of Nauvoo temple committee, 10 Oct. 1843. Participated in plural marriage during JS's lifetime. Murdered at Carthage, Hancock Co., Illinois.

Smith, John (16 July 1781–23 May 1854), farmer. Born at Derryfield (later Manchester), Rockingham Co., New Hampshire. Son of Asael Smith and Mary Duty. Member of Congregational Church. Appointed overseer of highways at Potsdam, St. Lawrence Co., New York, 1810. Married Clarissa Lyman, 11 Sept. 1815. Baptized into LDS church by Solomon Humphrey, 9 Jan. 1832. Confirmed and ordained an elder by Joseph Wakefield and Solomon Humphrey, 9 Jan. 1832. Moved to Kirtland, Geauga Co., Ohio, 1833. Ordained a high priest, June 1833. President of Kirtland high council. Served mission to eastern states with his brother Joseph Smith Sr., 1836. Appointed assistant counselor in First Presidency, 1837; member of Kirtland stake presidency, 1838. Left Kirtland for Far West, Caldwell Co., Missouri, 5 Apr. 1838. Appointed president of stake in Adam-ondi-Ahman, Daviess Co., Missouri, 28 June 1838. Expelled from Missouri; arrived in Illinois, 28 Feb. 1839. Moved to Commerce (later Nauvoo), Hancock Co., Illinois, June 1839. Appointed president of stake in Lee Co., Iowa Territory, 5 Oct. 1839. Member of Nauvoo

Masonic Lodge. Appointed to preside at Macedonia (later Webster), Hancock Co., Illinois, 1843–1844. Ordained a patriarch, 10 Jan. 1844. Appointed Nauvoo stake president, 7 Oct. 1844. Joined westward exodus of Latter-day Saints into Iowa Territory, 9 Feb. 1846. Arrived in Salt Lake Valley, 23 Sept. 1847. Presided over Salt Lake stake, 1847–1848. Ordained patriarch of church, 1 Jan. 1849. Died at Salt Lake City.

Smith, Joseph, Sr. (12 July 1771–14 Sept. 1840), cooper, farmer, teacher, merchant. Born at Topsfield, Essex Co., Massachusetts. Son of Asael Smith and Mary Duty. Nominal member of Congregationalist church at Topsfield. Married Lucy Mack, 24 Jan. 1796, at Tunbridge, Orange Co., Vermont. Joined Universalist Society at Tunbridge, 1797. Entered mercantile business at Randolph, Orange Co., ca. 1802, and lost all in a ginseng root investment. Moved to Tunbridge, before May 1803; to Royalton, Windsor Co., Vermont, 1804; to Sharon, Windsor Co., by Aug. 1804; to Tunbridge, 1807; to Royalton, 1809; to Lebanon, Grafton Co., New Hampshire, 1811; to Norwich, Windsor Co., 1813; to Palmyra, Ontario Co., New York, 1816; and to Farmington (later Manchester), Ontario Co., 1818. One of the Eight Witnesses of the Book of Mormon, June 1829. Baptized into LDS church by Oliver Cowdery, 6 Apr. 1830. Served mission to family of his father in St. Lawrence Co., New York, Aug. 1830. Lived at The Kingdom, unincorporated settlement near Waterloo, Seneca Co., New York, Nov. 1830–May 1831. Moved to Kirtland, Geauga Co., Ohio, 1831. Ordained a high priest, 4 June 1831. Ordained patriarch of church, 18 Dec. 1833, and assistant president, 6 Dec. 1834. Member of Kirtland high council, 1834. Labored on Kirtland temple. Served mission to eastern states with his brother John Smith, 1836. Sustained as assistant counselor to First Presidency, 1837. Moved to Far West, Caldwell Co., Missouri, summer 1838. Fled from Far West to Quincy, Adams Co., Illinois, winter 1839. Located at Commerce (later Nauvoo), Hancock Co., Illinois, spring 1839. Died at Nauvoo.

Smith, Lucy Mack (8 July 1775–14 May 1856), oilcloth painter, nurse, fund-raiser, author. Born at Gilsum, Cheshire Co., New Hampshire. Daughter of Solomon Mack Sr. and Lydia Gates. Moved to Montague, Franklin Co., Massachusetts, 1779; to Tunbridge, Orange Co., Vermont, 1788; to Gilsum, 1792; and to Tunbridge, 1794. Married to Joseph Smith Sr. by Seth Austin, 24 Jan. 1796, at Tunbridge. Moved to Randolph, Orange Co., 1802; to Tunbridge, before May 1803; to Royalton, Windsor Co., Vermont, 1804; to Sharon, Windsor Co., by Aug. 1804; to Tunbridge, 1807; to Royalton, 1809; to Lebanon, Grafton Co., New Hampshire, 1811; to Norwich, Windsor Co., 1813; to Palmyra, Ontario Co., New York, 1816–Jan. 1817; and to Farmington (later Manchester), Ontario Co., 1818. Member of Western Presbyterian Church of Palmyra, early 1820s. Baptized into LDS church, 6 Apr. 1830, at Seneca Lake, Seneca Co., New York. Lived at The Kingdom, unincorporated settlement near Waterloo, Seneca Co., Nov. 1830–May 1831. Led company of approximately eighty Fayette, Seneca Co., branch members from Seneca Co. to Kirtland, Geauga Co., Ohio, May 1831. Migrated to Far West, Caldwell Co., Missouri, summer 1838. Fled to Quincy, Adams Co., Illinois, during exodus from Missouri, Feb. 1839. Joined Female Relief Society, Mar. 1842, at Nauvoo, Hancock Co., Illinois. Lived with daughter Lucy Smith Millikin in Colchester, McDonough Co., Illinois, 1846–1853. Returned to Nauvoo, 1853. Died at Nauvoo. Her narrative history of Smith family, published as *Biographical Sketches of Joseph Smith*, 1853, has been an invaluable resource for study of JS and early church.

Smith, Samuel Harrison (13 Mar. 1808–30 July 1844), farmer, logger, scribe, builder, tavern operator. Born at Tunbridge, Orange Co., Vermont. Son of Joseph Smith Sr. and Lucy Mack. Moved to Royalton, Windsor Co., Vermont, before Mar. 1810; to Lebanon, Grafton Co., New Hampshire, 1811; to Norwich, Windsor Co., 1813; to Palmyra, Ontario Co., New York, 1816–Jan. 1817; and to Farmington (later Manchester), Ontario Co., 1818. Member of Western Presbyterian Church of Palmyra, 1820. Baptized by Oliver Cowdery, May 1829, at Harmony, Susquehanna Co., Pennsylvania. One of the Eight Witnesses of the Book of Mormon, June 1829. Among six original members of LDS church, 6 Apr. 1830. Ordained an elder, 6 Apr. 1830, at Fayette, Seneca Co., New York. Began mission to New York, 30 June 1830. Sent to serve mission to Kirtland, Geauga Co., Ohio, Dec. 1830. Migrated from New York to Kirtland; arrived Feb. 1831. Ordained a high priest by Lyman Wight, 4 June 1831. Served mission to Missouri with Reynolds Cahoon, 1831. Served mission to eastern states with Orson Hyde, 1832. Appointed member of first Kirtland high council, 17 Feb. 1834. Married first Mary Bailey, 13 Aug. 1834, at Kirtland. Committee member and general agent for Literary Firm in Kirtland, 1835. Member of Kirtland Safety Society, 1837. Appointed president of Kirtland high council, 2 Oct. 1837. Moved to Far West, Caldwell Co., Missouri, where he lived briefly before moving to Marrowbone, Daviess Co., Missouri, 1838. Participated in Battle of Crooked River, near Ray Co., Missouri, 25 Oct. 1838. Among first Latter-day Saints to seek refuge at Quincy, Adams Co., Illinois, 1838. Hired to farm for George Miller near Macomb, McDonough Co., Illinois, Mar. 1839. Moved to Nauvoo, Hancock Co., Illinois, 1841. Appointed a bishop at Nauvoo, 1841. Nauvoo city alderman, 1841–1842. Appointed guard in Nauvoo Legion, Mar. 1841. Married second Levira Clark, 30 May 1841, in Scott Co., Illinois. Appointed a regent of University of Nauvoo. Moved to Plymouth, Hancock Co., Jan. 1842. Member of Nauvoo Masonic Lodge. Member of Nauvoo City Council, 1842–1843. Died at Nauvoo.

Smith, William B. (13 Mar. 1811–13 Nov. 1893), farmer, newspaper editor. Born at Royalton, Windsor Co., Vermont. Son of Joseph Smith Sr. and Lucy Mack. Moved from Norwich, Windsor Co., to Palmyra, Ontario Co., New York, 1816–Jan. 1817. Baptized into LDS church by David Whitmer, 9 June 1830, at Seneca Lake, Seneca Co., New York. Lived at The Kingdom, unincorporated settlement in Seneca Falls, Seneca Co., by 1830. Ordained a teacher, 5 Oct. 1830. Moved to Kirtland, Geauga Co., Ohio, May 1831. Ordained an elder by Lyman Johnson, 19 Dec. 1832, at Kirtland. Served mission to Erie Co., Pennsylvania, Dec. 1832. Married first Caroline Amanda Grant, 14 Feb. 1833, at Kirtland. Ordained a high priest, 21 June 1833. Participated in Camp of Israel expedition to Missouri, 1834. Appointed member of Quorum of the Twelve, 14 Feb. 1835, at Kirtland. Moved to Far West, Caldwell Co., Missouri, spring 1838. Disfellowshipped, 4 May 1839. Restored to Quorum of the Twelve, 25 May 1839. Settled at Plymouth, Hancock Co., Illinois, ca. 1839, where he kept a tavern. Restored to fellowship. Member of Masonic lodge in Nauvoo, Hancock Co. Member of Nauvoo City Council, 1842–1843. Editor of Nauvoo newspaper *The Wasp*, 1842. Represented Hancock Co. in Illinois House of Representatives, 1842–1843. Wife died, May 1845. Ordained patriarch of church, 24 May 1845. Married second Mary Jane Rollins, 22 June 1845, at Nauvoo. Excommunicated, 12 Oct. 1845. Sustained James J. Strang as successor to JS, 1 Mar. 1846. Married third Roxey Ann Grant, 19 May 1847, in Knox Co., Illinois. Ordained patriarch and apostle of Strang's Church of Jesus Christ of Latter Day Saints, 11 June 1846, at Voree, Walworth Co., Wisconsin Territory. Excommunicated from Strangite movement, 8 Oct. 1847. Affiliated briefly with Lyman Wight, 1849–1850. Initiated a new movement with Martin Harris and Chilton Daniels, 1 Nov. 1855. Married fourth Eliza Elsie Sanborn, 12 Nov. 1857, at Kirtland. Moved to Venango, Erie Co., Pennsylvania, by 1860, and to Elkader, Clayton Co., Iowa, shortly after. Enlisted in U.S. Army during Civil War and apparently adopted middle initial *B* at this time. Spent active duty time in Arkansas. Joined RLDS church, 1878. Wife died, Mar. 1889. Married fifth Rosanna Jewitt Surprise, 21 Dec. 1889, at Clinton, Clinton Co., Iowa. Moved to Osterdock, Clayton Co., 1890. Died at Osterdock.

Snider, John (11 Feb. 1800–19 Dec. 1875), farmer, mason, stonecutter. Born in New Brunswick, Canada. Son of Martin Snyder and Sarah Armstrong. Married Mary Heron, 28 Feb. 1822. Baptized into LDS church, 1836, at Toronto. Ordained a priest, before 1837. Served mission to England, 1837. Moved to Far West, Caldwell Co., Missouri, 18 July 1838. Ordained a seventy, 19 Jan. 1839, in Far West. Moved to Hancock Co., Illinois, by 1840. Member of Nauvoo House Association. Appointed guard in Nauvoo Legion, Mar. 1841. Served mission to United Kingdom, 1842–1843. Migrated to Salt Lake City, ca. 1850. Died in Salt Lake City.

Snow, Eliza Roxcy (21 Jan. 1804–5 Dec. 1887), poet, teacher, seamstress, milliner. Born in Becket, Berkshire Co., Massachusetts. Daughter of Oliver Snow and Rosetta Leonora Pettibone. Moved to Mantua, Trumbull Co., Ohio, ca. 1806. Member of Baptist church. Baptized into LDS church, 5 Apr. 1835, in Mantua. Gave up patrimony for construction of Kirtland temple. Moved to Kirtland, Geauga Co., Ohio, 1837. Moved to Adam-ondi-Ahman, Daviess Co., Missouri, 1838. Moved to Commerce (later Nauvoo), Hancock Co., Illinois, 1839. "Married or sealed" to JS "for time and eternity," 29 June 1842. Lived with JS and family, Aug. 1842–1844. Acted as scribe for JS's journal, Sept. 1842. Served as first secretary of Female Relief Society, 1842–1846, in Nauvoo. Married Brigham Young as a plural wife, 3 Oct. 1844, in Nauvoo. Moved to Winter Quarters, unorganized U.S. territory (later in Omaha, Douglas Co., Nebraska), 1846. Migrated to Salt Lake City, 1847. Oversaw reestablishment and operation of ward relief societies, 1868–1880, in Salt Lake City. Served mission to Palestine to witness rededication of land for return of Jews, 1872–1873. Served as general president of Relief Society, 1880–1887. Known as Eliza R. Snow Smith, 1880–1887. Died in Salt Lake City.

Snow, Oliver (18 Sept. 1775–17 Oct. 1845), farmer, teacher. Born in Becket, Berkshire Co., Massachusetts. Son of Oliver Snow and Rebecca Wadsworth. Intention to marry Rosetta Leonora Pettibone in Congregational church dated 6 May 1800, in Becket. Moved to Tyringham, Berkshire Co., 1805. Moved to Mantua, Trumbull Co., Ohio, ca. 1806. Baptized into Baptist church, 1809; later affiliated with Campbellite movement. Portage Co. commissioner, 1809–1815. Baptized into LDS church, after 20 June 1836. Moved to Kirtland, Geauga Co., Ohio, 1837. Ordained an elder, before 24 Sept. 1837. Joseph Smith Sr. hid in Snow's home, 1837. Moved to Adam-ondi-Ahman, Daviess Co., Missouri, 1838; to Quincy, Adams Co., Illinois, 1839; to La Harpe, Hancock Co., Illinois, 1840; to Nauvoo, Hancock Co., 1841; and to Walnut Grove Township, Knox Co., Illinois, 1842. Died in Walnut Grove Township.

Spencer, Daniel (20 July 1794–8 Dec. 1868), rancher, merchant. Born in West Stockbridge, Berkshire Co., Massachusetts. Son of Daniel Spencer and Chloe Wilson. Moved to Savannah, Chatham Co., Georgia, ca. 1816. Operated a mercantile business in Savannah. Married first Sophronia Eliza Pomeroy, 16 Jan. 1823, in West Stockbridge. Returned to West Stockbridge, 1829. Married second Sarah Lester Van Schoonover, 30 June 1834. Baptized into LDS church by James Burnham, 3 Mar. 1840, in West Stockbridge. Moved to Nauvoo, Hancock Co., Illinois, 1841. Served mission to Canada, ca. 1841. Served mission to Cherokee Indian Nation, ca. 1842. Member of Nauvoo City Council, 1843–1844. Served mission to Canada, 1843. Served mission to Massachusetts, 1844. After murder of JS, served as interim mayor of Nauvoo, Aug. 1844–Feb. 1845. Ordained a high priest, 6 Oct. 1844, in Nauvoo. Moved to Winter Quarters, unorganized U.S. territory (later in Omaha, Douglas Co., Nebraska), 1846. Served as bishop at Winter Quarters. Migrated to Salt Lake City, 1847. Member of Utah territorial legislature, 1851. Died in Salt Lake City.

Spencer, Orson (13 May 1802–15 Oct. 1855), teacher, minister, university professor and chancellor. Born in West Stockbridge, Berkshire Co., Massachusetts. Son of Daniel Spencer and Chloe Wilson. Moved to Lenox, Berkshire Co., 1817; to Schenectady, Schenectady Co., New York, 1819; to Washington, Wilkes Co., Georgia, 1825; and to Hamilton, Madison Co., New York, 1827. Baptist minister in Massachusetts and Connecticut, ca. 1829–ca. 1841. Married Catherine Curtis, 13 Apr. 1830. Soon after, moved to Saybrook, Middlesex Co., Connecticut. Moved to Middlefield, Hampshire Co., Massachusetts, by 1840. Returned to West Stockbridge, 1841. Baptized into LDS church by Daniel Spencer, May 1841, in West Stockbridge. Moved to Nauvoo, Hancock Co., Illinois, 1841. Nauvoo city alderman, 1841–1845. Appointed professor at University of Nauvoo, 1841. Ordained an elder, before 6 Apr. 1843. Served mission to New Haven, New Haven Co., Connecticut, 1843. Ordained a high priest by George Miller, 6 Oct. 1844, in Nauvoo. Elected mayor of Nauvoo, 1845. Wife died, 1846, in Iowa Territory. Presided over British mission, 1847–1849. Migrated to Salt Lake City as captain of immigrant company, 1849. Member of Utah territorial legislature, 1851. Died in St. Louis.

Swazey, Ezekiel A. M. (9 Apr. 1808–3 Jan. 1863), soldier, attorney, farmer. Born in Vermont. Moved to what later became Iowa Territory, by 1830. Appointed brigadier general in Iowa territorial militia, 9 Jan. 1830. Elected member of first Iowa territorial legislature, 12 Nov. 1838. Resident of Van Buren Co., Iowa Territory, 1840. Married Phebe Squires, 15 Jan. 1851, in Farmington, Van Buren Co. Served in Civil War. Died in Farmington.

Taylor, James (21 June 1783–27 May 1870), government excise worker, farmer, joiner, carpenter. Born in Ackenthwaite, Westmoreland, England. Son of Edward Taylor and Elizabeth Saul. Christened Anglican. Moved to Lancaster, Lancashire, England, before 1805. Married Agnes Taylor, 23 Dec. 1805, in Kirkoswald, Cumberland, England. Moved to Milnthorpe, Westmoreland, by 1808; to Liverpool, Lancashire, by 1814; to Hale, Westmoreland, 1819; and to Toronto, 1832. Baptized into LDS church by son John Taylor. Moved near Oquawka, Henderson Co., Illinois, by Aug. 1842. Twice housed JS to hide him from his enemies, 1842. Ordained a high priest, by 1845. Migrated to Salt Lake City, 1847. Died in Salt Lake City.

Taylor, John (1 Nov. 1808–25 July 1887), preacher, editor, publisher, politician. Born at Milnthorpe, Westmoreland Co., England. Son of James Taylor and Agnes Taylor, members of Church of England. At age fifteen, joined Methodists and was local preacher. Migrated from England to York, York Township, York Co., Home District, Upper Canada, 1828–1829. Married Leonora Cannon, 28 Jan. 1833, at York. Baptized into LDS church by Parley P. Pratt, 9 May 1836, and ordained an elder shortly after. Appointed to preside over churches in Upper Canada. Ordained a high priest by JS and others, 21 Aug. 1837. Moved to Kirtland, Geauga Co., Ohio. Moved to Far West, Caldwell Co., Missouri, 1838. Ordained member of Quorum of the Twelve by Brigham Young and Heber C. Kimball, 19 Dec. 1838, at Far West. Served mission to England, 1839–1841. In Nauvoo, Hancock Co., Illinois, served as member of city council, judge advocate of Nauvoo Legion, and editor of *Times and Seasons* and *Nauvoo Neighbor.* Member of Nauvoo Masonic Lodge. Participated in plural marriage during JS's lifetime. With JS when JS and Hyrum Smith were murdered in jail at Carthage, Hancock Co., 27 June 1844. Served mission to England, 1846–1847. Arrived in Salt Lake Valley, 1847. Elected associate judge of provisional state of Deseret (later Utah Territory), 12 Mar. 1849. Served mission to France and Germany, 1849–1852; arranged for translation of Book of Mormon into French and published *L'Etoile du Deseret* (The star of deseret). In Germany, supervised translation of Book of Mormon into German and published *Zions Panier* (Zion's banner). Appointed to preside over branches in eastern states, 1854. Editor of *The Mormon,* New York City, 1855–1857. Member of Utah territorial legislature, 1857–1876. Following death of Brigham Young, presided over church from 1877 to 1887. Ordained president of church, 10 Oct. 1880. Died at Kaysville, Davis Co., Utah Territory. Buried in Salt Lake City.

Thompson, Mercy Rachel Fielding (15 June 1807–15 Sept. 1893), born in Honeydon, Bedfordshire, England. Daughter of John Fielding and Rachel Ibbotson. Immigrated to Toronto, 1832. Baptized into LDS church by Parley P. Pratt, 21 May 1836, near Toronto. Moved to Kirtland, Geauga Co., Ohio, 1836. Married Robert Blashell Thompson, 4 June 1837, in Kirtland. Moved to Far West, Caldwell Co., Missouri, 1838; to Quincy, Adams Co., Illinois, spring 1839. Husband died, 27 Aug. 1841. Moved to Nauvoo, Hancock Co., Illinois, by Apr. 1843. "Married or sealed" to Hyrum Smith "for time," 11 Aug. 1843, in Nauvoo. Moved to Winter Quarters, unorganized U.S. territory (later in Omaha, Douglas Co., Nebraska), 1846. Migrated to Salt Lake City, 24 Sept. 1847. Died in Salt Lake City.

Trumbull, Lyman (12 Oct. 1813–1896), teacher, lawyer, judge, statesman. Born in Colchester, New London Co., Connecticut. Son of Benjamin Trumbull and Elizabeth Mather. Moved to Greenville, Meriwether Co., Georgia, 1833. Admitted to bar, 1837, in Georgia. Moved to Belleville, St. Clair Co., Illinois, 1837. Elected to Illinois legislature, 1840. Served as secretary of state, 1841–1843. Married first Julia M. Jayne, 23 June 1843, in Springfield, Sangamon Co., Illinois. Served as justice of Illinois Supreme Court, 1848–1853. Moved to Alton, Madison Co., Illinois, 1848. Served in U.S. Senate, 1855–1873. Moved to Springfield, by June 1860. Moved to Chicago, 1863. Known as father of Thirteenth Amendment of U.S. Constitution, 1865. Instrumental in passing first Civil Service Act in U.S., 1870. Married second Mary J. Ingraham, 3 Nov. 1877, in Saybrook, Middlesex Co., Connecticut. Died in Chicago.

Turley, Theodore (10 Apr. 1801–12 Aug. 1871), mechanic, gunsmith, brewer, farmer, blacksmith, gristmill operator. Born at Birmingham, Warwickshire, England. Son of William Turley and Elizabeth Yates. Associated with Methodism, by 1818. Married Frances

Amelia Kimberley, 26 Nov. 1821, at Harborne, Staffordshire, England. Migrated to Upper Canada, 1825. Purchased land at Churchville, Chinguacousy Township, York Co. (later in Ontario), Upper Canada, 1834. Baptized into LDS church by Isaac Russell, 1 Mar. 1837, at Churchville. Ordained a priest, 24 Apr. 1837, in Churchville. Migrated from Upper Canada to Far West, Caldwell Co., Missouri, in Almon W. Babbitt company, July 1838. Member of Far West high council. Ordained a seventy by Heber C. Kimball, 22 Dec. 1838, in Far West. Appointed member of committee on removal from Missouri under Brigham Young, 29 Jan. 1839. Moved to Adams Co., Illinois, by May 1839. Accompanied Quorum of the Twelve on mission to Great Britain, 1839–1840. Moved to Nauvoo, Hancock Co., Illinois, by 1841. Member of Nauvoo Legion, 1841. Member of Nauvoo Masonic Lodge. Participated in plural marriage during JS's lifetime. Left Nauvoo during exodus, Feb. 1846. Moved to Winter Quarters, unorganized U.S. territory (later in Omaha, Douglas Co., Nebraska), by Nov. 1846. Member of Winter Quarters high council, 28 Nov. 1846. Arrived in Salt Lake Valley, 1849. Served colonizing mission to San Bernardino, Los Angeles Co., California, 1851. Appointed school commissioner, before 1853. Elected San Bernardino city treasurer, 1854. Appointed president of high council, 15 Mar. 1856. Returned to Utah Territory, 1857/1858. Moved to Washington, Washington Co., Utah Territory, by Dec. 1859. Died at Beaver, Beaver Co., Utah Territory.

Walker, Lorin (25 July 1822–26 Sept. 1907), carpenter, miller, housepainter. Born in Peacham, Caledonia Co., Vermont. Son of John Walker and Lydia Holmes. Moved to Ogdensburg, St. Lawrence Co., New York, by 1836. Baptized into LDS church by Abraham Palmer, June 1836, in Ogdensburg. Moved to Missouri, 1838; to Quincy, Adams Co., Illinois, by 1840; and to home of JS in Nauvoo, Hancock Co., Illinois, 1842. Ordained a seventy, before 1842. Married first Lavina Smith, niece of JS, 23 June 1844, in Nauvoo. Clerk of Fourteenth Quorum of the Seventy, 1844, in Nauvoo. Moved to Macedonia (later Webster), Hancock Co., 1847; to Florence, Douglas Co., Nebraska Territory, 1857; and to Farmington, Davis Co., Utah Territory, ca. 1860. Married second Mary Elizabeth Middlemas, 15 May 1879, in Salt Lake City. Moved to Rockland, Oneida Co., Idaho Territory, 1883. Died in Rockland.

Warren, Calvin Averill (3 June 1807–22 Feb. 1881), lawyer, businessman. Born in Elizabethtown, Essex Co., New York. Lived at Hamilton Co., Ohio, 1832. Moved to Batavia, Clermont Co., Ohio, by 1835. Married Viola A. Morris, 25 May 1835, at Batavia. Moved to Quincy, Adams Co., Illinois, 1836; to Warsaw, Hancock Co., Illinois, 1837; and to Quincy, 1839. Advised JS and other church members on bankruptcy cases, 1842. Identified by Jacob B. Backenstos as member of mob that killed JS and Hyrum Smith, 1844, at Carthage, Hancock Co.; served as counsel for defense of those tried for murder of JS, 1845. Married first Harriet W. Robbins Frierson, 30 Aug. 1849, in Adams Co. Married second Wady Ann Boswell, 25 Jan. 1866, in Adams Co. Moved to Melrose Township, Adams Co., 1880. Died in Melrose Township.

Warrington, Benjamin (1810–June 1850), wheelwright. Born in New Jersey. Married Sarah Horner, 16 Jan. 1834, in Preble Co., Ohio. Owned lots in Somerville, Milford Township, Butler Co., Ohio, 1835–ca. 1838. Moved to Hancock Co., Illinois, by 1840. Appointed quartermaster sergeant in Nauvoo Legion, 1 May 1841. Member of Nauvoo City

Council, 1843–1845. Only member of Nauvoo City Council who did not agree with council's resolution to suppress *Nauvoo Expositor*, 10 June 1844. Drowned in Platte River.

Wasson, Lorenzo D. (1819–28 July 1857). Born in New York. Son of Benjamin Wasson and Elizabeth Hale. Lived at Harpursville, Broome Co., New York, by 1836. Moved to Farmington, Fulton Co., Illinois, Aug. 1836; to Amboy, Ogle Co., Illinois, Dec. 1837; and to Nauvoo, Hancock Co., Illinois, Oct. 1840. Resided with JS in Nauvoo. Baptized into LDS church by JS, 20 Mar. 1842, in Nauvoo. Member of Nauvoo Masonic Lodge. Received elder's license, 18 Apr. 1842, in Nauvoo. Served mission to New Jersey and Pennsylvania, summer 1842. Moved back to Broome Co., before July 1843. Married first Marietta Crocker, 9 July 1843. Appointed member of Council of Fifty, 11 Mar. 1844. Escorted body of JS from Carthage, Hancock Co., to Nauvoo, 29 June 1844. Married second Aurelia H. Gaylord, ca. 1848. Died in Amboy.

Weld, John Fuller (11 Dec. 1809–28 July 1892), physician, surgeon. Born in Berkshire, Franklin Co., Vermont. Son of Daniel Weld and Lydia Fuller. Moved to Cornish, Cheshire Co., New Hampshire, by 1810. Moved to Sonora Township, Hancock Co., Illinois, 1827. Attended Dartmouth Medical School, at Hanover, Grafton Co., New Hampshire, 1833. Attended Castleton Medical College, at Castleton, Rutland Co., Vermont, 1835. Moved to St. Mary's, St. Mary's Township, Hancock Co., 1837. Moved to Nauvoo, Hancock Co. Reportedly friendly to Latter-day Saints, but no record of his baptism into LDS church. Appointed surgeon in Nauvoo Legion, Mar. 1841. Member of Nauvoo Masonic Lodge. Married first Frances Emiline Hibbard White, 4 July 1845, in Nauvoo. Married second Ruth Elizabeth Collins Rowe, 7 Apr. 1855, in Hancock Co. Moved to Sonora Township, by 1880. Died in Sonora Township.

Wells, Daniel Hanmer (27 Oct. 1814–24 Mar. 1891), farmer, teacher, ferry operator, lumber merchant, manager of nail factory, politician. Born in Trenton, Oneida Co., New York. Son of Daniel Wells and Catherine Chapin. Moved to Marietta, Washington Co., Ohio, ca. 1832. Moved to Commerce (later Nauvoo), Hancock Co., Illinois, 1834. Married Eliza Rebecca Robison, 9 Mar. 1837, in Hancock Co. Served as justice of the peace, 1840–1844, in Hancock Co. From 1841 to 1844, served as alderman, school warden, regent of University of Nauvoo, and commissary general in Nauvoo Legion. Nauvoo city alderman, 1841–1845. Baptized into LDS church by Almon W. Babbitt, 9 Aug. 1846, in Nauvoo. Leading participant in Battle of Nauvoo, 1846. Migrated to Salt Lake City in Brigham Young pioneer company, 1848. Attorney general for provisional state of Deseret, 1849. Member of legislative council, 1851. Ordained an apostle and appointed second counselor in First Presidency by Brigham Young, 4 Jan. 1857, in Salt Lake City. President of territorial legislative council, 1858–1863. Presided over European mission, 1864–1865, 1885–1887. Appointed counselor to Quorum of the Twelve, 6 Oct. 1877. Died in Salt Lake City.

Weston, Samuel (24 Oct. 1783–14 Dec. 1846), blacksmith, joiner, carpenter. Born in Belfast, Ireland. Moved to Ulverston, Lancashire, England, by 1812. Married Margaret Cleminson Gibson, 28 June 1812, in Ulverston. Joined British navy, 1812; captured by Americans and defected. Moved to Green Co., Kentucky, by 1816; to Malta Bend, Saline Co., Missouri, by 1820; to Lillard Co. (later Jackson Co.), Missouri, by 1821; and to what later became Independence, Jackson Co., by 1824. Elected deputy clerk of county court and recorder of deeds, contracted to build first courthouse, and served as election clerk, 1828, in Independence. Elected Jackson Co. judge, 1829. Justice of the peace, 1830–1833, in Independence. Member of Baptist church. Member of committee appointed to negotiate departure of Latter-day Saints from Jackson Co., July 1833. Involved in lawsuit over land against William W. Phelps and Oliver Cowdery, 1835, in Independence. Justice of the peace, 1838–1842, in Independence. Died in Independence.

Wheat, Almeron (7 Mar. 1813–12 June 1895), attorney. Born near Auburn, Cayuga Co., New York. Son of Luther Wheat and Elmira Marvin. Moved to Venice, Cayuga Co., by 1830. Moved to Ohio, before 1837. Served as prosecuting attorney in Marion Co., Ohio, 1837–1839. Moved to Quincy, Adams Co., Illinois, 1839. Married Laura Ann Harris, 9 June 1842, at Adams Co. Served as state representative from Adams Co., 1842–1844. Died in Quincy.

Whitmer, David (7 Jan. 1805–25 Jan. 1888), farmer, livery keeper. Born near Harrisburg, Dauphin Co., Pennsylvania. Son of Peter Whitmer Sr. and Mary Musselman. Raised Presbyterian. Moved to Ontario Co., New York, shortly after birth. Arranged for completion of translation of Book of Mormon in his father's home, Fayette, Seneca Co., New York, June 1829. Baptized by JS, June 1829, in Seneca Lake, Seneca Co. One of the Three Witnesses of the Book of Mormon, 1829. Among six original members of church and ordained an elder, 6 Apr. 1830. Married Julia Ann Jolly, 9 Jan. 1831, at Seneca Co. Migrated from Fayette to Kirtland, Geauga Co., Ohio, 1831. Ordained a high priest, 25 Oct. 1831, at Orange, Cuyahoga Co., Ohio. Served mission to Jackson Co., Missouri, with Harvey G. Whitlock, 1831. Driven from Jackson Co. by vigilantes, Nov. 1833; located in Clay Co., Missouri. Appointed president of church in Missouri, 7 July 1834. Left for Kirtland, Sept. 1834. Moved to Far West, Caldwell Co., Missouri, by 1837. Rejected as president in Missouri at meetings in Far West, 5 Feb. 1838. Excommunicated, 13 Apr. 1838, at Far West. Moved to Clay Co. and then to Richmond, Ray Co., Missouri, 1838, where he operated a livery stable. Ordained by William E. McLellin to preside over McLellinite Church of Christ, 1847, but later rejected that movement. Elected mayor of Richmond, 1867–1868. Later set forth his claims in *An Address to All Believers in Christ, by a Witness to the Divine Authenticity of the Book of Mormon*, 1887. Died at Richmond.

Whitney, Elizabeth Ann Smith (26 Dec. 1800–15 Feb. 1882). Born at Derby, New Haven Co., Connecticut. Daughter of Gibson Smith and Polly Bradley. Moved to Ohio, 1819. Married Newel K. Whitney, 20 Oct. 1822, at Kirtland, Geauga Co., Ohio. Shortly after, joined Reformed Baptist (later Disciples of Christ or Campbellite) movement. Baptized into LDS church by missionaries to unorganized Indian Territory under Oliver Cowdery, Nov. 1830. Left Kirtland for Far West, Caldwell Co., Missouri, fall 1838, but at St. Louis learned that Latter-day Saints were being driven from Missouri. Located at Carrollton, Greene Co., Illinois, winter 1838–1839. Moved to Quincy, Adams Co., Illinois, winter 1839–1840, and then Commerce (later Nauvoo), Hancock Co., Illinois, spring 1840. Appointed counselor in presidency of Female Relief Society at Nauvoo, 17 Mar. 1842. Moved to Winter Quarters, unorganized U.S. territory (later in Omaha, Douglas Co., Nebraska), Feb. 1846. Migrated to Salt Lake Valley, arriving 24 Sept. 1848. Second counselor to Eliza R. Snow in presidency of Relief Society, 1866–1882. Died at Salt Lake City.

Whitney, Newel Kimball (3/5 Feb. 1795–23 Sept. 1850), trader, merchant. Born at Marlborough, Windham Co., Vermont. Son of Samuel Whitney and Susanna Kimball.

Merchant at Plattsburg, Clinton Co., New York, 1814. Mercantile clerk for Algernon Sidney Gilbert at Painesville, Geauga Co., Ohio, ca. 1817. Opened store in Kirtland, Geauga Co., by 1822. Married Elizabeth Ann Smith, 20 Oct. 1822, in Geauga Co. Member of Reformed Baptist (later Disciples of Christ or Campbellite) faith. Entered partnership with Algernon Sidney Gilbert in N. K. Whitney & Co. store, by 1827. Baptized into LDS church by missionaries to unorganized Indian Territory, Nov. 1830. Appointed bishop at Kirtland, 1831. Traveled with JS to Missouri and then to New York City, Albany, and Boston, 1832. Member of United Firm, 1832, in Kirtland. En route to Missouri, fall 1838, when difficulties in that state were confirmed at St. Louis. Located his family temporarily at Carrollton, Greene Co., Illinois, and returned to Kirtland to conduct business. Moved family from Carrollton to Quincy, Adams Co., Illinois, and then Commerce (later Nauvoo), Hancock Co., Illinois. Appointed bishop of Middle Ward at Commerce, Oct. 1839. Nauvoo city alderman, 1841–1843. Member of Nauvoo Masonic Lodge. Member of Council of Fifty, 1844. Ordained a high priest, by Dec. 1845. Joined exodus of Latter-day Saints into Iowa Territory and Winter Quarters, unorganized U.S. territory (later in Omaha, Douglas Co., Nebraska), 1846. Sustained as presiding bishop of church, 6 Apr. 1847. Migrated to Salt Lake Valley, Oct. 1848. Bishop of Salt Lake Eighteenth Ward and justice of the peace, 1849. Died at Salt Lake City.

Wight, Lyman (9 May 1796–31 Mar. 1858), farmer. Born at Fairfield, Herkimer Co., New York. Son of Levi Wight Jr. and Sarah Corbin. Served in War of 1812. Married Harriet Benton, 5 Jan. 1823, at Henrietta, Monroe Co., New York. Moved to Warrensville, Cuyahoga Co., Ohio, ca. 1826. Baptized into Reformed Baptist (later Disciples of Christ or Campbellite) faith by Sidney Rigdon, May 1829. Moved to Isaac Morley homestead at Kirtland, Geauga Co., Ohio, and joined with other Reformed Baptist families having all things in common, Feb. 1830. Lived at Mayfield, Cuyahoga Co., when baptized into LDS church in Chagrin River, 14 Nov. 1830, and confirmed by Oliver Cowdery at Kirtland, 18 Nov. 1830. Ordained an elder by Oliver Cowdery, 20 Nov. 1830. Ordained a high priest by JS, 4 June 1831. Ordained JS and Sidney Rigdon high priests, 3 June 1831. Served mission to Jackson Co., Missouri, via Detroit and Pontiac, Michigan Territory, June–Aug. 1831. Joined by family at Jackson Co., Sept. 1831; located at Prairie branch, Jackson Co. Moved to and presided over Big Blue settlement, Jackson Co. Driven from Jackson Co. into Clay Co., Missouri, Nov. 1833. Recruited volunteers for Camp of Israel expedition to Missouri, 1834. Member of Clay Co. high council, 1834. Moved to Caldwell Co., Missouri, 1837. Elected colonel at organization of Caldwell Co. militia, Aug. 1837. Moved to Adam-ondi-Ahman, Daviess Co., Missouri, 1838. Member of Adam-ondi-Ahman stake presidency, 1838. Imprisoned with JS at Richmond, Ray Co.; Liberty, Clay Co.; and Gallatin, Daviess Co., Missouri, 1838–1839. Allowed to escape Missouri imprisonment during change of venue to Columbia, Boone Co., Missouri. Moved to Quincy, Adams Co., Illinois, summer 1839. Counselor in Zarahemla stake presidency, Lee Co., Iowa Territory, Oct. 1839. Member of Nauvoo House Association. Ordained member of Quorum of the Twelve, 8 Apr. 1841, at Nauvoo, Hancock Co., Illinois. Member of Nauvoo City Council, 1841–1843. Member of Nauvoo Masonic Lodge. Leader in procuring lumber for Nauvoo temple and Nauvoo House from Wisconsin pineries on Black River, Wisconsin Territory, 1843–1844. Served mission to eastern states to campaign for JS as candidate for U.S. president, 1844. Returned to Wisconsin Territory, 1844–1845. Led company of some 150 Latter-day Saints from Wisconsin Territory to Republic of Texas, arriving in Nov. 1845. Moved to Zodiac, Gillespie Co., Texas. Excommunicated, 3 Dec. 1848. Died at Dexter, Medina Co., Texas.

Wightman, William A. (12 Dec. 1807–Sept. 1842). Married Dolly Eaton, 31 Oct. 1832. Baptized into LDS church, by 1836. Ordained an elder, 27 Feb. 1836, in Geauga Co., Ohio. Laid out town of Ramus (later Webster), Hancock Co., Illinois, 1840. Served as bishop, 1841, in Ramus. Lived at Nauvoo, Hancock Co., after 1841. Member of Nauvoo Legion, 1841. Member of Nauvoo Masonic Lodge. Died in Nauvoo.

Woodruff, Wilford (1 Mar. 1807–2 Sept. 1898), farmer, miller. Born at Farmington, Hartford Co., Connecticut. Son of Aphek Woodruff and Beulah Thompson. Moved to Richland, Oswego Co., New York, 1832. Baptized into LDS church by Zera Pulsipher, 31 Dec. 1833, near Richland. Ordained a teacher, 2 Jan. 1834, at Richland. Moved to Kirtland, Geauga Co., Ohio, Apr. 1834. Participated in Camp of Israel expedition to Missouri, 1834. Ordained a priest, 5 Nov. 1834. Served mission to Arkansas, Tennessee, and Kentucky, 1834–1836. Ordained an elder, 1835. Appointed member of the Seventy, 31 May 1836. Married to Phoebe Carter by Frederick G. Williams, 13 Apr. 1837, at Kirtland. Served missions to New England and Fox Islands off coast of Maine, 1837–1838. Ordained member of Quorum of the Twelve by Brigham Young, 26 Apr. 1839, at Far West, Caldwell Co., Missouri. Served mission to Great Britain, 1839–1841. Member of city council, 1841–1843, in Nauvoo, Hancock Co., Illinois. Member of Nauvoo Masonic Lodge. Served mission to eastern states to raise funds for building Nauvoo temple, 1843. Served mission to eastern states to campaign for JS as candidate for U.S. president, 1844. Presided over British mission, Aug. 1844–Apr. 1846. Member of Brigham Young pioneer company that journeyed to Salt Lake Valley, 1847. Served mission to eastern states, 1848–1850. Member of Utah territorial legislature. Appointed assistant church historian, 7 Apr. 1856. President of St. George temple, Utah Territory, 1877. President of Quorum of the Twelve, 1880. Sustained as church historian and general church recorder, 1883. President of church, 7 Apr. 1889–2 Sept. 1898. Died at San Francisco.

Woodworth, Lucien (3 Apr. 1799–after 1860), architect, laborer, carpenter. Born in Thetford, Orange Co., Vermont. Married Phebe Watrous. Moved to Ellisburg, Jefferson Co., New York, by 1830; to Missouri, by 1839; and to Nauvoo, Hancock Co., Illinois, by 1841. Architect of Nauvoo House. Appointed aide-de-camp in Nauvoo Legion, May 1841. Member of Nauvoo Masonic Lodge. Member of Council of Fifty, 1844. Traveled to Texas to purchase land for Mormon settlement, 1844. Sent by JS to deliver letter explaining Mormon difficulties to Illinois governor Thomas Ford, 22 June 1844. Baptized into LDS church, by 1845. Ordained a high priest, by 1845. Moved to Pottawattamie Co., Iowa, by 1849; to San Bernardino, San Bernardino Co., California, by 1854; to Lehi, Utah Co., Utah Territory, by 1856; and back to San Bernardino, by 1860.

Woolley, Edwin (27 June 1807–14 Oct. 1881), farmer, coal miner, cattleman, builder, merchant. Born in East Bradford Township, Chester Co., Pennsylvania. Son of John Woolley and Rachel Dilworth. Raised in Quaker faith. Married Mary Wichersham, 24 Mar. 1831, in Columbiana Co., Ohio. Moved to East Rochester, Columbiana Co., by 1833. Baptized into LDS church by Lorenzo D. Barnes, 24 Dec. 1837, in West Township, Columbiana Co. Ordained a high priest, 6 May 1838, in West Township. Served as president of branch at East Rochester. Moved to Quincy, Adams Co., Illinois, 1839. Served mission to Pennsylvania, 1840. Moved to Nauvoo, Hancock Co., Illinois, 1840. Member of Nauvoo Masonic Lodge. Served mission to Massachusetts and Connecticut, 1842. Migrated to Salt Lake City, Sept. 1848. Elected to Utah territorial legislature, 1851. Died in Salt Lake City.

Young, Brigham (1 June 1801–29 Aug. 1877), carpenter, painter, glazier. Born at Whitingham, Windham Co., Vermont. Son of John Young and Abigail (Nabby) Howe. Brought up in Methodist household; later joined Methodist Church. Moved to Sherburne, Chenango Co., New York, 1804. Married first Miriam Angeline Works of Aurelius, Cayuga Co., New York, 8 Oct. 1824. Lived at Mendon, Monroe Co., New York, when baptized into LDS church by Eleazer Miller, 9/15 Apr. 1832. Wife died, 8 Sept. 1832. Served missions to New York and Upper Canada, 1832–1833. Migrated to Kirtland, Geauga Co., Ohio, 1833. Labored on Kirtland temple. Married second Mary Ann Angell, 31 Mar. 1834, in Geauga Co. Participated in Camp of Israel expedition to Missouri, 1834. Ordained member of Quorum of the Twelve, 14 Feb. 1835. Served mission to New York and New England, 1835–1837. Fled Kirtland, 22 Dec. 1837. Joined JS en route to Far West, Caldwell Co., Missouri; arrived with him 14 Mar. 1838. Member of presidency pro tempore of church in Far West, 1838. Directed Mormon evacuation from Missouri. Forced to leave Far West; reached Quincy, Adams Co., Illinois, Feb. 1839. Served mission to England, 1839–1841, departing from Commerce (later Nauvoo), Hancock Co., Illinois. Member of Nauvoo City Council, 1841–1845. Member of Nauvoo Masonic Lodge. Participated in plural marriage during JS's lifetime. Officiator in proxy baptisms for the dead in Nauvoo, 1843. Served mission to campaign for JS as candidate for U.S. president, 1844. With the Twelve, sustained to administer affairs of church after JS's death, 8 Aug. 1844, at Nauvoo. Directed Mormon migration from Nauvoo to Salt Lake Valley, 1846–1848. Appointed president of church, Dec. 1847. Superintendent of Indian affairs for Utah Territory, 1851–1857. Directed establishment of hundreds of communities in western U.S. Died at Salt Lake City.

Young, Richard M. (20 Feb. 1798–28 Nov. 1861), attorney, judge, politician. Born in Fayette Co., Kentucky. Moved to Jonesboro, Union Co., Illinois. Admitted to Illinois bar, 1817, in Jonesboro. Served as state representative from Union Co., 1820–1822. Married Matilda M. James, 25 June 1820, in St. Genevieve Co., Missouri. Served as captain in Illinois militia; as Illinois circuit judge, 1825–1827; and as presidential elector, 1828. Moved to Kaskaskia, Randolph Co., Illinois, before Apr. 1829. Served as Illinois circuit judge, 1829–1837. Moved to Galena, Jo Daviess Co., Illinois. Moved to Quincy, Adams Co., Illinois. Served as U.S. senator, 1837–1843. Justice of Illinois Supreme Court, 1843–1847. Served as clerk of U.S. House of Representatives, 1850–1851. Died in Washington DC.

Younger, Katharine Smith (28 July 1813–2 Feb. 1900), seamstress, weaver. Born at Lebanon, Grafton Co., New Hampshire. Daughter of Joseph Smith Sr. and Lucy Mack. Moved to Norwich, Windsor Co., Vermont, fall 1813; to Palmyra, Ontario Co., New York, 1816–Jan. 1817; and to Farmington (later Manchester), Ontario Co., 1818. Reported hearing JS's recitals concerning heavenly visitations and reported actually lifting gold plates. Baptized into LDS church by David Whitmer, 9 June 1830, at Seneca Lake, Seneca Co., New York. Migrated to Kirtland, Geauga Co., Ohio, from Seneca Co., May 1831. Married first to Wilkins Jenkins Salisbury by Sidney Rigdon, 8 June 1831, at Kirtland. After marriage, settled at Chardon, Geauga Co., 1831. Left Ohio for Far West, Caldwell Co., Missouri, May 1838. After expulsion from Missouri, located near present-day Bardolph, McDonough Co., Illinois, 1839. Moved to Plymouth, Hancock Co., Illinois, summer 1843. Moved to Nauvoo, Hancock Co., by 1845. Lived at Webster, Fountain Green Township, Hancock Co., fall 1847. Husband died, 28 Oct. 1853, in Plymouth. Married second Joseph Younger, 3 May 1857, in Hancock Co. Received into RLDS church, 1873, based on original baptism. Died at Fountain Green.

Ecclesiastical Officers and Church Appointees

The following charts show the general leadership of the Church of Jesus Christ of Latter-day Saints as well as local ecclesiastical officers in Nauvoo, Illinois, between 1839 and April 1843. The charts also identify the temple recorder and members of the Nauvoo temple committee and Nauvoo House Association. Readers wishing to conduct further research may consult the documented organizational charts posted on the Joseph Smith Papers website.

First Presidency, Quorum of the Twelve, and Patriarch

The following chart shows the members of the First Presidency and Quorum of the Twelve Apostles, as well as the church patriarch, with their dates of service. By 1839 the titles and offices of the First Presidency, which had varied in earlier years, were relatively stable, consisting of a president and two counselors; flexibility in its organization is evident, however, in positions held by Hyrum Smith, Amasa Lyman, and John C. Bennett. The responsibilities of the members of the Quorum of the Twelve, whose duties had been proselytizing and overseeing scattered branches of the church, expanded in Nauvoo as they took on significant administrative tasks. After the deaths of JS and Hyrum Smith on 27 June 1844, the First Presidency dissolved and the Quorum of the Twelve presided over the church until Brigham Young was sustained as church president in December 1847. For more information on the following individuals' terms of service, see the Biographical Directory in this volume.

Office	1839	1840	1841	1842	1843
First Presidency: President	Joseph Smith Jr. 6 Apr. 1830–27 June 1844				
First Presidency: Associate President[1]			Hyrum Smith 19 Jan. 1841–27 June 1844		
First Presidency: Counselors	Sidney Rigdon 8 Mar. 1832–27 June 1844				
	Hyrum Smith 7 Nov. 1837–19 Jan. 1841		William Law 19 Jan. 1841–before 8 Jan. 1844		
					Amasa Lyman Ca. 4 Feb. 1843–27 June 1844[2]
First Presidency: Assistant President			John C. Bennett 8 Apr. 1841–11 May 1842[3]		
Quorum of the Twelve: President	Brigham Young 14 Feb. 1835–27 Dec. 1847				
Quorum of the Twelve: Members	Heber C. Kimball 14 Feb. 1835–27 Dec. 1847				
	Orson Hyde 14 Feb. 1835–4 May 1839; 27 June 1839–28 Nov. 1878				

1. The term "associate president" was applied by later historians to describe Hyrum Smith's unusual office or role in the First Presidency, but it was not used during his lifetime. A revelation dated 19 January 1841 named Hyrum Smith church patriarch as well as "a prophet, seer, and a revelator" to the church. He was to "act in concert" with Joseph Smith, who would "show unto him the keys whereby he may ask and receive, and be crowned with the same blessing, and glory, and honor, and priesthood, and gifts of the priesthood, that once were put upon . . . Oliver Cowdery." Cowdery had received the keys of the priesthood in connection with Joseph Smith, had been sustained as "Second Elder of the Church" on 6 April 1830, and had served in the church's presidency from December 1834 to April 1838 under the titles "assistant president" and "assistant Councillor."

2. See 255n354 herein.

3. Bennett was appointed assistant president until Sidney Rigdon's health improved. On 15 June 1842, church leaders published a notice saying they had chosen to "withdraw the hand of fellowship from General John C. Bennett" effective 11 May 1842.

ECCLESIASTICAL OFFICERS AND CHURCH APPOINTEES

OFFICE	1839	1840	1841	1842	1843
QUORUM OF THE TWELVE: MEMBERS (CONT.)	Parley P. Pratt 14 Feb. 1835–13 May 1857				
	William Smith 14 Feb. 1835–4 May 1839; 25 May 1839–6 Oct. 1845				
	Orson Pratt 14 Feb. 1835–20 Aug. 1842; 20 Jan. 1843–3 Oct. 1881				
	John E. Page 19 Dec. 1838–9 Feb. 1846				
	John Taylor 19 Dec. 1838–10 Oct. 1880				
	Wilford Woodruff 26 Apr. 1839–7 Apr. 1889				
	George A. Smith 26 Apr. 1839–7 Oct. 1868				
		Willard Richards 14 Apr. 1840–27 Dec. 1847			
			Lyman Wight 7 Apr. 1841–3 Dec. 1848		
			Hyrum Smith 19 Jan. 1841–27 June 1844		
				Amasa Lyman 20 Aug. 1842–6 Oct. 1867[4]	
CHURCH PATRIARCH	Joseph Smith Sr. 6 Dec. 1834–14 Sept. 1840				

---

4. See 255n354 herein.

Presidents of the Seventy

The following chart lists the individuals who presided over the Quorum of the Seventy. Seventy was an office in the Melchizedek Priesthood patterned after the seventy individuals referred to in the New Testament (Luke 10:1–17) who were given certain powers and authority. According to a JS revelation, they were to "act in the name of the Lord, under the direction of the twelve . . . in building up the church and regulating all the affairs of the same, in all nations." Unlike most other Mormon ecclesiastical organizations, over which a president and two counselors presided, the Quorum of the Seventy was led by seven presidents.

Presidents of the Seventy
Josiah Butterfield
James Foster
Levi Hancock
Henry Harriman
Daniel Miles
Zera Pulsipher
Joseph Young

Nauvoo Ecclesiastical Officers

The following charts identify members of the Nauvoo stake presidency and high council as well as bishops in Nauvoo. In 1834 the Kirtland, Ohio, high council was organized and granted appellate authority over the disciplinary decisions made by other high councils and branches of the church. The high council of the church at Nauvoo also exercised this power, overturning on appeal multiple decisions that were first adjudicated by local branches outside of Nauvoo. On 20 August 1842 the Nauvoo high council divided Nauvoo and the immediate surrounding area into thirteen ecclesiastical wards and districts; the council also appointed ten new bishops to join currently serving bishops Newel K. Whitney, George Miller, and Isaac Higbee. Samuel Smith, Daniel Carn, and William Spencer were not ordained with the other appointed bishops on 21 August 1842, though Carn was serving as a bishop in Nauvoo by December 1843. For a time, Isaac Higbee and possibly Newel K. Whitney served as bishops of more than one ward. In addition to the individuals named below, Vinson Knight, Samuel Smith, and Shadrach Roundy were appointed on 19 January 1841 to preside over the Nauvoo bishopric, though it is unclear if they ever functioned in that capacity.

Stake Presidency	*High Council*	
William Marks, president	James Allred	Newel Knight
Austin Cowles, first counselor	Alpheus Cutler	Henry G. Sherwood
Charles C. Rich, second counselor	David Fullmer	Leonard Soby
	Thomas Grover	Lewis Dunbar Wilson
	George W. Harris	
	William Huntington Sr.	
	Aaron Johnson	

Bishops	
October 1839–20 August 1842	21 August 1842
Upper Ward Edward Partridge, died May 1840 George Miller, appointed Jan. 1841 *Middle Ward* Newel K. Whitney *Lower Ward* Vinson Knight, died July 1842 *Other* Isaac Higbee, ordained 19 Feb. 1841	Israel Calkins David Evans Jacob Foutz Jonathan H. Hale Isaac Higbee Tarlton Lewis George Miller John Murdock Hezekiah Peck Newel K. Whitney

CHURCH APPOINTEES

The following chart lists nonecclesiastical church appointees. Members of the Nauvoo temple committee were appointed at a church conference on 3 October 1840. The committee hired laborers, oversaw the construction of the temple and the disbursement of supplies and pay to laborers, and gave receipts to those who made donations for building the temple. Members of the Nauvoo House Association, who oversaw the construction of the Nauvoo House, were appointed by revelation on 19 January 1841. A month later, Illinois governor Thomas Carlin signed a bill incorporating the Nauvoo House Association and authorizing its trustees to issue stock to the value of $150,000 to finance the venture. The temple recorder was first appointed in December 1841; his primary responsibility was to record donations made by church members for the construction of the Nauvoo temple.

Temple Committee	*Nauvoo House Association*	*Temple Recorder*

Reynolds Cahoon
Alpheus Cutler
Elias Higbee
	Peter Haws
	George Miller
	John Snider
	Lyman Wight
		Willard Richards,
		   appointed 13 Dec. 1841
		William Clayton,
		   appointed 3 Sept. 1842

Nauvoo City Officers

The following chart identifies significant city offices in Nauvoo, Illinois, and the names of the individuals who held those offices between February 1841 and April 1843. The city charter for Nauvoo, approved 16 December 1840 to take effect the first Monday of February 1841, called for a city council consisting of a mayor, four aldermen, and nine councilors, who would be elected and serve for two years. The charter made provision for the city council to add to the number of aldermen and councilors if necessary. Other city officers were appointed or elected by the city council. The first city election was held 1 February 1841. An additional office of vice mayor was created 22 January 1842, though the holders of this office retained their seats as city councilors. Councilors and aldermen are listed in the order in which they most commonly appeared in municipal records.

The mayor and aldermen served as justices of the peace within the limits of the city of Nauvoo. The charter prescribed that the mayor's court "had exclusive jurisdiction in all cases arising under the ordinances of the corporation." The mayor also served as chief justice of the municipal court, and the aldermen as associate justices of that court, to which appeal could be taken "from any decision or judgement of said Mayor or Aldermen, arising under the city ordinances." From the municipal court, appeal could be made to the Circuit Court of Hancock County.

When council seats became vacant because of death, resignation, or appointment to other office, the vacancies were filled by election or appointment by the city council. If members of the city council were to be absent for significant lengths of time, substitute or temporary councilors were elected and sworn in to fill the vacancy. These temporary councilors are not listed in the following chart.

NAUVOO CITY OFFICERS

Office	1841	1842	1843
Mayor	John C. Bennett 3 Feb. 1841–19 May 1842		Joseph Smith Jr. 19 May 1842–27 June 1844
Vice Mayor		Joseph Smith Jr. 22 Jan. 1842–19 May 1842	Hyrum Smith 19 May 1842–6 Feb. 1843
			William Smith 19 May 1842–6 Feb. 1843
City Councilors	Joseph Smith Jr. 3 Feb. 1841–19 May 1842		
	Don Carlos Smith 3 Feb. 1841–7 Aug. 1841	Brigham Young 4 Sept. 1841–3 Feb. 1845	
	Hyrum Smith 3 Feb. 1841–27 June 1844		
	Charles C. Rich 3 Feb. 1841–6 Feb. 1843		
	John P. Greene 3 Feb. 1841–6 Feb. 1843		
	John Barnett 3 Feb. 1841–6 Feb. 1843		
	Vinson Knight 3 Feb. 1841–31 Jul. 1842		Amasa Lyman 5 Aug. 1842–6 Feb. 1843
	Wilson Law 3 Feb. 1841–6 Feb. 1843		
	Sidney Rigdon 8 Feb. 1841–1 Nov. 1841	William Law 1 Nov. 1841–6 Feb. 1843	
		John Taylor 30 Oct. 1841–3 Feb. 1845	
		Orson Pratt 30 Oct. 1841–3 Feb. 1845	
		Hugh McFall 30 Oct. 1841–19 May 1842	George A. Smith 19 May 1842–6 Feb. 1843

Office	1841	1842	1843
City Councilors (cont.)		**Heber C. Kimball** 30 Oct. 1841–3 Feb. 1845	
		Lyman Wight 1 Nov. 1841–6 Feb. 1843	
		Willard Richards 1 Nov. 1841–6 Feb. 1843	
		Wilford Woodruff 1 Nov. 1841–6 Feb. 1843	
		Samuel Smith 23 May 1842–6 Feb. 1843	
			Orson Hyde 6 Feb. 1843–3 Feb. 1845
			Sylvester Emmons 6 Feb. 1843–21 June 1844
			Benjamin Warrington 6 Feb. 1843–3 Feb. 1845
			Daniel Spencer 6 Feb. 1843–10 Aug. 1844
Aldermen	**Daniel H. Wells** 3 Feb. 1841–3 Feb. 1845		
	William Marks 3 Feb. 1841–6 Feb. 1843		
	Newel K. Whitney 3 Feb. 1841–6 Feb. 1843		
	Samuel Smith 3 Feb. 1841–23 May 1842		
	Gustavus Hills 23 Oct. 1841–6 Feb. 1843		

NAUVOO CITY OFFICERS

Office	1841	1842	1843
ALDERMEN (CONT.)		Orson Spencer 23 Oct. 1841–3 Feb. 1845	
		George W. Harris 30 Oct. 1841–after 8 Feb. 1845	
		Hiram Kimball 30 Oct. 1841–6 Feb. 1843	
			George A. Smith 11 Feb. 1843–10 Aug. 1844
			Samuel Bennett 4 Mar. 1843–3 Feb. 1845
MARSHALL	Henry G. Sherwood 3 Feb. 1841–21 Dec. 1843		
		Dimick Huntington 23 Oct. 1841–9 Apr. 1842	
TREASURER	Robert B. Thompson 3 Feb. 1841–27 Aug. 1841	John Fullmer 4 Sept. 1841–9 Sept. 1842	William Clayton 9 Sept. 1842–ca. 1846
CITY RECORDER AND CLERK OF THE MUNICIPAL COURT	James Sloan 3 Feb. 1841–12 Aug. 1843		
CORONER		Dimick Huntington 23 May 1842–ca. 1846	
SEXTON		William D. Huntington 4 Sept. 1841–ca. 1846	

Nauvoo Legion Officers

The charter for the city of Nauvoo, Illinois, approved 16 December 1840, allowed for the formation of the Nauvoo Legion, a unit of the Illinois state militia. The city council passed an ordinance officially organizing the Nauvoo Legion on 3 February 1841. The first meeting of the legion was held on 4 February 1841, when John C. Bennett, Don Carlos Smith, and other commissioned officers of the Illinois state militia elected the general officers of the legion. Other positions were filled during the following months.

The Nauvoo Legion comprised two brigades, or "cohorts," each headed by a brigadier general. The first cohort consisted of cavalry and the second of infantry and artillery troops. Officers retained their rank unless terminated by resignation, death, or cashiering out of the Nauvoo Legion. At its largest, the legion numbered between two thousand and three thousand men.

The following chart identifies the staffs of the lieutenant general, major general, and brigadier generals of the Nauvoo Legion, and the men who held the various offices between February 1841 and April 1843. Names are followed by the date of rank; dates of formal commission by the governor, when known, are provided in parentheses. Ending dates are not given except in cases of termination. Positions, dates of rank, and commission dates are taken from returns to the adjutant general of the state and records of the Illinois state militia.

NAUVOO LEGION OFFICERS

Lieutenant General's Staff

Office	1841	1842	1843
Lieutenant General	Joseph Smith Jr. 5 Feb. 1841 (11 Mar. 1841)		
Inspector General	John C. Bennett 5 Feb. 1841 (16 Oct. 1841)–12 Apr. 1842	James Arlington Bennet 12 Apr. 1842 (2 May 1842)	
Drill Officer	Albert P. Rockwood 9 Mar. 1841		
Judge Advocate	Sidney Rigdon 3 July 1841 (16 Oct. 1841)	John Taylor 6 Nov. 1841 (14 Dec. 1841)	
Aides-de-Camp	William Law 9 Mar. 1841		
	Robert B. Thompson 9 Mar. 1841–27 Aug. 1841		
	Isaac Morley 6 Apr. 1841 (16 Oct. 1841)		
	Zenos Gurley 6 Apr. 1841 (16 June 1841)		
	Jefferson Hunt 1 May 1841 (15 June 1841)		
			William Hall 15 Apr. 1843
			John Cowan 18 Apr. 1843
Guards	James Allred 9 Mar. 1841		
	Thomas Grover 9 Mar. 1841		

Office	1841	1842	1843
Guards (cont.)	C. M. Kreymeyer 9 Mar. 1841		
	John Butler 9 Mar. 1841		
	John Snider 9 Mar. 1841		
	Alpheus Cutler 9 Mar. 1841		
	Reynolds Cahoon 9 Mar. 1841		
	Elias Higbee 9 Mar. 1841		
	Henry G. Sherwood 9 Mar. 1841		
	William Marks 9 Mar. 1841		
	Samuel Smith 9 Mar. 1841		
	Vinson Knight 9 Mar. 1841–31 July 1842		
	Shadrach Roundy 6 Apr. 1841 (16 Oct. 1841)		
Herald and Armor Bearer		Edward Hunter 9 Sept. 1841 (14 Dec. 1841)	

Major General's Staff

Office	1841	1842	1843
Major General	John C. Bennett 5 Feb. 1841–30 June 1842		Wilson Law 13 Aug. 1842 (19 Sept. 1842)

Office	1841	1842	1843
Adjutant General	Hugh McFall 9 Mar. 1841		
Assistant Adjutant General—First Cohort		Hiram Kimball 3 June 1842	
Assistant Adjutant General—Second Cohort		Windsor Lyon 3 June 1842	
Surgeon General	Robert D. Foster 9 Mar. 1841		
Cornet		George Cooke 7 June 1842	Garrett Ivins 15 Apr. 1843 (8 June 1843)
Quartermaster General	George W. Robinson 9 Mar. 1841 / Wilson Law 9 Mar. 1841	Leonard Soby 1 May 1841 (15 June 1841)	
Commissary General	Daniel H. Wells 9 Mar. 1841		
Paymaster General	John Fullmer 9 Mar. 1841		
Chaplain	Hyrum Smith 9 Mar. 1841		
Assistant Inspector General—First Cohort	Carlos Gove 3 July 1841 (16 Oct. 1841)	John Bills 13 Nov. 1841 (14 Dec. 1841)	Davidson Hibbard 12 Mar. 1842
Assistant Inspector General—Second Cohort	David Smith 3 July 1841 (16 Oct. 1841)		
Aides-de-Camp	Carlos Gove 4 Mar. 1841 (16 Oct. 1841)		
	Lucien Woodworth 1 May 1841 (15 June 1841)		

Office	1841	1842	1843
AIDES-DE-CAMP (CONT.)		George Schindle 1 May 1841 (15 June 1841)	
		Lyman Wight 1 May 1841 (15 June 1841)	
		Chauncey Higbee 13 Nov. 1841 (14 Dec. 1841)	
			Jacob B. Backenstos 12 Mar. 1842
			John Eagle 12 Mar. 1842
			James Gordon Bennett 28 May 1842 (2 June 1842)
			Amos Dean 7 June 1842
			Francis Higbee 7 June 1842
			J. M. Binelo 7 June 1842
			Windsor Lyon 7 June 1842
			Robert Ivins 20 Apr. 1843 (8 June 1843)
WAR SECRETARY			James Sloan 12 Mar. 1842
QUARTERMASTER SERGEANT	James Robinson 9 Mar. 1841–20 Apr. 1841	Benjamin Warrington 1 May 1841 (15 June 1841)	
SERGEANT MAJOR	George Wyrick 9 Mar. 1841		

NAUVOO LEGION OFFICERS

Office	1841	1842	1843
Chief Musician		Edward Duzette 9 Mar. 1841	
Musicians		Levi Hancock 9 Mar. 1841	
		Dimick Huntington 9 Mar. 1841	
			Gustavus Hills 19 Mar. 1842
			William Pitt 2 Apr. 1842
Herald and Armor Bearer		Samuel Hicks 6 Apr. 1841 (16 Oct. 1841)	
First Cohort General Staff			
Brigadier General		Wilson Law 5 Feb. 1841–13 Aug. 1842	George Miller 23 Sep. 1842 (27 Apr. 1843)
Adjutant		(no record)	
Sergeant Major		(no record)	
Quartermaster Sergeant		(no record)	
Aides-de-Camp		Solon Foster 9 Mar. 1841	
			Erastus Derby 13 Nov. 1841 (14 Dec. 1841)
Assistant Quartermaster General			Windsor Lyon 1 Feb. 1842

Office	1841	1842	1843
Assistant Commissary General		Robert Ivins 1 Feb. 1842	
Surgeon	John F. Weld 9 Mar. 1841		
Assistant Chaplains		Brigham Young 3 July 1841 (16 Oct. 1841)	
		Heber C. Kimball 3 July 1841 (16 Oct. 1841)	
		Parley P. Pratt 3 July 1841 (16 Oct. 1841)	
		Orson Pratt 3 July 1841 (16 Oct. 1841)	
		Orson Hyde 3 July 1841 (16 Oct. 1841)	
		John E. Page 3 July 1841 (16 Oct. 1841)	
Herald and Armor Bearer		William Whitmarsh 1 Feb. 1842	

Second Cohort General Staff

Office	1841	1842	1843
Brigadier General	Don Carlos Smith 5 Feb. 1841– 7 Aug. 1841	Charles C. Rich 4 Sept. 1841 (14 Dec. 1841)	
Adjutant		(no record)	
Sergeant Major			Alanson Ripley 3 June 1842
Quartermaster Sergeant			Joseph B. Noble 3 June 1842

NAUVOO LEGION OFFICERS

Office	1841	1842	1843
Aides-de-Camp		Alexander McRae 9 Mar. 1841–1 Sept. 1842	
		Amasa Lyman 1 May 1841 (15 June 1841)–1 Sept. 1842	
Assistant Quartermaster General			John P. Greene 1 Mar. 1842
Assistant Commissary General			Joseph Young 1 Mar. 1842
Surgeon	James Kelly 9 Mar. 1841	Samuel Bennett 13 Nov. 1841 (14 Dec. 1841)	
Assistant Chaplains		John Taylor 3 July 1841 (16 Oct. 1841)–6 Nov. 1841	
		Wilford Woodruff 3 July 1841 (16 Oct. 1841)	
		William Smith 3 July 1841 (16 Oct. 1841)	
		Willard Richards 3 July 1841 (16 Oct. 1841)	
		George A. Smith 3 July 1841 (16 Oct. 1841)	
		William Marks 3 July 1841 (16 Oct. 1841)	
Herald and Armor Bearer			Philo Dibble 1 Mar. 1842

Glossary

This glossary defines terms appearing in this volume that have particular meaning in Mormon usage—especially ordinances, offices, and organizations. Terms are defined as they were used in the 1840s. Readers wishing to conduct further research may consult the fully documented glossary posted on the Joseph Smith Papers website.

Aaronic Priesthood. See "Priesthood."

Anointed. In this volume the term *anointed* is used in the metaphorical sense to mean chosen, elected, or otherwise designated by God to some position or responsibility.

Apostle. An office in the Melchizedek Priesthood. Responsibilities included being "special witnesses" of Jesus Christ. The Quorum of the Twelve Apostles was organized in February 1835 and given increased responsibilities in the early 1840s.

Baptism. Baptism by immersion, for the remission of sins, performed by one having the proper authority, was a requirement for church membership and an essential ordinance of salvation. Baptism was not to be performed for infants, but for those who had reached the age of accountability, which was defined as eight years old. During the JS era and beyond, some individuals were rebaptized for a remission of their sins after their initial baptism. Beginning in the 1840s, JS directed Latter-day Saints to perform vicarious baptisms on behalf of those who had died without having been baptized.

Bishop. Aaronic priesthood office whose duties included caring for church members' material needs, acting as a "judge in Israel" in settling disputes, and disciplining transgressors.

Branch. See "Stake."

Building committee. See "Temple committee."

Charter. See "Nauvoo charter."

Conference. Meetings dedicated to receiving reports, sustaining church officers, notifying members of appointments and ordinations, and providing instruction regarding policies and doctrine. Conferences provided an opportunity for assembled church leaders to counsel together and discuss substantive issues, and gave church members an opportunity to ratify leaders' decisions. Conferences for the whole church were held semiannually in Nauvoo and were attended by church leaders, lay members, and representatives from other branches of the church.

Confirmation. After baptism, new converts were "confirmed" members of the church and given the gift of the Holy Ghost through an ordinance performed by priesthood holders by the laying on of hands.

Consecration. A principle guiding church efforts to cooperatively and voluntarily share resources in building up communities and the church. Church members were encouraged to donate, or consecrate, money, goods, or labor to the church. During the early 1840s, most such offerings to the church went toward building the Nauvoo temple and Nauvoo House. See also "Tithing."

Dispensation. A period of God's work on earth, such as the "dispensation of the gospel of Abraham" (Vision, 3 Apr. 1836, in JS, Journal, 3 Apr. 1836, in *JSP*, J1:222 [D&C 110:12]). Latter-day Saints believed they were living in the "dispensation of the fulness of times" prophesied by the ancient apostle Paul, in which God will "gather together in one all things both which are in heaven and which are on earth" (Revelation, ca. Aug. 1830, in Doctrine and Covenants 50:3, 1835 ed. [D&C 27:13]; Ephesians 1:10). Revelation stated that JS was given "the Keys of this dispensation" (Vision, 3 Apr. 1836, in JS, Journal, 3 Apr. 1836, in *JSP*, J1:22 [D&C 110:16]). See also "Keys."

Elder. An office in the Melchizedek Priesthood signifying leadership and carrying no age requirement. The founding articles of the church outlined the duty of elders "to baptize, and to ordain other elders, priests, teachers, and deacons, and to administer bread and wine . . . to teach, expound exhort . . . and watch over the church; and to confirm the church . . . and to take the lead of all meetings" (Articles and covenants, 10 Apr. 1830, in Doctrine and Covenants 2:8, 1835 ed. [D&C 20:38–44]). All bearers of the Melchizedek Priesthood could be referred to as elders, regardless of the specific priesthood office they held. The term was also used to signify proselytizing missionaries generally.

Endow, endowment. The terms *endow, endowed,* and *endowment* were used to describe the bestowal of spiritual blessings upon the Latter-day Saints. First used during the Kirtland era, the terms came to refer to a specific temple ordinance introduced on 4 and 5 May 1842 in Nauvoo.

Female Relief Society of Nauvoo. An organization of women in the church founded by JS on 17 March 1842 in Nauvoo to provide relief to those in need and to prepare the women of the church to receive temple ordinances.

First Presidency. The presiding body of the church; consisted of a president (JS) and two or more counselors or assistant presidents.

Fulness of times. See "Dispensation."

Gathering. As directed by early revelations to JS, Latter-day Saints "gathered" in communities and congregations where they could receive instruction, take care of the poor, build temples, and prepare for the second coming of Christ. Latter-day Saints also anticipated a gathering, or restoration, of scattered Israel to the Holy Land.

High council. Each organized stake in the church generally had a high council, a group of twelve high priests organized "for the purpose of settling important difficulties, which might arise in the church, which could not be settled by the church, or the bishop's council, to the satisfaction of the parties" (Minutes, 17 Feb. 1834, in Doctrine and Covenants 5:1, 1835 ed. [D&C 102:2]). In addition to their judicial function, high councils played an important administrative role in the church. For congregations outside the jurisdiction of the standing high councils in Zion and her stakes, the Quorum of the Twelve constituted a traveling high council to regulate church affairs.

Keys. Early revelations equated "keys" with authority, which paralleled biblical use of the term. Keys were the governing authority in the priesthood and were therefore often associated with the First Presidency and the Quorum of the Twelve. JS stated that he received from divine messengers the several keys that constituted the authority necessary to lead the church. JS's revelations also connected the idea of keys to essential knowledge or understanding.

Laying on of hands. A ritual bestowing power, authority, or other blessings. One holding priesthood authority placed his hands upon another's head to confer the gift of the Holy Ghost, confer the priesthood, set apart to an office or calling, or offer a blessing for counsel, comfort, or healing.

License. The founding articles of the church instructed each holder of the priesthood to keep a certificate from the person who ordained him. Licenses were routinely issued to those ordained to the priesthood to certify their standing and authority in the church and could be revoked as a measure of church discipline.

Nauvoo charter. "An Act to Incorporate the City of Nauvoo," approved 16 December 1840 by the Illinois General Assembly, to legally organize the city of Nauvoo; provided for the creation of the city's executive, legislative, and judicial branches, as well as for establishing a university and militia. Nauvoo was the sixth city to be incorporated by the state of Illinois.

Nauvoo House Association. Incorporated 23 February 1841, the Nauvoo House Association oversaw the construction of the Nauvoo House (a boardinghouse) and financed its construction through the sale of association stock to those interested in investing in the project. See also "Nauvoo House," in Geographical Directory.

Nauvoo Legion. A contingent of the Illinois state militia, as provided for in the Nauvoo city charter. The legion, whose officers were to be commissioned by the governor, was to "be at the disposal of the mayor in executing the laws and ordinances of the city corporation, and the laws of the State, and at the disposal of the Governor for the public defence" (An Act to Incorporate the City of Nauvoo [16 Dec. 1840], *Laws of the State of Illinois* [1840–1841], p. 57, sec. 25).

Ordain, ordination. Priesthood offices were conferred on males, primarily adults, by the laying on of hands by those in authority. This conferral was frequently referred to as an *ordination*. Similarly, men or women could be "ordained" for a given calling or position by the laying on of hands in a sense later referred to as "setting apart." The term was also occasionally used in the generic sense, meaning to appoint, decree, or establish.

Ordinance. Religious rituals that early Latter-day Saints believed God had instituted for the blessing of humanity. Ordinances were performed by priesthood authority, were generally authorized by presiding officers holding the necessary priesthood keys, and often involved the making or renewing of covenants with God. Revelations singled out some ordinances, such as baptism and bestowal of the gift of the Holy Ghost, as necessary for salvation.

Patriarch. An office in the Melchizedek Priesthood with the authority and responsibility to give inspired blessings similar to those given by the Old Testament patriarchs. The blessings were recorded and preserved as church records.

Presidency. Priesthood quorums and various bodies of Latter-day Saints were overseen by presidencies. Presidencies generally followed the pattern of one president with two counselors, although the Quorum of the Twelve was presided over by a single president, and the original Quorum of the Seventy was led by seven presidents. Bishops and their counselors were designated in revelation as presidencies of the Aaronic Priesthood. See also "First Presidency."

Presiding elder. Priesthood leader responsible for a branch of the church. See also "Elder" and "Stake."

Priesthood. Power and authority from God delegated to man to govern the church and perform ordinances. Priesthood holders held responsibility for administering the sacrament of the Lord's Supper and other ordinances, overseeing pastoral duties, preaching, and proselytizing. JS oversaw the conferral of priesthood by the laying on of hands on ordinary adult male members of the church in good standing. No specialized training was required for ordination. Priesthood holders belonged to one of two general priesthood levels, which JS designated in 1835 as the Aaronic Priesthood and the higher Melchizedek Priesthood. Priesthood holders belonged to "quorums" organized by office. JS reported having received "keys," or governing authority in the priesthood, from resurrected biblical figures who appeared to him and to Oliver Cowdery. See also "Keys."

Quorum. Refers especially to a group to which individuals ordained to the Aaronic or Melchizedek priesthoods belonged. Quorums were organized by office, such as an "elders quorum." The organization of quorums provided leadership and a manageable structure for varied priesthood responsibilities.

Relief Society. See "Female Relief Society of Nauvoo."

Seal. To confirm, solemnize, or conclude. JS and other early Latter-day Saints used forms of the word *seal* when describing confirmations of religious proceedings, prayers, blessings, anointings, or marriages. Such sealings were performed in many ways: by the laying of hands on the person's head, with uplifted hands, by prayer, by announcement, with hosannas or amens, or by combinations of these. *Sealing* was also used in connection with the notion of power sufficient to bind (or loose) on earth and be recognized in heaven, or to consign to God's punishment or to salvation.

Stake. The ecclesiastical organization of Latter-day Saints in a particular locale. The terms *stake, branch,* and *church* were used in a roughly similar way, although the latter was also used to denote the church in its entirety or the Latter-day Saints generally in an area. Dozens of smaller branches, which were headed by a presiding elder or a high priest, existed throughout the eastern United States and Canada during the Nauvoo period. Stakes were typically larger local organizations of church members usually headed by a presidency, a high council, and a bishopric. Some revelations refer to stakes "to" or "of" Zion—places where substantial congregations of Latter-day Saints could be found outside the central place of gathering. This conceptualization drew on Old Testament imagery of the tent of Zion supported by cords fastened to stakes.

Temple. A building Latter-day Saints considered to be the House of the Lord, in which church members could hold worship services, conduct church business, and perform sacred priesthood ordinances essential for salvation. See also "Temple, Nauvoo," in Geographical Directory.

Temple committee. At a conference of the church on 3 October 1840, Alpheus Cutler, Reynolds Cahoon, and Elias Higbee were appointed as a committee responsible for managing the construction of the Nauvoo temple, which the Saints were commanded to build. The committee's duties included securing building materials, supervising construction, and managing the temple store, where hired workers could receive goods in exchange for their labor. See also "Temple, Nauvoo," in Geographical Directory.

Tithing. Tithing was defined in 1838 as a free-will offering of one-tenth of a person's annual interest or income, to be used for the construction of temples and other church needs. While church members in Nauvoo frequently contributed more than one-tenth, the "required" tithing for the Nauvoo temple was defined as "one tenth of all any one possessed at the commencement of the building, and one tenth part of all his increase from that time till the completion of the same, whether it be money or whatever he may be blessed with" ("Baptism for the Dead," *Times and Seasons,* 15 Dec. 1841, 3:626). Tithes could be paid in kind with such things as grain, produce, livestock, and donated labor. See also "Consecration."

Twelve Apostles. See "Apostle."

Urim and Thummim. Named in the Old Testament as an instrument or device of divination used by designated individuals; term was applied by Latter-day Saints to the "two stones in silver bows" JS used in translating the gold plates and to the "seer stones" he used for the same purpose.

Zion. In JS's earliest revelations, *Zion* was a synonym for God's work generally, but it soon came to mean the ideal society that JS sought to establish mirroring Enoch's righteous, unified, poverty-free community also called Zion. It also came to mean the place where God's people were to establish a holy city. On 20 July 1831, JS designated Independence, Jackson County, Missouri, as the site for the city of Zion—and Missouri generally as the "land" of Zion. Subsequent revelation made room for the expansion of Zion beyond a single city through the establishment of "stakes" where Saints would also gather. After the expulsion from Missouri, revelation described the stake at Nauvoo as the "cornerstone of Zion," allowing for a gathering to Nauvoo to take place without abandoning the prior geographical definition of Zion as centered in Missouri.

Essay on Sources

Historians' understanding of both the history of the Mormon church and JS's life during the Nauvoo era is greatly enhanced through the rich documentary record that exists for this period. Several of JS's close associates, including Wilford Woodruff, William Clayton, and Willard Richards, kept detailed journals during this time. These have been referenced repeatedly in this volume, generally to flesh out events and phenomena perfunctorily covered in JS's journal. Given the public nature of many of JS's activities, the editors of this volume made liberal use of several local contemporary newspapers for the same purpose. Of these, the *Times and Seasons* and *The Wasp* (later renamed the *Nauvoo Neighbor*)—two papers published in Nauvoo—have been most helpful, as they frequently carried detailed accounts of events JS's scribes could only briefly describe in the journals. The *Sangamo Journal* (Springfield, IL), *Quincy [IL] Whig,* and other contemporary papers have also been cited extensively, often for the light they shed on the movements and sentiments of anti-Mormons and dissenters affecting JS's life during this time.

The Nauvoo High Council Minutes, the Nauvoo City Council Minute Book, the Nauvoo Legion Minute Book, the Nauvoo Municipal Court Docket Book, and the Nauvoo Mayor's Court Docket Book are similarly invaluable for understanding JS's public and administrative roles in Nauvoo, the local militia, and the church. They also provide insight into how these various bodies were governed and into the issues that came before them. The Relief Society Minute Book provides the same type of information for the Female Relief Society of Nauvoo, as well as detailed accounts of several important discourses JS delivered to the leading women of the church. All of these, including the municipal records, are owned by The Church of Jesus Christ of Latter-day Saints today and are readily available to researchers. The Nauvoo Masonic Lodge Minute Book provides important information about JS and his associates' involvement with Freemasonry in Nauvoo and is an indispensable source for information on John C. Bennett's last days in Nauvoo.

Published collections of state statutes and various court decisions, as well as court records held in the LDS Church History Library and other locations, are instrumental in understanding the numerous legal issues raised in these journals. Records held in the Abraham Lincoln Presidential Library, in Springfield, Illinois, have been particularly helpful in explaining the resolution of Missouri's efforts to extradite JS for his alleged complicity in the 1842 assassination attempt on Lilburn W. Boggs. Additional light on other legal issues, as well as on numerous other issues raised in the journals, has been shed by various documents contained in the Joseph Smith Collection housed in the Church History Library. This collection contains many of JS's journals, correspondence, and legal records. Other collections held in the Church History Library and in Brigham Young University's L. Tom Perry Special Collections have been similarly useful. Documents generated as part of early church historians' efforts to compile a history of JS's life and the origins of the church have also been consulted, especially when evidence suggests that the historians—particularly Willard Richards—were eyewitnesses to the events they later described in the history. These include the manuscript history of the church and the rough draft notes upon which it is based. In general, these and other noncontemporaneous documents were used only when other sources were not available.

Works Cited

This list of sources serves as a comprehensive guide to all sources cited in this volume (documentation supporting the reference material in the back of this volume may be found on the Joseph Smith Papers website). Annotation has been documented with original sources where possible and practical. In entries for manuscript sources, dates identify when the manuscript was created, which is not necessarily the time period the manuscript covers. Newspaper entries are listed under the newspaper titles used during the time period covered by this volume. Newspaper entries also provide beginning and ending years for the publication. Since newspapers often changed names or editors over time, such dates typically approximate the years the paper was active under a particular editor; when it is impractical to provide beginning and ending publication dates by an editor's tenure, dates may be determined by major events in the paper's history, such as a merger with another sizable newspaper.

Some sources cited in this volume are referred to on first and subsequent occurrences by a conventional shortened citation. For convenience, some documents are referred to by editorial titles rather than by their original titles or by the titles given in the catalogs of their current repositories, in which case the list of works cited provides the editorial title followed by full bibliographic information.

Transcripts and images of a growing number of Joseph Smith's papers are available on the Joseph Smith Papers website.

Scriptural References

The annotation within volumes of *The Joseph Smith Papers* includes numerous references to works accepted as scripture by The Church of Jesus Christ of Latter-day Saints. The principal citations of Mormon scripture appearing in annotation are to JS-era published or manuscript versions. However, for reader convenience, these citations also include a bracketed reference to the current and widely available Latter-day Saint scriptural canon. All versions of scripture cited in this volume, early or modern, are identified in the list of works cited.

The church's current scriptural canon consists of the King James (or Authorized) Version of the Bible (KJV), plus three other volumes: the Book of Mormon, the Doctrine and Covenants, and the Pearl of Great Price. The following paragraphs provide more detailed information about uniquely Mormon scriptures and how they are cited in this volume.

Book of Mormon. The first edition of the Book of Mormon was printed for JS in 1830. He oversaw the publication of subsequent editions in 1837 and 1840. The Book of Mormon, like the Bible, consists of a number of shorter books. However, the present volume cites early editions of the Book of Mormon by page numbers because these editions were not divided into numbered verses. The bracketed references to the modern (1981) Latter-day Saint edition of this work identify the book name with modern chapter and verse.

Doctrine and Covenants. JS authorized publication of early revelations beginning in 1832 in *The Evening and the Morning Star,* the church's first newspaper, and initiated the publication of a compilation of revelations, which first appeared in 1833 under the title Book of Commandments. Revised and expanded versions of this compilation were published in 1835 and 1844 under the title Doctrine and Covenants. Since JS's time, The Church of Jesus Christ of Latter-day Saints has continued to issue revised and expanded versions of the Doctrine and Covenants, as has the Community of Christ (formerly the Reorganized Church of Jesus Christ of Latter Day Saints). The bracketed references to the modern (1981) Latter-day Saint edition of the Doctrine and Covenants, which cite by section number and verse, use the abbreviation D&C in the place of Doctrine and Covenants. A table titled Corresponding Section Numbers in Editions of the Doctrine and Covenants, which appears after the list of works cited, aligns the corresponding section numbers of the three JS-era compilations and the current editions of the Doctrine and Covenants published by The Church of Jesus Christ of Latter-day Saints and by the Community of Christ. For more information about the format of Doctrine and Covenants citations, see the Editorial Method.

Joseph Smith Bible revision. Beginning in June 1830, JS systematically reviewed the text of the KJV and made revisions and additions to it. JS largely completed the work in 1833, but only a few excerpts were published in his lifetime. The Reorganized Church of Jesus Christ of Latter Day Saints published the entire work in 1867 under the title Holy Scriptures and included excerpts from the writings of Moses in two sections of its Doctrine and Covenants. The Church of Jesus Christ of Latter-day Saints, which today officially refers to JS's Bible revisions as the Joseph Smith Translation, has never published the entire work, but two excerpts are canonized in the Pearl of Great Price and many other excerpts are included in the footnotes and appendix of the modern (1979) Latter-day Saint edition of the KJV. In the *Papers,* references to JS's Bible revision are cited to the original manuscripts, with a bracketed reference given where possible to the relevant book, chapter, and verse of the Joseph Smith Translation.

Pearl of Great Price. The Pearl of Great Price, a collection of miscellaneous writings that originated with JS, was first published in 1851 and was canonized by The Church of Jesus Christ of Latter-day Saints in 1880. The modern (1981) edition of this work consists of the following: selections from the Book of Moses, an extract from JS's Bible revision manuscripts; the Book of Abraham, writings translated from papyri JS and others acquired in 1835 and first published in the *Times and Seasons* in 1842; Joseph Smith—Matthew, another extract from JS's Bible revision manuscripts; Joseph Smith—History, a selection from the history that JS began working on in 1838; and the Articles of Faith, a statement of beliefs included in a JS letter to Chicago newspaper editor John Wentworth and published in the *Times and Seasons* in 1842. Except in the case of Joseph Smith—History, citations in this volume to early versions of each of these works also include a bracketed reference to the corresponding chapter and verse in the modern Latter-day Saint canon. The Pearl of Great Price is not part of the canon of the Community of Christ. References to the history JS began work on in 1838 are cited to the original manuscript of that history (see entry on "JS History" in the list of works cited).

Legal References and Court Abbreviations

Citations to legal cases in this volume usually reference the name of the case; the name of the legal reporter in which information about the case was published (when applicable), together with volume and page number; the deciding court; and the year of the court's decision. Legal reporters documenting state or federal supreme court decisions are referred to by an abbreviated title; full bibliographic information for each reporter is provided in the list of works cited, alphabetized under the abbreviated title. For example, in the citation "*In re* Clark, 9 Wendell 212 (N.Y. Sup. Ct. 1832)," the case name is *In re* Clark, information about the case is located on page 212 in volume 9 of the legal reporter abbreviated as Wendell, and the case was decided by the New York Supreme Court in 1832.

Whenever possible, legal treatises cited within this volume are the same editions referenced by JS and his contemporaries in Nauvoo; for those texts where the exact edition is unknown, a contemporary edition was substituted.

Jurisdictions and court names used in legal citations are contemporary to the year of the cited case and do not necessarily correspond to modern courts or jurisdictions. In accordance with Nauvoo's charter, Nauvoo's mayor and aldermen simultaneously held positions as justices of the peace within the limits of Nauvoo; cases decided in Nauvoo's municipal or mayor's court do not use the "J.P. Ct." designation.

C.C.D. Ill.	Circuit Court of the District of Illinois
C.C.W.D. Mo.	Circuit Court of the Western District of Missouri
Daviess Co. Cir. Ct.	Daviess County, Missouri, Circuit Court
Hancock Co. Cir. Ct.	Hancock County, Illinois, Circuit Court
Ill. Sup. Ct.	Illinois Supreme Court
J.P. Ct.	Justice of the Peace Court
Mass. Sup. Jud. Ct.	Massachusetts Supreme Judicial Court
Mo. 5th Cir. Ct.	Fifth Judicial Circuit Court of Missouri
Nauvoo Mayor's Ct.	Nauvoo, Illinois, Mayor's Court
Nauvoo Mun. Ct.	Nauvoo, Illinois, Municipal Court
N.Y. Sup. Ct.	New York Supreme Court
Warren Co. Cir. Ct.	Warren County, Missouri, Circuit Court

Abbreviations for Frequently Cited Repositories

BYU	L. Tom Perry Special Collections, Harold B. Lee Library, Brigham Young University, Provo, Utah
CCLA	Community of Christ Library-Archives, Independence, Missouri
CHL	Church History Library, The Church of Jesus Christ of Latter-day Saints, Salt Lake City
FHL	Family History Library, The Church of Jesus Christ of Latter-day Saints, Salt Lake City
MSA	Missouri State Archives, Jefferson City

Abraham (book of). See *Pearl of Great Price.*

Affidavits and Certificates, Disproving the Statements and Affidavits Contained in John C. Bennett's Letters. Nauvoo Aug. 31, 1842. [Nauvoo, IL: 1842]. Copy at CHL.

Albany Argus. Albany. 1825–1856.

Aldrich, Charles. Autograph Collection. State Historical Society of Iowa, Des Moines.

Allaman, John Lee. "Joseph Smith's Visits to Henderson County." *Western Illinois Regional Studies* 8, no. 1 (Spring 1985): 46–55.

Allen, Charles Hopkins. Autobiography, after 1920. Microfilm. CHL.

Allen, James B., Ronald K. Esplin, and David J. Whittaker. *Men with a Mission, 1837–1841: The Quorum of the Twelve Apostles in the British Isles.* Salt Lake City: Deseret Book, 1992.

Allred, William Moore. Reminiscences and Diary, 1885–1887. CHL.

Alton Telegraph and Democratic Review. Alton, IL. 1836–1855.

An American Dictionary of the English Language; Exhibiting the Origin, Orthography, Pronunciation, and Definitions of Words. Edited by Noah Webster. New York: Harper and Brothers, 1845.

American State Papers: Documents, Legislative and Executive, of the Congress of the United States. Edited by Walter Lowrie, Walter S. Franklin, Asbury Dickins, and John W. Forney. American State Papers: Naval Affairs. 4 vols. Washington DC: Gales and Seaton, 1834, 1860–1861.

Anderson, Richard Lloyd. *Joseph Smith's New England Heritage: Influences of Grandfathers Solomon Mack and Asael Smith.* Rev. ed. Salt Lake City: Deseret Book; Provo, UT: Brigham Young University Press, 2003.

Arnold, Isaac N. *Reminiscences of the Illinois Bar Forty Years Ago: Lincoln and Douglas as Orators and Lawyers.* Chicago: Fergus Printing, 1881.

Asbury, Henry. *Reminiscences of Quincy, Illinois, Containing Historical Events, Anecdotes, Matters concerning Old Settlers and Old Times, Etc.* Quincy, IL: D. Wilcox and Sons, 1882.

"Autobiography of Erastus Snow Dictated to His Son Franklin R. Snow, in the Year 1875." *Utah Genealogical and Historical Magazine* 14 (1923): 104–113, 161–170.

Bachman, Danel W. "New Light on an Old Hypothesis: The Ohio Origins of the Revelation on Eternal Marriage." *Journal of Mormon History* 5 (1978): 19–32.

Bankruptcy General Records (Act of 1841), 1842–1845. 7 vols. In Records of the U.S. District Courts, Southern District of Illinois, Southern Division (Springfield, IL), 1819–1977. National Archives–Great Lakes Region, Chicago.

Bassett, Samuel Clay. *Buffalo County, Nebraska, and Its People: A Record of Settlement, Organization, Progress, and Achievement.* 2 vols. Chicago: S. J. Clarke Publishing, 1916.

Baugh, Alexander L. "A Call to Arms: The 1838 Mormon Defense of Northern Missouri." PhD diss., Brigham Young University, 1996. Also available as *A Call to Arms: The 1838 Mormon Defense of Northern Missouri,* Dissertations in Latter-day Saint History (Provo, UT: Joseph Fielding Smith Institute for Latter-day Saint History; BYU Studies, 2000).

———. "'We Took Our Change of Venue to the State of Illinois': The Gallatin Hearing and the Escape of Joseph Smith and the Mormon Prisoners from Missouri, April 1839." *Mormon Historical Studies* 2, no. 1 (2001): 59–82.

Beecher, Maureen Ursenbach, ed. *The Personal Writings of Eliza Roxcy Snow*. Life Writings of Frontier Women 5. Logan: Utah State University Press, 2000.

Bennett, John C. *The History of the Saints; or, An Exposé of Joe Smith and Mormonism.* Boston: Leland and Whiting, 1842.

Bennett, Richard E. and Rachel Cope. "'A City on a Hill'—Chartering the City of Nauvoo." *John Whitmer Historical Association Journal* (2002): 17–42.

Berrett, LaMar C., ed. *Sacred Places: A Comprehensive Guide to Early LDS Historical Sites.* 6 vols. Salt Lake City: Deseret Book, 1999–2007.

Die Bibel, oder die ganze heilige Schrift des alten und neuen Testaments, nach der deutschen Uebersetzung D. Martin Luthers. Halle (Saale): der Cansteinischen Bibel-Anstalt, 1826.

A Bill Authorising the President of the United States to Cause Experiments to Be Made, to Test the Utility and Practicability of a Fire-Ship, the Invention of Uriah Brown. H.R. 296, 20th Cong. (1828).

A Bill Authorizing the Secretary of the Navy to Cause Experiments to Be Made to Test the Efficient Properties of a Liquid Fire Discovered by Uriah Brown. H.R. 621, 29th Cong. (1847).

Biographical Directory of the United States Congress, 1774–1989: The Continental Congress September 5, 1774, to October 21, 1788, and the Congress of the United States from the First through the One Hundredth Congresses March 4, 1789, to January 3, 1989, Inclusive. Edited by Kathryn Allamong Jacob and Bruce A. Ragsdale. Washington DC: U.S. Government Printing Office, 1989.

Black, Susan Easton, comp. *Early Members of the Reorganized Church of Jesus Christ of Latter Day Saints.* 6 vols. Provo, UT: Religious Studies Center, Brigham Young University, 1993.

Blackstone, William. *Commentaries on the Laws of England: In Four Books; with an Analysis of the Work. By Sir William Blackstone, Knt. One of the Justices of the Court of Common Pleas. In Two Volumes, from the Eighteenth London Edition. . . .* 2 vols. New York: W. E. Dean, 1840.

The Book of Abraham. See *Pearl of Great Price.*

A Book of Commandments, for the Government of the Church of Christ, Organized according to Law, on the 6th of April, 1830. Zion [Independence], MO: W. W. Phelps, 1833. Also available in Robin Scott Jensen, Richard E. Turley Jr., and Riley M. Lorimer, eds., *Revelations and Translations, Volume 2: Published Revelations.* Vol. 2 of the Revelations and Translations series of *The Joseph Smith Papers,* edited by Dean C. Jessee, Ronald K. Esplin, and Richard Lyman Bushman (Salt Lake City: Church Historian's Press, 2011).

Book of Doctrine and Covenants: Carefully Selected from the Revelations of God, and Given in the Order of Their Dates. Independence, MO: Herald Publishing House, 2004.

The Book of Mormon. 3rd ed. Nauvoo, IL: Robinson and Smith, 1840. The copy used for this volume is available at CHL.

The Book of Mormon: Another Testament of Jesus Christ. Salt Lake City: The Church of Jesus Christ of Latter-day Saints, 1981.

The Book of Moses (selections from). See *Pearl of Great Price.*

The Book of the Law of the Lord, Record Book, 1841–1845. CHL. JS's journal entries within this record book are transcribed on pp. 10–183 herein.

Bortle, John E. "Great Comets in History." *Sky and Telescope* 93, no. 1 (Jan. 1997): 44–50.

Boston Courier. Boston. 1824–before 1855.

Boston Daily Bee. Boston. 1842–1857.

Boston Investigator. Boston. 1831–1904.

Brewster, James C. *The Words of Righteousness to All Men, Written from One of the Books of Esdras.* . . . Springfield, IL: Ballard and Roberts, 1842.

Brigham Young Office Files, 1832–1878. CHL.

Brown, John. Letter, [Pleasant Grove, Utah Territory], to [John Taylor], [20 Dec. 1879]. Photocopy. Private possession. Copy at CHL.

Brown, Lisle G., comp. *Nauvoo Sealings, Adoptions, and Anointings: A Comprehensive Register of Persons Receiving LDS Temple Ordinances, 1841–1846.* Salt Lake City: Smith-Pettit Foundation, 2006.

Bulletin. St. Louis. 1842–1843.

Bushman, Richard Lyman. *Joseph Smith: Rough Stone Rolling.* With the assistance of Jed Woodworth. New York: Knopf, 2005.

Carlin, Thomas. Correspondence, 1838–1842. In Office of the Governor, Records, 1818–1989. Illinois State Archives, Springfield.

Chicago Express. Chicago. 1842–1844.

Christian Secretary. Hartford, CT. 1838–1896.

Christian Soldier. Providence, RI. 1842–1843.

Cincinnati Daily Gazette. Cincinnati. 1827–1883.

Clayton, William. History of the Nauvoo Temple, ca. 1845. CHL.

———. Journals, 1842–1845. CHL.

Cochran, Robert M., Mary H. Siegfried, Ida Blum, David L. Fulton, Harold T. Garvey, and Olen L. Smith, eds. *History of Hancock County, Illinois: Illinois Sesquicentennial Edition.* Carthage, IL: Board of Supervisors of Hancock County, 1968.

A Collection of Sacred Hymns for the Church of Jesus Christ of Latter Day Saints. Edited by Emma Smith. Nauvoo, IL: E. Robinson, 1841.

Collins, William H., and Cicero F. Perry. *Past and Present of the City of Quincy and Adams County, Illinois.* Chicago: S. J. Clarke Publishing, 1905.

A Confession of Faith, Which Contains a True Account of the Principles and Doctrines of the People Called Quakers, by Robert Barclay, First Published in the Year 1673, and Reprinted by the Society at Various Times; to Which Is Added, an Extract from the Letter of George Fox and Others to the Governor and Council of Barbadoes, in the Year 1671; and the Confession of Faith Presented by Friends to the British Parliament in 1693. Philadelphia: Joseph R. A. Skerrett, 1827.

The Congressional Globe, Containing Sketches of the Debates and Proceedings of the Third Session of the Twenty-Seventh Congress. Vol. 12. Washington DC: Blair and Rives, 1843.

Conkling, Alfred. *Treatise on the Organization, Jurisdiction and Practice of the Courts of the United States.* Albany: William and A. Gould, 1831.

The Connecticut Annual Register and United States Calendar, for 1837; to Which Is Prefixed an Almanack. . . . New London, CT: Samuel Green, [1837].

Cook, Lyndon W. "Isaac Galland—Mormon Benefactor." *BYU Studies* 19 (Spring 1979): 261–284.

———, comp. *Nauvoo Deaths and Marriages, 1839–1845.* Orem, UT: Grandin Book, 1994.

Copher, Charles B. "The Black Presence in the Old Testament." In *Stony the Road We Trod: African American Biblical Interpretation,* edited by Cain Hope Felder, 146–164. Minneapolis: Fortress Press, 1991.

Cranch / Cranch, William. *Reports of Cases Argued and Adjudged in the Supreme Court of the United States, in the Years 1805 and 1806.* 9 vols. Various publishers, 1804–1817.

Crawley, Peter. *A Descriptive Bibliography of the Mormon Church.* 2 vols. Provo, UT: Religious Studies Center, Brigham Young University, 1997, 2005.

Daily Atlas. Boston. 1832–1857.

Daily Missouri Republican. St. Louis. 1822–1919.

Daily National Intelligencer. Washington DC. 1800–1869.

D&C. See *Doctrine and Covenants of the Church of Jesus Christ of Latter-day Saints* (1981).

Davidson, Alexander, and Bernard Stuvé. *A Complete History of Illinois from 1673 to 1873; Embracing the Physical Features of the Country; Its Early Explorations; Aboriginal Inhabitants; French and British Occupation; Conquest by Virginia; Territorial Condition and the Subsequent Civil, Military and Political Events of the State.* Springfield, IL: Illinois Journal Co., 1874.

Decatur Daily Review. Decatur, IL. 1880–1887.

Deseret News. Salt Lake City. 1850–.

Deseret Weekly. See *Deseret News.*

Doan, Ruth Alden. *The Miller Heresy, Millennialism, and American Culture.* Philadelphia: Temple University Press, 1987.

Doctrine and Covenants, 2004 Community of Christ edition. See *Book of Doctrine and Covenants.*

Doctrine and Covenants of the Church of the Latter Day Saints: Carefully Selected from the Revelations of God. Compiled by Joseph Smith, Oliver Cowdery, Sidney Rigdon, and Frederick G. Williams. Kirtland, OH: F. G. Williams, 1835. Also available in Robin Scott Jensen, Richard E. Turley Jr., and Riley M. Lorimer, eds., *Revelations and Translations, Volume 2: Published Revelations.* Vol. 2 of the Revelations and Translations series of *The Joseph Smith Papers,* edited by Dean C. Jessee, Ronald K. Esplin, and Richard Lyman Bushman (Salt Lake City: Church Historian's Press, 2011).

The Doctrine and Covenants of the Church of Jesus Christ of Latter Day Saints; Carefully Selected from the Revelations of God. Compiled by Joseph Smith. 2nd ed. Nauvoo, IL: John Taylor, 1844. Selections also available in Robin Scott Jensen, Richard E. Turley Jr., and Riley M. Lorimer, eds., *Revelations and Translations, Volume 2: Published Revelations.* Vol. 2 of the Revelations and Translations series of *The Joseph Smith Papers,* edited by Dean C. Jessee, Ronald K. Esplin, and Richard Lyman Bushman (Salt Lake City: Church Historian's Press, 2011).

The Doctrine and Covenants of the Church of Jesus Christ of Latter-day Saints: Containing Revelations Given to Joseph Smith, the Prophet, with Some Additions by His Successors in the Presidency of the Church. Salt Lake City: The Church of Jesus Christ of Latter-day Saints, 1981.

Document Containing the Correspondence, Orders, &c., in Relation to the Disturbances with the Mormons; and the Evidence Given before the Hon. Austin A. King, Judge of the Fifth Judicial Circuit of the State of Missouri, at the Court-House in Richmond, in a Criminal Court of Inquiry, Begun November 12, 1838, on the Trial of Joseph Smith, Jr., and Others, for High Treason and Other Crimes against the State. Fayette, MO: Boon's Lick Democrat, 1841.

Documents of the Assembly of the State of New-York, Fifty-Ninth Session, 1836. Vol. 1, *From No. 1 to No. 42 Inclusive.* Albany: E. Croswell, 1836.

Dowrie, George William. *The Development of Banking in Illinois, 1817–1863.* University of Illinois Studies in the Social Sciences, vol. 11, no. 4. Urbana: University of Illinois, 1913.

Encyclopedia of Mormonism. Edited by Daniel H. Ludlow. 5 vols. New York: Macmillan, 1992.

Esplin, Ronald K. "The Emergence of Brigham Young and the Twelve to Mormon Leadership, 1830–1841." PhD diss., Brigham Young University, 1981. Also available as *The Emergence of Brigham Young and the Twelve to Mormon Leadership, 1830–1841*, Dissertations in Latter-day Saint History (Provo, UT: Joseph Fielding Smith Institute for Latter-day Saint History; BYU Studies, 2006).

Evening Post. New York City. 1801–.

"Ex Parte Joseph Smith—the Mormon Prophet" / "Circuit Court of the United States, Illinois, January, 1843. Before the Honorable Nathaniel Pope, District Judge. Ex Parte Joseph Smith—the Mormon Prophet." *The Law Reporter* 6 (June 1843): 57–67.

Flanders, Robert Bruce. *Nauvoo: Kingdom on the Mississippi.* Urbana: University of Illinois Press, 1965.

Fleming, Helen Vilate Bourne. Collection, 1836–1963. CHL.

Foote, Warren. Autobiography, not before 1903. CHL.

Ford, Thomas. *A History of Illinois, from Its Commencement as a State in 1818 to 1847. Containing a Full Account of the Black Hawk War, the Rise, Progress, and Fall of Mormonism, the Alton and Lovejoy Riots, and Other Important and Interesting Events.* Chicago: S. C. Griggs; New York: Ivison and Phinney, 1854.

[Fox, George]. *To the Protector and Parliament of England.* London: Giles Calvert, 1658.

Freedman, Paul. *Images of the Medieval Peasant.* Stanford, CA: Stanford University Press, 1999.

Freeman's Journal and Daily Commercial Advertiser. Dublin. 1806–1924.

General Church Minutes, 1839–1877. CHL.

"General Record of the 5th Quorum," 1844–1881. In Seventies Quorum Records, 1844–1975. CHL.

Goldenberg, David M. *Curse of Ham: Race and Slavery in Early Judaism, Christianity, and Islam.* Princeton, NJ: Princeton University Press, 2003.

Gregg, Thomas. *History of Hancock County, Illinois, together with an Outline History of the State, and a Digest of State Laws.* Chicago: Charles C. Chapman, 1880.

Hagerstown Mail. Hagerstown, MD. 1831–1890.

Haller, John S., Jr. *The People's Doctors: Samuel Thomson and the American Botanical Movement, 1790–1860.* Carbondale: Southern Illinois University Press, 2000.

Hamilton, Marshall. "'Money-Diggersville,'—The Brief, Turbulent History of the Mormon Town of Warren." *The John Whitmer Historical Association Journal* 9 (1989): 49–58.

Harris, Martin Henderson. Reminiscences and Journal, 1856–1876. CHL.

Harrison, S. B. *An Analytical Digest of All the Reported Cases, Determined in the House of Lords, the Several Courts of Common Law, in Banc and at Nisi Prius; and the Court of Bankruptcy: and also the Crown Cases Reserved, from Mich. Term, 1756, to Mich. Term, 1834, together with a Full Selection of Equity Cases, and the Manuscript Cases from the Best Modern Treatises Not Elsewhere Reported.* 3 vols. Philadelphia: Desilver, Thomas and Co., 1835.

Hawk-Eye and Iowa Patriot. Burlington, IA. 1839–1851.

Historian's Office. Brigham Young History Drafts, 1856–1858. CHL.

Historian's Office. Historical Record Book, 1843–1874. CHL.

———. Catalogs and Inventories, 1846–1904. CHL.

———. Histories of the Twelve, ca. 1858–1880. CHL.

———. Joseph Smith History Documents, ca. 1839–1856. CHL.

———. Joseph Smith History, draft notes, ca. 1839–1856. CHL.

Historical Department. Nineteenth-Century Legal Documents Collection, ca. 1825–1890. CHL.

The Historical Record, a Monthly Periodical, Devoted Exclusively to Historical, Biographical, Chronological and Statistical Matters. Salt Lake City. 1882–1890.

The History of Iowa County, Iowa, Containing a History of the County, Its Cities, Towns, &c. . . . Des Moines, IA: Union Historical Co., 1881.

The History of Lee County, Iowa, Containing a History of the County, Its Cities, Towns, &c. . . . Chicago: Western Historical Co., 1879.

History of Mills County, Iowa, Containing a History of the County, Its Cities, Towns, Etc. . . . Des Moines, IA: State Historical Co., 1881.

Hogan, Mervin B. *John Cook Bennett and Pickaway Lodge No. 23.* No publisher, 1983.

———. *Vital Statistics of Nauvoo Lodge.* Salt Lake City: By the author, 1976.

The Holy Bible, Containing the Old and New Testaments Translated Out of the Original Tongues: And with the Former Translations Diligently Compared and Revised, by His Majesty's Special Command. Authorized King James Version with Explanatory Notes and Cross References to the Standard Works of the Church of Jesus Christ of Latter-day Saints. Salt Lake City: The Church of Jesus Christ of Latter-day Saints, 1979.

Howe, Eber D. *Mormonism Unvailed: or, A Faithful Account of That Singular Imposition and Delusion, from Its Rise to the Present Time. With Sketches of the Characters of Its Propagators, and a Full Detail of the Manner in Which the Famous Golden Bible Was Brought before the World. To Which Are Added, Inquiries into the Probability That the Historical Part of the Said Bible Was Written by One Solomon Spalding, More Than Twenty Years Ago, and by Him Intended to Have Been Published as a Romance.* Painesville, OH: By the author, 1834.

Hunter, Louis C. *Steamboats on the Western Rivers: An Economic and Technological History.* Cambridge, MA: Harvard University Press, 1949.

Hunter, William E. *Edward Hunter: Faithful Steward.* [Salt Lake City]: Mrs. William E. Hunter, 1970.

Huntington, William D. Cemetery Records, 1839–1845. CHL.

Hyde, Marinda Nancy Johnson. Statement, [ca. 1880]. CHL.

Illinois Register. Vandalia, IL, 1836–1839; Springfield, IL, 1839–1846.

Indictment, Apr. 1839, State of Missouri v. James Worthington et al. for Larceny [Daviess Co. Cir. Ct. 1840]. Daviess Co., MO, Courthouse, Gallatin, MO.

Indictment, June 1843, State of Missouri v. Joseph Smith for Treason [Daviess Co. Cir. Ct. 1843]. Western Americana Collection. Beinecke Rare Book and Manuscript Library, Yale University, New Haven, CT.

"Inventory of President Joseph Fielding Smith's Safe," 23 May 1970. First Presidency, General Administration Files, 1921–1972. CHL.

Jennings, Warren A. "Isaac McCoy and the Mormons," *Missouri Historical Review* 61, no. 1 (Oct. 1966): 62–82.

Jenson, Andrew. *Latter-day Saint Biographical Encyclopedia: A Compilation of Biographical Sketches of Prominent Men and Women in the Church of Jesus Christ of Latter-day Saints.* 4 vols. Salt Lake City: Andrew Jenson History Co., 1901–1936.

Jessee, Dean C. "'Walls, Grates and Screeking Iron Doors': The Prison Experience of Mormon Leaders in Missouri, 1838–1839." In *New Views of Mormon History: A Collection of Essays in Honor of Leonard J. Arrington,* edited by Davis Bitton and Maureen Ursenbach Beecher, 19–42. Salt Lake City: University of Utah Press, 1987.

———. "The Writing of Joseph Smith's History." *BYU Studies* 11 (Summer 1971): 439–473.

Johnson, Jeffery O. *Register of the Joseph Smith Collection in the Church Archives, the Church of Jesus Christ of Latter-day Saints.* Salt Lake City: Historical Department of the Church of Jesus Christ of Latter-day Saints, 1973.

Johnstun, Joseph D. "'To Lie in Yonder Tomb': The Tomb and Burial of Joseph Smith." *Mormon Historical Studies* 6, no. 2 (2005): 163–180.

Jonesborough Whig and Independent Journal. Elizabethton, TN, 1839–1840; Jonesborough, TN, 1840–1849; Knoxville, TN, 1849–1861.

Joseph Smith Extradition Records, 1839–1843. Abraham Lincoln Presidential Library, Springfield, IL.

"Joseph Smith, the Prophet." *Young Woman's Journal* 17, no. 12 (Dec. 1906): 547–548.

Journal of Discourses. 26 vols. Liverpool: F. D. Richards, 1855–1886.

Journal of the House of Representatives of the Thirteenth General Assembly of the State of Illinois, at Their Regular Session, Begun and Held at Springfield, December 5, 1842. Springfield, IL: William Walters, 1842.

Journal of the House of Representatives of the United States: Being the First Session of the Thirtieth Congress; Begun and Held at the City of Washington, December 6, 1847, in the Seventy-Second Year of the Independence of the United States. Washington DC: Wendell and Van Benthuysen, 1847–1848.

Journal of the Senate of the Thirteenth General Assembly of the State of Illinois, at Their Regular Session, Begun and Held at Springfield, December 5, 1842. Springfield, IL: William Walters, 1842.

JS. In addition to the entries that immediately follow, see entries under "Smith, Joseph."

JS History / Smith, Joseph, et al. History, 1839–1856. Vols. A-1–F-1 (originals), A-2–E-2 (early security copies). CHL. The history for the period after 5 Aug. 1838 was composed after the death of Joseph Smith. Also available as *History of the Church of Jesus Christ of Latter-day Saints, Period 1: History of Joseph Smith, the Prophet, by Himself,* edited by B. H. Roberts, 6 vols. (Salt Lake City: Deseret News, 1902–1912).

JS Letterbook 1 / Smith, Joseph. "Letter Book A," 1832–1835. Joseph Smith Collection. CHL.

JS Letterbook 2 / Smith, Joseph. "Copies of Letters, &c. &c.," 1839–1843. Joseph Smith Collection. CHL.

JSP, J1 / Jessee, Dean C., Mark Ashurst-McGee, and Richard L. Jensen, eds. *Journals, Volume 1: 1832–1839.* Vol. 1 of the Journals series of *The Joseph Smith Papers,* edited by Dean C. Jessee, Ronald K. Esplin, and Richard Lyman Bushman. Salt Lake City: Church Historian's Press, 2008.

JSP, MRB / Jensen, Robin Scott, Robert J. Woodford, and Steven C. Harper, eds. *Manuscript Revelation Books.* Facsimile edition. First volume of the Revelations and Translations series of *The Joseph Smith Papers,* edited by Dean C. Jessee, Ronald K. Esplin, and Richard Lyman Bushman. Salt Lake City: Church Historian's Press, 2009.

Kent, James. *Commentaries on American Law.* 4th ed. Vol. 2. New York: By the author, 1840.

Kimball, James L., Jr. "The Nauvoo Charter: A Reinterpretation." *Journal of the Illinois State Historical Society* 44 (Spring 1971): 66–78.

King, Lester S. *The Medical World of the Eighteenth Century.* Chicago: University of Chicago Press, 1958.

Kronk, Gary W. *Cometography: A Catalog of Comets.* Vol. 2, *1800–1899.* Cambridge: Cambridge University Press, 2003.

Latter Day Saints' Messenger and Advocate. Kirtland, OH. Oct. 1834–Sept. 1837.

Latter-day Saints' Millennial Star. Liverpool. 1840–1970.

Laws of the State of Illinois, Passed by the Ninth General Assembly, at Their First Session, Commencing December 1, 1834, and Ending February 13, 1835. Vandalia, IL: J. Y. Sawyer, 1835.

Laws of the State of Illinois, Passed by the Tenth General Assembly, at Their Session Commencing December 5, 1836, and Ending March 6, 1837. Vandalia, IL: William Walters, 1837.

Laws of the State of Illinois, Passed by the Twelfth General Assembly, at Their Session, Began and Held at Springfield, on the Seventh of December, One Thousand Eight Hundred and Forty. Springfield, IL: William Walters, 1841.

Laws of the State of Illinois, Passed by the Thirteenth General Assembly, at Their Regular Session, Began and Held at Springfield, on the Fifth of December, One Thousand Eight Hundred and Forty-Two. Springfield, IL: Walters and Weber, 1843.

Laws of the State of Illinois, Passed by the Fourteenth General Assembly, at Their Regular Session, Began and Held at Springfield, December 2nd, 1844. Springfield, IL: Walters and Weber, 1845.

Laws of the State of Illinois, Passed by the Fifteenth General Assembly, at Their Session, Begun and Held in the City of Springfield, December 7, 1846. Springfield, IL: Charles H. Lanphier, 1847.

Leigh, P. Brady. *An Abridgment of the Law of Nisi Prius.* 2 vols. Philadelphia: P. H. Nicklin and T. Johnson, 1838.

Leonard, Glen M. *Nauvoo: A Place of Peace, a People of Promise.* Salt Lake City: Deseret Book; Provo, UT: Brigham Young University Press, 2002.

Leopard, Buel, and Floyd C. Shoemaker, comps. *The Messages and Proclamations of the Governors of the State of Missouri.* Vol. 1. Columbia, MO: State Historical Society of Missouri, 1922.

Letter of Transfer, Salt Lake City, UT, 8 Jan. 2010. CHL.

Letters regarding Freemasonry in Nauvoo, 1842. CHL.

Linder, Usher F. *Reminiscences of the Early Bench and Bar of Illinois.* Chicago: Chicago Legal News Co., 1879.

Liverpool Mercury. Liverpool. 1811–1904.

Lorimer, William A., ed. *History of Mercer County.* Historical Encyclopedia of Illinois, edited by Newton Bateman and Paul Selby. Chicago: Munsell Publishing Co., 1903.

Louisville Daily Journal. Louisville, KY. 1830–1868.

Lundeberg, Philip K. *Samuel Colt's Submarine Battery: The Secret and the Enigma.* Smithsonian Studies in History and Technology 29. Washington DC: Smithsonian Institution Press, 1974.

Lyman, Amasa. Journal, 1841–1844. Amasa Lyman Collection, 1832–1877. CHL.

Lyman, Eliza Maria Partridge. Journal, 1846–1885. CHL.

Macedonia Branch, Record / "A Record of the Chur[c]h of Jesus Christ of Latter day Saints in Macedonia (Also Called Ramus)," 1839–1850. CHL.

Madsen, Gordon A. "Joseph Smith as Guardian: The Lawrence Estate Case." *Journal of Mormon History* 36, no. 3 (2010): 172–211.

Maltby, Isaac. *A Treatise on Courts Martial and Military Law. . . .* Boston: Thomas B. Wait, 1813.

Martin, Charles, ed. *History of Cass County.* Historical Encyclopedia of Illinois, edited by Newton Bateman and Paul Selby. Chicago: Munsell Publishing, 1915.

Martyrdom and Ascension of Isaiah. In *The Old Testament Pseudepigrapha.* 2 vols. Edited by James H. Charlesworth. Garden City, NY: Doubleday, 1985.

Material Relating to Mormon Expulsion from Missouri, 1839–1843. Photocopy. CHL.

"Mary Elizabeth Rollins Lightner." *Utah Genealogical and Historical Magazine* 17 (1926): 193–205, 250–260.

McFarland, Philip. *Sea Dangers: The Affair of the* Somers. New York: Schocken Books, 1985.

McGregor, Malcolm G. *The Biographical Record of Jasper County, Missouri.* Chicago: Lewis Publishing, 1901.

McLaws, Monte B. "The Attempted Assassination of Missouri's Ex-Governor, Lilburn W. Boggs." *Missouri Historical Review* 60, no. 1 (Oct. 1965): 50–62.

Mendenhall, William. Diaries, 1842–1896. CHL.

Miller, William. *Evidence from Scripture and History of the Second Coming of Christ, about the Year 1843; Exhibited in a Course of Lectures.* Boston: Moses A. Dow, 1841.

Milwaukie Daily Sentinel. Milwaukee. 1844–1846.

Minute Book 1 / "Conference A," 1832–1837. CHL. Also available at josephsmithpapers.org.

Minute Book 2 / "The Conference Minutes and Record Book of Christ's Church of Latter

Day Saints," 1838–ca. 1839, 1842, 1844. CHL. Also available as Donald Q. Cannon and Lyndon W. Cook, eds., *Far West Record: Minutes of the Church of Jesus Christ of Latter-day Saints, 1830–1844* (Salt Lake City: Deseret Book, 1983).

Missouri, State of. "Evidence." Hearing Record, Richmond, MO, 12–29 Nov. 1838, State of Missouri v. Joseph Smith et al. for Treason and Other Crimes (Mo. 5th Cir. Ct. 1838). Eugene Morrow Violette Collection, 1806–1921, Western Historical Manuscript Collection. University of Missouri and State Historical Society of Missouri, Ellis Library, University of Missouri, Columbia.

Missouri, State of. Office of the Secretary of State, Commissions Division. Register of Civil Proceedings, 1837–1971. MSA.

Missouri Historical Society. Selected Papers Pertaining to Mormonism, 1831–1859. Microfilm. CHL.

Mormon War Papers, 1838–1841. MSA.

Nauvoo, IL. Records, 1841–1845. CHL.

Nauvoo City Council Minute Book / Nauvoo City Council. "A Record of the Proceedings of the City Council of the City of Nauvoo Handcock County, State of Illinois, Commencing A.D. 1841," ca. 1841–1845. CHL.

Nauvoo High Council Minutes, 1839–1845. CHL.

Nauvoo High Council Papers, 1839–1844. CHL.

Nauvoo House Association. Records, 1841–1846. CHL.

Nauvoo House Association. Stock Book, 1841–1845. Nauvoo House Association, Records, 1841–1846. CHL.

Nauvoo Legion Minute Book, 1843–1844. Nauvoo Legion, Records, 1841–1845. CHL.

Nauvoo Masonic Lodge Minute Book / "Record of Na[u]voo Lodge under Dispensation," 1842–1846. CHL.

Nauvoo Mayor's Court Docket Book / Nauvoo, IL, Mayor's Court. Docket Book, 1843. In Historian's Office, Historical Record Book, 1843–1874, pp. 12–50. CHL.

Nauvoo Municipal Court Docket Book / Nauvoo, IL, Municipal Court. "Docket of the Municipal Court of the City of Nauvoo," ca. 1843–1845. In Historian's Office, Historical Record Book, 1843–1874, pp. 51–150 and pp. 1–19 (second numbering). CHL.

Nauvoo Neighbor. Nauvoo, IL. 1843–1845.

Nauvoo Registry of Deeds. Record of Deeds, bk. A, 1842–1843. CHL.

Nauvoo Registry of Deeds. Record of Deeds, bk. B, 1843–1846. CHL.

Nauvoo Restoration, Incorporated. Collection, 1818–2001. CHL.

Nauvoo Temple. Record of Baptisms for the Dead, 1841, 1843–1845. CHL.

Nelson, David. *Appeal to the Church, in Behalf of a Dying Race, from the Mission Institute, Near Quincy, Illinois.* New York: John S. Taylor, 1838.

New-Orleans Bee. New Orleans. 1839–1844.

New York Daily Tribune. New York City. 1841–1924.

New York Herald. New York City. 1835–1924.

Niles' National Register. Washington DC. 1837–1849.

Northern Islander. St. James, MI. 1850–1856.

Oaks, Dallin H., and Joseph I. Bentley. "Joseph Smith and Legal Process: In the Wake of the Steamboat *Nauvoo*." *Brigham Young University Law Review*, no. 3 (1976): 735–782.

The Olive Branch, or, Herald of Peace and Truth to All Saints. Kirtland, OH, 1848–1849; Springfield, IL, 1849–1850; Kirtland, OH, 1850–1852.

The Oxford English Dictionary. Edited by James A. H. Murray, Henry Bradley, W. A. Craigie, and C. T. Onions. 12 vols. 1933. Reprint. Oxford: Oxford University Press, 1970.

Papers in the Case of Maxwell v. Cannon, for a Seat as Delegate from Utah Territory in the Forty-Third Congress. H.R. Misc. Doc. 49, 43rd Cong., 1st Sess. (1873).

Parkin, Max H. Collected Missouri Court Documents, 1838–1840. Photocopy. CHL.

Patriarchal Blessings. 1833–. CHL.

The Pearl of Great Price: A Selection from the Revelations, Translations, and Narrations of Joseph Smith, First Prophet, Seer, and Revelator to the Church of Jesus Christ of Latter-day Saints. Salt Lake City: The Church of Jesus Christ of Latter-day Saints, 1981.

Pease, Theodore Calvin. *The Centennial History of Illinois.* Vol. 2, *The Frontier State, 1818–1848.* Chicago: A. C. McClurg, 1922.

Pennsylvania Inquirer and National Gazette. Philadelphia. 1842–1859.

Perego, Ugo A., Jayne E. Ekins, and Scott R. Woodward. "Resolving the Paternities of Oliver N. Buell and Mosiah L. Hancock through DNA." *The John Whitmer Historical Association Journal* 28 (2008): 128–136.

Perego, Ugo A., Natalie M. Myres, and Scott R. Woodward. "Reconstructing the Y-Chromosome of Joseph Smith: Genealogical Applications." *Journal of Mormon History* 31 (Summer 2005): 70–88.

Perrin, William Henry, ed. *History of Cass County Illinois.* Chicago: O. L. Baskin, 1882.

Peters / Peters, Richard. *Reports of Cases Argued and Adjudged in the Supreme Court of the United States.* 17 vols. Various publishers, 1828–1843.

Peters Condensed / Peters, Richard, ed. *Condensed Reports of Cases in the Supreme Court of the United States, Containing the Whole Series of the Decisions of the Court from Its Organization to the Commencement of Peter's Reports at January Term 1827. With Copious Notes of Parallel Cases in the Supreme and Circuit Courts of the United States.* 6 vols. Philadelphia: John Grigg, 1830–1831; Desilver Jr., and Thomas, 1833–1834.

Phelps, William W. Diary and Notebook, ca. 1835–1836, 1843, 1864. CHL.

Philadelphia North American and Daily Advertiser. Philadelphia. 1839–1845.

Phillipps, S. March, and Andrew Amos. *A Treatise on the Law of Evidence. Fifth American, from the Eighth London Edition, with Considerable Additions.* Vol. 2. New York: Halsted and Voorhies, 1839.

———. *A Treatise on the Law of Evidence, from the Eighth London Edition, with Considerable Additions.* Vol. 1. Boston: Elisha G. Hammond, 1839.

Pickel, Leonard. Mormon Letters, 1841–1844. Western Americana Collection, Beinecke Rare Book and Manuscript Library, Yale University, New Haven, CT.

Platt, Lyman De. *Nauvoo: Early Mormon Records Series, 1839–1846.* Highland, UT, 1980.

Porter, Ray. *The Greatest Benefit to Mankind: A Medical History of Humanity.* New York: W. W. Norton, 1997.

Power, John Carroll. *History of the Early Settlers of Sangamon County, Illinois.* Springfield, IL: Edwin A. Wilson, 1876.

Pratt, Orson. Letter, [Nauvoo, IL], 14 July 1842. CHL.

Pratt, Parley P. *The Autobiography of Parley Parker Pratt, One of the Twelve Apostles of the Church of Jesus Christ of Latter-Day Saints, Embracing His Life, Ministry and Travels, with Extracts, in Prose and Verse, from His Miscellaneous Writings.* Edited by Parley P. Pratt Jr. New York: Russell Brothers, 1874.

———. Letter, Nauvoo, IL, to John Van Cott, Canaan Four Corners, NY, 7 May 1843. CHL.

Prayer, at the Dedication of the Lord's House in Kirtland, Ohio, March 27, 1836—By Joseph Smith, Jr. President of the Church of the Latter Day Saints. Kirtland, OH: 1836.

The Prophet. New York City. May 1844–May 1845.

The Public and General Statute Laws of the State of Illinois: Containing All the Laws . . . Passed by the Ninth General Assembly, at Their First Session, Commencing December 1, 1834, and Ending February 13, 1835; and at Their Second Session, Commencing December 7, 1835, and Ending January 18, 1836; and Those Passed by the Tenth General Assembly, at Their Session Commencing December 5, 1836, and Ending March 6, 1837; and at Their Special Session, Commencing July 10, and Ending July 22, 1837. . . . Compiled by Jonathan Young Scammon. Chicago: Stephen F. Gale, 1839.

The Public Statutes at Large of the United States of America, from the Organization of the Government in 1789, to March 3, 1845. . . . Edited by Richard Peters. 8 vols. Boston: Charles C. Little and James Brown, 1846–1867.

Quincy Herald. Quincy, IL. 1841–before 1851.

Quincy Whig. Quincy, IL. 1838–1857.

Quorum of the Twelve Apostles. Minutes, 1840–1844. CHL.

Racine Advocate. Racine, Wisconsin Territory. 1842–1888.

Randall, Ruth Painter. *Mary Lincoln: Biography of a Marriage.* Boston: Little, Brown, 1953.

"Recollections of the Prophet Joseph Smith." *Juvenile Instructor* 27, no. 6 (15 Mar. 1892): 173–174.

Record of Seventies / First Council of the Seventy. "General Record of the Seventies Book B. Commencing Nauvoo 1844," 1844–1848. Bk. B. In First Council of the Seventy, Records, 1837–1885. CHL.

"A Record of the Names of the Members of the Church of Jesus Christ of Latterday Saints, as Taken by the Lesser Priesthood, in the Spring of the Year 1842, and Continued, to Be Added as the Members Arrive at the City of Nauvoo, Hancock County; Illinois. Also the Deaths of Members, and Their Children, and Names of Children Under 8 Years of Age," after 1844–after 1846. In Far West and Nauvoo Elders' Certificates, 1837–1838, 1840–1846. CHL.

Records of the Solicitor of the Treasury / National Archives Reference Service Report, 23 Sept. 1964. "Record Group 206, Records of the Solicitor of the Treasury, and Record Group 46, Records of the United States Senate: Records Relating to the Mormons in Illinois, 1839–1848 (Records Dated 1840–1852), Including Memorials of Mormons to Congress, 1840–1844, Some of Which Relate to Outrages Committed against the Mormons in Missouri, 1831–1839." Microfilm. Washington DC: National Archives and Records Service, General Services Administration, 1964. Copy at CHL.

Relief Society Magazine. Salt Lake City. 1914–1970.

Relief Society Minute Book / "A Book of Records Containing the Proceedings of the

Female Relief Society of Nauvoo," Mar. 1842–Mar. 1844. CHL. Also available at josephsmithpapers.org.

Relief Society Record / "Record of the Relief Society from First Organization to Conference Apr 5th 1892. Book 1.," 1880–1892. CHL.

Reorganized Church of Jesus Christ of Latter Day Saints v. Church of Christ of Independence, Missouri, et al. (C.C.W.D. Mo. 1894). Typescript. Testimonies and Depositions, 1892. Typescript. CHL.

Reports Made to Senate and House of Representatives of the State of Illinois, at Their Session Begun and Held at Springfield, December 5, 1842. Springfield, IL: William Waters, 1842.

Republican Compiler. Gettysburg, PA. 1843–1845.

The Return. Davis City, IA, 1889–1891; Richmond, MO, 1892–1893; Davis City, 1895–1896; Denver, 1898; Independence, MO, 1899–1900.

Revelation Book 1 / "A Book of Commandments and Revelations of the Lord Given to Joseph the Seer and Others by the Inspiration of God and Gift and Power of the Holy Ghost Which Beareth Re[c]ord of the Father and Son and Holy Ghost Which Is One God Infinite and Eternal World without End Amen," 1831–1835. CHL. Also available in Robin Scott Jensen, Robert J. Woodford, and Steven C. Harper, eds., *Manuscript Revelation Books,* facsimile edition, first volume of the Revelations and Translations series of *The Joseph Smith Papers,* edited by Dean C. Jessee, Ronald K. Esplin, and Richard Lyman Bushman (Salt Lake City: Church Historian's Press, 2009).

Revelations Collection, 1831–ca. 1844, 1847, 1861, ca. 1876. CHL.

The Revised Code of Laws, of Illinois, Enacted at the Fifth General Assembly, at Their Session Held at Vandalia, Commencing on the Fourth Day of December, 1826, and Ending the Nineteenth of February, 1827. Vandalia, IL: Robert Blackwell, 1827.

Reynolds, Thomas. Office of the Governor, 1840–1844. MSA.

Richards, Willard. Journal, Apr. 1841–Jan. 1842. Willard Richards, Papers, 1821–1854. CHL.

———. Letter, Nauvoo, IL, to Jennetta Richards, Richmond, MA, 26 Feb. 1842. CHL.

———. Papers, 1821–1854. CHL.

Rigdon, Sidney. Collection, 1831–1858. CHL.

Robinson, Ebenezer, and Aaron Johnson. Docket Book, ca. 1842–1845. In Chicago Historical Society, Collection of Mormon Materials, 1836–1886. Microfilm. CHL.

Robison, Stephen D., comp. *Early Records Index: Adams County, Illinois.* 4 vols. [Salt Lake City]: Genealogical Society of Utah, [1994].

Rollins, Kyle M., Richard D. Smith, M. Brett Borup, and E. James Nelson. "Transforming Swampland into Nauvoo, the City Beautiful: A Civil Engineering Perspective." *BYU Studies* 45, no. 3 (2006): 125–157.

Rowe, David L. *God's Strange Work: William Miller and the End of the World.* Library of Religious Biography. Grand Rapids, MI: William B. Eerdmans, 2008.

Rowley, Dennis. "The Mormon Experience in the Wisconsin Pineries, 1841–1845." *BYU Studies* 32, nos. 1 and 2 (1992): 119–148.

The Saint Louis Directory, for the Year 1842; Containing the Names of the Inhabitants, and the Numbers of Their Places of Business and Dwellings; with a Sketch of the City of Saint Louis. . . . St. Louis: Chambers & Knapp, 1842.

Saints' Herald. Independence, MO. 1860–.

Salt Lake Daily Tribune. Salt Lake City. 1871–.

San Francisco Chronicle. San Francisco. 1865–1925.

Sangamo Journal. Springfield, IL. 1831–1847.

Saunders, Richard LaVell. "Francis Gladden Bishop and Gladdenism: A Study in the Culture of a Mormon Dissenter and His Movement." Master's thesis, Utah State University, 1989.

Scammon / Scammon, J. Young. *Reports of Cases Argued and Determined in the Supreme Court of the State of Illinois.* 4 vols. St. Louis: W. J. Gilbert, 1869–1870.

"Schedule Setting Forth a List of Petitioner[']s Creditors, Their Residence, and the Amount Due to Each," ca. 15–16 Apr. 1842. CCLA.

The Seer. Washington DC, Jan. 1853–June 1854; Liverpool, Jan. 1853–Aug. 1854.

Seixas, Joshua. *Manual Hebrew Grammar for the Use of Beginners.* 2nd ed., enl. and impr. Andover, MA: Gould and Newman, 1834.

Shurtleff, Stella Cahoon, and Brent Farrington Cahoon, comps. *Reynolds Cahoon and His Stalwart Sons: Utah Pioneers.* Salt Lake City: Paragon Press, 1960.

Signs of the Times and Expositor of Prophecy. Boston. 1840–1844.

Skousen, Royal, ed. *The Original Manuscript of the Book of Mormon: Typographical Facsimile of the Extant Text.* Provo, UT: Foundation for Ancient Research and Mormon Studies, Brigham Young University, 2001.

Smart, Donna Toland, ed. *Mormon Midwife: The 1846–1888 Diaries of Patty Bartlett Sessions.* Logan, UT: Utah State University Press, 1997.

Smith, Andrew F. *The Saintly Scoundrel: The Life and Times of Dr. John Cook Bennett.* Urbana: University of Illinois Press, 1997.

Smith, George Albert. Papers, 1834–1882. CHL.

Smith, Heman C. "Mormon Troubles in Missouri." *Missouri Historical Review* 4, no. 4 (July 1910): 238–251.

Smith, Joseph. In addition to the entries that immediately follow, see entries under "JS."

Smith, Joseph. Certificate, to Oliver Granger, 6 May 1839. CHL.

———. Collection, 1827–1846. CHL.

———. Indenture to Lydia Dibble Granger, Hancock Co., IL, 15 Mar. 1843. Henry E. Huntington Library, San Marino, CA.

———. Letter, Liberty, MO, to Emma Smith, Far West, MO, 1 Dec. 1838. CHL.

———. Letter, Nauvoo, IL, to James Arlington Bennet, Arlington House, Long Island, NY, 30 June 1842. CHL.

———. Materials, 1832–1844, 1883. CCLA.

———. Office Papers, ca. 1835–1845. CHL.

———. Power of Attorney, to Isaac Galland and Hyrum Smith, Hancock Co., IL, 1 Feb. 1841. Private possession. Copy at CHL.

Smith, Joseph, and Emma Smith. Indenture to Robert Peirce, Hancock Co., IL, 28 Feb. 1842. International Society Daughters of Utah Pioneers, Pioneer Memorial Museum, Salt Lake City.

Smith, Joseph, et al. Memorial to U.S. Senate and House of Representatives, 28 Nov. 1843.

In Records of the U.S. Senate, Committee on the Judiciary, Records, 1816–1982. National Archives, Washington DC.

Smith, Joseph F. Affidavits about Celestial Marriage, 1869–1915. CHL.

Smith, Lucy Mack. History, 1844–1845. 18 books. CHL. Also available in Lavina Fielding Anderson, ed., *Lucy's Book: A Critical Edition of Lucy Mack Smith's Family Memoir* (Salt Lake City: Signature Books, 2001).

Snow, Eliza R. *Biography and Family Record of Lorenzo Snow, One of the Twelve Apostles of the Church of Jesus Christ of Latter-day Saints.* Salt Lake City: Deseret News Company, 1884.

———. Journal, 1842–1844. CHL.

Snow, Erastus. Journals, 1835–1851, 1856–1857. CHL.

Snow, Lorenzo. Journals, 1836–1845, 1872. CHL.

Speech of Orson Hyde, Delivered before the High Priest's Quorum in Nauvoo, April 27th, 1845, upon the Course and Conduct of Mr. Sidney Rigdon, and upon the Merits of His Claims to the Presidency of the Church of Jesus Christ of Latter-day Saints. [Nauvoo], IL: John Taylor, 1845. Copy at CHL.

Staker, Mark L. *Hearken, O Ye People: The Historical Setting for Joseph Smith's Ohio Revelations.* Salt Lake City: Greg Kofford Books, 2009.

State of Missouri. See Missouri, State of.

Storrs, George. *The Bible Examiner: Containing Various Prophetic Expositions.* Boston: Joshua V. Himes, 1843.

Stover, Carl W., and Jerry L. Coffman. *Seismicity of the United States, 1568–1989 (Revised).* U.S. Geological Survey Professional Paper 1527. Washington DC: U.S. Government Printing Office, 1993.

Stuart, Moses. *Hints on the Interpretation of Prophecy.* 2nd ed. Andover, MA: Allen, Morrill, and Wardwell, 1842.

[Sumner, Charles]. "The Mutiny of the *Somers*." *North American Review* 57 (July 1843): 195–241.

Swan, Joseph R. *A Treatise on the Law Relating to the Powers and Duties of Justices of the Peace, and Constables, in the State of Ohio: With Practical Forms, &c. &c.* Columbus, OH: Isaac N. Whiting, 1837.

Taylor, F. *A Sketch of the Military Bounty Tract of Illinois....* Philadelphia: I. Ashmead, 1839.

Taylor, John. Collection, 1829–1894. CHL.

Taylor, Samuel. *An Universal System of Stenography, or Short-Hand Writing....* 6th ed. London: William Baynes and Son, 1826.

Thatcher, Luna Eunice Caroline Young. Collection, 1835–1876. CHL.

Thelen, David. "Memory and American History." *The Journal of American History* 75, no. 4 (Mar. 1989): 1117–1129.

Thomson, Samuel. *A Narrative of the Life, and Medical Discoveries of Samuel Thomson; Containing an Account of His System of Practice, and the Manner of Curing Disease with Vegetable Medicine: Upon a Plan Entirely New.* 9th ed. Columbus, OH: Jarvis Pike, 1833.

Thomsonian Recorder. Columbus, OH. 1832–ca. 1837.

Times. London. 1785–.

Times and Seasons. Commerce/Nauvoo, IL. Nov. 1839–Feb. 1846.

Tioga Eagle. Wellsboro, PA. 1838–1856/1857.

Tithing and Donation Record. 1844–1846. CHL.

Tracy, Nancy Naomi Alexander. Reminiscences and Diary, 1896–1899. Typescript. CHL.

Trumbull, Lyman. Letter, Springfield, IL, to James Pitman, Quincy, IL, Dec. [1842]. Secretary of State, General Correspondence, 1840–1846, 1850–1856, 1867–1918, 1923–1925, 1929–1960. Illinois State Archives, Springfield.

Trustee-in-Trust. Index and Accounts, 1841–1847. CHL.

Trustees Land Books / Trustee-in-Trust, Church of Jesus Christ of Latter-day Saints. Land Books, 1839–1845. 2 vols. CHL.

"Truthiana," 1843. Draft. CHL.

Tyng / Tyng, Dudley Atkins. *Reports of Cases Argued and Determined in the Supreme Judicial Court of the Commonwealth of Massachusetts.* 16 vols. Various publishers, 1808–1823.

U.S. and Canada Record Collection. FHL.

U.S. Bureau of Indian Affairs. Letters Received by the Office of Indian Affairs . . . Iowa Superintendency, 1839–1849. Typescripts. National Archives Microfilm Publications, microcopy 234, reel 363. Washington DC: National Archives, 1959.

U.S. Bureau of the Census. Population Schedules. Microfilm. FHL.

Vermont Chronicle. Bellows Falls, VT, 1826–1828; Windsor, VT, 1828–1862.

Vogel, Dan. "James Colin Brewster: The Boy Prophet Who Challenged Mormon Authority." In *Differing Visions: Dissenters in Mormon History,* edited by Roger D. Launius and Linda Thatcher, 120–139. Urbana: University of Illinois Press, 1994.

Von Wymetal, Wilhelm [W. Wyl, pseud.]. *Joseph Smith the Prophet: His Family and His Friends; a Study Based on Facts and Documents.* Salt Lake City: Tribune Printing and Publishing, 1886.

Walker, Ronald W. "Rachel R. Grant: The Continuing Legacy of the Feminine Ideal." *BYU Studies* 43, no. 1 (2004): 17–40.

Ward, Maurine Carr. "'This Institution Is a Good One': The Female Relief Society of Nauvoo, 17 March 1842 to 16 March 1844." *Mormon Historical Studies* 3 (Fall 2002): 87–203.

Warsaw Signal. Warsaw, IL. 1841–1843.

Washington's C.C. Reports / Washington, Bushrod. *Reports of Cases Determined in the Circuit Court of the United States, for the Third Circuit, Comprising the Districts of Pennsylvania and New-Jersey. Commencing at April Term, 1803.* 4 vols. Philadelphia: Philip H. Nicklin, 1826–1829.

The Wasp. Nauvoo, IL. Apr. 1842–Apr. 1843.

Wendell / Wendell, John L. *Reports of Cases Argued and Determined in the Supreme Court of Judicature and in the Court for the Correction of Errors of the State of New-York.* 26 vols. Albany: William and A. Gould, 1829–1842.

Western World. Warsaw, IL. 1840–1841.

Wheaton / Wheaton, Henry. *Reports of Cases Argued and Adjudged in the Supreme Court of the United States.* 12 vols. Various publishers, 1816–1827.

Whitney, Newel K. Papers, 1825–1906. BYU.

Whitney Family Documents, 1843–1844, 1912. CHL.

Whittaker, David J. "Brigham Young and the Missionary Enterprise." In *Lion of the Lord: Essays on the Life and Service of Brigham Young,* edited by Susan Easton Black and Larry C. Porter, 85–106. Salt Lake City: Deseret Book, 1995.

———. "East of Nauvoo: Benjamin Winchester and the Early Mormon Church." *Journal of Mormon History* 21 (Fall 1995): 30–83.

Whittemore Family, Papers, 1817–1978. Bentley Historical Library, University of Michigan, Ann Arbor.

Whorton, James C. *Nature Cures: The History of Alternative Medicine in America.* New York: Oxford University Press, 2002.

Wight, Lyman. *An Address by Way of an Abridged Account and Journal of My Life from February 1844 up to April 1848, with an Appeal to the Latter Day Saints.* [Austin, TX], [ca. 1848].

———. Petition, ca. 1839. CHL.

Woman's Exponent. Salt Lake City. 1872–1914.

Woodruff, Wilford. Journals, 1833–1844. Wilford Woodruff, Journals and Papers, 1828–1898. CHL. Also available as *Wilford Woodruff's Journals, 1833–1898,* edited by Scott G. Kenney, 9 vols. (Midvale, UT: Signature Books, 1983–1985).

Woods, Fred E. *Gathering to Nauvoo.* American Fork, UT: Covenant Communications, 2002.

"Workings of Mormonism Related by Mrs. Orson Pratt," 1884. CHL.

Yebamoth. Translated by Israel W. Slotki. Hebrew-English Edition of the Babylonian Talmud, edited by I. Epstein. London: Soncino Press, 1984.

Young, Brigham. Letter, Nauvoo, IL, to Parley P. Pratt, Liverpool, England, 17 July 1842. CHL.

Young, Emily Dow Partridge. Diary and Reminiscences, Feb. 1874–Nov. 1883. CHL.

Young, Joseph, Sr. *History of the Organization of the Seventies. Names of the First and Second Quorums. Items in Relation to the First Presidency of the Seventies. Also, a Brief Glance at Enoch and His City. Embellished with a Likeness of Joseph Smith, the Prophet, and a View of the Kirtland Temple.* Salt Lake City: Deseret News Steam Printing Establishment, 1878.

Zucker, Louis C. "Joseph Smith as a Student of Hebrew." *Dialogue: A Journal of Mormon Thought* 3 (Summer 1968): 41–55.

Corresponding Section Numbers in Editions of the Doctrine and Covenants

The Book of Commandments, of which a number of partial copies were printed in 1833, was superseded by the Doctrine and Covenants. Because the numbering of comparable material in the Book of Commandments and different editions of the Doctrine and Covenants varies extensively, the following table is provided to help readers refer from the version of a canonized item cited in this volume to other published versions of that same item. This table includes revelations announced by JS—plus letters, records of visions, articles, minutes, and other items, some of which were authored by other individuals—that were published in the Book of Commandments or Doctrine and Covenants in or before 1844, the year of JS's death. The table also includes material originating with JS that was first published in the Doctrine and Covenants after 1844. Such later-canonized material includes, for example, extracts of JS's 20 March 1839 letter written from the jail in Liberty, Missouri. These extracts, first canonized in 1876, are currently found in sections 121 through 123 of the Latter-day Saint edition of the Doctrine and Covenants.

The 1835 and 1844 editions of the Doctrine and Covenants included a series of lectures on the subject of faith, which constituted part 1 of the volume. Only part 2, the compilation of revelations and other items, is represented in the table. Further, the table does not include materials originating with JS that were not canonized in his lifetime and that have never been canonized by The Church of Jesus Christ of Latter-day Saints or by the Community of Christ. As only one of many examples, JS's journal entry for 3 November 1835 contains a JS revelation concerning the Twelve. This revelation has never been canonized and therefore does not appear in the table. More information about documents not listed on the table below will be provided in other volumes of *The Joseph Smith Papers* and on the Joseph Smith Papers website.

Some material was significantly revised after its initial publication in the canon. For instance, the revelation in chapter 28 of the Book of Commandments included twice as much material when it was republished in the Doctrine and Covenants in 1835. As another example, chapter 65 of the Book of Commandments stops abruptly before the end of the revelation because publication of the volume was disrupted; the revelation was not published in its entirety until 1835. These and other substantial changes of greater or lesser significance are not accounted for in the table, but they will be identified in the appropriate volumes of the Documents series.

The far left column of the table gives the standard date of each item, based on careful study of original sources. The "standard date" is the date a revelation was originally dictated or recorded. If that date is ambiguous or unknown, the standard date is the best approximation of the date, based on existing evidence. The standard date provides a way to identify each item and situate it chronologically with other documents, but it cannot be assumed that every date corresponds to the day an item was first dictated or recorded. In some cases, an item was recorded without a date notation. It is also possible that a few items were first dictated on a date other than the date surviving manuscripts bear. The dates found in this table were assigned based on all available evidence, including later attempts by JS and his contemporaries to recover date, place, and circumstances.

Where surviving sources provide conflicting information about dating, editorial judgment has been exercised to select the most likely date (occasionally only an approximate month), based on the most reliable sources. In cases in which two or more items bear the same date, they have been listed in the order in which they most likely originated, and a letter of the alphabet has been appended, providing each item a unique editorial title (for example, May 1829–A or May 1829–B). Information on dating issues will accompany publication of these items in the Documents series.

The remaining five columns on the table provide the number of the chapter (in the case of the Book of Commandments) or section (in the case of editions of the Doctrine and Covenants) in which the item was published in one or more of five different canonical editions, the first three of which were initiated by JS. Full bibliographic information about these five editions is given in the list of works cited. See also the Scriptural References section in the introduction to Works Cited for more information about the origins of the Doctrine and Covenants and other Mormon scriptures.

Key to column titles

1833: Book of Commandments
1835: Doctrine and Covenants, 1835 edition, part 2
1844: Doctrine and Covenants, 1844 edition, part 2[1]
1981: Doctrine and Covenants, 1981 edition, The Church of Jesus Christ of Latter-day Saints[2]
2004: Doctrine and Covenants, 2004 edition, Community of Christ[3]

Date	JS-Era Canon			1981	2004
	1833	1835	1844		
21 Sept. 1823				2[4]	
July 1828	2	30	30	3	2
Feb. 1829	3	31	31	4	4
Mar. 1829	4	32	32	5	5

1. The 1844 edition of the Doctrine and Covenants included one item written after the death of JS (section 111). That item is not included in this table.

2. The 1981 Latter-day Saint edition of the Doctrine and Covenants includes some items written after the death if JS. Those items are not included in this table. Any item for which information appears only in the "1981" column and in the "Date" column is a later-canonized JS item, as discussed in the first paragraph of the preceding introduction.

3. The 2004 Community of Christ edition of the Doctrine and Covenants includes two extracts from JS's Bible revision (sections 22 and 36) and items written after the death of JS. Neither the extracts nor the later items are included in this table.

4. This section, an extract from the history JS initiated in 1838, is here dated by the date of the event described in the section rather than the date of the document's creation.

Date	JS-Era Canon			1981	2004
	1833	1835	1844		
Apr. 1829–A	5	8	8	6	6
ca. Apr. 1829	9	36	36	10	3
Apr. 1829–B	7	34	34	8	8
Apr. 1829–C	6	33	33	7	7
Apr. 1829–D	8	35	35	9	9
15 May 1829				13[5]	
May 1829–A	10	37	37	11	10
May 1829–B	11	38	38	12	11
June 1829–A	12	39	39	14	12
June 1829–B	15	43	43	18	16
June 1829–C	13	40	40	15	13
June 1829–D	14	41	41	16	14
June 1829–E		42	42	17	15
Mar. 1830	16	44	44	19	18
6 Apr. 1830	22	46	46	21	19
Apr. 1830–A	17	45:1	45:1	23:1–2	21:1
Apr. 1830–B	18	45:2	45:2	23:3	21:2
Apr. 1830–C	19	45:3	45:3	23:4	21:3
Apr. 1830–D	20	45:4	45:4	23:5	21:4
Apr. 1830–E	21	45:5	45:5	23:6–7	21:5
10 Apr. 1830	24	2	2	20	17
16 Apr. 1830	23	47	47	22	20
July 1830–A	25	9	9	24	23
July 1830–B	27	49	49	26	25
July 1830–C	26	48	48	25	24
ca. Aug. 1830	28	50	50	27	26
Sept. 1830–A	29	10	10	29	28
Sept. 1830–B	30	51	51	28	27
Sept. 1830–C	31	52:1	52:1	30:1–4	29:1
Sept. 1830–D	32	52:2	52:2	30:5–8	29:2
Sept. 1830–E	33	52:3	52:3	30:9–11	29:3
Sept. 1830–F	34	53	53	31	30
Oct. 1830–A		54	54	32	31
Oct. 1830–B	35	55	55	33	32
4 Nov. 1830	36	56	56	34	33

---

5. This section, an extract from the history JS initiated in 1838, is here dated by the date of the event described in the section rather than the date of the document's creation.

Date	1833	JS-Era Canon 1835	1844	1981	2004
ca. Dec. 1830		73	74	74	74
7 Dec. 1830	37	11	11	35	34
9 Dec. 1830	38	57	57	36	35
30 Dec. 1830	39	58	58	37	37
2 Jan. 1831	40	12	12	38	38
5 Jan. 1831	41	59	59	39	39
6 Jan. 1831	42	60	60	40	40
4 Feb. 1831	43	61	61	41	41
9 Feb. 1831[6]	44	13:1–19	13:1–19	42:1–73	42:1–19
Feb. 1831–A	45	14	14	43	43
Feb. 1831–B	46	62	62	44	44
23 Feb. 1831	47	13:21–23, 20	13:21–23, 20	42:78–93, 74–77	42:21–23, 20
ca. 7 Mar. 1831	48	15	15	45	45
ca. 8 Mar. 1831–A	49	16	16	46	46
ca. 8 Mar. 1831–B	50	63	63	47	47
10 Mar. 1831	51	64	64	48	48
7 May 1831	52	65	65	49	49
9 May 1831	53	17	17	50	50
20 May 1831		23	23	51	51
6 June 1831	54	66	66	52	52
8 June 1831	55	66[7]	67	53	53
10 June 1831	56	67	68	54	54
14 June 1831	57	68	69	55	55
15 June 1831	58	69	70	56	56
20 July 1831		27	27	57	57
1 Aug. 1831	59	18	18	58	58
7 Aug. 1831	60	19	19	59	59
8 Aug. 1831	61	70	71	60	60
12 Aug. 1831	62	71	72	61	61
13 Aug. 1831	63	72	73	62	62
30 Aug. 1831	64	20	20	63	63
11 Sept. 1831	65	21	21	64	64
29 Oct. 1831		74	75	66	66

---

6. See also the following entry for 23 Feb. 1831.

7. The second of two sections numbered 66. Numbering remains one off for subsequent sections within the 1835 edition.

DATE	1833	JS-Era Canon 1835	1844	1981	2004
30 Oct. 1831		24	24	65	65
1 Nov. 1831–A		22	22	68	68
1 Nov. 1831–B	1	1	1	1	1
2 Nov. 1831		25	25	67	67
3 Nov. 1831		100	108	133	108
11 Nov. 1831–A		28	28	69	69
11 Nov. 1831–B[8]		3 (partial[9])	3 (partial[10])	107 (partial[11])	104 (partial[12])
12 Nov. 1831		26	26	70	70
1 Dec. 1831		90	91	71	71
4 Dec. 1831		89	90	72	72
10 Jan. 1832		29	29	73	73
25 Jan. 1832		87	88	75	75
16 Feb. 1832		91	92	76	76
ca. Mar. 1832				77	
1 Mar. 1832		75	76	78	77
7 Mar. 1832		77	78	80	79
12 Mar. 1832		76	77	79	78
15 Mar. 1832		79	80	81	80
26 Apr. 1832		86	87	82	81
30 Apr. 1832		88	89	83	82
29 Aug. 1832		78	79	99	96
22 and 23 Sept. 1832		4	4	84	83
27 Nov. 1832				85	
6 Dec. 1832		6	6	86	84
25 Dec. 1832				87	
27 and 28 Dec. 1832 and 3 Jan. 1833		7	7	88	85
27 Feb. 1833		80	81	89	86
8 Mar. 1833		84	85	90	87
9 Mar. 1833		92	93	91	88
15 Mar. 1833		93	94	92	89
6 May 1833		82	83	93	90
1 June 1833		95	96	95	92

---

8. See also the following entry for ca. Apr. 1835.
9. Verses 31–33, 35–42, 44.
10. Verses 31–33, 35–42, 44.
11. Verses 59–69, 71–72, 74–75, 78–87, 91–92, 99–100.
12. Verses 31–33, 35–42, 44.

Date	1833	1835	1844	1981	2004
		JS-Era Canon			
4 June 1833		96	97	96	93
2 Aug. 1833–A		81	82	97	94
2 Aug. 1833–B		83	84	94	91
6 Aug. 1833		85	86	98	95
12 Oct. 1833		94	95	100	97
16 and 17 Dec. 1833		97	98	101	98
17 Feb. 1834		5	5	102	99
24 Feb. 1834			101	103	100
23 Apr. 1834		98	99	104	101
22 June 1834			102	105	102
25 Nov. 1834		99	100	106	103
ca. Apr. 1835[13]		3	3	107	104
ca. Aug. 1835 ("Marriage")		101	109		111
ca. Aug. 1835 ("Of Governments and Laws in General")		102	110	134	112
26 Dec. 1835				108	
21 Jan. 1836				137	
27 Mar. 1836				109	
3 Apr. 1836				110	
6 Aug. 1836				111	
23 July 1837			104	112	105
Mar. 1838				113	
11 Apr. 1838				114	
26 Apr. 1838				115	
19 May 1838				116	
8 July 1838–A				118	
8 July 1838–C[14]			107	119	106
8 July 1838–D				120	
8 July 1838–E				117	
20 Mar. 1839				121–123	
19 Jan. 1841			[103]	124	107[15]

13. See also the preceding entry for 11 Nov. 1831–B.

14. This table skips from 8 July 1838–A to 8 July 1838–C because the revelation not shown here, 8 July 1838–B, has never been canonized.

15. The 2004 Community of Christ edition provides the following note regarding this section: "Placed in the Appendix by action of the 1970 World Conference: the Appendix was subsequently removed by the 1990 World Conference."

Date	JS-Era Canon				
	1833	1835	1844	1981	2004
Mar. 1841				125	
9 July 1841				126	
1 Sept. 1842			105	127	109[16]
7 Sept. 1842			106	128	110[17]
9 Feb. 1843				129	
2 Apr. 1843				130	
16 and 17 May 1843				131	
12 July 1843				132	

---

16. The 2004 Community of Christ edition provides the following note regarding this section: "Placed in the Appendix by action of the 1970 World Conference: the Appendix was subsequently removed by the 1990 World Conference."

17. The 2004 Community of Christ edition provides the following note regarding this section: "Placed in the Appendix by action of the 1970 World Conference: the Appendix was subsequently removed by the 1990 World Conference."

Acknowledgments

This volume, and the Joseph Smith Papers Project of which it is a part, are made possible through the help and generosity of many people and institutions. We give special thanks to administrators and officials of The Church of Jesus Christ of Latter-day Saints, Salt Lake City, which sponsors the project, and to management and staff of the Church History Library, Salt Lake City, where the majority of Joseph Smith's papers are located and where the project is centered. We also express special thanks to the Larry H. Miller and Gail Miller Family Foundation for their continued financial and emotional support of the project. Their generosity and encouragement have enabled the project to meet an ambitious production schedule while adhering to the highest scholarly standards.

In addition to the Church History Library, numerous other libraries and repositories have provided critical materials and assistance. These include the Family History Library, The Church of Jesus Christ of Latter-day Saints, Salt Lake City; the Community of Christ Library-Archives, Independence, Missouri; the L. Tom Perry Special Collections, Harold B. Lee Library, Brigham Young University, Provo, Utah; the Abraham Lincoln Presidential Library, Springfield, Illinois; the Beinecke Rare Book and Manuscript Library, Yale University, New Haven, Connecticut; the Bentley Historical Library, University of Michigan, Ann Arbor; the Daviess County, Missouri, Courthouse, Gallatin; the Illinois State Archives, Springfield; the International Society Daughters of Utah Pioneers, Pioneer Memorial Museum, Salt Lake City; the Missouri State Archives, Jefferson City; the National Archives and Records Administration, Washington DC; the National Archives and Records Administration, Great Lakes Region, Chicago, Illinois; the Quincy Public Library, Quincy, Illinois; the State Historical Society of Iowa, Des Moines; and the State Historical Society of Missouri at the Ellis Library, University of Missouri, Columbia.

This second volume of the Journals series had its genesis in two works by Dean C. Jessee: *The Papers of Joseph Smith, Volume 2: Journal, 1832–1842,* published by Deseret Book Company, Salt Lake City, in 1992; and the completed but unpublished third volume of that series. The earlier work of Jessee and those who assisted him is apparent throughout the volume presented here. Our understanding of Nauvoo and Illinois history in general has also benefited from conversations with several individuals, including Mark L. Staker, Emily Utt, and Donald L. Enders of the Historic Sites section of the Church History Department, The Church of Jesus Christ of Latter-day Saints; Glen M. Leonard, former director of the Church History Museum, Salt Lake City; Lachlan MacKay, Rene Romig, and Ronald E. Romig, historians and site directors of the Community of Christ; and Bryon Andreasen, Kathleen Thomas, Cheryl Schnirring, and Mary Michals of the Abraham Lincoln Presidential Library and Museum. Conversations with Jonathan A. Stapley, Samuel M. Brown, D. Michael Quinn, and Brian C. Hales helped sharpen our thinking and clarify issues surrounding Nauvoo plural marriage, ritual, and various other topics.

We express special thanks to several individuals whose special talents and dedicated efforts added materially to our understanding of these Nauvoo journals and the times in which Joseph Smith lived. LaJean Purcell Carruth, Church History Department, deciphered the shorthand that Willard Richards occasionally used; Joseph Johnstun, independent researcher and former director of tourism for the city of Nauvoo, provided valuable information for the maps and geographical directory; Derek Farnes, Andrew Thorup, Brent Beck, Ben Clift, Vania Hernandez, and Tyler Jones created the maps under the direction of Brandon Plewe, Brigham Young University; Sharon E. Nielsen, Joseph Smith Papers, collected and organized the information contained in the organizational charts; Gerrit Dirkmaat, Joseph Smith Papers, assisted with the organizational charts, helped identify obscure individuals who appear in the journal, and provided valuable insights into Nauvoo-era plural marriage; Jill Mulvay Derr, Church History Department, shed much-needed light on the lives of women in Nauvoo; Larry E. Morris and David Kitterman, Joseph Smith Papers, developed the volume chronology; and Gene A. Ware, Brigham Young University, utilized multispectral imaging techniques to restore faded or erased text. Special thanks are also due to Kay Darowski, Joseph Smith Papers, who oversaw a talented team of student researchers at Brigham Young University; David Grua, who was especially helpful with researching legal issues; Welden C. Andersen, who took the textual photographs featured in the volume and helped analyze multispectral images of damaged text; and Anna Staley and Viola Knecht, who served as administrative assistants for the project as a whole. The volume also benefited from careful review by the project's leadership, advisory board, and editors. We specifically thank Gordon A. Madsen and Larry C. Porter, who provided invaluable comments and feedback.

A number of other people contributed to the volume presented here, including employees, interns, and missionaries of the Church History Department; faculty and researchers at Brigham Young University; individuals associated with other academic and archival institutions; independent researchers and editors; and volunteers. We are especially grateful for the help of Linda Hunter Adams, Alex D. Braunberger, Lisse Brox, Jeffrey G. Cannon, Clark D. Christensen, Ethan J. Christensen, Lee Ann Clanton, Jared P. Collette, Justin Collings, Lia Suttner Collings, Renee Collins, Daniel J. Combs, Christopher K. Crockett, Joseph F. Darowski, Karen Lynn Davidson, Eric Dowdle, Vanessa Ann Dominica Dowdle, Patrick C. Dunshee, Jay R. Eastley, Naoma W. Eastley, J. Spencer Fluhman, Amanda Kae Fronk, James A. Goldberg, Angella L. Hamilton, Jared Hamon, Shirl Herget, Tyler Humble, Jeffery Ogden Johnson, Christopher C. Jones, Carma L. King, Cort Kirksey, Elias E. Kurban Sr., Jamie Layton, Mary-Celeste Lewis, Riley M. Lorimer, Jennifer L. Lund, Michael Hubbard MacKay, Allison Mathews, Winston Matthews, Chris McAfee, Colleen McDannell, Russell Jay McDonald, Kara Nelsen, Amy Norton, Sandy Olah, Jason M. Olson, Amanda Owens, Benjamin E. Park, Shauna Payne, Sarah Gibby Peris, Jennifer Peters, Josh E. Probert, Daren E. Ray, Mark Robison, Natalie Ross, Glenn N. Rowe, Ryan W. Saltzgiver, Leslie Sherman, Todd M. Sparks, Timothy D. Speirs, Virginia E. Stratford, Nathan N. Waite, Norman E. Waite, Chase Walker, Kathryn Jensen Wall, Stephen Whitaker, Kally Whittle, Julia K. Woodbury, and Ellen Yates.

We also thank the management and staff at Deseret Book for the professional help and advice they provided regarding the design, printing, and distribution of this volume. Special thanks are owed to Sheri L. Dew, Cory H. Maxwell, Anne Sheffield, Richard Erickson, Suzanne Brady, Gail Halladay, Derk Koldewyn, Ruth B. Howard, Jeffrey G.

Howard, Melissa Marler, Rachel Stauffer, and Whitney Hinckley. We are grateful to Scott Eggers, Scott Eggers Design, Salt Lake City, for designing the dust jacket and cover.